THE MODERN ANTHROPOLOGY OF
SOUTH-EAST ASIA

The culturally diverse and historically complex region of South-East Asia has played a vital role in the development of the concepts and methods of anthropology. It is a significant fact that many senior anthropologists of the post-war period who contributed to the development of anthropological theories and methods formulated their ideas and perspectives in their encounter with South-East Asia. Why, then, has this remarkable tradition of scholarship not yet provided the subject matter of a comprehensive introductory teaching text?

The present volume fills the need for such a text. It provides a succinct historical survey and analysis of the development of our understanding of the peoples and cultures of the region. It shows how social scientists have fully appreciated the value of an anthropological approach in understanding the dynamics of change in South-East Asia. Above all, this book addresses the major theoretical issues and themes that have emerged from the engagement of such anthropologists with South-East Asian communities.

This introductory volume is the prelude to a series of teaching texts on the peoples and cultures of South-East Asia. The series will give due emphasis to the responses to development, globalization and change of local communities in the region.

Victor T. King is Professor of South-East Asian Studies at the University of Hull, and author of *The Peoples of Borneo* (1993) and *Anthropology and Development in South-East Asia: Theory and Practice* (1999). **William D. Wilder** is Senior Lecturer in Anthropology at the University of Durham, and author of *Communication, Social Structure and Development in Rural Malaysia* (1982).

THE MODERN ANTHROPOLOGY OF SOUTH-EAST ASIA

Editors

Victor T. King, *University of Hull*
William D. Wilder, *University of Durham*

The books in this Series incorporate basic ethnographic description into a wider context of responses to development, globalization and change. Each book embraces broadly the same concerns, but the emphasis in each differs as authors choose to concentrate on specific dimensions of change or work out particular conceptual approaches to the issues of development. Areas of concern include: nation-building, technological innovations in agriculture, rural–urban migration, the expansion of industrial and commercial employment, the rapid increase in cultural and ethnic tourism, the consequences of deforestation and environmental degradation, the 'modernization of tradition', ethnic identity and conflict, and the religious transformation of society.

THE MODERN ANTHROPOLOGY OF SOUTH-EAST ASIA

An introduction
Victor T. King and William D. Wilder

THE MODERN ANTHROPOLOGY OF SOUTH-EAST ASIA

An introduction

Victor T. King and William D. Wilder

RoutledgeCurzon
Taylor & Francis Group

LONDON AND NEW YORK

First published 2003
by RoutledgeCurzon
11 New Fetter Lane, London EC4P 4EE

Simultaneously published in the USA and Canada
by Routledge
29 West 35th Street, New York, NY 10001

*RoutledgeCurzon is an imprint of the
Taylor & Francis Group*

©2003 Victor T. King and William D. Wilder

Typeset in Goudy by Wearset Ltd, Boldon, Tyne and Wear
Printed and bound in Great Britain by The Cromwell Press,
Trowbridge, Wiltshire

British Library Cataloguing in Publication Data
A catalogue record for this book is available
from the British Library

Library of Congress Cataloging in Publication Data
King, Victor T.
An introduction to the modern anthropology of South-east Asia/
Victor T. King & William D. Wilder
p. cm.
Includes bibliographical references and index.
1. Ethnology–Asia, Southeastern. 2. Anthropology–Asia,
Southeastern–History. 3. Asia, Southeastern–Social life and customs.
I. Wilder, William D. II. Title.

GN635.S58 K55 2003
306'.0959–dc21

2002068244

ISBN 0-415-29751-6 (hbk)
ISBN 0-415-29752-4 (pbk)

CONTENTS

ILLUSTRATIONS

Maps

Plates *(between pp. 192–193)*

1 Tropical rainforest, Central Kalimantan
2 Malay market scene, Bandar Sri Aman, Sarawak, Malaysia
3 Malay fishing village, Mersing, Peninsular Malaysia
4 Iban longhouse, Upper Embaloh, West Kalimantan, Indonesia
5 State mosque, Kota Kinabalu, Sabah, Malaysia
6 Shifting cultivation, Padawan, Sarawak, Malaysia
7 'Maloh' Dayak women chewing betel-nut, Upper Embaloh
8 Jame'Asr Hassanal Bolkiah Mosque, Gadong, Brunei
9 Main Buddhist temple complex, Grand Palace, Bangkok, Thailand
10 Main Buddhist stupa and monks at Nakhon Pathom, Thailand
11 Domestic Buddhist shrine of a Sino-Thai family, Bangkok
12 Offering prayers at a Buddhist temple in Phuket, Thailand
13 Thai temple at Phuket
14 Elephant shrine, Phuket
15 Sri Mahamariamman South Indian Hindu temple, Kuala Lumpur, Malaysia

vii

ABBREVIATIONS

ASEAN	Association of Southeast Asian Nations
CSSRC	Colonial Social Science Research Council
FTZ	Free Trade Zone
LSE	London School of Economics and Political Science
MAB	Man and Biosphere Program
MAS	Malay Administrative Service
MCA	Malay(si)an Chinese Association
MIC	Malay(si)an Indian Congress
MIT	Massachusetts Institute of Technology
PAS/PMIP	Parti Islam Se-Malaysia/Pan-Malay(si)an Islamic Party
PN	Parti Negara
RISDA	Rubber Industry Smallholders' Development Authority
SEAC	South East Asia Command
UMNO	United Malays National Organization

PREFACE

At the time of writing this book, the co-authors have between them 66 years as professional anthropologists. We hope – if we do not claim – that this experience has been intelligibly and instructively transmitted in this book. At the very least, we have attempted to establish what the 'directions' of the recognized traditions of the anthropology of South-East Asia have been, are, and will be in the near future. We have also emphasized certain traditions rather than others, and it may well be that other anthropologists would have chosen differently.

We hope to speed the acquisition of first-time knowledge of South-East Asian anthropology for undergraduates, and, in addition, we may have even provided ammunition for postgraduates, researchers and professional teachers when they debate among themselves the 'directions' of South-East Asian anthropology and the significance of its theoretical contributions. The ethnographic literature, and the theoretical debates based upon it, have enlarged dramatically in the last 20 years, and the growth of scholarly output shows no sign of slowing at the present time. This is both encouraging and daunting, and we have tried to show how the student and the researcher – who was once a student – can draw upon, and further enlarge, the accumulated experience of current anthropology, ideally 'without tears'. If that is the effect of our outline and critical survey of the field, we shall be gratified with work successfully undertaken.

It is perhaps a tacit acknowledgement of the rapid and continuing growth of South-East Asian anthropology that some topics for which we would have liked to have provided a separate chapter, most of all religious developments, we decided subsequently not to do so, because it would have made the book longer and more unwieldy than it already is and further postponed its publication. Nevertheless, we have endeavoured to cover what we consider to be the key literature in the main areas of anthropological concern, even in the anthropology of religion, in our historical examination of debates and contributions. In any case, we have also designed our book as part of a larger and continuing project in an attempt to make the newest South-East Asian anthropological researches accessible within an 'executive' framework, in short monographs not so technically cumbersome and costly that new students, and aspiring learners in South-East Asia itself, cannot utilize them conveniently and on demand. We expect that the full scope of anthropology will be exercised as these studies are assembled for the series. Several of these monographs – studies of specific local communities in today's South-East Asia – are due to be published soon by RoutledgeCurzon. They will be announced in due course.

In writing this volume we both owe a debt of gratitude to our respective institutions – the Universities of Hull and Durham – for granting us valuable periods of study leave, and in various ways providing us with funding and support to enable us to meet face-to-face from time to time to discuss progress, to secure materials through inter-library loan, and to produce such things as maps, illustrations and an index. We should also like to thank Jonathan Price of the then Curzon Press for showing interest and faith in the proposal and giving us the encouragement to press forward with our writing. Dr A.V.M. Horton, for many years an Honorary Research Fellow at Hull's Centre for South-East Asian Studies, has done a magnificent and meticulous job in compiling the index on our behalf. Dr Michael Parnwell, Reader in South-East Asian Geography at Hull, and an extraordinarily accomplished photographer, also kindly consented to allow us to use some of his excellent photographs of life and culture in South-East Asia. Two of his images grace the front cover of the book.

V.T.K. and W.D.W.
October 2002

INTRODUCTION

In our teaching in South-East Asian anthropology we had both been aware for some time of the lack of accessible, readable, thematic undergraduate teaching texts on the modern anthropology of the region, and specifically on the effects on local communities and societies of processes of modernization and globalization. We therefore decided to propose a series of short monographs on the main ethnic groupings of the region and to inaugurate the series with a jointly written introductory text. This introduction serves to provide an overview of the development of anthropology in relation to South-East Asia and addresses the main themes and issues which anthropologists have explored, and the theories and concepts employed, in their engagement with regional social and cultural realities. For our purposes, and particularly in our examination of the recent history of the subject, anthropology encompasses a rather broad field of studies, given that social and cultural life in colonial South-East Asia was often described and analysed not by professional anthropologists but by colonial administrators, missionaries, explorers and travellers, and by scholars whose training had been primarily in such subjects as linguistics, law, philosophy, theology, geography, archaeology or history. In other words, anthropology, or ethnology as it was usually called in continental Europe, was part of or embedded in other fields of study and more often than not undertaken as a spare-time activity by individuals working as civil servants, or as scientists or missionaries in European and American colonial dependencies in South-East Asia. It was only in the late colonial period and especially following the political independence of the South-East Asian territories that the study of anthropology became much more firmly, though not completely, a university-based discipline pursued full-time by scholars specifically trained in anthropological theories and methods.

While much of South-East Asia is now quite well represented in the current anthropological literature – ranging from Indonesia best of all to Indochina (Vietnam, Cambodia and Laos) least of all, with relatively good coverage of Malaysia, Singapore, Brunei, Thailand and the Philippines, and some detailed studies of Myanmar or Burma (generally in this text we use the term Burma) available from the 1950s and 1960s – we continue to lack a general textbook survey of the region. What is more, the rapidly increasing amount of ethnographic literature on South-East Asian peoples and cultures has tended to become ever more specialized and localized so that there is a real need for teaching materials with region-wide concerns and interests. In his review of South-East Asian Studies in the United States up to 1990, Charles Hirschman also remarked that one of the distinctive features of this field is 'the general absence of textbooks on Southeast Asia for university students' (1992: 49). Instead many of the scholars who work on the region, especially anthropologists, see themselves primarily as disciplinary specialists with an interest in a particular subject area and a particular community, country or subregion.

Our series is similar in concept to that of the well-known and successful Holt, Rinehart and Winston *Case Studies in Cultural Anthropology* which began in 1960 and is still active. However, this series is global in scope and only a handful of monographs on South-East Asia have appeared, most notably those by Robert K. Dentan (Semai, Peninsular Malaysia), Edward P. Dozier (Kalinga, northern Luzon), Thomas M. Fraser (Malays of southern Thailand), Alfred B. Hudson (Ma'anyan of southern Kalimantan), F. Landa Jocano (lowland Filipinos), Thomas Kiefer (Tausug, southern Philippines), J. Stephen Lansing (Balinese), and Thomas Rhys Williams (Dusun, northern Borneo). Many of these texts are now rather dated, although they are still extremely valuable as teaching tools. Another series, launched in 1993, which bears some resemblance to ours is Blackwell's *The Peoples of South-East Asia and the Pacific*, though, as the title suggests, its remit extends to the Austronesian populations of Melanesia and Polynesia as well. Specifically South-East Asian volumes have recently appeared by Victor T. King (Borneo peoples), Christian Pelras (Bugis), Ian Mabbett and David Chandler (Khmers), and Angela Hobart, Urs Ramseyer and Albert Leemann (Balinese), but these focus primarily on cultural history and archaeology, and are less concerned with the ways in which South-East Asian communities have responded to forces of change generated by processes of urbanization, industrialization, nation-building and the technological revolution in knowledge and information transfer.

In this context we have been firmly of the view that the monographs in our series should incorporate basic ethnographic description with a consideration of processes of and responses to development, globalization and change. The individual contributions in the series are intended to embrace broadly the same ethnographic concerns but the emphasis in each will differ as authors choose to concentrate on specific dimensions of change or explore particular conceptual approaches to the issues of development. For example, the currents of change may be bound up with planned social and economic development, or they may be seen as more diverse and unplanned in the context of the expansion of the market economy and opportunities for urban-based employment or commercial agriculture. Nation-building in South-East Asia is certainly one common factor in development and with it the incorporation of minority ethnic groups into the mainstream of national political, cultural and economic life and their progressive control and administration by central political and bureaucratic elites. New organizations and large-scale movements of many kinds also impinge on local communities: technological innovations in agriculture, rural–urban migration, the expansion of industrial and commercial employment and factory-based manufacture, the rapid increase in cultural, ethnic and environmental tourism, and the human consequences of deforestation and environmental pollution.

In this series current anthropological concerns with the 'modernization of tradition', ethnic identity and conflict, and religious conversion and the religious transformation of society may be blended with the analyses and debates which are already associated with particular South-East Asian societies, topics such as dual symbolic classification, the elementary structures of kinship, involution and shared poverty, economic dualism, cultural pluralism and polyethnic societies, peasant moral economy, the theatre state, religious syncretism and imagined communities.

In contemplating the shape and content of the series it struck us forcefully that the student reader interested in regional anthropology or in multidisciplinary area studies has very little to turn to by way of a consolidated introduction to the modern anthropology of South-East Asia. That is why we think it essential that our series commence with just such a general text. One has to go back some years to find suitable introductions to the anthropology of the region or at least a substantial part of it, and interestingly all of these earlier texts have been written by American anthropologists. Probably the best known is Robbins Burling's Hill Farms and Padi Fields: Life in Mainland Southeast Asia (1965 [1992 reprint]), although, in its treatment of archaeology, early history and the postwar period in particular, it is now very dated. As the title of the book suggests, it concentrates on the mainland states of Vietnam, Cambodia, Laos, Thailand and Burma, with some attention to Assam in north-east India, culturally part of South-East Asia proper, and Peninsular Malaysia, joined as it is to the mainland, but usually considered as culturally and historically part of the island world of South-East Asia. Burling's main personal and field experience of the region was among the Garo of the hills of Assam, where he spent two years in 1954–1956, and in Rangoon and lowland Burma in 1959–1960. Burling's introduction 'Hills and Plains' in which he posits a South-East Asian culture, embracing both mainland and islands, based on certain 'common threads' which underlie the obvious diversity, is still widely quoted by scholars of South-East Asia who are either searching for regional unity or arguing for its dissolution in the face of cultural, political and historical diversity (a theme which we shall address in our introductory statements in Chapter 1). Burling's central argument is that one element of diversity – the contrast between hill and lowland people – is paradoxically the most significant element of the region's unity because this persistent and long-established contrast, despite marked cultural discontinuities through time, is widespread and general in South-East Asia. Hill Farms and Padi Fields is a very readable introductory book, and, in its summary ethnographies and commentary on widely spread principles and patterns of socio-cultural organization, retains some value as a teaching text.

A complementary volume is Ben J. Wallace's *Village Life in Insular Southeast Asia* (1971), which arose out of Wallace's concern that he needed an introductory teaching text for his undergraduate course on the peoples and cultures of South-East Asia. Wallace's field experience was among the Gaddang, a hill population of northern Luzon, with whom he lived in the 1960s. He dwells on cultural diversity in the island world, but like Burling draws attention to broadly similar cultural elements found in the region and the general ecological and cultural contrast between highlands and lowlands. Socio-cultural systems are categorized and described by Wallace in terms of particular adaptations to different environmental opportunities and constraints, and in this regard Wallace's approach, in part, replicates Clifford Geertz's distinction, elaborated in his classic study *Agricultural Involution: The Processes of Ecological Change in Indonesia* (1963a) (see Chapter 3), between two ecotypes in Indonesia: the irrigated wet rice or *sawah* system of the lowland communities of inner Indonesia, particularly on Java and Bali, and the forest-based swidden or shifting agricultural (*ladang*) system of the upland tribal groups of the outer islands such as Sumatra, Kalimantan and Sulawesi.

There are also two later companion volumes in the Goodyear Regional Anthropology Series, which taken together cover most of the South-East Asian region: James L. Peacock's *Indonesia: An Anthropological Perspective* (1973) and Ronald Provencher's *Mainland Southeast Asia: An Anthropological Perspective* (1975). Peacock had considerable field experience in east Java in the 1960s and Provencher had undertaken research in Burma, Thailand and Peninsular Malaysia in the 1960s and early 1970s. Both texts, like that of Burling, pay considerable attention to the historical development of South-East Asian cultures from prehistory and early agriculture to the present, addressing the persistent theme of cultural and ethnic differentiation and diversification through time as people, ideas and traits entered the region from the neighbouring regions of China and India and further afield from the Middle East, Western Europe and North America, and South-East Asians responded to these external influences and to changing internal environmental and other circumstances. Additionally the texts devote some space to a consideration of the effects of major physical movements into South-East Asia of ethnic Indians and Chinese, especially during the European colonial period. Peacock, Provencher and Burling also have something to say about the relations between local peoples and the processes of state formation and nation-building in the period of political independence. However, the most recently published of these books, that by Provencher, is now 28 years old, and much has changed in the anthropology and the modern political, economic and cultural environment of South-East Asia in the intervening years.

The two Goodyear volumes, in addition to those of Burling and Wallace, as well as concentrating on historical narrative, also provide summary ethnographies of most of the main ethnic groupings of the region. Provencher considers the mainland plains peoples under the rubric 'Tai States' (lowland Thais, Laos and hill peoples including the Meo/Hmong and Yao), 'States of Burma' (including the Shan, Kachin, Chin, Karen, Mon, Arakanese and Burmans or lowland Burmese), 'Khmer State' (Khmers or lowland Cambodians, Chams and immigrant Chinese and Vietnamese), and 'Vietnamese States' (lowland Vietnamese, Chinese and various hill groups), and, in addition, 'Malay States' (Malays, Chinese, Indians and Borneo minorities including Ibans and Kadazans or Dusuns). Peacock, in his survey of Indonesian anthropology, spends two-thirds of the book on history, and then presents ethnographic summaries of the western islands – Java (Javanese, Sundanese), Bali and Sumatra (Toba Batak, Minangkabau, Acehnese) – and the eastern outer islands (Makassarese, Buginese, Western Sumbawans, Rotinese, Iban [of Malaysian Borneo], Ma'anyan, Ambonese, and, finally and rather oddly in this section, the Chinese).

We should also note that the volumes by Burling and Wallace cover some of the same ethnographic ground as the Goodyear texts, but with attention to certain of the other minority groups. Burling provides data on various mainland hill peoples, particularly the Garo of Assam and the Lamet of Laos, and the major lowland groups – the Burmese, Thais and Vietnamese – along with immigrant Indians and Chinese. Wallace considers insular South-East Asian groups according to ecological categories: hunter–gatherers (Andamanese, Semang); sea fishermen (Bajau, coastal Malays); shifting cultivators (Land Dayaks or Bidayuhs, Gaddang); and wet rice agriculturalists (Ifugao, Javanese). For the student who needs to gain a broad ethnographic knowledge of the region then these texts, along with the ethnographic surveys compiled by Frank Lebar *et al.* (1964, 1972, 1975) of mainland and island ethnic groups still provide us with convenient summaries of a range of different communities and a useful coverage of cultural histories, and it is not our intention to duplicate their efforts.

What strikes the reader about these books is that they are primarily descriptive, combining ethnographic and historical narrative in a straightforward way. There is very little attention given to anthropological concepts, methods, issues and debates in relation to South-East Asian data, although, as one might expect, the ways in which the material is presented and structured are informed and shaped by an anthropological perspective. Provencher also gives some thought to the problems of reconstructing cultural history, and Peacock makes brief reference to the relations between Islam and social change in relation to Max Weber's analysis of religion and economic change, to J.H. Boeke's concept of dualism and Clifford Geertz's concept of involution, and to the problems for the anthropologist of formulating socio-cultural categories or types.

We choose to remark on this lack of explicit attention to anthropological debates in these early texts, reminiscent in some ways of even earlier ethnographic surveys such as Fay-Cooper Cole's *The Peoples of Malaysia* (1945),

A.L. Kroeber's *Peoples of the Philippines* (1928), and the popular and discursive sociological commentary by Bruno Lasker, *Peoples of Southeast Asia* ([1944] 1945), because there is a noticeable change in style and content in two texts published soon after the appearance of Peacock's and Provencher's books. Donald Brown, after undertaking historical-ethnographical research on the sultanate of Brunei, published *Principles of Social Structure: Southeast Asia* (1976). It was one of the first attempts to say something more general about the region and to organize anthropological data on South-East Asia in conceptual terms. What he attempts to do is to define and analyse social structures and delimit generic social units and the principles (such as age, gender, ethnicity, stratification) on which they are based in terms of the socio-legal concept of the 'corporation'. Unfortunately his book has received relatively little attention among South-East Asianists and its emphasis on corporate, bounded units perhaps proved less attractive to American anthropologists, on the one hand, who were interested in modernization and cultural change, and to those European anthropologists on the other who were preoccupied with symbolic classification and alliance systems (see Chapters 2 and 3).

The other text is Charles F. Keyes's *The Golden Peninsula: Culture and Adaptation in Mainland Southeast Asia* (1977 [1995]), which as well as giving detailed ethnographic and historical attention to the cultures of Burma, Thailand and Indochina, also organizes the material more explicitly in conceptual terms and, in various parts of the text, addresses important theoretical discussions in anthropology. He makes reference to Robert von Heine-Geldern's work on cultural diffusion in South-East Asia; John F. Embree's notion of loosely structured Thai society; the models of hill tribe social structures formulated by Edmund Leach, F.K. Lehman and A. Thomas Kirsch; Claude Lévi-Strauss's elementary structures of kinship and Needham's development of these ideas in relation to various upland ethnic groups; analyses of the relations between Buddhism and the spirit cults in Thailand and Burma especially in the work of Stanley J. Tambiah and Melford E. Spiro; and Ruth Benedict's study of Thai culture and personality and Spiro's elaboration of this approach in his major studies of Burmese Buddhism and supernaturalism. Keyes draws on various of these theoretical strands in his concept of culture and its adaptive dimensions. He focuses on culture, 'both as adaptive strategies employed by people living in particular conditions and as systems of meaning to which humans must also adapt' (ibid.: 9). He therefore examines various cultural traditions – 'primitive and tribal', historic Theravada Buddhist and Sino-Vietnamese, and new mainland traditions of nationalism, socialism and communism

> as they are expressed in the everyday lives of people residing in specific places … [and] … how cultural traditions in the region have been transformed and, in some cases, supplanted by other traditions in the wake of radical changes in people's experiences.
>
> (ibid.: vii)

Like Keyes and Brown we shall be giving special emphasis to important concepts which have been developed and employed to understand South-East Asian social and cultural forms; in some cases, certain ideas and modes of analysis have also been significant for the general discipline of anthropology, such as Leach's pathbreaking examination of Kachin social structure in Highland Burma and Clifford Geertz's analyses of Javanese and Balinese culture, social organization and change. We shall not be dwelling too much on the details of social and cultural life in the region because these will be provided in the individual monographs which accompany this introductory book in the series. For this reason this introduction is not a simple and straightforward description of the anthropology of the region, nor is it necessarily an easy text to read, though we have tried to summarize difficult ideas and theories as plainly and intelligibly as possible. The text addresses concepts and analyses; it does not pretend to be ethnographically comprehensive; we have selected the literature which we consider to be important and to have made a difference to the subject and with which we think all students and scholars with an interest in South-East Asian anthropology should be familiar. We make no apologies for this, but we do think that it is essential that this literature is brought together for the first time in an introductory way. However, we have not devoted specific attention to the theoretical and empirical literature on development or applied anthropology which has already been the subject of a recent South-East Asia-wide survey by King (1999).

Aside from these early texts there are no recent general introductory volumes on modern South-East Asian anthropology which come to mind, though it is worth mentioning two valuable books of which the student who is new to the field should be aware: Roxana Waterson's *The Living House: An Anthropology of Architecture in South-East Asia* (1990) and Grant Evans's edited book *Asia's Cultural Mosaic: An Anthropological Introduction* (1993b). Both these texts do not adopt the sort of approach and coverage which we intend to provide in our introductory volume. Waterson's book is not, on the face of it, an introduction to South-East Asian anthropology. As the title suggests, it focuses on a key element in regional culture – the house. However, aside from an obvious interest in architectural forms, Waterson provides an immense amount of comparative detail from both mainland and island South-East Asia on the distribution of ethnic groups and their historical and cultural relationships as well as, most importantly, the socio-cultural context of the house, including information on kinship, descent, political organization and religion and cosmology. In this regard, Waterson examines a range of socio-cultural features of the region in comparative perspective by using the institution of the house as a focus. Yet, the book only approximates a general text, given that it is not intended to provide comprehensive information on all of the key features of South-East Asian cultures, the transformations which have taken place in the region in the modern period and the ways in which anthropologists have attempted to comprehend and describe these.

Grant Evans's substantial edited volume is a rather different sort of introduction to those which we have just considered. It contains a considerable amount of material on South-East Asia, no doubt because the majority of the contributors have solely or primarily South-East Asian expertise. However, it is a volume which covers the whole of Asia, from South through South-East to East Asia, and takes ethnographic illustrations particularly from India, China and Japan. Where it coincides with our present interests is that it is organized thematically, gives due attention to concepts and methods in anthropology and is concerned with current political, economic and cultural issues facing Asian communities. It has background chapters on archaeology, early history, languages and kinship and descent, but also considers debates in economic anthropology; analyses of social inequality, class, caste and status; anthropological approaches to state formations, ethnicity, gender, cosmology and urbanization; and the relations between anthropology, development and modernity. Despite the temptation to search for Asia-wide uniformities in an introductory text of this kind, Evans points out that 'Asia' is above all a Western creation, a product of Western perceptions of the 'other', a result of the European depiction and classification of other cultures, values and mentalities as radically different from the West. The construction of 'Asia' arose in the context of European contact and then the political and economic dominance of Asian populations and lands. These perceptions, now popularly embraced by the term 'Orientalism', were also intertwined with notions of biological and cultural evolution, categorizations based on race, commitments to economic progress and development and the values of liberal democracy in the context of Western nation–states, and the world-view associated with rational scientific enquiry and organization based on the central role of science and technology in society. Asian peoples and cultures were therefore contrasted with Western ones as less civilized and developed, and more mystical, spiritual and despotic. We shall see in Chapter 1 of this book how South-East Asia, a subregion of the Western construct 'Asia', has also been 'created', and the contribution of the anthropological imagination to this process of construction. Finally, Evans, though fully acknowledging the importance that anthropology attaches to cross-cultural comparison, warns that the 'use of the term Asia can be extremely misleading if it is used to denote some sort of cultural uniformity throughout the geographic area' (1993: 6). Instead he points to the diversity and complexity of Asian societies and cultures. The same warning must in turn apply to the subregion of South-East Asia, as we shall see in Chapter 1.

Map 1 South-East Asia in Asia

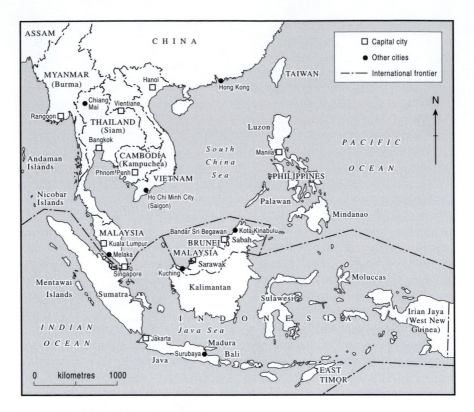

Map 2 South-East Asia: political divisions

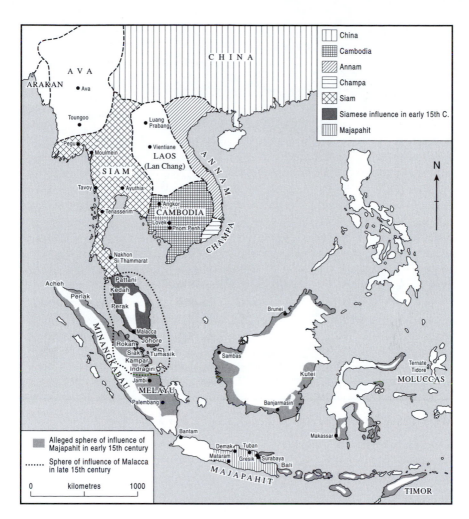

Map 3 South-East Asia: political divisions, fifteenth century AD

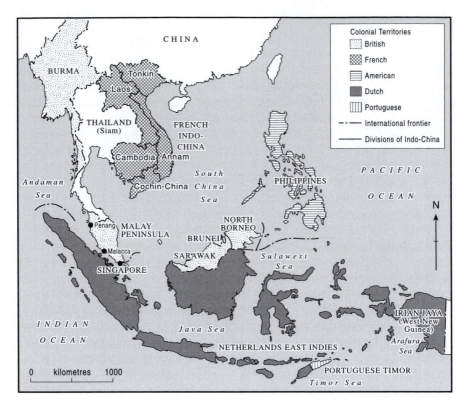

Map 4 Colonial South-East Asia on the eve of the Second World War

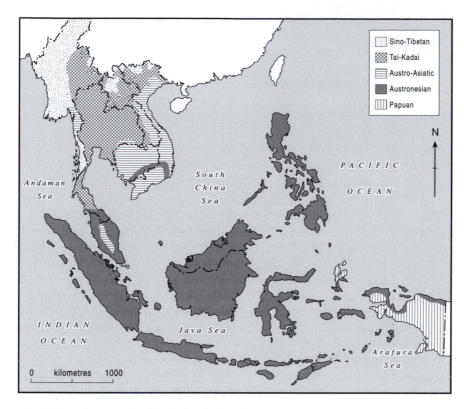

Map 5 Main language families in South-East Asia

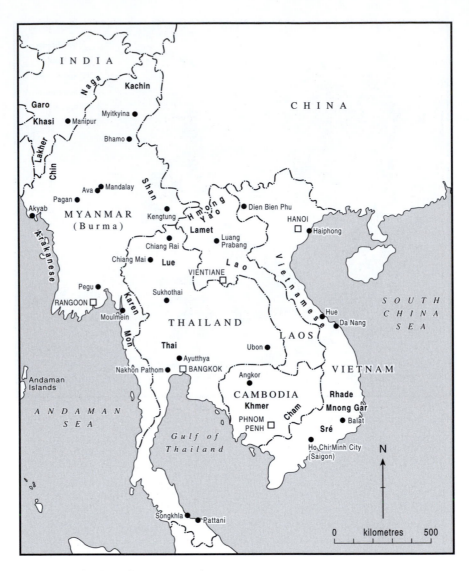

Map 6 Mainland South-East Asia: ethnic groups

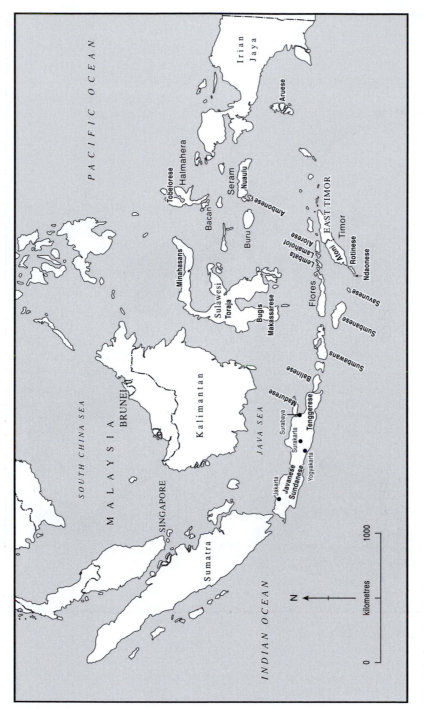

Map 7 Indonesia: ethnic groups

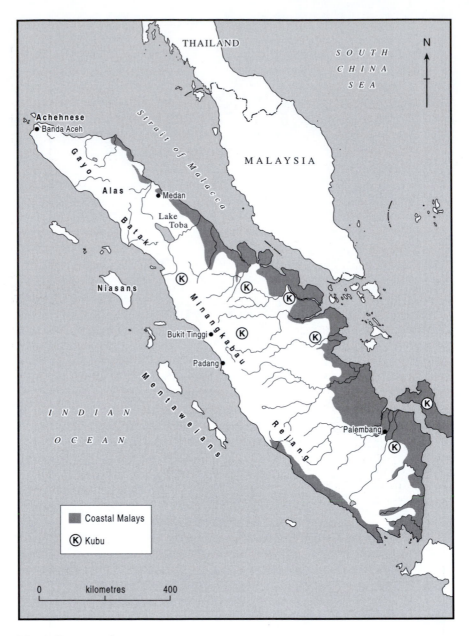

Map 8 Sumatra: ethnic groups

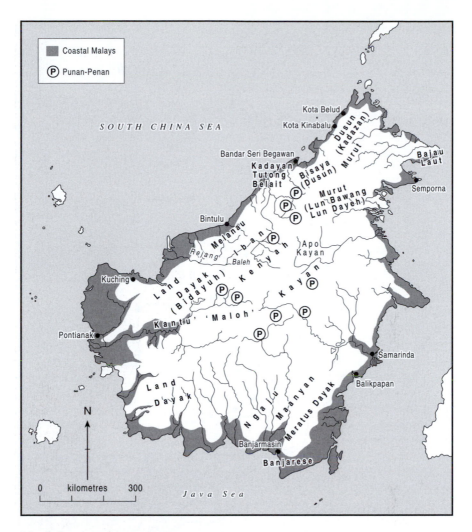

Map 9 Borneo: ethnic groups

Map 10 Peninsular Malaysia: ethnic groups

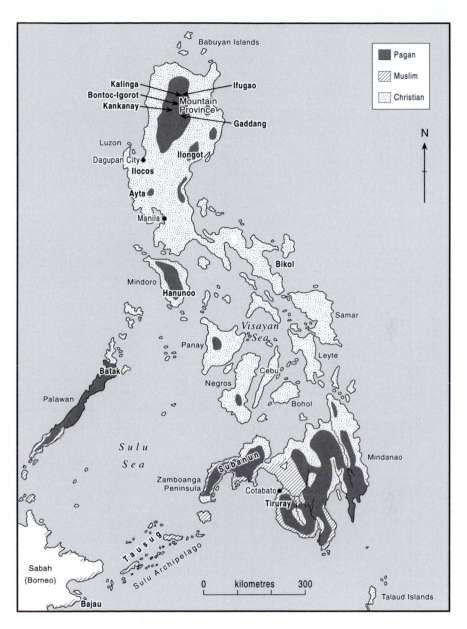

Map 11 The Philippines: ethnic groups

1

SOUTH-EAST ASIA

A field of anthropological enquiry?

In this introductory chapter we devote some attention to the reasons which have been deployed for denying South-East Asia an identity, which enables us to say something about the perspectives of anthropologists and of scholars from other academic disciplines. We also consider the arguments which have been mustered to endow South-East Asia with a positive status equivalent to the neighbouring continental land-masses of China and India.

Introduction

An anthropology of South-East Asia[1] requires us to give some consideration to the problems of defining the region and whether or not it makes sense to delimit this Asian part of the globe for anthropological enquiry and analysis. An immediate and obvious answer is that because several scholars before us have decided to address issues of social and cultural life, change and development in regional terms, and, like Burling in *Hill Farms and Padi Fields* ([1965] 1992), have claimed that South-East Asian communities do demonstrate certain region-wide cultural themes, then we can also safely adopt the same regional parameters. Yet we should be aware of the problems occasioned by taking on this area perspective for three major reasons. First, the distribution of societies and cultures does not map neatly on to the ten nation–states which are usually considered to comprise South-East Asia nor do classifications based on different cultural criteria such as religion or language coincide neatly one with another. Second, the region contains considerable social and cultural diversity so much so that there are always exceptions to certain general cultural themes. Third, the countries of South-East Asia have been subject to a long period of transformation and more recent rapid changes which have served to connect them as 'developing countries' or 'newly-industrializing economies' to wider political, economic and socio-cultural currents outside the region, particularly within the western Pacific rim. However, though we accept that it is by no means straightforward to define South-East Asia either in anthropological terms or from the perspectives of other scholarly disciplines, we have decided, for the purposes of our introductory comments on the anthropological literature, to

1

consider it as a unit separate from China and Japan to the north (usually considered along with the two Koreas, Taiwan, Macau and Hong Kong, under the umbrella of East Asia), India to the west (which along with Sri Lanka, Pakistan, Bangladesh, Nepal, Bhutan and the Maldives comprises South Asia), the Australasian continent to the south, and the Pacific island groups of Melanesia, Micronesia and Polynesia further east (see Map 1).

The South-East Asian region

So let us attempt to answer the question: What is South-East Asia? During the past 50 years or so since the end of the Second World War the answer to this question has apparently become rather more clear, even if there is still debate about some of the bases of the definition of South-East Asia as a geo-political, economic and socio-cultural area in its own right and about its place in the wider Asian region. In both scholarly and popular texts on South-East Asia it is now generally agreed that the region comprises the mainland states of Myanmar (Burma), Thailand (Siam), Laos, Cambodia (Kampuchea) and Vietnam, and the island or maritime countries of Malaysia, Singapore, Negara Brunei Darussalam, Indonesia and the Philippines. East Timor, a former Portuguese colony which was annexed and incorporated into Indonesia in 1976, has recently been established as a separate state (see Map 2). The South-East Asian region is therefore distinguished from the Indian subcontinent to the west and from the Chinese mainland to the north. The concept of a South-East Asia, comprising independent but interrelated nation–states, is given greater salience with the undoubted success of the Association of Southeast Asian Nations (or ASEAN). This regional organization was formed in 1967 by the Kingdom of Thailand, the Republics of the Philippines, Indonesia and Singapore and the Federation of Malaysia primarily to promote economic cooperation among its member states. The Sultanate of Brunei joined in 1984 and the Socialist Republic of Vietnam in 1996. The People's Democratic Republic of Laos and Myanmar (formerly the Socialist Republic of the Union of Burma) were admitted in 1997, and, Cambodia (formerly the People's Republic of Kampuchea) most recently in 1998. The current ASEAN leaders, though some more strongly than others, hold the conviction that an organization comprising all ten South-East Asian countries makes sense for a variety of economic, political, strategic and cultural reasons.

Anthony Reid, the distinguished historian of the region, has recently elaborated on the perspectives of ASEAN leaders in terms of what he calls a 'saucer model' of indigenous identity (1999: 7–23). He suggests that during the past 30 years a clear pattern has emerged in the context of such organizations as ASEAN of what he calls the 'low centre' of South-East Asia, that is Singapore and Malaysia, and to some extent Brunei and Thailand at the focal regional communications point and meeting place of the Straits of Malacca (Melaka). These states have pressed positively for the recognition and institutionalization of an indigenous South-East Asian identity. There is then the 'high periphery'

2

of Myanmar, Vietnam (Laos and Cambodia), and to some extent the Philippines and Indonesia, which have decided that they did not wish to be mere 'appendages of their larger and more threatening neighbours' (that is, India, China and the USA) and therefore South-East Asia 'became a kind of default option' for them (ibid.: 7). Thus for Reid, although there are differing local perceptions of regionalism and 'there is no dominant centre or common civilizational heritage' on which to base claims to 'Southeast Asianness', there is nevertheless an 'indigenous origin of the Southeast Asian idea' (ibid.: 8, 19). However, we should note that this indigenous conception of the region is a very recent phenomenon, it has emerged from a regional politico-economic organization and from strategic considerations, and that it is an historian who has firmly argued the case.

Diversity and external influences: the lack of definition

In his widely read introductory history of the region, Milton Osborne commences his survey by pondering the status of South-East Asia as a region (1985: 1–15). He notes that up until the Second World War the term 'South-East Asia' was not in general use, though, as Emmerson (1984: 5–6) and Reid (1999: 10) remind us, the concept 'Südostasien' was relatively commonly employed in German-language ethnological scholarship from the nineteenth century. Yet despite its earlier use by such Austrian ethnologists as Robert von Heine-Geldern (1923) (see Chapter 2), and its increasing occurrence in publications by European, American and Asian writers in the 1920s and 1930s, in a very real sense, the region did not exist until the 1940s as a distinguishable entity in the eyes of most scholars of Asia, nor was it thought about in these more general terms by local populations. What was emphasized instead was the cultural diversity and the geographical and political fragmentation of the area, and the fact that it had been subject to a variety of external influences over a very long period of time. The most important of these from early in the first millennium AD came from India and China, from the sixteenth century onwards Western Europe, and from the early twentieth century the USA. There were also long-established commercial and cultural contacts with the Middle East and the spread of Islam to the Malay–Indonesian world via India from the early centuries of the second millennium, as well as the Japanese occupation of South-East Asia during the Pacific War and the subsequent strong Japanese industrial and commercial penetration of the region over the past three decades. For all these reasons South-East Asia has been seen as a geographical bundle of countries, exhibiting only a spurious unity. The well-known geographer of Asia, the late Professor Charles Fisher, also referred to it as 'the Balkans of the Orient' (1962, 1964), a term which reflected the region's ethnic and socio-cultural complexity, its potential political fragility, its geographical fragmentation and its character as a meeting point of different external powers and cultures. More recently Charles Keyes, in rethinking the status of South-East Asian Studies in the USA, has remarked that 'there is no actual geo-political reality which constitutes Southeast Asia' (1992: 9), nor does it 'evoke, even for those who identify themselves as specialists in this area of the world, one of the great historic cultural traditions' (ibid.: 10). Indeed, Keyes and James Scott (1992: 2) have suggested that it is the very cultural differentiation and syncretism of the region, and long-standing cultural interactions through trade, migrations and political linkages which have proved such an attractive field of study for American cultural anthropologists.

Early Western perceptions

Until the 1940s various Western writers and observers often used the term 'Further India', 'Greater India', 'L'Inde extérieure' or 'Hinterindien' for those territories beyond the Bay of Bengal and the Indian Ocean, implying that they were merely an eastward cultural extension of the Indian subcontinent. Others referred to the countries of South-East Asia as the 'Far Eastern Tropics', suggesting that they comprised the southern tropical margins of China and other East Asian countries. Thus, in earlier texts on the region there are frequent references to the Indianized (or Hinduized) and Sinicized features of South-East Asian societies and cultures. To further emphasize the perceived significance of Indian and Chinese cultural influences and particularly the absorption of religions, modes of statecraft, material culture, literature and written scripts, South-East Asia was also sometimes designated as 'Indochina', though this term came to be firmly attached collectively to the French colonial dependencies of Vietnam, Cambodia and Laos. Among geographers another popular term was 'Monsoon Asia', which served to draw attention to the fact that the monsoon cycle of winds and rains is a dominant natural feature of the region, though, of course, not exclusive to it (Fisher, 1964: 3ff.).

Western scholarship therefore tended to view South-East Asia from the perspective of either India or China or both. What is more, the fact that various European powers and later the United States had colonial interests in specific parts of the region tended to constrain them from studying and attempting to understand South-East Asia as a whole (see Map 4). British writers, for example, commonly concentrated their attentions on their South-East Asian dependencies of Burma, the Malay States, the Straits Settlements (Singapore, Penang [Pulau Pinang] and Malacca [Melaka]) and the northern Borneo territories (including Brunei), and perceived these as an adjunct of the British Indian Empire and as part of the Indian Ocean strategic theatre. Indeed, until 1937 Burma was incorporated as a province of British India and had been the destination for substantial migrations of Indian citizens, particularly to the colonial capital Rangoon and the lower Irrawaddy Delta; the Straits Settlements had also been administered by the British Indian government until 1867.

Dutch scholars focused almost exclusively on their 'jewel in the crown' – the Netherlands East Indies or Indonesia – a vast territory stretching some 2,500

4

miles along the equator from Sumatra in the west to western New Guinea (Irian Jaya or West Papua) in the east. However, like the British, the Dutch also viewed their dependencies from an Indian Ocean perspective. Both colonial powers had established comparatively early on in their mercantile histories East India companies which traded with South-East Asia via India.

The French governed their colonies and protectorates as direct extensions of France overseas, hence the name for the French empire, 'la France d'outre-mer'. Thus, Vietnam, Laos and Cambodia were tied closely to the metropolitan country and its economy in the context of France's colonial policy of assimilation and later association. Again, as with British- and Dutch-administered territories the links with France were mainly westwards across the Indian Ocean. Partly as a consequence of Anglo-French rivalry in mainland South-East Asia in the nineteenth century, the Kingdom of Siam was left as a politically neutral buffer zone between British India and Burma to the west and French Indochina to the east. Nevertheless, Siam too was progressively drawn into a global economy dominated by Britain from the second half of the nineteenth century.

The Philippines is altogether a different case. Governed by the Spanish for well over 300 years from the latter part of the sixteenth century, the islands were linked closely to the Spanish American Empire, particularly Mexico, across the Pacific Ocean. Following the loss to Spain of its American colonies from the early part of the nineteenth century, the links between the Philippines and the metropolitan power were for a time re-routed via the Indian Ocean. But the orientation to the Americas was strengthened again when the USA took over the administration of the islands from Spain following the Spanish-American War in 1898. Unlike other territories in the region, the Philippines was incorporated decisively as an outlier of a wider trans-Pacific American economy and polity, and with the majority of its population embracing the Roman Catholic faith and the widespread use of American English, the Philippines has until recently been seen to be marginal to the South-East Asian region proper.

Another mercantile colonial power – Portugal – retained a vestige of its former sea-borne empire in South-East Asia until 1975 in the shape of the eastern part of the remote island of Timor. It was then annexed by military action and occupation into the Republic of Indonesia, only recently to be given its independence from Indonesia under the auspices of the United Nations. Prior to the decisive British and Dutch intervention in the region from the seventeenth century, Portugal had been a major commercial force in the Malay and Indonesian islands.

Thus, different parts of the region (and some for much longer periods than others) became part of the histories and perceptions of particular colonial powers, and the native elites of these dependencies were schooled in the relevant metropolitan language – English, French, Dutch, Spanish or Portuguese. Their world-views too were shaped to some extent by European concepts and preoccupations, and privileged members of native societies also had the opportunity to study at institutions of higher education in Europe or at colonial academies. Importantly, it was the exposure to Western political and social philosophies from the early part of the twentieth century that provided the rationale and impetus for the creation of indigenous political movements which ultimately demanded their independence from colonial rule and their right to social and cultural equality and autonomy.

It was during this period of late colonialism that we find the first real evidence of reflection and debate about the nature of South-East Asian societies and political systems, both in the writings of Western observers and of indigenous scholars, especially those who led nationalist movements. These writings usually focused on a particular colonial dependency rather than the region as a whole, and they began to concentrate on the effects of the interaction between Western and Eastern socio-cultural, economic and political systems. What is more there have been very few concepts which have managed to enjoy a lasting influence on the course of sociological and anthropological discussion and analysis after the Second World War (but see Evers, 1980a, 1980b). One such concept was that of social and economic dualism formulated by the Dutch scholar and colonial administrator, J.H. Boeke, in a doctoral dissertation submitted in 1910 (and see Boeke, 1953). Boeke observed that the Euro-American-dominated expanding world economy had brought great material benefit to the West, but at the expense of the impoverishment of rural communities in such places as the Netherlands East Indies (Evers, 1980b: 2–3). He saw colonial capitalism as socially and economically 'destructive' to native societies, though in his view there were also social and cultural reasons internal to Oriental peasant communities which contributed to their lack of capacity to respond to Western capitalism. Therefore, for Boeke colonial society was sharply divided between a modern, European-dominated capitalist sector and a traditional, Oriental subsistence sector, each characterized by a different set of economic and cultural values and features. We shall examine this concept of a dual society in Chapters 2 and 3 of this volume.

Another influential paradigm was that of pluralism or plural society presented by J.S. Furnivall, a British scholar and administrator, who produced detailed and insightful studies of the political economy of British Burma and the Netherlands East Indies (1939, 1956). He drew attention to the significance of the overseas Chinese and Indian trading communities in South-East Asian colonial society which functioned as economic intermediaries between the European and native populations. In particular, the developing urban areas or colonial entrepôts of the region like Singapore, Batavia (Jakarta), Rangoon and Saigon (Ho Chi Minh City) came to be increasingly dominated by Asian immigrants and Europeans. Furnivall's conception of a distinctive type of colonial system in which different ethnic groups comprise distinct 'economic castes' and keep to their own socio-cultural worlds, meeting only in the market-place, has been subject to detailed scrutiny, criticism and refinement in later studies of ethnicity in South-East Asia. Yet he, like Boeke, saw colonial society as sharply divided, although for Furnivall 'the conflict between rival economic interests tends to be exacerbated by racial diversity' (in Evers, 1980a: 88). We shall return to concepts of pluralism and ethnicity in Chapters 2 and 6.

Thus, the impact of European colonialism on native societies and cultures began to generate, prior to the Second World War, scholarly interest in the kinds of social transformations which had been taking place in the region and the consequences of these for the welfare of the local populations. The Dutch sociologist, Wim Wertheim, provides an excellent sociological overview of these processes and focuses especially on the utility of concepts from the great social philosophers Karl Marx and Max Weber in understanding the complexities of historical change in the region. He notes that the 'impact of nineteenth-century and early twentieth-century Western capitalism on South-East Asian societies was profound and lasting' (1980: 14), but it was not until the introduction and rapid expansion of large-scale Western-dominated cash-crop agriculture from the late eighteenth century that fundamental changes in local ways of life began to be set in motion. Osborne too notes that the 'eighteenth century was ... the last century in which the traditional world of Southeast Asia was dominant, if not universal' (1985: 38). Thereafter, the commoditization of land, labour and other resources and the expansion of a market economy, accompanied by increased European political, territorial and administrative control, transformed local social and cultural organization, and integrated even the remotest South-East Asian communities into a global economic and political system.

Indian and Chinese influence

Yet this colonial experience, which was enormously significant in its social impact and served to divide South-East Asia into separate political and cultural areas, was merely the later phase of a long period of contact with and influence from outsiders. This is hardly surprising given the fact that South-East Asia is a geo-politically fragmented, 'low pressure' area (Du Bois, 1964: 28), located at a crossroads between the Indian and Pacific Oceans and between the relatively heavily populated and solid continental landmasses of India and mainland China. In geographical terms mainland South-East Asia is cross-cut by rivers and mountain ranges, and the maritime regions comprise a scatter of islands, some large like Borneo and Sumatra, some small like Bali and Nias. In other words, South-East Asia has served as something of a vacuum to be filled by outside cultures and populations, and it has been torn, as it were, between the competing attentions of visitors from India, the Middle East and Europe to the west, the Americas to the east, and China and later Japan to the north.

Long ago South-East Asia was the focus of Indian and Chinese maritime trade – it was a land of gold, silver and exotic tropical forest produce; these commercial relations extending across the great sea routes between India and China began to increase in intensity and scale during the early part of the first millennium AD and they were by no means one way. South-East Asians were excellent mariners and they found their way not only to China and India, but also to Madagascar off the east coast of Africa. Furthermore, aside from China's maritime trade and tributary relations with its southern neighbours, which waxed and waned depending on its domestic political, military and economic circumstances, China also had intimate land contacts with the northern areas of Vietnam. The Sino-Vietnamese state of Nam Viet or Nan Yueh, located in the Red River Delta, was incorporated as a province of the Han Chinese empire in 111 BC and remained as an administrative unit of China for a whole millennium until AD 939. During that time the lowland Vietnamese communities concentrated in the northern regions of what is now Vietnam were open to relatively intense processes of Sinicization, involving the introduction of the Chinese classics, ideographs, Confucian principles and the mandarinate, and, from the fifth century AD, Mahayana Buddhism was also introduced to Vietnam via China by Chinese scholars and preachers. The Vietnamese kingdom of Dai Viet was established free from the Chinese yoke from AD 939, but despite its independence it subsequently adopted the Chinese administrative model of hierarchical bureaucracy. The Vietnamese ruler was conceived of as the 'Son of Heaven' who mediated between the earthly realm and the spiritual world. As Osborne has said, the bureaucracy was

> a pyramid with the ruler at the apex and with clearly defined links established between that apex and the lowest officials in the provinces who formed the base of this administration. The law was a written code, detailed in form and complete with learned commentaries. Strict rules covered the amount of authority possessed by each grade of official and the qualifications for each grade.
>
> (1985: 39–40)

In the rest of South-East Asia, with the exception of the Philippines and the remote highlands, the influence of Indian culture was readily apparent, though India never dominated the region politically nor occupied territories there. During the first millennium AD various kingdoms in the lowland areas of both mainland and island South-East Asia adopted certain Hindu-Buddhist precepts and Indian court culture; it is clear that the ruling groups of already established South-East Asian polities invited Indian Brahmins, knowledgeable in sacred lore, cosmology, ritual and legal and administrative procedures, to their courts as priests, advisers and astrologers. In particular, Indian cosmology and religion were used to legitimize and symbolize the position, status and rule of local monarchs, by presenting the latter as divine or at least as the mediators between the universe and the earthly world, in other words as a reincarnation of a Hindu deity or as a future Buddha (Heine-Geldern, 1963: 7–11). Again Osborne, in contrasting the Vietnamese political system with the Indianized polities, points out that in the latter the 'pattern of official relationships was in many ways much more complex, in part because it was a pattern lacking the clearly defined lines of authority that were so much part of the Vietnamese system' (1985: 40). Instead of a pyramid of authority, the Indianized systems were characterized by Osborne in terms of a series of concentric circles:

> it was only at the centre, where the smallest of these concentric circles is located, that the king's power was truly absolute. Beyond that central circle ... it was frequently the case that the king's power diminished in a clear proportion to the distance one moved away from the capital.
>
> (ibid.: 40)

In the first millennium AD and the first few hundred years of the second millennium many major Hindu and Mahayana Buddhist kingdoms emerged in South-East Asia such as Srivijaya in the Palembang region of Sumatra, Majapahit in east-central Java, Angkor in central Cambodia, Pagan in interior Burma, and Champa in central and south Vietnam. Remarkable monuments such as Borobodur in Java, the Vishnu temple of Angkor Wat and the Khmer Buddhist temple, the Bayon, at Angkor Thom in Cambodia were constructed, and provided evidence of substantial and powerful states capable of mobilizing large numbers of people to erect royal and religious buildings to the glory of the ruler. Most of the states of island South-East Asia, with the partial exception of those in east-central Java, were oriented primarily to sea-borne trade, while the majority of those of the mainland depended significantly, though not exclusively, on irrigated wet rice cultivation on the vast lowland plains.

Subsequently these states gave way to new dynasties and kingdoms, which were again adopting religious concepts, symbols and political structures from India, and, for much of the island world of South-East Asia, from the Middle East via India (see Map 3). Theravada or Hinayana Buddhism was spread from Ceylon (Sri Lanka) and adopted by the lowland Mons and Burmans, particularly from the eleventh century. Important Theravada Buddhist states were therefore established in central and southern Burma, and later by Tai-speaking peoples in Thailand and Laos and by the Khmers of Cambodia. In island South-East Asia and southern Vietnam Islam began to expand along the trade routes, especially in the context of India–China commercial relations and the Indonesian spice trade from the tenth century. However, it was the founding of the Muslim sultanate of Malacca in the southern Malay Peninsula and its control of the spice trade which led to the rapid dissemination and consolidation of Islam throughout the Malay–Indonesian world and even into the southern Philippines. Both Theravada Buddhism and Islam gave expression to more egalitarian socio-religious principles and they penetrated more decisively to the rural peasantry in contrast to the relatively hierarchical, court-oriented political systems of the earlier Hindu and Mahayana Buddhist states.

Various sociological–anthropological studies have attempted to describe and analyse the socio-political structures and underlying organizational principles of these indigenous states. Probably it was the work of the Dutch historian, Jacob van Leur, on these traditional states which has had a lasting influence (1955). Van Leur conceived of the empires founded primarily on intensive irrigated rice cultivation and the organization and management of hydraulic works as 'patrimonial bureaucracies', using a concept first developed by Max Weber (ibid.: 56–57). He argued that political control, exercised through an administrative bureaucracy, and expressed in the divine, semi-divine or sacred ruler, depended principally on the mobilization of village labour and the extraction of surplus agricultural products, particularly rice. However, the Indianized land-based states were not highly centralized units; rulers and their retinues depended on various political, administrative, legal and cultural practices to counter the 'ever-threatening centrifugal tendencies' (Wertheim, 1980: 9). A well-known Dutch sociologist, Bertram Schrieke, also undertook detailed studies of the organization of traditional patrimonial Javanese polities and the nature of statecraft in decentralized systems of personal rule based on patron–client relations and personal entourages (1955–1957). We shall take up this theme again a little later in our discussion of the work of O.W. Wolters.

A competing sociological concept which has been used to understand traditional Oriental state structures is that based on Karl Marx's notion of an 'Asiatic mode of production' (Marx, 1964), though this has been subject to detailed criticism (see, for example, Christie, 1985). Marx's characterization of these states as relatively stable structurally, highly centralized politically, comprising closed village communities, and based on 'a lack of private ownership of land and the complete subjection of the individual peasant to village authority' now seems untenable, given our increased knowledge of these systems, though superficially his model probably has more relevance to the Chinese-influenced Vietnamese state than to the Indianized polities (Wertheim, 1980: 9). In contrast to Marx's unitary model of a mode of production, it is now accepted that there were variations in the structure of these states; they were also subject to changes generated by both internal contradictions and conflicts as well as external socio-cultural, economic and political forces. This was even more so for the so-called 'harbour principalities', also described and analysed in Weberian terms by van Leur (1955), which were not based on hydraulic agriculture but on 'sea trade and international traffic' as well as the control of hinterland commerce; the orientation of these riparian states to the outside world for purposes of trade 'generated a more cosmopolitan atmosphere and a greater receptivity to foreign cultural influences' (Wertheim, 1980: 11). Although the role of the royal aristocracy and the court was considerable, these mercantile states comprised a relatively mobile, ethnically mixed population of small traders and 'sea nomads', artisans and large-scale merchants. Rather than the control of land and villagers exercised by the hydraulic states of the region like Cambodian Angkor, the maritime states such as Srivijaya in southern Sumatra depended on the control of strategic port-centres and sea routes.

Thus, on the eve of European intervention in South-East Asia from the early sixteenth century with the Spanish and Portuguese in the vanguard, there were numerous indigenous states, both large and small, fragmented and scattered throughout the mainland and island regions. Some of these were very powerful, incorporating other states as their clients and tribute-payers, though the political and economic fortunes of a given state obviously waxed and waned considerably over time (Winzeler, 1976: 26). With the exception of the Hindu Balinese and the Filipinos of the northern two-thirds of the Philippines who also continued to follow their village-based folk religions, Muslim communities and sultanates controlled major coastal regions of the archipelago; in the mainland lowlands of Burma, Thailand, Laos and Cambodia, apart from the Sinicized Mahayana Buddhist state in north Vietnam, Theravada Buddhist polities held sway. Finally, away from the main trade routes and rice-bowl areas, animist hill peoples practised forest-based agriculture, horticulture and hunting–gathering; in some cases these marginal communities were also linked to the large states through trade and tribute. But as Wertheim notes the 'most striking feature of these tribal peoples ... is that they were generally not integrated into larger political units' (1980: 10). It is no surprise then that outside observers were impressed by the diversity of South-East Asian societies and cultures, their cultural debt to India and China, and the lack of wider political unity. External influences from India, China and the Middle East, in particular, also served to sharpen the distinctions between the upland and lowland communities of the region, and served to separate Sinicized northern Vietnam from the rest of the Theravada Buddhist mainland states, and these in turn from the Muslim-dominated archipelago.

Western influence: increasing ethnic diversity

The era of European involvement in the affairs of South-East Asia began in earnest with the Portuguese conquest of the Muslim spice emporium of Malacca in 1511, situated at a key strategic point on the Malay Peninsula overlooking the Straits of Malacca. However, it was to be well into the nineteenth century before the European powers began significantly to take over and administer territories and populations. Their main concern up until then had been to control strategic port-centres and trade routes like the Malay–Indonesian harbour principalities before them, though from the seventeenth century the Spanish in the Philippines and the Dutch in Java did begin to establish a more substantial territorial and administrative presence.

Aside from the gradual introduction of European cultural elements into South-East Asia, seen most dramatically in the Spanish-directed conversion of the majority of lowland Filipinos outside the Muslim south to Catholicism, the Western presence contributed to another aspect of cultural diversity. The European colonial powers encouraged and facilitated Chinese and Indian migration to the region. Even prior to European intervention South-East Asia had received visits from Indian and Chinese traders, adventurers, scholars and religious travellers, and some had settled in the region in small numbers; but as a favourable environment under the Western powers was established for the conduct of trade, commerce and economic production, migration from southern China especially, but also from India, increased. From the nineteenth century, following the establishment of colonial dependencies, this physical movement into the region to the centres of economic activity became a flood. The Chinese settled in coastal ports, in the tin- and gold-mining areas from southern Burma through the western Malay Peninsula and the northern Indonesian islands to western Borneo, and in centres of commercial crop production such as the large rice-growing areas of the plains of mainland South-East Asia around Bangkok, Phnom Penh, Hanoi and Saigon. The Indians were concentrated mainly in the British-administered territories, especially as traders, shopkeepers and money-lenders in the urban areas, and as labourers in the rice-bowl of lowland Burma and the rubber plantation belt of western Malaya.

This cultural and ethnic complexity continues to this day. The large nation–states of Indonesia and the Philippines, for example, comprise a diversity of ethnic groups, spread over numerous islands and large distances, while Malaysia is a classic example of a plural society with its three main ethnic groupings of Malays, Indians and Chinese and a substantial minority of non-Muslim indigenes including the Dayaks of the Malaysian Borneo states of Sarawak and Sabah. Even the small city state of Singapore, over three-quarters of whose population comprises ethnic Chinese, has significant minorities of Malays and Indians; and in Vietnam, though by far the largest community of citizens comprises ethnic Vietnamese, there are also considerable numbers of Chinese as well as indigenous hill populations, popularly called by the French term 'montagnards'.

South-East Asia's geographical openness and fragmentation, its cultural and ethnic diversity with no dominant cultural tradition, and the variety of external influences to which the region has been subject over a long period of time resulted in it being perceived by Western observers and writers, and indeed by local residents, as a loose bundle of territories and peoples with no common defining features.

The creation of South-East Asia

Political and strategic issues

What was it then which changed these perceptions and led to the general acceptance of the term 'South-East Asia' to define a specific part of Asia? We should note that the main impetus for this recognition came not from anthropologists or ethnologists, although they certainly contributed to the efforts to give shape and content to this emerging South-East Asian identity. The watershed was the Pacific War and the Japanese occupation of the region, or in Japanese terms, the 'southern resources area' of their 'Greater East Asia Co-prosperity Sphere'. From a strategic and military standpoint, both from a Western and a Japanese perspective, it became clear that the territories surrounding the South China Sea and at the meeting point between the Indian and Pacific Oceans constituted a unit separate from India and China. Although the creation in 1943 of Admiral Lord Louis Mountbatten's allied South-East Asia Command (SEAC), which was based in Sri Lanka during the Second World War, was certainly not the first occasion when the term 'South-East Asia' was used, it did serve to raise the visibility of the area in official and scholarly circles (Emmerson, 1984: 5–9; Smith, 1986: 7ff.; Reid, 1999: 9–11). However, it should be noted that Mountbatten's Command did not cover precisely the area which subsequently came to be called 'South-East Asia'; it excluded the Philippines, for example, and included Sri Lanka.

After the war various Western governments, and particularly the USA, accepted the need to understand the region in its own right, and further impetus was given to this emerging regional interest with the foundation in Europe and America of university departments, programmes and centres specializing in South-East Asian Studies (Mohd. Halib and Huxley, 1996: 1–9). In a recent reflective paper on the development of South-East Asian Studies, Ruth McVey gives special emphasis to the role of America in the 'creation' of Southeast Asia as a concept and the promotion of post-war regional scholarship (1995). For the USA the defeat of the Japanese signalled 'the liberation of the Southeast Asia peoples' and the beginning of their journey on the road to 'national self-realization' and 'progress to modernity' (ibid.). These two central concepts of nation-building and modernization were to form the core of modernization theory, the dominant American post-war social science paradigm in the analysis of South-East Asia, which embraced the disciplines of politics, economics, sociology and psychology in particular.

Post-war decolonization and the creation of independent nation–states, accompanied by the increased need to promote social and economic development in the former colonial dependencies, and to counter the perceived threat posed by the rise of Third World socialist and communist movements and governments, resulted in Western nations, particularly the USA with its perceptions of its national security interests, developing a broader and more general view of South-East Asia as a region. For Britain, for example, the need to sustain its economic presence in Malaya, Singapore and Brunei, and further afield in Hong Kong, after the independence of India and Pakistan, meant that it had to think much more in regional terms. South-East Asia assumed even greater strategic importance during the Cold War, after the emergence of a mainland Chinese communist government, the defeat of the French by the Vietnamese communists at Dien Bien Phu in 1954, the British struggle against communist insurgency in Malaya in the 1950s, and the increasing involvement of the Americans in the Vietnam War in the 1960s. The USA, in its attempts to encircle and thus contain the expansion of Asian communism, came to see the destinies of the South-East Asian countries as interlinked. What is more, the region was rich in such natural resources as oil, tin and timber, and a vital source of industrial raw materials including natural rubber. After all, it was the promise of profit and the desire to control resources which had first attracted the Western powers and then Japan to South-East Asia.

South-East Asia as a socio-cultural area?

Nevertheless, these larger political, economic and strategic considerations which came to the fore in the mid-twentieth century should not cause us to assume that South-East Asia was merely constructed and 'imagined', to use Benedict Anderson's term (1991), by America and Western Europe. Ananda Rajah, though critical of the attempts to identify the common criteria which define South-East Asia as a region, suggests that 'having been so constructed, it nevertheless possesses a reality for scholars and people in the region alike' (1999: 42).

Despite differences among scholars in the attempts to put cultural flesh on the concept of South-East Asian identity, there are certainly various social and cultural elements which serve to unite large parts of the region and distinguish them from China and India, although they do not constitute general unifying features of all ten South-East Asian nation–states nor do they establish clear and unambiguous boundaries. Despite outside influences these elements have shown a remarkable resilience and adaptability, and they demonstrate that South-East Asia is by no means a pale acculturated imitation of India and China. In this connection historians and archaeologists, and to a lesser extent anthropologists, have mustered evidence to show that South-East Asians did not simply absorb outside cultural traits. They actively sought elements of Indian and Chinese culture for their own purposes; they selected and adapted them, and in the process transformed them into something distinctively South-East Asian. For example, despite the long period of Indian influence, South-East Asian communities never adopted the Hindu caste system, while Hindu-Buddhist art and architecture were infused with South-East Asian styles and aesthetic values, just as religious values and practices were accommodated to pre-existing beliefs and rituals. Furthermore, archaeological research in the 1960s and 1970s began to reveal that 'agriculture and metallurgy appeared in Southeast Asia much earlier than had previously been supposed' (Miksic, 1995: 47). In other words, the region was not merely a marginal backwater which had received technological innovations from neighbouring areas. It was itself an area of independent invention and development, and recent research in archaeology and anthropology suggests that there were cultural themes which were relatively widespread in the region in pre- and protohistory up to the beginning of the first millennium AD, when Indian influences began to be apparent.

In linguistic terms large numbers of people in island South-East Asia are speakers of Austronesian languages (see Map 5). This non-tonal language family is said to have originated from a Taiwanese source about six thousand years ago, and ultimately from southern China (Bellwood, 1985). Austronesian speakers then spread over the Malay–Indonesian archipelago from about 3000 BC onwards. They also populated the Pacific Islands commencing about 3,000 years ago; they found their way to central and southern Vietnam, which settlement eventually gave rise to the kingdom of Champa, and some travelled across the Indian Ocean to Madagascar off eastern Africa (ibid.). This language family now provides the basis for the national languages of Malaysia, Brunei, Singapore and Indonesia (Malay/Indonesian) and the Philippines (Tagalog). It is also spoken by minority groups in southern Thailand, Vietnam and Cambodia.

In mainland South-East Asia the linguistic patterns are rather more complex, but languages of the Tai-Kadai family are very widely spoken in Thailand, the Shan States of Burma, lowland Laos, southern China, and on the northern fringes of Cambodia, Vietnam and Malaysia. The other major set of mainland languages comprises the Austroasiatic family spoken by the Vietnamese, the Khmers or Cambodians, the Mons of Burma, certain of the hill groups of northern Burma, Assam, Vietnam and Laos, most of the aboriginal groups of the Malayan Peninsula and the Nicobarese. Finally, there is the Sino-Tibetan language family of which Chinese is a member; its speakers comprise the lowland Burmese or Burmans, and various hill peoples in Burma and the neighbouring mainland South-East Asian countries, as well as in northern and north-eastern India, Bangladesh, southern Tibet and Nepal (Prasithrathsint, 1993; Burling, 1965: 162–165).

Although it is still a subject of much dispute amongst linguists, it has been suggested that there might be very remote connections between these four large Asian language families, and particularly between Tai-Kadai and Austronesian. The archaeologist, Peter Bellwood, also suspects that the ancestors of all these four families, who were of Mongoloid physical stock, might have inhabited contiguous areas of southern and central China from the early period of agricultural development about 8,000 years ago (1995). He further suggests that these Neolithic revolutions then led to the expansion of settlement, and, over a very long period of time, the complex movements of populations and cultural traits into other parts of Asia, including the regions to the south. Some thirty-five years ago Burling, though suggesting that some of the 'typological resemblances' among several of the mainland languages are likely to have been the result of contact and exchange, also poses the question 'Could it be that all these languages are, even if only very remotely, related to each other in one great super-family?' (1965: 168).

As with languages, although various other traits do not serve to define all of South-East Asia as a distinguishable category, there are some cultural features which emerged during this early period of linguistic and agricultural development which are nevertheless found very widely in the region. In their forms of social organization South-East Asian peoples generally exhibit differences from those of India and China. A widespread feature of South-East Asian family life is the principle of bilateral or cognatic reckoning of kinship (Burling, 1965; Murdock, 1960b; Wolters, 1999). In other words, ideally the ascription of status is based on kin ties traced equally through both the maternal and paternal sides, or it allows a choice of affiliation between the mother's or the father's kin. Interestingly, Winzeler, in his perceptive analysis of the relations between ecology, culture, social organization and state formation in South-East Asia, also remarks that 'kinship is generally reckoned bilaterally, corporate descent groups are absent, marital residence tends to be bilocal or neolocal, and inherited property tends to be divided equally between males and females and between older and younger siblings' (1976: 628). This form of family and kinship organization also tends to be associated with relative gender equality, and South-East Asian women do indeed play vital active roles and are involved in decision-making in agriculture and trade, as well as in domestic activities (see Chapter 8). However, though cognatic social organization is widely distributed in the region – among most of the majority lowland communities, and among the hill populations of Borneo and the Philippines – there are also sizeable minorities, again mainly in the hill regions of mainland South-East Asia, certain of the main islands of Indonesia such as Sumatra, and in much of eastern Indonesia, organized on the basis of lineal descent and corporate descent groups.

Be that as it may, Wolters, in his heavily nuanced consideration and subsequent reconsideration of the possible ingredients of a regional history of early South-East Asia up to the fifteenth century, also discovers certain 'cultural commonalities' (1999: 11). He cautions that this does not mean that all societies and cultures in South-East Asia possess these or, for those that do, that they have identical characteristics. However, like Burling and others, he draws attention to the importance of cognatic social organization and its association with the comparable status of men and women (ibid.: 17–18). In addition, he notes the widespread occurrence of the politico-cultural institution of 'big men' or as he prefers to call it 'men [and women] of prowess' (ibid.: 18–19). Leadership then is characterized by flexibility, instability and achievement, and the personal qualities of a leader have to be demonstrated and continually renewed; they comprise, among others, skills and accomplishments in negotiation, diplomacy, public oratory and military action, and spiritual powers expressed in supernatural support and favour. Thus, according to Wolters, leaders have to create and sustain personal ties and allegiances among their followers. Wolters further proposes that this form of leadership in early South-East Asia provided a cultural environment conducive to the adoption of Indian, and specifically Hindu elements focused on the devotional and personalized cults of Siva and Vishnu in which a leader or ruler could achieve through 'ascetic practices and the pious cultivation of his faculties of volition and imagination, . . . a close relationship with the god of his affection' (ibid.: 22). These god-like rulers therefore had to concentrate spiritual power, and demonstrate in word and deed that they were fit to occupy their position and be someone to remember and honour after their death.

The organizational and cultural features associated with this kind of leadership comprised patron–clientship, personal entourages, factions and cliques, marriage alliances and tributary and ritual relations with followers, and the need constantly to disseminate knowledge and present evidence of the leader's prowess as well as gather information on behalf of the political centre about local conditions and the opinions of one's subjects. With regard to the conceptualization of time and space in this kind of politico-cultural order, Wolters argues that the importance of demonstrating and actively sustaining prowess meant a 'preoccupation with the present that came from the need to identify in one's own generation those with abnormal spiritual qualities' (ibid.: 21). There was, therefore, not a dominant concern with the past, with descent and ancestry, but with what was happening in the present and what needed to be done here and now to preserve one's status and position. Social groupings and political units were also not enclosed within a defined and fixed territory, but were focused on centres which radiated indefinitely outwards, and waxed and waned in their fortunes, influence and extent. The concept which Wolters uses is that of the 'mandala' (the circle of kings); polities were dynamic, multi-centred and overlapping; they were not fixed, exclusive and defined in territorial terms.

In his earlier formulation, Wolters presented exceptions to this cultural complex; they comprised Vietnam with its adopted Chinese model of organization and more clearly defined, bounded and fixed political centres and sub-centres, and the tribal populations who lived in the 'distant highlands' beyond recorded history (ibid.: 36–39). In his re-evaluation of his earlier paper Wolters suggests more recently that, although the Vietnamese polity did differ from the Indianized states, the dividing line is not as sharp as he originally proposed since the early Vietnamese 'empire' did demonstrate the importance of personal rule, clientage, men of prowess, and an orientation to the present (ibid.: 143ff.). As for those communities in the distant uplands or hinterlands, Wolters recognizes subsequently that they were not as distant from the lowland centres as he had supposed. There were various political, economic and cultural linkages and interrelations between upland and lowland populations, as well as

> [certain] shared assumptions about themselves such as the existence of innate prowess, the need to compete for personal prestige, the tendency for the less successful to affiliate themselves with the more successful by joining the latter's entourage, and familiarity with open social systems. The uplands could also be a place of refuge when conditions in the lowlands were disorderly or harsh.
>
> (ibid.: 161–162)

Wolters also adds another element to his South-East Asian cultural complex which does make sense in terms of the importance attached to cognation, personal prowess, status achievement and the preoccupation with the present. This is the concept of 'heterarchy', rather than hierarchy, which he adopts from

17

Joyce White's re-examination of materials from prehistoric burial sites in north-eastern and central Thailand. Heterarchy refers to 'an organizational structure in which "each element possesses the potential of being unranked (relative to other elements) or ranked in a number of different ways"' (cited in Wolters, ibid.: 122). Clearly, heterarchy, as White indicates, is associated with a flexible, competitive status system in pluralistic, multi-centred polities.

Finally, returning to Burling's work, he has drawn our attention to other broad South-East Asian cultural features which bear on the gradual differentiation between lowland and upland cultures (1965: 3–4). He points to similarities in ancient South-East Asian folk religions and symbolism, based on spirit propitiation, and ancestor and fertility cults. Elements of these religions are now principally to be found among the minority tribal groups. However, aspects of them are also still actively observed in the great lowland traditions of Hinduism, Buddhism, Islam and Christianity. There was also traditionally a focus on the sacred qualities of the human head and the widespread practice of tribal head-hunting; again the special reverence for the head is evident in both highland and lowland cultures, but the dramatic significance of heads in fertility rituals can be seen most directly in various upland tribal communities. Certain house-forms, particularly the large, rectangular multi-family dwellings raised on stilts were also found widely in the region, and these too are still preserved primarily in various minority hinterland communities in such places as Borneo, Sumatra and Sulawesi (see also Waterson, 1990). Finally, tattooing of the body was relatively common, as were various items of material culture and decorative motifs on pottery, iron- and woodwork, costume and jewellery. Yet again evidence of these cultural motifs is to be found most clearly among the hill and interior populations of South-East Asia.

Thus, despite the diversity, Burling (and others like Wolters) discerns 'numerous common threads', among them 'aspects of family organization, a respected position for women, the propitiation of malignant spirits, and similar technological habits' (1965: 2). More than this for Burling 'the most important unifying theme' is that 'each country has both hill people and plains people, and the contrast – and sometimes conflict – between the two ways of life can provide a theme which helps to bring order into our understanding of the area' (ibid.: 4).

The support for 'cultural continuities' has been expressed very recently by John Bowen, an anthropologist who has undertaken field research in Sumatra, in his emphasis on 'relative gender equality', 'hierarchical reciprocity' between rulers and ruled (expressed in marriage alliance systems, patron–clientship and centre–periphery relations), and 'outward orientation' (2000: 6–11). Yet these widespread cultural themes and motifs most definitely present us with a dilemma in our conceptualization of South-East Asia as a region. Let us now turn to these problems, and consider, in addition, some of the issues in defining the region which have been the preoccupation of disciplines other than anthropology.

Within and beyond South-East Asia: different disciplinary perspectives

Anthropology

The cultural features outlined above provide some additional, though qualified substance to the post-war, mainly American-generated political and strategic definition of South-East Asia as a distinct region, but they do not set clear cultural boundaries to it nor do they coincide with the definition of the region as delimited by political scientists and in terms of the constituent states of the Association of Southeast Asian Nations. Depending on the particular criterion chosen, the unit or category we call South-East Asia differs; it expands, contracts or shifts ground accordingly. As we have seen, linguistic similarities serve to unite large parts but not all of South-East Asia, and they also connect communities within the region to populations politically outside it. Mainland South-East Asian languages spill over into southern China and the northern and north-eastern regions of the Indian subcontinent; Austronesian languages are found beyond South-East Asia in Taiwan, eastern Africa and most of the Pacific islands. Cultural traits also link South-East Asia with regions beyond; Heine-Geldern, in his 1923 monograph, includes parts of north-eastern India, the Andaman and Nicobar islands and Taiwan within the South-East Asian cultural area. On the other hand, although western New Guinea, as a constituent province of Indonesia, is part of the region politically, in cultural terms it belongs to the Australo-Melanesian area; the indigenous populations of New Guinea are also of Australoid stock while most South-East Asians are of Mongoloid physical type, with the exception of small pockets of surviving Negrito populations and Negrito elements in Peninsular Malaysia, southern Thailand, eastern Indonesia and the Philippines. These latter are also part of an Australoid substratum which was once widespread in island South-East Asia before the arrival of Austronesian-speakers (Bellwood, 1985).

South-East Asia is also home to significant numbers of ethnic Chinese and Indian communities, and, despite their having undergone some changes in their interactions with indigenous peoples, they still retain cultural, social, economic and other connections with their ancestral lands to the north and west. Furthermore, students of comparative religion will draw attention to the linkages between the Theravada Buddhist cultures of South-East Asia and Sri Lanka, the similarities between Vietnamese and Chinese Mahayana Buddhism, the shared features of Malay–Indonesian and southern Philippines Islam and that of northern India and the Middle East, certain parallels between Hinduism in Bali and India, and between Philippine Catholicism and that of the Christian world of the Americas and Europe. Thus, the cultural, ethnic and racial boundaries of South-East Asia are not coincident; they are permeable and they have changed and shifted over time. The problem is compounded because in addition, and '[u]nlike South Asia or China, Southeast Asia has no discrete geographical features to mark its boundaries' (Miksic, 1995: 62). What is clear, however, is that the various South-East Asias of anthropologists, ethnologists and cultural historians are not the South-East of the political scientist.

We shall also see in the following three chapters that, with few exceptions, the definition, conceptualization or social construction of South-East Asia as a region has never loomed large in anthropology. The absence of region-wide anthropology texts is a symptom of this lack of interest. By and large anthropologists have concentrated on specific societies and cultures often to explore particular methodological and theoretical issues or to fill ethnographic gaps. Some have also extended their interests to a set of socially, culturally and historically interrelated populations in a sub-region of South-East Asia or have defined a 'type' society or culture which embraces several communities; these can be relatively localized like Edmund Leach's 'Kachin Hills social structure' ([1954] 1970), Jérôme Rousseau's 'Central Borneo society' (1990), and Fred Eggan's 'Mountain Province (Luzon) societies' (1941, 1967), or more extensive like J.P.B. de Josselin de Jong's 'Malay archipelago as an ethnological field' ([1935] 1977), or A. Thomas Kirsch's 'hill tribe society of mainland South-East Asia' (1973).

Most of the major figures in the post-war anthropology of South-East Asia have usually seen themselves as anthropologists working within certain subject areas of the discipline (for example, political or economic anthropology, symbolism, kinship or ecology) and not primarily as South-East Asianists. In saying this we should beware of discriminating and opposing too sharply discipline/subject interests and area studies because as Bowen has argued 'the two have shaped and do shape each other' (2000: 3). Nevertheless, we should recognize that the overwhelming majority of anthropologists have been marginal to the debates about South-East Asia as a region, and if they do conceive of a unit relevant to their interests they tend to refer to a sub-region or to a country not to the region as a whole.

There is a further problem to which we shall return at the end of the chapter and to which we referred in our introductory statements, and that is that the societies and cultures of South-East Asia have been subject increasingly to outside forces of change, particularly since political independence. Some of those anthropologists interested in these wider transformations have therefore turned to the literature on the sociology of development and political economy to help locate their local studies in broader processes of modernization and globalization. Again, this perspective has led to the breaking down of South-East Asia's boundaries as it has become incorporated into what was once called the 'Third World' or the 'developing world', and, more recently, for certain of the countries in the region like Singapore, the 'newly industrializing world'.

History

There continue to be lively debates among historians about the possibility and value of identifying a South-East Asian regional history and unity, and the nature of the region's links with and responses to the wider world. However, recent exchanges have tended to concentrate much more on the possibility of constructing a 'regional history' as against the desirability of pursuing the detailed study of South-East Asia's diverse 'local or subregional histories'. A major recent contribution to our thinking is Anthony Reid's two-volume *Southeast Asia in the Age of Commerce 1400–1680* (1988–1993). In the first volume, *The Land below the Winds* (1988), Reid identifies and explores the 'deep-seated structures' of South-East Asian societies, and identifies the 'early modern' period from about 1450 to 1680 as a crucial phase in the region's history. According to Reid, during this time there was a dramatic increase in commercial interaction and this, in company with broad linguistic linkages, similar ecologies and shared socio-cultural elements, served to define and unify South-East Asia as a region, though it was also a time of significant change. The second volume, *Expansion and Crisis* (1993), examines in particular the economic and religious changes experienced during the sixteenth century onwards; by the seventeenth century local societies, cultures and economies had become integrated into a wider international commercial system increasingly linked to Europe. For Reid the emergence of European dominance was then the occasion of South-East Asia's break with the past, its gradual division into separate spheres of foreign influence and the commencement of its underdevelopment and dependency.

However, Reid's attempt to identify unifying features in the 'age of commerce' has been the subject of scrutiny and criticism. Attention has been drawn to the fact that he focuses mainly on the maritime Malay–Indonesian populations of South-East Asia, and for historians like Victor Lieberman, who have examined in detail mainland history, this historical unity is not so obvious (1995: 796–807). As Barbara Andaya has recently observed of Lieberman's 'thoughtful disagreement' with Reid's thesis, the features emphasized by Reid 'cannot apply in the mainland, where political and economic patterns reflect, albeit weakly, trends in Europe, Japan, and in the developing Dutch and Spanish colonial structures' (1997: 164). Furthermore, the significant cultural shifts identified by Reid in the island world of South-East Asia in the 'early modern' period seem not to be so evident in the mainland Buddhist cultures. Therefore, some historians of the region press for the importance of examining the variety of local societies, cultures and sub-regions rather than attempting to generalize and 'homogenize'. Andaya suggests, for example, that in the certainty of South-East Asia's contemporary recognition as a 'global unit' historians of the region 'might be emboldened to press more strongly the view that Southeast Asia owes its regional identity as much to internal diversity as to cohesion' (ibid.: 170); there are echoes here of Burling's notion of cultural unity in hills–plains diversity.

21

In Wolters's earlier paper he too, despite identifying 'some widespread cultural traits inherited from prehistory' (1999: 38), and arguing that he has discerned certain continuities in early South-East Asian history up to the fifteenth century, nevertheless, concludes that, given the obvious cultural diversity in the region and the increase in this diversity through time, it is the 'locality or sub-region [which] should remain the focus for studying history in earlier Southeast Asia' (ibid.: 55). This is for the simple reason that until we have accumulated much more knowledge and information on South-East Asia's local or sub-regional cultural diversities and their transformations (in legal codes, art styles, language and language use, religious beliefs and practices, social forms and identities), then it is extremely difficult to establish similarities and dissimilarities between them and establish whether or not there is a regional shape to their several histories. Wolters does examine, and more so in his later re-evaluation of his earlier statements, historical continuities, and intra-regional political and commercial relations and the ways in which the common cultural characteristics of South-East Asia have shaped the perceptions, processes and forms of 'localization' of outside models and ideas, particularly from India. He says that he is now not 'so fastidious in defining a "region" and can now recognize a more "regional" shape to the history of early Southeast Asia', but he remains 'as convinced as ever that the characteristics of subregional, or local, cultures are as significant as the shared cultural traits' (ibid.: 106).

Politics, international relations and economics

Political scientists mainly define South-East Asia in terms of its constituent nation–states, and therefore its territorial boundaries appear to be clear-cut. Indeed, American post-war political science defined South-East Asia as a collection of independent nation–states and promoted 'the political character of the regional idea' (Emmerson, 1984: 12). However, even in this regard some students of politics, particularly those concerned with international relations and security issues, have become increasingly interested in the developing connections between South-East and East Asia within the wider western Pacific Rim. Strategic specialists now talk much more in terms of a Pacific Asian or East Asian strategic theatre which embraces South-East Asia, China and Japan; and some have begun to examine the strategic importance of India to the region in the context of the Indian Ocean theatre.

Processes of political liberalization and democratization, and the intertwining of commercial relations between the countries of Pacific Asia have also resulted in the realization among political scientists that various Asian countries share similar experiences and problems and should be studied together and comparatively. The rapid growth of many of the Asian economies has also meant that development economists and political economists increasingly tend to examine processes of industrialization and economic change across the wider Asian region. The phenomenon of the 'Asian tiger economies' links Singapore with Taiwan, Hong Kong and South Korea. In addition, the shared Confucian heritage of these four countries has led some observers to suggest the importance of cultural factors in encouraging economic development. As Huxley has said, in a recent survey of studies of the international relations of South-East Asia:

> paradoxically, at a time when many mainstream international relations specialists are beginning to take more than a polite interest in the contribution of Southeast Asian states to international cooperation, the late 1980s and 1990s have brought questioning of Southeast Asia's very meaning as a 'region' in economic and security terms.
>
> (1996: 242)

Broader anthropological and sociological concerns

As we have indicated at various points it is by no means clear that anthropological and more especially macro-sociological analysis of the societies which have only relatively recently emerged from the shadow of Western colonialism and embarked on the path of economic growth and development should be confined within a regional perspective. In recent years the countries of South-East Asia have been seen increasingly as part of a wider western Pacific Asia economic and political community, and, of course, as part of a global economy and a globalizing world; and such social effects of modernization that accompany urbanization and industrialization, technological innovations in agriculture, intra- and international labour migration, and the increase in wealth and consumerism, have encouraged sociologists in particular, and some but not all anthropologists, to think in terms of more general patterns of social change in Asia. These include, for example, the development of the 'new rich' and the middle classes, modern urban lifestyles, factory employment, and changing gender relations. What is more, the earlier perspectives adopted by social scientists to understand the processes and problems of development of newly independent countries in the two decades or so after the Second World War were not constrained within any particular regional parameters. They were concerned to formulate general theories of modernization, economic growth and development, or of underdevelopment and dependency, which would apply to the whole developing world, though their empirical material was often selected from a particular part of that world. For example, most of the case studies used in the early formulation of theories of underdevelopment and dependency were taken from the Latin American experience (Frank, 1967). These were only subsequently applied in detail to South-East Asia (see, for example, Catley, 1976; Higgott and Robison, 1985; Taylor and Turton, 1988; Schmidt et al., 1997).

We shall obviously keep these cross-regional perspectives in mind in our focus on the anthropology of South-East Asia and acknowledge that the changes taking place there are in part generated by general forces beyond the region (Nas, 1998). However, we have now arrived at a period of history, characterized by processes of globalization, in which, almost paradoxically, regional economic and trading blocs such as the Association of Southeast Asian Nations have taken on an increasing importance and have a clear role to play in the global economic and political system. Thus, in our view the ten countries which together comprise South-East Asia will continue to have an identity and a rationale separate from the rest of Asia. Furthermore, globalization and the spread of American popular culture to other parts of the world have also generated an increased consciousness of the importance of local cultural identities. Therefore, an understanding of South-East Asia as a region, especially in anthropological terms, given its linguistic and cultural complexity and its rich and varied history, will require specific specialist area expertise and, as Wolters proposes, will need the detailed study of local and sub-regional cultures. Of necessity, these special features and the scholarly requirements which flow from them will continue to set South-East Asia apart from East and South Asia. As we have said, the region is not and never has been a pale reflection of India and China and it should not be viewed through an Indian or Chinese cultural and historical lens (Evans, 1993a). Furthermore, various of the anthropological concepts and debates on which we shall focus in this text have emerged from analyses of empirical material from community-based, country-specific or sub-regional studies within South-East Asia, and, although we shall not lose sight of the general processes of social change and development at work, it seems sensible to locate them in the real-life experiences of one particular part of the world and its various constituents.

Overall, for us, South-East Asia constitutes a convenient unit of study, and it coincides very roughly with the ten ASEAN nation–states. But we have to emphasize that we should not then think of it in terms of a bounded, unified and homogeneous socio-cultural area. It is a diverse region and, depending on the definitional criteria employed, its boundaries shift. Nevertheless, anthropological endeavour in this region has generated an interesting and valuable theoretical and ethnographic literature which does deserve attention in its own right, and it is to this literature that we now turn.

Note

1 We prefer the hyphenated rendering of 'South-East Asia'. On occasion the acceptable alternative – 'Southeast Asia' – is used when it appears specifically in quotations from other authors.

2

ANTHROPOLOGY AND THE COLONIAL IMPACT (1900–1950)

This chapter covers the period from the late nineteenth century through to 1950, a time when anthropological ideas began to be adopted for the analysis of ethnographic data and for its possible use by colonial administrations. We also witness the beginnings of academic anthropology. During this period anthropology had only a small personnel and much ethnographic study was undertaken by keen amateurs and spare-time researchers whose reports were mainly published in the journals and monographs of various Orientalist societies which also embraced scholarly interests in languages, literatures, archaeology, philosophy, history, folklore and geography. The similarities and differences in the relationships between the study of non-Western societies and cultures and the structure and direction of colonial administration as it was found in the British South-East Asian dependencies, the Netherlands East Indies, French Indochina and the American Philippines are examined as are the different perspectives and approaches employed in gathering and analysing ethnographic material. These approaches comprise classification and ethnographic description; evolutionary theories; diffusionism; functionalism, principally a British-derived approach; Dutch structuralism; American culture and personality studies; and analyses of acculturation and socio-economic change.

Introduction

In order to provide a historical backdrop for the discussion in later chapters of the concerns of contemporary and modern anthropology it is necessary to consider in which directions anthropology developed in colonial South-East Asia – its main interests, subject matter, perspectives and methods – so that we are able to determine how recent anthropological work has built on, responded to or reacted against 'colonial anthropology', or rather the different anthropologies which developed in the context of Western colonialism. We shall limit the discussion roughly to the studies undertaken from the beginning of the twentieth century when anthropological ideas began to be adopted and used actively in the analysis and organization of data, when the notion of anthropology's usefulness to colonial administrations was promoted, and when anthropology or ethnology as a separately defined field of scholarly enquiry had managed to begin to gain a firm presence in institutions of higher education in the West and South-East Asia. Furthermore, during the past fifty years or so of colonialism the inclusion of anthropology in the training programmes of colonial civil servants and other officers began to be expressed in detailed studies of South-East Asian societies and cultures by those employed in the administrative services (see King, 1999: 12–31, for a recent survey of colonial anthropology).

Since the 1970s there has been an increasing interest in the anthropological profession in the history of the discipline and, in particular, its colonial antecedents. Grant Evans, in his Introduction to *Asia's Cultural Mosaic*, poses the matter in the following terms: 'Just how much anthropology was caught up in the process of colonial domination is debatable ... but the history of colonialism clearly had an important impact on the evolution of anthropology as a discipline' (1993a: 26–27). Some anthropologists, critical of the uncomfortably close relations between the development of anthropology and the exercise of colonial governance, have argued variously that colonial interests directed and gave shape to the perspectives and subject matter of anthropology, and that anthropology was the 'child of imperialism' (Gough, 1968) and an 'agent' of dominant societies (Diamond, 1980). Talal Asad also proposed that during the colonial period anthropologists 'contributed, sometimes indirectly, towards maintaining the structure of power represented by the colonial system' (1973: 17). Clearly there was a complex relationship between the emerging discipline of anthropology and colonialism which operated at different levels in different ways at different times in different places, though we think that van Bremen and Shimizu have the sense of it when they suggest that anthropology certainly 'thrived in the colonial period' but was not 'inherently of it' (1999: 2). Indeed, the roots of anthropology go back much earlier to the philosophers of the eighteenth-century Enlightenment and their concerns with the nature, origins and development of human society and culture.

An additional complication in considering the relations between anthropology and colonialism is that much of the anthropological research and writing on other cultures was undertaken not by academic anthropologists but by colonial officials and missionaries, who lived and worked in the dependent territories, who were fluent in the mainstream vernaculars, and who recorded social and cultural life in their spare time. Some had acquaintance with anthropological literature either through personal interest or more often formal colonial training programmes provided in universities, academies and colleges, while others did not. Many individuals who made substantial contributions to the anthropological literature of South-East Asia were specialists in such subjects as linguistics, law, geography, archaeology or history, and would not have identified themselves primarily as anthropologists or ethnologists. Research findings were often published in colonial journals which were regional and multidisciplinary in orientation rather than discipline-specific; these included in the British territories the journals of the *Malayan* and *Straits Branches of the Royal Asiatic*

Society, The Sarawak Museum Journal and the *The Federation Museums Journal;* in the Dutch East Indies *De Indische Gids, Koloniaal Tijdschrift, Koloniale Studiën* and *Bijdragen tot de Taal-, Land- en Volkenkunde van Nederlandsch-Indië,* and in French Indochina *Bulletin de l'Ecole Française d'Extrême-Orient* and *Bulletin de la Société des Etudes Indochinoises.* In other words, the boundaries of the discipline of anthropology and the definition of practitioners of anthropology as well as the distinctions between 'pure' (or theoretical) and 'practical' anthropology were much more indeterminate during the earlier development of the subject than in the post-Second World War period when colonial territories increasingly gained their political independence (Pels and Salemink, 1999: 1–5). The demise of colonial administrations meant that data on local communities were no longer required by them nor did Europeans have privileged access to field-sites, support and funds, and the discipline of anthropology had established a firm institutional and professional presence in universities. Indeed, 'the image of a "pure" academic anthropology was partly constituted in a direct struggle with nonacademic ethnographic traditions that largely emerged from colonial practice' (ibid.: 7).

Anthropology and colonial relations

Usefully, Eyal Ben-Ari distinguishes three kinds of linkage between anthropology and colonialism (1999: 382–405; and see also Pels and Salemink for a detailed examination of the colonial contexts of ethnographic practice, 1999: 1–52). First, there is the relationship between anthropology as an applied or practical social science and the use or potential use of its knowledge and expertise by colonial administrations. Second, there is the matter of the relations between anthropology's concepts and theories, particularly with regard to the prominent position of functionalist perspectives in anthropology in late colonialism (see below), and the interests, needs and 'logic' of colonial regimes; and, third, the relation between the products of anthropology (and their dissemination through scholarly publications, reports, surveys, cultural inventories, lectures for learned societies, popular writings and the media, teaching and training) and the development and maintenance of a 'colonial discourse' about those 'others' who were governed and administered (ibid.: 383).

Practical anthropology and colonial policy-making

The role of anthropologists as advisers of colonial government and as specialist practitioners who apply their skills and knowledge to the solution of administrative problems seems generally to have been minimal and primarily a phenomenon of late colonialism, though some senior academic anthropologists argued explicitly that the discipline had practical value and therefore should be given support and patronage (see, for example, Malinowski, 1929), and several anthropologists were employed by governments for this purpose. Even those

27

who were concerned about the ethical and intellectual consequences of working for colonial governments sometimes provided a rationale for this activity by proposing that improvements in administration could be encouraged if those employed in it knew something about the culture and sociology of those whom they administered (Leach, 1950). However, from the evidence before us, it would appear that, despite the rhetoric, anthropology provided very little of practical value for colonialism; their findings were often ignored in policy terms and were often thought to be presented in a form which was not amenable to implementation. There was sometimes acute tension between academic anthropologists and administrators based on differences in career, interests, outlook, experience and lifestyle, and not infrequently a suspicion that fieldworkers living among native communities ran the risk of becoming too closely identified with and sympathetic to the interests, and possibly unrealizable demands of the subject populations. Professional anthropologists were in any case mainly interested in the academic and intellectual rewards which flowed from their work and not so much its practical consequences.

Notwithstanding this low level of positive interaction between applied anthropology and administration in policy and project terms, anthropology as a young, developing, fieldwork-based discipline oriented primarily to the study of non-Western cultures, benefited considerably from the association with officialdom; it provided research opportunities, it offered financial support in grants and sponsorship, sometimes employment as research officers or museum personnel, it furnished other facilities for research like transport and interpreters, and it gave a measure of security and protection in undertaking field-studies in often remote locations. In other words, anthropology flourished in the interstices of a relationship of political, economic and cultural inequality between the representatives of the colonial state on the one hand and the indigenous subject populations on the other.

Anthropological theory and colonial governance

The second dimension of the anthropology–colonialism interface is that of the relationship between anthropological theories and modes of analysis and the 'logic of government'. Did the conceptual framework of functionalism, in particular, 'fit' colonial interests, especially in the operation of the system of indirect rule, favoured particularly by the British, which depended on the articulation of an alien administration with native politico-legal systems and therefore knowledge of indigenous cultural and social values and practices? The focus in functionalist analysis on how small-scale indigenous social and cultural systems function, cohere, sustain order and re-establish stability following periods of conflict and change did tend to depict them as timeless or changeless. There would appear to be a plausible connection to be made between studies which identified the structures and mechanisms which enabled local communities to sustain a functioning harmony and equilibrium and colonial preoccupations with establishing and maintaining law and order, identifying factors which generate conflict and instability, and managing the actual and potential destabilizing effects of the incorporation of small-scale societies into wider political and economic systems.

Nevertheless, functionalism was not directly, if at all, the product of a colonial system. It was above all a general intellectual movement in the social sciences and was, among other things, a reaction against the previous dominant social theories of evolutionism and diffusionism. The concept of a system, whether it be a tribe, ethnic group, lineage, family group or a village, comprising interrelated parts which operated in some way to sustain the whole, provided a convenient way of arranging and ordering complex data, usually gathered orally and by observation from different spheres of social and cultural life. As we shall see in our selective survey of anthropological studies in colonial South-East Asia, functionalism was by no means the only or even dominant paradigm. It was especially important in British anthropology in Africa, and was not particularly significant in Dutch ethnology, for example, where customary law studies and structuralism tended to dominate the field (Ellen, 1976: 319).

Functionalism co-existed with other approaches; evolutionist and diffusionist theories persisted; some observers contented themselves with straightforward ethnographic description of a particular community, with little, if any attention to analysis guided by theory; others were concerned to survey and gazette a large number of ethnic groups in a given territory, usually accompanied by some attempt at ethnic or racial categorization; interest in experimental psychological methods, especially in American social science, resulted in some studies on the relationships between culture, personality and character; the influence of French Durkheimian sociology led to the development of a particular 'school' or approach in Dutch colonial ethnology, usually referred to as 'structuralism', which was concerned, among other things, to reveal general principles of social and symbolic classification in Indonesian societies which could, in turn, be deployed to reconstruct an ancient Indonesian social structure; studies of the effects of European colonialism on indigenous communities, especially in the later colonial period when there was a shift to concerns with native welfare and development, led to the formulation of concepts such as economic dualism and cultural pluralism to understand how colonial societies, comprising foreign and local populations, were organized, and the prospects for the development of colonial subjects. Therefore, far from a concentration on order and stability, a substantial part of the 'anthropological' literature during the colonial period was concerned with processes of change, albeit usually in schematic and speculative fashion and based on evolutionary and diffusionist assumptions. It should also be borne in mind that contributions to anthropological knowledge were not the exclusive preserve of scholars from those countries which possessed colonies. In South-East Asia, for example, important studies were undertaken by Austrians, Germans and Scandinavians, among others, and it is reasonable to suppose that their studies would have been unlikely to have been guided by the preoccupations of the colonial powers.

Anthropology and colonial discourse

It is probably in its contribution to a 'colonial discourse' that anthropology generally had the most significant, though often indirect influence. In the course of their engagement with the indigenous populations, anthropologists constructed 'other cultures'; their subject matter was, as Adam Kuper has indicated, the 'colonial subject, and they allowed him to be identified with the erstwhile "primitive" or "savage" of the evolutionists' (1983: 147–148). In this connection Evans-Pritchard, in his influential introduction to the subject matter and methods of social anthropology in 1950, discusses what anthropologists mean by 'primitive societies', and though he suggests that the term is perhaps 'unfortunate' he nevertheless states that 'it has now been too widely accepted as a technical term to be avoided' (1962: 7). 'Primitive societies' are then 'small in scale with regard to numbers, territory, and range of social contacts, and ... have by comparison with more advanced societies a simple technology and economy and little specialization of social function'. He continues, 'Some anthropologists would add further criteria, particularly the absence of literature, and hence of any systematic art, science, or theology' (ibid.: 8).

Therefore, it is not so much anthropology's assumed or claimed practical contribution to policy and decision-making that is significant, '[r]ather, it is the concepts, definitions, classifications, and theoretical perspectives of anthropology that permeate the social climate within which policy making takes place' (Ben-Ari, 1999: 388). Certainly anthropologists also helped raise cultural awareness among colonial civil servants of native cultures. This is not to say that the representations and images which anthropologists helped create comprised a unified and agreed perspective on the 'colonial others'. However, through such channels as the provision of training programmes for colonial cadet officers and in engaging in debates and information exchange with a range of observers and scholars of indigenous societies and cultures, the emerging discipline of anthropology helped construct a variety of images of the 'native' or 'primitive', and, in the South-East Asian context in particular, the lowland 'peasant' and the upland 'tribesman'. In this connection, there were those who were concerned to preserve and protect the interior minorities against encroachment from the majority lowland populations and in this endeavour they reconstructed traditional cultures, the 'noble savage', in part to demonstrate the value of cultures under threat (see Salemink, 1999).

Brief country surveys

Britain

The concept of a practical or applied anthropology in the context of colonialism had only really gained currency in Britain by the 1920s. From the early twentieth century a few anthropologists had begun to be employed by some British colonial administrations, particularly in Africa, and training programmes for colonial civil servants were introduced at Oxford, Cambridge and London, although there was no general policy to recruit academic anthropologists to work in the dependent territories. Both Bronislaw Malinowski (1929) and A.R. Radcliffe-Brown (1931), the two leading figures in British anthropology at that time, contributed positively to the case for anthropology as a practical science and they provided university courses in applied anthropology. Edmund Leach also notes that, in the late 1930s, several of the participants in Malinowski's seminar programme at the London School of Economics were colonial administrators on home leave (1977: 56). The LSE had introduced a special programme on Colonial Administration in 1932 which included an anthropology component, and was intended mainly for administrators, educationalists and missionaries. One administrator who attended Malinowski's LSE seminars was H.N.C. Stevenson of the Burma Frontier Service, who subsequently published an important study of economics and feasts of merit among the Chin of Highland Burma (1945); the influence of Malinowski, and another of Malinowski's students, Raymond Firth (see below), is very clear.

The relationship between anthropology and colonial administration was strengthened following the establishment of the International Institute of African Languages and Cultures in 1926, which was to become the International African Institute. It was to be expected that Britain's main focus would be Africa – its backyard – rather than Asia or the Pacific. The Institute, sponsored by various colonial governments in the region and the International Missionary Council, adopted a research policy which was based on the close cooperation between researchers and administrators; the policy was directed to making available research findings on such matters as land tenure, property rights, customary law, and legal institutions to assist in addressing administrative problems and improving governance in Africa. In 1937 another significant development in African anthropology was the foundation of the Rhodes–Livingstone Institute in the then Northern Rhodesia which undertook much practical research in central and eastern Africa in the context of the increasing colonial policy orientation to the welfare and the development of the colonial populations. However, these contributions were relatively modest, they occurred on the eve of decolonization, and they did not loom large in the main intellectual preoccupations of the anthropologists of the time.

The Colonial Development and Welfare Act was passed in 1940 for the support and organization of social and economic development in the dependencies, and the Colonial Social Science Research Council (CSSRC), as a branch of the Colonial Research Committee, was established in 1944. In South-East Asia the Council was requested by the first Governor of the newly established Crown Colony of Sarawak, ceded to the British Crown in 1946 by the last Rajah of Sarawak, Sir Charles Vyner Brooke, to commission a socio-economic survey of the state. Raymond Firth, as Secretary of the CSSRC, and Edmund Leach as the anthropologist designated to undertake the general survey and make recommendations, worked out the details of the study with the Governor. Leach was already familiar with South-East Asian cultures, having spent a considerable period of time in Highland Burma just prior to and during the Japanese war. The results of his field research and his travels as a British army officer in the Kachin Hills were published as a pathbreaking monograph in 1954 (see Chapter 4).

Leach's excellent Sarawak report, based on his visit there in 1947, was submitted to the Council in 1948 (published in revised form in 1950). The main objective of the survey was 'to suggest projects for sociological research' in order to 'provide Government with data for gauging the probable local response to the various schemes of development [then] under consideration' (Leach, 1950: 7, 16–17). Leach's recommendations resulted in the Council's decision to support four major anthropological projects: these comprised J.D. (Derek) Freeman's study of Iban pioneer shifting cultivators of the Rejang river (1955a, 1955b [1970]), W.R. Geddes's work on the Sadong Land Dayaks (Bidayuh) who were more permanently settled shifting cultivators (1954), H.S. Morris's examination of Coastal Melanau sago cultivators of the Oya and Mukah region (1953), and T'ien Ju-K'ang's mainly urban-based field research on the Chinese (1953). In our view, these studies proved to be an important landmark in the post-war development of South-East Asian anthropology, and are widely quoted, particularly Freeman's publications on the Iban.

At the same time that Leach was engaged in his Sarawak survey, Raymond Firth undertook a parallel reconnaissance of Malaya (1948). He and his wife, Rosemary Firth, had, like Leach in Burma, undertaken research in South-East Asia in 1939–1940, immediately prior to the Japanese occupation, and were therefore also acquainted with the region. Raymond Firth's seminal work on the Malay peasant fishing economy of the east coast Malayan state of Kelantan appeared in print in 1946 (1966, revised edition), and Rosemary Firth's complementary study of housekeeping among Kelantan peasant households had been published in 1943 (1966, revised edition). Unfortunately Firth's recommendations in his post-war Malayan survey could not be implemented because of the insecure and unstable conditions caused by the Malayan Emergency and Communist insurrection. However, important research was commissioned in the neighbouring colony of Singapore and studies were completed successfully by Maurice Freedman on urban Chinese family and marriage (1957), his wife, Judith Djamour, on Malay kinship and marriage (1959) and by Alan J.A. Elliott on Chinese religion (1955).

Aside from the studies of Leach, Firth and their colleagues and students very few other studies were carried out by university-based academic anthropologists during the late colonial period. Unlike the situation in Africa, the scholarly field in Asia tended to be dominated by Orientalist scholars interested in the archaeology, history, languages and literatures of the 'great traditions' of Hinduism, Buddhism and Islam. There was little professional, full-time anthropological research among the lowland peasant 'little traditions' of the region or the minority interior or upland tribal populations. The field was left mainly to scholar-administrators and officials in Burma, Malaya and northern Borneo, who pursued their anthropological interests during their spare time. Some of them were acquainted with anthropological ideas and methods, though they tended to content themselves with recording detailed ethnographic data, in some cases of encyclopaedic proportions, formulating ethnic classifications and constructing cultural histories. They included, among many others, Ivor H.N. Evans's work on northern Borneo and the Malayan Peninsula (1922,1937, 1953), Charles Hose's ethnographies of Borneo cultures (Hose and McDougall, 1912), J.H. Hutton's monographs on the Nagas (1921a, 1921b), James George Scott's survey of the Shan States of Upper Burma (Scott and Hardiman, 1900), Walter Skeat's compendium on Malayan aborigines (Skeat and Blagden, 1906), and Richard Winstedt's wide-ranging studies on Malay culture and history (1925, 1947). We shall consider some of these contributions later in this chapter.

After the Second World War Burma gained its political independence within three years, and there was very little anthropological research undertaken during that time. The Federation of Malaya was granted independence in 1957, and the colonies of Singapore, Sarawak and Sabah followed suit in 1963 when they joined Malaya to form the wider Federation of Malaysia. Singapore left the Federation in 1965 to form an independent republic. As we have seen, Britain did sponsor anthropological fieldwork in Sarawak and Singapore in the late 1940s and early 1950s, but the Malayan Emergency made it difficult to conduct research in rural areas of the Peninsula. Finally, the Sultanate of Brunei remained a British protectorate until 1984, but there had been no interest shown by British anthropologists in conducting social science research in the post-war years; there were a few important studies undertaken by American anthropologists.

The Netherlands

The interrelationships between colonialism and the study of native cultures and societies are nowhere better illustrated than in the Dutch administration of the Indonesian archipelago. Ellen has argued that, unlike the origins of British anthropology, 'the Dutch tradition is very strongly rooted in a particular set of colonial relations'. More than this Ellen suggests that the 'importance of the Indonesian experience in shaping the character of Dutch anthropology cannot be overemphasized', and that 'it is impossible to understand its creation, development and institutionalization as a professional discipline except in relation to colonial policy there' (1976: 304). From the early nineteenth century the Dutch placed increasing emphasis on the need for its administrators to have a sound grasp of the customs, institutions and languages of the local populations. The Dutch established training courses for colonial civil servants and military officers well before the British developed training facilities in Oxford, Cambridge and London. The first courses were begun in Surakarta in 1832, Breda in 1836, and most importantly in Delft in 1842 where training in ethnology and geography was attached to the Royal Academy of Civil Engineers; T. Roorda was appointed to Delft in the same year as Professor of Oriental Linguistics, Geography and Ethnology (van Bremen, 1999: 362). In 1864 an Academy was established in Leiden, and remained a separate institution until it was closed and its staff absorbed into the University there in 1877 (Prager, 1999: 330). Up until 1877 ethnology had been a subsidiary subject in the training programmes, but it then became a university subject in its own right, though still a component of general instruction on the East Indies, and a Chair was established at Leiden University in the Geography and Ethnology of the East Indian Archipelago. Its first occupant was P.J. Veth (1877–1885), whose early training had been in theology and who had then studied Hebrew, Malay language and literature and Indonesian Islam. From 1891 the instruction of colonial civil servants was focused decisively in Leiden, but in the late colonial period a training facility was also opened in Utrecht in 1925.

The rationale of the training courses on the East Indies was to provide a grounding in what was considered to be the essential practical knowledge that colonial servants had to command: geography, history, Islamic and customary law, and ethnology, along with instruction in the major languages of Javanese and Malay. This broad field of studies within which the study of ethnology was embedded was called Indology (Indologie or Indonesian [East Indian] studies), and its practitioners wrote mainly in colonial journals for an audience interested not in any specific discipline but in Indonesian affairs. In the spirit of this broad multidisciplinary perspective on the Dutch East Indies, Veth, for example, published substantial encyclopaedic studies of various parts of the archipelago: West Borneo (1854–1856, 2 volumes), Java (1875–1884, 3 volumes) and Central Sumatra (1881–1897, 9 volumes). These were major compendia of largely undigested geographical, historical, linguistic and cultural material gathered from miscellaneous sources, and in the case of Sumatra from a major expedition organized by Veth in 1877–1879 (Koentjaraningrat, 1975: 25–27).

Veth's successor to the Leiden Chair was G.A. Wilken (1885–1891), the founder of Dutch comparative ethnology and a major exponent of evolutionary theory in The Netherlands (see below). Wilken was born in northern Sulawesi, the son of a missionary; his early career as a colonial civil servant in the Moluccas, Sulawesi and Sumatra gave him a broad perspective of the diversity of cul-

tural forms in Indonesia. Subsequently he lectured on the civil servant training course at Leiden in 1883 and two years later was appointed Professor at
the University. Wilken was followed by the Sinologist, J.J.M. de Groot
(1891–1903), and then the Chair was occupied for over thirty years by A.W.
Nieuwenhuis (1904–1935), the distinguished scholar of Borneo cultures and
former medical officer in the Dutch East Indies army. The title of Nieuwenhuis's Chair was changed and it demonstrated even more forcefully the underlying philosophy of Indology. He was designated the Professor of the History,
Literature, Manners and Customs of the Peoples of the East Indian Archipelago, and the Physical Geography of that Region (see below).

We should also mention here an important contribution to the ethnography
of the Dutch East Indies which arose from the problems which the Dutch were
experiencing in pacifying the Muslim Achehnese in northern Sumatra with
whom they had been engaged in hostilities for much of the latter half of the
nineteenth century. The colonial government engaged Christiaan Snouck Hurgronje, a distinguished scholar of Islam, to undertake a study of the Achehnese
in the early 1890s with a view to providing the authorities with information on
their social, political and religious life so that the Dutch might both quell the
resistance and establish an effective administration. Snouck Hurgronje's study
provided in effect a general ethnography of the Achehnese, which is still widely
quoted, but also an analysis of the role that religion played in Achehnese resistance ([1893–1894] 1906; and see Siegel's critical commentary on Snouck Hurgronje's interpretation of Achehnese society, [1969] 2000).

As we shall see later, the direction of the development of Dutch anthropology took a decisive turn on the publication of a paper in 1918 by F.D.E. van
Ossenbruggen entitled 'The origin of the Javanese concept of *monca-pat* in relation to primitive classification'. Van Ossenbruggen, a Leiden-trained lawyer,
played an enormously influential role in the development of Indonesian customary law studies (*adatrecht*), along with another distinguished lawyer, C. van
Vollenhoven, who, as Professor of Islamic Law and other Folk Institutions and
Customs in the Netherlands Indies at the University of Leiden, succeeded in
establishing customary law studies as a separate subject of study in Dutch law
schools. In our view one of the outstanding case studies exemplifying this focus
on *adatrecht* is Victor Korn's detailed work on Balinese customary law (1924,
1932), and Korn, more than any other ethnographer presented a construction
of 'traditional' Bali (uniquely Hindu, integrated, and based on the village, irrigation society and caste) which was to have a profound influence on subsequent
ethnographic studies, including those by American anthropologists (Schulte
Nordholt, 1999).

Customary law studies played as central a role in Dutch colonial anthropology
as did functionalism in British anthropology, given that it was Dutch policy to
preserve, but modify native law, in association with Islamic and European law
(Ellen, 1976: 319; Schulte Nordholt, 1999: 269–270). However, though van
Vollenhoven did magnificent work in compiling and classifying a large amount

of data on customary law and securing its scholarly importance and recognition, it was van Ossenbruggen who was to have a major impact on the course of Dutch anthropology. Like many other scholars of Indonesia, van Ossenbruggen was born and raised in the colony. He spent much of his life there working first as a lawyer, then in the administration and finally as a lecturer in the training school for native administrative officers at Malang in Central Java (Koentjaraningrat, 1975: 94). Van Ossenbruggen wished to promote the understanding of native customary law by studying its cultural background and local world-views and mentalities. In this endeavour, and after an initial interest in Wilken's unilinear evolutionary theories, he subsequently applied certain structuralist ideas on 'primitive classification' developed by Emile Durkheim and Marcel Mauss. It was the marrying of Durkheimian concepts with empirical material from Indonesia that was to have a profound effect on Dutch anthropology.

These ideas, introduced into Dutch scholarship by van Ossenbruggen, concerning the principles on which social and cultural forms were ordered, arranged and classified were then developed by W.H. Rassers, who was a student of Indonesian languages and literatures. He spent his entire career at the Leiden Museum of Ethnology and was extremely knowledgeable on Javanese culture. In a series of publications which appeared between 1922 and 1941 (some of which were brought together in English translation in 1959), he applied notions of classification to analyses of Javanese drama, literature and folklore, particularly the Panji epics, carving, the sacred dagger (keris), batik and ornamental designs, and architecture. The work of van Ossenbruggen and Rassers was then absorbed, refined and promoted by a key figure in the development of Dutch anthropology, J.P.B. de Josselin de Jong. De Josselin de Jong was appointed to a supernumerary Chair in General Ethnology at Leiden University in 1922, and then succeeded to Nieuwenhuis's Chair in 1935, which was redefined as the Cultural Anthropology of Indonesia and its connection with General Anthropology. The nephew of de Josselin de Jong says the following about this change of title:

> [It] is significant and realistic, for now at last, for the first time since Wilken, the subject was in the hands of a man who was in the main stream of anthropological thinking; who maintained close contacts with his colleagues in the U.S.A., Britain, Germany, and France; and who carried out, and trained his pupils for, fieldwork in North America, the Caribbean, and Indonesia. With him, the structuralist trend takes a firm shape.
>
> (P.E. de Josselin de Jong, 1977: 5)

It is important to note that de Josselin de Jong also taught and supervised several students who pursued careers in the East Indies civil service.

Structuralism continued to play a significant role in post-war anthropology in The Netherlands, but the Dutch preoccupation with Indonesia as a field of anthropological study waned following full Indonesian independence in 1949.

An exception was the research undertaken in western New Guinea, retained by the Dutch after the transfer of sovereignty in all the remaining territories of the former Dutch East Indies. J. van Baal, who served as one of the post-war Governors of New Guinea, published substantial ethnographic studies and encouraged field research in the territory in the 1950s. New Guinea ethnology was also included as a compulsory element in the training of Dutch administrators (Visser and van der Wiel, 1981: 228), and several government servants, including J. Pouwer, J.W. Schoorl and A.C. van der Leeden, undertook anthropological research in New Guinea prior to its eventual transfer to Indonesia in 1962 (Kloos, 1975: 18; Pouwer, 1966).

Ellen makes two important overall remarks about Dutch colonialism and anthropology: first, that the 'level of educational organization for the training of those destined for the colonial bureaucracy has not been equalled by another European imperial power, including Britain'; and, second, that '[m]ost of the ethnographies [on Indonesia] were not written by anthropologists at all, but ... by missionaries and government officials, and most importantly, by customary-law scholars' (1976: 316). These circumstances in turn resulted in both a 'strength and weakness' of Dutch anthropology, namely 'its emphasis on painstaking description, the attention for the minutiae of life' (Blok and Boissevain, 1984: 335). The descriptive, applied and practical orientation in Dutch anthropology was continued after the loss of the Indonesian possessions and became the core of what came to be known in the post-war period as 'non-Western sociology', linked very closely to Dutch foreign aid programmes and the broad multidisciplinary field of development studies.

France

Rather later than the Dutch, the French established a training school for administrators in 1889 at the École Nationale de la France d'Outre-Mer. It offered instruction in the ethnology of South-East Asia and Africa. The Ecole had originally been founded in 1885 to provide education for natives from the colonies and dependencies. However, like the Dutch experience in the East Indies, the contribution of academic anthropologists to colonial government in the French-administered territories of Vietnam, Laos and Cambodia was not particularly significant. Instead ethnology's relationship to colonial affairs was mediated through the training of colonial officals and the research which they carried out in the countries in which they served. Indeed, the French

maintained a distinction between academic ethnologists producing synthesizing works in the metropole and colonial (amateur) ethnographers whose work was taken seriously in the academy. The latter would provide the former with research data, which could then be used for scientific abstraction.

(Salemink, 1999: 283–284)

It took many years before the organization of ethnographic research was institutionalized in France, and fieldwork was never as important in the French tradition as it was in that of Anglo-Saxon anthropology. The Institut d'Ethnologie of the University of Paris was established in 1926 and the Paris Museum of Mankind (Musée de l'Homme) in 1937 (Bayly, 2000: 582). The general study of the Orient, particularly French Indochinese archaeology, was promoted by the Hanoi-based École Française de l'Extrême Orient, founded in 1898, although an ethnographic branch, headed by Paul Lévy, was not established until 1937, and the Institut Indochinois de l'Étude de l'Homme came into being in 1938 (ibid.: 583). Of special interest to the French in Vietnam were the interior populations of the central and northern highlands, originally referred to as 'Moi', a Vietnamese word meaning 'savages', and then by the French term 'Montagnards', or hill peoples. The highlands were also considered to be of strategic importance to French rule in the wider Indochinese context and ethnographic research had been undertaken in the process of 'pacifying' the hill regions (Salemink, 1999: 282–283). Some senior French military officers had argued for the need to understand the cultures and identities of these upland tribes so that appropriate forms of administration could be instituted. Ethnographic studies were therefore undertaken from the 1890s by French military personnel garrisoned in outposts in the Military Territories along the border with southern China and north-east Laos. Of special note was the work in Upper Tonkin of Commandant and later Lieutenant-Colonel Auguste Louis-M. Bonifacy and Commandant Emile Lunet de Lajonquière and his colleagues. French policy was largely devoted to maintaining loose control over these difficult, unstable, remote upland regions, but, as Michaud says:

> [D]espite the military background of these early observers and the obvious issue of security lying behind these ethnographic investigations, the writings of these officers are remarkably free from the excessive ethnocentrism and blatant racism that characterised Western *mission civilisatrice* at the time.
>
> (2000a: 64)

In the Central Highlands another very well-known early ethnographer was Henri Maitre who had conducted several military expeditions in the Darlac area between 1905 and 1914 and wrote a substantial work, *Les jungles moi*, on the culture and history of the hill peoples there (cited in Salemink, 1991: 247).

French colonial government increasingly concentrated on these upland groups in the 1920s and 1930s because of the policy decision to administer them separately from the lowland majority Vietnamese. It was probably Léopold Sabatier, a French colonial official who served in Darlac for many years until 1926, who made a singular contribution to French colonial ethnology (Salemink, 1999: 286). Sabatier was, in effect, the French counterpart of the Dutch customary law specialists, van Vollenhoven and van Ossenbruggen. He recorded the customary laws (*coutumiers*) of the Rhadé, an Austronesian-speaking minority (Salemink, 1991: 248ff.). He also worked to modify elements of their politico-legal system and culture for the purposes of French administration. Sabatier argued from a cultural relativist position for the importance of understanding Rhadé (or Edê) customs in their own terms – a radical departure from the prevailing evolutionist perspective – and he believed that these, or at least those which did not conflict with French administrative aims, should be protected. He was eventually forced to resign from his post when he tried to resist the plans of the colonial government to open up the highlands to commercial exploitation and colonization.

The significance of Sabatier's work was acknowledged after 1937 when the École Française, in cooperation with the medical faculty at the University of Hanoi, established the Indochinese Institute which took an increasing interest in ethnographic research. This combined activity focused particularly on the compilation of material on customary law and ethnolinguistic research (see, for example, Guilleminet, 1952; Lafont, 1963). The research was related to the government's policies to promote the social and economic development of the native populations, especially in the highland areas, under French protection and guidance. As Salemink has said: '[E]thnographic practice concentrated on the possibilities of political management of the ethnic groups' (1999: 288).

The French orientation to development, with the explicit separation of the majority lowlanders from the hill minorities, linked to protection of the minorities and the recognition of the value of preserving their cultures, though in modified form, continued to influence the perspectives of professional anthropologists in the immediate post-war years up to the defeat of the French by the North Vietnamese army at Dien Bien Phu in 1954. Jacques Dournes's studies of the Koho Sré/Jarai of the Central Highlands is a case in point (1972, 1977, 1980) as is Georges Condominas's detailed field research on the Mnong Gar (1977; and see Lafont, 1963). Both anthropologists contributed to the construction of Montagnard culture as an ethnographic category separate from the lowland Vietnamese and continued the French tradition of detailed ethnohistorical and empirical investigation. What is also clear is that earlier classifications of the hill peoples into bounded, separate tribal groups, typified in Sabatier's focus on the Rhadé, gave way to the French construction and reification of a generalized upland ethnic category or 'nation' (that is 'Montagnard'), in opposition to the lowland Vietnamese (or Kinh) (Salemink, 1999: 294–298).

Of the small number of French professional anthropologists who worked in Vietnam in the immediate post-war years, Georges Condominas is certainly the best known. His research was commissioned by the Office of Colonial Scientific Research in France in 1947, and he undertook detailed field research on the Austroasiatic-speaking Mnong Gar in 1948–1949. As Salemink indicates, Condominas 'positioned his ethnographic work firmly in colonial governmentality, conceived as the scientifically informed management of native populations' (1999: 308). His monograph on the Mnong Gar, published in 1957 and then in

English in 1977 with a new Preface was an innovative study in the form of an ethnographic diary, which presented ethnographic data and described the observer's involvement in gathering field material in a work of high literary quality (ibid.: 309).

We should also note that there was another stream of French colonial writing, which demonstrated significant differences from its British counterpart. Some French observers like Paul Mus concentrated especially on Indochinese politics and religion 'as domains of modernity, rupture and revolutionary initiative', and came close to the concerns of French metropolitan social science in its studies of instability, revolution and insurrection in French domestic politics (Bayly, 2000: 585). In contrast to British functionalism there was a much greater French concern with history, change and conflict.

America

The American colonial experience is closer to that of the British than of the French and Dutch. American academic anthropology had early on expressed an interest in the practical application of its expertise and knowledge to the administration, development and welfare of native subjects, and the issues which had confronted the United States in relation to its own native Indian populations obviously played an important role in this early realization. Fred Eggan notes that 'in the Philippines anthropological viewpoints and knowledge were applied to the solution of administrative problems long before applied anthropology was recognized as a profession' (1974: 196). The American Society of Applied Anthropology was not founded until 1941 when the American colonial presence in the Philippines was all but at an end.

In the very early years of the establishment of American colonial rule in the Philippines there was a recognition of the need for detailed information on various of the native communities which had now to be administered and assisted in their development. The Bureau of Non-Christian Tribes was established in October 1901 within the Department of the Interior; an explicit distinction was made between the particular issues facing the minority communities and those of the lowland Catholic majority. After independence in 1946 the Bureau became known as the Commission on National Integration (Zamora, 1976: 316). Its first Chief was David P. Barrows, who, assisted by Merton L. Miller and Albert Jenks, organized and administered the Ethnological Survey in the Philippines. They were also charged with the task of coordinating the establishment of an administration for the hill minorities in Mountain Province, Luzon and the Muslim regions of the southern Philippines. All three had obtained doctoral degrees in anthropological subjects – Barrows and Miller at Chicago and Jenks at Wisconsin. Jenks is probably the best known of the three in anthropology circles for his major study of the Bontoc (1905), and his general study of the hill populations. On the transfer of power from

Spain to the United States in 1898 very little was known about the hill popula-tions because the Spanish had never effectively administered large parts of this remote upland country.

Yet, as with anthropology in the other colonial territories in South-East Asia, there was little in the way of direct involvement of professional anthro-pologists in the affairs of colonial government. Ethnographic studies were mainly undertaken by those who were employed by the American administra-tion in the Philippines. Among the American school teachers who were engaged to staff the expanding school system in the remoter parts of the archi-pelago, two individuals deserve special mention: Roy Franklin Barton and Henry Otley Beyer. Barton, in particular, made an outstanding contribution to American anthropology in the Philippines through his studies of the culture, social organization and customary law of the Kalinga and Ifugao of northern Luzon (1919, 1949). As in Indonesia and Indochina there was an urgent colo-nial need for information on the indigenous legal systems and institutions, and Barton provided detailed material on traditional laws and their socio-cultural context. This was of special interest to the administration because of the wide-spread practice among the hill tribes of self-help in the redress of wrongdoing, and its expression in the institutions of the blood-feud, head-hunting and arbiters or go-betweens. Barton and others therefore described what for them were embryonic legal forms and this focus of interest in the anthropology of law and social order was to persist in post-war American field research in the Philip-pines. A key institution in the USA for post-war research on the Philippines was Chicago University, primarily through the presence there of Fred Eggan (see Chapter 3).

Beyer, on the other hand, played a vital role in the development of anthro-pology as an academic discipline in the Philippines. A Department of Anthro-pology was founded at the University of the Philippines in 1914 (Lynch and Hollnsteiner, 1961: 1), and Beyer was appointed to a post in anthropology in that year. He became Professor of Anthropology there in 1925 and eventually retired in 1954; among his many achievements was the setting up of the Insti-tute and Museum of Ethnology and Archaeology at the University and his training of a generation of local scholars in Manila (Zamora, 1976: 316; and 1967).

Beyer promoted a broad-based, eclectic anthropology which ranged over archaeology, prehistory, physical anthropology, museum studies, customary law and folklore. Given the American administration's interests in its minority populations, it is no surprise that Beyer concentrated his attention on these, ini-tially the hill peoples of northern Luzon, and then the minorities of the central and southern Philippines. He was heavily involved in the work of the Ethnological Survey and the series of ethnographies which emerged from it. He had also been influenced by the diffusionist and migration theories of Heine-Geldern, and on that basis he attempted to reconstruct the racial ancestry and the prehistory of the Philippines (see below).

Anthropological perspectives in colonial South-East Asia

Despite the post-war criticisms of functionalist anthropology and its suggested association with colonial administrative interests during the late colonial period, this mode of analysis was one among many approaches adopted by anthropologists and other scholars interested in the societies and cultures of the region from the late nineteenth century through to the immediate post-Second World War years. Functionalism had very little influence, for example, on Dutch anthropology, and was much more influential in British research in Africa and to a lesser extent in the Pacific.

Having provided a brief overview of the main developments in anthropology and ethnographic research in South-East Asia as they related to the progress of colonial administration, it remains to consider some of the key concepts and approaches employed in understanding social and cultural life in the region and the main contributions to the anthropological literature. Some of these contributions, either in ethnographic description or in analysis or both, continued to have an important influence on the debates within the anthropology of South-East Asia after political independence (see Chapters 3 and 4). It is difficult to categorize this literature on the basis of particular perspectives or modes of description and analysis because some of our authors embrace more than one theoretical orientation and some changed their position through time as they encountered other approaches and re-evaluated their earlier work. For example, certain of the attempts to describe and classify ethnic or racial groups in a given region are based on evolutionary or diffusionist assumptions, and some writers abandoned earlier commitments to evolutionary theories in favour of functionalist analysis. Nevertheless, there are some clearly identifiable organizing ideas or interests: the main ones are classification and ethnographic description; evolutionism; diffusionism; functionalism (and its variant, structural-functionalism); Dutch structuralism; culture and personality studies; and studies of acculturation and socio-economic change.

Classification and ethnographic description

As the European powers and the United States extended their reach to the geographically remotest parts of South-East Asia, especially into the northern upland ranges of mainland South-East Asia, and the interior hill regions of the large islands of the archipelago, there was an increasing need to gather ethnographic data and classify these often culturally and linguistically diverse minority populations (see Maps 6 to 11 for the main ethnic groups referred to in the text). Often information was gathered in the context of major scientific expeditions commissioned and supported by the government or learned societies. These were also a means of staking a claim to a particular territory as colonial powers competed for control of the indeterminate frontier zones of mainland South-East Asia and the great island of Borneo. Given the lack of knowledge of many of the cultures of the region, it was to be expected that considerable effort would have to be devoted to basic ethnographic description and the categorization of different groups, partly for the purposes of colonial administration. For British social anthropology as it was promoted under the guidance of Malinowski and Radcliffe-Brown, the task of classification and comparison on the basis of racial and cultural critera, and the study of the distribution of peoples and cultures by recourse to diffusionist theories were usually labelled 'ethnology' and were seen as a discipline separate from social anthropology (Evans-Pritchard, 1962: 4–5). However, in continental Europe the term ethnology was often used interchangeably with anthropology (Ellen, 1976: 303).

Some of our best examples of ethnographic compilation, particularly in association with scientific expeditions, comes from the Dutch East Indies. We have already referred to the Central Sumatra expedition organized by P.J. Veth in 1877–1879. It comprised twenty-three scientists, though Veth did not participate personally in the explorations. The production, editing and publication of Veth's nine-volume compendium of the findings of the expedition, in addition to material gathered from all manner of other sources, was spread over seventeen years between 1881 and 1897. Ethnographic data jostled with geographical, historical, linguistic and administrative information. Ellen refers to it as 'ethnographic encyclopaedism', a concern with 'essentially empirical and . . . descriptive ethnography of the Dutch territories' (1976: 312).

A similar enterprise was that of A.W. Nieuwenhuis, a later occupant of Veth's Chair at the University of Leiden. Having joined the first Central Borneo expedition in 1893–1894 led by Gustaaf Molengraaff, Nieuwenhuis took the opportunity to collect a large amount of ethnographic material on the Mendalam Kayan, a Dayak group of the Upper Kapuas region of West Borneo among whom he lived for a period of three months. Three years later he organized a second expedition (1896–1897) which succeeded in crossing Central Borneo from Pontianak on the west coast to Samarinda in the east (Nieuwenhuis, 1900). He revisited the Mendalam Kayan at this time, but also recorded information on other groups in the Upper Kapuas and in the Upper Mahakam river. Then in 1898 Nieuwenhuis undertook a third expedition to the heart of the island, this time travelling from the east coast to the interior Apo Kayan where he studied Kenyah communities as well as Kayans. His massive two-volume compendium, *Quer durch Borneo* (1904–1907), records the results of his last expedition and included ethnographic material from his second expedition.

Koentjaraningrat observes that despite this relatively detailed knowledge of the peoples of Central Borneo

> [Nieuwenhuis] did not appear to develop any degree of sophistication in his anthropological methodology and theories. As a result, his several volumes on the various ethnic groups of Central Kalimantan were essentially little more than travel accounts giving rather superficial descriptions of the people encountered.
>
> (1975: 46)

Nieuwenhuis was a confirmed empiricist, holding to the importance of correct observation and recording of the facts as he saw them. His ethnographies therefore tend to concentrate on directly observable phenomena such as items of material culture and overt behaviour and practices, as well as anecdotal material and stories about particular individuals and events, with little attempt at uncovering the principles underlying the patterning and ordering of social and cultural life, nor the complex context of political behaviour and relations. He held to a cultural relativist position and, in his record of his sojourn among the Mendalam Kayan, demonstrates a degree of empathy with the people, although his underlying assumptions were guided by an evolutionist frame of reference. He attempted to account for, as he described it, the low level of civilization of the Dayaks of Borneo, and he did so by recourse primarily to environmental factors, specifically the difficulties presented for survival and eking out a livelihood in a harsh tropical rainforest habitat. Later in his academic career he became interested in theories of animism and critically addressed various proposals offered by the English evolutionist E.B. Tylor, including Tylor's explanation of the origin of the belief in souls from dream interpretations. But he held to Tylor's view that animism is 'a religion based on beliefs in personal spirits' (Koentjaraningrat, 1975: 67). Overall Nieuwenhuis's views fitted well with the Dutch colonial ethical ideology of the time, that colonial governance and protection were necessary for the development of backward, uncivilized populations (de Wolf, 1999: 321).

A similar approach to ethnographic recording is found in Albert C. Kruyt's studies of various of the Toraja groups of Central Sulawesi. Kruyt spent over forty years among the Toraja working there as a missionary, particularly among the Bare'e Toraja. He produced a three-volume work on the Bare'e with a fellow missionary, N. Adriani (1912–1914; and see Downs, 1956), and towards the end of his career wrote a four-volume record of the West Toraja (1938). Kruyt, like Nieuwenhuis, was content to compile detailed 'factual' information on the more overt elements of Torajan culture, with little analysis or interpretation. However, being deeply interested in native religion and having had a very long acquaintance with the Toraja, he did develop a theory of animism, based on the notion of 'soul-substance' (1906). He discovered that this substance is concentrated in certain parts of the human body and in bodily excretions, as well as in various animals, insects and objects. It could be harmful or beneficial to humans, and it was the goal of magical practice to increase its beneficial properties and guard against or diminish its dangerous aspects. Kruyt suggested that primitive thought distinguished soul-substance from spirits which are derived from the souls of the deceased. These, unlike soul-substance, had personalities and they had to be gratified or appeased so that they worked on behalf of human society or at least did not harm humans in any way. Kruyt also posited an evolutionary transition from animism associated with a 'communistic' way of life to what he called 'spiritism' (the beliefs and practices concerning spirits) which coincided with an 'individualistic' lifestyle. Subsequently he discarded this concept of soul-substance and concentrated on the notion of an abstract 'magical power' which needed to be kept in a condition of equilibrium through human ritual action.

In the British territories of Burma, the Malay States and northern Borneo there were several outstanding examples of administrators who undertook major projects of ethnographic compilation and ethnolinguistic classification. In Burma it is probably J.G. Scott's and J.P. Hardiman's *Gazetteer of Upper Burma and the Shan States* in five volumes, compiled primarily by Scott, which demonstrates more than any other exercise the work of the detailed colonial gatherer and recorder of data. Scott arrived in Malaya in 1875 and found work as a foreign correspondent for the London newspaper, the *Evening Standard*. He then took up a college teaching post in Rangoon while continuing to pursue his enthusiasm for journalism by serving as the correspondent for various London newspapers. During his time in Rangoon he also penned sketches of lowland Burmese cultural values and practices for the *St James's Gazette*, which were brought together as a book under the title *The Burman: His Life and Notions* (1882) under his school-master's nickname Shway Yoe. He also travelled to Mandalay in Central Burma and beyond to the hill areas of Upper Burma. For the next few years he then spent time to-ing and fro-ing between London and the hill areas of mainland South-East Asia as a journalist, specifically in the frontier regions of the expanding French Indochinese territories (Dalby, 1995: 108–157).

Given his experiences in this part of the world Scott took up a post as a district administrator with the Burma Commission in 1886, stationed first at Mandalay. He was then assigned to various parts of the Shan States where he organized several major and minor expeditions and journeys, following the destruction of the Burmese monarchy in the third Anglo-Burmese War and the annexation of Upper Burma by the British in 1886. He was therefore very much involved in the process of 'pacification' in the Shan States and the establishment and extension of British administration and control in the expanding frontier zone. He also participated in the first and second Anglo-Siamese Border Commission and the Burma–China Boundary Commission of 1898–1900. It was in this capacity that he travelled very widely among the hill communities and assembled a prodigious amount of data on their geography, history and culture. Dalby says of Scott's *Gazetteer*:

> [T]his remarkable work ... is, in many ways, still the last word on the topography of Upper Burma, on the history of Burmese districts and of Shan States, and on local legends, both religious and secular. Numerous state histories and temple histories are translated at length or summarized in its pages.
>
> (1995: 153)

Examples of ethnographic classifications, surveys and cultural descriptions of the populations of the Malayan Peninsula and northern Borneo are numerous.

Three which stand out are W.W. Skeat's and C.O. Blagden's *Pagan Races of the Malay Peninsula*, comprising some 1,600 pages of text in two volumes (1906), Charles Hose's and William McDougall's *The Pagan Tribes of Borneo*, in two volumes (1912), and Henry Ling Roth's *The Natives of Sarawak and British North Borneo*, also in two volumes (1896). All three are in the same genre: encyclopaedic compilations of materials from diverse sources, using the same kinds of descriptive ethnographic categories (among others: racial characteristics, language, manners and customs, morals, food, medicine, habitation, livelihood [agriculture, hunting, gathering, fishing], trade, arts and crafts, weapons and warfare, decorative arts, rituals of the lifecycle [birth customs, initiation rites, marriage customs, funeral rituals], music, song and dance, religion and magic, myths and folklore, and social organization). The first two compendia were written primarily by colonial administrators, Skeat and Hose, who both had a passion for studying and recording local cultures. They both also relied on specialist assistance, Skeat on the linguist Blagden, who subsequently lectured in Malay language at the School of Oriental and African Studies in London, and Hose on the anthropologist McDougall, who had participated in the Cambridge Torres Straits Expedition of 1898–1899. Roth, on the other hand, was an amateur ethnographer, who for many years occupied a curatorial post at the Bankfield Museum in Halifax, West Yorkshire. He had never resided in the East, but was stimulated to compile material on northern Borneo when a collection of unpublished materials of a colonial administrator in Sarawak came into his hands by chance. Roth, in his cultural encyclopaedia, does not provide a commentary on the material; instead he extracts, gathers, reproduces and orders it, along with an enormous collection of illustrations and diagrams. It is above all an ethnographic reference work.

Skeat and Blagden state honestly in their introductory remarks that theirs is a 'descriptive ethnography', with 'many facts, but few hypotheses' (1906: viii). Like Hose, they adopt the position of the enlightened administrator, emphasizing the importance for good colonial governance of 'intimately studying and carefully considering the peculiarities of the alien and less civilised races committed to our care' (ibid.: x). Indeed, Skeat and Blagden compare official British support and encouragement for ethnographic research in Malaya unfavourably with the efforts of the Dutch, French and Americans in their South-East Asian territories. On the the basis of racial characteristics and cultural and linguistic criteria they classified the 'pagan races', sometimes referred to as 'wild tribes' or 'savage tribesmen' into three broad racial–physiological categories: the Semang Negritos; the Sakai/Senoi Veddoids or Australoids; and the Mongoloid proto-Malay Jakun or 'savage Malays' specifically contrasted with the Muslim 'civilised Malay'. Of course, this classification has been subject to much subsequent criticism and modification, but it provides an excellent illustration of the kind of approach to ordering and arranging native cultures. What is more, there is a strong sense of colonial paternalism in the ways in which customs, values and characters are depicted. Skeat and Blagden conclude: 'every portion of the primitive social fabric reared by these tribes bears the clear impress of the child-like simplicity and trustfulness that lies at the root of their character' (1906, i: 495).

This is not to say, however, that the society and culture of the traditionally dominant lowland people of the Peninsula – the peasant Malays – were neglected. Skeat's *Malay Magic* (1900), a compendium of Malay folk religion, in the same format and with the same encyclopaedic ambitions, proved to be a landmark in the study of Malay religious shamanism, and undoubtedly stimulated Winstedt's later study of Malay syncretism (1925). The rich data in these studies and several others were subsequently analysed by Endicott in the light of modern structuralist perspectives (1970; and see Chapter 4).

Charles Hose was an avid observer, classifier and collector of ethnographica, but also a keen naturalist who collected and wrote much about the fauna and flora of Borneo. In his *Pagan Tribes* one discerns the intimate relationship between the concerns of the enlightened, paternal colonial administrator and the amateur ethnographer, though local cultures were also of interest and importance to Hose in their own right. *The Pagan Tribes* has remained a major reference work and introduction to the native cultures of Borneo. Hose, like many other colonial observers in the period of late colonialism, argued for a sympathetic understanding and treatment of other lifeways, the value of studying other cultures for our more general understanding of the human condition and, for Europeans, appreciating aspects of their own social and cultural life, and for the appreciation of the rationality of other practices and values when comprehended in their overall cultural context. Hose was a prolific writer, and in his later books *Natural Man* (1926), which was, in effect, an abridged version of *The Pagan Tribes* and *Fifty Years of Romance and Research or a Jungle-Wallah at Large* (1927), he describes and presents other cultures sympathetically to a wider non-specialist reading public, and expresses the 'progressive idea that subject peoples cannot be considered savages since their mental processes are like those of Europeans' and that 'the best way to rule is through example and understanding' (Durrans, 1988: xv).

Finally, a classic example of the colonial ethnographer, and an idiosyncratic one at that, is Ivor H.N. Evans. Evans spent much of his career in Malaya from 1912 until 1932 as curator and ethnographer at the Perak Museum in Taiping, but prior to that he had seen brief service in the North Borneo Chartered Company as a cadet in the district administration in 1910–1911. He was temperamentally unsuited to a bureaucratic life. In his *Among Primitive Peoples in Borneo*, he says:

> To my mind the most enjoyable part of district work is the travelling
> ... there is freedom from all official routine ... change of scene, inter-
> course with the natives, for whom I cherish a great affection, and a
> feeling of having almost cast off the shackles of a paid servant.
>
> (1922: 74)

After his long period of residence in Malaya Evans took early retirement and returned to a quiet life of writing and contemplation in Suffolk, England. However, he missed the East and in 1938, a few years before the outbreak of the Pacific War, he decided to return to North Borneo and continued to undertake ethnographic research, especially on the religious beliefs, practices and folklore of the Dusun of the Kota Belud area. Evans deliberately set himself against theory and analysis, though he was acquainted with developments in Cambridge anthropology and studied under Alfred Haddon. During his long career he wrote and produced several ethnographies on the peoples, cultures and archaeology of North Borneo and the Malayan Peninsula. His publications usually comprise a series of largely unconnected, piecemeal, diffuse descriptions of cultural traits, beliefs, ritual activities, material culture, folk-stories and myths, spiced with the personal observations, experiences, motivations and views of the informed author. His last book, *The Religion of the Tempasuk Dusuns of North Borneo* (1953) is a detailed and painstaking study of the rituals, beliefs and folk-stories of Dusun communities in North Borneo. But perhaps his best-known and admired ethnography is *The Negritos of Malaya* (1937), which, though a compilation, does at least address some of the ethnographic difficulties generated by earlier studies of such groupings as the Senoi and Semang, and tries to make sense of the interrelations and distributions of the different aboriginal populations.

Yet above all, Evans was concerned to observe and record 'facts' and to construct as comprehensive a cultural account as possible. He worked in the Malay language, not in Dusun, and relied heavily on key informants and interpreters, usually men. Although he was aware of the variations and changes in cultural beliefs and practices, and those between different performances of the same ritual, and between individual perceptions and interpretations of religious belief and practice, he was determined to get at what he perceived to be the correct order, sequence and interpretation. Rarely did he attempt to explain cultural differences and locate them in a context of interacting social groups and individuals. Indeed, Evans remained firmly within the tradition of British empiricism, and although he resided for long periods of time in exotic communities, he worked through interpreters to pursue tirelessly the ethnographic 'facts'.

The French too had their ethnographic compilers and classifiers in their attempts to capture the cultural diversity of Indochina. Among the best-known were J. Harmand's survey of the Indochinese 'races' (1882) and Henri Maitre's work on the upland minorities (1912). French ethnography was especially concerned with racial differences and physical typologies, and this focus also translated into evolutionist assumptions about those lowland groups in Indochina such as the Sino-Confucian Vietnamese and before them the Muslim Chams of the once great central and south Vietnamese 'Indic' empire of Champa as of superior and more vigorous racial stock and the highland and interior 'primitives' without civilization and statehood who were considered inferior physiologically and mentally (Bayly, 2000: 589, and see pp. 49–52).

Evolutionism

The existence of diverse cultures and societies in South-East Asia, various racial–physical types, very different ecologies and habitats from hunting–gathering to the cultivation of wet rice by irrigated methods, a variety of forms of kinship and descent, and diverse ethnolinguistic groups and religio-political systems, proved to be a fertile laboratory for evolutionary theory. The basic premise of evolutionists was that more complex or advanced cultural elements or indeed whole cultures are derived from earlier simpler forms through such processes as adaptation to the natural environment, demographic expansion or cultural exchange. Evolutionists often differed in their views on the precise factors underlying evolutionary change. What is more, early writers assumed that this evolutionary process operated according to certain laws of development in a unilinear fashion, in other words, all cultural forms, perceived as natural or organic systems, passed through broadly the same stages, though later modifications to evolutionary theory suggested the possibility of diverging evolutionary pathways or multilinear evolution. Victorian evolutionists and philosophers like Henry Maine, J.F. McLennan, John Lubbock, Lewis Henry Morgan, Edward Tylor and James G. Frazer were especially preoccupied with finding explanations for changes in family and marriage organization and discovering the origins of religion (Evans-Pritchard, 1962: 29–32).

Probably one of the best-known exponents of evolutionary perspectives in relation to South-East Asian ethnography was the Dutch scholar and Leiden Professor, G.A. Wilken. Much of his work was brought together in four volumes, *De Verspreide Geschriften* (1912), after his death and edited by F.D.E. van Ossenbruggen, one of the most distinguished of Wilken's students. Wilken was familiar with the writings of various evolutionists, Tylor, McLennan, Morgan and Lubbock, as well as Darwin's theory of the origin of species. These influences and Wilken's personal acquaintance with a range of different societies and cultures during his residence in the East Indies led him to try to explain the variations between different kinds of organization by recourse to the premise that one type of society had evolved into another, and that one could detect residues or 'survivals' of previous forms in certain existing societies. Wilken also believed that colonial officers and lawyers would benefit from a comparative understanding of the social and cultural background of the various customary law systems in Indonesia, given that the Dutch were committed to codifying, modifying and using native law in conjunction with European legal practice. Wilken's early career had been in the colonial civil service, and he was the son of the missionary, P.N. Wilken, who had worked in northern Sulawesi (Koentjaraningrat, 1975: 28ff.).

Wilken embraced widely held views of the time, articulated particularly by J.J. Bachofen, that the earliest form of human family life had been based on 'primitive promiscuity' and communal marriage within the family group, though he subsequently had doubts about this early stage. Promiscuous relations between male and female kin gave way to the matriarchal family group headed by the mother when men desired to have exclusive access to their wives; they were then prohibited from marrying their female relatives within the group but had to seek partners and marry outside it. Incest prohibitions required exogamy or marriage with partners from other groups. Continuity through the generations gave rise to the formation of large corporate groups based on the principle of matrilineal descent. However, once men began to desire closer identity with their children and control over them they began to bring women to live with their own group or form a separate group under male control. Thus the matriarchal family gave way to the patriarchal family, and, with the continuity and expansion of the size of the group through time, patrilineal descent came to be the central organizing principle of society. Ultimately, though the reasons are obscure, the large patriarchal family breaks down and gives rise to the independent parental or nuclear family of husband, wife and children.

Wilken used this four-stage unilinear evolutionary model to explain variations between forms of kinship and descent in Indonesia, given that on the island of Sumatra alone, for example, one could find the matrilineal society of the Minangkabau, the patrilineal Batak and Rejang and the cognatic coastal Malay groups. Using the notion of the evolutionary transition from one family system to another Wilken attempted to explain the origins and development of a range of related institutions and practices: incest prohibitions, exogamy, brideprice, the levirate (where a man is obliged to marry the wife of a deceased brother), teknonymy (where parents are addressed by the name of their children, as 'Father of ...' or 'Mother of ...'), and the couvade (where the father has to participate in the trials and tribulations of his wife's pregnancy and childbirth and observe various prohibitions and restrictions).

Wilken also explained other variations between Indonesian societies in evolutionary terms. He examined the differences between customary law systems based on self-help, vengeance and personal retribution, which he proposed were the earliest stages in the development of law, and those with legal codes and judicial and legal institutions, which, he argued, represented advanced evolutionary stages. He also devoted considerable energy to the study of Indonesian religions and, following Tylor's theory, maintained that animism represented the earliest form of religion, and that notions of the soul and spirits had emerged from human contemplation and comparison of the conditions of life, death, sickness, dreaming, visions and trance. His studies of totemism, ritual offerings and rituals of bodily mutilation were also premised on a movement from primitive forms of magical belief and practice to more advanced religious forms.

Elements of evolutionary theory were certainly to be found very widely in ethnographic writing of the late nineteenth and early twentieth centuries, in the work of A.C. Kruyt and A.W. Nieuwenhuis, for example, and in various publications on Malaya and Borneo by British observers. Given the syncretic nature of religions in South-East Asia, evolutionary and diffusionist explanations seemed to be especially apt. Probably one of the best-known examples is that of R.O. Winstedt, of the Malayan Civil Service, and his study of Malay magic and its relationship to Islam (1925). Winstedt had been influenced both by the theories of Tylor and Frazer on the evolution of religion from earlier stages of animism and shamanism, though he was also interested in tracing the diffusion of ideas and practices from the Middle East and India to the Malayan Peninsula, and examining what he termed 'survivals' from earlier periods and degraded elements of early beliefs and practices. He says, 'from fear of local spirits and godlings [the Malay] passed through acceptance of the Hindu pantheon to the worship of Allah' (1947: 1).

Another exponent of evolutionary theory was the well-known British anthropologist, A.C. Haddon, who had organized the Cambridge University Expedition to the Torres Straits between New Guinea and Australia in 1898–1899. This expedition, which included W.H.R. Rivers, C.G. Seligman, C.H. Myers and W. McDougall, marked a turning point in British anthropology. There was now an increasing emphasis on the importance of collecting data from direct observation and contact with other cultures, and anthropology became increasingly a professional rather than a part-time activity. Most of the members of the expedition went on to conduct more detailed field research in other locations or sent their students to do so. For example, Haddon and Rivers supported Radcliffe-Brown to undertake research on the Andaman Islanders in 1906–1908, and in his monograph Radcliffe-Brown demonstrated the influence of the Durkheimian perspective in the interpretation of the function of customs in expressing collective sentiments and contributing to community solidarity (1922). Haddon, during his return journey from the Torres Straits, detoured to Sarawak, spent some time examining, photographing and sketching native woven cloths in the Sarawak Museum, and with the assistance of the administrator and amateur ethnographer, Charles Hose, undertook field trips into the hinterland of Borneo (Haddon, 1932). Haddon relied heavily on Hose's advice and guidance on the naming of designs on Iban ritual cloths, and Hose collected and subsequently sent several specimens of cloths to Haddon for the Cambridge Museum. Haddon's book, co-authored with the textile specialist, Laura Start, *Iban or Sea Dayak Fabrics and their Patterns* (1936), became a classic in the study of the material culture of South-East Asia, but it was heavily influenced by evolutionary ideas. Haddon, perceiving primitive society as representing an earlier stage of evolution, relied on this notion to explain the relations between different motifs, and that of survivals of earlier designs in later patterns. One problem he faced was that various named motifs such as 'deer', 'shrew' and 'hawk' did not demonstrate any resemblance to the creatures so named. Haddon assumed that the later designs were merely derivations or stylizations of earlier more realistic designs. He was preoccupied with the explanation of the original meaning of the designs on the assumption that the primitive society which created them is ignorant of their significance or can no longer account for their origin. Through evolutionary processes the design becomes increasingly detached from its original form and name so that realism 'degenerates' into stylization.

We shall examine briefly in the later section on 'functionalism' various of the problems of evolutionary theory. Some of the same shortcomings were also to be found in theories of diffusion, though diffusionists also rejected various of the assumptions of evolutionism, as we shall see in the next section.

Diffusionism

The theory usually known as diffusionism emerged partly in reaction to evolutionary perspectives and the doubts which came to be cast on their unsatisfactory explanations of socio-cultural change. Diffusionists argued that the concept of unilinear evolution was far too speculative. It was conjectural history based on inadequate data, and, even on the basis of the available evidence, evolutionary processes could not be firmly demonstrated. More importantly evolutionism did not take sufficient account of the interconnections between cultures and societies. Differences between cultures at the same point of time did not indicate necessarily that one form had evolved into another through time. On the other hand, for the diffusionists one of the most obvious mechanisms of change was the transfer of ideas, traits and artefacts from one society to another. If similar cultural elements and complexes are found in different societies it was postulated that this was either the result of contact between them or diffusion to these societies from a common source. Different complexes were therefore considered to be the result of different waves of influences or migrations.

Diffusion had an obvious appeal among some early twentieth-century scholars, given that there was evidence that different groups had indeed migrated into various parts of South-East Asia, and that there had been the spread of cultural traits. However, diffusionist theory tended to become the preoccupation not of those involved in colonial administration or in providing training for civil servants, but of university-based scholars. Specifically, a substantial contribution was made by the so-called 'Vienna School of Historical Ethnology' of P.W. Schmidt (Keyes, 1977: 3). Schmidt developed a theory, which was subsequently heavily criticized by various Dutch ethnologists, including W.H. Rassers, of the diffusion of mythological themes concerning sun and moon symbolism on the basis of their distribution among the Austronesian peoples of the Indonesian archipelago, Melanesia and Polynesia (1910). He suggested that two cultural complexes could be discerned: one in the western part of the archipelago, including Sumatra, Java, Kalimantan and Sulawesi, in which moon symbolism associated with elements of what he referred to as the belief in a 'high god' or a supreme being was dominant; the other complex in the eastern regions of Indonesia through to Melanesia and Polynesia had a preponderance of sun symbolism. Schmidt argued that the first cultural complex to enter the region focused on moon myths; this complex had its origin somewhere in mainland South-East Asia. It later gave way in the eastern regions to a complex focused on the sun, which originated from New Guinea. Schmidt was of the view that the belief in a creator or 'high god' was an early cultural element in Indonesia, which had been replaced by the belief in a variety of spirits and magical power, and the remnants of the original monotheistic religion could only be found in remote and isolated societies there.

One of the most distinguished of Schmidt's students was Robert von Heine-Geldern, who, according to Keyes, 'was the first anthropologist to attempt a general systematic ordering of Southeast Asian ethnography within a broader framework informed by anthropological theory' (1977: 4). Heine-Geldern's theory has some merit in explaining some of the connections between and distributions of various cultural elements, art styles, material artefacts and languages. Heine-Geldern was by no means an uncritical advocate of diffusion as a mechanism of cultural change, but certain of his ideas have been revised subsequently on the basis of new archaeological evidence from Asia.

Heine-Geldern put forward a detailed and complex scheme for the movement of peoples and cultures into and through South-East Asia (1928, 1932). A key definitional element in his cultural complexes was types of axes in what he called the South-East Asian 'High Neolithic' period. He proposed: (1) an 'oval-axe' culture of Mongoloid peoples with plank boats, and particular pottery styles, had moved from eastern Asia through the Philippines and eastern Indonesia to New Guinea and Melanesia and had influenced Papuan and Melanesian cultures; (2) a 'shouldered-axe' culture of probably Mongoloid peoples speaking Austroasiatic languages moved from an unknown homeland to South-East Asia, southern coastal China, north-eastern Korea, Japan, Taiwan, the Philippines, northern Sulawesi and perhaps part of India; (3) a 'quadrangular-axe' culture of Austronesian-speakers moved from China into South-East Asia; other elements of the cultural complex included particular pottery styles, stone and shell ornaments, pile-dwellings, megaliths and head-hunting; (4) there was an emigration of a seafaring Austronesian branch from the southern Malayan Peninsula through the Indonesian archipelago and its interaction with Papuan-speakers in the east of the archipelago; (5) the movement of a second Austronesian branch through Borneo, the Philippines and Taiwan to Japan; and (6) the emergence of Polynesian culture from the intermixture of the Austronesian 'quadrangular-axe' culture with the Austroasiatic 'shouldered-axe' culture. Heine-Geldern (1965) also distinguished two broad pre-Indian tribal art styles in South-East Asia: the earliest to spread into South-East Asia in the second millennium BC was characterized by monumental, sculptural forms associated with commemoration and magic, a megalithic culture and the quadrangular stone axe, evidence for which is to be found among the upland tribes of Assam and western Burma, certain Torajan groups of Sulawesi, on Nias off the coast of Sumatra, and in the hill areas of northern Luzon; the later style is ornamental, and although associated with religion and magic, is much more a product of aesthetic considerations; it is represented in the cultures of the Batak of Sumatra, the hinterland tribes of Borneo and Mindanao, some of the Torajan groups, and in eastern Indonesia. Heine-Geldern links this complex with the Late Bronze–Early Iron Age Dongson culture of northern Indochina and Yunnan and its spread into the island regions of South-East Asia from about 700 BC.

In his paper on the archaeology and art of Sumatra appended to Edwin Loeb's survey of Sumatra, Heine-Geldern provides details on the monumental art, megalithic culture, ancestral cults of the early quadrangular axe culture of Nias, and the later 'wave' of culture which spread from mainland South-East Asia comprising ornamental Dongson influences, elements of which are to be found in Batak and Minangkabau art (1935: 305–331). Loeb's work also shows evidence of the influence of diffusionist theory, though mixed with evolutionist ideas and American cultural anthropology (1935). In his compilation of ethnographic materials of Sumatra, Loeb embraces earlier theories based on racial categorizations and migrations: South-East Asia was populated by Negritos no longer represented in Sumatra, then Veddoids of which the Kubu of the Palembang region are an example, and then the Mongoloid Austronesians divided into an earlier Proto-Malay migration wave represented by the Bataks (and elsewhere, the Dayaks of Borneo, Torajas of Sulawesi and the Igorots of northern Luzon) and the later Deutero-Malay migration represented by such groups as the coastal Malays and the Javanese (1935: 14–17).

Although diffusionary explanations had some value, they tended to be discredited by the more extreme views presented by such writers as W.J. Perry, who adapted the ideas of G. Elliot Smith on the ancient Egyptian origins of a megalith-building, sun-worshipping cult, to examine what he called the 'megalithic culture' of Indonesia (1918). Perry argued that a cultural complex was carried into South-East Asia by an ancient population which used and carved stone, erected stone structures for ritual purposes and worshipped the sun. Other elements of the complex included irrigated rice agriculture, gold and metal working, certain pottery styles, belief in 'soul-substance' and a sky-world, fertility rites and a hereditary and initiated priesthood, with a social system comprising elaborate strata, chiefs, totemic clans and matrilineal descent. The occurrence of some of these traits together is evidence of their survival from the earlier total complex of stone-using sun-worshippers. Perry had undertaken his research in South-East Asia on the advice of W.H.R. Rivers to whom he dedicates his book. Rivers, in his work on Melanesian ethnohistory, had emphasized the processes of migration and cultural interaction, and that megaliths in Melanesia were the work of sun-worshipping immigrants (1914).

Though rather less far-fetched than Perry's and Elliot Smith's views, Charles Hose also could not resist speculating on the origins of Borneo peoples. Interestingly the 'Preface' to his *Natural Man* was provided by the diffusionist Professor Elliot Smith who suggests the possibility of the transmission to Borneo of certain customs known among the ancient Egyptians, Romans, Babylonians, Etruscans and Persians (1926: ix). Hose, however, was attracted to the notion of physical migration, and based on what he perceived to be significant racial and cultural differences between various major indigenous groups, proposed three 'invasions' into Borneo, the first being the ancestors of the Kayan peoples of central Borneo whom he suggests had migrated from the Irrawaddy Basin in Burma via Sumatra; the Muruts had then followed from the Philippines or Annam, and the most recent arrival, which Hose supposed took place in the seventeenth century, were the ancestors of the Ibans who were brought from Sumatra as 'pagan fighting men' by Malay noblemen (1926: 3ff.). Groups such as the Punans, Kenyahs and other smaller groups were then assumed to have been the original populations of the island 'going back possibly to the time when Borneo was still continental' (ibid.: 9). Of course, other than the supposed racial and cultural differences within Borneo and the assumed similarities with populations outside Borneo, Hose had no firm evidence for his migration theory.

Even among professional anthropologists interested in the Philippines the lure of explanations for cultural differences based on notions of diffusion and physical migration proved irresistible. Alfred Kroeber produced a handbook entitled *Peoples of the Philippines* guided by the exciting discovery that the islands 'furnish an unusual story to the student of the development of civilization. Layer after layer of culture is recognizable, giving a complete transition from the most primitive condition to full participation in Western civilization' (1928: 11). He attempted to demonstrate that cultural variation in the Philippines could be interpreted in terms of 'waves of civilization', and, in particular, the arrival in the islands of three racial types which he labels 'Negrito' (an 'excessively simple' culture represented by small pockets of population in northern Luzon, Mindanao and Palawan [ibid.: 39, 226]), 'Mongoloid-Indonesian or Proto-Malayan' (their culture was best preserved among the hill peoples of northern Luzon, and represented an ancient South-East Asian civilization spread across both the mainland and island regions [ibid.: 226, 228]), and a 'Mongoloid-Malaysian or Deutero-Malayan' (found mainly in the lowlands and influenced by Indian culture and then by Spanish Catholicism and Islam [ibid.: 225]).

The problem with Schmidt's, Heine-Geldern's, and indeed Hose's and Kroeber's argument, and even more so with that of Perry, is to demonstrate that the distribution of cultural traits has been generated by their diffusion. Some of the distributions could equally well have been the result of local and internal changes in cultural elements without movement of traits from one place and culture to another. There are also difficulties in establishing the criteria and methods on which diffusionists determine similarity and difference between cultures. Nor is it clear why and how certain elements occur together in a complex. Nevertheless, there has clearly been physical movements and the movement of traits into and through South-East Asia, though the wave theory of the diffusionists, the migration routes proposed and the precise content of the cultural complexes are far too simply drawn and have been criticized on the basis of subsequent research and findings from archaeology and ethnolinguistics (Bellwood, 1985).

Functionalism

The functionalist perspective and the subsequent combination of this with a concern to understand how particular societies are structured emerged in part as a reaction to the general speculative historical reconstructions of the evolutionists and diffusionists, which were usually based on superficial, unreliable data gathered by observers who were not generally skilled in ethnographic research. Instead such anthropologists as Bronislaw Malinowski and A.R. Radcliffe-Brown argued for the importance of collecting detailed data through sustained field research in the vernacular in specific communities and to further this understanding by then conducting controlled comparisons of cultural and social institutions. What is more, the need for direct participant observation and the careful documentation of social and cultural life was of even greater importance in pre-literate societies without written histories and records. However, Malinowski and Radcliffe-Brown did not abandon certain elements of evolutionary theory.

The requirement that information be recorded in much more detail therefore meant that the studies had to be undertaken either by university-trained anthropologists, with full-time support for a long period of fieldwork, or by those like missionaries and district administrators, with the appropriate training in anthropology, who resided for long periods of time in close contact with local communities and who had the opportunity to collect data on the spot. In South-East Asia it was usually the latter category of observers which was more directly involved in data collection, and only in the dying years of colonialism did academic anthropologists begin to undertake field research there, more often than not among those minority groups at a physical and social distance from the administrative capitals of the dependent territories.

The basic assumption of Malinowski's functionalism was that cultures are integrated wholes; they are 'working units' and cultural elements have to be understood in the context of their use or function, not, as in evolutionist analyses, their origins and development. What is important is to establish connections between institutions. For Malinowski '[e]very custom exists to fulfil a purpose and so all customs have a living, current meaning for members of a society', but he tended not to prioritize particular relations, customs or institutions so that for him 'any set of connections constituted a system' (Kuper, 1983: 26, 29). Malinowski also argued that customs existed to fulfil human needs, and he tended to see these in psychological and biological terms, specifically in terms of individual interests, needs and sentiments. Individuals, according to Malinowski, were also calculating, choice-making cultural beings pursuing their particular interests and goals; he therefore focused on the individual rather than developing an understanding of social systems. But above all he argued for the reasonableness of individuals in 'primitive' small-scale societies once one understands the social and cultural context within which they make decisions and choices in the pursuit of their interests.

There were clear differences in perspective and emphasis between Malinowski and Radcliffe-Brown, although both of them were usually lumped together as functionalists. It was Radcliffe-Brown who was to take the functionalist perspective to a more sophisticated level of analysis by combining the notion of function with that of social structure and developing the concept of an integrated, ordered social system of formal rules and abstracted patterns. For him the social system comprising the sets of relations between individuals performing social roles was the focus of analysis rather than the Malinowskian study of the cultural and biological individual and behaviour and customs. Thus, the function of a social instititution is the contribution it makes to the total activity or social system of which it is a part; it contributes to the maintenance and survival of the whole. Radcliffe-Brown's emphasis on social structure became dominant in British social anthropology in the late 1930s and was carried forward by Edward Evans-Pritchard and Meyer Fortes, particularly in the study of small-scale political organization and relations of kinship and descent.

With regard to South-East Asian research, the impact of functionalism was modest, and was much more evident in British research on Africa. Fortes had some influence on the research of Derek Freeman (1955a, 1955b [1970]) on Iban cognatic social organization; Fortes distinguished the politico-jural domain of clan and lineage organization from the domestic domain of kinship and family relations, and it was the latter which had particular relevance for anthropologists interested in cognatic relations. Raymond Firth, however, kept to a modified version of Malinowski's functionalism, and with his students, some of whom undertook research in South-East Asia, concentrated on individual interests, action and choice in its socio-cultural context. Firth and his colleagues at the LSE were especially interested in the study of small-scale peasant economic systems in Malay(si)a and Java (see Chapter 5).

Functionalism, and particularly Radcliffe-Brown's emphasis on functioning social systems, drew its inspiration from the theories of Emile Durkheim and his associates, especially Marcel Mauss and Robert Hertz, the group of Paris-based scholars known as the *Année Sociologique* after the name of the journal which they founded and in which they published their key ideas. The influence of the French school was mediated particularly through Radcliffe-Brown in Britain, Australia and the USA, Malinowski to a lesser extent, and J.P.B. de Josselin de Jong in The Netherlands (see next section), and guided some of the research in the British, American and Dutch territories in South-East Asia. We shall also consider in Chapter 4 the contribution of French-influenced structural anthropology to the post-war development of South-East Asian anthropology. Nevertheless, Durkheim's insistence on the importance of gathering and analysing social facts and his concern with religion as an expression of collective social life and values can be seen in the work of Antoine Cabaton on the Muslim Chams of southern Vietnam, though Cabaton, a researcher with the Ecole Française, combined Durkheimian insights with old-style French racial theories (Bayly, 2000: 596–597). A better-known Durkheimian, at least in his earlier work on the culture, cosmology and architecture of the Chams, was Paul Mus, who was the son of a colonial educator, brought up in Hanoi, and also a researcher at the Ecole (ibid.: 602–611). Among other things, Mus compared the level and kind of social integration which existed between the Sinicized Vietnamese whose culture he considered to possess a greater degree of 'sociality', and the Indianized Chams 'who were less solidly "rooted" and "integrated" . . . within their collective social units' (ibid.: 609). Subsequently, however, Mus became increasingly interested in the cultural roots of Vietnamese nationalism and the 'social pathologies' engendered by colonialism (ibid.: 621).

Some of the best examples of the British functionalist approach, although, as we have seen there is considerable variation in approaches within functionalism and structural–functionalism, is to be found in the work of the anthropologists who worked in Malaya, Sarawak and Singapore during the late 1930s and in the immediate post-war colonial period. The Colonial Social Science Research Council studies of Freeman ([1955a] 1955b, 1970), Geddes (1954), Morris (1953), Freedman (1957) and Djamour (1959) are good examples, and the Firths' studies in east coast Malaya. In the USA the studies undertaken on the Philippines sponsored both through the University of Chicago programme established in 1952 and headed by Fred Eggan, who had been a student of Radcliffe-Brown, and by the Anthropology Department at the University of the Philippines, provide illustrations of the approach there. However, a slightly earlier contribution is that of de Moubray (1931) in his study of customary law among the matrilineal Malays of Negeri Sembilan. De Moubray was an administrative officer in the Malayan Civil Service who was concerned to provide a basic ethnography and explanation of matrilineal society, or as he refers to it 'matriarchal custom' for his fellow civil servants in Negeri Sembilan. He argued for its value, based as it was on a strong local identity and 'a firm body of tradition' (ibid.: 193). In piecing together often 'chaotic and conflicting evidence', he examines legal rights and obligations and the administration of ancestral and acquired property. De Moubray states that he was 'gradually forced to adopt this [functional] method' which he 'stumbled across . . . without knowing that it was a recognized anthropological method' (ibid.: 10). However, he insists that the diffusionist, evolutionist and historical methods are required in conjunction with functionalism to understand fully Negeri Sembilan society. He also cannot resist speculating about the origins of matriarchy, and the reasons for its decay. But in trying to reach an understanding of how the matrilineal system coheres and the logic of its operation, he adopts a functionalist perspective.

What characterized functionalist studies above all was detailed ethnographic narrative based on long-term field research and an analytical approach concerned to demonstrate how societies maintain order and sustain continuity, and the key units, groups and relationships which comprise the social structure. Thus, as with similar studies undertaken in Africa and the Pacific Islands especially, there is a concentration on such areas of life as kinship, marriage, descent, village life and organization, and social stratification. A major preoccupation in the cognatic societies of much of South-East Asia, among the Malays, the lowland Filipinos and the hill or hinterland minorities of Borneo and the Philippine archipelago was the identification of organizational mechanisms and elements which would provide order and structure in the absence of large-scale corporate descent groups. The analysis of descent groups had reached a high level of sophistication in African anthropology, but many of the nonunilineal or cognatic societies of South-East Asia presented a different set of problems for those anthropologists interested in principles of social structure. They did not have large-scale corporate unilineal descent groups providing social coherence and continuity. Thus, a significant feature of the work of such anthropologists as Freeman, Geddes and Eggan was to examine group formation and the ways in which large numbers of people can be mobilized for particular activities. South-East Asian anthropology has therefore produced a fund of material, debate and discussion, which has influenced a generation of post-war anthropologists, on the nature and structure of small family units (domestic, nuclear and stem famil-ies), on the village as a kinship, residential and corporate unit, on networks of relationships focused on individuals (usually termed 'personal' or 'bilateral kin-dreds' or 'kinship circles' in the literature), on bilateral descent groupings, on the social consequences of employing the principle of cognatic or bilateral descent in organizing property relations and political life, among other things, and, where they are found, the structure and operation of social strata or ranks in cognatic societies.

Leach's (1950) social science survey of Sarawak addresses the main issues in the investigation of cognation and social structure, as do the general statements in George Murdock's influential edited book *Social Structure in Southeast Asia* (1960a). Murdock's text, which resulted from a symposium held in Bangkok in late 1957, contains, among others, contributions by Derek Freeman (Iban of Borneo), Fred Eggan (Sagada Igorots of northern Luzon), Charles Frake (eastern Subanun of Mindanao), Edmund Leach (Sinhalese of northern Sri Lanka) and Koentjaraningrat (Javanese). Murdock's introduction to the book entitled 'Cog-natic Forms of Social Organization' (1960b: 1–14) has probably been one of the most widely quoted statements in the anthropology of South-East Asian cog-natic kinship. The problem to be confronted was set out by Murdock in the following terms, that for those societies which 'do not employ either patrilineal or matrilineal descent as a major organizing principle in the grouping of kinsmen ... there still exists no solid consensus regarding organizational prin-ciples, typology, or terminology comparable to that achieved for unilineal social systems' (ibid.: 2).

In a classic structural–functionalist statement, Eggan, in his study of Sagada Igorot social organization states that 'social structures have jobs to do', and that bilateral societies like unilineal ones have to 'cope with the problems of trans-mission and continuity without too much confusion' (1960: 49). Eggan finds this order and continuity in the kinship network, bilateral descent groups and residential wards, which are corporate groups. Freeman, too, in his dialogue with Radcliffe-Brown, and in addressing the problem of order in cognatic societies analysed in detail the Iban family corporation and the 'ramifying cognatic kinship structure' based on personal kindreds. He says that, on the basis of what we know of bilateral societies, 'there are a number of solutions alternative to unilineal descent all of which result in ordered social systems' (1960: 85). We shall return in Chapter 3 to this issue of social order in cognatic societies with reference to the Philippines, and then in Chapter 4 we shall examine the ways in which so-called structural anthropologists, influenced especially by the ideas of Claude Lévi-Strauss, have analysed unilineal societies in South-East Asia.

Malinowskian functionalism, as we have said, was continued in the work of Firth and various of his students. Firth's study of Malay fishermen in 1939–1940 was intended, in part at least, as a contribution to practical anthropology, to provide 'a body of factual inquiries' for policy-makers concerned with the improvement of the economic conditions of peasant communities (1966: xi). However, its main aim was to offer a contribution to economic anthropology and to understand 'how a Malay fishing economy ordinarily functions', the mechanisms of adaptation to both internal and external conditions and the 'value of their traditional forms of cooperation' (ibid.: xii). In particular, Firth examined the socio-cultural context of economic decision-making and activity in the use of labour and capital, and also provided a large amount of detailed ethnographic material on the technical and organizational aspects of fish production, marketing and distribution. Firth shows how the fishermen make choices in economic matters given the opportunities and constraints they face, and the ways in which economic transactions are embedded in personal, social, kinship and residential networks. He says that the economic decisions of the producers and consumers in an exchange are 'governed by their total relationship to one another, not simply by their immediate relationship in the exchange situation' (ibid.: 7). Therefore, he demonstrates, as did Malinowski in his study of the Trobriand economy, that apparently irrational decisions and behaviour have to be understood in the total socio-cultural context and with regard to the constraints, opportunities, interests and preferences that individuals have to address (and see Chapter 5).

This is precisely the approach which H.N.C. Stevenson adopts in his study of the economics of the Chin of Upper Burma on the basis of field research in 1934–1936. He acknowledges his debt to Malinowski and Firth; he proposes that his study is a contribution to applied anthropology for his 'brother officers on the frontiers of Burma' in that the understanding of economic production, distribution and consumption is of crucial importance to the administration of the hill populations (1945: vii). In addition, economic choice is exercised from 'a given range of preferences' which for 'primitive' societies include social and psychological factors, and that the 'economic disposal of resources', given the importance of social and cultural considerations in small-scale communities, 'has the same basic meaning in Chin economy as in western economy' (ibid.: 3).

Dutch structuralism

As we have said, the origins of a particular approach to the understanding of the structures of indigenous societies in Indonesia can be found in the work of F.D.E. van Ossenbruggen. His most influential paper, inspired by Durkheim and Mauss's work on 'primitive classification' ([1903] 1963), focused on the structure of the Javanese village and the origin and nature of the *monca-pat*, an archaic form of village confederation or unity, which comprised a central village and four symmetrically arranged outer villages associated with cardinal points ([1918] 1977). Van Ossenbruggen noted that the four–five arrangement occurred very frequently in Javanese culture and proposed that the system was based on the major Javanese social divisions which provided a conceptual framework for classifying the cultural and natural world. More particularly, these principles relate to an earlier form of society whose structure and character can now only be detected in surviving cultural domains. He concludes that in Java, therefore, 'tribal divisions once served as the basis for the organization of images and perceptions' (1977: 45).

It was then W.H. Rassers who took this perspective a stage further in his wide-ranging analyses of various dimensions of Javanese culture, particularly the Hindu-Javanese Panji epics (1959). He detects a pervasive dualism in Javanese culture and world-view, and the arrangement of cultural categories into opposed pairs associated with such divisions as male–female, sun–moon, good–evil, upperworld–underworld. He argued that these are 'reflections' of the structure of ancient Javanese society which comprised exogamous moieties which were in turn divided into four clans linked by a system of asymmetric cross-cousin marriage and organized on the basis of bilineal descent (see also Chapter 4). The Panji stories also recorded the cosmic initiation rituals of the common ancestor of both moieties, who also exhibits markedly dualistic features.

The crucial link in the development of analyses of social and symbolic classification was J.P.B. de Josselin de Jong, who brought together Malinowski's work on the function of myth in primitive society and Rasser's and van Ossenbruggen's ideas on the principles of Javanese classification. De Josselin de Jong was dissatisfied with evolutionary theories, and argued that ancient social forms could be reconstructed by revealing the structural principles underlying the classification of current diverse social, cultural and natural forms in existing societies. He argued furthermore that ancient Indonesian society was based on a bilineal or double unilineal clan system, the clans intermarrying in a circle, each giving brides to one clan and taking brides from another. Ritual gifts were also exchanged in marriage. The clans were arranged into moieties, associated with a dualistic cosmology. De Josselin de Jong maintained that these principles were widespread in the Indonesian archipelago, justifying the study of Indonesia in comparative terms as an anthropological or ethnological field of study ([1935] 1977). In some sense it comprised a unit of analysis exhibiting common cultural features which could be related back to an unspecified earlier time when there was a common social structure across Indonesia. This structure has subsequently been affected by internal changes and external influences and become increasingly differentiated. But the traditional culture was remarkably resilient and able to assimilate and 'Indonesianize' outside influences.

De Josselin de Jong trained a whole generation of Dutch ethnographers, many of whom had followed programmes in Indonesian languages and literatures, or, as colonial office cadets, training programmes in Indology. Many language students were destined for posts as government linguists and philologists, or missionaries and Bible translators, and it is significant that Dutch structuralism owes much to the interests and expertise of linguists, philologists and textual scholars. One of the most influential writers in pre-war structural anthropology was F.A.E. van Wouden, who followed the Leiden training course for the East Indies civil service, and then studied Indonesian languages and anthropology before taking up a post in northern Sulawesi in 1935. His doctoral thesis of 1935, under de Josselin de Jong's supervision, was subsequently translated by Rodney Needham and published in English as *Types of Social Structure in Eastern Indonesia* (1968). Van Wouden attempted to make sense of what he referred to as the 'erratic distribution and intermingling of patrilineal and matrilineal forms of social organization and of unilateral circulating marriage systems' in eastern Indonesia, and he explained this phenomenon 'as the expression of a specific type of social structure characterized by double descent' (1977: 184). His perspective was very much in line with Dutch structuralist thinking, and the attempt to identify unifying principles which underlie different social and cultural forms across a range of societies. Other notable contributions in this genre were G.J. Held's research on the Indian epic, the Mahabharata (1935), and Hans Schärer's study of Ngaju Dayak religion (1963). Both scholars worked in Christian mission enterprises in the East Indies.

These Leiden studies were to have a significant influence on post-war Dutch anthropology and continued to be promoted in Leiden by P.E. de Josselin de Jong in particular (see, for example, 1951, 1965, 1977). They pre-dated the work of Claude Lévi-Strauss on the 'elementary structures of kinship' ([1949] 1969) and symbolic classification (1966) and were also to help guide the research in Indonesia and in other parts of South-East Asia of several Oxford-based anthropologists under the supervision of Rodney Needham (see Chapter 4). Dutch structuralist analyses and customary law studies of Indonesian cultures provoked criticism from various American cultural anthropologists, including Clifford and Hildred Geertz, who had worked in Indonesia from the early 1950s (e.g. Clifford Geertz, 1961; Hildred Geertz, 1965; and see Chapter 3). Dutch ethnologists were criticized for their tendency to describe and analyse village communities as closed systems, separate from wider political and economic contexts; their concentration on standardized customs and social rules and norms; the assumption that there is a congruence between symbolic and social classification; and the speculative reconstruction of an ancient and general Indonesian society which was assumed to comprise a dual organization. Be that as it may, many Leiden-trained administrators and anthropologists were certainly fully conscious of the negative consequences of colonialism for native societies, and were 'haunted by questions of acculturation and culture change', even though one of the core elements in the characterization of an ancient Indonesian society comprised its ability to incorporate or absorb external cultural influences (Prager, 1999: 328; Schulte Nordholt, 1999: 267ff.).

Culture and personality studies

Concepts and theories from psychological studies have played an influential role in the development of anthropology, particularly in attempts to understand and explain so-called 'primitive mentalities' and the origins of magic and religion. These were very important in the work of eighteenth- and nineteenth-century philosophers and social thinkers in their use of 'associationist psychology' and then 'introspective psychology'. However, the influence of psychological perspectives has always been more pronounced in American than in British, French and Dutch anthropology, though Malinowski, for example, had been trained in experimental psychology, and his work, in contrast to that of Radcliffe-Brown, carried the clear imprint of psychological concepts. In this perspective cultural behaviour is explained in terms of certain 'feelings', 'emotional states', 'needs' or 'instincts' and behaviour 'arises in situations of emotional stress, frustration, or intensity and its function is cathartic, expletive, or stimulating' (Evans-Pritchard, 1962: 44–45). However, in the interwar years a particular focus in American anthropology, associated with Franz Boas, Ruth Benedict and Margaret Mead, emerged with the development of psychoanalysis and gestalt theory. This was not a prominent perspective in colonial anthropology in South-East Asia but there were a few American studies undertaken on Indonesia and Thailand of the ways in which individual personality and behaviour are shaped by culture, especially as a result of child-rearing practices.

Probably the best-known study is that of Gregory Bateson and Margaret Mead in Central Bali in 1936–1937 (1942; as well as Jane Belo, 1970). They concentrated on the process of growing up in the Balinese village of Bajung Gde and the ways in which both general patterns of behaviour and individualistic behaviour are interrelated with the process of social and cultural learning and instruction. In what was a unique study for its time the researchers took some 25,000 photographs of a sample of eight children over a period of a year. The conclusions drawn were that the Balinese character was shaped and based on fear instilled by the mother, and the reassurance of protection by the father if an individual followed the culturally delineated pathways. The emphasis was on constructing a picture of the character of the average Balinese rather than studying individual personalities, and, according to Bateson and Mead, the Balinese character was detached and unemotional in interpersonal relationships; overall Balinese society was described in terms of stasis, equilibrium and balance. This study was also one element in a broader series of studies undertaken by Mead in the Asia Pacific region 'framed as experiments in cultural variability' (Bowen, 2000: 12).

Another study of culture and personality was undertaken by the American anthropologist Cora du Bois in 1938 on the eastern Indonesian island of Alor (1944). Various psychological tests were administered on a sample of the population to examine processes of infant-feeding and child-rearing, and attitudes towards such matters as food, sex and religious beliefs. Du Bois concluded that the Alorese male experienced deep feelings of insecurity, a lack of self-worth and enterprise and 'an unconscious distrust of women' which arose primarily from his early childhood experience of maternal neglect (Koentjaraningrat, 1975: 132). Interestingly Du Bois's general, though brief study, in three lectures delivered in 1947, on the social forces at work in South-East Asia, was far more perceptive and prescient (1964). She adopts the standard American cultural anthropology paradigm of the time, defining the concept of culture in very broad terms, as well as examining cultural integration, conflict, diffusion, adaptation, survival, and so on; but she does not use psychological perspectives overtly in her attempt to understand the then current problems of the South-East Asian region and its prospects for the future.

The problems with the culture and personality studies were significant, given that psychological tests administered in non-Western cultures were in their infancy at that time, and that these tests and more general psychological and psychoanalytical perspectives were based largely on Western preoccupations. On the basis of the methods used, the limited sampling, and the relatively superficial treatment of the socio-cultural and historical context of behaviour, it was difficult to accept the character stereotypes presented by Western anthropologists. What is more, such anthropologists as Mead, Ruth Benedict and John Embree also undertook even more far-fetched and generalized 'national character' studies during the Second World War, in an attempt to advise American policy-makers on both war-time and post-war strategies. Studies were especially focused on Japan, but Benedict also produced a study of Thai national character (1952). We shall return to a more detailed examination of American cultural and psychological anthropology in Chapter 3.

Studies of acculturation and socio-economic change

Given the dominance of functionalist, customary law and structuralist studies in the anthropology and ethnology of late colonialism, there was very little room for analyses of social change and acculturation. The analysis of change tended to be located within general speculative evolutionary and diffusionist frameworks, or in cultural–historical narratives. The most enduring work on socio-economic and cultural transformations was undertaken by administrators and scholars who had come under the influence, not of anthropology, but of sociological concepts, particularly from Max Weber, and who had accepted that processes of socio-cultural change could only be understood in a politico-economic context.

The main focus was the consequences of Western colonialism and capitalism for native societies. Of special importance in this connection is J.H. Boeke's concept of 'dual society' or 'dual economy' (1953). Boeke, who had had long service in the Dutch colonial administration, was concerned to explain the distinctive character of the Indonesian rural economy, and he did so by emphasizing the 'sharp, deep, broad cleavage' which divided Indonesian society into two separate segments: an Eastern, traditional, non-capitalist sector, and a Western, modern, capitalist sector. In his view, local communities do not respond to capitalist-generated economic stimuli, given that they possess only limited economic needs; they are averse to risk-taking, capital accumulation and continuous profit-seeking and lack discipline and organizational abilities. In his explanation of the Oriental predicament he examines the persistence of the influence of 'traditional culture' and 'personality', but, according to Koentjaraningrat, for Boeke the fundamental causes of local backwardness and poverty were

> the intrusion of a Western economic system into the previously balanced social equilibrium of the village community; the disruption of village autonomy by central government interference; the exploitation of the village population for the benefit of Western economic enterprises, and the great gap that consequently existed between the rural and urban society.
>
> (1975: 76)

The concept of dualism has exerted a significant influence on post-war sociological and economic analyses of South-East Asia, but it has also been criticized for its misleading characterization of Oriental peasant economy. Indeed, the work of Firth and his colleagues on South-East Asian peasant communities suggests that there is not such a marked difference between Oriental and Western economic motivations, decision-making and organization, and that Boeke has a too narrow and formal conception of Western economic theories and principles. And therefore, second, Boeke's emphasis on a sharp distinction between two social and economic types is insufficiently sensitive to the interconnections between different economic sectors, communities and groups, to the variations within sectors and communities, and to the dynamic processes of change and response. We shall see in Chapter 3 how Boeke's concept has been taken forward and revised in relation to post-war studies of Indonesian society.

Another analytical concept of some significance for post-war social science is that of the 'plural society' first formulated by J.S. Furnivall in his study of colonial Burma and its comparison with the Dutch East Indies (1939, 1948). For Furnivall, like Boeke, a novel concept was required to understand the particular circumstances of colonial tropical dependencies. He too considered tropical society to be sharply divided internally, but, he added another social, economic and indeed cultural element to that society: the 'alien' Asian communities of

Chinese and Indians wedged between Boeke's modern, Western capitalist sector and traditional native society. These then formed, in hierarchical fashion, 'distinct economic castes' which lived cheek by jowl, but which did not meet and mix socially and culturally other than in their engagement in the market-place in economic transactions.

Furnivall, like Boeke, overstated the cleavages in colonial society, and he also held a too simple view of the relations between ethnicity or race, economic function and social class. Whereas he assumed overall a coincidence of these, in his concept of an economic caste, the relations between class, and indeed power and status relations, and ethnic identity are exceedingly complex. However, a major difficulty with Furnivall's concept is that it does not provide us with the analytical means to address processes of change and inter-group conflict, though it does, importantly, draw our attention to the ethnic dimension of social organization in South-East Asia, and the fact that ethnicity has consequences for economic activity and organization (see Chapter 6).

There were several other studies of processes of socio-economic change in South-East Asia, though these had very little impact on post-war social science research. The Indologist, sociologist and colonial civil servant, Bertram Schrieke, edited an important volume on the effects of Western colonialism on native societies, prompted by the colonial government's desire to utilize anthropological and sociological information and expertise for the improvement of the welfare of the indigenous populations (1929). Overall the several contributors to the volume demonstrated both the beneficial and deleterious effects of colonialism; there were also examples of the supposed Indonesian tendency to absorb external influences, as well as instances where outside traits and ideas had been rejected. Nevertheless, Schrieke was one of the few scholars with a commitment to sociology and to the sociological interpretation of history. His interest in Weberian perspectives provides one of the foundations for the post-war development of Dutch historical sociology, whose main champion was Wim Wertheim.

Finally, an interesting contribution to the study of change came from a rather unlikely source. J.P. Duyvendak, a student of J.P.B. de Josselin de Jong, undertook doctoral research on Kakean society on the island of Seram, eastern Indonesia, and analysed his material in structuralist terms. From 1929 he worked as a teacher in Java and in the late 1930s became Professor of Anthropology at the Law School at Batavia (Prager, 1999: 337–338; Koentjaraningrat, 1975: 177). In 1935 he published his introductory text on the ethnology of Indonesia, and, although it included ethnographic summaries of most of the major traditional cultures in Indonesia within a broadly Leiden structuralist framework, 'a large part of the book . . . was devoted to the problems of acculturation and culture change' in the East Indies (Prager, 1999: 337). The analysis was phrased in terms of the movement from a traditional, unified, integrated society to a modern one; the process entails social disequilibrium and crisis. Duyvendak proposed that the colonial government should therefore protect and guide traditional communities through this difficult period of transition. As Prager notes, for Duyvendak, traditional Indonesian cultures could not be preserved from Westernization and modernization, but at least the application of anthropology to the understanding of these processes might help to cope with 'the disintegrative influences of colonialism' (ibid.: 338).

We have therefore come full circle, and it is illustrated in a perspective on South-East Asian cultures, that is Dutch structuralism, which appears to have had very little to do with colonialism in the development of its ideas. Yet, because many of its practitioners were intimately involved in the colonial administration, or in Christian missions or in training civil servants, they were ultimately presented with a dilemma. Their actions on behalf of colonialism or in accepting it as a reality led to the destruction, as they saw it, or at least the radical transformation, of the very cultures which they were seeking to understand and reconstruct. Ironically therefore '[t]he observers of the decay were the very agents of that process' (ibid.: 348).

3

ANTHROPOLOGY IN THE PERIOD OF DECOLONIZATION (1950–1970)

The American tradition

This chapter examines the important contribution which American anthropologists made to the study of social, cultural and economic change in South-East Asia during the period when the colonial powers were withdrawing from the region. American anthropology concentrated mainly on the lowland, cognatic or bilateral, wet rice-cultivating peasant societies in Thailand, Burma, Indonesia and the Philippines and was organized in a small number of well-funded multidisciplinary programmes based at such universities as Chicago, Cornell, Yale and the Massachusetts Institute of Technology. Four outstanding figures in this period were Clifford Geertz, Manning Nash, Lauriston Sharp and Melford Spiro. Although there was some continuity with the colonial period in the dominant perspectives and approaches used, interests began to shift to the processes of modernization and nation-building, how small-scale communities were affected by these changes and how (and if) indigenous values and practices were responding to the challenges of political independence, urbanization and commercialization. Of particular importance was Geertz's studies of 'agricultural involution' and syncretic religion in Java, Sharp's and Hanks's ethnographies of the social and economic organization of a Central Thai village and the utility of the notion of 'loose structure' in understanding Thai social forms, and Nash's study of religion and modernization and Spiro's analysis of the relationships between Buddhism and folk religion in the Mandalay region of Burma. On the other hand, interest in the upland minorities of the Philippines and the analysis of cognatic organization was sustained by Eggan and his students at Chicago. Much of the work undertaken by local anthropologists at this time also adopted the perspectives and concerns of American anthropology, given that many of them had received their training in Manila and the United States.

Introduction

Anthropology had to adjust to a new political and economic order after the Second World War. Some of the major dependent territories of the region – Burma, Indonesia and the Philippines – secured their political independence shortly after the end of the Japanese occupation, although, in the case of such countries as Indonesia, not without a bitter struggle. Vietnam and the neighbouring territories of Laos and Cambodia became embroiled in widespread and prolonged military conflict in which the French and then the Americans and other allies were involved, and it was not until 1975 that Vietnam became a united and independent country. Even then political turmoil in the Indochinese countries continued until recently. Given its shared borders with Laos and Cambodia, Thailand too was not immune from these conflicts. The remaining British-controlled territories in South-East Asia – Malaya, Singapore, Sarawak and North Borneo – secured their independence in 1957 and 1963 relatively smoothly, although Communist insurrection in Malaya and active Indonesian confrontation in the Borneo territories posed threats to that process. The Sultanate of Brunei's protectorate status continued uninterrupted until December 1983, with its stability endangered only once during the 1962 uprising. As one might have expected, the process of decolonization was therefore relatively peaceful in some cases, and in others violent and destabilizing. In various parts of the region anti-colonial struggles, inter-ethnic conflicts and super-power confrontations meant that conditions were unsuitable for anthropological research. Nationalist sensitivities in newly independent nations also contributed to the difficulties of securing research permission and undertaking fieldwork. Increasingly anthropology became a professional, university-based discipline and anthropologists full-time practitioners whose status in former colonial countries, as visiting researchers there on sufferance, could be decidedly fragile and uncertain.

The pattern of anthropological research reflects these local and international conditions. Very little anthropological research was conducted in large areas of mainland South-East Asia in the post-war period. Apart from scattered studies undertaken in the 1950s and 1960s in Indochina, mainly by Americans, the circumstances of war prevented any sustained research there. Burma closed its doors to the outside world in 1962 and so there was no practical possibility of continuing the important studies which had been carried out there in the 1950s and early 1960s. The bulk of the work was concentrated in Thailand, Indonesia, the Philippines and Malaysia, in other words mainly in the Austronesian-speaking island world. On the mainland the influence of anthropological perspectives developed in the context of Thailand was overwhelming. Yet there is one central theme in the two decades of research up to 1970 and that is the importance of American social scientists and American-sponsored fieldwork in the region, and the training of young native social scientists in American universities, sponsored by American foundations. Decolonization had not only resulted in the political and administrative withdrawal of the Europeans from South-East Asia but also their partial displacement in the academic field. Even where such countries as Britain retained some scholarly interests, they increasingly recruited American doctoral students to undertake primary research, most notably at Oxford and in London. Koentjaraningrat also says specifically of Dutch Indology that '[w]hen the independent Republic of Indonesia disposed of the Dutch civil servants, the opportunity for Dutch indologists to carry out social research while serving in small sub-district areas at various places all over Indonesia simultaneously disappeared' (1975: 180).

This development was obviously one element in the emergence of the USA as a world power with strategic, political and economic interests in such developing regions as South-East Asia. Not that one can necessarily establish direct connections between anthropological studies and American involvement in what came to be known as 'the Third World', although in certain cases there were relations between anthropologists and American political and military agencies (King, 1999: 39ff.). But certainly America's power and wealth in the context of an increasing confrontation between Western capitalism and Soviet and Chinese Communism to win hearts and minds in the ex-colonial territories provided a context for an expansion of academic activity. The presence of the USA in South-East Asia was based in part on its continuing economic and security interests in the Philippines, its former colony, but it was this region that presented particular ideological, strategic and military threats to Western capitalism. In order to ensure the containment of Communist China, North Korea and North Vietnam, and to counter the growing strength of indigenous South-East Asian socialist and communist movements, the USA became very much involved in the political and economic affairs of Indochina, especially South Vietnam, as well as Thailand, Burma (up to 1962), and Indonesia and to a lesser extent, given the continuing British presence there, the Malay Peninsula, Singapore and the northern Borneo states. Some social science research was also linked closely with American economic development aid.

We have already discussed in Chapter 1 the creation of South-East Asia as a region in its own right from the 1940s and the significant American involvement in that process. The USA also invested substantially in the development of various research centres focused on South-East Asia; its rapidly expanding international role demanded that it have expertise in the languages, cultures, societies, histories and geographies of the developing world as well as scholars well versed in the politics, economics and international relations of non-Western areas. The dominance of American scholarship in major parts of the South-East Asian region during the 1950s and 1960s is exemplified in the well-funded Cornell Southeast Asia Program which promoted team research projects in Thailand dating from 1948 under the direction of Lauriston Sharp (Skinner and Kirsch, 1975; Bell, 1982) and The Modern Indonesia Project under George McT. Kahin (Koentjaraningrat, 1975: 192). Some Cornell scholars such as Robert Textor and G. William Skinner undertook research on both Thailand and Indonesia (see pp. 73–77 on Thailand and for Indonesia, Skinner [1959, 1963] and Textor [1954]). Another high profile research team worked in Java and Bali, under the auspices of the Center for International Studies at the Massachusetts Institute of Technology (MIT) out of which the writings of Clifford and Hildred Geertz and Robert Jay emerged (Higgins, 1963; Koentjaraningrat, 1975: 198–207). Yale University established a Southeast Asia Program and sponsored a considerable amount of anthropological work on the outer islands of Indonesia by E.M. Bruner on the urban Batak of Medan in Sumatra (1959, 1961), F.L. Cooley in Ambon (1962), Clark Cunningham among the Toba Batak of Sumatra (1958, and see Chapter 4 for his work on the Atoni of Timor), Robert Knox Dentan among the Semai of Malaya (1968), P.R. Goethals in Sumbawa (1961), and Leopold Pospisil among the Kapauku of West Irian (1958).

The University of Chicago continued its pre-war research interests in the Philippines under Fred Eggan (1941, 1967). For obvious reasons, American researchers dominated both sociological and anthropological research in the Philippines, and an important figure in bridging the two disciplines was Frank Lynch who had trained in anthropology under Otley Beyer at the University of the Philippines in the late 1940s and with Eggan in Chicago from 1954 to 1959. Lynch, a Jesuit priest, resided permanently in the Philippines from 1959 until his premature death in 1978. He played a crucial role in *The Philippine Sociological Review*; he established a Department of Sociology and Anthropology at the Ateneo de Manila and founded the Institute of Philippine Culture at the same university in 1960. As the Institute's first director he played a pivotal role in the development of field research in sociology and anthropology in the 1960s and 1970s (Yengoyan and Makil, 1984). Finally, the major post-war anthropological research in Burma up to 1962 was undertaken not by the British but by Americans such as Manning Nash, Melford Spiro, Michael Mendelson and F.K. Lehman; again Chicago provided an important institutional focus for this research, but also the University of Illinois.

The dominant paradigms in the post-war period, which anthropology embraced, demonstrated a continuity with conceptual frameworks common in the colonial period – structure, function, evolution, diffusion and culture and personality. The main pre-war fieldwork-based ethnographic studies had been carried out in Africa, North America and some of the Pacific Islands, primarily among what were then considered to be 'tribal' populations. Very little had been done in South-East Asia, though colonial observers had tended to concentrate on upland or interior minorities. It was clear that anthropologists were having to address what for them were novel social and cultural arrangements. We shall shortly see an example of this in the Cornell studies of Thai social organization, in Geertz's study of Javanese agriculture and Manning Nash's work on the Burmese of the Mandalay region.

Western social science also had to address the processes of modernization, development, decolonization and nation-building, and American social scientists concentrated on the hitherto neglected lowland or 'peasant' communities of South-East Asia – Javanese, Balinese, Thai, Burmese or Burman, Vietnamese, Filipino or Tagalog, Ilocano and Bisayan. It was no longer very easy to focus on the small-scale, closed village community separate from the wider sets of changing relations of which it was a part. American students usually adopted neo-evolutionary schemes in their study of socio-cultural change based on the assumption that newly independent, less developed societies were on the path of progress from tradition to modernity. For obvious reasons American anthropologists especially were disinclined to embrace any radical or Marxist explanatory framework. Instead traditional societies, based on idealized constructions of less advanced, small-scale, socially relatively undifferentiated, non-specialized, and technologically simple societies in which family, ethnic and religious ties played important roles were contrasted with modern ones, exemplified by Western large-scale, rational, industrialized, socially differentiated democracies oriented to 'more universalistic symbols of nation and community' (Hefner, 1990: x). Modernity would be achieved primarily by the diffusion or transfer of modern values, institutions and practices, as well as capital, technology and knowledge from the West to the developing world. In other words, the examination of and explanation for the dynamic processes of change, transformation and economic growth in such regions as South-East Asia were framed in a very generalized, relatively static model which assumed a gradual shift or progression from one integrated system to another and the transfer of traits from the more advanced to the less advanced to assist the transition to sustained economic growth.

Some post-war, mainly American, anthropological studies subscribed broadly to this paradigm. However, there were those like Clifford Geertz who rejected simple evolutionary, typological, acculturative models and instead revised, elaborated and developed our understanding of the socio-cultural dimensions of modernization and development. He used both detailed local level case studies and an anthropological perspective on nation-building to examine the variety of possible directions and forms of change and their underlying processes. Others, both American and European, continued to focus on what were assumed to be relatively closed small-scale societies or cultures, the modes of integration of village- or community-based social systems, and the structural principles that order ideas, values and social relations in 'other cultures'. A significant amount of attention was devoted to ethnographic investigations, building up empirical knowledge of hitherto little-known societies and cultures using the fieldwork methods of modern anthropology or updating, revising and filling the gaps in colonial ethnographies. With few exceptions, it was only from the 1970s that more radical interpretations of social change in the postcolonial world gained ground, and even by this time there were still very few native anthropologists contributing to the debates (see Chapter 5). Therefore, despite dramatic global political and economic changes, anthropological perspectives on South-East Asia, which were mainly promoted by Western scholars, were generally locked into established, conventional paradigms.

Let us now turn to the main themes and significant contributions of post-war anthropology up to about 1970, focusing in particular on American anthropology in South-East Asia, and devoting specific attention to the Cornell studies in Thailand, the MIT research programme in Java and Bali; the contributions of American anthropologists to the understanding of lowland Burmese society and culture, and a selection of research on Philippine societies, which concentrated especially on the traditional legal systems and social organization of minority groups. Many of these studies focused on processes of change and the relations between small-scale 'peasant' or 'tribal' communities and wider social, economic, cultural and political systems. They also had a major interest in cultural syncretism, specifically understanding the ways in which the great religious traditions of Buddhism, Hinduism, Islam and Christianity, which had been imported into South-East Asia from India, China, the Middle East and Europe, accommodated earlier folk or 'animistic' traditions. In Chapter 4 we shall then turn to European structuralist studies which represented a coming together of French, British and Dutch anthropological interests in particular kinds of South-East Asian 'traditional' society and which contrasted quite markedly with the dominant American concerns of the time. Their central concern was the internal structure and classification systems of the minority hill or interior populations of South-East Asia. The main inspiration for these studies came from the work of Emile Durkheim and Marcel Mauss, which was in turn given a new, post-war lease of life by Claude Lévi-Strauss. The Geertzes and Spiro in particular were very critical of the structural anthropology of Lévi-Strauss, which was to have a significant influence on British anthropology, as well as of Dutch structuralism. For their part British anthropologists like Rodney Needham were dismissive of American kinship studies and the use of cultural and psychobiological paradigms.

Thailand, Sharp and Hanks

In the immediate post-war period a series of important studies was instigated and organized by Lauriston Sharp at Cornell, including field research on rice-growing villages in Central, North and North-East Thailand, the Chinese community in Bangkok, Thai society in historical perspective, modern politics, and minority upland groups in Northern Thailand. Among those social scientists participating in the programme were Lucien Hanks (1972), Kamol Janlekha (1957), Herbert Phillips (1965), G. William Skinner (1957, 1958) and Robert Textor (1973). Other important contributors were Jane Hanks and Hazel M. Hauck (Sharp and Hanks, 1978: 15).

Sharp carried out his first field research in Thailand in 1947–1948; he initiated the Cornell–Thailand Project in 1947, and in 1948 decided to focus primarily on the settlement of Bang Chan (Sharp et al., 1953). Although Sharp became especially well known for his association with Thailand and more generally Asian Studies, he had also undertaken field research in North America, North Africa and Australia. He was an important figure in the development of multidisciplinary area studies programmes in the USA, and was the Director of Cornell's Southeast Asia Program from 1950 to 1960. He argued for the importance for anthropology of understanding the history and language of a given population, as well as placing small-scale community studies in a national

and regional context. This broader interest in regions was obviously strengthened by his period of study at the University of Vienna in 1930–1931 where
Robert von Heine-Geldern was teaching. He also focused specifically on 'the
interplay of the cultural forces of modernization as they have impinged on
indigenous cultures' (Smith, 1974: 8), and Bang Chan was chosen for long-term
investigation as a Central Thai 'rice village' on the north-eastern margins of the
expanding metropolitan area of Bangkok. Sharp also had a particular interest
in the application of anthropological expertise to real-world issues. Nevertheless, he tended to adopt the American social science paradigms of the time,
focusing on the processes of cultural modernization experienced by small-scale,
less developed societies, and initially at least he was preoccupied with structural–functionalist notions of bounded groups and defined communities, or
more popularly 'village societies' (Sharp and Hanks, 1978: 26ff.).

Unlike some Western sociologists, political scientists and economists of the
time, the Cornell team did not subscribe to a simple evolutionary model of the
modernization process. They attempted to demonstrate that it was not inevitable that Thai society would develop in the same direction and in the
same way as Western society, that it had its own peculiar genius, and that we
should not try to squeeze Thai categories, concepts and arrangements into a
Western frame of reference. Lucien Hanks, one of Sharp's closest colleagues,
says, for example, with reference to his research on Thai society that he 'would
like to avoid the implication that some societies are more "advanced" than
others by dint of greater specialization and differentiation' (1975: 197).
However, the Cornell researchers did impose a particular interpretation on the
material from Bang Chan which was to lead to intense debate about its validity
and value.

Among the most prominent of Sharp's team was Lucien M. Hanks. Hanks
made a significant contribution to the anthropology of Thailand, though he is
probably known best for a relatively slim volume entitled *Rice and Man* (1972)
in which he explores the ecology and history of rice cultivation and the changing relations between culture and the environment (and see Chapter 7). He
locates his study of Bang Chan in the 1950s in a wider consideration of the
characteristics of riziculture in South-East Asia. He was concerned to examine
and explain human adaptations to changing environments, and, particularly for
Bang Chan the impact of the market, technology and communications on the
methods of rice agriculture. He chronicles the steady enlargement and improvement of Bang Chan's village system, particularly transformations in its social
structure, in line with the modernization of its productive potential, concentrating on 'what happens to rice growers when they increase their output of rice'
(1972: 1).

Hanks's study also had a directly practical intent as did so much of Sharp's
anthropology. Hanks argued that detailed knowledge of the physical, technical,
social and cultural dimensions of rice agriculture will enable us better 'to assess
the extent of the social and psychological changes that any new agricultural

technique implies', especially in the process of increasing rice yield and output (Hanks, 1972: 1). Hanks's interest in cultural ecology echoes the classic works of Geertz on irrigated and swidden rice agriculture in Indonesia (1963a), and for the Philippines Harold Conklin's study of Hanunoo shifting cultivation (1957) and Charles Frake's examination of Subanun social organization and shifting agriculture in Zamboanga del Norte, western Mindanao (1955). We shall take up this theme of ecological relations again in Chapter 7, but it is worth noting here that in contrast to Geertz's discovery of a steady process of 'involutionary development', 'stagnation' and 'shared poverty' among wet rice cultivators in Java (see below), Hanks sees a process essentially of 'evolutionary development', 'progress' and 'commercialization' in central Thailand.

So dominant were the studies of Sharp and Hanks in Bang Chan in social science circles in the 1950s and 1960s that it was suggested even in the 1970s that the 'world's view of rural Thailand is biased by Bang Chan' (Moerman, 1975: 151). The Cornell team were also among the first anthropologists to describe relationships in a bilateral or cognatic society, one of the most wide-spread forms of social organization in South-East Asia. Hanks examined both Thai kinship as comprising 'a set of voluntary reciprocities between pairs of people'; he also pointed to the lack of fixed, perpetual bounded groups (1972: 80ff.) and developed the hierarchical-based concepts of patron–clientship and entourage in understanding wider dimensions of Thai social organization (1962, 1975). The notion of patron–clientship as comprising unequal, flexible, multi-functional, bilateral relations between a superior patron, and an inferior client, provided yet another way of understanding how cognatic societies without corporate kinship groups operate.

Much of the early post-war research on Thai social organization, particularly that stemming from Cornell, also addressed a paradigm which had first been proposed by John Embree in 1950. Indeed, it remained a major preoccupation in Thai studies well into the 1970s. It led to a wide-ranging set of comparative studies which debated whether or not the paradigm continued to have heuristic value (Evers, 1969) and its status was subsequently enhanced when it was chosen as one of a very few distinctive concepts which had emerged from socio-logical work on South-East Asia (Evers, 1980b). An American anthropologist whose main experience had been in Japan, Embree, in a relatively cursory and impressionistic comparative paper on East Asian, Vietnamese and Thai social organization, suggested that the latter should be characterized as 'loosely struc-tured' (1950: 181–193). By this he meant that the Thais from his perspective have a high tolerance for variations in individual behaviour, they do not commit themselves to the continuing fulfilment of obligations in the longer term, nor do they have a strong sense of familial duties and expectations. Overall rights, duties and reciprocal obligations are less clearly defined, of less importance, and less regular in Thai society than in Japan. Discipline, regimen-tation, tidiness, solidarity, allegiance and formality are not given a high priority.

It so happened that some of Embree's observations seemed to offer an explanatory framework for the relatively diffuse community of Bang Chan studied by Lauriston Sharp, Lucien Hanks and their colleagues in the late 1940s and the 1950s. The Cornell team had been looking for an organized village. Instead they found a settlement which had neither clearly delineated physical boundaries nor administrative ones (Sharp and Hanks, 1978: 23, 140–141). It had only been founded in the mid-nineteenth century, its population came from diverse social and ethnic origins, and, in close proximity to Bangkok, it was subject to rapid change (ibid.: 24; Hanks, 1972). The first major study of Bang Chan seemed to lend detailed empirical support to Embree's paradigm. In *Siamese Rice Village* we are informed that 'the exceptionally amorphous, relatively unstructured character of all Thai society is clearly reflected in the undifferentiated social organization of Bang Chan' (Sharp *et al.*, 1953: 26). Even in the 1970s Hanks continued to refer to the 'very looseness' of Thai household organization (1972: 151–152).

The loose structure model began to be questioned seriously from the late 1960s but it was effectively demolished by another American anthropologist, Jack Potter, in the 1970s. Potter remarked, in his study of a northern Thai village near the provincial capital, Chiangmai, that, although Sharp had modified his view in his later work, several of Sharp's colleagues recognized considerable variation in Thai society and that Hanks had demonstrated, in his analysis of patron–clientship, that Thai society is structured. Nevertheless, the endorsement of Embree's loose structure model in 1953 'greatly influenced subsequent work on rural Thailand, most of which was carried out by Sharp's colleagues and students at Cornell' (1976: 4). Among others Potter refers to the later research of Herbert Phillips in Bang Chan (1965) and Phillips's observations that the villagers are 'individualists' and that 'their kinship institutions tend to be amorphous, and kinship relations are unpredictable and inconsistent' (1976: 5). Steven Piker was another influential supporter of the paradigm in its early days (1968).

Potter devotes his 1976 book to demonstrating, on the basis of ethnographic detail, that the northern Thai village in which he worked does not conform to the loose structure paradigm. Interestingly the village, which he refers to as Chiangmai, had already been studied by the American anthropologist Konrad Kingshill under its real name Ku Daeng ([1960] 1965). Potter argues that Chiangmai/Ku Daeng is 'a highly structured society' (ibid.: 148), and he indicates that later studies of rural Thailand, mainly undertaken in the north and north-east in the 1960s and early 1970s, suggest that his findings are by no means unique. He further suggests that like the Balinese villages described by the Geertzes, in terms of the notions of 'form and variation', 'Thai villages are extremely variable and no two are exactly alike' (ibid.: 149). However, they are 'constructed from a limited number of structural principles' located in the family and kinship, residential arrangements, labour exchange, differences in age, class and status, political and administrative patterns and religious organization. He therefore concludes that the loose structure model overall is 'inaccurate and misleading' and has to be replaced by a 'more accurate and realistic portrayal of Thai peasant social structure' (ibid.: 11). Potter also suggests that there is sufficient evidence in the Bang Chan ethnographies to confirm his view that the researchers there were far too preoccupied with the loose structure perspective and therefore 'overlooked basic features of social structure that Bang Chan shared with all other Thai villages at that time' (ibid.: 204). In addition, he notes that studies undertaken in Thai villages in northern Thailand (DeYoung, 1955) and even in the neighbourhood of Bang Chan in the Central Plain (Kaufman, 1960) at the time the Cornell team were active demonstrate that the model of loose structure and the particularities of Bang Chan do not apply elsewhere (1976: 8ff.).

Subsequently, as one might anticipate, Potter's own work came under criticism from a group of anthropologists, Thai and non-Thai, who in the later spirit of rethinking and deconstruction suggested that the concepts of 'village', 'community' and 'shared space' also needed questioning, as did the methodological tendency to study a single village community and draw more general conclusions from it. Such anthropologists as Jeremy Kemp (1989, 1993) and Chayan Vaddhanaphuti (1993) emphasized that much of the anthropology of rural Thailand, embracing not only the Bang Chan studies but also the work of Potter, used as their basic frame of reference the conventional and inappropriate notion of the 'village' or 'community', equated with some kind of defined social group, and often perceived as a territorially bounded unit. Kemp and others pointed out that the concept as formulated by earlier anthropologists is profoundly ambiguous and that different principles underlying social and cultural life frequently do not coincide to delineate neatly bounded groups. Furthermore, the concept of village should be recognized as an ideological construct: villages as administrative units have often been 'created' by governments in the process of defining, controlling, taxing and administering rural populations just as communities have been 'created' by anthropologists searching for 'social groups', 'holistic units' and 'corporate entities' (and see Chapter 6). What is more, rural settlements have increasingly been brought within the purview of the state and often what is assumed to be traditionally or authentically rural is in fact the result of changes set in train by outside forces (Kemp, 1993: 89ff.; and see Manning Nash below on the notion of 'multiple society' and modernization of the peasantry in Burma and Malaysia).

Another set of ideas which implicitly addresses the notion of 'loose structure' was based on the concepts of ego-focused social networks, dyadic ties and strategies of choice. We examined some of these ideas briefly in Chapter 2 in relation to the literature on cognatic social organization and we shall take them up again later when we discuss social organization and traditional legal institutions in the Philippines. Let us now turn to another very influential paradigm in the anthropology and sociology of South-East Asia and a body of work which has been widely referred to and criticized in the anthropological literature. We refer to the studies of Clifford Geertz and his colleagues and in particular the concept of 'involution' and more briefly the more general concept of 'culture'.

Java, Bali and Geertz

There is a no more prolific scholar than Clifford Geertz, and it is difficult to summarize and do justice to his major contributions to South-East Asian anthropology and anthropology in general (Inglis, 2000). He has ranged over several fields of interest, and although his central preoccupation has been the concept of culture and its relation to social action, he has made contributions to the study of economic development, ecology, comparative history, nationalist politics and social organization. Nevertheless, two of his early classic studies must be *The Religion of Java* (1960), for Geertz an example of an ethnographic report (ibid.: 7), and the more theoretical *Agricultural Involution: The Processes of Ecological Change in Indonesia* (1963a). We shall devote our primary attention to his concept of 'involution' since, like the 'loose structure' paradigm, it was a novel concept which emerged specifically from research on South-East Asia.

The parallels between Sharp's research in central Thailand and Geertz's programme in east-central Java are striking. In both cases well-funded team projects were directed to increasing the understanding of a segment of very complex lowland irrigated agricultural societies and cultures in the context of modernization, development and nation-building. Although of lesser significance in its impact on anthropology, we might also mention here the research of the Michigan State University, Vietnam Advisory Group in the 1950s on the village of Khanh Hau in the Mekong Delta out of which Gerald Hickey's study *Village in Vietnam* (1964) emerged. Hickey's study was very much in the mainstream of American cultural anthropology and functionalism, taking its inspiration from American work on peasant 'little communities' as part of a larger society and examining 'the fabric of interrelated social institutions' (ibid.: xxv). We shall refer to Hickey's more important body of writing on the upland peoples of southern and central Vietnam in Chapter 4.

In many respects this multidisciplinary research team approach marked a distinct break with much of the pre-war anthropological research conducted by lone students. The MIT team in Java comprised eleven fieldworkers funded by the Ford Foundation. Nevertheless, the focus of this team research tended to remain the defined social unit: in Thailand, Bang Chan, in east-central Java, Modjokuto, but whereas the Thai village, though of mixed origins comprised a relatively small agricultural population of 1,600, Geertz's Modjokuto (or 'Middletown'; its real name is Pare) was a markedly multi-ethnic town of 24,000, the majority Javanese, with some 2,000 Chinese who comprised 'the heart of the economic circulatory system' (1960: 2). Following the Modjokuto research in 1952–1954, Clifford and Hildred Geertz visited Bali in 1957–1958, sponsored by the Rockefeller Foundation, and focused on the town of Tabanan in the south-west of the island which had a population of 12,000 with over 800 Chinese residents. The Geertzes also made a brief return visit to Java at this time.

One of the main objectives of the MIT team, under the direction of the economist, Benjamin Higgins, was to examine the problems and prospects of Indonesian economic development, with specific reference to socio-cultural factors. Geertz's study of agricultural involution needs to be read in relation to Boeke's work on Indonesian dualism discussed in Chapter 2. It is in part a revised and more dynamic version of Boeke's dual economy thesis in which Geertz questions Boeke's interpretation of the relations between peasant 'mentality' and Dutch colonial policies. It should also be read along with three of Geertz's companion volumes: *The Development of the Javanese Economy* (1956), *Peddlers and Princes* (1963b) and *The Social History of an Indonesian Town* (1965). Two other members of the Modjokuto team, Hildred Geertz and Robert Jay, provided important and detailed complementary ethnographies or reports on the structure and functioning of a cognatic society, Hildred Geertz specifically on the Javanese family (1961a) and Jay on the wider Javanese social organization, including kinship, status and patron–clientage (1969).

One of Clifford Geertz's major preoccupations in these four publications is to understand processes of change and the trajectory of social and cultural transformation in post-independence Indonesia, a country, which at that time, was attempting to recover from war, conflict and economic dislocation following the Japanese occupation and the revolutionary struggle against the Dutch for self-determination. *Agricultural Involution* is the more theoretical piece which emerged from the lengthy detailed, historical paper of 1956. It is an ecological and historical analysis of the emergence and development of dualism in Java, or more accurately 'inner Indonesia', which for Geertz comprises parts of Java, Bali and Lombok, under Dutch colonialism and its contrast with transformations in the Outer Islands. Geertz's study is also located firmly in the post-war sociological literature on modernization because he is concerned to explain why Indonesia, in contrast to Japan, had not managed to embark on the path to industrialization, modernization and sustained economic growth. He attempts to explain this failure, or to uncover the 'obstacles' to growth, in terms of a particular kind of colonial experience acting upon a particular kind of village economy and ecology. He therefore also addresses the ways in which Javanese 'culture' – human motivations, values, behavioural patterns, and social action and relations – shapes and is shaped by these wider forces and processes. How, then, did the Javanese cope with these pressures of change?

With his interests in historical explanation Geertz's views demonstrate some similarities with later underdevelopment and dependency approaches (see Chapter 5), though overall *Agricultural Involution* is firmly in the tradition of American cultural anthropology and neo-evolutionary modernization perspectives. Geertz's main explanatory framework is based not on neo-Marxist theories nor on notions of a single world system but instead on the concept of ecosystem. His approach stems from cultural ecology (see Chapter 7). He examines some of the detailed connections between certain Javanese social and cultural forms, economic organization and the environment, and the ways in which these relations change in the context of wider sets of economic and political relations.

Geertz argues that the colonial government integrated Javanese peasant agriculture into a capital-intensive, commercial system which produced cash crops for the Dutch, simultaneously confining the farmers to the subsistence sector while excluding them from the commercial sector, and using some of their land and labour for profit. The Javanese therefore reproduced their labour power in the 'traditional' subsistence sector and cultivated sugar and coffee for the Dutch in the 'modern' sector. This 'dualistic' activity was in turn made possible by the properties of irrigated rice agriculture which, Geertz argued, could support increasing population densities and agricultural intensification. Improved irrigation facilities for sugar cultivation, which was suited to the lowland environment, benefited rice agriculture on adjacent land, and enabled an increase in rice production. However, with population increase and a lack of access to alternatives in other sectors of the economy, the rice yield per hectare increased but not production per capita.

According to Geertz, the Javanese response to this predicament was quite simply to squeeze more and more of their number into the rice sector, dividing up and redistributing work and production, and increasing communal rather than individual rights to land. The result was a high level of peasant socio-economic homogeneity and 'shared poverty', an unlikely set of circumstances for achieving modernization and the transition to capitalism. Rather than an accelerating process of evolution (as depicted by Hanks in Bang Chan) and then a revolutionary transformation from tradition to modernity, Javanese social, cultural and economic forms turned in on themselves; they became 'involuted', internally over-elaborated, intricate and complex and locked into a 'permanent transition'. Although the concept of 'involution' is taken from Alexander Goldenweiser, Geertz's thesis is close to that of Furnivall in his book *Netherlands India* (1939) which argues that peasant social differentiation and the capacity of rural society to modernize were undermined by the transformation of rights to land occasioned by the demands of the Dutch Cultivation System or forced cultivation of commercial crops introduced in 1830. These involutional tendencies continued after 1870 when the Cultivation System was replaced by Dutch private enterprise and commercial plantation agriculture. However, in his imaginative use of the concept of 'involution' Geertz presents us with the characteristics of a generic process of 'systemic' or 'organic ageing', a process of ' static expansion', of infilling which accompanies advanced maturity.

Geertz pursues this theme, among others, in *The Social History of an Indonesian Town* which is, in part at least, the urban companion volume to his study of Javanese agrarian transformation. His general theory of involution is here given 'body' by its application to case material. Again Geertz uses a cultural-historical perspective and focuses on the change from a colonial urban structure in Modjokuto comprising 'self-contained status communities' to something approximating larger scale politico-cultural groupings or 'streams' (*aliran*) focused on modern political party organization, although this transition is far from complete (1965: 4). He argues that the colonial town – a 'hollow town', a 'social composite' – comprised 'a collection of impermeable strata living, one might almost say, side by side' (ibid.: 4). It emerged from the introduction of social groups (Dutch, Chinese and various categories of Javanese: *priyayi* civil servants, *santri* traders, landless *santri* and *abangan* migrant workers) from outside rather than as a product of local organic growth (see below). This colonial order began to be dissolved decisively from the 1930s but a new stable structure had yet to emerge. Therefore, Geertz sees the contemporary urban system, as in the rural areas, as 'incomplete', 'contradictory', 'inconstant', 'loose' and 'unstable' (ibid.: 8), as 'an unbroken advance toward vagueness' (ibid.: 5), though ultimately he isolates five 'vaguely comprehended' groupings which cross-cut the politico-cultural groupings; they comprise the intelligentsia, literati, town mass, village sub-elite and the rural mass (ibid.: 140–141). In his view Indonesia has yet to complete the transition from a traditional to a modern order. It is betwixt and between, 'a sociological jumble' (ibid.: 121). What is more, in his general appreciation of post-independence political development and nationalism, the developing nations overall fare little better; having secured independence the 'forward movement' of nationalism 'has been replaced by a complex, uneven, and many-directioned movement by its various parts, which conduces to a sense less of progress than of agitated stagnation' (1973: 236–237; and see Inglis, 2000: 58, 61–62).

In his *Peddlers and Princes*, Geertz examines another dimension of change. He identifies, both in eastern Java and Bali, two specific socio-economic groups involved in commercial activities which, if they can overcome certain constraints, might contribute to the process of modernization, economic rationalization and the ultimate realization of take-off into sustained economic growth. His 'entrepreneurial group of Islamic [*santri*] small businessmen' in the individualistic, face-to-face bazaar economy of Modjokuto have the economic motivation and an available market, but lack the larger-scale organizational forms and the capacity to accumulate capital necessary to make '[p]rogress toward more effective patterns of economic activity' (1963b: 29). Geertz's focus on *santri* traders should also be placed in the context of the more comprehensive study by Alice Dewey, another member of the MIT team, of the range of small-scale marketing in Modjokuto and the relations between Javanese and Chinese traders (1962, and see Chapter 5). On the other hand, Geertz argues that the 'nascent entrepreneurial class of displaced aristocrats' in Tabanan, Bali, have collective forms of organization on which to build derived from pre-existing agrarian-based gentry–peasantry relations, but these have to be adapted flexibly to the needs of the market-place and the entrepreneurs' struggle to overcome the problems of operating relatively large, unwieldy, inefficient, collectivist, welfarist companies (1963b: 121–127). In other words, Geertz, in this study, is filling in and exploring the variety of socio-cultural contexts within which economic modernization can and does take place. His comparative micro-sociological study makes us aware of the problems occasioned by a too economically focused perspective on modernization and a too generalized view of the social and cultural changes which are assumed to accompany it. He advises us that the 'transition to a modern [Indonesian] society has begun' but 'whether – or perhaps better, when – it will be completed is far from certain' (ibid.: 4). Indeed, for Geertz, Modjokuto in the 1950s was a 'curious mixture of borrowed fragments of modernity and exhausted relics of tradition' in which 'the future seemed about as remote as the past' (1983: 60).

Let us then return to Geertz's analysis of involution in Java, which does attempt to formulate a more general conceptual framework for considering the prospects for Indonesia's economic growth and modernization. Such a closely argued, audacious and compelling thesis, eloquently expressed and structured, has had a profound influence on Indonesian studies and has also had some impact on the general sociology of change and development (Wertheim, 1974) as well as on analyses of rural social structures in such neighbouring countries as the Philippines (van den Muijzenberg, 1975). The main areas of criticism of Geertz's analysis are usefully summarized by the Alexanders (1978, 1979, 1982), White (1983a, 1983b) and van Niel (1992: 181–201). In addition, Larkin (1971: 283–295) has elaborated Geertz's thesis in relation to historical data from Pampanga in Central Luzon (see below). Geertz also replied to most of his critics, claiming that they had largely failed to grasp the main point of what he had attempted to do, especially with regard to his analysis of the importance of cultural processes in their relationships with socio-economic and environmental change (1984).

An overall difficulty is that Geertz's thesis, based in part on observations made during the 1950s when there was clear evidence of rural stagnation in parts of Java, tends to have been presented theoretically 'in timeless terms and for all Java' (van Niel, 1992: 183). What is more, the detailed historical evidence of the nature of Javanese society prior to 1830 when the Dutch set major changes in motion is not to be found in *Agricultural Involution*, though it is sketched out in the 1956 paper (ibid.: 185–187). There are five main areas of criticism of Geertz's study as follows: first, Geertz's two ideal types of ecosystem, each associated broadly with a particular region of Indonesia, present an over-simplified picture of the country's ecology (Koentjaraningrat, 1975: 202–204). Second, Geertz's views on peasant social homogeneity and shared poverty have been questioned on the basis of evidence that lowland Javanese villages were characterized, and increasingly so from the 1870s, by marked inequalities in landownership and differentiation of wealth and power, and the presence of a large number of landless and land-poor residents (Elson, 1978; Hüsken, 1979; Hefner, 1990). Some critics have argued that, even if there had been involutional processes operating in colonial Java up to the 1950s, the effects of the Green Revolution and the introduction of new technologies in lowland rice agriculture in Indonesia from the 1970s, have led to increased inequalities in land distribution and an increase in landlessness and non-farm employment (see

Kahn, 1985, for a summary of the criticisms, and see Chapter 5). Third, it has been argued that, in contrast to Geertz's conclusion, rice production gradually stagnated during the nineteenth century and did not absorb ever-increasing amounts of labour; instead sugar cultivation placed tremendous demands on local labour. Thus the wet rice ecosystem in the sugar districts, certainly up until the 1860s, did not witness a process of increasing intensification (Hefner, 1990: 43–44; van Schaik, 1986). Fourth, several scholars have demonstrated considerable variations in the relations between population density, rice cultivation, cash crop agriculture and land tenure across Java, in contrast to Geertz's more general thesis of involution there (Elson, 1984; Lyon, 1970; Stoler, 1977; van Niel, 1992). Finally, though Geertz was finely tuned to the dynamism of Javanese rural society, later writers indicated just how much more dynamic, durable and flexible it was than the 1950s and 1960s' notion of a passive, involuted, dispirited peasantry suggests (Lyon, 1970) and that in the nineteenth century there was a general increase in prosperity in rural areas, particularly among those who controlled land, and the development of capitalist relationships (van Niel, 1992).

Overall, Geertz assumes a tightly interrelated ecosystem in parts of rural Java focused on the properties of wet rice agriculture and a relatively uniform Cultivation System; his postulated link between high levels of sugar cultivation, wet rice agriculture, high rice yields and high population densities appears not to be borne out generally by the Dutch archival evidence on east and central Java. Instead it has been demonstrated by later writers that the impact and implementation of Dutch policies were more varied, that there were activities other than sugar cultivation which affected peasant households, that some of the possible reasons for population growth do not seem to square with Geertz's framework and that the consequence of these processes was not social homogeneity and shared poverty. In addition, Koentjaraningrat (1975) points to certain difficulties occasioned by Geertz's method of analysis which depends on the construction of ideal types. Geertz then compares and contrasts these ideal types 'on the basis of a fixed number of characteristics' and tends to sacrifice empirical detail and complexity, and sometimes even inconvenient evidence, in favour of conceptual clarity and theoretical ingenuity (ibid.: 199–200). Van Niel concludes his studies of Javanese agriculture by proposing that 'as far back as we can see into Java's past there have always been Javanese types which do not fit Geertz's model' (1992: 201), and Hefner demonstrates the lack of fit for the Javanese in the Tengger highlands of East Java (1990). Koentjaraningrat, in his overall appreciation of Geertz's studies of social and cultural change in Modjokuto, suggests that Geertz's preference for the construction of contrasting ideal types over-simplifies complex processes and that his view of the Javanese in particular as 'stranded' between tradition and modernity cannot be supported by the evidence (Koentjaraningrat, 1975: 204–205).

Nevertheless, this is not to deny the importance of Geertz's study, particularly the significance which he attaches to historical and ecological analysis, and the emphasis he places on a generic type of change – involution – which does capture appositely certain kinds of response to external forces and to the need to use a fixed resource more and more intensively. Geertz rightly draws our attention to the introduction of new economic and social pressures into the Javanese village under Dutch colonialism – especially the pressures on land generated by the dramatic increases in population from about 6 million at the beginning of the nineteenth century to over 20 million by 1900 – and the most important fact that the Javanese overall managed to respond to these challenges. Indeed, there is still some dispute about when and to what degree the capitalist transformation of agriculture occurred as against, in Geertz's thesis, the development and persistence of small family farms and peasant forms of production and redistribution, a process which Kahn has referred to as 'peasantization' (1985: 69–96, and see Chapter 5).

The value of Geertz's work has also been recognized by many commentators despite their criticisms. For example, John Larkin, the socio-economic historian of Philippine rural life, explicitly adopted the concept of involution as an antidote to conventional historical analysis in his examination of the sugar- and rice-producing region of Pampanga in the nineteenth century; he argued that this perspective on agrarian change helped make sense of the necessarily limited data available to the historian on certain long-term changes in the past (1971). In his study of land usage he discovered that there was neither population pressure nor land shortage in Central Luzon to affect the production of rice and sugar, as a literal reading of Geertz's hypothesis would demand. Rather, he found that an acute shortage of finance throughout the nineteenth century did produce stagnation and over-elaboration of social relations, and therefore 'some manifestations of an involuted society' (ibid.: 795). Larkin then reformulated and expanded Geertz's concept with three propositions: first,

> when an agricultural society with a substantial peasant base is subjected to significant economic deprivation of an important resource, be it land, cash, or something else, that society may well develop complex social and economic arrangements and mechanisms to share as far as possible those scarce resources.

Second, 'the more shortages of resources that exist, the more involuted that society may become'; and finally, 'individual scarcities produce specific kinds of social response' (in Java 'elaborate social and ritual behavior'; in Pampanga 'various complex contractual schemes involving land transferral and harvest splitting') (ibid.: 795).

Geertz's four major studies of social change and development which we have just reviewed rather cursorily have a rather different focus from his ethnographic masterpiece, *The Religion of Java*, although this study underpins his other work by presenting the sets of religious ideas which inform Javanese social action (Inglis, 2000: 60–61). Again Geertz constructs ideal types in attempting to arrange and order his data. *Religion* is primarily a detailed ethnography and not specifically devoted to the analysis of change. He addresses the theme of the relations between religion and social change much more directly in his later comparative and historical study *Islam Observed: Religious Development in Morocco and Indonesia* (1968). In this book he examines religious responses, more particularly the development of Islamic modernism and reformism, to the 'secularization of thought' and the transformations set in train by industrial capitalism and scientific thought.

In his *Religion of Java* Geertz formulates a now famous triadic division focused on 'three main social-structural nuclei … the village, the market and the government bureaucracy' (1960: 5). Each is broadly although not exclusively associated with a variant of Javanese religion, the village with the *abangan* tradition, the market with the *santri*, and the bureaucracy with the *priyayi*. The village *abangan* system is said to comprise 'a balanced integration of animistic, Hinduistic, and Islamic elements, a basic Javanese syncretism which is the island's true folk tradition'; its main elements are animistic: the ritual or communal feast (*slametan*) to mark rites of passage and other significant events, and a set of beliefs about spirits, curing, sorcery and magic associated with a range of different, though primarily magical practitioners or specialists called *dukun* (ibid.: 5, 86ff.). The *santri* religious system of the market or more specifically the domestic trade network consists primarily of 'a careful and regular execution of the basic rituals of Islam – the prayers, the Fast, the Pilgrimage' as well as various 'social, charitable, and political Islamic organizations' (ibid.: 6). Finally, the *priyayi* white-collar elite has its historical connections with the old Hindu-Javanese courts, and therefore its religious system is focused on elements of court culture – dance, drama, music and poetry – and 'a Hindu-Buddhist mysticism' (ibid.).

Geertz argues that these three types are not 'constructed', but rather emerge from the Javanese perceptions of their own religious system in the vernacular terms they use to talk about it. Geertz also insists that his study is a 'report', 'a simple description' and in that spirit he provides the details, the 'facts' about beliefs, practices, and institutions of the three sub-systems one by one, liberally sprinkling the text with edited quotations from his field-notes. It remains one of the standard reference works on Javanese religion, although it has been reviewed and commented on extensively, sometimes critically. One of the major criticisms again came from Koentjaraningrat (1975: 200–201) who argued that nowhere does Geertz define religion and there are many elements in the book which have very little if anything to do with Javanese religion. In this connection, Koentjaraningrat argues that the *priyayi* sub-system is not a religious variant at all in that the *priyayi* are a socio-cultural elite and not a religious community. He therefore proposes that there are only two religious sub-systems, the *santri* who adhere to Islamic doctrine, and reject heterodoxy, and the *abangan* or Javanists who are heterodox. Therefore, religious variation is conceived of in terms of the degree of participation in and the kind of orientation to Islam (1975: 200–201; and see Hefner, 1985: 3–4). Geertz himself remarks that the *priyayi* 'religious orientation is more difficult to set off from the *abangan* than is the *santri*' and that *priyayi* and *abangan* 'orientations, from the point of view of culture content, are in part but genteel and vulgar versions of one another' (1960: 234). In his final chapter (ibid.: 355–381), Geertz examines the conflicts and tensions between the three subsystems, noting that these are moderated in various ways because the Javanese embrace a set of overarching cultural values, ideas and ethics, and nationalist aspirations, and participate in a common set of social relations. Again Geertz suggests that the 'strain is clearly greatest between *santris* and the other two groups' (ibid.: 356). In support of Geertz's own observation Mulder too notes that 'most priyayi are abangan in the sense that they do not take their (Islamic) duties seriously' and that they are both 'religiously only defined by their not being santri', though he qualifies this by saying that 'even then there are exceptions!' (1989: 4). Thus, 'Javanism' with its emphasis on pre-Islamic traditions is counterposed to Islam. A further development of the two sub-system framework is that proposed by Mark Woodward who like others draws attention to Javanist–Islamic distinctions but subsumes 'Javanism' under an over-arching Islamic umbrella (1989). He argues that popular and mystical traditions are in effect related to Islamic Sufism and therefore are simply different aspects of Islam.

Probably Andrew Beatty's recent book is one of the most thoughtful studies of the 'varieties of Javanese religion' and it provides a commentary on both Geertz's work and that of some of his critics (1999). Interestingly, Beatty notes that the structure of his own book, 'wittingly or unwittingly', is broadly the same as that of Geertz's *The Religion of Java*. In other words, Beatty begins with an analysis of the focal ritual (*slametan*), followed by folk traditions, then orthodox Islam and finally Javanist mysticism (ibid.: 9–10). He agrees with Geertz, in contrast to various of his critics, that Javanese religion 'can best be grasped from three contrasting vantage points'. But he states that he conceives of the three forms in a rather different way – 'more relationally, less identified with particular groups, and in a single social context quite unlike the disparate, semi-urban setting of Geertz's field-work' (ibid.: 9–10). He is therefore less concerned with clearly defined ideal types and more concerned with interactions at religious boundaries and how differences are both maintained and overcome in practice.

Beatty undertook his field research in Banyuwangi in the easternmost part of Java and analysed religious or ideological pluralism and diversity in the context of the dominant religion, Islam. However, he examines how elements of Javanese folk religion and mysticism make different kinds of compromise with Islam. On the common ground where those of different religious orientation intermingle, compromise is made possible because differences are played down or smoothed over. He also concentrates on practical village Islam and emphasizes the ways in which *santri* and *abangan* interact and the fact that there are villagers who are 'neither clearly santri nor abangan but something in between' (ibid.: 115). The *slametan*, which Beatty unlike Geertz does not associate specifically with the *abangan* tradition, contains 'all three of Geertz's variants' (ibid.: 30), and, despite their differences, the participants, whether pious Muslim, animist or mystic, reach compromises. Ritual symbols are multivocal and ambiguous; differences of religious orientation are both 'expressed and muted' (ibid.: 51) by employing different interpretations of symbols, wordplay, situational flexibility and varying emphases. The *slametan* therefore is an occasion in which there is a 'temporary accommodation' (ibid.: 49), 'a refusal to contest meanings in public' (ibid.: 43), and 'a recognition of common social values and common humanity which override doctrinal differences' (ibid.). However, following the events of 1996–1997 and the downfall of President Suharto, Beatty indicates that Javanese syncretism is being rethought and he suggests the possibility but not the inevitability of 'a more prominent role for Islam' (ibid.: 247).

Before moving on to consider Geertz's general contribution to the study of culture we need to indicate some of his significant observations on Balinese social organization and cultural forms. Undoubtedly one of his most important early pieces was his attempt to make comprehensible and analyse variations in village organization across southern Bali (1959). In a wonderfully lucid paper he argues that Balinese village structure is not a constant; it is remarkably variable in time and space. But what are constant are the components, elements or 'planes' which comprise the structure and which intersect and overlap in complex and variable ways. These are based on a set of principles of group affiliation and comprise separate membership in a temple, a hamlet (*banjar*), an irrigation society (*subak*), and voluntary associations, shared caste status, ties of kinship, descent and affinity, and a subordinate relationship to a particular government official. Each of these elements performs a different social function and, in a book jointly written with his wife Hildred, Geertz subsequently explores in detail the dimension of kinship and marriage as one of those autonomous yet intersecting domains (Geertz and Geertz, 1975).

This persuasive rendition of Balinese village society and the cultural ethos on which it is based has been questioned by Fredrik Barth, in his extraordinarily detailed 'synthetic account of society and culture' in Buleleng, northern Bali, where he carried out a total of fifteen months' field research between 1984 and 1989 (1993: 3). Barth argues that, in Geertz's image of a society which comprises functional parts, each part of which 'goes about its business calmly and correctly, without assertive leadership and command, in an intricately ordered but independent way', the emphasis is placed on consensus, formal institutions and the acceptance by individuals of a set of cultural rules about order and the appropriate performance of roles (ibid.: 109–111). Instead Barth proposes that, if one focuses on individuals pursuing their interests and purposes (that is on individual rather than structural variation), and if one examines the processes by which social and cultural forms are created 'from particular combinations of ideas, material circumstances, and interactional potentials' (ibid.: 4), then the Balinese village can also be seen as an arena of political factionalism, unrest, violence, rivalry and struggles for power where individuals strive to realize particular ambitions and where collective decision-making and cooperation are frequently problematical (ibid.: 111–121). With reference to subsequent studies on South Bali where Geertz had worked in the late 1950s, Barth suggests that this depiction of village life also holds there (ibid.: 121–122). Barth's perspective comes close to postmodern analyses (see Chapter 6) in his interest in the ways in which societies and cultures are represented and in the deconstruction of images which argue for inherent coherence, boundedness and order. But he suggests that he differs from postmodernism in his stress on the processes of construction of social and cultural 'realities' in the arena of individual variation and interaction (ibid.: 4–7).

Geertz's late classic on Bali is undoubtedly his relatively short essay, though with a roughly equivalent number of semi-detached notes, on the nineteenth-century Balinese state, the 'negara' of his title (1980). Geertz points out that this Sanskrit loanword with its original meaning of town is used 'more or less simultaneously and interchangeably' in Indonesian languages to refer to 'palace', 'capital', 'state', 'realm' and 'town', and it is counterposed to another Sanskrit loanword 'desa' which refers to 'countryside', 'region', 'village', 'place', 'dependency' or 'governed area' (ibid.: 4). His analysis attempts to demonstrate how these two categories of existence were interwoven and mutually interdependent. He formulates the concept of a 'theatre state' in which 'the kings and princes were the impresarios, the priests the directors, and the peasants the supporting cast, stage crew, and audience'; in short, '[c]ourt ceremonialism was the driving force of court politics' (ibid.: 13), and the state was in effect the king – the 'exemplary centre' (ibid.: 11–18).

Geertz's study of the culture of politics, the poetics of polity and the symbolism of power has also evoked much critical commentary, but it is clear that this is a thought-provoking work, and according to Inglis, Geertz's 'noblest' (2000: 155). What Geertz does is present and dissect persuasively one of the most significant dimensions of state action – its theatrical or symbolic expressions – and, though it is much more immediate in the Balinese state and more generally in the Indianized states of South-East Asia, it is an aspect of all states. He therefore attempts to redress the balance between conceptions of the state which emphasize it as the locus of power, strength, force, control, subjection and decision-making, and his own perspective which focuses on the state as 'a structure of thought' or 'a constellation of enshrined ideas' (ibid.: 134–135).

Despite this important analytical orientation, some of his critics have argued that Geertz shifts the balance too much in the direction of 'the cultural' and 'dramatic' and away from the 'political' and 'economic' premises and actions of the state. Barth too raises the issue of what precisely the Balinese state was expressing and acting out, and importantly who precisely embraced the ideas which were presented and orchestrated by kings, princes and priests. He says that the 'attitudes of Balinese subjects to their rulers, even in South Bali, may have been at best ambiguous' (1993: 222). What is more, the characterization of certain acts as drama or 'pageant' might well under-state the dimensions of violence, honour, anger and bravery which they also enshrine and portray, and

Barth argues that what the state conveyed or 'taught' was a 'conception of caste', 'a comprehensive model of human rank differences and hierarchy' embodied in descent groups (ibid.: 226–235). Above all, and as with criticisms of Geertz's work on Javanese religion and Indonesian agriculture to the effect that his all-embracing models tend to underplay variation, Barth too suggests that the model of the Balinese theatre state, based on South Balinese experience, cannot incorporate 'the many forms of organization and the many strands of tradition that flourish today in North Bali' (ibid.: 21).

We shall dwell finally but briefly on Geertz's other wide-ranging writings on the concept of culture and his analyses of various cultural events and expressions in Indonesia. We intend to return to some of his findings and observations in later chapters. But it is worth noting here that his commitment to the understanding and exploration of 'culture' runs consistently through his work, though it is more subdued in some pieces than in others. He also indicates that, aside from this his 'most persistent interest', he has also worked, as we have seen, in other areas of the social sciences, particularly in the field of social and economic change and development. His collection of selected essays entitled appropriately *The Interpretation of Cultures* (1973) and the more recent *Local Knowledge* (1983) provide us with his major statements on the subject and include case material on Java and Bali. The best-known of these studies are '"Internal Conversion" in Contemporary Bali' (1973: 170–189), 'Person, Time, and Conduct in Bali' (ibid.: 360–411), 'Deep Play: Notes on the Balinese Cockfight' (ibid.: 412–453), 'Ritual and Social Change: A Javanese Example' (ibid.: 142–169), and 'Religion as a Cultural System' which includes his analysis of the encounter or 'ritual combat' between the frightening Balinese witch Rangda and the 'endearing monster' Barong (ibid.: 114–118). In much of this Geertz tackles the small rather than the large picture – the minutiae of everyday life – rituals, pastimes, person-categories, though always with an eye on general cultural themes.

Geertz's very personal, amusing yet deeply analytical account of a Balinese cockfight is a must for any student of anthropology interested in the ways in which ethnography is constructed. As Inglis says, 'it is accessible to the commonest reader, vivid, pungent, moving and profound' (2000: 85). In Geertz's hands we see how the cockfight provides an opportunity for the Balinese to display their other selves to themselves; 'a people of unusual blandness and obliquity in ordinary dealings present a tale of themselves as wildly clamorous and murderously cruel' (ibid.: 87).

For Geertz culture comprises human-generated 'webs of significance' and anthropology's task is to search out, reveal, interpret and explain the 'symbolic dimensions of social action' (1973: 30). Humans are 'symbolizing, conceptualizing, meaning-seeking' creatures (ibid.: 140). In his discussion of religion as a cultural system, Geertz presents us with one of his most measured definitions of culture: 'it denotes an historically transmitted pattern of meanings embodied in symbols, a system of inherited conceptions expressed in symbolic forms by means of which men communicate, perpetuate, and develop their knowledge about and attitudes toward life' (ibid.: 89). Or expressing it in another way and adding other dimensions to the definition, as Geertz invariably does, culture comprises '[s]ymbol systems, man-created, shared, conventional, ordered, and indeed learned, [and they] provide human beings with a meaningful framework for orienting themselves to one another, to the world around them, and to themselves' (ibid.: 250). Or putting it very simply, the primary task of cultural anthropology is 'to determine what this people or that take to be the point of what they are doing' (1983: 4).

It is this concept of culture as a system of meanings and symbols in terms of which social relations are engendered, conducted, sustained and transformed which Geertz uses to examine dynamic socio-cultural changes in post-war Indonesia, and although, in his earlier work on processes of modernization and development, it does not play a dominant analytical role, it still serves to inform Geertz's overall perspective in that he wishes to understand economic and political changes in their 'meaningful' cultural context. For one of the most thought-provoking studies of 'culture as meaning' and its relations to social action using an ethnographic, historical, comparative and regional perspective in the tradition of Geertz, then Robert Hefner's work on the highland Javanese is essential reading (1985, 1990). But before leaving Geertz we should keep in mind Barth's detailed critique of Geertz's tendency to seek 'systematics' and coherence in cultural materials (a cultural 'ethos' or 'essence') and congruence between formal institutional rules, observed patterns of behaviour, and the goals, interests and priorities of individuals. As we have seen, Barth's emphasis on individual interaction and the influence of 'positioning' on individual inter-pretations and knowledge requires us to recognize that 'the outcomes of inter-action are usually at variance with the intentions of the individual participants' so that 'we cannot judge people's interpretations and intents directly from the observable consequences of their acts' (1993: 170, 343).

Burma, Nash and Spiro

As in American work on Java, Bali and Thailand the preoccupation with mod-ernization and development and its relationships to social and cultural processes can also be found in Manning Nash's study of two villages in the vicinity of Mandalay in Upper Burma (1965). The tone and focus of the book are captured in Nash's opening statement:

> The new nations of Asia and Africa are in the foreground of current history. The emergence of a host of new nations since the end of World War II is one of the most dramatic and portentous phenomena of this era. Breaking loose from colonial domination the new nations of Asia and Africa are discovering ways and means of transforming traditional societies into modern ones.
>
> (ibid.: 1)

Nash wished to uncover 'the sources of susceptibility and resistance to social change in a newly developing nation, to point out the range of opportunities that appear to the ordinary villager in a modernizing society' (ibid.: 2), and in this sense he had a very practical purpose in providing social data 'needed for planning' (ibid.: 323). His preoccupation with the possibility of Burma achieving modernity within the political context of liberal democracy is also apparent. Although he recognized the uncertainties and difficulties which Burma faced, he tended to view Burmese nationalism from the perspective of the lowland Burmese rather than the nation as a whole and with reference to a Western view of modernity. In the early 1960s there might well have been some justification for proposing that 'some of Burma's real assets in working toward a regime of civil liberties and representative institutions capable of promoting modernization cannot be overlooked' (ibid.: 102). Yet, given the political and economic developments in Burma following the establishment of military rule in 1962 and the brutal way in which the State Law and Order Council (SLORC) consolidated its control from 1988, Nash's optimism has proved to be largely unfounded.

In the 1950s and 1960s the circle of American South-East Asianists was relatively small; in his acknowledgements to his 1965 book, Nash indicates that Clifford Geertz read his manuscript and, in considering processes of socio-cultural change, Nash refers to Geertz's *Peddlers and Princes* in its attempt to address issues of socio-cultural variation between different communities. In an introductory comment very reminiscent of Geertz, Nash says of village Burma that the 'traditional and the modern are side by side in an odd and unstable mixture' (ibid.: 4). Nash also relied on the advice and suggestions of two other major figures in post-war studies of Burma – Lehman and Spiro. We shall consider Lehman's contribution in the next chapter when we examine structural anthropology and Leach's work on Highland Burma; Lehman provides an important connection between American cultural anthropology and European structuralism, which has never enjoyed much popularity in the United States. But it is worth noting here, that though Lehman's main ethnographic focus was the Chin, an upland minority in Burma, he was well versed in Buddhism and lowland Burmese culture; he read Nash's and Spiro's book manuscripts and proffered advice to them, particularly in the romanized transcription of Burmese words using a system which Lehman himself had developed. It should also be mentioned that both Nash and Spiro worked in other societies outside Burma; Nash in Mexico–Guatemala and Kelantan (Malaysia) and Spiro in an Israeli kibbutz and in Micronesia.

What was especially intriguing about the study of modernization in Burma and indeed Thailand was that change was taking place in societies which held to a philosophy of other-worldliness and to the principle that one's current life is the result of one's good deeds and misdeeds in all previous lives; it is an ethic, in contrast to Western Protestantism, which proposes that humans should ultimately remove themselves from the world of suffering and achieve the extinction of self or at least seek to secure a better rebirth in future lives. How could such an ideology accommodate itself to processes of modernization and secularization? It was an issue in the sociology of religion which Max Weber had examined in his ambitious comparative studies of European and Asian religious traditions, and both Nash and Spiro attempted to address it from the perspective of village Burma, just as Geertz was concerned to understand the relations between modernization and Islam in small-town Java. In other words, following Weber, the major question to be examined is: 'Does Buddhism inhibit economic growth, and, if it does, to what extent and in what ways?'

Fortunately Nash managed to complete his fieldwork in Burma in 1960–1961 not long before the military coup of March 1962 and the subsequent exclusion of all foreign researchers from the country. His compatriot, Melford Spiro, who also conducted research in the Mandalay region in 1961–1962 and who met Nash during fieldwork, had hoped subsequently to undertake 'a series of trips' to Burma to provide as comprehensive a study as possible. In the event this proved impossible and Spiro advised that his material and research for his two major studies of Burmese religion (1967, 1970) remained incomplete because of the 'visa policies of the ... military Government' (1967: 9). However, he did work with Burmese immigrants and refugees in Thailand during the summers of 1969–1972 which helped him fill certain gaps for his third volume on Burmese kinship and marriage (1977). Both Nash and Spiro made the point that the absence of any substantial ethnographies on lowland Burmese society and culture also required them to provide basic information on their study villages. Nash states firmly that his over-riding concern was to 'explain or account for real behavior in real societies', in short, he sought 'facts' (1965: 313), and he sought them in the context of defined village units, though recognizing that they were elements in a larger and more complex whole. In a later edited collection of comparative essays on Theravada Buddhism, Nash emphasizes that all his contributors 'show an awareness of the fact that their unit of study forms but part of a larger social and cultural system' (1966: vii).

Nash, as with Geertz's comparison of communities in Java and Bali and more generally of different agricultural systems in Indonesia, studied two villages in the dry zone of lowland Upper Burma with rather different ecosystems: 'Nondwin', a village practising mixed cropping and 'Yadaw', one cultivating rice using irrigated methods. He also visited several other villages to obtain as full a picture as possible of the range of social and cultural variation across Upper Burmese rural communities and the different responses to externally generated change, though he notes that variations are relatively minor.

Nash, familiar with Boeke's concept of dualism, and indeed critical of it (1965: 16–17), and with Furnivall's concept of a plural society, formulated his own concept of a 'multiple society' to help him understand local rural communities or 'peasants' within fast-changing and newly created national societies (and see Nash, 1964). Reminiscent of the notion of pluralism, Nash's concept never enjoyed the academic popularity and recognition accorded the paradigms of pluralism, dualism, involution and indeed loose structure. He argued, like Furnivall, that a multiple society is held together by 'a single political network and a national economy' (1965: 3, and 321–322). In outline, Nash's concept is not so different from that of Furnivall, though it attempts to address the social organization of a new nation rather than a colonial state. The multiple society therefore comprises a small urban-based, modernizing 'national' elite or class which wields political and economic power; it holds sway over a poorly articulated range of differently organized regional and local 'segments', including 'agrarian villages' which have different world-views and goals. Essentially he draws a distinction between the elite and the peasantry, and eschews any kind of class analysis of Burmese society. To accommodate the phenomenon of pluralism, Nash also argues in a rather untidy fashion that some segments of the multiple society comprise 'plural cultures', in effect the tribal minorities of Burma (ibid.: 321; 1964: 420–421). The main impetus for change comes from the political and economic centre while local villages are 'exhorted, ordered, or coerced'; the capacity for local level changes tends to be modest, constrained by the rural economic structure (1965: 3, 29–33, 93–101). Nash also addresses the concept of 'loose structure' and while accepting that the Burmese social system, like that of the Thai, permits flexibility and choice, nevertheless argues that Burmese village society is structured on the basis of 'conventional understandings' which give form to various groupings, roles, relations and social persons (ibid.: 73). These understandings are rooted primarily in village Buddhism which gives rise to different kinds of 'perduring groups' (ibid.: 151).

Nash's main concerns are focused on a description and relatively low-level analysis of economic activities and social organization and their relationships to Buddhism and spirit or animistic (nat) beliefs as they are practised and understood in his study villages. He argues convincingly that one must examine empirically particular activities to determine whether or not and to what extent and in what ways religious values are institutionalized and give rise to or shape behaviour (and see 1963). Above all he concentrates on individuals as exercising choice and formulating strategies. He therefore, for example, investigates areas of religious life where there is a degree of freedom in the interpretation and implementation of basic precepts. His investigations, again given his preoccupation with a particular kind of modernization, led him to suggest that generally Buddhism is neither a facilitator of nor an obstacle to economic development. He also acknowledges that Buddhism developed in tune with 'a society where structural change was minimal'. Nash concludes that Buddhism is ambiguous in its effect and therefore it requires the Burmese elite to reduce 'this ambiguity to make Buddhism come to grips with the prospect of a modern, industrial, and ever-growing society' (1965: 164). In other words, he is of the view that Buddhism is not a positive force for development and will need to be adapted to accommodate the needs and character of a modern society.

As we shall see in a moment, Nash carried forward and developed this style of analysis from the mid-1960s in his study of politics, religion and modernization in the predominantly Malay state of Kelantan in east coast Peninsular Malaysia (1974). In introducing his subsequent research he points to his continuing interest in 'complex', changing societies, and West Malaysia appeared to offer a 'promising' research site. He says, 'I had already worked in Burma and hence had a feel for former British colonies and modern Southeast Asia. Burma, at that time, was closed to anthropological investigation', and the Pasir Mas district of Kelantan gave him the opportunity to examine 'the patterns of a complex segment of a nation state and also to contribute something to the understanding of social change' (ibid.: ix).

Let us now turn to the work of Melford Spiro, probably the most outstanding anthropologist of post-war Burmese society and culture and certainly the most prolific. Like Nash the focus of his research was the dry zone area of Upper Burma, specifically the village of 'Yeigyi' some ten miles from Mandalay. His research was not directly concerned with matters of modernization and development in contrast to Nash, though he did address issues of religious change in Burma. His interests come close to those of Geertz in the latter's study of Javanese religion; Spiro focuses on the world of the sacred and spiritual. However, although Spiro, in his analysis of Burmese supernaturalism and Buddhism, employed a concept of culture which approximates that of Geertz in that he is concerned to understand and interpret a transmitted system of shared public symbols and their meanings, and to examine the interrelationships between culture, social action and social structure, Spiro differs from Geertz in combining 'functionalist cultural theory' with 'psychodynamic personality theory' (1977: xi–xii). It should be noted that Spiro subsequently presented a more refined definition of culture which explicitly distinguishes 'symbol' from 'meaning' and considers culture as 'a system of interrelated propositions . . . encoded in public signs' (1992: 4, 43).

Nevertheless, for Spiro the anthropologist also has to examine the 'cognitive, motivational, affective and perceptual systems', in short, the personality of individual actors in that the meanings of cultural symbols can only be accessed by studying what 'actors think, feel, believe, desire' (ibid.: xii), and by investigating the relationships between social processes, particularly the socialization of children by parents, peers and teachers, and individual motives, emotions, perceptions and needs. In contrast to Geertz, Spiro proposes that underlying cultural diversity, which is in turn a response to diverse ecological and historical contexts, there is a 'common psychobiological "human nature"' (1967: 6). Using this psychological-functionalist perspective therefore Spiro argues that culture, and here specifically religion, satisfies a restricted set of common human needs (desires, beliefs, drives, emotions, aspirations, tensions). In this regard, in his description and analysis of Burmese supernaturalism, he focuses on the problem of suffering, and how it is explained and addressed (ibid.: 2–3, 8). We shall examine his two major studies of religion in more detail in a moment.

First, we need a brief mention of his later book on Burmese kinship and marriage. It presents us with a relatively detailed exposition of a bilateral or cognatic kinship system, and in that respect provides us with useful comparative data for the studies of Thai 'loose structure' and Javanese society undertaken by the Cornell and the MIT teams respectively. However, Spiro's central tenet is that underlying cultural diversities there is a common set of principles which cut across cultures. In the examination of kinship these comprise the biological facts of human reproduction and the dependency of infants and children on their parents, which in turn are related to certain patterns and processes both sociological (such as the biparental family, the incest taboo and socialization) and psychological (such as ambivalence towards parents). Spiro examines in particular the relations between 'sentiments' or 'attitudes' (or affective and cognitive meanings) developed in small families, social experience and kinship behaviour, and these in turn with kin terms, categories and jural norms. Although Spiro examines in some detail the formal properties of Burmese kinship, his main concern is with attitudes, emotions, tensions, motivations and sexual behaviour.

Subsequently Spiro published a miscellaneous collection of previously printed analytical and ethnographic papers on Burma (including material on the Burmese world-view, marriage payments, household composition, economic action and religion, politics and factionalism, social change and gender ideology). It also includes two introductory theoretical papers (one an expanded version of a previously published paper) which restate and develop further his views on cultural diversity, cultural relativism and the unity of human nature (1992). His argument, which of course has been contested, is posed in straightforward terms; cultural diversity is an accepted fact but it is anthropology's task to explain, understand and 'know' other cultures. Although there are dangers in interpreting other cultures, not least the problems of ethnocentrism, cultural hegemony and explanations based on one's own standards and values, interpretation is possible because 'we share a common humanity' (ibid.: xi, 17). Therefore, Spiro argues that, despite the obvious differences between Burmese and Western culture, 'Burmese actors are not "Other", but "Brother", whose beliefs and actions are susceptible, in principle, of the same types of explanations that are employed to explain the beliefs and notions of Western actors' (ibid.: xiii). The task of the anthropologist is to make 'the strange familiar' and conversely 'the familiar strange' (ibid.: 57).

In his *Burmese Supernaturalism* (1967) Spiro examines beliefs in supernatural beings or spirits and the preventive, therapeutic and offensive rituals related to them. He considers beliefs in witches, ghosts and demons, and *nats*, particularly the important cult of the Thirty-Seven Nats. Very like Geertz's attempt to explain how a great tradition, in his case Islam, can operate side by side with a religious system whose basic premises are different, Spiro concentrates on the relationships between supernaturalism and Buddhism which he concludes are 'in a state of tension' (ibid.: 247). According to Spiro, this tension is perceived in both doctrinal and ethical terms: doctrinally the belief in the inevitability of *karma* (Pali: *kamma*; Burmese: *kan*) and the determination of one's present and future existences on the basis of merit and demerit accumulated in previous lives does not square with the practice of spirit propitiation in order to effect a change in one's physical and spiritual well-being in this life; and ethically Buddhism and the *nat* cult give expression to different orientations to the world – while Buddhism is in ideal-typical terms characterized as a philosophy of morality, asceticism, serenity, rationalism and otherworldiness (at least in its concern with the extinction of existence), the *nat* cult is amoral, sensual, emotional, turbulent, nonrational and thisworldly (ibid.: 257–263). Obviously the tension or incompatibility between two different, distinguishable but coexisting religious systems needs to be managed, and Spiro argues that this is achieved by legitimizing the *nats* in Buddhist terms and assimilating Buddhist supernaturals to non-Buddhist ones. In this process the prominence of Buddhism over the *nat* cult is affirmed: Buddhism confers legitimacy on supernaturalism, and rituals are sequenced and sacred space so arranged as to place the *nat* cult in an inferior position. Spiro also points out that despite the tension between Buddhist rationalism and *nat* superstition, canonical Buddhism does not ignore beliefs in spirits. Indeed it acknowledges their existence and indicates ways of exorcizing them or pressing them into service by reciting sections from the Buddhist scriptures (ibid.: 251–252). In contemporary Burmese Buddhism as in other Theravada Buddhist countries some monks also practise as exorcists, and Buddhist relics and ritual paraphernalia are believed to have magical power to ward off evil.

In a very valuable concluding chapter Spiro reviews previous attempts to characterize the relationships between Buddhism and supernaturalism. He rejects the notion that animism is the real religion of the Burmese; instead he argues that Buddhism has primacy with regard to the resources, time and energy devoted to it, its position and status in Burmese values and norms, and the sacred power it possesses. 'Far from being a veneer, Buddhism is deeply embedded in Burmese culture and deeply rooted in Burmese personality. And rather than being indistinguishable, Buddhism and the nat cultus are in most, but not in all, respects distinctive systems' (ibid.: 266). Nevertheless, he argues that the importance of supernaturalism for the Burmese lies in its capacity to meet human needs which remain unfulfilled in Buddhism. For him the belief in spirits provides an alternative explanation for the problem of suffering and furnishes the means to cope with and address current personal predicaments. It also accommodates those 'impure' impulses, thus ensuring that Buddhism, as an ethical and moral religious system, remains 'pure' and uncontaminated by them (ibid.: 3–5, 279–280). We shall see in Chapter 4 how Stanley Tambiah's analysis of the relations between Thai Buddhism and the spirit cults from a structuralist perspective (1970) compares with that of Spiro. But we should also note at this juncture that Spiro has not interpreted correctly the concept of *karma* in relation to supernaturalism since in normative doctrinal Buddhism *karma* does not completely determine one's present and future status in life; there is some flexibility in that *karma* works along with wisdom and effort in framing one's destiny.

Although Spiro's study of supernaturalism is among the most thought-provoking of the post-war anthropological studies of folk religions in South-East Asia, it is surpassed in its quality and scholarship by his major study of Burmese Buddhism, published three years later. *Buddhism and Society* (1970), reissued in a second expanded edition in 1982 (references below are to the second edition), presents us with one of the most comprehensive anthropological studies of Theravada Buddhist doctrine and practice in mainland South-East Asia. In this text of over 500 pages Spiro gives a careful and informed exegesis of canonical Buddhism and its relationship to or rather its discrepancies with actual Burmese Buddhist beliefs, including supernaturalism; he provides a detailed description of Buddhist ritual in village Burma, including calendrical, life-cycle and crisis rites; he also describes the main features and organization of the monastic system, paying particular attention to the personal characters and motivations of monks and the relations between the state and the monkhood; and finally he considers the relationships between Buddhism and Burmese society, and spends some time commenting on Weber's sociology of religion and his specific analysis of Buddhism. In particular, he discerns, using a Weberian ideal-type framework of analysis, three sub-types of normative or scriptural Buddhism, which he refers to as 'nibbanic' (a religion of radical salvation), 'kammatic' (a religion of proximate salvation), and 'apotropaic' (a religion of magical protection). He also examines a fourth system, 'esoteric Buddhism' (a religion of chiliastic expectations) which is 'only marginally related' to the scriptures (ibid.: 162) and comprises combinations of occult beliefs and Buddhist doctrines located in 'quasi-secret sects'. In broad outline his three major sub-systems are, he says, abstracted from local native classifications, and are found to varying degrees in all Buddhists. His triadic division is reminiscent in some respects of Geertz's three ideal types of Javanese religion. As with his approach in his study of the tension between supernaturalism and Buddhism, Spiro argues that the discrepancies between Buddhist textual doctrine, belief, conception and practice are 'a product of cognitive orientations and motivational dispositions that are pan-human in their distribution' (ibid.: xix). In more concrete terms religious ideas are 'used to provide hopes, to satisfy wishes, to resolve conflict, to cope with tragedy, to rationalize failure, to find meaning in suffering' (ibid.: 6), and, although culture to some extent shapes human nature and gives rise to the phenomenon of cultural diversity, there are limits to this process in that there are 'certain universal needs which will not for long be frustrated' (ibid.: 14; 1992: xv).

Spiro, mainly following J.H. Bateson (ibid.: 7–11), summarizes Buddhist doctrine in terms of five concepts: materialism (there is no human soul and certainly no spiritual essence which survives death); atheism (there is no God, no saviour God, and no Creator; one seeks and achieves salvation by one's own efforts alone and not with divine assistance); nihilism (there is no permanent existence and humans should seek to end the cycle of rebirths); pessimism (life is suffering, and the only way to eliminate suffering is to eliminate worldly desire and ultimately existence); and renunciation (detachment and renunciation of worldly existence and desires). However, in the process of becoming a popular or mass religion within the embrace of large rural populations, Spiro argues that the message of salvation in terms of the attainment of 'nothingness' or the extinction of self, *nirvana* (Pali: *nibbana*; Burmese: *neikban*), has of necessity been changed; elements of Buddhist ideology have been selectively emphasized, and others reorganized, reinterpreted, ignored or rejected, given the life circumstances of most ordinary people. For the majority of lay Buddhists their goal is the attainment of a more satisfying rebirth, an increase in merit over demerit so that suffering is diminished and pleasure increased in future existences. The basis of this goal is that there are degrees of suffering and pleasure and by certain prescribed actions one can decrease the first and increase the second. In other words, it is 'the frustration of desire' which is viewed by the Burmese as the source of suffering, and 'its fulfilment as the essence of salvation' (ibid.: 73). In his examination of kammatic Buddhism, Spiro therefore focuses on the concept of merit and demerit and its relationship to *karma*, and the acquisition of merit by giving or charity, particularly in the support of monks, moral behaviour and meditation.

Finally, in his examination of what he calls 'apotropaic Buddhism', Spiro indicates that it is concerned not with otherworldly affairs but with mundane matters of fortune and misfortune which can be addressed by 'specific magical acts', including spells taken from the Buddhist scriptures, and rituals involving offerings to Buddhist images, pagodas, relics, saints and gods (ibid.: 140); in this regard supernatural beings can be called on to render assistance and Buddhism overall is conceived of as 'a protective shield against the dangers ... of the present existence' (ibid.: 140). The dangers include attack by evil spirits, ghosts and demons, illness and crop failure. In apotropaic Buddhism, which has close links with Burmese supernaturalism and magical practice, a major preoccupation derived from a 'universal psychological need' is to explain and address immediate suffering (ibid.: 141). According to Spiro this variant or system also has a basis in the Buddhist canon and is sanctioned by it (ibid.: 144–147), although, as might be anticipated, his Burmese informants had only 'loose and vague conceptions of supernatural assistance' (ibid.: 154).

As one might anticipate Spiro has been criticized for his explanation of religious phenomena in terms of psychological variables, especially by scholars who prefer social structural explanations and analyses and are unconvinced by Western-derived psychological frameworks. In his analysis of the personalities of monks, for example, Spiro contends that monasticism helps meet certain conscious and unconscious needs 'developed in childhood' (ibid.: 27); these include the need for dependency and relief from social responsibilities, an excessive preoccupation with oneself ('narcissism' and 'vanity'), and emotional 'timidity' or detachment (ibid.: 337–350). Like Freud, Spiro focuses on childhood experiences as the main locus for the development of psychological structures (e.g.

ibid.: 70–71). Notions of self-help, the unpredictable occurrence of fortune and misfortune, beliefs in hostile witches and *nats*, the uncertainty about the availability and effectiveness of supernatural assistance based on the concepts of *nirvana* and *karma* are all said to correspond with certain childhood socialization experiences, particularly, so Spiro maintains, emotional and physical indulgence in infancy followed by an unpredictable and unexplained general withdrawal of this support in childhood and its subsequent inconsistent provision (ibid.: 132–133, 137–139, 154–155). Spiro's claim that people only hold to certain religious ideas and practices if they are psychologically functional or satisfying appears not to be testable on the evidence he himself presents, and, when he does present evidence on Burmese character, he appears to do so selectively to confirm his hypotheses (Gombrich, 1972: 484–488). There is also evidence of variations in child-rearing practices and personalities in Burma as well as in the commitment to certain beliefs and practices, but these remain unexplained in Spiro's *general* explanation of Burmese character and culture. Furthermore, Spiro does not compare his data with other cultures which provide similarities with the form and content of Burmese processes of socialization and character formation and those which do not, in order to begin to determine whether or not his causal propositions hold. Indeed, evidence from other neighbouring Theravada Buddhist cultures suggests that, in some areas of religious belief and action, child-rearing practices have no or very little bearing at all.

As we have seen in Geertz's work, there is also a danger in constructing ideal types, of drawing out differences between different complexes too sharply. Spiro does this in his distinction between the 'great tradition' of Buddhism and the 'little tradition' of supernaturalism, even assigning separate studies to them. In *Buddhism and Society* he presents his three types of Buddhism primarily as separate but related complexes of ideas or 'cognitive structures', and in his characterization of kammatic Buddhism, he sees it as deviating in certain respects from normative nibbanic Buddhism. He proposes at one point that attainment of *nirvana* 'is achieved by the extinction of karma' (1982: 68). But, as Gombrich states in his review of Spiro's book, progress towards *nirvana* is achieved by accumulating good *karma* through good intentions, not by eliminating it, though *nirvana* is ultimately attained by the extinction of craving as a result of the full realization of the Buddhist truths (1972: 491). Gombrich goes on to argue that Spiro's three kinds of Buddhism

> are really not fully-fledged independent *cognitive* structures at all. Apotropaic Buddhism consists mainly of the ritual use of Buddhist sacra for magical purposes, with a poorly developed rationale, and attitudes and values little or no different from those of kammatic Buddhism. As for kammatic Buddhism, part of it is good nibbanic Buddhism, part of it (like apotropaic Buddhism) is an extrapolation from people's behaviour.
>
> (ibid.: 493)

Instead of Spiro's three cognitive sub-systems Gombrich prefers to use the straightforward and simple distinction 'between what people say they believe and what they act as if they believe' (ibid.: 493). This for him helps explain much more about the development of canonical and practical Buddhism, its paradoxes and contradictions, and the ways it has interacted with other religious traditions.

Despite these criticisms of Spiro's work there is no doubt that he and other American anthropologists working in mainland South-East Asia in the 1950s and 1960s contributed greatly to our understanding of the ideas and practices of village Buddhism and the ways in which it relates to both canonical and historical Buddhism and the non-Buddhist tradition of spirit cults. These researchers were also concerned to examine the social and cultural responses of small-scale societies to the forces of modernization, although they tended to work with a relatively simple distinction between tradition and modernity.

A widely read volume, edited by Manning Nash and arising from a conference at the University of Chicago in 1963, brought together a number of the anthropologists who had been working in Burma, Thailand and Cambodia (and indeed Ceylon) in the immediate post-war years to consider both the common features of Buddhism as a 'practised' religion and the reasons for variations in beliefs and behaviour in different communities (1966). The contributors included Nash and his wife, June, along with David Pfanner who had worked in villages in the Pegu district of Lower Burma in the 1950s, Jasper Ingersoll who lived in the village of Sagatiam near the provincial capital of Nakhon Pathom in Central Thailand during 1959–1960, and Michael Moerman who, at roughly the same time, had studied the Thai-Lue of Ban Ping in Chiengrai province, Northern Thailand.

The collection provided a mainly empirical record of local level religion, and, among other things, emphasized first, the pre-eminence of Buddhism in mainland South-East Asia as against the spirit cults, and, second, began to question the utility of the concept of 'loose structure', given the obvious organizational requirements of Buddhism, the focal coordinating role of the Buddhist monk, and the community-wide obligations to participate in ritual. Manning Nash presents succinctly the justification and purpose of the volume: the papers

> constitute a first attempt to provide an empirical basis for the serious comparative study of Theravada Buddhism as a living religious system. Indeed, most of the information in them is new and expands our grasp of what it means to be a Theravada Buddhist in the varying communities where that system is dominant.
>
> (ibid.: xii)

Malaysia, Nash and Provencher

Following his field research in the interior dry zone of Burma, Manning Nash turned his attention to the east coast of Peninsular Malaysia and periodically from 1964 to 1970 he spent some fifteen months working on aspects of social and cultural change in the Pasir Mas district of Kelantan, 'one of the bastions of Malay culture on the peninsula' (1974: 5, 7). The central township of Pasir Mas is situated on the banks of the Kelantan river 12 miles from the state capital, Kota Bharu, and Nash and his research assistants surveyed twenty villages (*kampong*) in the district, and studied one community, Tasek Berangan, in more detail. He wished to gain a regional rather than a localized village perspective on change. The regional economy was dominated by small-holding subsistence rice and commercial rubber cultivation along with the growing of vegetables, fruit and coconuts (ibid.: 19–20). The average rice plot was just over 2 acres in extent, and the largest holding was about 50 acres so that there was a degree of socio-economic homogeneity in the countryside. Nevertheless, Nash discerned four broad groupings or classes in Pasir Mas, though, as we shall see shortly, he is less concerned with social classes (he sometimes calls them 'economic group-ings' (ibid.: 113), and more interested in political factions, and at times his delineation of classes seems confused and contradictory, and his economic cate-gories jostle with those based on status. Overall, these stratified groupings com-prised the urban-based 'educated, official and commercial class' or 'notables' (including bureaucrats, politicians, merchants, secular and religious teachers), possibly including the old aristocracy, some of whom owned land in the coun-tryside; a small group of rural rich who employed others to work their land; a middle class (who owned about 5 acres of rice land), and the 'poor' (who had little or no land, generally laboured for others or on others' land as tenants, or worked as artisans and petty traders, or migrated seasonally or semi-permanently in search of work (ibid.: 20, 42–43, 84). In Chapter 5 we shall see how this system of social stratification compares with a variety of cases studied by other, mainly British-based researchers in rural Peninsular Malaysia.

Nash wanted to understand how Kelantanese Malays had responded to the challenges of nation-building and economic change in Malaysia, and he saw the main impulses for change being generated from outside the district. His frame-work is yet again a modified version of modernization theory, combined with the concept of individual choice and decision-making, which he had already employed in his Burma research. In addition, in examining the mechanisms and processes of change, he identifies key secular and religious roles (or 'brokers') at the local level which connect to the wider systems, and 'the domains and activities that place kampongs like Tasek Berangan, towns like Pasir Mas, and cities like Kota Bharu in a single dynamic and strife-ridden social arena' (ibid.: 68). Two of his key mediation or brokerage roles comprise the mosque official and prayer-leader (*imam*) and the *penggawa*, the individual who occupies the lowest rung of the civil service below the District Office; he receives a salary and is primarily responsible for local administration, law and order, and the co-ordination of sub-district heads (*penghulu*) and village heads with the District Office (ibid.: 70ff.). Nash argues that these roles connect the peasantry to 'hier-archical structures which govern them securely and inform their faith'; they are primarily directed to the maintenance of order and continuity (ibid.: 77). He looks for the primary sources of change in other arenas, specifically in politics, religion and the economy, and how these might affect social and cultural life.

His general perspectives are revealed succinctly in his introductory chapter 'Social Change in a New Nation'. He says of Malaysia in the 1960s that the 'indices of modernization ... are all moving in the proper directions ... [and] ... the fundamental aspects of modernization, institutional modification and innovation in basic belief systems ... are well under way' (ibid.: 2). For Malays, Pasir Mas is also 'a stronghold of tradition' (ibid.: 7), and Nash conceptualizes 'tradition' as 'social process', and as comprising those cultural elements which 'are worthy of psychic attachment and social defense' by their 'association with the heritage of the culture' and with relationships within Malay communities and especially between Malays and non-Malays (ibid.: 8). He also recognizes that there was debate among the Malays of Kelantan about what their tradition or life style should be (ibid.: 65). Despite this more dynamic concept of 'tradi-tion', Nash is still concerned with the detailed empirical exploration of the 'large and abstract dichotomy supposedly existing between "traditional" and "modern" societies' (ibid.: 8), the 'uneasy mix' between 'the old and the new' (ibid.: 65) and the social consequences of 'traditional' and 'modern' roles (ibid.: 84). It is important to compare Nash's work with the research of Raymond Firth and his colleagues which is discussed in detail in Chapter 5, and which is less preoccupied with the transition from tradition to modernity.

Nash points out that the anthropologist tends to focus on micro-level changes, the small incremental shifts in organization and deviations in patterns of behaviour, and for him this is done by examining 'a segment of a society whose form, function, and dynamics are in great measure determined not by its interior mechanisms but by the workings of the larger society in which it is embedded' (ibid.: 6). However, the first task is 'to search for regularities in the flow of experience and to attribute meaning to those regularities' (ibid.: 10). As with Geertz the sets of meanings attached to behaviour and action – the inter-connected symbolic systems uncovered – constitute for Nash 'the culture of the social unit studied' (ibid.: 11). Nash explains that this does not mean that culture is fully integrated nor social structure in balance and harmony; indi-viduals make choices which are not completely determined nor constrained by social structure and culture. The actions and behaviour based on these choices in relation to the individual desire to maximize control over resources or people provide the seeds of change and transformation (see Chapter 4 for Edmund Leach's and his critics' discussion of the major human motivational orientation of the desire for power and wealth). Nash acknowledges that, in capturing the main features and principles of the social and cultural life of the rural Kelantanese Malays, he first of all artificially freezes them in time and isolates them from their surrounding environment (ibid.: 63). He then widens the frame to examine interactions between the different levels of a complex society and the tensions and conflicts generated. The focus of the interactions comprise 'actors in role sets striving to meet their ends, and as they strive they change themselves, others, and eventually the cultural and social system in which their striving takes place' (ibid.: 69).

One area of tension and the potential for change which Nash identified in Kelantan in the 1960s was the conflict, both political and religious, between, on the one hand, the United Malays National Organization (UMNO), the pro-Malay party of government, comprising mainly Western-educated moderate Malay accommodationists who had formed an alliance with political parties representing the other two major ethnic groups in Malaysia, the Chinese and Indians, and, on the other hand, the opposition Pan-Malay(si)an Islamic Party (PMIP or PAS), staunchly Islamic, vigorously pro-Malay, and, despite Malaysia's multi-ethnic constituency, in support of the establishment of an Islamic State. The complicating factor in Kelantanese politics was that PAS, in opposition to the UMNO-dominated alliance government at the federal level, was in control of the state government (ibid.: 86ff.). This conflict penetrated to the local level through party organization of rural branches, and was directed to issues of Malay identity and their national position and status in Malaysia. It also had a class dimension in that UMNO support was largely drawn from the urban areas and the educated rural population while PAS had a predominantly 'traditional' rural constituency, though Nash argues that '[t]rue class or interest politics, as opposed to communal politics, has not developed in Kelantan' (ibid.: 109). Rather, it was based on patron–clientship and factionalism between 'traditionalists', including a religiously-based, Malay-oriented literati and 'modernists', including a Westernized elite.

In addition to political conflict Nash also examines the 'economic arena' in Pasir Mas, and the impacts of capitalist production and the market. This is primarily phrased in communal terms, and centres on the contrast between the perceived wealthy and dynamic Chinese population and the relatively poor and backward Malay, and for Nash specifically the differences between the dynamic Chinese-dominated shophouse sector ('true businesses', ibid.: 118), directly connected to the national and international economy and the small-scale Malay bazaar sector ('slow-growing and non-innovative', ibid.: 123). Much of this is reminiscent of Geertz's observations in *Peddlers and Princes* (see above). However, for the rural Malays Nash suggests that there are two primary sources of change: government development programmes, particularly targeted at rural areas and agriculture, and increasing numbers of unemployed and underemployed youth (ibid.: 128ff.). The first is, of course, highly politicized, and especially in Kelantan where the allocation of resources for development are closely linked to winning and sustaining support in the competition between UMNO and PAS. The second is a result of population growth, land fragmentation, and low returns to agriculture. Nash points to a process of 'involution' taking place both in rural and urban areas to provide at least some kind of livelihood for more and more people (ibid.: 139). However, Nash argues that the spread of education, changing aspirations and the increase in political mobilization make it unlikely that an involutional process will continue in the longer term. Nash predicted, and, given Malaysian government policies from the 1970s, was proved right, that increasing resources would be invested in development interventions to move more Malays from the 'traditional' sector to the 'modern' sector of the economy, and to redress the economic imbalances between Malays and Chinese (ibid.: 142–143). He also anticipated that modernist Islam would gain ground against fundamentalist Islam, but that the shape and tone of Malaysian politics – with its emphasis on communalism and ethnicity – would continue (ibid.: 147).

For Nash, Malaysia in the early 1970s was 'poised on the edge of full modernization', and its major challenge then was

> [the] orderly induction of most of the Malay peasantry into a modern economic sector with all of the implications of modernity: increased occupational differentiation; class structures based largely on economic performance and education; reduced familial networks; and loss of some sense of community in return for spatial and social mobility.
>
> (ibid.: 148)

This theme of modernization and its relationship to rural traditionalism was taken up by Ronald Provencher in his research in west coast Peninsular Malaysia at roughly the same time that Nash was working in the rather remote state of Kelantan (1971). Provencher worked in Malaysia in 1964–1965, using Fred Eggan's method of controlled comparison (1954), examining two historically, socially and culturally related communities, one urban (Kampong Bharu), established in 1899 within the inner city boundaries of Kuala Lumpur, and one rural (Kuang), some twenty miles distant and founded in 1924 on Malay reserved land. Provencher's findings were based on a sample of 185 urban and 181 rural households and he proposed that the two communities were 'representative' of both west coast rice- and rubber-growing Malay villages and established Malay urban settlements whose economy relied on government employment, small-scale trade and wage labour (1971: 2). Provencher focused on unbounded 'personal networks' and 'personal communities' to order his data, in other words ego-based networks of interaction, support and approval (ibid.: 3), and he wished to determine how different environments (in terms of population density, composition and heterogeneity, social and physical mobility, and economic differentiation) corresponded to differences in social and cultural behaviour and interaction. He was not primarily interested in studying change, but in the process of understanding rural and urban socio-cultural variations, he argued that this would assist in our understanding of the role of urban areas in

social and cultural change (ibid.: 1). With reference to the debates in the literature on Thai social behaviour and organization, Provencher maintains that west
coast Malay society, with its absence of 'sociocentric groups', could also be characterized as 'loosely structured', though formal, predictable behaviour between
those of unequal rank he describes as 'tight' (ibid.: 204–207).

As we might anticipate, patterns of interaction (manners, etiquette or courtesy) did differ between the two 'worlds', particularly given the greater social
and physical mobility, sub-ethnic heterogeneity and inter-ethnic interaction of
urban Malay residents, the fact that many Malays – especially young, unmarried
men – rented property in Kampong Bharu and were much more transient, and
that workplace was usually separated from residence in contrast to the more
established, close, multi-stranded, face-to-face relationships in the rural
community. For Provencher 'the urban setting provides a wider range and
greater contrast in the use of the Malay interaction system than the rural setting
does' (ibid.: 172). Nevertheless, Provencher concludes that, although urban
communities were subject to processes of Westernization and modernization,
these processes were not uniform and linear affecting all categories or groupings
of people to the same degree and in the same way. Rather, certain sub-
populations in urban areas also demonstrated important elements of 'traditional'
formal behaviour and interaction, specifically among urban property owners and
in relation to the frequency of holding and attending ritual feasts (khenduri)
(ibid.: v, 143).

The Philippines: law and violence in cognatic societies

In the post-war Philippines the focus of American anthropological interest was
much more balanced and spread between lowland and upland populations and
there was no dominant figure nor paradigm in post-war anthropology there.
Some senior American anthropologists, like their European counterparts elsewhere in South-East Asia, continued the tradition which had been established
during the colonial period of working among minority communities. Davis and
Hollnsteiner remark that the 'first four decades of Philippine anthropology
[1900–1940] are characterized by a nearly exclusive concern for two primary
interests, culture history and non-Christian peoples, especially the so-called
"tribal" peoples' (1969: 60; and see Keesing's survey, 1962). However, after
1950 there was a noticeable shift of attention to the study of lowland Christian
Filipino society both in rural and lower-class urban communities (Hart,
1977: 3).

Yet, despite the changing emphasis towards lowland majority populations
exemplified in the 1950s' research by Donn Hart among the Cebuan Filipino of
southern Negros in the Bisayan islands, central Philippines (1954, 1977), and
Frank Lynch's study of a Bikol town in south-eastern Luzon (1959), the influence of Fred Eggan and his Philippine Studies Program at Chicago was important in continuing to direct field-research to Mountain Province and to

minorities elsewhere in the archipelago. Among other research themes, Eggan and his students concentrated on the form and functioning of cognatic or bilateral societies, the nature of dyadic relations within the domestic family or household and the kindred, and the structure of bilateral descent groups, which had been neglected fields of study up to the 1950s. As Eggan says, 'The Philippines provides one of the important regions of the world for the study of bilateral social systems' (1967: 186).

Interest in bilateral kinship did, however, take American anthropologists into both lowland and highland communities. Ethel Nurge, a student of Eggan, carried out field-research in north-east Leyte, one of the Bisayan islands, in 1955–1956, and focused on household composition, dyadic relations in the family, and specifically the relationship between mother and child (1965). As we have seen in Spiro's work and in Chapter 2, socialization processes have been a significant concern in American anthropology, especially the interaction between certain kinds of behaviour and the encouragement of certain personality types. Nurge explicitly contrasts Leyte child-rearing practices with those of American mothers with regard to such traits as succorance, achievement, responsibility, dominance, obedience, sociability and aggression (ibid.: 82–86). In addition to Nurge's well-known monograph, there was a spate of child-rearing, socialization and personality studies undertaken in the 1950s and 1960s; on authoritarian attitudes and Filipino school experience (Guthrie, 1961); Filipino child-rearing and personality development (Guthrie and Jacobs, 1966); and enculturation and socialization in Panay (Jocano, 1969a) and the Ilocos region (Nydegger and Nydegger, 1966). The Nydeggers' study took its inspiration from the work of Mead and Benedict, among others, and was part of an international cross-cultural study of child-rearing and personality formation conducted in the 1950s by social scientists from Cornell, Harvard and Yale.

Nevertheless, alongside research on bilateral social organization, the pre-war concerns of Barton and others in studying traditional legal institutions and practices occupied a special position in Philippine anthropology. Indeed, it was in the post-war Philippines that much of the significant anthropological field research on South-East Asian legal concepts and practices was undertaken, especially among minority ethnic groups which, in the absence of written legal codes, courts, judges and a police force, were considered to pose special problems for the understanding of how social order is maintained in small-scale societies.

Probably one of the best-known of the American students of the anthropology of law was Edward P. Dozier who acknowledges that his interest in the Mountain Province was first stimulated by Fred and Dorothy Eggan. Dozier studied primarily amongst the Northern Kalinga in 1959 and 1960 (1966, 1967). Barton on the other hand had worked among the Southern Kalinga (1949), and Dozier uses Barton's material for comparative purposes, as well as his own data collected during several weeks' research in the southern area of Lubuagan. Dozier investigated modern adaptations in the mechanisms for maintaining law and order and ensuring punishment for wrongdoing. The traditional Kalinga system, as described by Barton, had been based on self-help, head-hunting, revenge killing and feuding. But with the expansion of American administration, educational institutions, communication networks, trade and wage-work, there was an increasing need for Kalinga to cooperate with their neighbours and to travel widely through their territories. Therefore, a more secure and stable system of peace-keeping had to be devised. The institution of the peace pact (*bodong*) was established, and it is this and the 'arbiters' who operated it, which Dozier analyses in some depth, particularly in his first monograph (1966), and then more briefly in his second (1967). His first major publication *Mountain Arbiters* (1966) provides a detailed historical and sociological treatment of the Kalinga peace pact system, their customary law, social and economic organization and religion, as well as comparing the two divisions of Northern and Southern Kalinga.

Like the major lowland populations of the Philippines, Thailand, Burma, Malaysia and Indonesia, and the natives of Borneo (see, for example, Hudson [1972] for an excellent ethnography of a Bornean society), the upland Philippine communities also organize their social life on a cognatic or bilateral basis. As we saw in Chapter 2, in the work of such writers as Eggan, there was an early preoccupation among American anthropologists with the study of kinship and marriage. In contrast to those minority groups in South-East Asia which were organized on a unilineal basis, and especially those like the Kachin and Chin of Burma which had prescriptive marriage rules (see Chapter 4), the cognatic societies of the Philippines without corporate unilineal descent groups appeared to those Western anthropologists who studied them to present special organizational problems. Dozier devotes considerable attention to Kalinga social organization and describes and analyses residential units including villages, hamlets and households, as well as examining what Barton referred to as the 'kinship circle' and Eggan the 'personal kindred'. Dozier notes that '[t]his grouping is found among all the mountain peoples of northern Luzon' (1967: 20). In Kalinga this grouping comprised an individual's siblings, first, second and third cousins, and all those ascendants to great-grandparents and descendants to great-grandchildren. Apart from siblings no other individual has the same kinship circle. A first cousin, for example, shares some common relatives with a given ego, but there will be other relatives of the cousin who will not fall within ego's own kindred range.

The Kalinga kinship circle is therefore a ramifying network of individually focused relationships, and traditionally it played an important role in disputes and conflicts. Members of a kinship circle were 'obligated to avenge any member who is killed, wounded, or wronged in any manner' (ibid.: 22). In the past serious wrongdoing often resulted in revenge in the form of woundings or head-taking. On the other hand, should a member of one's own kindred commit an offence against someone of another kinship circle, then all members were expected to contribute to any compensation or reparation due. With regard to marriage rules, while marriage to first cousins is strictly forbidden in Kalinga and there are objections to marriage with second cousins, marriage to third cousins and beyond is quite permissible. Therefore, the kindred is cross-cut and reinforced by affinal ties, and individuals from different kinship circles also intermarry. The complications occasioned by systems of self-help to address wrongdoing in a cognatic society in which kindreds overlap endlessly and are cross-cut by marriage ties are considerable. In a community without discrete social groups a given individual might find that his loyalties were divided in a dispute, and it is precisely this situation of divided allegiance which helped resolve conflicts. There were always those who sooner or later would wish to seek mediation, particularly in a local area in which the network of relationships was at its most dense. Beyond the 'home region' where relations of kinship and affinity were less common or more attenuated, there was usually a situation of feud and hostility expressed in warfare and sporadic head-hunting raids.

Dozier argues that the peace pact system was built upon earlier Kalinga institutions of kinship and arbitration. Traditionally the path to social esteem for a Kalinga man was to demonstrate prowess in warfare and success in head-hunting. A brave warrior earned the title of *mangol* and it was these men who achieved rank, influence and wealth, and ultimately could act as 'arbiters' of disputes in their home region. Among the Southern Kalinga there were also wealthy 'aristocratic' families (*kadangyan*) from which mediators would be drawn (ibid.: 74–76). With the gradual disappearance of head-hunting and warfare, following the establishment of the American colonial state, the path to power and influence came increasingly to depend not on warriorship but on the accumulation of wealth and involvement in modern political activity. Nevertheless, at the time that Dozier carried out his research, the values associated with personal revenge and bravery in war were still in evidence, and he notes that, though head-hunting had 'virtually disappeared, private revenge in the form of killings and woundings is common' (ibid.: 78).

What the Kalinga did, however, was to translate their mechanisms of mediation within a region with the use of influential 'arbiters' to the wider interregional arena to provide a means both to maintain peace and to settle disputes without recourse to personal revenge. The peace pact is based on a mutually agreed set of provisions (*pagta*) between two regions drawn up by the respective regional leaders; these latter serve as arbiters and upholders of the provisions. The *pagta* are in turn derived from the complex body of Kalinga customary law which exhibits variations across regions. However, the peace pact is in effect initiated by two individuals, often in the context of a trading agreement, who hold the pact on behalf of their respective kinship circles, though the provisions are binding on all members of the two regions represented through the two kindreds to the agreement (ibid.: 84). Spears are exchanged between the two pactholders as a sign of good faith, and the regional leaders hold a follow-up meeting to negotiate and agree the provisions. The pact is then periodically reaffirmed at a major feast or celebration.

Dozier concludes his study by emphasizing that the peace pact adheres 'closely to traditional concepts and practices revolving around the key principles of kinship and the blood feud' (ibid.: 96). Despite the fact that he is concerned with 'traditional' institutions and their recent adaptations, he is also, like most other post-war American anthropologists who undertook field-research in South-East Asia, interested in the effects of modernization and the growth of the modern nation–state on minority populations and small-scale communities. It should be noted here that a valuable complementary study on the peace pact by a Filipino anthropologist reached broadly similar conclusions to those of Dozier and placed the Kalinga in the wider context of the colonial and the postcolonial state (Bacdayan, 1967).

A similar set of issues is addressed by Thomas Kiefer in his study of the Tausug, a Muslim population of the southern Philippines, whose political centre is the island of Jolo, in the Sulu Archipelago (1972). The Tausug were the dominant ethnic group in the former Sulu Sultanate and they incorporated into this political system ethnically distinct Samal-speaking communities which included the so-called Bajau 'sea gypsies' or 'sea nomads' (Nimmo, 1972; Sather, 1971) and the Jama Mapun of Cagayan de Sulu and southern Palawan (Casiño, 1976). Unable to undertake fieldwork in Indonesia because of the troubles there in 1965, Kiefer chose to reroute to the Philippines where he stayed for two years from 1966 until 1968. His main interests were 'traditional law' and Islamic societies, and he adopted a relatively straightforward framework to investigate Tausug law, that is to discover what principles are employed to recruit people to groups, how the groups function once formed, and what values inform individual and group action. Like Dozier he studied the ways in which wrongdoing is redressed and order maintained in a cognatic society based on personal kindreds. Kiefer says that Tausug culture is 'heavily preoccupied with the problems of violence and its control. Law, political activity, feuding, and conflict comprise the major focus of an adult man's concern' (1972: 2). The values associated with this cultural focus are personal responsibility (for redress), shame, honour, bravery and male friendship (ibid.: 52–75).

The Tausug recognize an ego-centred personal kindred (*usbawaris*) extending to first cousins and upwards and downwards from this genealogical level; this is the grouping which has the main responsibilities towards an individual in the case of a dispute, and provides the core of the feuding group, particularly if brothers and male first cousins are residing in close physical proximity to one another (ibid.: 29–30). An individual might also involve close friends in his 'minimal alliance group', though these provide a rather more unstable set of relationships (ibid.: 71–75). Unlike the informal Kalinga arbitration system, the Tausug rely on the mediation of disputes through established community and regional headmen, religious officials and aristocrats, whose authority ultimately stems from the Sultan, though in practice it is the headmen who are the most crucial in the mediation process. However, in practice, the headmen's authority will vary depending on the level of their local and regional support, their wealth, titles, wisdom and judgement.

Kiefer locates the Tausug in the Philippine nation–state in the 1960s, particularly given their status as a Muslim minority in a predominantly Catholic country. There were and clearly still are Muslim secessionist tendencies in the south, and the 'violent' nature of Tausug society in which '[a]ll Tausug men have a fascination with guns' (ibid.: 75) presented problems for the government in Manila. Nevertheless, at the time of his research Kiefer did not foresee political separation as a possibility, though he did point out the major differences (and conflict) between Tausug legal perceptions and practices and those of Manila to the extent that there was a stand-off between the national Constabulary stationed in the south and armed bands of mainly rural Tausug youth (ibid.: 138–139). Yet armed conflicts between Muslims and Christian immigrants had escalated elsewhere in many parts of Mindanao in the early 1970s when Kiefer was engaged in writing his book. In the case of the Tausug, Kiefer could only hope for 'the development of a kind of working misunderstanding between Tausug law and government law, ... supplemented by an increase in the quality and sensitivity of the Filipino officials who are forced to deal with the Tausug' (ibid.: 141). Subsequent events in the Philippines have, however, taken a rather different turn with persistent conflict and violence between Christians and Muslims.

Still on the subject of indigenous systems of law, the study by Stuart Schlegel of the Tiruray of the Cotobato Cordillera in south-western Mindanao also deserves to be mentioned (1970). Again Schlegel acknowledges the support of Fred Eggan, among others, in his research. Schlegel had worked as the principal of a high school in Upi, Cotobato from 1960 to 1963 and subsequently undertook field-research for a further two years in Figel, a neighbourhood in the Tran Grande. His study, like those of Dozier and Kiefer, focuses on native customary law and the methods employed by the Tiruray to address and resolve disputes in a cognatic society organized on the basis of households and personal kindreds. There are striking similarities between the Tiruray and the Kalinga and Tausug in respect of the responsibilities which kinship groupings carry to seek redress on behalf of their members, ultimately through blood revenge, as well as to contribute to compensation and fines for any wrongdoing committed by one of their number. However, Schlegel's approach differs from that of his colleagues in that he concentrates not so much on the organizational aspects of law and order, but on the relationship between social action and the realm of morals and values. In this regard he is particularly influenced by the cultural anthropology of Clifford Geertz, and investigates the moral, evaluative and emotional basis of Tiruray legal thought (hence his use of the term 'justice' in the title of the book).

Schlegel demonstrates the difficulty of formulating a cross-cultural definition of law. However, he, like Dozier and Kiefer, draws attention to the central importance of social rules which 'create obligations upon the members of [a] society, either by exacting behavior which contributes to the society's welfare or by prohibiting behavior which would be harmful' (ibid.: 154). These rules are then applied to particular contexts, and they are subject to adaptation, change and adjudication. As obligations they also carry a moral load; they concern what is proper, respectful and good, and the moral propositions about appropriate action comprise the 'normative implications of Tiruray common sense' (ibid.: 158). It is taken for granted, in the nature of things, that one should behave in a certain way and that, above all, one should respect others and their feelings, though it is also recognized that men are by their very nature 'potentially violent' (ibid.: 29–31). A social situation and social relations are evaluated in terms of the concept of *fiyo* (the way things should be), and when the world is right and proper then so is one's *fedew* (state of mind or rational feelings, literally translated as 'gallbladder') (ibid.: 31–32).

The focus of Schlegel's study is the *tiyawan*, which is a formal encounter between two or more kindreds at the time of marriages, disputes and deaths in which there is 'speaking' or 'discussion', and property as bridewealth or in fines is transferred, presided over by specialists (legal authorities) called *kefeduwan* (ibid.: 23, 58–68). The *tiyawan* provides the mechanism for settling disputes peacefully. *Kefeduwan* are experts in customary law and act as mediators in adjudication proceedings. They use highly metaphorical language in their exchanges and their purpose is to 'settle the case properly; to recognize all appropriate rights and to accept all appropriate fault, to the end that every *fedew* will become again good (*fiyo*), which, to Tiruray, is the state of justice' (ibid.: 122). The *kefeduwan* do not have coercive power; they cannot punish. But they represent and express the moral order of the Tiruray and by this means carry authority. Schlegel demonstrates in detail the principles of Tiruray justice by describing numerous cases of *tiyawan*.

Schlegel also addresses the national context within which Tiruray justice operates. He is pessimistic about the prospects for the survival of this system of customary law under the onslaught of modernity. He argues that, although it can adapt, it does so slowly, and those Tiruray who are incorporated into new economic, political and moral systems gradually abandon their traditional legal–moral order. In order to preserve it they have to 'retreat farther and farther into the mountains and forests' (ibid.: 172). Schlegel says that, in these circumstances, 'it seems very doubtful that in another twenty years it will be possible to locate a single Tiruray community where isolation and ecological conditions remain to permit the traditional Tiruray way of life' (ibid.: 25). The Tiruray 'are becoming ... ever less Tiruray and ever more Filipino' (ibid.: 26). We shall take up issues of nationhood, globalization and the relations between small-scale communities and states in more detail in Chapters 5, 6 and 7.

Local anthropologists and American anthropology

Given the importance of American anthropology in post-war South-East Asia, it is perhaps not surprising that much of the research undertaken by local anthropologists also operated within the paradigms and interests of senior American researchers. Small numbers of local students were sent to American universities, especially in the 1950s and 1960s for graduate studies. Philippine academe, for example, for a long time led by a close-knit network of American scholars and funded by American research foundations and universities, provides unequivocal evidence of this pattern. Philippine sociology and anthropology had been directed by a handful of American professors; in sociology Chester Hunt and Frank Lynch were pre-eminent, and in anthropology H. Otley Beyer, at the University of the Philippines, Fred R. Eggan at Chicago, Harold Conklin at Yale and Donn V. Hart at Syracuse University, New York. Hart had carried out field research in the Bisayas in the early and mid-1950s and was appointed to Visiting Professorships at the University of the Philippines and subsequently Silliman University. Otley Beyer in particular had early on concentrated on the hill peoples of Mountain Province, specifically the Ifugao, and subsequently extended his research, on the government's request, to the minorities of the central and southern Philippines; this focus of interest was sustained by several American and Filipino anthropologists (Zamora, 1967). Conklin, for example, remarked that Otley Beyer had introduced him to Ifugao ethnology as early as 1945 (1967: 204–205).

The University of the Philippines was the first institution of its kind in South-East Asia to establish a Department of Anthropology, which from 1921 to 1951 was a combined department with Sociology. Otley Beyer presided over it from 1914 until his retirement in 1954. It provided the channel for sending promising young Filipino graduates to the USA, mainly to Chicago and Cornell. The first Filipino anthropologist to pursue graduate studies in the USA was Marcelo Tangco, who studied at Harvard and Berkeley in 1921–1925 and succeeded Beyer as chairman of the Department in 1954. In that year Moises Bello was sent to Chicago to study for his master's degree and subsequently E. Arsenio Manuel followed Bello on a scholarship to study for his doctorate in 1960. At the same time Mario D. Zamora was (unusually) undertaking research on an Indian community in Uttar Pradesh and completed his PhD in cultural anthropology at Cornell in 1963; Eudaldo Reyes finished his doctorate at Cornell a few years later. The National Museum of the Philippines also had anthropological interests; Robert Fox and F. Landa Jocano were there in the 1960s and both had received their doctorates from Chicago.

This small number of local scholars produced mainly functionalist ethnographies of a range of minority populations with particular attention to bilateral social organization, folklore and ethnohistory, beliefs and rituals, and customary law. Among the ethnic groups covered were the southern Kankanay of Benguet, Northern Luzon (Bello, 1967, 1972), the Sulod or 'Bukidnon', a mountain people of central Panay (Jocano, 1968), and the Malitbog of Panay (Jocano, 1969b). The dominant paradigm in Philippine anthropology at this time was behaviourist and positivist with an interest in the study of social norms and roles, social values and the processes and mechanisms of integration and institutionalization, and the relations between cultural patterns and personality. Jocano, for example, says of his Sulod study undertaken in 1957–1958, that it is based on the twin concepts of social structure and function and is concerned with the institutions and relationships which conduce to social cohesion and integration (1968: 3). Bello's study of the Kankanay also concentrates on social structure and mechanisms of integration, and the relatively smooth and 'mild' process of acculturation (1972). Jocano's later research on traditional medicine among lowland Filipinos provides a straightforward ethnographic account of folk healers and curing practices, concentrating on overt behaviour, customs and rituals (1973).

Even the more sociological studies of social stratification tended to focus on integration and stability rather than on social class conflict and contradiction. Frank Lynch's study of social class in a Bikol town exemplifies this approach (1959) in his formulation of a two-class patron–client model comprising 'big people' and 'little people'; the two classes need each other; they are 'functionally related' and the reciprocal relations between the upper class and the lower class contribute to community stability and solidarity. Yengoyan says that Lynch's 'view of class as a series of mutually overlapping, and thus cohering, interest groups is based on a firm commitment to behaviorism in conjunction with ... the rigor of positivism' (1984: 12). Studies of social inequality and social change were therefore tempered by a focus on personalistic, cross-cutting patron–client relationships (Hollnsteiner, 1963) and the interaction between modernization processes and Philippine values (Carroll, 1968). Both Lynch and Mary Hollnsteiner, Lynch's student and successor as director at the Institute of Philippine Culture, promoted the importance of the concept of 'smooth (i.e. conflict-free) interpersonal relationships' (SIR) in Philippine social values. Conflicts and tensions are under-played.

Chester Hunt and Dylan Dizon, in a general survey of Philippine sociology, conclude: 'Relatively little in the way of distinctive theoretical development has emerged from Philippine sociological research and publications' (1978: 132). They attempt to explain the emphasis on functionalist perspectives and the 'pragmatic and relatively conservative' stance of Philippine scholarship in the three decades after the Second World War; and they argue that, following Philippine independence, it was of paramount importance for the new nation to increase the store of ethnographic information by studying 'local customs' and to address practical social problems and policy issues (ibid.: 106–107). They note that 'American sociologists who know the country best have offered little encouragement to radical tendencies' (ibid.: 107). Indeed, Hunt and Dizon were themselves very much preoccupied with the traditional–modern paradigm in their review, though noting that the Philippines did not 'quite fit' either pattern (ibid.: 132). In this environment there seemed to be little inclination to indulge in theoretical speculation, although it has to be said that, within the parameters which were set by American scholarship, the Filipino-trained students did take issue with particular interpretations of the data and some of the details of the ethnographies presented by American anthropologists (see the papers in Zamora, 1967).

The same pattern can be found in Indonesia where local students, supervised by American scholars, adopted the paradigms of the day, and were especially attracted to modernization theories and functionalism, and to the possibilities offered by the practical application of sociological research. From the 1950s relatively small numbers of Indonesian students were trained not in The Netherlands but in the USA, particularly in Cornell's Modern Indonesia Project which developed out of the wider Southeast Asia Program. Of those Indonesians trained at Cornell who rose to prominence following their graduate studies, three deserve special mention: Koentjaraningrat (1961, 1967, 1968, 1975), Selosoemardjan (1962) and Harsja Bachtiar (1967). However, if anything, there was a greater concentration in local Indonesian research, in comparison with that in the Philippines, on issues of nation-building and development and their consequences for local communities. Topics examined included community and agricultural development, and ethnic identity in the context of Indonesian national unity. Koentjaraningrat emphasizes the lack of division and distinction between anthropology and sociology in Indonesia (1975: 217–221); and in this connection the research of Selosoemardjan and Harsja Bachtiar was much more sociologically oriented, although they were both very familiar with anthropological perspectives. After his early work on Minangkabau social organization (1967), Harsja Bachtiar devoted his main attention to issues of national integration, bureaucracy, youth movements and development (1968, 1972), while Selosoemardjan, in his study of social change in Yogyakarta, examined 'change from a closed to an open class system' and the passage or move of urban Javanese 'away from tradition' to embrace 'progress' and 'modernity' (1962: 411–412).

It was really Koentjaraningrat who kept to a much more anthropologically oriented research agenda. Following Indonesian independence, he played a central role in the task of collecting ethnographic studies of the country's diversity within an overall national unity, and taking stock of what had been achieved in research on its societies and cultures. Of special note is his monumental bibliographical and critical review of the cultural anthropology of Indonesia, broadly defined, to meet 'an urgent need for a definition of the field and scope of anthropology, not only for academic but also for practical reasons' (1975: vii). It provided the first relatively comprehensive account, from the perspective of a Javanese scholar, of Dutch colonial studies of East Indian peoples and cultures as well as post-war anthropological research, both Western and local. Koentjaraningrat also notes that because of their 'inadequate training and experience, the anthropological research done by Indonesian anthropologists during the two post-war decades, has usually consisted of little more than fact- and data-gathering, and has mainly been simple description in its form' (ibid.: 253). Koentjaraningrat's edited volume *Villages in Indonesia* (1967) was also the first major attempt to bring together post-war studies from first-hand field research of a range of ethnic groups undertaken by local and foreign, mainly American, anthropologists. The list of contributors reads like a 'Who's Who' of anthropologists of Indonesia in the 1950s and 1960s: including Harsja Bachtiar, Frank Cooley, Clark Cunningham, Clifford Geertz, Alfred and Judith Hudson, Peter Goethals and Masri Singarimbun. The collection provides basic descriptions of economic activities and organization, social structure, including kinship, stratification and leadership, and religious life, though other than in Geertz's chapter (1967a: 210–243), there is little questioning of the appropriateness of the concept of the 'village' as a unit of analysis.

Both in his own chapter in the book on the Javanese village of Tjelapar and in a number of other papers on Javanese social organization (e.g. 1961, 1968), Koentjaraningrat has contributed significantly to the debates about the nature of cognatic societies and the ways in which social life is structured in communities without corporate descent groups. We have already mentioned in Chapter 2 his contribution to the collection of essays in George Murdock's *Social Structure in Southeast Asia* (1960a). Nevertheless, the theme of the challenges and opportunities facing local communities (in all their diversity) within a newly independent, developing nation continually surfaces in Koentjaraningrat's work; in this respect he also takes over the dominant American paradigm of modernization and progress, and conceives of peasant villages as 'part-societies' incorporated into larger wholes. Let us leave this chapter on the American tradition with a quotation from him:

> The interplay between local and national loyalties in village communities ... is of basic importance ... The villagers' knowledge and perception of the wider world, however, must be improved constantly. The organizers of community development thus have to take into consideration the sharp distinction between the awareness, the perception, the relations, and the loyalties of the Indonesian villager in reference to the world beyond the village and in reference to the Indonesian nation.
>
> (1967: 405)

4

ANTHROPOLOGY IN THE PERIOD
OF DECOLONIZATION (1950–1970)

The European tradition

This chapter covers the work of British, Dutch and French anthropologists in the immediate post-war period and emphasizes the differences between the interests and perspectives of American cultural anthropologists and European structural anthropology. It takes up the discussion of Dutch structuralism again and its later developments under P.E. de Josselin de Jong. The theories of Lévi-Strauss are considered and their connections with Durkheimian sociology, along with Lévi-Strauss's influence on British anthropology, particularly in Edmund Leach's study of Kachin social structure and Rodney Needham's and his students' analyses of classification, symbolism and social structure among a range of Indonesian/Malay and northern mainland South-East Asian communities. Given the importance of Leach's work on Highland Burma, the response to and revisions and criticisms of his approach and conclusions are discussed in detail, among them Lehman's ethnography of the Chin of Highland Burma. Finally, we examine Tambiah's structural analysis of the relations between Buddhism and the spirit cults in North-East Thailand and Peacock's study of a Javanese proletarian drama form as a 'rite of modernization'.

Introduction

The general preoccupation of American anthropology during the 1950s and 1960s with the majority lowland populations of South-East Asia and the processes of socio-cultural, economic and political change within the context of nation-building to which these peoples were responding was not replicated to any great degree by anthropologists from the European traditions of structural anthropology. Interestingly while many Americans were working in communities which were constituent parts of 'great traditions' and of large-scale political systems, the majority of their British and British-trained counterparts who adopted a structuralist framework of analysis, particularly those who were attracted to the theories of Claude Lévi-Strauss, usually undertook research among and/or studied the secondary literature on the descent, marriage and symbolic systems of the 'exotic' minority populations of the hill areas of mainland South-East Asia and the outer islands of Indonesia.

116

Nevertheless, there were some US-based social scientists who did employ structuralist perspectives in their work and we shall consider F.K. Lehman's study of the Chin of Highland Burma and James Peacock's research on Javanese drama in this connection. We shall also examine Stanley Tambiah's study of North-East Thai religion (1970) as an example of a British structural analysis of lowland village religion rather different from the studies of Burmese and Thai Buddhism and supernaturalism undertaken by American cultural anthropologists.

We have already referred in Chapter 2 to the emergence and development of Dutch structuralism and the inspiration given to Dutch Indology by Emile Durkheim and his colleagues in their studies of classification, moral values and ideas, the principles underlying the relationships between social and symbolic categories, and the emphasis which they placed on social structures and social forms. As Evans-Pritchard has said of the central thesis of Durkheim and his followers, 'Ideas and values were not for them a mere ideological reflection or superstructure of the social order. On the contrary, they rather tended to see the social order as an objective expression of systems of ideas and values' (1960: 16–17). Marcel Mauss's essay on 'the gift' ([1924] 1954), Robert Hertz's two essays on the 'pre-eminence of the right hand' and the 'collective representation of death' (1960) and Durkheim and Mauss's *Primitive Classification* ([1903] 1963) were especially influential. In the post-war period it was Claude Lévi-Strauss ([1949] 1969), Rodney Needham (1958, 1962, 1973b, 1977, 1979), Edmund Leach (1952, [1954] 1970) and P.E. de Josselin de Jong (1951, 1965, 1977, 1984) who were foremost in applying the ideas and methods of the French sociological school primarily, though not exclusively to South-East Asian empirical data, and energetically promoting them to a wider anthropological audience. Needham also supervised a number of American students at Oxford who embraced the structuralist paradigm.

This European approach was very different from that of American anthropologists reared in the 'culturalism' of Franz Boas, Alfred Kroeber, Ruth Benedict and Margaret Mead. The Boasians were preoccupied with the examination of cultural patterns and the explanation of cultural variations in terms of the influence of environment rather than heredity; or to put it another way the pre-eminence of 'nurture' over 'nature'. Margaret Mead's study of female adolescence in Samoa is a classic example of this genre (1928). More especially it was Mead and Benedict who brought pyschology or personality studies into relationship with culture and argued for the influence of culture (through such processes as child-rearing) on the shaping of individual and collective personalities.

In the European structuralist tradition it was Needham who was to play an especially significant and pivotal role by bringing together and disseminating to an English-speaking audience the ideas and findings of the various streams of Dutch, French and British structuralism. In so doing he made a major contribution to the anthropology of South-East Asia. In his early research career he had studied in Leiden and was very conversant with the Dutch literature on

Indonesia. Among many other scholarly activities, he translated van Wouden's study of eastern Indonesian social structures from Dutch (1968) and Schärer's work on dual symbolic classification in Ngaju religion from German (1963). He supervised the English translation of Lévi-Strauss's *Elementary Structures*, translated into English Lévi-Strauss's *Totemism* and Durkheim's and Mauss's essay on 'primitive classification', and with his wife Claudia Needham, provided an English version of Hertz's two essays on death and the right hand. He supervised a number of anthropologists at Oxford, many of them Americans, who worked in this structuralist tradition and who undertook detailed research in Indonesia and Malaysia. Among the most prominent of them are R.H. Barnes, Kirk Michael Endicott, James J. Fox and Clark E. Cunningham. Needham also carried out his own structural analyses of a range of societies in mainland South-East Asia and the Malay–Indonesian archipelago (see, for example, 1957, 1960a, and see below). A dramatic illustration of the differences and disagreements between the European structuralist position and American cultural and psychological approaches is provided by Needham's polemical essay *Structure and Sentiment* (1962) in which he presents a defence, though with several qualifications, of Lévi-Strauss's analysis of social institutions, specifically unilateral cross-cousin marriage, contained in *Elementary Structures* (1969a), and a comprehensive critique of George Homans and David Schneider's 'sentimental', psychological explanations of the same phenomenon in their *Marriage, Authority, and Final Causes* (1955). Let us first of all summarize Lévi-Strauss's treatise on marriage alliance and its relations to Durkheim and Mauss's ideas.

Lévi-Strauss and French structuralism

In his *The Elementary Forms of the Religious Life* ([1912] 1995), Durkheim explores the social roots of religion. He argued that its elementary or early forms in society are 'collective representations' or expressions of a 'group mind'. Members of a collectivity infuse moral principles with sacredness and come to render these as real or concrete by realizing them in social activities. It is in the interactive experience – the sharedness of collective ritual – that individuals come to accept that there is something which exists outside of them – a greater power or reality – which is conceived of as a supernatural agent, a god or gods, and which is in turn made real through concrete representation in the form of effigies, icons or totems.

Marcel Mauss, Durkheim's nephew, then examined one elementary social principle, which was to inspire Lévi-Strauss to present a major reorientation of kinship studies and apply these insights to several dozen ethnographic cases, all distributed in eastern Asia and western Oceania, among them the marriage arrangements of various minority communities of South-East Asia. Mauss (1954) pointed to the universal practices of gift-giving and ceremonial exchange, and the principle of reciprocity which underpinned them. Gift-giving, he argued, is a vital means of creating and sustaining social solidarity.

Mauss drew attention to the beautifully simple social fact that the receipt of a gift entails a repayment, and more specifically that 'exogamy is an *exchange* of women between clans' (Needham, 1962: 7; emphasis Needham). Lévi-Strauss then elaborated Mauss's insight. In the first ten chapters of *Elementary Structures*, he seized on the uniquely human incest taboo as the 'single fact' accounting for the supreme form of gift exchange in the transfer of women from one group to another in marriage. All human societies recognize as a consequence the fundamental distinction between 'own group' (non-marriageable women) and 'other groups' (to provide possible spouses). This distinction manifests itself in complementary dualism, reciprocity and exchange.

Lévi-Strauss took three elements of Durkheimian and Maussian sociology – solidarity, reciprocity/exchange and collective representations – and argued that certain kinds of descent system, which he refers to as 'elementary', can be understood from this perspective. Women as 'gifts' in marriage are transferred from one social group or clan to another; an exchange is transacted. Marriage then serves as a means of forging alliances, providing a medium for social interaction and more generally securing society-wide solidarity or integration. The tendency or propensity for reciprocity or gift-giving between two parties and the apprehension of the opposition between oneself and others in this process of exchange are also innate in the human mind and are but one aspect of a universal logic of duality – a structural logic – in terms of which the mind operates, and which serves to structure both social relations and cultural categories. The creation of social and cultural institutions and the meanings attached to them are therefore unconscious products of 'certain fundamental structures of the human mind' (1969a: 84). In other words, the mind 'thinks' in contrasting yet linked pairs, and by counterposing one item or element with its opposite it creates a relational meaning; meaning is generated by the relations between items in a structure, and these structures of the human mind are discoverable by anthropological analysis.

Lévi-Strauss elaborates this dimension of his theory by drawing on the concepts and methods of structural linguistics, a field of study developed by Roman Jakobson and the Prague School. In this linguistic paradigm phonemes comprise the primary contrasting pairs of sounds that create linguistic meaning, and this methodology can be applied by the structural anthropologist to the analysis of social groups and cultural symbols to discover unconscious underlying structures. The anthropologist seeks then a 'grammar of culture' (cf. Leach [1954] 1970). With regard to social relations, just as two social groups – A and B – can be brought into a relationship of opposition and connection through the medium of marriage exchange, so a host of cultural categories can be given symbolic meaning by and through their contrasting relationship and by processes of mediation. For Lévi-Strauss, among the most important and pervasive instances of dual symbolic categorization are life and death, male and female, upperworld and underworld, right and left, cooked and raw, and culture and nature, and for him relations, the forms or structures so generated and their modes of mediation, are more important than their cultural content. Drawing on the work of Durkheim and Mauss on 'primitive classification', he explores the general principles of social and cultural categorization and their manifestations, first in his case study of *Totemism* (1969b), a distinctive kind of classification in which social groups are brought into relationship with natural categories or 'totems', and then in his highly theoretical and philosophical treatise *The Savage Mind* (1966).

In *Elementary Structures* Lévi-Strauss distinguishes two kinds of system: 'elementary structures' in which marriage is prescribed with a certain category or kind of relative (specifically a cross-cousin) and explicitly forbidden with other relatives, and 'complex structures' in which the choice of marriage partner is left to other mechanisms or criteria in that there are prohibitions on certain kinds of marriage but no 'positive' marriage rule. Elementary structures are then further subdivided on the basis of two broad forms of marriage exchange: (1) 'restricted exchange' in which a society is divided into pairs of units which exchange women in marriage directly; in its simplest form a society comprises two exogamous marriage classes integrated by the reciprocal and symmetrical exchange of women. Lévi-Strauss says that these '[symmetrical] systems can operate mechanisms of reciprocity only between two partners or between partners in multiples of two' (1969a: 178). The main cases of restricted exchange are to be found in aboriginal Australia; and (2) 'generalized exchange' in which descent groups are engaged in indirect 'asymmetrical' relationships through matrilateral cross-cousin marriage and which, for Lévi-Strauss, provides an appropriate mechanism for the maintenance of social solidarity; in other words, at a minimum, kinship group A passes its women to kinship group B which passes theirs to kinship group C, and C in turn passes their women to group A. However, conceptually this 'marriage in a circle' or 'circulating' or 'asymmetric connubium' as Dutch ethnologists called it, though capable of operation with a minimum of three groups, can be extended to include several more groups. The main cases of generalized exchange occur in 'Outer' or 'Peripheral' Indonesia (especially Sumatra and the Lesser Sunda islands) and the hill regions of the northern mainland (Assam, northern Burma, Laos), as well as ancient China and its northern neighbours (see map 'The Axis of Generalized Exchange' in Lévi-Strauss 1969a: 460).

The logic of this system of matrilateral cross-cousin marriage is that all transactions are conducted in the same direction so that two groups are consistently related to one another as 'wife-givers' and 'wife-takers'. Many examples of this type are to be found among the minority populations of mainland South-East Asia and the outer islands of Indonesia. Lévi-Strauss also discusses a third type of marriage system which he labels 'closed' involving 'patrilateral cross-cousin marriage' (prescribed marriage to the category of father's sister's daughter). He notes a greater prevalence of matrilateral cross-cousin marriage in the ethnographic record and suggests that this conduces to greater solidarity than the patrilateral type. In this connection the patrilateral type is difficult in practice to operate because it generates 'discontinuous' relationships between groups; in other words, with each generation the direction of the transfer of women in marriage is reversed. It 'forces the interruption and reversal of collaborations from generation to generation and from lineage to lineage' (1969a: 450). Subsequently, Needham has shown that, though a theoretical possibility, there are in fact no extant ethnographic examples of the patrilateral type; and that 'a hypothetical patrilateral system would be so obviously difficult to work as to be reckoned for practical purposes socially impossible' (ibid.: 115). More particularly, the change in the direction of the transfer of women in alternate generations and the resulting alternation of the statuses of wife-givers and wife-takers decisively undermine the solidarity of the descent group.

It should also be noted that, though the details of the argument cannot be addressed here, on the preparation of the English edition of *Elementary Structures* under the editorship of Rodney Needham, Lévi-Strauss 'indirectly' charged the editor with 'a "fundamental misunderstanding" of the very title and subject matter of the book, and imputes to him ... a fallacious assimilation of elementary structures to prescriptive marriage' (Needham, 1969: xix). The intricacies of the debate about the distinction between prescription (where there is lack of choice of a marriage partner) and preference (where there is choice of partner), and the application of both at the level of the indigenous model and at the level of empirical reality (or actual marriage choices), have been set out clearly by Needham in several publications (e.g. 1962: 8; 1963). Eventually he provides a precise specification of prescription as a 'formal property of a system of categories of social classification' (1973a: 174). It is clear that Needham correctly interpreted Lévi-Strauss's original meaning and intention insofar as it can be deciphered, although Needham indicates that there are indeed ambiguities, confusions and self-contradictions in Lévi-Strauss's treatment of prescription and preference and uncertainty about whether he was primarily concerned with 'what people say or with what they do' (Kuper, 1983: 172; Needham, 1973a; and see Lounsbury's review of *Structure and Sentiment*, 1962) .

Specifically Lévi-Strauss begins the Preface to the first edition of *Elementary Structures* with the following sentence:

> Elementary structures of kinship are those systems in which the nomenclature [kinship terminology] permits the immediate determination of the circle of kin and that of affines, that is, those systems which prescribe marriage with a certain type of relative, or, alternatively, those which, while defining all members of the society as relatives, divide them into two categories, viz., possible spouses and prohibited spouses.
>
> (1969a: xxiii)

With this simple and straightforward statement, and despite the subsequent Anglo-French quarrels, Lévi-Strauss inspired a large body of research on the kinship, marriage and symbolic systems of many societies in South-East Asia and elsewhere, though we should note that several Dutch scholars, including van Wouden, Rassers and J.P.B. de Josselin de Jong, had already traversed some of the ethnographic and analytical ground that Lévi-Strauss was subsequently to cover in the 1940s (see below and Chapter 2). Unfortunately these publications in the Dutch language had escaped Lévi-Strauss's attention, which he acknowledges in the second French edition of 1967 (1967: 360 n.9), and in any case they had not been brought together in any comprehensive nor theoretically sophisticated fashion. J.P.B. de Josselin de Jong, for his part (1977), issued a 60-page English-language digest of *Elementary Structures* as early as 1952, three years after the book was first published, and in recognition of its outstanding importance to anthropologists.

The complexities of Lévi-Strauss's writings can be off-putting for those of a more empirical and ethnographic persuasion. Nevertheless, we must acknowledge that his analytical framework, based on reciprocity and binary opposition, which he developed to heady levels of abstraction, did stimulate a whole generation of anthropologists to examine in detail South-East Asian social and cultural classification systems and the principles which order them, especially among various minority communities in eastern Indonesia, Sumatra and the highlands of mainland South-East Asia. The occurrence of these unilineal societies in the more marginal areas of the region also tended to direct the attention of European anthropologists away from the majority lowland populations.

Lévi-Strauss himself analyses several South-East Asian cases; he devotes considerable attention to the Kachin of Highland Burma as a type case of 'generalized exchange', and his analysis of their system of matrilateral cross-cousin marriage prompted Edmund Leach (1951) to take up various problematical issues posed by Lévi-Strauss's study, and in *Political Systems of Highland Burma* ([1954] 1970) to situate the Kachin alliance system in a more general framework of political, economic and cultural change. Lévi-Strauss also examines or at least makes summary reference to a range of other upland societies from the Nagas of north-eastern India through various of the other Assam/Burma frontier groups including the Purum, Aimol, Chiru and Chawte, and several frontier groups comprising the Garo, Khasi, Mikir, Lakher and Chin. Needham takes up this particular mantle and in a series of articles analyses social and cultural classification in many of these societies of the north-east India-Burma borderlands (Aimol [1960b], Chawte [1960c], Kom [1959a], Vaiphei [1959b]), as well as concentrating specifically on the Purum case in his *Structure and Sentiment* (1962).

Needham and Oxford structuralism

Marriage, structure and sentiment

There is a direct connection between Lévi-Strauss's theory of kinship and Needham's and his students' wide-ranging analyses of South-East Asian cultures. The most obvious connection is provided by Needham's 'methodological essay' *Structure and Sentiment*. But before summarizing his argument there we should briefly consider his inaugural lecture at Oxford delivered in May 1977 which refers back to his earlier work and that of his colleagues and students. In this brief address he identifies decisively the remarkable fact that in spite of the variations and contingencies of social phenomena and the restlessness and unpredictability of the human spirit, we humans (as members of social and cultural communities) 'so regularly end up with highly similar institutions' (1977: 17). Among the primary factors relevant to these regularities and of importance for our purposes in reviewing South-East Asian material are: (1) a restricted range of symbolic resources or elements used to convey meaning (colours, animals, birds, sounds, inanimate objects, mythical figures); (2) the frequency with which categories and symbols are ordered in binary pairs (right and left, male and female, strong and weak, king and priest), the common means of marking boundaries and representing social and ritual transitions, and the formal properties – symmetry, asymmetry, alternation and so on – which define systems; (3) the common principles which structure relationship terminologies (descent and affinity) so that, for example, 'descent systems can be compared universally by reference to only six elementary modes' (ibid.: 19); and (4) the characterization of modes of classification as falling into two main types: hierarchical and analogical (ibid.: 17–19). Needham then sets out these issues in a clear and concise way in his guide or handbook *Symbolic Classification* (1979) in which he defines and explains the concepts of 'symbol', 'category', 'classification', 'abstract relations' (opposition, transition, prestations/exchange) and 'transformations', and the perspective which has come to be referred to as 'structural' analysis.

Needham's *Structure and Sentiment* is intended to demonstrate the value of structural as against psychological explanation. He does so in relation to the social institution of 'unilateral cross-cousin marriage' or specifically marriage to the category mother's brother's daughter. Put very simply and briefly, the American anthropologists George Homans and David Schneider argued against Lévi-Strauss's structural explanation of this institution and his apparent concern with the effectiveness or utility of institutions in creating and maintaining 'organic solidarity'. They maintained instead that the explanation of regular or preferential (not specifically prescriptive) marriage with cross-cousins, and the more frequent occurrence of matrilateral cross-cousin marriage in comparison with patrilateral cross-cousin marriage can be explained by the sentiments and personal affinities between the individuals so related in the context of the locus of jural authority. Their main assumption is that matrilateral cross-cousin marriage is coincident with a patrilineal organization and that an individual's mother's brother is a kind of indulgent 'male mother' whereas his father exercises jural authority over his son, and relations between them are thereby characterized by respect and restraint. Therefore, an individual especially fond of his mother's brother, visits him often, sees much of his maternal uncle's daughter and becomes fond of her; '[t]heir marriage will be sentimentally appropriate' (Homans and Schneider, 1955: 23). Homans and Schneider support their position partly on the basis of Radcliffe-Brown's propositions about the tendency for sentiments generated in a close familial or domestic context between two individuals (in this case, mother and son) to be extended to a closely related set of individuals (in this case, mother's brothers). Needham demonstrates that Radcliffe-Brown's argument is invalid 'or, at very least undemonstrated' on several counts (1962: 32–40).

Likewise Needham's criticisms of Homans and Schneider are clear and unambiguous and so numerous that we do not have the space to rehearse them all here. The main ones are first that Homans and Schneider have wrongly attributed to Lévi-Strauss the formulation of a causal theory to explain the origin of particular social institutions and have entirely misinterpreted the nature of his understanding and explanation of structural relationships. Second, they 'confuse prescription and preference' (ibid.: 53; and see 1963, 1973a). Third, and more particularly Needham effectively demolishes their proposition that the institution of unilateral cross-cousin marriage and the more common occurrence of one type of cross-cousin marriage as against another can be explained by recourse to predispositions and sentiments which are supposed to have been nurtured by the personal and behavioural relationships conducted and developed between individuals. As Needham demonstrates with reference to Lévi-Strauss's theory and to the relevant empirical data, the relationships upon which Lévi-Strauss focused are between corporate groups and categories of relative within a social system; they are structural not interpersonal; they concern primarily 'alliances' between groups and not a personal union between two individuals, and therefore they and their nature cannot be determined by sentimental predispositions. What is more, the additional complicating factor which presents problems for a theory based on sentiments is that in a given alliance relationship the descent group which provides women in marriage to another group is considered to be in a socially superior position; wife-givers are of higher status than wife-takers. Finally, Needham demonstrates that Homans and Schneider offer no direct empirical evidence to support their theory (1962: 53–73).

For our purposes Needham's Chapter 4 of his essay is most important in that he presents an analysis, on the basis of the available published material, of one South-East Asian society. The Purum of Manipur on the Indo-Burma border are a Tibeto-Burman-speaking population (and see Needham, 1958, for a more extended analysis). In the early 1930s when they were the subject of study by Tarak Chandra Das, from whose work Needham derives much of his empirical material, they comprised just over 300 individuals in four villages and were divided between five named exogamous patrilineal clans; four of the clans were subdivided into named lineages or descent groups. Following a period of brideservice by the husband, marriage was patrilocal. These groups were related through a marriage system which prescribes marriage with a bride belonging to the category mother's brother's daughter (more specifically with a woman from the clan of the mother's brother) and strictly forbids it with the category father's sister's daughter so that a given group is permitted to 'take wives from certain groups but not from others' (1962: 78). Furthermore, as Needham says, 'The relationship terminology . . . accords with the rule of descent and with the marriage prescription' (ibid.: 76).

In this system it is not entailed that a man marries specifically and singularly his actual mother's brother's daughter, his first cross-cousin. Instead he may marry any woman who falls within the classificatory category 'mother's brother's daughter', or wife-giver (potential spouse's home group), the relationship term being used to cover a large class of women. The society is thereby divided for any given individual into three broad categories: lineal relatives (speaker's own group), wife-givers and wife-takers. Groups are related, as Lévi-Strauss's model of generalized exchange depicts, in 'cycles of alliance', but as Needham so clearly demonstrates, the situation on the ground is far more complex, even for such a small-scale society as the Purum (1962: 79–82). Nevertheless, the structural principle crucial to an understanding of this complexity is that the 'tripartite categorization orders relations between individuals, between groups, and between the component local descent groups of the village, and creates ties between the politically independent villages' (ibid.: 82). It seems unlikely that Needham, as some of his critics claim, 'showed a rather literal faith in the ideal model, and assumed that it corresponded to the practices of actual societies in a direct fashion' (Kuper, 1983: 174). Indeed, he makes an explicit distinction between behaviour, jural rules and social classification (1973a).

A particularly significant feature of such societies as the Purum which order social categories and groups into a system governed by the principles of opposition, asymmetry, complementarity and connectedness, is that they may also do so analogically in the symbolic and cultural realm. Needham goes on to show that the Purum house is divided into sections which accord with the division into kin and affines and into superior (*phumlil*) and inferior (*ningan*) sections or parts (1962: 87–90). The arrangements of rituals and the prestations exchanged between wife-givers and wife-takers are also ordered in terms of a pervasive dualism which relates consistently to the conceptual division between right and left, and male and female – right and male being superior in status to and more auspicious than left and female. Needham therefore reveals the principles of classification which underlie both social and symbolic orders in a 'total structural analysis', and he presents 'a mode of classification by which things, individuals, groups, qualities, values, spatial notions, and other ideas of the most disparate kinds are identically ordered within one system of relations' (ibid.: 95).

Subsequently Needham and his students were to undertake a range of studies of the social and symbolic organization of South-East Asian societies employing a structuralist framework. The most detailed analysis in this mode is undoubtedly Robert Barnes's study of the patrilineal Kédangese of eastern Indonesia and the relations between descent, marriage and symbolic classification (1976). Among many of the other studies which deserve mention are Iwabuchi's analysis of the ethnically complex society of Alas in the Special Province of Acheh, northern Sumatra. He demonstrates the 'rupture' of an asymmetric prescriptive system under the possible influence of coastal Malay or Achehnese cognatic social organization (1994: 246–255). In addition, Andrew Beatty, in his analysis of Nias social structure and feasts of merit, explores the relations between marriage alliance, social stratification and ceremonial exchange, and he says, in contextualizing his study, that '[t]he same complex of institutions has been analysed before in a number of societies of Southeast Asia, from highland Burma to eastern Indonesia. The present study is intended to be both an ethnographic analysis and a contribution to theoretical discussions in that tradition' (1992: 1).

Oxford anthropologists have also provided analyses of symbolic classification in particular, developing the seminal work of Durkheim's student, Robert Hertz. The cases are too numerous to consider here and so we propose to select a few of the best examples of this work.

Death and the right hand

Rodney and Claudia Needham translated Hertz's two classic essays into English (1960): 'A Contribution to the Study of the Collective Representation of Death' (1907) and 'The Pre-eminence of the Right Hand: A Study in Religious Polarity' (1909). Hertz's essay on death focused on the complex of ideas which underlies secondary treatment of the dead (in which the corpse is given a 'temporary burial' and then subsequently undergoes a full funeral ceremony); his main examples are taken from the literature on the Dayaks of Borneo, specifically the Ngaju of south-eastern Kalimantan. He examined the complex of ideas and values surrounding death, and the interrelationships between three crucial elements in funerary rites: the non-material aspect of the dead person (the 'soul') and its passage to the afterworld; the condition of the corpse and its ritual treatment; and the living and their adjustment to death in mourning and other ritual observations. The central analytical notion employed is that of a passage or transition from one state or condition to another. Hertz goes to the heart of the problem when he describes death as 'an initiation' which is 'exactly analogous to that by which a youth is withdrawn from the company of women and introduced into that of adult men' (1960: 80). It comprises a 'change of status in the individual' which 'implies a deep change in society's mental attitude toward him, a change that is made gradually and requires time' (ibid.: 81). With this extraordinarily simple but analytically powerful concept of transition Hertz enables us to make sense of a whole host of ideas, values and actions focused on death and its consequences for society. His work provides valuable connections with that of another French anthropologist, Arnold van Gennep, who presents a general framework for the analysis of rites of passage (1960). For van Gennep rituals of transition comprise three phases or stages, viz. separation, transition or liminality and reincorporation. The analytically powerful ideas of Hertz and van Gennep are examined in detail by Huntington and Metcalf using a considerable amount of case material from South-East Asia (1979), and in Metcalf's extraordinarily richly textured study of the death rites and world-view of the Berawan of Sarawak (1982). In particular, Huntington and Metcalf demonstrate the usefulness of the concept of transition and the observation of Hertz that 'death throws into relief the most important cultural values by which people live their lives and evaluate their experiences' (ibid.: 2).

Let us now spend a little more time here on Hertz's other essay on the pre-eminence of the right hand, a paper which inspired a substantial amount of research on dual symbolic classification not only in South-East Asia where Hertz's ideas seem particularly appropriate but in many other parts of the world as well (see Parkin, 1996: 59–87). Aside from the Needhams' translation of the essay, the key text which brought Hertz's essay to prominence is Rodney Needham's later edited book *Right and Left* (1973b). This contains Needham's new English translation of Hertz's essay and a collection of papers, most of them republished, on lateral symbolism produced from 1916 to 1971, covering societies from Asia to Africa to South America, and including significant contributions from Cunningham on the Atoni of Timor and Fox on the Rotinese of eastern Indonesia.

Hertz examines the phenomenon of dualism, polarity or opposition, and poses the question why in culture after culture there is a preference for the right hand or the right side of the body as against the left. Hertz concludes that the asymmetry between right and left is in part to do with the structure of the brain and the nervous centres, and the connection between right-handedness and the 'greater development in man of the left cerebral hemisphere' (Hertz in Needham, 1973b: 4). However, he proposes that 'organic tendencies towards asymmetry' (ibid.: 5) cannot wholly explain the overwhelming emphasis of the right hand or right side in human cultures. He demonstrates that commonly there is a concordance between various opposed or contrasted qualities, values, powers, beings and objects, particularly oriented to the religious polarity of the sacred and the profane. Therefore, the right side is normally associated with the sacred, good, life, superior, high, sky, noble, male, light, and the left with the opposed properties or qualities. These dual categories are also frequently connected analogically to social groups, which Hertz refers to as sections or halves ('moieties') of a tribe. He proposes that 'The obligatory differentiation between the sides of the body is a particular case and a consequence of the dualism which is inherent in primitive thought' (ibid.: 20); the very general distinction between right and left and its association with other cultural categories therefore appears to be 'a fundamental feature of thought and imagery' and the classificatory principles so identified seem to be 'natural proclivities of the human mind' (Needham, 1973b: xiv, xxxiii). Needham notes, however, that it is a matter for investigation whether or not the principle of complementary opposition is a general feature of a given culture or confined to certain areas of social and cultural life. We shall see below that in Malay culture, for example, the principle of triadic division is said to be especially significant and among the Atoni dualisms seem to be embedded in a quadripartite classification. What is more, Needham advises that the specific symbolic opposition between right and left may be prominent in certain cultures but of less importance in others (ibid.: xx–xxii). Again we shall see in the case of the Rotinese that the distinction between inside and outside seems to be of overriding concern.

Clark Cunningham's paper on the symbolism of the Atoni house in the princedom of Amarasi is without doubt one of the finest article-length analyses of an Indonesian classification system. It was first published in 1964 and then revised for inclusion in Needham's edited volume. Cunningham suggests that the house 'like ritual, may be an effective means to communicate ideas between generations in a preliterate society' (1973: 204) and it serves as a model of the cosmos in that the principles of order and the symbols expressed in the house also extend to a whole range of other cultural categories in Atoni to do with space and time, and human relations with animals, plants and the supernatural. The house (*ume*) is ordered by certain principles of classification which express unity and difference, though Cunningham indicates that Hertz's stress on opposition or difference in the division between right and left should be adjusted to take account of the importance of unity in the Atoni case, and the mediation or connectedness between opposites. The house is a vitally important element in Atoni life; it is, of course, a residential unit providing shelter for an elementary family; but it is also an economic and a ritual unit and is the centre for prayer, sacrifice and feasts. Although the arrangement of the main sections and elements of the house is complex, it is clear that there is a pervasive dualism underlying this order. The Atoni, like the Purum and the Kachin, comprise patrilineal descent groups, prescribe marriage with the category matrilateral cross-cousin, and are divided into wife-giving and wife-taking groups. Divisions and areas of the house are also apportioned to particular categories of kin.

The door of the house faces southwards and this direction is referred to as 'right'; north is 'left' and these divisions are in turn associated with good and evil, and the colours red and yellow respectively. Prayers are offered to the Divinity (the Lord of the Sun, Sky or Day) to the east which is also associated with origins and the colour white; the west is the 'way of the deceased' and is associated with the colour black. Men wear red and white coloured cloth and women black. The house is also divided into an inner section or centre, and an outer section. Elements such as the door, water jar, hearth and platforms for storage and sleeping (two or three in number) provide the main points of order in the house and their locations are 'invariable' or variable within certain fixed limits. There is also an ordered disposition of support posts ('mother posts', 'chicken posts' and 'feet'), beams, rafters and spars. Cunningham demonstrates that, although the classification system underlying the spatial order in the house is based on divisions into right and left and inner and outer, there is in the arrangement of space and elements the 'use of the number four, expressing unity' as well as 'concentric circles' and 'intersecting and concentrically arranged crosses' (ibid.: 216). There is also a vertical arrangement of space in which upper portions are associated with male and lower ones female. Overall within the house

> male activities and symbols are regularly associated with the right side generally, the outer section, the right side of the inner section, and the attic; female activities and symbols are associated with the inner section (or back) and, particularly, the left side of the inner section.
>
> (ibid.: 222)

It is difficult to do justice to Cunningham's succinct yet sophisticated and complex analysis of Atoni symbolism as it is expressed in a central element of their culture. But it demonstrates what can be done to further our understanding of the ways in which social and cultural categories are ordered in terms of a restricted number of underlying formal principles and relations.

The paper by James Fox on Rotinese classification draws attention to the crucial significance of the differentiation and connection between the categories inside and outside. These order domestic, social and political space, and more especially they serve as the basis for the categorization of the spirit world into spirits of the inside, centre or house (the spirits of the ancestors) and those of the outside which are 'a disordered collection of individual roaming spirits' (1973: 349). The latter 'frighten' and 'terrify'; they are 'dangerous'. Fox also indicates that the spirits of the outside have 'died a bad death' suddenly, violently and inauspiciously as in childbirth or by drowning (ibid.: 351, 352). The concept of good and bad death associated with other opposed categories such as right and left, south and north is widespread in the Indonesian world.

It is also worth mentioning at this point Fox's important edited *The Flow of Life: Essays on Eastern Indonesia* (1980) which brings together beautifully the various strands of European structuralism. The book is dedicated to the memory of J.P.B. de Josselin de Jong and F.A.E van Wouden; it contains papers by Dutch scholars including P.E. de Josselin de Jong, Oxford structuralists including Rodney Needham, and French anthropologists. It relates its interests back to the Durkheimian tradition and to the work of Lévi-Strauss and focuses on 'a number of crucial social categories employed by the various peoples of eastern Indonesia' (ibid.: 10). Its main concerns are to re-evaluate and develop the seminal ideas of van Wouden in particular and to examine comparatively marriage, alliance and exchange as well as social and symbolic classification (in house forms, textile designs, spatial organization, state structures, rituals of life and death, and in forms of speech based on dyadic pairs [Fox, 1971a]) across a range of culturally related societies within a field of ethnological study.

Importantly the collection links alliance relationships between groups with the 'flow of life' and that women, as the 'providers' of life constitute a pathway in marriage along which life is transmitted (1980: 12–13). An important mode of expression of origins, life and growth resides in plant and more generally botanic imagery (Fox, 1971b). Fox, in conclusion, proposes that various societies in eastern Indonesia 'despite the intricacies of their patterns of alliance, . . . seem to share certain common ideas about the nature of life, of society, and of the human person' (1980: 14).

Malay magic and Orang Asli world-views

This is a convenient point to consider another study which Needham has often referred to as a model of the Oxford approach: Kirk Michael Endicott's *An Analysis of Malay Magic* (1970). Like Fox, Endicott considers the classification of the spirit world in an Austronesian culture. His study of the popular as against the Muslim religion of the Malays was based on a thorough examination of secondary sources originally for the Bachelor of Letters degree at Oxford. It demonstrates how a structural perspective can provide a synthetic understanding of a complex set of ideas and practices, 'a complexity bordering on chaos' (ibid.: 1). Malay folk religion had been described by several authors from the late nineteenth century to the 1950s, including Nelson Annandale and Herbert Robinson, Jeanne Cuisinier, Walter Skeat, Frank Swettenham, R.J. Wilkinson and R.O. Winstedt. Their ethnographic material covered several states of the Malayan Peninsula from Patani to Perak to Kelantan, illustrating the heterogeneity of the Malay population and the influences from various religious traditions. Endicott subjects this earlier work to critical scrutiny. His working assumption is that 'there is some order to be found at some level of analysis' in Malay 'magic' or folk religion despite the lack of cultural homogeneity (ibid.: 2). His two main analytical concepts comprise what he calls the 'traditional order' (people's specific ideas, values and cultural categories and the relationships between them) and the 'structural order' or 'model' (which 'translates the specific categories and relations of the traditional order into formal and universal ones' [ibid.: 5]). Endicott points out that even the traditional order is an abstraction and is not presented as such by the people themselves, or at least lay people; it is a product of anthropological analysis and is not a product of individual thinking and perception. It is composed of 'meaningful' elements and relations, and meanings are either inherent (in that they define the essential qualities or content of something and provide it with its identity), or relational (in that they derive from structural positions in a network or system of relations, in short a classification), or symbolic (in that they derive from analogy having similar positions in different systems of classification). The structural order is at a yet higher level of abstraction and operates with universal logical categories familiar to structural analysis, viz. opposition, identity, homology, analogy, inclusion and complementarity.

130

The central organizing concept of Malay magic is *semangat* which Endicott translates as 'soul' or 'vital principle', though he indicates that the term has multiple meanings depending on context. It can refer to one aspect of the human soul, or the human soul overall, or all-pervading generalized essence. According to Endicott there are two mental operations of relevance in understanding Malay magical ideas and practice, that is, first the principles by which generalized essence is differentiated, and, second, the ways in which it is concentrated in distinctive parts of bodies and 'outstanding classes of things' (ibid.: 95). Endicott shows how the process of differentiation generates three aspects of the human soul: *semangat* (which maintains the body's boundaries and ensures its integrity), *nyawa* (the 'breath of life' which distinguishes the living from the dead) and *roh* (which leaves humans when they sleep and distinguishes humans from the rest of creation). These three dimensions of the human soul differentiated from generalized essence are also distinguished from, yet connected to, other elements of the spiritual world: free spirits (*hantu* and *jin*), ghosts, familiar spirits (*polong* and *pelesit*), birth demons or vampires (*bajang, langsuir, pontianak* and *penanggalan*), animals and were-tigers. Free spirits are then categorized into the various major divisions of the physical world: earth, jungle, water and human habitation; and non-physical divisions to do with society, time and space. Importantly the differentiation between the human soul and various kinds of spirits depends to an important degree on the kinds of relationship which the spiritual essence has with material bodies.

The procedures and ritual paraphernalia employed by the magician can be understood in terms of the Malay categorization of the spiritual, physical and non-physical worlds and the relationships between spiritual essence and matter. The magician seeks to control and manipulate spirits and souls by modifying these categories, by strengthening and maintaining boundaries when necessary or by weakening boundaries to facilitate the passage of spiritual essence across them. Endicott presents a detailed description of the magician, the process of becoming one and acquiring the appropriate knowledge (*ilmu*), the maintenance of secrecy, and magical practices and the contexts in which they are deployed. The magician has recourse to 'spells' (to plead, command, threaten, locate and name); 'boundary strengtheners' such as iron, gold, silver, stones, candle-nuts and cockle-shells; 'boundary weakeners' including water and multi-coloured thread; 'essence receptacles' such as limes, eggs, cloths and leaf brushes 'for absorbing spirits or for acting as a substitute body for a soul' (ibid.: 137); 'communicators' like incense, candles and percussion instruments; 'offerings' mainly of food; and magical 'numbers', particularly three and four.

Endicott concludes his perceptive structural analysis by proposing certain key principles which underlie Malay ideas and classifications. These comprise: (1) the distinction between the material and essential planes of existence and their interconnections; (2) differentiation of these planes into hierarchical sets and their successive inclusion; (3) differential attribution of power depending on the relations between categories of matter and essence; (4) and the tendency to differentiate categories at each level into triadic sets and the lack of prominence of dual classifications. Endicott suggests that divisions into three – for example, *semangat, nwaya* and *roh* – would seem to be especially appropriate in such cases as Malay folk religion in which conflicting or contradictory ideas are brought together into a syncretic whole (ibid.: 178–179).

A rather different kind of study, though demonstrating continuities with his analysis of Malay magic, is Endicott's ethnography of the religion of the hunting–gathering Batek Negrito based on seventeen months of field-research in Kelantan, Peninsular Malaysia, between 1971 and 1976 (1979). Endicott provides a vivid record of Batek ideas about the form, content and functioning of the natural and supernatural worlds and their place within them. In particular, he considers central coordinating ideas about deities, superhuman beings and were-tigers. He adopts what he calls a 'literalist' approach in his attempt to describe Batek religion as near as possible in terms of the people's own concepts. These latter, he says, 'make sense in their own right' (ibid.: 28) as a system of interrelated elements. In this respect his perspective comes close to his description of the 'traditional order' of the Malays – the unities, distinctions and relations found within their 'collective representations'. However, Endicott departs from his earlier work, by exploring not so much the structural principles underlying that order but rather how concepts are used in practice. He concludes that the Batek generally live in harmony with their rainforest environment and perceive it and the supernatural which permeates and maintains it as essentially beneficent. In short, Batek religious ideas allow the people more easily to grasp, handle and render comprehensible certain 'natural' processes and events and their causes which are rather unpredictable but of 'continuing practical importance' (ibid.: 199).

Before leaving our brief consideration of Endicott's contribution to the study of 'collective representations', it is worth noting that other significant studies of South-East Asian aboriginal religions emerged from the Oxford school under Needham's tutelage. Among them Erik Jensen's careful analysis of Iban religion, the principles of classification, particularly that of balanced and symmetrical dual opposition, which order diverse realms of Iban thought, and the spiritual conceptions which underlie their agricultural fertility cult (1974). There is also Signe Howell's extraordinarily richly textured ethnography of the hunting–gathering Chewong of central Pahang, in which, like Endicott's study, she presents the principles and perspectives which appeared to be of significance to the Chewong themselves in thinking about and understanding themselves, their society and their cosmology, and in working in and using the surrounding natural environment (1989). She stresses Chewong egalitarian values; the importance of consciousness and action according to rational principles which this entails (importantly the principle of reciprocal exchange); and the principle of separation of classes of beings or 'things', and specifically 'the necessity of keeping specified things, or acts, apart' (ibid.: 245).

P.E. de Josselin de Jong and post-war Dutch structuralism

We have already examined the main ideas and interests of pre-war Dutch structuralism based at Leiden and associated especially with the study of Indonesian cultures which 'proved so eminently suitable for that particular approach' (P.E. de Josselin de Jong, 1977: 10). Nevertheless, it is worth noting that a structuralist interest continued in The Netherlands after the war despite the fact that, following Indonesian independence and the deterioration in Dutch–Indonesian relations, the previously close links between Dutch structuralism and Indonesia weakened considerably. The structuralist tradition was sustained primarily by J.P.B. de Josselin de Jong's nephew, Patrick de Josselin de Jong, who succeeded to the Chair of Cultural Anthropology in Leiden on his uncle's retirement in 1956. Other notable post-war contributors were J. van Baal (1971), R.E. Downs ([1977] 1955), G.W. Locher (1961), and, in his detailed study of the Atoni of Timor and his balanced criticisms of the work of F.A.E. van Wouden, H.G. Schulte Nordholt (1971, 1980). The achievements of the Dutch structuralists are amply demonstrated in *Structural Antropology in the Netherlands: A Reader*, which was published in 1977 and edited by P.E. de Josselin de Jong. The editor draws attention to significant themes, elements and preoccupations in this work up until the 1950s: these comprise detailed ethnographies of Indonesian cultures based primarily on the analysis of indigenous texts and official reports and the corresponding lack of interest in theory and method; the examination of territorial and political classifications; the broader study of native cognitive systems, especially religion and mythology, based on binary or dual oppositions; the analysis of descent and affinal alliance, particularly those based on what was called 'limited cross-cousin marriage', or 'asymmetric connubium' and double descent; and the assumption that certain underlying principles of order operate within the Malay–Indonesian culture area (see J.P.B. de Josselin de Jong, [1935] 1977).

The close connections between the interests of these Dutch scholars and those of Lévi-Strauss are illustrated in the early reactions of the Dutch, particularly J.P.B. de Josselin de Jong ([1952] 1977), to the publication of *The Elementary Structures of Kinship*. Many of Lévi-Strauss's ideas (exchange, reciprocity, alliance, cosmic dualism, mediation) are anticipated in de Josselin de Jong's classic statement on the Malay Archipelago as 'a field of ethnological study' delivered as an inaugural lecture in 1935. In his 1952 commentary on Lévi-Strauss's theory of kinship, J.P.B. de Josselin de Jong draws attention to the significance of the principle of double descent or bilinealism in helping explain some of the features of affinal arrangements, a form of descent which Dutch ethnologists had previously explored in some detail in relation to Indonesian material (1977: 291, 307–310). He also emphasizes (contra Lévi-Strauss who is concerned with the primacy of the act of exchange and not with what is actually transferred) the importance of the nature of the goods which are exchanged in marriage transactions based on the very common distinction in Indonesian cultures between 'male' and 'female' goods (ibid.: 311, 314).

P.E. de Josselin de Jong, in his doctoral thesis on the socio-political structure of the matrilineal Minangkabau of Sumatra and the related Negri Sembilan Malays of the Malayan Peninsula (1951), also explores the relationships between descent and affinal alliances, and presents a detailed analysis of relationship terminology, descent group structure, property rights, kingship and political organization, and 'connubial' relations. The study is based on published and unpublished sources and not on primary field research, and de Josselin de Jong attempts to cast light on several features of Minangkabau organization: among other matters, the fact that the traditional rulers of Minangkabau were organized patrilineally in an overall matrilineal society, that the original four matriclans of Minangkabau are organized into two major sections or phratries – Koto-Piliang and Bodi-Tjaniago – and the role and position of matrilateral cross-cousin marriage in the wider society. The study provides a detailed examination of various issues raised by Lévi-Strauss to do with elementary structures (eg. ibid.: 184ff.), as well as a presentation of the Dutch structuralist perspective on double descent and dual classification as it was developed by such writers as van Wouden and Rassers.

De Josselin de Jong argues that the Minangkabau, though matrilineal, also recognize patrilineal descent and that it was a much more prominent social organizational principle in the past. He indicates that the matrilineal principle has prominence in socio-political matters and in the inheritance of material possessions and the patrilineal in religious and sacred life and the inheritance of prestige (ibid.: 109, 168). He concludes that 'we can still observe traces of true double descent, which system affords an explanation of some phenomena which must remain inexplicable from an exclusively matrilineal standpoint' (ibid.: 82). He also disagrees with Lévi-Strauss that generalized exchange requires a co-incidence between the rules of descent and residence. Instead he proposes that asymmetrical connubium 'can quite well operate in an organization with double descent' (ibid.: 191).

Even in the 1970s and 1980s P.E. de Josselin de Jong continued to play an important role in developing and re-evaluating structural analyses of South-East Asian societies, and taking stock of what had been achieved. One such exercise deserves brief mention. In his editorial introduction to the volume on *Unity in Diversity: Indonesia as a Field of Anthropological Study* (1984), a modern adaptation of his uncle's concept of the 'Malay Archipelago as a Field of Ethnological Study', P.E. de Josselin de Jong indicates that the interrelated formal elements of the 'structural core' or rather the 'basis for comparison' of the Malay/Indonesian archipelago presented by J.P.B. de Josselin de Jong in his inaugural lecture in 1935 were subsequently modified on the basis of new field data, especially during the 1950s (1984: 6). What is more, he notes that the work of Lévi-Strauss exerted a considerable influence over Dutch structuralism as anthropology became increasingly professionalized and much less the preserve of Indologists. Lévi-Strauss's notion of 'basic elements' in one system being transformations of those within another in the same cultural area of comparison has been particularly influential, and Leiden structuralists have also refined their notion of structural principles to discriminate between principles as 'rules' and principles as 'ideas' (ibid.: 7–8). P.E. de Josselin de Jong also indicates that, given the premise that societies within a field of study should be 'genetically' related in linguistic terms, for future research the boundaries of the field might well have to be circumscribed in the first instance to sub-regions within Indonesia rather than attempts being made to compare societies across the whole 'Indonesian' region.

Structuralism: some problems and variants

As we have already noted, structural anthropology has contributed much to our understanding of the ways in which social and cultural categories are ordered and given meaning within a system of interrelationships governed by a small number of formal principles and properties. Analyses usually concentrate on the detailed exploration of the ways in which a variety of elements in a given community are arranged and related one with another; they provide a synthetic model of a complex reality. Nevertheless, there have been several major criticisms of this mode of analysis in relation to such matters as the status of the structural models which are presented, their importance or otherwise to members of the culture in question and to other features of the culture, and whether and how they can be validated if they are 'unconscious' models. In other words, is too much being read into the materials? Are valid connections being made? Can the model be tested? (See, for example, Beattie, 1968, 1976, 1978; though Needham has responded to various of Beattie's specific points of criticism in his editorial introduction to *Right and Left* [1973b] and see 1976.) In Endicott's analysis of Malay magic, for example, the arrangement and ordering of cultural elements into an over-arching triadic classification by bringing together material from different 'Malay' communities, at different points in time, and from different regions of the Malayan Peninsula seem contrived; using different criteria some of the categories could well have been ordered into dual or quadripartite classifications (see also Wilder [1998] on cosmic images in Malay tradition).

Some critics have suggested that the methods used by structuralists to depict classification systems by using two-dimensional tables and lists, and a variety of graphic devices tend to over-simplify complex realities (in terms of process, context, continuity, subtlety, ambiguity, creativity and change) and seem to be more appropriate for literate cultures rather than to convey different forms of oral communication and action in pre- or non-literate cultures (Goody, 1977). The work of the structuralists also has something of a timeless quality; although they are obviously aware of social and cultural change and the transformation of classification systems and they sometimes incorporate this concern into their analyses, usually this is not a focus of their work as it is among post-war American cultural anthropologists. The larger contexts of political and economic change, of the incorporation of small-scale communities into nation–states are obviously not of prime interest.

Hildred Geertz has been especially critical of the Dutch variant of Durkheimian sociology as applied to Indonesian cultures and states baldly that she has not found the model of binary oppositions illuminating for the analysis of her own fieldwork materials (1961b, 1965). Clifford Geertz also argues for an understanding not of formal properties and principles of classification and the internal structure of symbols but instead the analysis of symbolic forms in relation to social action. In other words, he wants to understand the function and use of symbols in concrete events and activities and how they organize perceptions, meanings and emotions (1961). With regard to dual symbolic analysis his point is that complementary opposition is so common to human thinking, why bother to examine it in such minute detail (1961), and he is especially critical of Lévi-Strauss's distanced, intellectualist analyses of other cultures, remote from the realities of their everyday lives; he has created, in Geertz's view, 'an infernal culture machine' (1967b: 25–32). Melford Spiro too, though he differs from Geertz in analytical perspective, argues that religion is not something which individuals primarily 'think about' and 'classify with', rather they live and act by it (1982: 6).

In some ways anthropologists who, in the wake of the masterly essays by Hertz, Needham and Lévi-Strauss, enthusiastically and, as we have said, with great success demonstrated the 'total order' of the social and cultural universe displayed by the Purum, Balinese, Rotinese and numerous other South-East Asian groups became their own worst enemies. By their employment of the lemon-squeezer technique of rigorous and apparently elegant structuralist analysis they ran the risk of denaturing and straitjacketing the data so that people were actually found to violate their own marriage rules, to clutter their symbolic classifications, and to be oblivious to structural changes in their own social organization.

For a start, their analyses often failed to take full advantage of what is already known both of South-East Asian world-views (microcosm and macrocosm, natural symbols) and the theory of symbols. As to symbolic theory, a source which seems never to have been consulted in anthropological discussions of dual symbolic classification is a 1932 study by C.K. Ogden (a psychologist known to Malinowski), *Opposition: A Linguistic and Psychological Analysis*. Ogden explains the multiple formal possibilities of dichotomous categorization (binary opposites). And the well-known essay by Lévi-Strauss – 'Do dual organizations exist?' ([1956] 1963), in which he experimentally manipulates oppositions to produce two forms of dualism (diametric and concentric) and one of triadism (the 'Indonesian' form) – has, surprisingly enough, never been tested on ethnographic cases.

And then – as to South-East Asia and the venerable, long-established organizing principle of *microcosm-macrocosm* (*Hooykaas on Bali [1974]: bhuvana agung* [cosmos] and *bhuvana alit* [human world]; Rawson [1967] on art, cf.

Waterson 1990) – it has been overlooked that dual symbolic classification is only a special form of it. Laterality ('right' and 'left') is a property of the human body, as is gender dichotomy; so too are the phonenic binaries ('front–back', 'oral–nasal', and so on) shown by the structural linguist Jakobson to be inherent in the human vocal organs and therefore in speech; and so are other spatial binaries ('inside–outside', 'high–low', and so on). The human anatomy, in turn, is an analogue of the dwelling-house on which so much attention has been focused recently, and the house is a microcosm of the village, the territorial hierarchical state (*negara*), and the universe itself (the cosmos). The body can generate or transmit symbols in addition to simple binaries – centred space, the body as plant, and so on, and connect these various layers in dominant cultural–symbolic images (see Wilder [1998] for a study of the body and its expressions in the Malay cosmos).

Nevertheless, the structuralist perspective has been a major influence in South-East Asian anthropology and it has been used in quite novel ways. Let us examine three variants of the approach in the work of Edmund Leach on the Kachin of Highland Burma (including Lehman's Chin research), Stanley Tambiah on the relations between Buddhism and spirit cults in North-East Thailand, and James Peacock on a Javanese genre of popular theatre (*ludruk*). Leach and Tambiah were Cambridge-based anthropologists, and Peacock, an American anthropologist, who brought ideas together from both European structuralism and American cultural anthropology.

Leach and the Kachin of Highland Burma

A major contribution to the anthropology of South-East Asia and to anthropology more generally is Edmund Leach's study of the socio-political organization of the Kachin of Highland Burma, their relations with the valley-dwelling Shan, and the transformation over time of relatively egalitarian Kachin communities (*gumlao*) to stratified, state-like ones (*gumsa*) and vice versa ([1954] 1970). Leach gathers together several strands of analysis in his work: it is at one and the same time a study of social and political change among a tribal minority population, examining historical materials spanning some 100 years from the mid-nineteenth century and bringing them into relationship with field observations between 1939 and 1945; an examination of inter-ethnic relations in a complex multi-ethnic situation which embraces what were considered to be separate 'tribes' and ethnic units by earlier writers; a critique and an attempt to go beyond the British functionalism of Firth and the structural-functionalism of Radcliffe-Brown and their immediate followers by using insights from French structuralism and linking it with a dynamic though 'idealist' and 'rationalist' social theory; and an analysis within a political (and economic) context of a particular case of matrilateral cross-cousin marriage or prescriptive alliance which Lévi-Strauss had also examined in some detail in *The Elementary Structures of Kinship*.

Critical of the dominant paradigm of early post-war British anthropology and its preoccupation with models of organic equilibrium and with the mechanisms by which social systems are maintained, Leach argues instead that an anthropologist's description of a social system is an abstraction or model. To impose an order or structure on the complexities or 'confusions' of everyday life the model makes it appear that the system so described is in equilibrium; it provides insights into the organization of social life by presenting it as if it were ordered and integrated ([1954] 1970: ix–x, 4). The description is after all composed of inter-related linguistic elements and interconnected concepts, but the attempt by the anthropologist to grasp the realities of social life must always be an imperfect 'fictional' rendering, a 'figment' of the imagination. Leach stresses that we must not confuse the model of an integrated system with reality and assume that equilibrium, stability and order are intrinsic or 'natural' features of social systems (ibid.: xi–xiii). Nevertheless, he indicates reassuringly that, although the anthropological model is fictional, this is more or less the way in which the Kachin think about their own society through the medium of their own symbolic language. More specifically, this ideal model is made explicit from time to time in rituals when Kachin express symbolically the approved or proper status relations between individuals and groups. Leach adopts a broad definition of ritual and its counterpart, myth: 'Ritual acts are ways of "saying things" about social status' (ibid.: 279). The difference between the anthropologist's model and the native's model is that the categories of the former are drawn with much greater precision using sociological concepts than those of the latter which are expressed in myth and ritual. He demonstrates this distinction in his detailed examination of the structural categories and relations of one Kachin *gumsa* community, Hpalang, an analysis which takes up about one-third of Leach's book.

Leach inserts the dynamic element into his analysis when he points out that the Kachin categories which comprise the social structural model can be evaluated differently and rearranged because rituals, myths and symbols which are used to express social relations and talk about social structures are inherently ambiguous and elastic in their meanings. Kachin exploit this ambiguity in the process of making choices between alternative courses of action and in competing one with another for political power (ibid.: 10). The driving force in Leach's analysis is the desire for power, political office and social esteem and the social structure 'consists of sets of ideas about the distribution of power between persons and groups of persons' (ibid.: 4). Individuals in the *gumsa* and *gumlao* systems 'use the same words to describe the categories of their own political system and that of their opponents but they make different assumptions about the relations between the categories in the two cases' (ibid.: xiii).

Leach's analysis is therefore devoted to examining the relationships or rather the inconsistencies within and between model and reality through time and across ethnic groups or tribes and to demonstrating that over a long period of time there has been change, movement or 'oscillation' between Kachin *gumsa* and *gumlao* organization. In other words, relatively egalitarian communities have transmuted into stratified ones, and stratified, state-like structures have 'collapsed' and reverted to egalitarian ones. Leach characterizes this as a 'moving equilibrium' in which the Kachin *gumsa* system is inherently unstable and shifts towards either a state-like Shan order or reverts to an egalitarian *gumlao* order. It does so because in making choices between alternative political ideals ('aristocracy' and 'democracy') a collectivity of individuals acting together alters the structure of society. Yet among the Kachin these alternative models (or ideals) of organization coexist and can be used by individuals to justify different courses of action in everyday political life.

On the basis of his research between 1939 and 1945, Leach isolated two broadly separable elements in his arbitrarily defined area of the Kachin Hills: (1) the Shan who are Buddhists; they are relatively culturally homogeneous, valley-based wet rice cultivators, possessing socially stratified state or 'feudal' structures (*möng*) headed by princes (*saohpa*), cognatically organized, moderately urbanized and, with few exceptions, Tai speakers; and (2) the Kachin who comprise a much more culturally heterogeneous population with diverse languages and dialects and elements of material culture, although the language of one of the Kachin groups – Jinghpaw – serves as the lingua franca; the Kachin are defined to some extent in relation to the Shan in that they are not Buddhists; they are mainly hill rice cultivators, though some communities grow rice on irrigated terraces; they are organized in patrilineal descent groups distinguished between wife-givers and wife-takers and linked in marriage alliances. Kachin socio-political organization can be categorized into two kinds or 'species' – a 'democratic' form (*gumlao*) with the primary political unit comprising a single village community and with no class differences, and an 'aristocratic' form (*gumsa*), comprising a state or territory (*mung*) headed by a prince (*duwa*) or chief with the population divided hierarchically into social classes. Leach indicates that among the Kachin it is problematical to sort Kachin communities into discrete ethnic groups or 'tribes'. The different criteria of definition (language, dress, ecology, political organization/territory) cross-cut one another in a complex fashion.

Leach's solution to this problem of ethnic and temporal diversity is to treat Shan and the two main varieties of Kachin as constituents of a single system or social structure; they are interdependent sub-systems or 'variations on a theme' (ibid.: 60). Despite the fact that it is relatively straightforward to demarcate Shan as an ethnic unit because of their greater socio-cultural homogeneity and their territorial and political integrity, even here there is a problem. Leach points out that Shan and Kachin are close neighbours and have been engaged in political and economic interaction over a very long period of time; nearly all Shan states include a variety of Kachin hill villages; some Kachin have intermarried with Shan, converted to Buddhism and over time have 'become' Shan; some Kachin consider themselves simultaneously to be Kachin and Shan. Furthermore, Leach demonstrates that in understanding Kachin political behaviour and organization one must realize that the Shan 'feudal' state serves as a model for ambitious Kachin princes or chiefs; they attempt to make themselves like Shan and some of them succeed in so doing. The Kachin *gumsa* system is therefore an approximation of a Shan state, and this is a quite crucial feature of Leach's extended model of social structure; structural relations cut across ethnic groups and help explain behaviour, events and changes in one sub-system by recourse to the organizational features of another sub-system. Elements of Lévi-Straussian structuralism are clearly demonstrated in this aspect of Leach's model.

Another crucial element which Leach analyses is the relationships between Kachin patrilineages, which are interrelated through both lineage segmentation or fission and marriage alliances based on the prescription of matrilateral cross-cousin marriage. As we have seen in Lévi-Strauss's structural analyses of alliance systems based on the prescription that one can only marry women from the category mother's brother's daughter, descent groups are linked as wife-givers to wife-takers; in this system it is not permitted to give a woman in marriage to a group from which brides are received and vice versa. Leach argues that in the Kachin case the relationship or rather the contradiction between lineage and rank is the key to explaining the oscillation between a hierarchical and an egalitarian system, and both *gumlao* and *gumsa* are 'structurally defective' (ibid.: 204). In a *gumlao* order all lineages are considered to be equal; they marry in a circle and brideprice is low. There may be little difference in rank status between wife-giving (*mayu*) and wife-taking (*dama*) lineages. Yet implicit in the terminological distinction between *mayu* and *dama* is that there is asymmetry and wife-givers are superior to wife-takers. In a *gumsa* system the *mayu–dama* relationship is used to legitimize the ranking of lineages in a political hierarchy. Wife-takers are the vassals of wife-givers.

The contradiction is one between equality as expressed in descent and affinity in that lineages linked by marriage 'in a circle' are considered equal, and at the same time ranked because wife-givers are superior to wife-takers. Leach says:

> Rank implies an asymmetrical relationship. The overlord extorts services from his subordinate without obligations of reciprocity. Kinship implies a symmetrical relationship; a *mayu–dama* (affinal) or *hpu–nau* (lineage brother) relationship between a chief and his follower may imply one-sided obligations from the follower towards his chief, but it also implies that the chief has obligations towards his follower. The weakness of the *gumsa* system is that the successful chief is tempted to repudiate links of kinship with his followers and to treat them as if they were bond slaves (*mayam*). It is this situation which, from a *gumlao* point of view, is held to justify revolt.
>
> (ibid.: 203)

Leach's examination of the structure of Kachin society reveals the essential internal mechanisms which explain the ways and direction in which social forms change, but he emphasizes that the impetus or ultimate causes of change are 'nearly always to be found in changes in the external political and economic environment' (ibid.: 212). These comprise: (1) variations in the availability of resources and the means of production, in other words, environmental variables; (2) external political influences including the effects of British colonialism as well as relations with the Shans and other neighbouring populations; and (3) the actions of individual chiefly leaders and *gumlao* 'revolutionaries' (ibid.: 227–263).

Finally, Leach also comments in his monograph on the connections, similarities and differences between the Kachin and such neighbouring populations as the Chin and the Naga, and in his conclusions proposes that his 'type of analysis is capable of considerable further development and that it might usefully be applied to many parts of the ethnographic map' (ibid.: 292). In his 'Introductory Note' to the 1964 reprint of his book he refers approvingly to the research of F.K. Lehman on the Haka Chin (1963) and its relevance to his Kachin research. He says 'Viewed overall, Chins turn out to be even more like Kachins than most of us would have expected' ([1954] 1970: xv). Before briefly summarizing the major criticisms of Leach's study, it is worthwhile considering Lehman's work because it adds interesting dimensions to Leach's analysis.

Lehman and the Chin

Lehman obviously took some inspiration from Leach's analysis but his study of the Chin provides in its own right an important contribution to the understanding of the different dimensions of hill–lowland relations in mainland South-East Asia. In particular, he relates variations in Chin socio-political organization primarily to the different relationships which different Chin communities have with lowlanders. We should also remember that Lehman made a more general contribution to American studies of Burmese culture and society, given his close academic relations with such anthropologists as Manning Nash and Melford Spiro. However, Lehman certainly differs from Spiro in his intellectual interests and is closer to European structuralists in his approach. He acknowledges an 'intellectual debt' to Edmund Leach and Rodney Needham, although his work also demonstrates affinities with European cultural–historical studies and American concerns with cultural ecology and evolution. He dedicates his book to his former tutor, Robert von Heine-Geldern, and the 'Foreword' to the volume was written by the American cultural ecologist, Julian H. Steward (1963: vii–x). Steward draws specific attention to Lehman's main argument that variations in Chin social organization were primarily a product of their perceptions of and their different relations, both direct and indirect, with lowland Burman civilization (ibid.: viii) as well as local adaptations to the environment. Various of the Chin groups have long had trading, political and military relationships with the Burmans or ethnic Burmese (ibid.: 5). Lehman coins the term 'subnuclear' for populations like the Chin which reside on the margins of state formations, and he suggests that this category of societies is widespread in the upland regions of mainland South-East Asia. The Chin are, according to Lehman, neither a fully 'tribal' nor 'peasant' society; they possess characteristics of both (ibid.: 3–4, 221–223).

Interestingly the Chin–Burman relationship was not one-sided, and it should be noted that there were also Chin who resided on the plains in close proximity to the Burmans and were subject to more intense acculturation processes. Lehman indicates that from the early eighteenth century the Northern (hill) Chin, more distant from plains populations, were raiding into the lowlands and taking Burmans as slaves, as well as plundering neighbouring regions of Assam and Manipur; they also absorbed lowland refugees who fled into the hills as a result of Shan–Burman conflicts (ibid.: 27). Raids provided the Northern Chin with material goods which fed into their local prestige networks and 'led to a concentration of wealth in the hands of powerful families' (ibid.: 28). Apparently it was these families which coordinated and controlled the movement of goods into the hills, and their prominent position in trade enabled them to control land and to establish an alliance system in which they were able to demand higher marriage prices from the lineages which received their women as brides. However, overall the Chin saw themselves at a disadvantage in relation to the civilized Burmans, particularly with regard to the latters' 'quantity of cultural possessions, material and nonmaterial'; this 'evoked both envy and respect' (ibid.: 30).

Lehman carried out fieldwork in the Chin Hills between February 1957 and August 1958, travelling very widely through the region. He spent most of his time among the Haka Chin in the Central Chin Hills, with a briefer period among the southern Matupi division. The Chin, Tibeto-Burman-speakers and part of a wider Kuki–Chin ethno-linguistic subgrouping (see also Needham, 1959a, 1960b, 1960c, 1962), dwell in the mountainous areas lying along the borders of western Burma, north-east India and Bangladesh; they mainly practise hill or swidden cultivation, and, depending on the location, rice, maize or millet are the staple crops with a range of supplementary vegetable crops. Chin society, like that of their neighbours the Kachin, comprised a segmentary patrilineal system of clans and maximal and minimal lineages. On the basis of significant differences in social and cultural organization, Lehman makes a distinction between the Northern Chin (which comprises those of the northern and central hill regions) and the Southern Chin. Those in the north, including the so-called Central Chin whose economic organization had been studied previously by H.N.C. Stevenson, were more distant from lowland Burman populations, and they developed supralocal political organization with hereditary chiefs, specialized political offices, lineage stratification, exchanges of prestige goods, status displays in merit feasts, and a more elaborate technology and material culture as a result of their more indirect trading relations with lowlanders and the greater uncertainty in the flow of trade goods (1963: 103ff.). This political system was reticulated by a complex web of asymmetrical affinal alliance in which higher status lineages gave women in marriage to lower status ones in an overall system of prescriptive matrilateral cross-cousin marriage. For Lehman, in contrast to Lévi-Strauss and Needham, these affinal relationships are to be understood primarily in political terms, not in terms of their formal structural properties and as systems of exchange. Nevertheless, his analysis of descent and affinal relations comes much closer to the structuralism of European anthropologists than it does to the psychological interpretations of American social scientists interested in culture and personality (ibid.: 103–156). His excursion into Chin attitudes and psychological orientations comprises a chapter of only three pages (ibid.: 195–197).

According to Lehman, in contrast to their cousins to the north, the Southern Chin in closer proximity to the Burmans conducted peaceful trading relations with them and did not need to elaborate their social organization and develop an overarching political system to secure trade goods and technology from the lowlands; these were relatively freely and regularly available (ibid.: 44–46). The Southern Chin social system therefore did not exhibit any marked stratification or ramifying alliance system with established and hereditary political offices. Lehman proposes that there may well be a general principle at work among mainland South-East Asian hill populations which is that 'the farther the group is from direct contact with the plains culture, the more elaborate is its own' (ibid.: 45).

In this regard several other writers have adopted Leach's framework – wholly, in part, in modified form or radically altered – to examine other minority hill populations in mainland South-East Asia, with mixed results. As we shall see in a moment, Kirsch (1973) posits a general 'hill tribe society' on the basis of shared religious concepts and practices. Yet he finds it difficult to determine whether certain communities should be classified as 'autocratic' or 'democratic', and he does not include upland–lowland relations in his model of change. Friedman ([1979] 1998: 12–15) notes, in response to one of his critics, that his original model of a Kachin-type system does not accommodate the chiefly structures of Konyak Nagas and that these might represent a 'new trajectory' of change. He too, in his initial formulation, did not consider Kachin–Shan relations as germane to his analysis. Finally, in a review of the work of Izikowitz, Kunstadter and Durrenberger on upland–lowland relations in northern Thailand and Laos, Cooper (1978: 60–63) suggests that either the ethnic groups considered to be in interaction are too broadly, uniformly and misleadingly drawn, or that the specific 'autocratic'–'democratic' categories and political processes presented and deployed by Leach are not evidently used, or that the assumed interrelationships between upland minorities and lowland majorities are simply not investigated or demonstrated.

Leach's critics

Comments on and criticisms of Leach's analysis are legion, and Leach has responded to some of these (1983; and see Friedman, 1998: 11, 341, 353–354). But it is important that the broad outlines of these criticisms be provided here, and Raymond Firth hints at some of them in his 1954 'Foreword' to Leach's monograph (1970: v–viii). First, Thomas Kirsch, an American cultural anthropologist, re-evaluates the ethnography of the religious life of the upland minorities of mainland South-East Asia (1973), and explores some of Leach's blind-spots occasioned by his emphasis on political motivations. Second, there is the structural Marxist critique of Jonathan Friedman ([1979] 1998), which concentrates on modes of production and economic organization, and which has some connection with Talal Asad's criticisms of the 'market model' of political behaviour (1972) used by Leach and indeed other anthropologists like Fredrik Barth. Third, David Nugent (1982, 1983) argues, from what might loosely be termed a 'political economy' perspective (see King, 1983 and Friedman, 1998: 341ff.), that there are inadequacies in Leach's analysis of the historical data, that Leach cannot demonstrate that an oscillation between two social forms occurred during the nineteenth century, and that pre-British Kachin hierarchy depended primarily on the chiefly control of the production and trade in opium, mainly with southern China.

In his 'Foreword' Raymond Firth draws explicit attention to Leach's emphasis on power in his analysis (1970: vii–viii). Leach has said: 'I consider it necessary and justifiable to assume that a conscious or unconscious wish to gain power is a very general motive in human affairs' (ibid.: 10). Firth, however, suggests that when one looks generally at social behaviour 'it would seem that valuations of a moral and religious order enter and jostle the power and status-seeking elements' (ibid.: viii). It is precisely this dimension which Kirsch takes up in his study because he says it is clear that, as Leach himself indicates, a Kachin *gumsa* chief 'bases his claim to power primarily on his control of religious ritual' (1973: 1), and various of the structural categories which Leach analyses in political and territorial terms are in fact religious and ritual categories. A chief, for example, has exclusive rights in his domain to sacrifice to the earth and sky spirits controlling fertility in the area, and status is sustained and enhanced by holding 'feasts of merit' in which food and other goods are redistributed to clients and followers.

Kirsch acknowledges that Leach has focused on a most important set of changes among the Kachin and that is the shift backwards and forwards between egalitarian and hierarchical orders. Indeed, Kirsch attempts to demonstrate that these transformations are characteristic of several upland communities in mainland South-East Asia, including various Naga groups, the Zahau Chin and the Lamet, which comprise 'autocratic' and 'democratic' forms. Nevertheless, in contrast to Leach, who assigns primacy to the 'social structure' based on the distribution of political power and relegates 'culture' to the status of a 'frill', 'accident' or 'accretion', Kirsch, in the tradition of American cultural anthropology, argues, like Geertz before him, that culture, and particularly religion, is far more central. He says that religion is the 'repository of cultural values and conceptions which provide the cognitive and affective framework within which social action takes place' (ibid.: 3); cultural values 'shape and control human behavior' (ibid.: 36). Kirsch does not suggest that there is a simple cause–effect relationship between religion and political power, rather there are complex interrelationships and feedbacks (ibid.: 6). Yet, he maintains, the structural variability across these upland areas contrasts with a basic similarity and continuity in religious values, and religion is a powerful motivational force in 'hill tribe society'. Individuals therefore seek to increase and maximize their ritual efficacy, potency and fertility; rather than hunger for power it is hunger for enhanced ritual status. This emphasis on the fertility-enhancing roots of political organization echoes A.M. Hocart's more general theory that the seeds of the state should be sought in ritual and religion; he argues that the state was originally an organization for 'life', and its ruler's primary task was to enhance his citizens' fertility and health (1970).

Kirsch provides a valuable corrective to Leach's single-minded analysis of political power, but it has to be said that once Kirsch establishes the primacy of religion, he tends to want to explain everything in these terms. He frankly admits that, while Leach has focused on the Machiavellian, conspiratorial motivations of the Kachin, he has portrayed upland peoples 'as if they were some sort of religious fanatics' (1973: 37). He argues, for example, that religious goals provide a strong motivation to maximize food production, and 'feasts of merit' serve as a means to redistribute surplus production to the less fortunate. Yet the ethnographic evidence does not seem to be sufficient to support this interpretation. Nor is it entirely clear how competition for ritual potency and well-being works out in practice (ibid.: 7). Kirsch argues that competition for it in a *gumlao* system is perfect and in a *gumsa* system there is a tendency to absolute monopoly. Yet there appears to be no theoretical upper limit to the amount of fertility and potency that can be harnessed nor is it clear at what point, in religious terms, an egalitarian revolt against a chief's monopoly of ritual is likely and quite how dissatisfaction is generated. Finally, Kirsch, as he himself admits, does not really address the important matter of the relations between tribal societies and the larger-scale state-based political systems of the lowlands. He concentrates on internal motives and mechanisms of change.

At this juncture it is also worthwhile referring to the work of Gerald Hickey on the minorities of the Central Highlands of Vietnam (1993, and 1982a, 1982b). Hickey follows closely Kirsch's model of 'hill tribe society' and the importance that these upland groups attach to specific religious ideas and motivations. Hickey argues that '[d]espite variations among their societies, the highlanders have a common culture that shares a great many characteristics of the Southeast Asian upland culture described by Kirsch' (1993: xvii). More particularly, with regard to 'the man-nature-cosmos triad, fertility and potency are intertwining themes that flow through all aspects of highland life' (ibid.: xxv). Yet Hickey's work was also powerfully influenced by French colonial ethnology which from the 1930s began to create or construct a category of upland culture in opposition to the lowland Vietnamese (Salemink, 1999; and see Chapter 2).

Leach and Kirsch tell us much about the political and religious dimensions of social action, but there is yet another area of social life which requires attention – the economic – and this is provided by Jonathan Friedman in his structural Marxist model of hill tribe society ([1979] 1998). It is difficult to to do justice to the complexity of Friedman's systems model which presents in detail how modes of production and social formations come to be transformed as a result of internal contradictions and processes. Indeed, Friedman subsequently re-evaluated, in 1979, his original analysis presented in a doctoral thesis in 1972, and he has suggested recently that even the revised model is no longer adequate in interpreting changes in tribal societies (1998: 32–33). He confirms, in the recently published second edition of his 1979 monograph, that he has continued to move from 'structuralist Marxism' in the direction of 'global anthropology' (ibid.: 11). We shall return in Chapter 5 to consider various neo-Marxist contributions to the analysis of socio-economic change in small-scale societies in South-East Asia and their incorporation into modern nation–states and a global economic and political system. Suffice it to say here that Friedman does draw our attention to the importance of examining the ways in which the Kachin exploit their environment with the level and kind of technology at their disposal and with due regard for the constraints which the environment imposes upon them. He also analyses the organization of labour and the work process, the forms of realization, distribution and utilization of surplus, and the relationship between economic processes and political and ideological ones. He emphasizes that his model does not assume that technology or productive relations are causal, rather in a system of production there is 'reciprocal causality' and relations of correspondence and contradiction. In this respect his structural model in its formal properties and relations bears some similarity with Lévi-Strauss's conceptual framework.

Friedman concentrates on the properties of Kachin shifting or 'slash-and-burn' cultivation and notes that its critical features are that it is an extensive form of agriculture. It requires that, following cultivation usually for one or two years, the land should be left fallow for a long period of time to allow the vegetation to recover. This requirement also sets limits to demographic density, and if population increases and the environment is over-exploited, then the agricultural system starts to break down, the level of production decreases, while the demands on labour to address a deteriorating economic situation increase. Another significant feature of the Kachin system of production and exchange is that women are given a 'value' and that a one-way circulation of women in marriage requires the flow of goods and prestations (in the form of such items as cattle, mats, cloth, gongs, ironware, silver jewellery, cash) in the opposite direction. Surpluses are therefore converted into wives and through 'feasts of merit' into political and religious status; chiefly households establish close relations with supernatural beings and the offerings made to them are perceived to contribute to further economic, political and ritual success. Chiefs are granted tribute and labour; they accumulate slaves as war-captives and debtors, and they can press them into service on their behalf. Chiefly women are also valued more highly than others and command higher brideprice.

The critical contradiction which Friedman identifies is that increasing rank differentiation leads to demographic and territorial expansion, and demands an increasing surplus. Unfortunately a shifting cultivation system cannot continue indefinitely to respond to these increasing pressures; chiefs take an increasing proportion of a decreasing level of production. This system, now under extreme strain, results in increasing dissatisfaction among the chief's subjects and provides the context for a *gumlao* revolt. Rank and brideprice are devalued, the need for surplus is reduced and the population disperses.

Friedman's model, though we have presented it in a necessarily very simplified form and stripped it of its Marxist technical jargon, appears to make sense of most of the data. However, what his initial study did not do, though he recognizes the problem in subsequent work, is to address the issue of Kachin relations with lowland populations. He argues that the Kachin system, as it relates to surrounding states, is 'predatory' and 'expansionist' in nature, developing under its own momentum and *subsequently* tapping into external, lowland exchange networks (ibid.: 32–37). Indeed, Friedman sees external relationships more as a logical extension of internal exchange and circulation within Kachin *gumsa* society. Yet, in certain circumstances, some *gumsa* communities might be transformed into more 'dependent' or 'peripheral structures' or 'prestige-good' economies whose survival does rely to some extent on external trade with larger state economies.

Nevertheless, a point which needs to be borne in mind is whether or not in practice surplus production in lineages and subsequent developments occur quite in the way in which Friedman's model suggests; surely the process and its location are likely to vary depending on variations in environmental factors, and to proximity to particularly valued raw materials and trade routes, as well as to the intervention of individual actors committed to the acquisition of position, status, power and wealth (King, 1981)? Friedman notes recently that his work was directed to 'explicit model building and theorizing' and not so much to 'concrete' ethnography nor to issues of 'personal agency, the constitution of personal experience and motivation, and the relation between agency and structure' (1998: 24–25). He may not be far from Leach's, or indeed Kirsch's, approach in his recent reference to agency and motivation. Furthermore, in this connection, Friedman also points out that while, in the Introduction to his 1979 monograph, he was concerned to place Kachin in a regional and global context, he failed to place them in a concrete historical context, particularly that resulting from the British pacification and administration of Burma (ibid.:

26). After all, the British directed the exploitation of the environment in various ways by establishing forest reserves for the extraction of teak and by restricting shifting agriculture, as well as by opening up markets for opium poppy and tea cultivation, and disrupting and changing the patterns and content of trade. In these areas of concern Leach's doctoral thesis is especially perceptive (1947), and Friedman's analysis would have benefited from an examination of other kinds of resource exploitation and the importance of controlling trade routes. Finally, Friedman does tend to establish a direct connection between social esteem and economic production, and as Leach demonstrates, claims to rank and prestige and the evaluation of social position may not be based directly on the control over material resources.

Another criticism from a Marxist perspective of the kind of political model which Leach uses comes from Talal Asad, who, in his critique of Barth's work on Swat Pathan political organization, addresses the question of competition for political power and the assumption that individuals make choices in terms of the desire to gain power and esteem (1972). The general thrust of Asad's analysis lends support overall to Friedman's position. Asad points out that the model which Barth (and Leach) employs assumes that individuals make choices on an equal basis; securing power becomes an end in itself and it is by no means clear what motivates others to accept the position of those who gain power. Asad draws attention to the close relationship between this perspective and that of Thomas Hobbes who proposed that there was 'a general inclination of all mankind' and this was 'a perpetual and restless desire of Power after power, that ceaseth only in Death' (cited in Asad, ibid.: 80). Asad argues that there is an implicit assumption of consensus between leaders and followers in this 'market model' based on individual motivation, choice and dyadic relationships. There must be consensus for them to act together to change the social structure. However, Asad suggests that political choice for some is restricted by inequalities which are already established, and that there is control and regulation of some by others who have greater economic power and control over material resources (and see Cooper, 1978: 60).

Leach maintains that: 'In the last analysis the power relations in any society must be based upon the control of real goods and the primary sources of production.' Nevertheless, he still maintains that 'this Marxist generalization does not carry us very far' ([1954] 1970: 141). The difficulty which Leach's analysis occasions is that it does tend towards an idealist interpretation of social change and at times there is a lack of clarity in determining precisely what is changing and what the relations are between 'ideal order' and 'empirical fact'. In his analysis of the Kachin community of Hpalang, for example, Leach indicates that the *gumsa* categories used were largely a 'pretence' on the part of the local leaders, and had Hpalang been based on *gumlao* principles, then the facts on the ground 'would have been almost the same'. He concludes therefore in this instance that the difference between the two forms is largely a matter of ideology and not of both theory and fact (ibid.: 97).

Finally, Nugent expresses some uncertainty about Leach's use and interpretation of the historical data (1982). This is hardly surprising when Leach himself says that 'the recorded facts of Kachin history are so fragmentary as to be capable of almost any interpretation' ([1954] 1970: 227). Nevertheless, Nugent maintains that the historical sources do not indicate a long-term *gumlao–gumsa* oscillation, that the evidence up to the latter part of the nineteenth century suggests that all Kachin communities were *gumsa*, they were based significantly on trade with Yunnan, and especially though not exclusively trade in opium, and that the 'democratic' alternative only appeared thereafter as a result of major disruptions in the political and economic environment in Burma and neighbouring parts of southern China reinforced by the expansion of Western colonialism in the region.

Both Leach (1983) and Friedman (1987, reprinted in 1998) responded to Nugent's criticisms and questioned his interpretation of the historical data. They both emphasize that opium production was not as important nor as widespread in the nineteenth century as Nugent claims. More particularly 'trading and opium are primarily associated not with *gumsa* but with *gumlao* Kachin' and the powerful chiefs of the Triangle Area were not (or very little) associated with opium production and trade (Friedman, 1998: 343–348). Furthermore, Nugent does not really explain why social changes among Kachin took the form they did because he does not demonstrate how trade relates to social structure (King, 1983; Friedman, 1998: 343ff.). Indeed, Friedman, referring to the work of Maran La Raw (1967), suggests that Nugent fails to appreciate that there is not a simple dichotomy between *gumsa* and *gumlao*; nor does Leach's monograph explore this issue in detail. Instead there are two kinds of *gumsa* organization – one of hereditary paramount chiefs (*gumchying gumsa*), the other of 'proud and free' anti-hereditary chiefs (*gumrawng gumsa*) – as well as *gumsa* polities, tied into Shan domains, which are 'not to be considered thoroughly Kachin' (ibid.: 349). With regard to the *gumlao* order there are non-hereditary *gumlao* chiefs dependent on a *gumsa* polity, and truly independent, chiefless *gumlao* communities. Friedman argues that it is this complexity which has to be explained by an internal model of change related to a regional and 'global' economic and political system. What does bring Leach, Friedman and Nugent together is their appreciation of the importance of examining Kachin social structure in the context of wider sets of political and economic relationships and forces, although they disagree about the ways in which these relate precisely to structural changes among the Kachin, and the priority which should be accorded to both particular external and internal social elements and forces.

Tambiah and North-East Thai buddhism

In contrast to the dominance of structuralism in Oxford, Stanley Tambiah was one of the few Cambridge anthropologists of the 1960s who adopted a structuralist perspective in the analysis of the relations between religion and society.

He acknowledges his debt to Edmund Leach in the Preface to his 1970 book on Thai Buddhism and the spirit cults, noting that Leach 'has taught me most of the anthropology I know' (1970: v).

Prior to Tambiah's study of Buddhism and 'animism', or, in his terms, 'spirit cults', in North-East Thailand (1970), different researchers had formulated several different ways of conceptualizing the interrelationships between a 'Great Tradition' and a 'Little Tradition'. As we have seen in the Islamic world of South-East Asia, Clifford Geertz had described and analysed Javanese religion in terms of three sub-systems which gave emphasis to the different major religious influences in Java: Islam, Hinduism-Buddhism and folk religion. However, in the mainland Theravada Buddhist societies there appear to be four major perspectives which researchers have used to characterize the relationships between Buddhism and 'animism' and in some respects Hindu Brahmanism.

First, there are those like DeYoung (1955) and Kaufman (1960) who argue that Buddhism and animism are so intertwined that they are almost indistinguishable, particularly from the perspective of the layperson. Second, there is the 'layered' model which sees Buddhism as the dominant religion superimposed upon a pre-Buddhist animistic base. Kirsch, for example, conceives of Thai religion in this way (1965), and in emphasizing doctrinal differences between religious traditions, depicts Buddhism and animism as in functional conflict one with another with Brahmanism serving as an intermediate buffer and integrating mechanism between the two. Animism is 'localized', 'lower', 'inferior', a 'survival'. Earlier colonial observers, however, also using a 'layered' model, often saw Buddhism as a 'veneer', resting on the real belief system which was 'animism'. Third, some observers emphasize the tension, conflict or incompatibility between Buddhism and animism. Spiro, though he states that spirit cults are not incompatible with Buddhism and are complementary to it and sanctioned by it (1967: 251–253), nevertheless concentrates on the central doctrinal contradiction posed by the law of *karma* which, he says, predetermines good and bad fortune in this life, and the propitiation of supernatural agents in order to avoid misfortune or remedy it. Spiro also points to the ethical tension between Buddhism and the amoral, turbulent, non-ascetic character of 'supernaturalism'. Finally, there are those who, while recognizing the differences and contradictions between Buddhism and animism, see them as operating on a continuum and in a relationship of complementarity. Mandelbaum, for example, demonstrates that in some cultures two of the general functions of religion are separated with different duties, rituals and practitioners being assigned to each (1966: 1174–1193; and see Mendelson, 1960). One complex is oriented to the transcendental function of religion while the other attends to pragmatic concerns.

In this connection, Leach, in his structuralist analysis of the position and role of the Buddhist monk, also notes that in religion there is a central concern with the distinction between this world and the continuation of life, which is socially equivalent to 'youth', and the other world, death and reconciliation to it, associated with old age (1962: 81–102; and 1968). Buddhism addresses other-worldly concerns and animism thisworldly ones. In this regard the monk, who follows an ascetic, serene, celibate life-style in the separate confines of a monastery, who cannot take life, nor conduct commercial transactions, and receives alms from the laity, is structurally 'marginal' and in behaviour, dress and appearance is symbolically separate from everyday life. Leach argues that the monk is therefore ideally placed to serve as a bridge between this world and the next; he performs an important role in mortuary rites, and serves as a means for laypeople to make merit to secure a better rebirth. On the other hand, spirit cult practitioners, symbolically opposed to the monk, but also marginal persons, actively and ecstatically through trance and possession bring the supernatural into this world to help address immediate problems.

Tambiah, in his study of the north-eastern Thai village of Baan Phruan Muan in 1961–1962, and again in 1965 and 1966, examines the different kinds of relations which operate between Buddhism and 'animism' (1970). However, he overcomes the problems which earlier observers experienced by concentrat-ing on 'ritual complexes' in practical village religion, and the ways in which these relate to the historical traditions of Buddhism both generally and specifi-cally in Thailand. He therefore recognizes the crucial importance of distinguish-ing and relating practice and doctrine. What he also does is demonstrate how the system of religious categories expressed in thought (speech) and action are interwoven with the social structure of the village. He therefore locates the 'collective representations' of these Thai villagers in 'practical' religion and in social structure, and examines historically the continuities and transformations of village religion in relation to Buddhist philosphical, canonical and literary traditions. Tambiah claims that he is making a specific contribution to the study of the interrelationships between sacred words and acts in ritual as well as between myth and ritual.

He presents four ritual complexes: rites performed by Buddhist monks to do especially with 'good death and good rebirth'; *sukhwan* ritual performed by village elders to recall villagers' escaped spirit essences to do with 'prosperity and orderly progression in life', and associated with elements of Hindu Brah-manism; the cult of the village guardian spirits or deities presided over by special officiants and to do with 'protection and fertility'; and rituals to do with 'bad death and bad or delayed rebirth' and addressed to malevolent spirits which cause illness and affliction. The latter two complexes would come under the umbrella of 'animism' in the work of earlier writers. Tambiah obviously builds upon previous literature, but though he acknowledges that in several respects the four ritual complexes demonstrate contrastive or opposed features, they are also ordered in terms of complementarity, linkage and hierarchy (ibid.: 2).

The four complexes cover much of what we might call 'village religion' but not all of it. Tambiah then step-by-step constructs an overall model of Thai village religion which he refers to as a 'kaleidoscopic view of the religious field' (ibid.: 337). He presents this 'total field' diagramatically as a circle divided into four sectors (corresponding to the ritual complexes), and the circle then divided into five concentric circles or bands (ibid.: 338). The innermost circle contains the primary religious concepts of the villagers concerning merit, demerit, life and death; the next, the main supernatural agents or entities addressed; then the ritual officiants responsible for engaging with the supernaturals; then the rituals conducted by the officiants; and finally the social groupings which participate in the rites. Tambiah examines each of these segments in relation to the others using the four concepts of opposition, complementarity, linkage and hierarchy. He points out that the model is a structural model; it is not constructed by the villagers themselves, though they would in various situations and contexts make distinctions between the categories and sectors which comprise the total model. In other words, it is built up from the thoughts and actions of the players; it comprises their 'collective representations' (ibid.: 339–340).

Tambiah, like other structuralists, has come in for criticism particularly from American cultural anthropologists. The major matter at issue is the relationship between Tambiah's model of village religion as a 'total field' and the perceptions and distinctions of villagers. Do the distinctions, relationships and interpretations of the structuralist have any basis in the empirical evidence or are they merely clever manipulations of the anthropologist? Local differences and conflicts in interpretation of religious categories and ritual elements do tend to be resolved and subsumed in the overall structural model, and sometimes much more is read into the material than is warranted. What is more, relations between religious categories and ritual complexes are expressed as logical relations and it is unclear how, for example, changes in one category or complex might affect another.

Peacock and Javanese drama

Peacock's study of a Javanese dramatic form bridges the divide between European structuralism and American cultural anthropology concerned with the effects of modernization and nation-building on small-scale communities (1968). Peacock also subsequently wrote a more general theoretical book on symbolic anthropology (1975) in which he draws on Durkheim, Leach, Lévi-Strauss, Mauss, Needham, Rassers and van Gennep as well as Clifford and Hildred Geertz, Margaret Mead and Max Weber. His main focus is the relationships between the symbolic and the social order, and for that reason he finds Anglo-French structuralism a useful framework and deploys Needham's concept of 'symbolic classification'. However, he sees this primarily as a static frame of reference in which symbols gain meaning in relationship to one another and to the social order; they also ritualize, display and legitimize social relations and statuses, reminding people of their shared values. An excellent example of this concordance between the social and the symbolic orders is the Javanese shadow play (*wayang kulit*) in that it mystically orders and symbolically depicts fundamental social relations and associated moral values in traditional Javanese society. Peacock, however, is critical of the 'intellectualist' approach of Lévi-Straussian structuralism, in that it views classification as an end in itself rather than a means to an end. He therefore grafts on to this concern with the structural relations between different orders or categories of phenomena, a Weberian perspective which examines the ways in which symbols are used in action, and how they might encourage and influence the form and direction of social change by imbuing certain kinds of activity and orientations to the world with positive meanings and values. In this regard his work comes close to Clifford Geertz's analyses of ritual performance.

Peacock studied what he refers to as a 'proletarian' drama form in the port city of Surabaya in eastern Java in 1962–1963. He discovered that there were 594 *ludruk* troupes in the province of East Java in 1963 and along with a range of other expressions of dramatic life in Java concluded that the 'sheer amount of dramatic activity ... and the venerable role of drama there suggest that drama has something significant to do with the lives of Javanese' (1968: 5). Drama is ubiquitous in Javanese life, and it is also a lived tradition.

Interestingly, Peacock conceptualizes *ludruk* as a 'rite of modernization', following Arnold van Gennep's structuralist analysis of rites of passage. It serves then as a symbolic expression of a transition or passage from one state or condition to another. But, according to Peacock, it does more than mark or define a transition because it plays a role in the modernization process in Java and assists those who participate in the performances, both audiences and actors, 'to apprehend modernization movements in terms of vivid and meaningful *symbolic classifications*'; it also encourages participants to empathize and identify with modern modes of social action, and it involves them in artistic forms which 'structure their most general thoughts and feelings in ways stimulating to the modernization process' (ibid.: 6). In other words, the participants internalize what the symbols are expressing – the messages which are being conveyed – but often in an indirect, subtle and sensory way. More than an analysis of the structure of the symbols portrayed on stage and the principles which order them, Peacock explores the emotional, motivational, moral and sensory load of symbols and suggests that operating as they do through psychological processes symbolic forms have consequences for certain kinds of social action.

Peacock therefore examines in detail *ludruk* plots, their structure and progression; speech, music, dance, action, gesture and behaviour on stage; costumes and props; and audience reactions and their socio-economic backgrounds. *Ludruk* is a coarse, common, lewd and vulgar kind of entertainment popular among Javanese *abangan* communities, but not among *santri* and *priyayi* (cf. Geertz, 1960). Peacock indicates that its roots go back to an earlier nineteenth-century Javanese song-and-dance performance which had associations with *abangan* religion and had as its main characters a female impersonator or transvestite and a clown. These are still the two dominant figures in modern *ludruk* but the performance has been elaborated to include an introductory 'rapture dance' in which a man 'dressed in bizarre black men's or women's clothes' simulates love-making (1968: 61); there is a sequence in which two clowns – 'downtown types' – engage in a dialogue followed by a 'comic skit'; then a female impersonator sings and dances; and finally there is the story or melodrama interrupted by transvestite and clown interludes (ibid.: 62–64).

Participants in *ludruk* are Javanese proletarians and the 'under-class' who live in the urban 'villages' (*kampongs*) of Surabaya; there were also close interrelations between *ludruk* and the Indonesian Communist Party. Peacock discovers two major schemes of symbolic classification among these lower-class urban dwellers, which order cultural and moral categories from diverse spheres of Javanese life: one which has its roots in ancient Javanese cosmology associated with traditional cultural forms such as the shadow-play, and that is the distinction between *alus* (refined) and *kasar* (coarse or crude) behaviour and thought; and the other which has emerged from postcolonial Indonesian nationalist discourse and that is the socio-political distinction between *maju* (progressive) and *kuna* (conservative) attitudes and behaviour. Peacock presents a structuralist analysis of the symbolic representations of the transvestite and the clown in terms of these two major classificatory axes: the transvestite is associated with the *alus–maju* axis and the clown with the *kasar–kuna* axis. However, both actors are also profoundly ambiguous in symbolic terms and constantly collapse and mediate these distinctions. Peacock detects in *ludruk* performances, particularly in the melodrama sequence, a gradual move away from interest in the *alus–kasar* opposition to a concern with the *maju–kuna* distinction, which in turn serves to encourage predispositions towards the modernization process among lower-class Javanese.

Peacock's absorbing and stimulating study extends the analysis of symbolic action in interesting directions. He is certainly not dogmatic about the connections between dramatic forms and social processes. What he does seem to be suggesting is that the functional role of *ludruk* in assisting the modernization process is highly probable on the basis of his field research data; there is not a simple cause–effect relationship between aesthetic forms and social action, but instead *ludruk* in this case demarcates, defines, crystallizes and clarifies modernization and the movement from rural to urban and from agriculture to factory. It does so in a symbolically powerful and meaningful way so that the Javanese who participate in performances can both comprehend what is being said and portrayed, internalize it and identify emotionally with it. One particular difficulty with his analysis is that his audience does not generally comprise the potentially socially mobile, young 'modernizers', but instead older generations, usually above 30 years of age, for whom mobility is more problematical. It is therefore uncertain how the experiences generated in *ludruk* are then translated into action outside of the performances through such processes, we assume, as socialization; and Peacock indicates some of the practical difficulties of encompassing such a broad range of social interaction beyond *ludruk* (ibid.: 276–279). What is more, the socio-political context within which *ludruk* flourished in the early

1960s was radically transformed following the events of 1965 and the emascula-
tion of the Indonesian Communist Party. It appears that the freedom which
ludruk performers had to express their views about the character and direction
of Indonesia's modernization was significantly curtailed with the inception of
President Suharto's New Order government in 1966.

It is not surprising that Peacock's study is a somewhat unusual contribution
to this primarily European structuralist tradition in that, as an American
scholar, he shared one of the major interests of post-war American cultural
anthropology. He was concerned with social and cultural processes in the
context of a modernizing, newly independent nation. Nevertheless, there was
another stream of European research which began to establish itself during the
1970s. It took its inspiration from the writings of Marxist, dependency and
political economy theorists, but in addressing processes of modernization it
examined small-scale communities within an expanding and exploitative international capitalist system. We shall turn to this work in the next chapter but we
shall also need to consider as a prelude to this neo-Marxist literature an earlier
collection of studies on peasant economies associated principally with Raymond
Firth and the London School of Economics.

5

SOCIAL AND ECONOMIC CHANGE
'Peasants' as part-societies

As we saw in Chapter 3, American post-war anthropology did not neglect the political and economic relations between small-scale societies and the wider systems of which they are a part. Indeed, anthropologists like Sharp, Hanks, Nash, Provencher and Geertz were concerned, among other things, to address and understand the responses of rural and small town communities to the processes of modernization, economic growth and development occasioned by decolonization and the building of new nations. Geertz was especially interested in imaginative local reactions to nationalism and modernization, and the potentially problematical interactions between primordial loyalties – the commitment to local identities, traditions and communities – and the generalized ideologies of nationhood and modernity (1963c) (see Chapter 6). On the other hand, European structuralists were much less exercised by the wider context within which the communities they studied, usually upland 'tribes' and outer islanders, were located, and instead continued to focus predominantly on the internal relationships between social and symbolic structures. Nevertheless, there were several studies undertaken by British-based anthropologists of socio-economic and cultural change among 'peasant' societies primarily in Malaysia. In this connection we shall examine the work of Raymond Firth and his colleagues and students at the LSE on peasant economies. We then turn to a parallel stream of work in the USA on peasant societies which emerged in the 1970s and which had important theoretical connections with British studies. It was undertaken primarily by political scientists like James Scott and Benedict Kerkvliet who had an acute sense of the value of historical and anthropological analysis and who examined peasant responses to change in the context of the nature and prerogatives of peasant socio-economic organization. Finally, we consider the later development of neo-Marxist and political economy analyses of peasant societies by Joel Kahn, Kathryn Robinson and Andrew Turton among others and the concepts of 'peasantization', 'proletarianization' and 'agrarian differentiation'.

Introduction

In Chapter 2 we introduced the concept of 'functionalism' and referred to the studies of Raymond and Rosemary Firth on Malay peasant fishing communities in 1939–1940. This interest in small-scale Malay peasant societies and economies was sustained into the 1960s until Raymond Firth's retirement from the LSE. He and his fellow anthropologists devoted particular attention to 'peasant' societies as part of wider processes of change, though primarily with regard to social and economic rather than political organization. One area of interest, albeit somewhat muted, was economic differentiation in peasant societies, the ways in which new social classes emerged, and the characteristics of these. This focus in their work became ever stronger as Malaysia modernized and rural societies were drawn into national programmes for development and economic growth; their emphasis was rather different from American anthropological work on the Malay peasantry which was concerned rather more with religious and political change (see Chapter 3). The more general American interest in peasant politics, particularly in forms of resistance and protest and more broadly in the cultural expression of local identities in the face of changes generated by the increasing incorporation of small-scale cultivators into national and international political and economic systems, was then carried forward by Scott (1976) and Kerkvliet (1977) and their critics (e.g. Popkin, 1979, and see King, 1978). Eric Wolf's seminal work on peasantries (1966) and their defining characteristics (in social, economic, cultural and political terms), has also been especially influential in much subsequent work in anthropology. Wolf defines peasants as constituent parts of 'a larger, compound society' and as

> rural cultivators whose surpluses are transferred to a dominant group of rulers that uses the surpluses both to underwrite its own standard of living and to distribute the remainder to groups in society that do not farm but must be fed for their specific goods and services in turn.
>
> (ibid.: 3–4)

Nevertheless, 'functionalist' economic anthropology up to the 1970s largely avoided any engagement with Marxism and Marxist class analysis, and rather than examine links between peasant societies and the global economy, they tended to concentrate on, at the most, regional and national level changes. There was also a tendency to delineate local bounded units (villages, communities) in relation to external links rather than seeing boundaries as problematical and as artificial creations. On the other hand, Scott, while more directly addressing Marxist theories, argued in favour of an analysis which embraced local level perceptions of exploitation and justice – in other words perceptions, values and experiences framed in terms of a peasant 'moral economy' – rather than more general and abstract notions of exploitation, the extraction of surplus value and false consciousness (1976: 7, 31, 158–160).

Scott too, at least in his early work, tended to downplay the role of classes and class conflict in small-scale societies in favour of an emphasis on shared values, reciprocity between unequals and patron–clientship (ibid.: 3).

After a consideration of Raymond Firth and his colleagues' work on Malay peasantries and James Scott's concept of 'moral economy', we then turn to neo-Marxist approaches to peasant economies, inspired by French philosophical and anthropological thought in the 1960s and 1970s, and, finally, the literature on agrarian differentiation of the 1980s. To varying degrees and in different ways all these studies have been concerned with changing economic and political relations in rural societies and the primary forces of change. A consideration of this literature, devoted to the understanding of change, enables us to gain some appreciation of how anthropologists began to examine the processes and con-sequences of decolonization, the globalization of economic life and the increas-ing incorporation of village communities into large-scale economic and political systems. This increasing concern with 'the economic' also acted to establish closer links with the study of political economy and the sociology of development (Clammer, 1985a: 7–11), and one of the few South-East Asia-wide edited volumes which took account of these developments in the 1970s and 1980s includes anthropological material together with studies from the macro-perspectives of development sociology and political economy (Taylor and Turton, 1988).

The context

Even during the colonial period many rural dwellers in South-East Asia had seen their lives change significantly, though the direction and pace of change varied considerably depending on locality and accessibility, environmental opportunities and constraints, local histories and demographies, pre-existing social, economic and political structures, and the differences in colonial philo-sophies and administrative approaches (Geertz, 1963a; Adas, 1974; Scott, 1976; Kerkvliet, 1977; Popkin, 1979). Yet overall the context of the changes which the Firths were to witness towards the end of Western colonialism in the region, and which others saw gathering pace during the period of decolonization was one of increasingly commercialized agriculture and other economic activities, the expansion of markets in land, labour and agricultural and other rural pro-ducts, the opening up of opportunities for social and physical mobility with the availability of work outside agriculture, especially in towns, improvements in educational provision, the development of infrastructure, particularly road and rail transport, the introduction of technological innovations, and the incorpora-tion of rural communities, and their leaders, into state-wide bureaucratic systems.

Villages in South-East Asia had always been open to the outside world, but external contacts and links increased in extent and intensity so that the divide between 'rural' and 'urban' became much less marked (Rigg, 2001: 25–41) .

New social classes also began to emerge as some rural dwellers accumulated land and others were rendered landless, or as some acquired education and positions in the local and regional administrations, or developed business interests in trade and retailing. Yet 'peasant' family farms and craft enterprises continued to survive, indeed, in some areas increased in number. Anthropologists turned their attention to these small-scale, 'peasant' societies and, while studying their internal organization, also had to try to understand the changing relationships between subsistence production and market-oriented activities, in what ways relationships within rural communities were being affected by external links, the varied trajectories of change, and the local tensions and conflicts set in train by the penetration of capitalism and the modern state.

Malay peasants

Malay fishing communities and the Firths

Raymond Firth and his wife, Rosemary, undertook research in 1939–1940 in Malay fishing communities in Kelantan and north Trengganu on the east coast of Peninsular Malaysia (Firth, 1966). Firth returned briefly in 1947 while he was engaged in a general survey of the 'social and economic conditions of the Malay peasantry', and again, in the company of his wife, for some six weeks in 1963. He examines how the fishing economy functions and adapts to its environmental circumstances and the relations between technology and social and economic organization. Rosemary Firth, in a complementary study, considers the ways in which households, and specifically women as the main 'housekeepers', distribute and utilize the fruits of production (1966: 1), since '[a]ll money earned by the fisherman is given to the woman both to spend and to save' (ibid.: 27). The Firths attempt to reveal the 'rationality' of peasant economic action once it is understood in its own terms. In this chapter we intend to take up certain issues of peasant social and economic organization which Raymond Firth in particular explores, and the relationships between small-scale economies and wider forces of change.

An important feature of a fishing economy is that it usually requires communities to enter into some form of market exchange to obtain other foodstuffs, particularly rice and vegetables, which they do not produce themselves. Nevertheless, in the villages which Firth studied about one-third of households had a mixed economy and owned rice lands, some of which were leased to agriculturalists; agriculturalists were also hired to do the ploughing; and most fishing households were involved in a range of other activities, either in the agricultural sector or in various forms of labouring and handicraft production. Firth indicates differences between peasant agriculture and fishing in that in the latter there tended to be a relatively sharp gender division of labour because men worked at sea, while women kept house, reared children, and undertook onshore activities like making foodstuffs, clothes and nets, gutting fish and operating as small-scale vendors; in fishing economies there was more scope for day-to-day cooperation in 'moderately large groups', which was in turn associated with 'complex systems of distributing the earnings'; and finally higher risks attached to investment in boats and gear because they were 'more liable to sudden damage and loss' and the amount of capital tied up in equipment was considerable (1966: 3).

Firth points out that the concept of 'peasant economy', in the sense in which he uses the term, does not apply exclusively to farmers; certain kinds of fishing and artisanal economies can also be deemed to be peasant-like. He defines a 'peasant economy' as one with 'relatively simple, non-mechanical technology; small-scale production units; and a substantial production for subsistence as well as for the market'. However, 'the economy does not function mainly by its dependence on foreign markets' (ibid.: 5). Firth argues that there are elements of this economy which conform to principles recognizable in capitalist or market-based economies, given that there is some attention to market-exchange, but there are other elements which do not. Some capital goods are produced over which there is some individual control and there may be certain persons whose primary role is to provide capital goods for production; some goods may be loaned out; the practice of taking interest in money or kind on a loan is present; money is used as a medium of exchange. What is more, peasants also recognize the principle of 'economizing'; in other words, they have to make decisions about the allocation of their scarce resources, whether it be land, labour or capital, between their different needs, wants and goals. Elsewhere, in a general essay on economic anthropology Firth argues that it is misleading to draw too sharp a distinction between small-scale economies and capitalist ones because it is assumed that the former do not operate in accordance with market principles and calculations of profit-maximization and economic advantage (1967: 5ff.). He says, 'On the basic principles of choice in the use of resources and perception of relative worth in an exchange, there is a continuum of behaviour over the whole range of human economic systems' (ibid.: 6). What Firth does is import certain ideas from conventional economics, particularly with regard to decision-making and choices, into economic anthropology and then modifies them appropriately in relation to non-Western, small-scale economies (Clammer, 1985a: 48–53).

However, Firth does point out that there is no developed class division of labour (into capitalists/rentiers/owners, managers and labourers) in a peasant economy nor the separation of workers from their means of production. Indeed, such practices as free borrowing and the exercise of communal rights have a dampening effect on the development of inequalities and class relations, and there is no clear-cut division of the proceeds of production into such capitalist categories as rent, interest, profits and wages. Nevertheless, in the case of the Malay fishing economy there were some fishermen who were more wealthy and influential than others; these were the lift-net experts or leaders (*juruselam*); they located the fish and organized lift-net crews; they usually provided the major capital contribution to a fishing association in the form of at least one of the boats and the net, and they frequently had financial interests in other boats. Firth also identifies certain fish dealers or middlemen as well as entrepreneurs in net manufacture whose level of ownership and disposal of capital were greater than most ordinary fishermen.

In small-scale, face-to-face peasant communities individuals also interacted one with another not merely in economic terms as producers, consumers, owners and coordinators of production, but also as relatives, neighbours and friends. Economic relationships, therefore, in contrast to capitalist society, were embedded in social networks; they had a more 'personal' and 'social' content (Firth, 1966: 7), and in a peasant economy individuals made choices and took decisions not simply or exclusively on the basis of economic calculation for the simple reason that relationships and groups were multifunctional and multi-dimensional. Returning to Marcel Mauss's seminal idea, the important principle underlying transactions is one of reciprocity, though the transactions involved in giving and receiving are much more complex than Mauss allowed (Firth, 1967: 8–17).

Firth's view of the Malay peasant fishing economy in Kelantan and Trengganu and its relationship to a modern capitalist one is provided succinctly in the following terms:

> it is incorrect to apply the term 'pre-capitalistic' to such an economy except in a special sense – that is, only in regard to the small magnitude and different form of its capital operations and to the almost complete absence of a class of 'capitalists'. As far as function is concerned, the system uses capital in ways that are frequently strictly parallel to those in a modern business economy.
>
> (1966: 127)

This characterization certainly applied to Malay fishing communities in the late 1930s and the 1940s. The Firths describe a society which, though part of a much larger world – the world of the market, colonial government administration, the traditional Malay court headed by the Sultan, the Islamic faithful – nevertheless, maintained a significant degree of social cohesion and equality. Fishing methods relied on locally made, shallow, undecked sailing craft and, depending on location and type of fish, seines or hauling nets, drift-nets, gill-nets and lift-nets. Other equipment such as curing trays and baskets were made locally, usually by women.

Yet even in the 1940s there were signs of change afoot with improvements in communications, particularly roads and motor transport, so that larger markets were becoming available for the sale of fish; there was also a gradual introduction of technological innovations into the fishing industry, and widening opportunities for investment and purchase. On their return visit to the east coast in 1963, the Firths witnessed even greater transformations and obtained clear evidence of economic differentiation. The major generators of change were the mechanization of fishing with the introduction of motorized, diesel-powered fishing boats and the use of ice for preserving fish. The first development enabled large purse-seine nets to be used, reduced the dependence on weather conditions, opened up more distant fishing grounds, and decreased the travelling time to them; the availability of ice, which was manufactured in government-planned ice factories, meant improvements in fish preservation and access to more distant markets. The greater need for capital to invest in boats and modern nets and the increase in the scale and speed of marketing also resulted in some fish dealers, nearly all of whom were Malays, acquiring financial interests in boats and nets, and the elimination of smaller beach-dealers. Firth proposes that this seemed to signal the 'emergence of a category of larger-scale capitalist fish dealers' (1966: 309). Some local Malay entrepreneurs, who had made their money in trading or who had inherited rice and rubber land, and some who were *juruselam*, also invested in the new technologies. Often they joined together in a combine (*konsi*). Chinese merchants had become involved in that they supplied new purse-seine nets on credit through suppliers in the local towns such as Kota Bharu, but Firth did not identify a significant intrusion of Chinese capital into the industry at that time. The new Malay entrepreneurs were known as *orang kaya* or 'the rich men' and the economic and social distance between them and ordinary villagers was much greater than that between the well-to-do and commoners in 1940.

Changes in the capitalization of the industry also resulted in higher running costs of equipment, as well as more of the returns going to owners of capital and less to labour in comparison with the 1940s. Some of the lift-net experts and boat-owners in lift-net groups had also been driven out of business in competition with the more efficient purse-seine system and began to serve as crew members in purse-seining. Overall the economic position of ordinary crew or labourers in the industry had deteriorated by the early 1960s and there were clear signs of the emergence of class divisions and of a rich and a poor class. From his sample of 177 households and 823 individuals Firth discovered that about two-thirds of the fishermen 'had no significant capital at all' (ibid.: 342).

Rosemary Firth drew attention to other kinds of change, especially from the perspective of women: the increasing availability of manufactured consumer goods in Kelantan, the development of new demands on income, the centralization of marketing facilities, and the widening contacts which women had with towns and markets (1966: 175–184). However, another area of significant change was indicated by Raymond Firth, specifically in the arena of politics and administration. The administration of the newly independent country had now directed itself to promoting economic development, and 'education had come to the villages' with the possibility of increased social and physical mobility for young, bright educated people (1966: 305). One complication in Kelantan's political life, however, was that the Pan-Malay(si)an Islamic Party (PMIP) or Parti Islam Se-Malay(si)a (PAS) which controlled the state government was in opposition to the Alliance Government at the federal level. This resulted in some problems in the allocation of central funds for economic development and some conflicts between state and federal officials. But Firth considered that by the early 1960s these political changes, in contrast to the impact of technology, had still not affected the ordinary Kelantan fishing household unduly. The main consequence of the establishment of a modern state apparatus was that it provided avenues for advancement for the educated and also another locus of socio-political leadership above the village level outside traditional territorial and court-based aristocratic leadership.

Finally, Firth suggests that some individuals of the more wealthy entrepreneurial sector, given the increased availability of education as well, were likely to move into other fields of activity, including the bureaucracy and electoral politics. By the 1960s and within the space of only thirty years the wider world had therefore impacted on these villages and resulted in increasing economic and political differentiation, a feature which Rosemary Firth also remarked on forcefully in her restudy of Malay housekeeping. She, like Raymond Firth, emphasizes the effects of technological change in particular and its associated 'economic compulsions', especially on 'traditional hierarchies' of wealth and skill, and the clear evidence of the increase of poverty among significant sections of the community and the accumulation of wealth in others (1966: x).

Negeri Sembilan Malays and Swift

Michael Swift, who carried out doctoral research under Firth's supervision in Jelebu in the Peninsular Malaysian state of Negeri Sembilan during the mid-1950s, provides complementary data on agriculturalists. Like Firth he also examines, among other things, the effects on a peasant economy of the expansion of market relations and commercialization and the establishment of government administration (1965). At the time that Swift undertook his research the economy in Jelebu comprised rice cultivation, mainly for subsistence needs, in the narrow valleys, and rubber and fruit growing on the neighbouring hill slopes. Swift's initial working hypothesis was that economic changes had resulted in increasing socio-economic individualization and had undermined the importance of the traditional matrilineal organization of the Minangkabau Malays of Negeri Sembilan, particularly the control of ancestral land by matrikin (ibid.: 2). The majority of the rice lands were in the hands of women in the 1950s, although sons could inherit land in the absence of a daughter, and men could also purchase land. Women were the main contributors of labour to rice agriculture. Swift discovered that there was a tendency to withdraw from rice agriculture in competition with rubber cultivation, especially when rubber prices were good (ibid.: 50–51), and that increasingly local farmers were coming to depend on rubber production to meet all their main consumption needs (ibid.: 174).

Like the fishing communities of Kelantan, the Malay farmers were tied into a wider system of market exchange; they sold primary products such as rice, fruit and rubber in return for imported consumer goods. However, in contrast to the situation which Firth observed in Kelantan where Malay entrepreneurs had a significant stake in finance and fish marketing, in Jelebu '[a]ll economic functions other than primary production are carried on by other races, above all by the Chinese' (ibid.: 28).

With regard to his initial hypothesis Swift ultimately concludes that the major factor of change had not been agricultural commercialization but rather the growth and development of a modern government administration. The need for an efficient centralized bureaucracy comprising educated and trained officials to administer justice and land, and also implement government development policies such as irrigation projects had resulted in the displacement of the traditional political system based on the Sultan's family, a non-royal aristocracy and the leaders of kinship groups. The authority of the clan chiefs, who were responsible in the past for the administration of customary law, had been especially undermined. Swift's expectation that rubber planting would result in an increased demand by men for individual ownership of land was not borne out, principally because much of the land on which rubber was cultivated had already been removed from the control of matrilineal kin by a government act of 1891 and the separation of the categories of matrilineal land and newly granted land (ibid.: 86, 173). Commercial agriculture merely reinforced trends which had already been set in motion by political and administrative changes.

Like Firth, Swift discovered a process of economic differentiation taking place, though in Jelebu it was only in its early stages; there was evidence of land concentration and the emergence of a group of more wealthy landowning farmers who also comprised the local political elite, and a class of tenants, labourers and share-croppers. This in turn had been exacerbated by land scarcity as a result of population growth and the government's land alienation policies. Swift also identifies the emergence of a bureaucratic class (schoolteachers, clerks, officials, technical staff), some members of which had emerged from the ranks of the village wealthy (ibid.: 157–161).

Malay leadership and Husin Ali

The issue of class differentiation was taken up in a much more direct and substantial way by Syed Husin Ali, another doctoral student of Raymond Firth who had also been supervised in his early postgraduate career at the University of Malaya by Michael Swift. For his Master's thesis at the University of Malaya Husin Ali undertook field research for four months from late 1959 to early 1960 in Kampung (Kampong) Bagan (1964). He then carried out a study of three agricultural communities between 1964 and 1969 for his doctoral thesis at the LSE (1975). In his earlier study Husin Ali focuses on constructing an overall picture of the class and status structure of one Malay community, Bagan. His study included 149 Malay households; he excludes resident Chinese households from his analysis (1964: 12). He notes that Bagan, which was divided between two administrative villages led by 'village headmen' (*ketua kampung*), was incorporated into a national administrative structure through the institution of the *penghulu*, a traditional leadership position, which had been co-opted to provide leadership at the *mukim* level (the smallest administrative unit below the District) and a local point of contact with the District Officer. The *penghulu* was a salaried government official, responsible for collecting land revenue and maintaining law and order, while the lower level *ketua kampung*, who reported to the *penghulu*, were community leaders and not full-time government functionaries, and received only an allowance or honorarium (ibid.: 23).

In addition to being part of a nation-wide administrative structure the Bagan villagers were also part of a market economy; they cultivated mainly rubber and coconuts for sale, and provided smaller quantities of areca nuts, nipah palm leaves, and coffee for the market (ibid.: 34–35). The village class structure was based importantly around land ownership and agriculture, and Husin Ali demonstrates that land was very unevenly distributed. In part, this was the result of the historical development of the region and the importation into Johore of Javanese bonded agricultural labourers through Singapore (ibid.: 29–31).

His analysis of class, taken to refer to

> a group of people who are in the same station of life and who share a common interest, owing to the similar position they occupy in relation to the means of production and/or the similar roles they play in society, particularly as regards economic production
>
> (ibid.: 10)

revealed two main classes: 'landlords' (*tuan tanah*), who did not work on the land themselves, and 'farmers' or 'farm operators' (*petani*), who to a greater or lesser extent did work the land (ibid.: 36–37). Nevertheless, the situation was much more complicated than this and there was also the non-farm sector to take into account. In the agricultural sector, based on a sample of 124 household heads, there were five classes: landlords, landlords-cum-owner operators, owner operators, owner operators-cum-tenants or farm labourers, and tenants or farm labourers. The significant finding was that landlords comprised only 16.1 per cent of the household heads but controlled over two-thirds of the land, while tenants/labourers constituted nearly 30 per cent of the sample yet owned only 3.8 per cent of the land (ibid.: 40). The remaining 25 household heads were not primarily engaged in agriculture, and were either in government service in such occupations as teaching or administration, or in non-government service mainly as wage-earners in the nearby town. Even among these individuals there were some who owned pieces of land (ibid.: 48), and they constituted a rather mixed bag in class terms. Husin Ali assigns some of them to the main agricultural-based classes, as for example, labourers, but the majority he designates as 'white-collar' 'middle class' below the landlords (ibid.: 56).

The analysis of status provides a slightly different picture. Status, defined in terms of 'the way members of a community differentiate and rank each other according to such factors and criteria which reflect the social values, attitudes and beliefs in the community' (ibid.: 58, and see 1975: 71ff.), delineated four groupings which were accorded different levels or degrees of respect: Muslim religious functionaries, village officials, government servants such as teachers, and those who had good incomes such as landlords (1964: 69). Although status cross-cut class position in that, for example, mosque officials and religious teachers were drawn from different classes, and the relative status ranking between landlords and the middle class was not drawn precisely, there was also considerable overlap between class and status which overall ranked landlords and those of the middle class above others. In particular, landlords tended to occupy high status and influential positions in village society (ibid.: 76–79). Husin Ali says, 'Ten out of 16 members of the middle class are in some committee or other ... Three are chairmen and seven are secretaries. As for the landlords 12 out of 20 are active in the kampong' (ibid.: 98).

Husin Ali detects clear lines of class tension in the village between landlords and tenants/labourers, and between the landlords who were also shopkeepers and the non-owning farmers who were their customers (ibid.: 107–119). But there were various social ties of kinship and neighbourhood coupled with the values of village harmony and respect for those of higher status which served to prevent open conflict breaking out. In addition, a situation of labour surplus existed which placed labourers in a rather precarious position in relation to landowners (ibid.: 119–121). However, Husin Ali also points to some social mobility in the community as a result of land accumulation or the subdivision or loss of land. One increasingly important element in enhancing an individual's life-chances was education, though at the time of Husin Ali's research there was still a distinction between English language education, which was really only open to the wealthy, and Malay medium education which, even for the best graduates from Malay schools, only gave access to school teaching as a career or a lowly clerkship (ibid.: 137).

The effect of modern politics, expressed in the *mukim* elections for the *penghulu*ship in 1959 and the campaign for the parliamentary representative in the Federal General Election in 1956, also demonstrated various fault-lines between influential individuals and their supporting clients or cliques, but these did not form around class interests. Traditionally the position of the *penghulu* was an hereditary one, but in 1956 the Johore State Government decided that it should be subject to election. The conflict, which Husin Ali argues was generated by conflicting values and not class interests, formed around a young forward-looking radical group which supported an educated owner-farmer and a more conservative group defending 'old traditions' and supporting the son of the retiring *penghulu* (ibid.: 103). In the federal election of 1956 there was a split between a group supporting the established Malay political party, the United Malays National Organization (UMNO), and those supporting the strongly Malay party, Parti Negara (PN), which enjoyed a relatively short-lived political existence. Husin Ali remarks that this too was a conflict of values and '[m]ost of the *kampung* folk did not understand the manifestoes put forward by the rival parties, or the implications that those manifestoes had or did not have on their lives' (ibid.: 106).

Overall Husin Ali points to the opening of Kampung Bagan to the outside world, and the influence of 'educational, administrative and economic' changes on its social structure. Although outside influences such as the commercialization of agriculture had had some impact on social class and status within the village, an important feature of this small-scale society was the emergence of a non-agricultural middle class, the increasing availability of other forms of occupation outside agriculture, and the movement of some village residents to the nearby towns in search of work (ibid.: 146).

Husin Ali then takes this initial study of social stratification forward by concentrating on leadership in three Malay peasant communities: Kangkong, Kerdau and Bagan (Kangkong, a rice-growing and fishing community in coastal Kedah; Kerdau, a rice and rubber *kampung* in Pahang; and again Bagan, a rubber- and coconut-growing community in east coast Johore) (1975). He points out that in all three cases it was by no means an easy task to define the 'village' (ibid.: 39ff.). His discussion of the difficulties of conceptualizing the Malay village shows some similarities with the later debates about the Thai village and whether or not it is a natural or artificial unit (see Chapter 3). He argues that communities could be delineated on the basis of territorial arrangements, kinship and descent, and various cooperative activities, but what marked out peasants as a type, other than that they were 'people who work on land, irrespective of whether they own it or not' (ibid.: 87), were that they were also oriented outwards or beyond the local community to the larger society of which they were a part (ibid.: 70). Nevertheless, drawing social, cultural, economic and political boundaries around variously clustered houses and hamlets and relating these to 'administrative villages' was problematical even though Husin Ali says it could be done. In a similar vein, Wilson, in his study of the Malay community of Jendram Hilir, Selangor in 1964–1965, suggests that '[t]he use of the village as a unit of study and description is more for convenience than it is a reflection of the social structure of Malay society' (1967: vii; and 112–113, 145–146); there was an 'imposed unity' in that villagers were members of a religious congregation and the village was an administrative unit, but it was not 'self-contained' because 'villagers relate to persons outside the village in their various role capacities' (ibid.: 38). Masuo Kuchiba and his colleagues in their comparative study of three Malay rice-growing villages also remarked that generally 'village boundaries are not distinct and most of the inhabitants do not know exactly where they are located. The same is true of the boundaries of the *kampung* as an administrative unit' (1979: xii). Like Husin Ali, Wilson examines the opening up of local communities to the outside world, and this was particularly so for Jendram Hilir because of its close proximity to urban areas including Kuala Lumpur and such local towns as Bangi, Kajang and Seremban.

Husin Ali notes that in the Malay language there are two terms which refer to leadership: *pemimpin* (from the root-word *pimpin* meaning 'to go hand in hand' or 'to lead a person by the hand'), which was generally used by villagers to refer to supra-village positions, and *ketua* (from the word *tua* meaning 'old') used for such institutions as *ketua kampung* (headman of the village as an administrative unit) and for those who 'headed' or led groups or units of individuals (1975: 12–13).

Important processes in the transformation of Malay institutions of leadership were set in train during the British colonial period and these included the replacement of the sultanates and traditional chiefs with a modern, qualified, specialized bureaucracy. It was staffed at the lower levels by an English-educated Malay elite, the Malay Administrative Service (MAS), initially recruited from the Malay aristocracy, but then increasingly opened up to educated commoners as well. Malay reactions to colonial rule also resulted in the formation of cultural, religious and political movements and associations seeking improvements in the status and economic position of the Malay population. The desire for political independence was championed after the Second World War by the moderate, accommodationist Malay political party, UMNO, led by Tungku Abdul Rahman, a member of the royal family of the state of Kedah, and supported by English-educated civil servants and professional people, 'many of whom were from families with aristocratic backgrounds' (ibid.: 29). The Pan-Malay(si)an Islamic Party, however, mainly led by those who had received religious and Malay medium or Arabic education, made its appeal to the more strongly Islamic, traditionalist Malays, predominantly in the northern and eastern Malay states of Kedah, Perlis, Kelantan and Trengganu (ibid.: 30). Following Malayan independence in 1957 and then the independence of the wider Federation of Malaysia in 1963, increasing opportunities were opened up for educated Malays in administration and politics both at the state and federal levels.

Husin Ali makes a simple distinction between 'traditional' and 'new' leaders, although the boundary between them has become increasingly blurred. Of the traditional leaders the most prominent were the 'village elders' (*orang tua kampung*), elderly villagers who were accorded respect (ibid.: 102ff.). Apparently they still had some influence over customary law (*adat*), religion and family matters, usually in times of crisis, dispute and marriage in the 1960s. This was especially so for those who also performed roles as religious teachers and mosque officials, *penghulu*, village officials, or were landlords or shopkeepers (ibid.: 106–108). However, their position of authority was being increasingly questioned by some of the younger educated, physically mobile villagers, and in no sense did they constitute a village council. Whether elderly or not, 'religious functionaries' as a category also provided traditional leadership: both Islamic specialists – *imam* (prayer leaders in the mosque or prayer house), *lebai* (person knowledgeable in Islam), *ustaz* (religious teacher) – and folk religion specialists – *bomoh* and *pawang* (magician) (ibid.: 108–116). Again Husin Ali points out the consequences of change, education and mobility: 'Proportionately more young people are sceptical about magic and they are also more indifferent towards Islam than the older people' (ibid.: 116). Finally, there were the secular functionaries, the *penghulu* and *ketua kampung*. These had been traditional offices which were usually hereditary, though from the 1950s elections were gradually being introduced and for the *penghulu*ship there was even the possibility of selection; both positions had become subject to the authority of the District Officer, though village headmen were responsible to the *penghulu* in the first instance and were often delegated duties by him (ibid.: 117–119). The *penghulu* in particular had become a salaried government official, and drawn especially into assisting the District Office in land administration (registration of titles, collection of revenue, settlement of land disputes) and from 1959 had taken on responsibilities to do with rural development through the chairmanship of the Mukim Development Committee (ibid.: 121–122). The *penghulu* undertook these tasks with the assistance of village headmen in the *mukim*. Therefore, traditional positions had become local level elements in a nationwide bureaucratic and, as we shall see in a moment, political system.

The new rural leaders began to emerge in the 1950s specifically connected to political party activity and the increasing involvement of national political parties in rural affairs. Husin Ali describes the situation after independence in the late 1950s and the 1960s and there have obviously been further changes since then with accelerating modernization in the countryside and the expansion of educational and other opportunities for rural Malays. UMNO and PAS, for example, began to establish rural branch parties and frequently these were initiated by those with influence and status, including *penghulu*, *ketua kampung* and school and religious teachers. Support for political parties was usually secured by using kinship, neighbourhood and client networks and such organizations as religious schools. The rural branches generally had a small core of committed registered members who served on the branch committee and assisted in election campaigns and in organizing a range of welfare, educational and recreational events, some of which were party-related (ibid.: 132–136). Subsequently the ruling that government servants could not hold office in a political party meant that ex-government officials such as retired school teachers, or well-to-do landlords or educated individuals from ordinary farming households became increasingly involved in local level politics as 'party functionaries'. Yet in the 1960s government officials still tended to play influential backroom roles in rural party activity, and rural leaders often occupied more than one leadership position in village society. Husin Ali identifies among the landlord and middle class in village society numerous cross-cutting ties of kinship and marriage. Interestingly, in his study of a Malay village in central Pahang, Wilder too points to close interconnections through descent and affinity of *penghulu* and *ketua kampung* in the Bera region, with evidence of continuity in the occupation of political offices, wealth, a high level of kin and class endogamy, and advantages in education in that several of them were also teachers, clerks and administrators (1982a: 67).

Husin Ali notes that at the time of his research there was evidence of some continuity in new leadership positions in that rural Malays still accorded some importance to traditional factors in electing certain individuals to political party office. However, considerations of education and wealth were increasingly prominent: 'Ex-officials, landlords and teachers are often chosen by the villagers to be their leaders and some of these people do not have any link at all with the past' (1975: 143). One significant element in local level leadership was the ability to build and sustain a following, and the organizing principle of patron–clientship played an increasingly crucial role in mobilizing grass-roots support. Wealth and landownership obviously provided resources to enable patronage to be offered to a clientele, but the support of more powerful patrons outside the village, usually with political power and the resources which this commanded, was also of vital concern to local leaders (ibid.: 152). The provision of material assistance to rural Malays by the governing party UMNO in the form of rural development programmes became an important agency for retaining political support and for ensuring that local UMNO leaders, associated with this largesse as 'brokers', performed as effective patrons (ibid.: 163–164).

Husin Ali argues that it was the *penghulu* and the party functionaries who were the 'leader-brokers' in rural Malay society in the 1960s, and that through government support and the political and economic rewards which this carried, they were also becoming more wealthy. He detects increasing class polarization and social tensions in this process of 'accelerated modernization' and rather than providing genuine rural leadership members of the village elite become 'brokers' for those more powerful state- and national-level politicians and bureaucrats. He returns to the notion of a peasantry and suggests that, although there have been significant changes in the countryside, a key feature of the peasantry remains; it is a 'part society' and a 'part culture' (ibid.: 164).

Pahang Malays and Wilder

Perhaps the logical end-point of this set of studies of the Malay peasantry is W.D. Wilder's study of Kampung Kuala Bera in Pahang, based on field research in 1964–1966 and 1976 (1982a). Wilder was also a graduate student at the LSE with Raymond Firth. In effect, Wilder opens up the Malay village even further to the outside world, and employs the concept of 'communication' or modes of message-exchange, information flow, and the facilities or devices for generating, sending and exchanging messages, in order to analyse social interaction, group formation and boundary markers within the community, but importantly also the connections between Kampung Kuala Bera and the wider world through such devices as the mass media and intermediaries (ibid.: 2). Here his interests overlap to some extent with Husin Ali's on rural leadership.

Kampung Kuala Bera, a 'well-defined territorial unit' (ibid.: 33), was the capital village of the *mukim* of Bera in central Pahang, and therefore the seat of its *penghulu* (ibid.: 23). The main elements of its economy were swamp rice cultivation, fresh-water fishing, animal husbandry (water buffalo, goats, chickens and ducks), and fruit and vegetable growing. Rubber was the main cash crop and was 'one reason accounting for a strongly monetized economy in the village' (ibid.: 122). The villagers' involvement in small-scale commercial agriculture also lends support to Firth's observations on peasant economy in that Wilder points to the fact that notions of price, capital, loss on investment and purchase by instalments were 'commonplace' in the village (ibid.: 124). Goods such as radios, sewing machines and outboard motors were purchased, but a major and highly valued investment was the pilgrimage to Mecca (*haj*).

Up until the mid-1950s the village was 'a traditional riverine settlement' (ibid.: 118), but from 1956 it began to be connected more extensively and firmly to the outside world, particularly the towns, by roads and motorized transport. Education had also become more widely available and some individuals, particularly men, went on to secondary education and to salaried posts in government; the village had a postal service, and transistor radios had arrived in the early 1960s. The local community was also linked into a far-flung network of relatives who had left the village for work and who kept in contact with their kin through correspondence, periodic visits and cash remittances (ibid.: 136). Wilder also demonstrates the ways in which national party politics in 1965 had penetrated to the village level and examines this in relation to the rival business networks of two full-time village shopkeepers, both of them local religious figures, one a member of UMNO and the other of the PMIP or PAS. These opposed, competitive coalitions involved prominent village personages (retired schoolteachers, businessmen, leading party functionaries) linked to influential individuals beyond the village (ibid.: 143–147). Because these two factions carried considerable economic and political weight, much of the village communication was channelled through them, and '[a]s a result, religion, politics and enterprise in Kampung Kuala Bera all bore the stamp of the – at the time explosive – national political rivalry between UMNO and PMIP' (ibid.: 147). According to Wilder, the branch organizations of the two main Malay political parties 'had considerable effects on village social structure' (ibid.: 176).

Another medium of contact between the village and the outside world, which we have touched on earlier in this chapter, was that of government-sponsored rural development. Wilder also examines the introduction of rubber planting schemes in Pahang from 1956 to 1965 and the problems which certain of these experienced in Kampung Kuala Bera because of the 'lack of communication' with villagers and their resultant resistance to them (ibid.: 155ff.). His work emphasizes the importance of understanding the social organization of state-generated transformation and provides a healthy warning against a too

171

'economistic' approach to the analysis of development programmes and the changes resulting from them (see Geertz, 1984, and Chapter 7).

The government had devised several schemes to assist smallholder rubber cultivators (mostly on holdings of 3 to 10 acres), either providing cash grants and tree seedlings for replanting new high-yielding rubber stock on existing old holdings (the Rubber Replanting Programme which was begun by the colonial government in 1952), or new planting ('extensification') in large blocks on additional cleared forest land near the village (New Block Planting and Fringe Alienation schemes begun in the 1960s by state governments using federal government loans). The first programme was relatively straightforward in planning and implementation, given that replanting took place in phases on existing land and was in the hands of the peasant cultivator under supervision; information was channelled directly to and from the cultivator. The Programme, which was taken over by the newly formed Rubber Industry Smallholders' Development Authority (RISDA) in 1972, supplied farmers with seedlings, technical advice, inspections and direct finance. Payments to compensate the cultivator for lost production until the new trees had matured were provided but were tied to performance standards supervised by the Replanting Office inspectors.

Wilder demonstrates that the replanting scheme – based on the principles of 'intensification', renewal and rehabilitation – was generally successful since it was a gradual, monitored, manageable programme dependent on negative feedback directly to the cultivator to ensure that any necessary adjustments were made. In addition, the decision to replant, based primarily on the ability of the smallholder to afford to remove the acreage of old trees from production, was taken by the farmer himself and implemented on a small piece of land of 1 to 5 acres. In its first twenty-five years of operation the majority of older or first generation rubber smallholdings had been replanted and the main objectives of the programme met. The replanting process worked with almost clinical, microscopic accuracy because of its small scale and intensely local interest.

On the other hand, the alternative of new block planting was a failure. It required an exceedingly cumbersome, lengthy sequence of administration and more intermediaries to handle the processes of site-selection, clearing and planting the new land, the recruitment of settlers or smallholders and supervision of maintenance. The project was larger scale with a new block consisting of 60 or more 5 to 6-acre lots planted with rubber by outside contractors. Overall, because the scheme relied on the local *penghulu* as the intermediary to gather information and transmit and interpret messages, implementation was too slow, field inspections inadequate, regulations too rigid, local cooperation and involvement patchy and government officials, without due regard for local circumstances, over-estimated the demand for new rubber land in Pahang (Wilder, 1982a: 160–164). Above all there was greater scope for conveying faulty information, and there was an assumption on the part of government development agents that the *penghulu* was the most effective and knowledgeable channel of communication while the *ketua kampung,* in closer contact with ordinary villagers, was likely to be too traditionalist and a hindrance to development, and in consequence was ignored. In reality inadequate and faulty information was gathered and in consequence too much land was allocated.

Wilder's finding was that where 'villagers' attitudes and decisions are treated as information relevant to the development process', then support was more likely to be forthcoming in contrast to those schemes, dependent on a bureaucratic process, in which villagers felt themselves to have been largely ignored (ibid.: 173). It seemed that in 1965–1966 the government had begun to recognize this shortcoming and to place more emphasis on the involvement of *ketua kampung* and villagers in the implementation of development programmes. Interestingly villagers were also increasingly aware of the need to organize themselves formally into associations and registered societies with committees to enable more effective interaction with outside bodies and to come to terms with a modernizing, developing, bureaucratizing state in which they were small players, but in which the major plank of the Malay-dominated government was to bring development and prosperity to the Malay peasantry (ibid.: 178–179). Wilder says:

> The point to be emphasized, I think, is how well aware the villagers are of the government's overall objectives and of certain of the formal means of attaining them through the formation of committees, action and pressure groups, and the like.
>
> (ibid.: 184)

Wilder's approach seems to be a logical development of the earlier studies of peasant communities in his attention both to social fields within and beyond the village, but he brings them within one conceptual field by the use of the concept of 'communication'.

The studies which emerged from the Firths' early interest in peasant economies certainly help draw our attention to the processes affecting village communities in a newly independent Malaysia, and along with various studies from American anthropologists in Thailand, Burma, Indonesia and the Philippines, confirm that early post-war anthropology had to move away from its preoccupation with the defined, self-contained, autonomous social and cultural unit. Nevertheless, the horizons of these anthropologists, using mainly functionalist, structural-functionalist and cultural analyses, usually only extended to the surrounding region or in rare cases to the nation–state; they continued to concentrate primarily on the local situation. They were also concerned most directly with the here and now rather than with the historical context of the societies under study. Something more seemed to be needed, and it was James Scott who from the 1970s began to examine the historical context of agrarian change and the political culture of small-scale cultivators in relation to the expanding power of the state, while neo-Marxist anthropologists analysed economic organization, class relations, conflict and exploitation in a nation–state and global context using concepts from the literature on imperialism, capitalism as a mode of production, and underdevelopment and dependency.

Scott and the moral economy of the peasant

Like Geertz's *Agricultural Involution* (1963a) and Hanks's *Rice and Man* (1972) (and see Chapters 3 and 7), Scott's *The Moral Economy of the Peasant* (1976) compiles and synthesizes extensive historical and numerical data available from the colonial period. It was during the rapid global expansion of capitalism and the colonial state in the nineteenth and early twentieth centuries that land tenure and land usage in much of South-East Asia were transformed, and this, in turn, dramatically altered the economic horizons of the land-dependent peasantry and began to establish the foundations of today's rural society. While it can be argued that Scott's thesis is not as original as those of Geertz and Hanks, given that the notion of, and indeed the term 'moral economy' is taken from E.P. Thompson's classic study of the English working class (1966), and the topic of peasant protest, within and beyond South-East Asia, is a well-worn one (see, for example, Moore, 1966; Wolf, 1969; Sartono, 1973; Sturtevant, 1976), it argues with a persuasiveness, lucidity and elegance at least equal to theirs. It also explores a rather different dimension of rural life; while Hanks paints a crisis-free picture of rice-growers in Thailand, and Geertz a crisis-coping one for Java, Scott mainly portrays the effectiveness or otherwise of crisis-prevention in Burma and Vietnam.

Scott starts from the material conditions of rural livelihood, specifically the characteristics of peasant subsistence economy, and links these with various social, cultural and technical arrangements designed to enhance the chances of meeting the basic material requirements of existence and lessening the risks of not meeting them or averting them altogether. He therefore identifies a crucial and over-riding concern for certain sectors of the peasantry in South-East Asia and elsewhere, and that is 'the desire for subsistence security' or alternatively 'the fear of dearth' (1976: vii, 6). This concern helps explain the 'safety-first principle' in agriculture and in related economic spheres; the adherence to a variety of local and trusted seeds and plants, the preference for consumable rather than commercial crops, the dependence on time-worn planting, sowing and cultivation methods, and the reliance on a variety of agricultural and non-agricultural activities in order to spread risks. The 'subsistence ethic' which comprises the moral principles of 'the right to subsistence' and 'the norm of reciprocity' also helps us understand various social arrangements and institutions and the standards by which behaviour is judged (ibid.: 167). Scott says: 'Patterns of reciprocity, forced generosity, communal land, and work-sharing helped to even out the inevitable troughs in a family's resources which might otherwise have thrown them below subsistence' (ibid.: 3). It should be noted that he warns against the notion of a rustic idyll, a too romantic view of the altruism and harmony of village life and the implied egalitarianism in social relationships (ibid.: 5), though he does emphasize reciprocity, cooperation, shared values, redistribution, altruism, welfarism, paternalism, anti- or non-market transactions, and actions to defend or restore the status quo, in short he presents a picture of village 'traditionalism' (Popkin, 1979: 5–17). We shall see in Chapter 6 how and why 'traditional' values and practices are constructed, recreated and transformed rather than their being fixed and immutable.

Scott draws on a wide range of literature from South-East Asia and elsewhere to construct his image of precapitalist rural society and his focus on security, redistributive mechanisms and risk insurance within the village echoes the work of Firth and his colleagues, to whom Scott refers explicitly in his text, and the studies, among others, of Geertz (1963a) on Java, Hanks (1972) and Moerman (1968a) on Central Thailand, and Takahashi (1969) on Central Luzon. Scott also acknowledges that his emphasis on subsistence economics applies generally and with much greater force to the 'poor peasant or tenant', to those 'with very low incomes, little land, large families, highly variable yields, and few outside opportunities' rather than the richer peasantry (1976: 25). Nevertheless, at times he does not appear to take sufficient account of class relationships in rural society, the tensions and conflicts to which these give rise, the implications of social inequality for power structures, leadership and political mobilization at the local level, and risk-taking and social mobility among the peasantry.

That having been said, Scott does draw attention to some very important features of village socio-economic and cultural organization, particularly with regard to the poor, and he throws considerable light on their responses to the penetration of the state and the market during the colonial period. Let us look in a little more detail at his findings. Using the examples of rural change and peasant protest in lowland Burma and Central Vietnam, Scott argues that peasant perceptions and their experiences of injustice and inequity were strengthened and exacerbated as the colonial state increased its presence in and its hold on rural communities in South-East Asia; the direct expression of this increasing control came in the form of fixed taxes (particularly head-taxes), fluctuating prices for primary commodities (specifically rice), land registration and its commoditization, landlordism, economic specialization and individualism, and class polarization. Scott's historical focus is captured appositely in the following quotation:

> The transformation of land and labor (that is, nature and human work) into commodities for sale had the most profound impact. Control of land increasingly passed out of the hands of villagers; cultivators progressively lost free usufruct rights and became tenants or agrarian wage laborers; the value of what was produced was increasingly gauged by the fluctuations of an impersonal market.
>
> (ibid.: 7)

175

What is more, the colonial state contributed to this process:

> Not only did it provide the legal and coercive machinery necessary to
> ensure that contracts were honored and the market economy retained,
> but the state was itself a claimant on peasant resources. Much of its
> administrative effort had been bent to enumerating and recording its
> subjects and their land for tax purposes.
>
> (ibid.: 8)

Scott analyses these processes in the context of British Lower Burma and French
Cochinchina and their expression in the so-called 'depression' or 'tax rebellions'
of 1930–1931 associated with the Saya San uprising in the Irrawaddy Delta and
the Nghe-An and Ha-Tinh revolts in Annam. Similarly Benedict Kerkvliet, in
his detailed study of the Huk unrest in Central Luzon which raged on and off
from the 1930s through to the 1950s, employs a 'moral economy' framework and
argues that '[a] major cause for the unrest was the dramatic deterioration of traditional ties between local elites and peasants' and the loss of the protection, sponsorship and financial assistance which those ties afforded (1977: 250).

Although Scott and Kerkvliet do identify some of the mainsprings of peasant
discontent, two important considerations in evaluating their work are, first, the
extent to which their findings are generalizable, especially with regard to their
concentration on poor peasants and tenants, and, second, the extent to which
their emphasis on 'traditional' values, behaviour and relationships based on the
principles of reciprocity and the right to subsistence capture appropriately the
nature of rural society in South-East Asia. One of the most incisive critiques of
the 'moral economists' is Samuel Popkin, another political scientist with historical and anthropological interests (1979). Popkin accepts that peasants are preoccupied with security and 'the constant threat of falling below the subsistence
level', indeed, some of his data support Scott's argument (ibid.: 5, 145–154,
156–157, 165, 182), but, contrary to Scott, he argues that the small-scale cultivator rather than being cooperative and altruistic is 'a rational problem-solver,
with a sense both of his own interests and of the need to bargain with others to
achieve mutually acceptable outcomes' (ibid.: ix). Thus, 'exchanges between
peasants are shaped and limited by conflicts between individual and group
benefits' (ibid.: 4). Popkin then sees individual farmers as rational, self-inter-
ested strategists, risk-takers and gamblers motivated by personal gain and applying 'investment logic' to short- and long-term as well as public and private
investments. He argues that traditional rural life was far from being rosy and
harmonious and instead welfare and insurance arrangements were imperfect and
limited, patrons were not essentially paternalistic, and village-based practices
and arrangements reinforced rather than levelled social inequalities. Furthermore, local farmers, particularly the better off among them, manipulated and
even rejected some colonial decrees in order to maintain former patterns of
inequality and exploitation. For Popkin, exposure to a money economy and

markets was not necessarily disadvantageous to the peasantry, nor could the desire to re-establish previous traditional institutions be the prime reason for the emergence of peasant movements during the colonial period.

What Popkin does demonstrate, in his use of examples of peasant responses to change in colonial Vietnam, is that Scott's framework does not apply to peasant society generally. It is much less relevant to those peasant-based movements which were forward-looking, well-organized and led, firmly established, institutionalized, supra-local and involving richer peasants and other members of the rural elite, and which, rather than constituting defensive and restorative actions in relation to 'traditional' socio-cultural values and practices sought to remake, transform or replace elements of the local social and cultural order, to grasp the new opportunities on offer and to engage with capitalism and the market (ibid.: 17–31).

Scott is also rightly critical of certain premises of Marxist theories with regard to exploitation and the appropriation of surplus value, though he perhaps understates the subjective and dynamic elements in Marx's labour theory of value. Scott himself uses concepts which are part of the stock-in-trade of Marxist-oriented social scientists; these include 'class', 'proletariat', 'feudalism' and 'capitalism', and he isolates and describes particular rural and urban classes including the peasant classes (poor, middle and rich, tenants and sharecroppers), landholders and money-lenders, and rural wage labourers. Unfortunately his use of these terms is rather imprecise so that at times the peasantry appears as a unitary class and at other times as differentiated into several classes. His concepts of feudalism and the transition from a feudal to a capitalist order are also problematical and too broadly sketched; overall Scott's notion of 'feudalism' appears to refer to an assumed established traditional order in the various lowland rice-growing areas of South-East Asia. Yet it is clear that, in certain parts of the region, this 'feudal' order based on landed property was itself primarily the product of colonial intervention, and that precolonial society was not one constituted by private property, large estates or fiefs and the judicial and administrative structure of the European manorial system. Furthermore, social, economic and political relations were rather variable in different parts of the region and it is difficult to lump them together as 'traditional' or 'feudal' in order to embrace such pioneer or frontier areas as Lower Burma and Cochinchina (see King, 1978: 131–141).

Nevertheless, an important contribution of Scott's work was that it began to locate rural cultivators in a broader historical, socio-economic and political context and it attempted to understand the moral and cultural dimension of peasant communities and their responses to change in terms of particular economic imperatives. The problems with his study were that the concept of 'moral economy' applied with more force to certain categories of peasant and to certain kinds of peasant behaviour and not to others and that his particular use of such categories as 'feudalism' and 'capitalism' resulted in a misleading characterization of certain processes of change affecting South-East Asian rural communities from the later nineteenth century onwards. It did not take sufficient account of the fact that what appear to be 'traditional' social, economic, political and cultural forms may well be relatively recent creations of specific historical circumstances under colonialism (see Chapter 6). Let us now turn to Marxist-influenced perspectives to evaluate their contribution to the study of rural social transformations, specifically with regard to such concepts as class.

Indonesian peasants and Kahn

In searching for perspectives and paradigms which might equip them with the necessary analytical tools to address issues of social change and locate peasants and tribes not only within the nation–state but also within a wider global economic and political system, some anthropologists embraced more radical frameworks. From the 1960s onwards this comprised a direct attack on the ideas and methods of economic anthropology. The inspiration came from two streams of French Marxism, first Claude Meillasoux's much more empirical approach to understanding small-scale, pre- or non-capitalist economic organizations ('economic types' as he calls them) and the relevance of a reformulated Marxism for this, and, second, Maurice Godelier's more theoretical combination of Marxism and Lévi-Straussian structuralism (Bloch, 1975). There were then attempts to synthesize some of these ideas in the work of Emmanuel Terray and Pierre-Philippe Rey, though much of French Marxism was also influenced by Louis Althusser's rethinking of Marx's historical materialism and his use of the analytical categories, 'mode of production' and 'social formation'. In addressing the interrelationships between small-scale societies and wider systems, the anthropology of South-East Asia does not provide many examples of neo-Marxist and political economy analyses, though there are certainly some excellent examples of this genre. We have already referred to Jonathan Friedman's work on Highland Burma in this connection in Chapter 4, and we shall shortly examine the work of Joel Kahn. These studies in turn complemented an increasing interest among political economists and sociologists in the work of André Gunder Frank and others on under development and dependency and the consequences for the nation–states of South-East Asia of their integration into a global economic and political system (Higgott and Robison, 1985; Clammer, 1985a).

It must be said from the outset that there was not one agreed Marxist position in anthropology, rather, there were several Marxisms, sometimes arguing very fine points of theory and emphasis. We do not have the space to consider the details of the arguments here, but the development of and debates within Marxist anthropology up to the end of the 1970s, when it was at its most popular, have been nicely summarized by Kahn and Llobera (1981) in a general theoretical paper and by Clammer (1985a) specifically in relation to Asian material. However, certain themes or elements are common to all. There is an emphasis on the importance of historical analysis, on social change and on understanding relationships of inequality (social class), and relations of exploitation and conflict between groups which have different material interests and occupy different positions with regard to property, exchange and the economy. There is a concern to examine and understand, in non-capitalist societies, 'modes of production', which comprise the forces of production (such as technology and the environment) and the social relations of production including the division of labour, and how these interconnect with other dimensions of society such as kinship, descent and religion. One central focus is therefore on what Firth refers to as peasant economic organization. Another interest is the analysis of the ways in which different modes of production (for example, capitalism and petty commodity production) interrelate and the consequences of these interactions in an overall society or 'social formation'. An important conclusion from many different Marxist analyses of non-capitalist societies is that once one understands the material conditions of existence ('the economic infrastructure'), specifically the importance and the nature of labour or work, then one recognizes the ideological, or some might say 'illusory' character of such institutions as religion, ethnicity, politics and kinship, or alternatively the ways in which kinship relations, for example, function as relations of production (Kahn, 1978). Furthermore, Marxist anthropology has also helped demonstrate how production is variously represented and also mis-represented culturally in different societies (Bloch, 1975: xiii–xiv).

Where there is disagreement between Marxist and non-Marxist anthropology, and what is emphasized firmly by Raymond Firth in his critical commentary on Marxist anthropology is the degree of primacy that should be given to work, labour and production (1975: 34–47), and Firth also addresses Marx's too simple and sketchy model of primitive society or primitive communalism. Firth argues that '[o]ne has as much right to assert that human culture was born with symbolization and with exchange . . . as with labour' (ibid.: 34). There is much else which Firth criticizes in Marx's work, principally from his conventional or 'liberal' economics perspective, but he also recognizes the analytical value of certain Marxist ideas. He notes that, in non-capitalist or non-Western societies, it is partly because of the processes of radical social change set in train from the colonial period, the expansion of market relations, the development of wage labour and the emergence of new social classes and class conflict that Marx's ideas have acquired a greater salience in anthropology (ibid.: 31). Of special interest to our discussion in this chapter is that Firth emphasizes the relevance of Marxist theories for the study of peasant societies and economies (ibid.: 49), and the 'set of hypotheses' about social relations and particularly about social change. He draws attention to

> the basic significance of economic factors, especially production relations; the relations to structures of power; the formation of classes and the opposition of their interests; the socially relative character of ideologies; the conditioning force of a system upon individual members of it.
>
> (ibid.: 52–53)

For a contrasting approach from that of Firth to the study of social relations among Malays, Halim Salleh's neo-Marxist analysis of a residential ward of Kota Bharu, Kelantan, provides an excellent example (1981). He examines the change from a social hierarchy based on notions of royalness (*daulat*) to capitalist relationships in which inequality and exploitation are still expressed in non-capitalist status terms to do with honour and respect (ibid.: 151ff.).

Let us now turn to Joel Kahn's work on Indonesia (1974, 1975, 1978, 1980, 1981) to establish how a neo-Marxist frame of reference has been employed to understand the structure and changes in the matrilineal Minangkabau society of West Sumatra, and broader transformations in Indonesia from the beginnings of Dutch contacts with the East Indies in the seventeenth century. Kahn, a student of Maurice Bloch, did fieldwork in 1970–1972 in the highland district of Agam with its capital at Bukit Tinggi. Kahn is especially concerned to place the Minangkabau in a historical context, as well as in the wider Indonesian society, or 'social formation' as he calls it (1974), and 'to assess the degree to which conditions in West Sumatra are and have been the product of the integration of the region into a world capitalist system' (1980: 2). His emphasis therefore is rather different from the studies of Firth and his colleagues both in historical depth and socio-spatial breadth.

Kahn makes reference to other studies of peasant socio-economic organization in South-East Asia, and in an earlier article takes issue with some of Swift's observations (1975: 153). With regard to Swift's comment on the Malays of Jelebu in Peninsular Malaysia to the effect that their economy was small in scale (1965: 26), Kahn suggests that, though this was indeed the case, its scale was not fixed; it varied, or rather developed cyclically, according to specific historical circumstances, but there was no inevitability about the repetition of cycles (1975: 138; 1980: 190). Nor, Kahn suggests, is Swift able to explain satisfactorily why certain economies remain small in scale, specifically with reference to the Minangkabau of West Sumatra, other than to suggest that it has something to do with personality types (fatalism), cultural drives (nurtured in childhood) and individual motivation. Swift argues, for example, that the Minangkabau were individualists oriented to short-termism and therefore best suited to petty trading and small-scale operations (Swift, 1971: 263–267; 1965: 170). Kahn, on the other hand, searches for an explanation in the structure of changing economic relations both within the local region and beyond (1980: 184–199). He also argues that the popular and established conception of a 'traditional', culturally unique matrilineal Minangkabau society 'disintegrating' in the face of a Western market economy and nationalist politics, and moving towards 'modernity' is misleading because what are perceived to be 'traditional' social and cultural features, both by present-day Minangkabau and several outside observers, have been created and shaped by 'specific forms of European domination which evolved from the seventeenth century onward' (ibid.: 6–7, 151–171; 1975: 147–151). Up to the late nineteenth century Dutch interests in the East Indies were predominantly mercantile and their position in commerce and production was secured by establishing monopolies and fixed exchange rates, extracting tribute from local political allies, imposing controls and quotas on production of such items as spices, instituting tax-farming, and introducing forced or 'servile' labour for the cultivation of sugar and coffee (1981: 185–213). The general process of controlling labour was one which Kahn terms 'peripheralisation' (ibid.: 197–198), but the key issue is that the various forms of production were non-capitalist, though interlinked with a world market in commodities. These forms, he argues, were also the result of class struggles between merchants, landowners/aristocracies and direct producers (ibid.: 208–211).

Kahn's focus is the local Minangkabau blacksmithing industry, concentrated in one of the sections of the community or township (*nagari*) of Sungai Puar in highland West Sumatra. It was here that metal goods (axes, sickles, hoes, ploughs, machetes, knives) were forged and finished from scrap steel in small workshops (*apa basi*) to supply a wider Sumatran market. Each forge usually specialized in a particular type of ware; it had a head smith (*nangkodoh*) who owned and managed the operation, bought in the raw materials and sold the finished products. He was simultaneously the owner of the means of production, the manager and a worker; he employed wage-labourers and extracted a small surplus from the enterprise (1975: 142). In this regard he was analogous to Firth's lift-net expert in Kelantan. Workshops and earned property were usually inherited in the male line while rice-lands, houses and house-plots were considered to be ancestral property and usually passed down through matrilineal groups. Smithing was labour-intensive, in other words there was a relatively large contribution of 'living labour' to the value of the final product; it operated at a low level of technological development (productive forces), with limited capital accumulation and 'atomistic', individual productive units; there was little cooperation or rationalization above the *apa* level and therefore considerable duplication of activities (ibid.: 140–141; 1980: 85ff.). The units comprised from one smith, usually knife-makers, up to four in such operations as the forging of hoes and axes. The blacksmithing section of Sungai Puar had a mixed economy, not only comprising blacksmiths, but also small traders, merchants, shopkeepers, carpenters, seamstresses, farmers and government employees (1975: 138). Many young villagers especially aspired to jobs in government service or in the armed forces (1980: 103).

Kahn characterizes blacksmithing as a form of peasant economic activity which he refers to as 'petty commodity production' (ibid.: 4), and like Firth's application of the notion of 'peasant' to non-agricultural activities, Kahn too proposes that artisanal, small-scale production (and indeed exchange) of commodities can also be seen as 'peasant-like'. However, he argues that the concept of a peasantry should not lead us to assume that it is some sort of unchanging or fixed type or a universal evolutionary stage; instead the task is to determine how peasant economic forms emerge and are sustained, and how processes of 'peasantization' operate. He suggests that economic differentiation of peasantries, class polarization, and capitalist forms of production are not the necessary results of the expansion of capitalism and its incorporation of non-capitalist economies; in certain circumstances petty commodity production and individual enterprises can emerge (a process of 'peasantization') and continue as the predominant form of economic activity under the umbrella of capitalism. What is more, various forms of subsistence production can also be sustained. Indeed, in Minangkabau the result of the commoditization of land, labour and products during the late Dutch colonial period, particularly from the 1870s onwards with the shift in emphasis from mercantile to large-scale corporate and finance capitalism and the dismantling of the Cultivation System, was the increasing predominance of petty commodity production (ibid.: 179ff.). In addition, the Dutch created a commercial-cum-political elite closely associated with the colonial state and European economic activities (ibid.: 172). Kahn draws attention to a similar process of 'peasantization' identified by Geertz in the context of agricultural involution, though he also notes that several critics of Geertz have pointed to the opposite trend of social and economic differentiation in Java. We have also seen that, among rural Malay communities in Peninsular Malaysia, the Firths, Husin Ali and Swift all pointed to similar processes of capital accumulation, and the emergence of social classes (ibid.: 126–127; and see Kahn's own references to the unequal distribution of land in Minangkabau, and the existence of wage labour, share-cropping and renting, ibid.: 66–74).

In response, Kahn proposes, on the basis of his own findings in the Sumatran province as a whole and indeed in parts of Peninsular Malaysia, that differentiation is not inevitable and that wage labour and new technologies are often deployed to 'maintain a viable peasant existence' (1985: 88); that, though differentiation does take place in agriculture, its scale and degree may not be as significant as class formation outside the peasant sector; Kahn says for Indonesia as a whole that 'there are vast class differentials between peasant producers and the upper reaches of the bureaucracy, armed forces, owners of plantations and those involved in the largely foreign-controlled capitalist sector'; that, even where there is differentiation there is still evidence of the importance of the small individual enterprise; and that, finally, processes of differentiation and peasantization are historically specific and may operate in a cyclical and not a unilinear fashion (1980: 128). We can agree with Kahn that class differences among peasants are relatively modest when compared with the substantial differences between peasants and those beyond the village. But this should not cause us to lose sight of the fact that, within rural South-East Asian societies, ownership of even 3 to 5 hectares of land, which is often classified as a 'large' farm in various parts of the region, does provide significant surpluses, enables the employment of wage labour, and opens access to locally influential and powerful positions (White, 1989: 25). It is often these farmers who are also the crucial political allies and brokers of higher level political actors and bureaucrats in their relations with the rural majority. Therefore, in rural terms the unequal distribution of land and life-chances are still considerable and they do not depend solely on landownership and the distribution of rights in land.

Kahn attempts to explain why Minangkabau blacksmiths had been unable to increase the scale of their operations and their profitability and productivity. He examines the characteristics of the industry itself but more importantly he relates the petty commodity sector both to the capitalist sector and ultimately to the world economy, and to what he refers to as 'a form of lineage production' (i.e. primarily irrigated rice agriculture). Kahn notes specifically that black-smiths (as well as carpenters and merchants) depended both on the national and international economy to sell their goods, while 'most families are at the same time subsistence cultivators *and* commodity producers' (1980: 122). In other words, Kahn analyses the interrelationships of different modes of produc-tion within what he calls the 'Indonesian social formation', and the contradic-tions between the forces and relations of production. For example, an important advantage for a blacksmith was to have access to land and to subsistence rice production: '[a] constant supply of rice makes it relatively easy for an entrepre-neur to keep the financing of his enterprise separate from the consumption demands of his own family ... [and] land can act as a form of insurance' (ibid.: 122). Furthermore, a man's class position in relation to commodity production 'seems to be affected by the amount of land to which he has access through either his wife or his own family of origin' (ibid.: 122).

The small size of the operation, of course, meant that, given the amount of capital which the *nangkodoh* had at his disposal and the risks he carried, it was difficult to increase the capacity and workforce of the operation appreciably, and, if he did reduce the share of income allotted to the workers he would have found it difficult to keep his workforce (1975: 144). The labour supply was simply not available in sufficient quantities to attract capital investment. Small improvements in the quality of the goods, though technically feasible, would not have commanded an increased price sufficient to warrant the costs of the necessary investment. The market price which smiths could have charged for their goods was low, and Kahn suggests that this was because it was determined by the price of imported metal goods which sold at prices 10 to 15 per cent above domestically manufactured goods. In other words, the market and prices for Minangkabau metal goods were affected by the incorporation of local black-smiths as small-scale, low-value, low-quality producers into a world capitalist market for steel products (ibid.: 145). Petty commodity production was also influenced by the level of production and the price of the basic foodstuff, rice. Kahn demonstrates from the Dutch colonial period onwards that when there was a rise in world commodity prices with stable rice prices, there was an increase in the scale of blacksmithing and other forms of commodity produc-tion; additional labour was then drawn into petty commodity production from rice agriculture; in consequence there was a decrease in efficiency and produc-tion in the rice sector which resulted in an increase in rice prices; this put pres-sure on wage levels and the petty commodity sector, and in turn precipitated a decrease in the size of productive units and their individualization (ibid.: 150–154).

Kahn also points to a brief period in the late 1950s and early 1960s in Indonesia when there was a resurgence in the blacksmithing sector. There was evidence of increasing capital investment, mechanization, the growth of larger factory-type productive units, and the entry into the industry of investors. This coincided with Sukarno's Guided Democracy, nationalist economic policies, the nationalization of foreign-owned enterprises, a partial Indonesian withdrawal from the world economy and a consequent decline in imported goods. These changes had the effect of raising prices for various commodities and opening up a larger domestic market for local blacksmiths. However, with the hyper-inflation of the 1960s which included a dramatic rise in rice prices, and the post-Sukarno reorientation of economic policies under Suharto's New Order with the re-integration of Indonesia into the world economy, blacksmithing in Minangkabau returned to earlier petty commodity forms with the collapse of larger-scale units and the re-emergence of individual enterprises (1980: 186–199).

The importance of Kahn's contribution to our understanding of peasant economies lies especially in his attention to the ways in which national and international economic forces affect economic activities and organization at the local level. However, his acknowledgement of the problematical nature of the category 'peasant' at times leaves us a little unclear about what it comprises. For Kahn it appears to be equivalent to rural petty commodity production so that peasants are seen as a specific rural detachment of the urban 'petite bourgeoisie'. Yet he also refers in Minangkabau to 'peasant agriculture' and 'peasant farms' and states that farming is 'truly the work of peasants' (ibid.: 103), and in a subsequent paper examines the movement of peasants into petty commodity production (1982). However, rice agriculture in the district of Agam was devoted to subsistence production, and though the subsistence sector, dominated by relations of kinship and marriage, was intimately interrelated with blacksmithing, there is a degree of uncertainty in Kahn's work whether the concept of a 'peasantry' refers only to rural petty commodity production as a distinctive mode of production, or to an economic structure which embraces and unites both small-scale subsistence and commodity production. In another paper Kahn appears to favour the latter definition (1978: 113–114). It is clear that Clammer also sees the notion of petty commodity production and its relationship to the definition of a peasant economy as problematical in that he defines a peasant mode of production not in terms of petty commodity production as such but primarily with reference to the domestic family farm as a small-scale unit of production, consumption and ownership (1985a: 140–141, 148).

Another difficulty is in Kahn's conception of 'class'. He shows that while there were wealth differences among Minangkabau producers, petty commodity production was characterized by 'an economic equality among economically independent entrepreneurs' since 'no one is tied by relations of property to another' (1980: 89). Nevertheless, Kahn does delineate social classes primarily in terms of productive relations, though he notes at one point that 'class differentiation is partly the result of age' (ibid.: 92). In blacksmithing there were six 'class' positions: a head blacksmith employing four to five labourers, a head smith with two to three labourers, an independent producer, a wage worker, a worker with close kinsman, and a wage worker with a large enterprise (ibid.: 93). He notes that a head smith 'can extract a slight surplus from his labourers' (ibid.: 91), and elsewhere in his analysis he collapses 'employers of labour' into one upper category (ibid.: 119). His main scheme is a class categorization of men only. Most women were located in the subsistence sector, but, in the commodity sector, there were seamstresses and women mat-makers who were mainly tied into larger enterprises as wage-workers (ibid.: 110). Kahn also refers, at another point, to 'white collar workers' as a class (ibid.: 124–125), and then 'peasants' as a class (ibid.: 128, 129) in relation to classes beyond the local area which comprised the upper echelons of the bureaucracy and the armed forces, as well as plantation owners and 'varied factions of the international bourgeoisie' (ibid.: 128, 211). There does seem to be a difficulty for Kahn in defining classes in a situation in which there was a quite marked gender division of labour and where a subsistence sector was linked to (and sustained by) a petty commodity sector and in turn to a national and international capitalist economy. We shall see below just how fluid class relations can be in the work of those who have used the concept of agrarian differentiation. But let us briefly turn to another study of Indonesian social change which demonstrates even more dramatically the effects of the penetration of capitalism on rural societies and their incorporation into a global economy as wage-workers.

From farmers to mine-workers in Indonesia

Using perspectives from underdevelopment and world-systems writers such as André Gunder Frank and Immanuel Wallerstein combined with neo-Marxist anthropology, Kathryn Robinson examines what happened when a foreign-owned nickel mining and processing operation, P. T. Inco (International Nickel of Canada), was established in central Sulawesi on the agricultural land of the Torajan highland village of Soroako and incorporated the village into a new mining township called Desa Nikkel ('Nickel Village') (1986). She carried out research in this Indonesian mining town in 1977–1979 and for two months in December 1980 to January 1981. The title of her book *Stepchildren of Progress* 'derives from the evaluation the Soroakans make of the new order' (ibid.: xiii); they considered themselves to have been marginalized by the mining enterprise and rather than deriving real benefits from it, which they felt was their due as the original 'children' of the region, they were 'pushed aside', and treated like 'stepchildren' while outsiders and newcomers reaped the rewards (ibid.: 15). The region saw a large influx of immigrant workers along with expatriate, mostly Canadian, Australian, Filipino and Korean personnel, and what was originally a rural community of some 1,000 people was transformed into a bustling multi-ethnic mining town with about 8,000 residents.

We have already seen how the influence of the outside world has impinged upon fishing communities, peasant cultivators, and petty commodity producers in Malaysia and Indonesia up to the 1970s. In the case of Soroako, however, the changes were rapid and dramatic when much of the village rice land was appropriated, with compensation, by the Indonesian government in 1972 for the construction of the plant and township and, by 1978, a multinational mining company was in full production (ibid.: 102–103). Robinson shows how capitalist relations of production had transformed previously subsistence Muslim rice cultivators, lake fishermen and forest gatherers and hunters into irregularly employed, low-paid, unskilled wage-labourers for the company, and how the Soroakans attempted to make sense of and respond to their dispossession. In contrast to Kahn's Minangkabau petty commodity producers, the majority of Soroakans, who prior to the project had been self-sufficient in rice, lost their means of production. Nevertheless, this proletarianization was the culmination of a long period of gradual incorporation into the world economy which really commenced during the second half of the nineteenth century when the Dutch opened up central Sulawesi to trade (ibid.: 70–81); there were inequalities in land ownership and wealth in Soroako prior to the commencement of mining and a small group of large landowners who were also involved in external trade in forest products (ibid.: 122–123, 130–131).

Most Soroakans as 'semi-proletarians' depended primarily on the company for their livelihoods, but, given the intermittent and unstable nature of their employment, fluctuating in response to the world market for nickel, about one-third of villagers continued to derive their main income from agriculture. However, the terms and conditions of agriculture and where it could be undertaken were also determined to a large extent by the presence of the mining company and its domination of the local economy. In addition to direct employment in mining and processing, most of the other economic activities in the area had been generated by the presence of the company, and some Soroakans had become involved in the provision of services, particularly the sale of food, to the company and its employees (ibid.: 153–155). Robinson examines class relations in the township determined principally by the company's categorization of its staff into professional and managerial (senior and junior) positions (senior positions were mainly occupied by expatriates and junior positions by Indonesians), skilled Indonesian workers (foremen, skilled tradesmen, nurses and teachers), and unskilled labourers (manual workers and machine operators) (ibid.: 21–24). This differentiation was also expressed in residential terms, in that different categories of staff, excluding unskilled labourers, had different company housing allocated to them in different parts of the township, while the approximately 1,000 Soroakans continued to live nearby in their traditional wooden stilted houses, and immigrant unskilled labour occupied dwellings adjacent to the established village (ibid.: 36–37). The majority of

Soroakans were employed by the company as unskilled labourers, though there were a few who were skilled workers.

Robinson shows how the introduction of wage labour, including the increasing commoditization of goods and services in Soroako, affected a whole range of social relationships, separating work from home, transforming gender, kinship and status relations and encouraging a consumerist ethos. The new class structure based primarily on capitalist production was also expressed in racial and ethnic terms in that expatriates – 'Whites' – occupied the higher echelons of the company hierarchy and the Indonesians the lower positions. The reasons given for this differentiation by expatriate managers were often phrased in racial terms (ibid.: 262–263), while the Indonesians made distinctions among themselves on the basis of assumed differences in socio-cultural identities reinforced by a degree of residential segregation (ibid.: 263ff.). The Soroakans and other workers from Sulawesi comprised the majority of unskilled workers, while Indonesians from West Java and Sumatra were concentrated at the higher skilled and management levels. Robinson identified an increase in the consciousness of 'being Soroakan' among the local indigenous population under threat from outsiders and their distinction between themselves and immigrants, though many of them shared the same class position as unskilled workers.

There is certainly much of value in Robinson's and indeed Kahn's work, although the neo-Marxist and underdevelopment paradigms which they and others have used, have generally gone out of fashion. Kahn himself, as we shall see in Chapter 6, while retaining some interest in 'peasants' has moved increasingly to a concern with cultural politics, globalization and postcolonial theory (1993, 1995). Nevertheless, neo-Marxist analyses have drawn our attention to the ways in which 'peasantries' have been created, sustained and transformed, the importance of historical analysis, the interrelationships between different kinds of economic system and how small-scale societies are affected by the wider systems of which they are a part. Robinson says that the process of capitalist expansion 'has been characterised by increasing loss of community autonomy and increasing dependence on economic relations with the world outside the village' (1986: 288).

Agrarian differentiation

A field of research which emerged at least in part from neo-Marxist and underdevelopment approaches was the study of the processes, causes, mechanisms and indicators of rural change, or 'agrarian differentiation', in the context of wider political and economic systems, and how these wider forces shape and are shaped by local processes (Hart, 1986: xv). It is exemplified in the work of Gillian Hart, Benjamin White and Andrew Turton among others, and brings together the multidisciplinary expertise of anthropologists, rural sociologists, agricultural economists and economic historians. They have focused on lowland rice-growing societies of South-East Asia, particularly in the context of the

Green Revolution and the introduction of high-yielding rice varieties and its associated technology into irrigated rice cultivation. The theme of the interaction between local and wider processes has been sustained in this literature as well as an interest in the exploration of the category 'peasant society and economy'. The analytical categories used are not essentially Marxist ones (such as modes of production and their articulation, social formation, forces and relations of production), but as in the neo-Marxist literature, the emphases are on understanding social change, the changing relations between groups in the control of labour and resources (as in land accumulation and dispossession), economic exploitation and the appropriation of surpluses, processes of capital formation, local struggles, dissent and everyday resistance, and the action of the state (Hart *et al.*, 1989; Turton, 1989b: 70–72).

The importance of 'the exercise of power at different levels of society' and in different historical contexts is seen to be a key mechanism by which the local is connected to the larger system (Hart *et al.*, 1989: xiv), often through forms of patronage between those at the higher levels of the state apparatus and 'dominant rural groups' (ibid.: 3). There is also an interest in the ways in which technological development and commercialization interact with power structures so that it is not just a matter of the expansion of the commodity economy but also the differing ways in which the state (comprising a hybrid mix of different interest groups such as high-level military personnel, bureaucrats, politicians, capitalists) has sought to exercise control over rural populations in order, for example, to prevent their political mobilization in anti-government movements and to secure supplies of essential foodstuffs and rural commodities for export (ibid.: 2). An important mechanism to achieve these aims, though it varies in content and form between different South-East Asian countries, is to form alliances with rural elites who 'become, in essence, political and economic agents of the state in the countryside and are co-opted into the larger structure of power as preferred but dependent clients' (Hart, 1989: 33).

Turton refers to the main rural and subdistrict beneficiaries of state support and largesse as 'local powers' (1989a: 66–67; 1989b: 70–97). However, he notes that it is difficult to make a clear distinction between 'a rural sector' and a 'higher level' district, provincial and regional sector since alliances are formed across these boundaries (1989b: 81). Like some of the LSE peasant studies and Kahn's work, Turton, in his studies on rural Thailand, identifies a small minority of villagers who were 'well-to-do' and had greater control over resources, prestige and power than others, though they were not an entirely closed group, and some previously wealthy households had not managed to maintain their position. Rather than a 'peasant elite', Turton refers to them as a 'village-level upper stratum', which was closely intertwined with a 'supra-village sector' (ibid.: 84). They included 'larger landowners, commodity dealers, shopkeepers, village officials, some teachers, rice millers, moneylenders, owners of small-scale transport and machinery, [and] large-scale employers of wage labor'; usually various of these roles were combined in the same household (ibid.: 82). This stratum linked other villagers to the state and market beyond and took advantage of their position to secure state benefits in the form of credit and agricultural inputs as well as various payments for official duties, political handouts, and preferential access to education, health and office. They were involved in both capitalist relationships within and beyond the village and more 'traditional' kinds of patronage. Crucially they were linked to 'district level' bureaucrats and capitalists. They also exercised power and influence, as clients of the state in such organizations as the subdistrict council through which funds for local development projects began to be channelled from 1975, agricultural coopera-tives and Farmers' Groups handling rural credit schemes in particular, and various local militia, volunteer defence forces and Village Scouts which per-formed local intelligence gathering, surveillance, security and ideological roles (ibid.: 91–93). In Thailand the rather more loose and less centralized state bureaucracy gave village leaders room for manoeuvre and it required state repre-sentatives to invest considerable resources and time in their recruitment and retention (Hart, 1989: 33–36).

In the studies by Hart and others on other countries in the region, a village upper stratum can also be identified, but there are considerable differences between them in their relationships with the state. In Suharto's Indonesia, for example, the highly centralized military–bureaucratic state structure resulted in the village elite being incorporated as minor state functionaries; this was com-bined with a higher level of repression and control of the rural masses in con-trast to Thailand. In Malaysia, on the other hand, the UMNO-dominated state had concentrated on providing resources (fertilizer, rice price support, irrigation technology) to those village leaders willing to support the government against the orthodox Islamic opposition of PAS, thereby dividing the rural population politically and economically; various benefits had also been spread rather more widely to ordinary rice producers, though, in the large irrigated rice-growing schemes, the introduction of mechanization in broadcast sowing and harvesting meant that much labour (and therefore political support) was displaced and the need for large landowners to cultivate patron–client relations with those with little or no land had decreased.

In the Philippines under President Marcos, the power of the established landowners who constituted a large, mainly town-based landed oligarchy was affected by the Marcos land reform programme, but instead they were given 'preferential access' to various commercial opportunities in managing rural credit programmes and rice processing and marketing operations. Village-level leaders were provided with certain of the benefits from the Green Revolution, and even small peasants had access to state-subsidized credit (Hart, 1989: 40–46). However, the economic crisis in the Philippines under Marcos meant that rural capitalists with resources to invest shied away from any direct involvement in rice production, given low rice prices and low profitability, and rice producers, though not necessarily losing their land, had to give up more of their rice crop to their creditors. Fegan suggests, therefore, that it is likely that the smallholding farmer will continue as an important unit in rice cultivation (1989: 159ff.).

Gillian Hart and her colleagues explicitly draw attention to the perceived shortcomings in the neo-Marxist literature, specifically the lack of adequate empirical material to support their theoretical formulations, the increasingly involuted debates about the definition of capitalism and the nature of the inter-relationship of other modes of production with it, and the generally uncritical transplantation of European models (particularly in relation to Russian and East European peasantries) to non-Western cases on the assumption that there is a universal form of agrarian differentiation (Hart et al., 1989: 2; White, 1989: 15–30). In contrast the proposal is not for theoretical sophistication but for flexibility and openness in analysing and understanding concrete local situations, for not formulating general laws of change, and for appreciating that the state is not a monolithic entity serving a particular class interest or pursuing a coherent set of policies; its intervention in the countryside varies historically and between countries. The diversity in the cases from Thailand, the Philippines, Malaysia and Indonesia is considerable as we have seen, but echoing the findings of Kahn earlier, the authors draw attention to the persistence of 'petty production' and the small or middling family-owned or tenanted farm, and also the diversification of activities into non-agricultural pursuits (Hart et al., 1989: 9; Turton, 1989a: 53, 57–58). The most dramatic example of diversification has been the large outflow of Philippine labour to other parts of the world in tourism-related activities, construction work and domestic employment. Another interesting development in the countryside of Java and Thailand has also been the creation by landlords of permanent tied-worker contracts providing for more secure employment and generally a higher annual income for a group of the landless to the exclusion of others who have to endure much more insecure, casual arrangements (Hart, 1989: 36–40). The results of this have been to create divisions among rural labourers, and to encourage hard work, reliability and discipline among tied-workers in case they lose their privileged status.

The studies by Hart, Turton and others reveal the complexity of changing social, economic and political relations between individuals and groups, given that an individual and his/her household might well be involved in a range of activities – among them, working their own land, renting or share-cropping land of another owner, hiring labour, on-farm or off-farm wage-labouring, or petty trading. With the commercialization of agriculture and the penetration of capital there has not been a general polarization into large farmer-manager capitalists and landless tenants and wage-labourers in South-East Asia, rather, there has been the emergence of a range of different groupings with different relationships to production and exchange. Nevertheless, in all the four countries under study there is still concentration of land and the presence of a significant level of landlessness, poverty, tenancy and wage-labouring, and there are usually quite marked regional disparities between more and less prosperous communities. Hart and her colleagues also question the utility of such units of analysis as households and villages or communities in that the household is itself composed of individuals who have different production and consumption relations with each other (especially based on gender and age), and the mobility of capital and labour extends beyond the village (see, for example, White, 1989: 21–23).

An important conclusion, which throws into relief the considerable changes which have taken place among peasant communities in South-East Asia, particularly during the past half century and since the studies undertaken by the Firths, is that even the independent rural producer, let alone the tenant and agricultural labourer, has become more and more dependent. As Turton notes, in his examination of the Thai peasantry, small owner-producers have been brought into wider circuits of commodity exchange on which they have become reliant to sustain their livelihoods. Therefore, although they own their means of production, specifically land, and they deploy their own labour to work it, their ability to control their own social and economic lives has been drastically reduced. Those outside the production process, who control markets, prices, agricultural processing, storage, transport, finance, technical inputs and information, have rendered the small farmer as 'wage-labour equivalent producers of surplus value' (1989b: 74–75). The concept of a 'small farmer' or 'peasant producer' also conceals a high degree of diversity in the life chances of those so designated, and for many of them the precariousness of their situation (ibid.: 76–79). What is more, the penetration of the state and the market, and especially the incorporation of rural producers into state-generated development programmes, has created increasingly complex social arrangements. Again as Turton says, 'many new divisions have been created, by branch of production, forms of labor process, etc., which fragment and cross-cut lines of class, community, and household' (ibid.: 75). In this situation, and despite attempts by both earlier functionalist anthropologists and neo-Marxist scholars of peasant societies to delineate social classes, Turton suggests that class formation and the consciousness of class interests are 'in an inchoate and fluid state' (ibid.). Other non-class or non-class specific factors, which neo-Marxist analysts have tended to consign to the ideological or superstructural – national, regional, local, personal and religious loyalties – may also play a significant role in social interaction and social arrangements.

Conclusion

In considering this literature on peasantries it therefore makes less sense to consider local communities as bounded units. We have seen the gradual widening of the perspectives and scope of anthropologists and other anthropologically oriented social scientists like Scott as they have attempted to come to terms with the issue of 'incorporation' – the involvement of small-scale communities in forces and processes not only of regional and national scope but of global import. In this chapter we have tended to concentrate on economic organization and change and the values (or 'morality') and behaviour associated with it. In the next chapter we shall see a similar situation in anthropological studies of ethnicity and identity as anthropologists have moved increasingly from a concern with specific and local identities and ethnicities to the examination of them in terms of nation-building and globalization, processes associated with such agents as a supranational media and mass tourism.

Plate 1 Tropical rainforest, Central Kalimantan

Source: courtesy V.T. King

Plate 2 Malay market scene, Bandar Sri Aman, Sarawak, Malaysia
Source: courtesy V.T. King

Plate 3 Malay fishing village, Mersing, Peninsular Malaysia

Source: courtesy V.T. King

Plate 4 Iban longhouse, Upper Embaloh, West Kalimantan, Indonesia

Source: courtesy V.T. King

Plate 5 State mosque, Kota Kinabalu, Sabah, Malaysia

Source: courtesy V.T. King

Plate 6 Shifting cultivation, Padawan, Sarawak, Malaysia

Source: courtesy V.T. King

Plate 7 'Maloh' Dayak women chewing betel-nut, Upper Embaloh
Source: courtesy V.T. King

Plate 8 Jame'Asr Hassanal Bolkiah Mosque, Gadong, Brunei
Source: courtesy V.T. King

Plate 9 Main Buddhist temple complex, Grand Palace, Bangkok, Thailand
Source: courtesy V.T. King

Plate 10 Main Buddhist stupa and monks at Nakhon Pathom, Thailand
Source: courtesy V.T. King

Plate 11 Domestic Buddhist shrine of a Sino-Thai family, Bangkok

Source: courtesy V.T. King

Plate 12 Offering prayers at a Buddhist temple in Phuket, Thailand
Source: courtesy V.T. King

Plate 13 Thai temple at Phuket

Source: courtesy V.T. King

Plate 14 Elephant shrine, Phuket

Source: courtesy V.T. King

Plate 15 Sri Mahamariamman South Indian Hindu temple, Kuala Lumpur, Malaysia
Source: courtesy V.T. King

Plate 16 Decaying Chinese shop-houses ready for redevelopment, Kuala Lumpur, Malaysia

Source: courtesy V.T. King

Plate 17 Chinese shop-houses and high-rise development in 1980s' Singapore

Source: courtesy V.T. King

Plate 18 Central business district by the Singapore River

Source: courtesy V.T. King

Plate 19 Oil palm plantation, Selangor, Malaysia

Source: courtesy V.T. King

Plate 20 Tea plantation, Ranau area, Kinabalu, Sabah

Source: courtesy V.T. King

Plate 21 Balinese market trader

Source: courtesy M.J.G. Parnwell

Plate 22 Local girl, Inle Lake, Shan States, Myanmar
Source: courtesy M.J.G. Parnwell

Plate 23 Lowland wet rice cultivation, Sintang, West Kalimantan
Source: courtesy V.T. King

Plate 24 Sultan Mosque, Singapore

Source: courtesy V.T. King

Plate 25 Public housing estate, Singapore
Source: courtesy M.J.G. Parnwell

Plate 26 Vietnamese woman street trader in Ho Chi Minh City
Source: courtesy V.T. King

Plate 27 Thai traffic warden, Kanchanaburi, Central Thailand

Source: courtesy V.T. King

Plate 28 Transplanting rice, North-East Thailand

Source: courtesy M.J.G. Parnwell

Plate 29 Terraced rice-fields, Tana Toraja, Sulawesi, Indonesia
Source: courtesy M.J.G. Parnwell

Plate 30 Traffic jams in Bangkok

Source: courtesy M.J.G. Parnwell

Plate 31 The Temple and the Central Business District, Bangkok
Source: courtesy M.J.G. Parnwell

Plate 32 Getting around in busy Bangkok traffic

Source: courtesy M.J.G. Parnwell

Plate 33 Akha girl, Chiang Rai, Northern Thailand

Source: courtesy M.J.G. Parnwell

Plate 34 Fisherman, Inle Lake, Shan States, Myanmar
Source: courtesy M.J.G. Parnwell

Plate 35 Transplanting rice in Kampung Kuala Bera, Pahang, Malaysia
Source: courtesy W.D. Wilder

Plate 36 Malay life on the water, Pahang
Source: courtesy W.D. Wilder

Plate 37 Malay agricultural work-crew at Kampung Kuala Bera
Source: courtesy W.D. Wilder

Plate 38 Village scene from Kampung Kuala Bera
Source: courtesy W.D. Wilder

Plate 39 Malay swamp padi fields (*padi paya*)
Source: courtesy W.D. Wilder

Plate 40 Use of the dibble stick for planting, Pahang

Source: courtesy W.D. Wilder

6

ETHNICITY, IDENTITY AND NATIONALISM

The anthropology of South-East Asia has been concerned with issues of ethnicity and the formation and transformation of cultural identities. Although problems of ethnic unit definition have also been addressed by anthropologists in other parts of the world, it is in South-East Asia that much of the pioneering work has been done. In Chapter 1 we discussed the difficulties of defining South-East Asia as a region in large part because of its marked ethnic diversity, outside contacts, and its increasing cultural differentiation through time, and then suggested in our review of colonial anthropology that this complexity provided an ideal laboratory for theories about social evolution and cultural diffusion. The region then, characterized by ethnolinguistic and cultural variation, especially in the hinterland and upland areas where minorities reside, provides an arena in which ethnic groupings intermingle, identities change, and the various criteria used to delineate groupings often do not coincide or demonstrate sufficiently marked discontinuities to establish clear ethnic boundaries. This chapter examines the problems anthropologists have addressed in delimiting ethnic units for analysis and the ways in which identities and cultures are constructed, constituted and transformed. It also considers criticisms of Furnivall's concept of plural society drawing on examples from Burma and Malaysia; issues surrounding ethnic labelling in Borneo and the concept of a 'Brunei society'; relationships between the construction and reconstruction of identity in the context of the development of cultural tourism in Bali and Torajaland; and studies of the interaction between national culture and minority cultures in Indonesia with reference to the Meratus Dayaks, the Bemunese of Aru and the Minangkabau.

Introduction

Attempts to apply cross-cultural definitions of ethnic unit identification to South-East Asia have usually failed; for example, Naroll's general definition of a 'cultunit' or 'culture-bearing unit' as 'People who are domestic speakers of a common distinct language and who belong either to the same state or to the same contact group' (1964: 283–284; 1968) has been criticized by anthropologists such as Moerman, in his study of the ethnolinguistic mosaics of northern Thailand and particularly the problem of demarcating the Lue population of that region (1965, 1968b). Moerman argues that attempts to formulate an unambiguous, consistent cross-cultural definition for comparative purposes fails to address the difficulties of drawing discrete boundaries around ethnic units, often ignores local circumstances, and downplays what is stressed by a given collectivity of people in defining themselves to outsiders. Here Moerman draws attention to the distinction between definitions constructed by outsiders and assumed to be 'objective', and the so-called 'subjective' definitions or 'folk models' of those who are the object of study (Moerman, 1965: 1215–1216, 1221). In this connection too Nagata warns that 'social scientists need to be more sensitive to what their subjects consider to be meaningful categories and reference groups, rather than imposing a western taxonomy whose meaning, even to westerners, is often obscure' (1975a: 3). However, we shall see in a moment that even relying on self-definition is not without its problems.

In Chapters 1 and 2 we also referred briefly to the concept of the plural society formulated by J.S. Furnivall in his studies of the political economy of colonial Burma and Indonesia. Furnivall was one of the first scholars to attempt to construct an analytical framework for understanding the ethnic complexity of the region, and to focus on some of the socio-economic consequences of the economic migrations of Chinese and Indians into Western-controlled 'tropical dependencies'. What he emphasized was the market as a meeting-place of different societies and cultures and the primacy of trade and commerce which at the same time served to reinforce ethnic divisions and delineate 'economic castes'. The colonial state provided both the context for interaction between immigrant communities and indigenous populations, and the means, through its exercise of political power, to sustain an ethnically divided society. In other words, outside the affairs of the market and the polity, cultural diversity flourished in religious, family and domestic activities.

As we shall see, the concept of pluralism was debated and revised in post-war studies of the newly independent countries of South-East Asia, especially in Malaysia and Singapore with their substantial immigrant communities. Nevertheless, another dimension of identity began to be introduced in post-war anthropological studies and that is the relationships not so much between indigenous peoples and immigrant Asians, but between indigenous plains and valley dwellers, the majority of whom were wet rice cultivators and members of the great civilizations and state structures of South-East Asia (Hinduism, Buddhism, Islam and Hispanized Roman Catholicism), and the minority interior or hill peoples who were predominantly forest-based shifting cultivators, hunters and gatherers. In simple and popular terms the distinction was made between lowland 'peasants' and 'upland tribespeople', and it was probably the volume edited by Peter Kunstadter (1967) on the relationships between lowlanders and uplanders, and specifically the interaction between tribes, minorities and nations which began to mark South-East Asia out as a region of ethnic complexity which required special attention and the development of concepts to do with cultural identity and difference.

As we have seen in Chapter 4 it was those anthropologists mainly working in the European tradition, or at least influenced by it, and who focused on minority hill peoples in mainland South-East Asia, notably Edmund Leach and F.K. Lehman, who drew attention to the difficulties of delineating 'tribal' units, the ways in which upland–lowland interactions influence identity formation and change, and the problematical nature of cultural boundaries. During the post-war period there is a noticeable shift away from the notion of pluralism, a notion tied particularly to the social structures created by the colonial powers and often associated with 'racial' categories, to the more all-embracing and versatile concept of ethnicity or ethnic identity. This latter concept in turn began to be examined with regard to the phenomenon of nationalism in South-East Asia, the relationships between national 'communities' (Anderson, [1983] 1991) and the identities of the ethnic groupings which comprised them. Finally and most recently identities, whether national or sub-national, have been considered increasingly in the context of processes of globalization and from the perspective of postmodern or postcolonial theory; the concerns in this field of study are to understand multiculturalism, cultural otherness or 'alterity' and marginality, and the ways in which 'other cultures' are constructed or constituted (Kahn, 1993, 1995; Pemberton, 1994; Tsing, 1993).

It is perhaps no coincidence that one of the most influential post-war social science studies of the origins and spread of nationalism – Benedict Anderson's *Imagined Communities* (1991) – emerged significantly from reflections on the processes of identity formation in South-East Asia (see, for example, ibid.: 116–133, 155–162, 163–185). Although primarily working within the discipline of political science, Anderson has been finely tuned to the intimate interrelationships between politics and culture, and, his work on Indonesian, and particularly Javanese political culture and concepts of power, has evoked considerable interest among anthropologists, especially American cultural anthropologists. His perspective on nations as 'imagined communities' also owes much to 'an anthropological spirit' (ibid.: 5) and relates directly to anthropological studies of ethnicity and identity formation. He examines the cultural roots of nationalism, the meaning attributed to and the values associated with nationness, and he is concerned to explore how a sense of identity, of belonging, of 'fraternity', is invented or created and sustained through time, and how boundaries are drawn, maintained and changed (ibid.: 6–7). In short, Anderson looks at how nationhood has been thought about, represented and given meaning, and the key factors and processes in its emergence; for him these are the development of printing and publishing ('print-capitalism') and the associated creation, privileging and standardization of particular 'national' print-languages; the creation of administrative units and their unification through markets in the context of the expansion of Europe overseas; the development of capitalism, bourgeoisies and rational bureaucracies; and the importance in colonial territories of the 'census, map and museum' (ibid.: 163–185). An extreme example of this process of creating a nation in South-East Asia is Laos, and though it might be thought that the lowland Laotians constitute a separate ethnic group expressing Lao nationhood (see Halpern, 1964), Evans argues that 'the modern state of Laos only exists because of French colonial occupation' (1999: 21). Without European intervention, 'it is almost certain that at least the lowland areas of Laos would have become part of the Thai state', indeed the populations of what is now north-eastern Thailand were formerly known as Lao, while various of the upland groups in present-day Laos 'would probably have been absorbed by Vietnam' (ibid.: 21).

In this chapter we shall present a selection of studies on various aspects of ethnic identity, and as in Chapter 5 where we examined primarily the economic relationships between small-scale communities and the wider systems of which they are a part in the context of rural transformations, we shall consider here the more recent perspectives on ethnicity and the relations of local communities to the nation–state and to processes of globalization, and the ways in which identities are created, sustained and transformed. We also intend to provide some Indonesian case studies on the ways in which the development of international tourism has influenced ethnic identities and their representation. The study of ethnic identity has been an ideal subject of study for anthropologists of a postmodern persuasion in that rather than being fixed and immutable ethnicity and culture have come to be seen as flexible, negotiable, contested, relative and subject to change. Furthermore, anthropologists have increasingly questioned the ways in which they represent and have represented 'cultural otherness'.

What is ethnicity?

From what we have said already it is clear that the concept of ethnicity, which we shall be using here, jostles and has been used synonymously with such concepts as race, nation, identity, community, culture, society and tribe, among others, and in situations of ethnic diversity such alternative concepts as multi-ethnic, multiracial, multicultural and plural have been employed. Indeed, dictionary definitions often gloss 'ethnic' with such terms as 'tribal', 'racial groups' or 'nation'; Nagata indicates that the term is often misused and ambiguous and sometimes equated with 'primordialism' (1975a: 2, 1979: 188–189) in, for example, the work of Geertz (1963c) where 'plural groups' are conceived of in terms of basic loyalties stemming from ties of kinship, descent, race and place of origin. The problem in concentrating on the 'basic givens' of identity is that, as Dentan indicates, they translate too easily into a notion of ethnicity which sees ethnic groups as static, homogeneous, exclusive and bounded, and as carrying their own sets of cultural values and practices (1976: 71ff.). On the contrary, when we study ethnicity we are concerned with the social and cultural processes and factors which give rise to similarity and difference, and the ways in which groupings of people construct, maintain and transform their social and cultural identities. In this process of construction, or as Anderson proposes 'invention', boundaries are created for the purposes of social interaction and avoidance. It is in this connection that Lehman, for example, sees ethnic identities or categories as rather like 'roles' which people adopt and play out (1967: 106–107), and Barth proposes that ethnic groups can be conceptualized as an 'organizational type' which involves social processes of 'exclusion' and 'incorporation' and the choice by the actors themselves of those socio-cultural features which are deemed to be significant for purposes of identity and boundary construction (1969: 13–15). Shared ethnicity is not only premised on biological self-perpetuation but also on membership of a shared field of interaction and communication based on shared values and behaviour (ibid.: 10–12).

In examining the relationships between ideas of identity and social relationships some anthropologists have also made the distinction between an 'ethnic category' (as the conceptual dimension of identity by which individuals assign themselves and are assigned by others to a particular unit within a classification system of units) and 'ethnic group' (as pertaining to the dimension of social interaction and communication) (Rousseau, 1990). Nagata says, for example, that 'many of the "ethnic groups" known to anthropologists are really only categories, which may undergo periodic or episodic transformations into groupness under the pressure of compelling issues and needs' (1979: 203). Under certain circumstances, then, such as population pressure and demographic imbalances, or competition for economic resources and political power, ethnic identities often crystallize and boundaries are drawn more sharply.

It is also worth noting that many anthropologists who have studied ethnicity do not see it, unlike those of a Marxist persuasion, as merely ideological or superstructural, disguising or mis-representing class relationships, but as a principle of organization which has direct consequences for modes of behaviour and interaction. Nevertheless, there are circumstances in which social class differences are expressed as ethnic or cultural differences, or appeals to ethnic unity and identity override class inequalities, or ethnicity is used to explain or 'talk about' political and historical relationships (Rousseau, 1975: 32–49). In particular, ethnic identities are often created by functionaries of the state, reworked and re-presented by those so categorized, and implicated in discourses about the ways in which state domination can be secured and sustained (Kahn, 1993: 278–280; Tsing, 1993: 5–37).

Ethnic identity is first and foremost a matter of self-identification (Moerman, 1965; Dentan, 1976: 75–76; Nagata, 1979), and it is premised on assumed common origins; people of the same ethnic category claim that they share the same roots, and that their identity is a basic 'given'; it is fixed, firm and unbreakable. In this respect ethnicity closely resembles the anthropological category 'kinship' (including descent) (King and Wilder, 1982: 1–6). As with kinship, ethnicity commands primary loyalty; descent is claimed from common ancestors and frequently uses biological justification including shared 'blood' or other kinds of natural imagery such as common 'roots', 'soil' and 'branching' or 'spreading' 'plants' or 'trees'. Often in South-East Asia, when people are asked to identify themselves, they provide the most direct kind of identification, which is both natural and cultural, that they are 'a man', 'a woman' or a 'person'; in other words, they and their kind are 'human' and physically share 'human-ness', with the implication that 'other people' different from them are in some sense less than human. Interestingly, ethnic terms that have been applied by majority lowland populations to interior or hill populations have come into general usage, but frequently have pejorative connotations, and mean something akin to 'savages', 'barbarians', 'primitives', 'slaves', 'hicks' or 'hillbillies'.

Origins can also be expressed in terms of shared physical or territorial space or real or presumed birthplace. Again in South-East Asia people might claim a common geographical origin, that they came to their current residence from the 'upstreams' or from the 'coast' or from 'across the sea' or from a named location such as a river or a mountain. Alternatively, migration and movement may not be an identified but rather physical fixity; ethnic identity in this case is expressed and claimed in terms of indigenousness, of one's continuous occupation of 'this place', that 'We have been here from the beginning'. The criterion of place is also often associated with a particular habitat and ecology so that individuals might identify themselves or be identified by others as coastal dwellers, as hill or sea people, as forest dwellers, or as gardeners or fishermen. Indeed, Barth argues that ecological circumstances 'mark and exaggerate differences' (1969: 14), and often give rise to the development of complementary and interdependent trading and other relationships.

Ethnicity is obviously expressed as a product of the past, evoking common origins, social linkages and shared cultural values and traits like language and religion. However, the historical dimension of identity also demonstrates that rather than identities being fixed, constant and immutable, they frequently change and can be acquired. This aspect of 'passing' or 'crossing' ethnic boundaries is something Barth explores in his edited volume *Ethnic Groups and Boundaries*, arguing that rather than focus on the social and cultural content of identity one should be examining the mechanisms of boundary maintenance and how boundaries are not only crossed but transcended. Barth makes the important point that identities are created, maintained and transformed through interactions and relationships between those defined as 'us' and others defined as 'them' (ibid.: 9–10). In other words, ethnicity is relative, and ethnic categories and groups do not exist in isolation one from another. Nagata too, in her analysis of ethnicity in Malaysia, indicates that, as her research progressed she moved from a concern with 'ethnic groups' to 'a preoccupation with the boundaries themselves' (1979: 3).

As we have already seen in Chapter 4, Leach, in his Highland Burma study, demonstrates that Kachin identity is to a significant extent both created and transformed in relationship with the valley-dwelling Shan so that importantly the Kachin define themselves and are defined as 'other than Shan'. In addition, in his monumental three-volume study of the ethnohistory of the populations of the Central Highlands of Vietnam up to the mid-1970s (1982a, 1982b, 1993), Hickey argues that a developing, educated inter-ethnic elite was 'instrumental in the rise of highlander ethnonationalism' and a sense of 'montagnard' ethnicity in response to the pressures from and increasing interaction with lowland-dominated states (1982a: xvii).

Leach also has evidence to show that over time some Kachin have 'become Shan' through the process of conversion to Buddhism and gradual assimilation, often through intermarriage, into Shan society and culture, and that depending on circumstances some Kachin assume a Kachin identity and at other times claim to be Shan. Change in ethnic identity can also involve individual or group conversions or both. Similarly Kunstadter, in his examination of hill ('tribes') and valley ('peasant') populations in north-western Thailand, states that there have always been connections between them and that 'social systems have *never* been sharply defined nor impermeable'. He adds that 'Perhaps we anthropologists are to blame for the idea that "tribes" are well-defined, bounded, self-integrated units' (1969: 70).

Parallel processes can be seen at work in the Muslim world of South-East Asia where some formerly pagan populations have converted to Islam and over time changed their overall ethnic identity to 'become Malay'. In Borneo, for example, many of those now identified as 'Malay' have non-Malay ancestry and at various times transitional communities can be identified which are in the process of changing their identities but continue to follow customs from their pre-Islamic past (King, 1993: 31ff.; and see below). Often it is the self-identity of minority groups which is most clearly created in relation to a dominant majority. In this connection Dentan, in his study of an aboriginal population of Peninsular Malaysia, poses the interesting question 'If there were no Malays, who would the Semai be?' because '[w]hat unity the Semai feel they have seems to come from their constant contrast of how they live with how Malays live' (1975: 54). He also suggests that the switching and manipulation of identities are not unusual in South-East Asia, especially among the hill populations and that 'multi-culturation ... provides many people with a series of identities which they can don and doff as particular interactions dictate' (1976: 78). The important volume edited by Nagata explores various relationships between the politically and culturally dominant Malay population in Malaysia and demonstrates that for the Malays, as well as the 'settled' Chinese and Indians, 'identity ... is considerably more rigid' than it is for the 'tribal populations' who tend to be more fluid in ethnic affiliation, and more susceptible to ethnic role switching and to forming their identities in relation to dominant reference groups (1975a: 4–10).

Religious conversion and intermarriage are obviously two important mechanisms involved in changes of ethnic identity. Others comprise the practice of adoption of children between different ethnic groupings, the assimilation of clients and slaves taken from other populations, the incorporation of foreign groups into a state political structure, and shifts in economic activities, when for example previously nomadic populations settle down and adopt the agricultural way of life of their neighbours. Often several of these processes are operating simultaneously. In addition, Kahn points to the processes involved for South-East Asian populations in contact with the West and the effects of 'culture contact', 'Westernization' and 'globalization' (1993: 17–18, 22–23). In this regard what were assumed to be 'traditional' markers of identity by earlier anthropologists, and indeed often presented as such by the people themselves, are instead discovered to be 'inventions' or creations of colonialism and the West. We have already seen in Chapter 3 how the institution of the Thai village was a recent administrative creation, and in Java the studies by Breman (1982) among others have shown that the closed, corporate village community was developed by the Dutch for administrative purposes and to enable the colonial state to implement and sustain the cultivation system in the nineteenth century. However, Kahn argues that we should beware over-drawing the distinction between 'invented' traditions and 'authentic' cultures since all traditions are created in certain social and historical contexts and experienced as authentic or 'real' by those who carry them, and that they are not simply the creations of outsiders since local populations (both elites and masses) were also actively involved in making their own cultures (1993: 28–29).

Pluralism reconsidered

Burma

In the context of Burma it was to be political scientists and historians who primarily employed and revised Furnivall's concept of plural society. Two of the best known are probably Robert Taylor (1987) in his study of the colonial and postcolonial state in Burma and its relationship to civil society, and Michael Adas (1974) in his examination of colonial economic development and the growth of the rice industry in the Irrawaddy Delta from the mid-nineteenth century. Both writers consider Furnivall's concept to have some utility in understanding the social structure of British Burma and in emphasizing the way in which a multi-ethnic society had been created and held together politically by the colonial state in its quest 'to create and free wealth' (Taylor, 1987: 68). However, they were of one mind in their criticism that Furnivall had failed to demonstrate the complexities and dynamics of a plural society. He had presented a far too 'stagnant image' of social relations (ibid.: 79). Furnivall's plural society comprised 'separate racial groups' (Europeans, Indians, Chinese and native Burmese), the sharp divisions between them coinciding broadly with separate economic functions; they were divided culturally and socially, with no common social and political will; each group was an aggregate of people and not an organic, integrated whole; most non-Burmese were footloose migrants, temporary residents, whose homelands were elsewhere and whose commitment to the territory within which they resided was slight; they sought economic gain, and their social life was incomplete.

Taylor, however, demonstrates that the relations between ethnicity and social class (or economic function) were much more complex than Furnivall allowed, and this helps explain the nature of the relationships between the different groups (ibid.: 123–147). Far from being economically homogeneous, the lowland Burmese developed new class formations under British rule; a Burmese middle class of mainly urban-based white-collar workers emerged which served primarily in public administration and was tied closely to the colonial state. Another fraction of the Burmese middle class was rural-based, comprising larger landowners, money-lenders, agricultural creditors and rural shopkeepers. However, the mass of the Burmese were peasants or owner cultivators, tenants and rural labourers, and the level of landlessness and proletarianization increased as the rice industry became ever more closely tied into the world market, and population pressures on land grew. As jobs became more difficult to find, especially during the Depression years of the 1930s, Burmese labourers moved into urban occupations and competed in Rangoon with Indians in, for example, the docks, transport and manufacturing. Indians too were class divided into a mainly urban-based proletariat; but as commercial rice agriculture expanded Indian workers also drifted into the countryside in search of work, and there came into contention with Burmese agricultural labourers. An Indian middle class, unlike that of the Burmese, but like the Chinese, was not white collar, but was mainly concentrated in urban-based trade, commerce and industry, though Indian money-lenders also became involved in financing the rice industry in areas around the capital and the main urban centres. Taylor demonstrates that it is not the coincidence of class and ethnicity (Furnivall's 'economic castes') which explains inter-ethnic conflict, but rather competition between members of different ethnic groups occupying the same class position. For example, communal tensions erupted in 1930 in the Rangoon docks between Burmese and Indian labourers competing for work. Most importantly, Taylor argues that this social structure was created by a colonial state which encouraged a *laissez-faire* economic system but monopolized all the instruments of coercion, sanction and control.

Adas also examines the changing interrelationships between different 'cultural groups' and notes that what was a symbiotic relationship in the second half of the nineteenth century when land was plentiful and generally rice prices were rising on the world market, gradually turned into a conflictual one up to the Second World War as population and the labour supply increased, the rice frontier closed and rice prices fell (1974: 104–106, 122–123, 166ff.). Adas argues that the plural society is 'an extremely vulnerable and unstable form of social organization' (ibid.: 192), and requires direct political control to keep it in being. Yet, he states that the threat of physical force by an authoritarian regime was not the only means of sustaining a sharply divided society. Members of the elites of the various non-British 'cultural groups' were drawn into the British sphere through the institutions of English education and law, and various areas of the economy encouraged relationships of interdependence. In addition, the boundaries between the different groups were not as impermeable as Furnivall's concept of pluralism suggests; there was intermarriage, inter-ethnic concubinage and religious conversion which gave rise to hybrid or mixed groups such as the Anglo-Indians and Anglo-Burmese (ibid.: 108). Like Taylor, Adas also emphasizes the divisions within the various 'cultural groups', particularly class divisions and the fact that the main Burmese-Indian communal violence broke out not at all levels of society, and not between ethnic segments of the middle class, but primarily among agricultural labourers and dock-workers (ibid.: 166ff.). He also draws attention to cultural divisions within groups which did not coincide neatly with class divisions. Particularly in the Indian community there were significant cleavages between Hindus and their constituent castes, Muslims, Sikhs and Jains (ibid.: 106), and among the natives of Burma Furnivall's cover term 'Burmese' disguised the fact that in addition to the lowland Buddhist Burman majority there were also lowland Mons and Arakanese, and the numerous minorities – Karens, Chins, Kachins, Nagas, Shans – mainly inhabiting the valleys, hills and mountains surrounding the rice-growing plains. What he also shows is that the characterization of Asian peasantries as passive and unresponsive to market stimuli, as depicted in Boeke's concept of a dual society, is a product of political, economic and historical circumstances. The Burmese, when presented with the opportunities to grow rice for the market and expand production, embraced the profit motive, sought consumer goods with alacrity, and became involved in a physically and socially mobile society (ibid.: 210–213).

Adas also indicates that the 'cultural' differences in the plural society were expressed in terms of racial and physical differences, and the four broad 'racial groups' were based on stereotypes which were incorporated into British colonial-administrative policies and practices. These four groups were in fact not groups at all in the sense that they provided arenas of interaction and communication on the basis of shared values, but rather ideological categories which were used for politico-administrative purposes and which expressed relationships of class, status and power as well as assumptions about racial superiority and inferiority and the suitability of the different 'races' for different kinds of economic activity in the colonial economy.

Malaysia

Elsewhere in South-East Asia the concept of pluralism was applied and reconsidered in greatest measure with reference to Malaysia, though the concept is also often used interchangeably with notions of race, ethnic relations and communalism. There is a burgeoning literature on Malaysian pluralism for obvious reasons. Nowhere in the region, other than Singapore, are there relatively large communities which have resulted from immigration into these formerly British colonial territories from homelands outside South-East Asia. In both Malaysia and Singapore, though Indian populations are significant, it is the Chinese who comprise the largest community. Indeed, in Singapore they constitute over three-quarters of the population, while in Malaysia they make up just over one-quarter of Malaysians.

It was the British anthropologist Maurice Freedman who was one of the first post-war researchers to examine the history and structure of the Chinese community in the Malayan Peninsula and Singapore. Given the insecure conditions in the Peninsula during the Malayan Emergency (1948–1960), Freedman, as one of the anthropologists commissioned by the Colonial Social Science Research Council in the late 1940s to undertake basic ethnographic research in Britain's South-East Asian territories, concentrated his attention on the Chinese of Singapore (1957, 1961, 1962). T'ien Ju-K'ang carried out a parallel study among the Chinese of Sarawak (1953). However, Freedman's article on the creation of a plural society in Malaya (1960) stimulated subsequent reflection on the appropriateness of the concept for understanding the social structure of Malaysia.

As in Burma ethnic identities were constructed within the British colonial state. The three major nation-wide or macro-level ethnic categories (sometimes referred to as 'races') in Malaysia (Malays, Chinese and Indians) are a relatively recent creation. Although there were obvious cultural differences between local populations and immigrant Asians, these did not really crystallize into broad ethnic categories until the emergence of political organizations and the politicization of ethnicity in the two decades before the Second World War and in the run-up to the independence of the Federation of Malaya in 1957. Ethnicity became increasingly interrelated with political identity in that the Malays, Chinese and Indians all formed their own ethnic-based or communal parties (the United Malays National Organization, the Malay(si)an Chinese Association and the Malay(si)an Indian Congress), and differences between these categories came to be expressed in terms of economic imbalances, specifically between the Chinese and the Malays, and in terms of the 'special rights' of the Malays as indigenes or 'sons of the soil' (*bumiputera*) in public sector employment, education and the general economic field (Lee, 1986a: v; 1986b: 28–33). Nagata also points out that it is urban areas of Malaysia where 'ethnic categories and relations have come to be most conspicuous and most problematic' (1979: 4), and it is here where one finds interesting examples of attempts by Malays, with their predominantly rural and agricultural roots, to define and construct their identity as modern, urban Malays living in a multicultural environment (Kahn, 1997: 118–119).

Nevertheless, the overarching ethnic or plural framework began to be established by the British from the late nineteenth century, and through census-taking, classification and stereotyping there was a continuous process of rationalization and simplification, bringing a multitude of ethnic groupings together into a few major ethnic categories. The colonial state also separated ethnic identities economically and administratively. The Malay sultans and their retinues were incorporated into a system of indirect rule and Malays were brought into various areas of administration, the army and police force. The British confirmed and 'protected' the position of the mass of the rural Malay population on 'reserved' land as small-scale rice and rubber cultivators, while encouraging Chinese immigration to support the mainly urban-based commercial and business needs of the colonial economy. Many Chinese also became wage-labourers in tin-mining, commercial agriculture, transport, manufacturing and urban services. Indians, mainly from north India, arrived to take up various urban occupations in trade, retailing, money-lending and the professions. Mainly Tamil labourers from southern India worked on foreign-owned rubber plantations, and Sikhs in particular took up positions in the police and army. Boundaries between the ethnic groupings hardened progressively as the newcomers continued to increase in numbers and threatened to overwhelm – economically and demographically – the local populations. The large-scale immigration of both men and women in the late colonial period also provided the opportunity for marriage within one's own ethnic grouping rather than marriage across ethnic boundaries and encouraged cultural self-sufficiency and resilience especially among the Chinese (Nagata, 1979: 30–31). The colonial government as the ultimate inter-ethnic arbiter, and by means of an ideology of racial differences, a system of indirect rule and the maintenance of an ethnic division of labour, acted to separate the members of the various ethnic groupings one from another and bring into being a plural society (Nagata, 1975b: 117–121). The suitability or otherwise of particular groups for certain tasks and occupations came to be explained in terms of 'innate' racial characteristics or 'traditional' cultural values, specifically Malay conservatism, fatalism and dependence as against Chinese rationalism, risk-taking and self-reliance (Nagata, 1979: 81–82). The minority groups of the Malayan Peninsula and British Borneo were subject to similar processes of ethnic rationalization; the diverse non-Malay native communities of the Peninsula were lumped together as 'Orang Asli' (aboriginals) and administered separately (Dentan, 1997: 98–134), and those of Borneo were gradually rearranged into a small number of broad categories under the general label 'Dayak' (Winzeler, 1997: 1–29) (and see below).

However, historically intra-ethnic divisions were just as significant, if not more significant than those between the three major categories, and even today at the local level the bases of intra- and inter-ethnic interaction are much more complex and variegated than at the national level. As we have seen in the case of Burma, the Indian community is divided in terms of religion, caste, place of origin in India, occupation, class, language and other cultural attributes. Indeed, throughout much of the colonial period British administrators in Malaya and the Straits Settlements tended not to lump 'Indians' together under that label, but differentiated them into sub-groupings of Tamils, Bengalis, Gujeratis, Sikhs,

Chulias (Muslims from the Coromandel coast), Parsees (from Bombay), Malay-alis (from Malabar) and so on. With regard to the Chinese, again there are internal cultural and linguistic divisions between, for example, Hokkien, Teochiu, Cantonese, Hakka, Hainanese and Foochow, and, as Freedman, T'ien and others have demonstrated, a tendency for the clustering of dialect groups, in particular occupations and economic specialisms. The category 'Malay' too embraces class and status distinctions and comprises a range of different sub-regional groupings, some long-established in the Peninsula and others relatively recent migrants such as the Javanese and Madurese, the Minangkabau and Achehnese from Sumatra, the Banjarese from Kalimantan and the Bugi-nese from eastern Indonesia (Clammer, 1986: 54ff.). The definition of 'Malay' in terms of religion, language and custom, has become increasingly fixed and is now set firm in constitutional terms. Yet the groupings which are now included under this ethnic umbrella were much more diverse and fluid than the current political, constitutional and administrative definition presents (Nagata, 1979: 14).

Again as in Burma there were also hybrid populations in Malay(si)a resulting from intermarriage and cultural exchange which blurred boundaries between groups. Among the best known are the Straits, Peranakan or Baba Chinese, who have been long settled in Malacca (Melaka) and Penang (Pulau Pinang), and who combined elements of Chinese and Malay culture; the Eurasians of mixed predominantly Portuguese and Malay descent who reside in Malacca; the Jawi Peranakan or Indian Muslims of mixed Indian-Malay ancestry; and the Indian Babas or Malacca Chittys who are of Hindu Indian descent but have absorbed much of the local Malay culture (Clammer, 1980, 1986; Nagata, 1979: 25–49).

Among those who undertook studies on post-1963 ethnic relations in the newly formed Federation of Malaysia with reference to the concept of pluralism, Judith Nagata is probably the most outstanding researcher (1974, 1975b, 1979). Like the commentators on Burmese pluralism, she too explores the relationships between ethnicity and social inequality, though, under the umbrella of 'stratifi-cation', she considers both class and status relationships (1975b: 114–115, 121–130; 1979: 144–183). She undertook fieldwork in 'colonial' Georgetown, Penang and the Malay royal town of Bintang in Kedah. Unlike Taylor and Adas, this entails her drawing the distinction between 'objective' analyses of inequality (class) and 'subjective' ones (status, rank and prestige) and examin-ing how members of different ethnic groups perceive social hierarchy. This enables her to demonstrate that in objective terms there are emerging class rela-tionships which cut across ethnic boundaries in modern Malaysia, although Malaysians subjectively do not perceive of their society in class terms. Instead they commonly express 'social differences in an ethnic idiom', and emphasize the plural nature of their society rather than an inter-ethnic class consciousness. For this reason Nagata prefers to call these emerging classes, or 'occupational and functional strata', 'quasi-groups', which comprise businessmen (merchants, entrepreneurs), professionals, civil servants, and workers or labourers (1975b: 130–133; 1979: 164–172). What is more, the three broad 'ethnic groups' (Malays, Chinese, Indians) have their own ethnic-specific status systems and they have different perceptions of the overall Malaysian social structure. In this sense an ethnic group is also in some respects like a status group 'associated with a particular evaluation of honour and ideal style of life' (1975b: 117). Lee also argues that conflicts between ethnic groups frequently take on the character of status conflicts in which 'each group seeks to degrade the other and to reinforce what it perceives as a morally justified stance' (1986b: 29).

The internal Malay status system was traditionally oriented around the distinction between a secular ranking system which placed royalty and aristocracy at the top, and a religious hierarchy which accorded most prestige to those with Arab descent and/or descent from the Prophet, and then religious leaders and teachers and those who had undertaken the pilgrimage to Mecca (Nagata, 1979: 147–150). There was a complex and finely graded set of status positions, many of them carrying specific titles and attached to particular offices. However, a broad distinction was made betweeen rulers (*rajah*) and commoners or ordinary people (*ra'ayat*). In modern Malaysia the internal Malay status system continues to grant the highest status to royalty and aristocracy and then to those of high religious standing. In terms of status ranking within the wider Malaysian society senior government officers occupy the highest position followed by businessmen and professionals, yet, when other ethnic groups are included, the Chinese are placed overall above the Malays and Indians. Nagata suggests that Malays do not perceive their own ethnic grouping or the wider Malaysian society in class terms (1975b: 122–123). They are preoccupied with the subtleties of ranking which comprises an eclectic, continuous series of statuses, and wherever possible the Malays attempt 'to preserve a semblance of congruence between these [statuses] and other social attributes such as wealth and power' (1979: 158).

For the Chinese, status is based heavily on wealth, urban occupations and English education. Therefore, businessmen are accorded the highest prestige above professionals and political and government officers. Rural occupations are placed at the bottom of the scale. Interestingly with regard to the wider society Malay royalty and aristocracy are considered to be the most prestigious, though 'in a category by themselves ... almost detached from "real" society' (1975b: 124). Then come the Malay political elite; the Chinese did not see themselves as having a Chinese national elite. At the lowest level was the Malay peasantry. Within their own system the Chinese tended to emphasize clan affiliation, dialect and region of origin rather than class differences (1979: 160).

Among the Indians Nagata states that the primary principle of categorization is religious affiliation followed by regional and linguistic differences rather than an Indian-wide status hierarchy (ibid.: 162). When asked specifically about status they accorded greatest importance to wealth, followed by professional position and qualifications and the English language. Businessmen are given the which is particularly evident in the increasing Westernization of the political, bureaucratic and business elites. However, overall, Nagata sees the 'mosaic' of pluralism being sustained and argues for the continuing importance of understanding Malaysian society in terms of the interrelationships between ethnicity, class, status and power.

Ethnicity in Indonesian Borneo and Brunei: self-identity, ethnic names and social systems

Indonesian Borneo

Let us now turn to examine an especially problematical case study of ethnic labelling in Borneo, and the problems of self-definition. Michael Moerman, in his work on the Lue of northern Thailand, argues for the importance of self-identity and self-naming in delimiting ethnic groupings, but recognizes that even native classifications and names may not provide clear and unambiguous evidence for the identification of separate units for analysis (1965). Folk or indigenous classifications, which constitute local attempts to bring order to complex and dynamic socio-cultural relations, often provide overlapping and conflicting sets of ethnic categories and names. Neighbouring communities might have very different classification systems to locate and define themselves and their neighbours, and these are then usually extended beyond the local context in an *ad hoc* way to embrace more physically and culturally distant communities; they may also comprise an amalgam of self-generated and externally derived categories and labels which do not fit neatly one with another. Some units may be more easily defined and clearly bounded than others and it is often minorities or marginal groupings which prove more problematical to delimit and denote.

Problems of ethnic identification and nomenclature have loomed large in the ethnographic study of Borneo societies, with many different and often contradictory anthropological schemes of classification on offer. Rousseau focuses precisely on this dilemma in his attempts to understand the relationships between ethnic categories and social relations in central Borneo (1975, 1990). He says:

> It was very difficult to identify recognizable ethnic units, because groups with the same name might speak different languages, while groups with distinct names seemed to be identical. Central Borneo appeared as a checkerboard pattern of ethnic units distributed randomly through the vagaries of migration. It was not even possible to assume neat boundaries between hunter–gatherers and swiddeners, because they sometimes spoke the same languages and were in close contact with each other.
>
> (1990: 1)

Rousseau's approach is to argue that 'people use an idiom of ethnic categories to explain political realities' (1975: 350). A good example is the cover term 'Dayak', a perjorative term of disputed derivation used by coastal dwellers to refer to interior and upriver pagans, and then adopted by British and Dutch colonial administrators. After independence it has come to be appropriated by indigenous political elites and incorporated into the names of various political parties both to distinguish natives who are not Muslim-Malay from the politically dominant Malays and to create and develop wider political consciousness and support (King, 2001a: 3). In addition, the term 'Iban', now so well known in the anthropological literature of Borneo, was not accepted by the far-flung populations so named until relatively recently. Those communities now called 'Iban' did not begin to perceive themselves as a relatively homogeneous and explicitly defined ethnic category until the second half of the nineteenth century when the English Brooke family, the 'white rajahs' of Sarawak, brought them into wider administrative, legal and educational systems and established communications between relatively isolated communities. It gained further impetus in the post-war period when native populations began to mobilize politically in response to the formation of Malay and Chinese political parties. It is suggested that the term 'Iban' was derived from the word 'ivan' (meaning 'wanderer'), which was coined by the Kayan, the former enemies of those who came to be called 'Iban', to refer to migratory and aggressive head-hunters who were encroaching on their territory from the mid-nineteenth century. The term 'Iban' gradually replaced the local river-based terms used by the people themselves and even the general labels of 'Sea Dayak' or 'Dayak' used by British colonial administrators (Wadley, 2000: 86).

An especially interesting and problematical case of ethnic definition and nomenclature is that of the 'Maloh' of the Upper Kapuas region of West Kalimantan (King, 1985; the ethnic term is placed in inverted commas because it is not a generally agreed term). The 'Maloh' are not a culturally homogeneous population with clearly defined boundaries, although there are cultural markers which permit us to distinguish a cluster of communities in the upper Kapuas region of Indonesian Borneo from differently named neighbours. The 'Maloh' language is distinctive in Borneo, though its speakers have borrowed from neighbouring languages like Iban and Malay; they had a craft specialization – silver- and gold-smithing – which was made much of as a distinctive feature of 'Maloh' culture, though this is no longer practised; there are also elements of material culture and ritual and the values which underpin them which serve as boundary markers, though again the 'Maloh' have absorbed much from their neighbours so that some observers have claimed that major features of 'Maloh' social organization are derived from contact with and incorporation into a Muslim–Malay cultural and political world (Thambun, 1996; Bernstein, 1997). Some communities have also been significantly acculturated by the neighbouring Iban. What is particularly problematical about the 'Maloh' is that they are a stratified, minority population located historically in a cultural contact zone

between dominant central Borneo groupings such as the Kayan, migratory Iban and Iban-related communities, and the expanding coastal and riverine-based Muslim–Malay states. Therefore, there has been considerable cultural exchange, intermarriage, religious conversion and assimilation in this ethnically diverse region. In addition, internally the 'Maloh' adopted different identities depending on their situation, purposes and the level of contrast they wished to make. Aside from the identification with specific named communities or villages and the rivers along which they lived, an important higher level identity was that which has been referred to as 'divisions' or 'sub-groupings' of which there are three: Embaloh (or Tamambaloh), Taman (or Kapuas) and Kalis (King, 1985: 33–34). These divisions were based mainly on linguistic and other cultural distinctions, and they clustered more or less geographically.

A major difficulty which King faced during his field research in the early 1970s was deciding what ethnic term or 'ethnonym' to use to denote these people of interior Borneo because 'there is no generally accepted, internally derived name appropriate for them as a whole' (ibid.: 35). What is more, the Dutch colonial literature on this part of Borneo reflected this observation in that Dutch writers generally used river-based names in their classifications of the population as a whole or its constituent parts. To add to the difficulties, members of the Embaloh/Tamambaloh division maintained that it was the term for their division which should be extended to cover the other two as well, while those of the Taman division stated that everyone was 'Taman'. The Kalis, on the other hand, did not accept the labels 'Embaloh' or 'Taman' as appropriate to them. There were also different versions of origin myths and oral histories of migration which were employed as a means of supporting particular claims to cultural and historical ascendancy.

Rather than select from one of these disputed internal names, King opted for the term 'Maloh' which was 'a general name . . . used by the neighbouring Iban to refer to distinctive Dayak people in the Upper Kapuas who are widely known for their skills in fashioning metals' (ibid.: 35). At the time this externally derived ethnic label (or 'exonym') adapted from the name 'Embaloh', the river complex closest to Iban settlement in the borderlands between West Kalimantan and Sarawak, appeared to be accepted by those so named. The Iban comprised the main market for 'Maloh' decorative silver- and goldware; 'Maloh' smiths travelled widely through Iban country, and some had settled down and married Iban women; they frequently brought Iban-made trade goods such as woven cloth back to their home villages. Many 'Maloh' were fluent in the Iban language and the gradual Iban expansion and encroachment into 'Maloh' territories had resulted in considerable 'Maloh' assimilation into Iban communities and culture. The term 'Maloh' enjoyed wide currency in Sarawak and the Kalimantan borderlands; it was a term well known in the post-war English language literature on Borneo; and 'Maloh' smiths accepted it as a valid designation of an overall cultural identity which, despite processes of assimilation and cultural exchange, marked them off from their neighbours. However, rarely

did the 'Maloh' use the term themselves; their most frequent points of reference were river-based names.

Since the 1970s the issue of ethnic labelling has become much more contentious. The craft of metal-smithing was on the wane in the 1960s and had all but disappeared in the 1970s because of competition from imported bazaar jewellery. Thus, the context within which the term 'Maloh' had flourished was no longer relevant. Its use became much more problematical and it became increasingly unacceptable to those so named. In other circumstances and as with the externally derived labels 'Dayak' and 'Iban' the designation 'Maloh' might have been adopted by the people themselves. Some of King's publications were also read by young 'Maloh' intellectuals who began to debate the term. Wadley has said that at the present time 'educated "Maloh" are making efforts to find a common indigenous ethnic label and at the same time to challenge Western ethnography about their group' and to assert their own 'intellectual authority over outside, Western scholarship' (2000: 92, 94). One of the early challenges came from Jacobus Frans, a government official and politician, who is of mixed 'Maloh'-Iban ancestry and hails from the Embaloh division. He and other supporters have vigorously promoted the ethnonym 'Dayak (or 'Daya') Banuaka' which is itself an interesting combination of a general external referent for non-Muslim natives, usually translated as 'interior' or 'inland person', and the 'Maloh' word *banuaka*, which means 'our people' or 'people of our place' (King, 2001a: 15). This latter term is widely used to refer to institutions and practices which are distinctively 'Maloh', but until recently it was not used specifically as an ethnonym. Interestingly the term has also been challenged by another local scholar from the Taman or Kapuas division. Thambun Anyang, in his Dutch doctoral thesis, is not convinced that the term *banuaka* is sufficiently discriminating since he argues that its primary meaning is 'us together' and it can be extended to those who are not culturally 'Maloh' (1996: 4). Instead he prefers the term 'Taman' or 'Taman family' as the most appropriate general ethnic label (ibid.: 18ff.). Apparently the Kalis continue to reject both labels. This difference of view seems to be a recent expression of long-standing differences between the three 'Maloh' divisions and the internal disagreements about historical and cultural priorities. Wadley argues that the internal debates among young educated 'Maloh' about the general ethnic label appropriate to them is likely to take interesting turns, depending on the political and administrative position and influence of the key local players, and that 'the search for a common ethnic label that is agreeable to both anthropologists and native politicians may actually be in vain' (2000: 96, 97–98). What appears to be happening at the moment is that anthropologists are either content to confine their attention to a 'Maloh' river-based grouping or division and use the local term appropriate to it without venturing beyond (Arts, 1991; Diposiswoyo, 1985; Okuno, 1997) or employing a combined term such as 'Maloh/Banuaka' (Bernstein, 1997: 19). We are therefore qualifying certain of the ethnic labels we use, recognizing that they are subject to dispute, negotiation, rejection and replacement.

What this debate also raises is the problem of cultural homogeneity as against cultural variation and the ways in which ethnic categories interlink with social relations. In writing about a particular named population there is still a tendency to assume that what defines them to outsiders is more important than what divides them internally. The problem of ethnic labelling among the 'Maloh' is, in part at least, to do with the significant internal differences among them and the fact that the ethnic category 'Maloh' is not coterminous with a 'society' or 'social group', nor does it correspond with a unified and homogeneous cultural grouping. For example, although for certain purposes anthropologists and the 'Maloh' themselves distinguish 'Maloh' from the neighbouring Malays, Iban, nomadic Punan and others, in important respects all these separately named groupings are part of the same social system and we cannot understand the 'Maloh' without reference to social relationships within a wider system. This also recognizes that a not inconsiderable number of 'Maloh' communities enjoy closer relations with their non-'Maloh' neighbours than they do with other 'Maloh'. This is especially so in their relationships with Muslim-Malays since the upriver Malay states, established from the early nineteenth century, have been an important point of reference for the 'Maloh'; we have seen that Leach describes a similar situation in Highland Burma where the Buddhist Shan states played an important role in Kachin socio-political and cultural life ([1954] 1970).

In his study of Taman ethnomedicine, Bernstein observes that 'in the most distant Taman villages ... Malay healers ... play an important role' and that the Taman have 'incorporated many of the Malays' practices' (1997: 41, 430). What is also clear is that from the nineteenth century many 'Maloh' converted to Islam and over time changed their ethnic identity to ' become Malay'. Members of the 'Maloh' aristocracy or upper rank formed alliances with the ruling families of the Malay states to sustain their political and economic position, and this usually involved intermarriage and conversion to Islam. There is also evidence of certain 'Maloh' aristocrats seceding from a longhouse with their followers and settling down in Malay trading centres. Some 'Maloh' commoners also intermarried with Malays and moved to Malay settlements sometimes out of dissatisfaction with their social and political position in their own community and to realize opportunities elsewhere (King, 1985: 61; 2001a: 22–27). Therefore, the ethnic categories 'Malay' and 'Maloh' are best seen as constituent parts of the same society or social system; each depends on and is integrated with the other. The same point can be made about 'Maloh' relations with neighbouring Iban and nomadic Punan.

Brunei

This situation parallels the relationships between native non-Muslim and Malay communities in Brunei. The Brunei sultanate has been an important centre for the dissemination of Islam and Malay culture for some five hundred years at least, and was a significant international trading emporium in the fifteenth and sixteenth centuries (King, 1994). It has also provided a major political, economic and cultural focus for surrounding populations. What King has called 'Brunei society' is therefore, in contrast to the views of Brown (1970, 1998), not coincident with the Brunei Malays as an ethnic category because the Brunei sultanate comprised and still comprises a stratified plural social order (King, 1996a). The concept of a Brunei society must include not only the ethnic Bruneis but the Muslim Kadayan and non-Muslim Dayak ethnic groupings such as the Dusun (or Bisaya), Murut (or Lun Bawang/Lun Dayeh), Tutong and Belait. Historically, before the creation of the separate states of Brunei Darussalam and Malaysian Borneo, Brunei society also shaded into more distant communities such as the Iban and the coastal Melanau (King, 1994, 1996a).

This notion of a Brunei society which cuts across ethnic categories and groupings, a concept of 'society' or 'social structure' which Leach first developed in relation to his study of the Kachin, makes sense for four main reasons. First, the roots of the Brunei Malays as an ethnic category and group can be traced to the pagan aboriginal populations of the Brunei Bay region. Rather than the ethnic Bruneis and other non-Malay peoples constituting separate groups with distinct origins, they share a common cultural heritage and myths of origin. Second, there has been a continuous and dynamic interrelationship between Brunei Malays and others through the conversion of various communities to Islam, especially through intermarriage, the practice of conferring titles and offices on pagan leaders and incorporating them into a common political and administrative system, and the use of the Malay language as a lingua franca. There have also been processes of interaction and assimilation operating between non-Malay populations, particularly between the Kadayan and the Murut, so that while in theory some communities might be presented as clearly defined, in practice they shade into one another. Third, there existed a common set of principles of social organization and shared social categories, comprising ranks, ethnic categories/groups and local units which brought together and ordered the several populations of the Brunei Bay region. However, different communities interpreted these categories and the interrelationships between them in different ways depending on interests and circumstances. Finally, the Brunei social system was underpinned by a variety of economic relationships in which different groupings tended to fulfil different functions in the division of labour. In the case of the Kadayan, for example, they were important providers of food, especially rice, in the Brunei polity and exchanged this with Brunei Malays who mainly comprised administrators, traders, craftspeople and fishing folk (King, 2001a: 31).

The Upper Kapuas and Brunei cases demonstrate the importance of Malay centres of trade, commerce, court ritual and administration as nodal points in overarching social systems and that these were not alien implants but derived primarily from transformations of locally established non-Malay communities.

They also show that territorial boundaries, ethnic and cultural distinctions, and social divisions are not coterminous.

Ethnicity, the Indonesian 'culture state' and Dutch colonialism

We now want to take the issue of identity formation of marginal or minority populations further by examining case studies from Indonesia which adopt a postmodern perspective. We start, however, with Pemberton's study of Indonesian nationalism under President Suharto and its basis in a Javanese identity which was forged during the Dutch colonial period (1994). We then move to a consideration of the ways in which marginal populations are created and how they respond to their marginality in the modern Indonesian nation–state by referring to two case studies: Tsing's study of the Meratus Dayaks of southeastern Kalimantan (1993) and briefly Spyer's work on the Aruese of the Moluccas (2000). The theme of the creation and transformation of identities is then pursued in a slightly different direction with a consideration of tourism development with regard to the cultures and identities of the Balinese and the Toraja of highland Sulawesi. We end with Kahn's analysis of the 'constitution' of Minangkabau identity in the context of Dutch colonial policies (1993). Kahn's work demonstrates the ways in which the Dutch colonial state contributed to the creation of images and identities of its subject populations and it links in nicely with studies of the 'touristification' of Balinese culture, which commenced during the colonial period, and with Pemberton's study of the Javanese.

On the subject of 'Java'

Pemberton's postmodern analysis of the culture of Javanese-dominated Indonesian politics reveals in considerable detail how the Indonesian political elite deployed such concepts as 'traditional values', 'ritual' and 'cultural inheritance' to maintain centralized control and order in the country (1994). It tells us something about the ways in which Javanese identity has been created and transformed, but more importantly it sets the scene for our case studies by considering the practices and ideologies of those who held the reins of power in Jakarta. State action affected the most out-of-the-way places and the identities of minority populations like the Meratus Dayaks, the Bemunese of Aru, the Balinese, the highland Toraja and the Minangkabau through the national education system, the use of the Indonesian national language, the promotion of symbols of nationhood on radio, television and in the press, the introduction of vigorous programmes of regional and local development, including tourism development, and intervention in local level politics and administration. What is more, Indonesian political leaders and administrators built upon the Dutch legacy in adopting colonial definitions and classifications of ethnic groups and European depictions of 'traditional' cultures.

Pemberton originally studied gamelan music in Indonesia in 1971 and again in 1975–1977 but was increasingly drawn into a wider interest in cultural matters and returned to Central Java for further field research in 1982–1984, focusing specifically on the interrelationships between history, politics and culture as these were played out in the sultanate of Surakarta (Solo) (ibid.: ix–xi). His sojourn in Java coincided with the third national Indonesian elections in 1982. As well as ranging over the politics of culture of New Order Indonesia, Pemberton also examines in some depth, through Javanese manuscripts and Dutch archives and published work, the creation of the culture of the Central Javanese court of Surakarta and 'the centrality of the construct "ritual" in Javanese cultural discourse' (ibid.: 1). What especially exercises his research is the fact that, up until the recent collapse of the Suharto regime, the New Order had been generally untroubled by protest and opposition. Social unrest was relatively rare, particularly in Java, and when it occurred it was rather quickly dealt with. Politics, including the holding of elections, was in effect de-politicized in Indonesia and was expressed publicly in the realm of culture and rituals. Pemberton notes that the Suharto government whose official political party, Golkar, always won national elections had styled the 1982 elections, a 'Festival of Democracy', a grand 'national ritual'. Although Suharto's authoritarian regime deployed the full force of the state to sustain itself in power, it presented itself in quite other terms. And it is this image-making, cultural representation and ideology-construction (or in postmodernist terms 'discursive practices') which Pemberton explores.

Pemberton argues that 'culture' is used in Indonesia to transcend political and class interests and to express the essential character and consequences of New Order rule; social stability and the steady state are expressed and explained by reference to 'traditional values', 'cultural inheritance' or 'origins', and 'ritual', so that political events and actions like elections are styled as ritual and ceremony. Pemberton also locates the origins of the wider concept of Indonesian 'traditional culture' focused on social order specifically in Java and in an invented Javanese past, which is not surprising given the dominance of the Javanese in Indonesian politics. These cultural expressions embrace not just those official ones generated by the central government and acted out in public spaces, but various local or village-based practices which the government supports, preserves and promotes as examples of 'tradition'. A key local level ritual, on which Geertz concentrated in his *The Religion of Java*, is the *slametan* (see Chapter 3), a communal event associated with such matters as weddings and tutelary spirits which, as Geertz says, expresses and strengthens 'the general cultural order and its power to hold back the forces of disorder' (1960: 14). What is more the search for and reaffirmation of 'traditional order' is an open-ended affair; Pemberton refers to 'the haunting sense of incompleteness' in the 'process of recovering "tradition"' because in New Order Indonesia it is expressed in such generalized terms (Pemberton, 1994: 10–11). This incompleteness demands attention to repeated ritual performances, the presentation of offerings, and supplications and prayers directed to capturing and fulfilling 'tradition'.

New Order discourse, as well as presenting some sense of cultural unity focused on Java, also acknowledges diversity not only among Javanese villages but also more generally in Indonesia. In this connection Pemberton draws attention to the enormous theme park, 'Taman Mini', constructed on the out-skirts of Jakarta. The idea of Taman Mini 'Indonesia Indah' or the 'Beautiful Indonesia'-in-Miniature Park, came from the First Lady, Mrs Suharto, after a visit to Disneyland just before the 1971 national elections (ibid.: 12). The Park was opened in 1975 and was designed, as its name suggests, to be Indonesia-in-Miniature. Aside from a host of recreational and leisure facilities including a hotel, there is a lake with islands representing the archipelago, examples of 'ancient monuments' harking back to a glorious Indonesian past, and an area with twenty-six display houses designed to represent the customary architectural styles of each of Indonesia's twenty-six provinces (ibid.: 152–161). It is import-ant to note that it is regional cultures which are depicted thus and not the cul-tures of specific ethnic groups, and, as we shall see in our discussion of Bali, the Indonesian state defines culture in terms of overt, standardized elements such as material artefacts, costume, dance, music and ceremony. The centrepiece of the Park is predictably an audience hall of Central Javanese aristocratic design, not miniaturized, indeed grander than the originals, where 'traditional' ceremonies are performed. As Pemberton says, this Java-centred Taman Mini, close to the national capital, collapses Indonesian past and present and its vast expanse and diversity of peoples into an organized, ordered and manageable cultural space.

For the origins of Indonesian cultural discourse focused on Java, Pemberton goes back to the foundation of the Palace of Surakarta, drawing attention very importantly to the role of the Dutch East India Company in the establishment of this Javanese kingdom in 1745. What he also demonstrates is that, in their attempt to distance and distinguish themselves from the intruding foreign power, the Surakartans, presented and in part created a 'Javanese style', which during the nineteenth century came to be seen as a typically Javanese cultural identity. In the Surakartan chronicles, in its literature and customs such as wed-dings, emerges a distinctively Javanese identity which harks back to earlier pre-colonial times (ibid.: 22–23). This idea of Javanese culture was further con-firmed as authentic, traditional and original by Dutch scholars working in the field of 'Javanologie' and through the Java Institute, established in Surakarta in 1919, and the Institute's scholarly journal, *Djawa*, published between 1921 and 1941. It is this identity and authenticity and these origins of Java which the New Order recovered, re-worked and presented as authentically Javanese, and at the core of Indonesian national identity. Yet this was an identity created by court chroniclers in the context of a kingdom which had become increasingly subject to Dutch rule, without real political power particularly from 1830, but which retained for itself and elaborated court ceremonial (especially weddings), dress, status and etiquette in a remarkably ordered and hierarchical cultural space (ibid.: 28–147). Interestingly, in Malaysia a similar process has been at work; Kessler notes that present-day Malay culture is grounded in the traditional Malay polity, in the relationships between the ruler (*raja*) and the people (*ra'ayat*), and 'it derives from and finds its "traditional" or historical model in the Melaka sultanate. Its charter is to be found in how that paradigmatic historical epoch or experience is known' (1992: 146). Nevertheless, as we have already seen, that identity is a negotiable and open-ended one and not fixed and homogeneous.

The Indonesian government's 'construction of a New Order cultural dreamland' (Pemberton, 1994: 318) in the process of creating and promoting an Indonesian identity, and the exercise of control over its culturally diverse populations have, quite naturally, had consequences for those minorities outside Java. We shall now turn to examine the various ways in which these latter have responded to the penetration of the agents and forces of the state – a process set in motion during the Dutch colonial period – and the identities which have been created in that process, both by the state and the people themselves. As Kahn has said, 'Very few analysts have recognized that just as Indonesian-ness is a constructed or created identity, so are the lower-level ethnicities of the Balinese, the Javanese, the Minangkabau, and so forth' (1998: 13).

People on the margins: the Meratus Dayaks and the Bemunese of Aru

The following two case studies demonstrate the responses of outer island populations to the actions of the Indonesian state under Suharto, and the ways in which the identities of minorities have been constructed and expressed in relationship to the state's promotion of national unity and development in the pursuit of maintaining social control and order.

Anna Tsing's study undertaken between 1979 and 1981 and again in 1986 focuses on the Dayaks of the Meratus Mountains of south-eastern Kalimantan and the 'cultural and political construction of marginality' (1993: 5). It is not only about how the Meratus Dayaks are marginalized by the powerful forces of the state and the actions and perceptions of neighbouring lowland majorities such as the Banjar Malays but also how the people themselves respond to their marginal identity through protest, challenge, negotiation, and the reinterpretation and explanation of their status in stories, songs and narratives of people and events. Tsing also examines the different perspectives of men and women on marginality, given that women generally 'are disadvantaged political actors' (ibid.: 8). In particular, she records the conversations and encounters with an elderly female informant, Uma Adang. Tsing's postmodern, postcolonial perspective therefore involves her in an analysis of 'marginalizing discourses, institutions, and experiences' about domination and difference and concerned with the distinctions between civilization, modernity, progress, order and power on the one hand and the primitive, traditional, backward, nomadic, disordered, untamed and displaced on the other (ibid.: 5–6). She examines the limitations and weaknesses of state authority and power at its margin, on the periphery.

Interestingly as in the 'Maloh' case the Meratus communities are not easily labelled. With the help of a local graduate student Tsing decided on the term 'Meratus' to designate those she studied; this was not a term which was used by the people themselves, but one created by the anthropologist and her adviser. She justifies this because of the absence of an 'authentic' internally derived label of local identity. Other general terms were considered perjorative and derogatory; the lowland Banjar coined the term 'Bukit', which has been used frequently in the ethnographic literature, but with its connotation of 'hillbilly' was obviously unacceptable locally. Tsing therefore decided on 'Meratus Dayaks' because, she says, 'it refers to Dayak inhabitants of the Meratus Mountains', and for her graduate student its root *ratus* (which means 'hundreds' in Indonesian) 'evoked the diversity of the people'; it is 'a kind of anti-ethnic label ... for a group of people who are all very different from each other' (ibid.: 52). It appears that marginalization had generated local diversity, dispersal, mobility and until recently a retreat into isolation so far as this was possible, and not a Kachin-, Kajang- or Semai-like coming together of minorities in opposition to a dominant majority. Meratus are shifting cultivators and forest foragers, and the primary social unit is the *umbun* or the group which makes a swidden farm together, and which are 'proud of their autonomy' (ibid.: 64). Tsing says that the Meratus 'value the autonomy to travel and farm where they please and to form diverse, shifting identities and affiliations in conjunction with this mobility' (ibid.: 63). She did not discover any stable, clearly defined 'village' communities to study and found that it was best to travel around the region, staying in different places with 'loosely connected' *umbun*. In this connection she came to know Meratus relationships as ramifying, shifting and re-forming, and their culture as not fixed and stable but as open-ended, variable and negotiable. 'Travel' was a central concern of her study.

Yet the main categorical distinction is between lowland Banjar Malays and upland Meratus and by giving them a general ethnic label. Tsing does accord the Meratus Dayaks some kind of identity separate from others. The issue is nevertheless further complicated because even the means used to make ethnic distinctions are contested, the Banjar, for example, arguing these on the basis of 'profound racial and cultural differences' while the Meratus deny these Banjar claims and many of them say that they speak the same language as the Banjarese (ibid.: 53). It was state policies, colonial and postcolonial, which tended to divide one from another and create the Meratus as a separate, marginal category (ibid.: 41ff.). However, though the 'state' or 'government' (the 'exemplary centre' organizing and performing national rituals of power) is counterposed to the 'people' and to 'local politics' (the 'disorganized periphery') as external, authoritarian and dominant, the two are intimately interrelated (ibid.: 22–26), and Tsing shows how the Meratus conceive of, talk about and represent state power in terms of violence, terrorism, government 'head-hunting', ceremonial building projects in the name of development, and the preoccupation with establishing 'order' (in diet and cuisine, fixed settlements and resettlement schemes, family planning) (ibid.: 76ff.).

Similar concerns exercise Patricia Spyer in her study of the 'backcountry' Aruese of Bemun on Barakai island in the south-eastern Moluccas, a community of pearl divers and collectors of marine products long involved in far-flung international seaborne trade (2000). She carried out research there in 1984, 1986 to 1988 and again in 1994. However, here we are dealing not with land-locked, relatively isolated Dayak communities, but with trade- and sea-oriented maritime people. Spyer explores the construction of identity and the relationships of the Bemunese with the two categories 'Aru' and 'Malay' as well as their 'entanglements' with modernity and the world beyond Aru. For the Bemunese, like the Meratus Dayaks, they were incorporated into the Dutch colonial state and then the independent Indonesian nation yet also marginalized within this wider economic and political system. They were subject to and participated in a discourse of power and displacement. For the Bemunese the expression of their problematical relationship with modernity and the state and the conceptualization of the relationships between here and there, between the 'local' and the 'distant', and between 'community' and the 'world beyond' was in terms of 'expectancy', 'desire', a 'diffuse sense of deficit and longing' and an 'incompleteness' (ibid.: xix, 4, 28, 33, 35). Specifically they questioned Spyer about their long-lost or 'misplaced' kin across the seas and their desire to re-establish contact with their descendants. The consequence of these entanglements was, according to Spyer, 'the perception that the world in certain crucial respects resides in another place, more often than not across the sea' (ibid.: 4).

Let us now turn to another kind of engagement with the Indonesian nation–state in the context of tourism development and the ways in which local identities are expressed and changed.

Tourism and ethnicity: the Balinese and Toraja

The recent development of ethnic and cultural tourism in South-East Asia has had important consequences for the ways in which those populations targeted as objects of tourist interest perceive themselves and others, and particularly how they have responded to national programmes of development and identity formation.

During the past two decades anthropological studies of tourism development and its relationships to culture and society have assumed an increasingly important position in the discipline. It was probably Valene Smith's edited volume *Hosts and Guests: The Anthropology of Tourism* (1977), subsequently published in a revised edition (1989), which more than any other contribution stimulated interest in the effects of tourism on local identities and cultures. It also contained papers by Philip McKean on the Hindu Balinese and Eric Crystal on the upland Toraja of central Sulawesi. McKean, in particular, had argued against an earlier pessimistic view that mass tourism destroys traditional cultures; more specifically he cast doubt on the claim that cultural performances and items of material culture produced for the Indonesian tourist market become commodities and lose their meaning for those who 'package' and sell them to tourists. McKean, on the other hand, proposes that tourism in Bali, far from undermining Balinese culture, led to its sustenance and revitalization (1976, 1989). He suggests that the Balinese separated and distanced the cultural products for tourism from their 'authentic' local versions which were therefore not despoiled by the process of 'staging'. McKean points out that tourism also provided a considerable source of income for the Balinese, some of which was reinvested in the training and upgrading of music and dance troupes and in the development of craft skills. Overall, tourist interest in their culture served to instil a sense of pride in the local performers and artists and helped reinforce Balinese identity in the context of the Indonesian nation–state.

A similar thesis is presented by Crystal in his analysis of a central element of Torajan identity, the Aluk To Dolo, or 'the ceremonies of the ancestors', which include elaborate funeral rituals (1989). In the early 1970s Indonesian government planners began to consider the possibility of developing tourist interest in Torajan culture and formed the view that it had the potential to become another Bali; funeral ceremonies were identified as a potential major attraction, along with carved effigies of the dead displayed in rock shelters, distinctive house architecture and a dramatic highland scenery (Volkman, 1984, 1990; Adams, 1997: 159). A transport infrastructure and other tourist facilities such as hotels and guest-houses were developed and tourism increased rapidly, indeed so rapidly that Toraja moved within the space of a few years from elite, ethnic tourism to mass or charter cultural tourism. Until the efflorescence of tourism, Crystal suggests that Torajan culture seemed likely to disappear under the pressures of Christian missionary activity, the spread of modern education, and the promotion of an Indonesian national identity. However, following the government's endorsement of Torajan religion as the focus of a tourist spectacle, Torajan leaders embraced the 'tourist ethic'. Crystal says that 'death ceremonies especially came to be reassessed in light of regional economic planning potential and national priorities' (1989: 148), and on the strength of these 'exotic' rituals the Toraja gained the status of a 'touristic *primadona*' and secured 'an esteemed place in the Indonesian hierarchy of ethnic groups' (Adams, 1997: 159).

Like McKean's assessment of Balinese culture, Crystal identifies the positive effects of tourism development in providing incentives for the Toraja to maintain and renew their rituals and artistic traditions, and to present their identity in terms which both contributed to Indonesian national development and emphasized a distinctive 'Torajaness' within the Indonesian nation. During the 1980s tourism in Torajaland had 'clearly become a phenomenon of international significance' (Crystal, 1989: 161), and some of the tourist revenue as well as income earned in labour migration away from Torajaland was channelled back into financing ever grander funeral rituals (Volkman, 1985). However, though the foreign package holiday market increased considerably, the majority of tourists to Torajaland have comprised Indonesians from other ethnic groups and the attention devoted to the Toraja by fellow Indonesians has 'added new fuel to long-simmering ethnic antagonisms', especially between these highlanders and the neighbouring lowland Buginese and Makassarese living in the shadow of a high profile Torajan culture (Adams, 1997: 174). In spite of the positive influence on Torajan culture and identity, Crystal also points to the negative consequences of the very rapid growth in tourist numbers: the loss of precious heirlooms and artefacts, stolen and sold on the international 'primitive art' market, and the potential loss of cultural integrity as ceremonies become more and more 'staged' and separated from any meaningful value complex.

Interest in the positive and negative effects of tourism development on local cultures and identities has subsequently led to attempts to re-evaluate the notion of culture. The work of Robert Wood (1984, 1993) and Michel Picard (1990, 1993, 1996) has been especially important in this regard. In addition, the increasing importance of the efforts of governments in both promoting a sense of nationhood and national identity as well as encouraging local cultural activities for tourists in the interest of economic development, has also resulted in studies of the relationships between tourism, ethnicity and the state (Picard and Wood, 1997). Wood has said in relation to the Asian and Pacific societies considered in his 1997 co-edited volume with Picard that 'the state plays a central role not only in structuring the tourist encounter but also in shaping and controlling the visible contours of ethnicity' (ibid.: 5). States may, for example, officially support certain cultural markers and labels of local ethnicity and discourage or prohibit others in relation to the construction and promotion of national identity. In this regard Wood refers to the 'domestication' and 'sanitizing' of ethnicity in such places as Singapore where local residents define their own identity primarily in terms of specific sub-groupings of Chinese such as Hokkien or Cantonese and Indians such as Tamil or Sikh but the Singapore government and the tourism industry divide all Singaporeans into four major ethnic categories or 'races': Chinese, Indian, Malay and Other (ibid.: 12). In other words, officially self-identity is denied, the 'races' are seen as unique, separate and bounded, and 'individuals are pressured to identify with one ethnic group, to search for their respective ethnic roots, and to act according to the official stereotypes of their cultural traditions' (Leong, 1997: 94).

As we have seen, the assumption that ethnicity, and of course the 'cultural stuff' which makes up ethnic identity, is primordial, fixed, handed down and inherent, has been called into question, and in the anthropology of tourism too Wood has argued that what we call 'traditional culture' is subject to continuous reformulation and 'on-going symbolic construction' (1993: 60); in other words, culture is constantly being contested and symbolically recreated in interactions between different ethnic groupings and increasingly in relation to state policies and actions. This also applies to notions of cultural authenticity with regard to tourist experiences in that the central problem is to understand the processes by which certain elements or items of culture are assigned and thereby acquire authenticity, which will in turn depend on the different criteria used to determine authenticity in different tourist circumstances. Cohen argues that authenticity like the notion of 'traditional culture' and 'ethnic identity' is not fixed but negotiable, and this helps explain why a 'cultural product, or a trait thereof, which is at one point generally judged as contrived or inauthentic may, in the course of time, become generally recognized as authentic' (1988: 379).

The Balinese, through the detailed research of Michel Picard, provide one of the best examples of a population which has dynamically transformed its cultural identity in the context of tourism development and the policies and programmes of the colonial and the postcolonial state (1996, 1997). Picard, like Wood, addresses the debate between those who argue that tourism debases and undermines local culture and those who maintain that it preserves and promotes it; he also examines McKean's claim that the Balinese are able to establish boundaries between the sacred (culture for the gods) and the profane (culture for tourism). Picard suggests instead that these observers have been asking the wrong kinds of questions (1996: 8). It is not so much whether or not Balinese culture has been able to withstand the onslaught of tourism, but how it has been shaped and transformed by tourism from within. Picard coins the term 'touristic culture' in his Balinese research to make it plain that tourism is not an external force for change impacting on Balinese culture from without, but rather a process changing Balinese society from within, and that the Balinese have been actively engaged in transforming their own culture and ethnic consciousness in response to tourism opportunities.

Nevertheless, this process of the 'touristification' of Balinese culture, of 'blurring the boundaries between the inside and the outside, . . . between that which belongs to "culture" and that which pertains to "tourism"' (1997: 183), was brought into being by Dutch colonial administrators and Orientalist scholars who regarded Bali as a 'living museum', as the only surviving repository of Hindu-Javanese civilization which had been swept away from other regions of the East Indies by Islam (ibid.: 185; and Schulte Nordholt, 1999). It should be noted that the Dutch had completed their 'pacification' of Bali, which was often described by nineteenth-century observers as a 'wild', 'savage' and 'warlike' place, by 1908 'after a long and bloody struggle' (Vickers, 1989: 2, 11–36). After taming it the 'wild' image of Bali was no longer appropriate and the Dutch set about protecting, preserving and celebrating its culture.

The Dutch defined Balinese identity and the cultural integrity of the Balinese essentially in Hindu terms, and in opposition to Islam; they also tended to over-emphasize the importance of caste hierarchy and Hindu kingship (Boon, 1977: 41–46, 68, 70). The policy of cultural protection and patronage was known as the 'Balinization of Bali' (*Baliseering*) and it was directed to promoting a renaissance of Balinese culture and to ensuring that the people of Bali remained 'authentically Balinese' (Picard, 1997: 186). The political context of this policy was the Dutch concern to put behind them their 'ruthless conquest of the island' and to combat the spread of Islamic radicalism and Indonesian nationalism by supporting the Balinese nobility and reinforcing the 'traditional' administrative order (Vickers, 1989: 3; Picard, 1997: 186). Nevertheless, it was the Dutch and not the Balinese nobility who ultimately held the reins of power, and in the process of preserving Balinese culture and society in a fixed and time-less form, they transformed it, reorganized village administration, codified cus-tomary law, created a Dutch-educated Balinese intelligentsia, and emphasized particular aspects of Balinese culture at the expense of others. 'They banned slavery and widow sacrifice, disapproved of activities such as cockfighting, phased out the use of opium, and altered the structure of state organisation' (Vickers, 1989: 92). In other words, 'the Dutch set the framework within which the Balinese were going to define themselves' (Picard, 1997: 186), and they also began in earnest to open the island to tourism during the 1920s and 1930s.

Bali came to be presented variously in tourist brochures, guides and travel books as both 'exotic' and 'erotic', the 'Gem of the Lesser Sunda Islands', the 'Last Paradise', the 'Enchanted Isle', the 'Island of Artists' or the 'Island of Bare Breasts' (Picard, 1996: 23, 27–32; Vickers, 1989: 77–130). Anthropologists like Margaret Mead, Gregory Bateson and Jane Belo, and foreign artists, aesthetes and writers like Gregor Krause, Walter Spies, Beryl de Zoete, Colin McPhee, Vicki Baum and Miguel Covarrubias who sojourned in Bali in the 1920s and 1930s also contributed to this exoticism in their descriptions of the 'Island of Gods and Demons' (Picard, 1996: 32–33). Yet these images were rooted in another Western-derived image of noble rice-cultivating peasants living in village republics and embodying the essence of Balinese culture (Vickers, 1989: 89–91, 107, 110, 117). As Picard says, it was depicted

> as the homeland of a traditional culture insulated from the modern
> world and its vicissitudes, whose bearers, endowed with exceptional
> artistic talents, devote an outstanding amount of time and wealth
> staging sumptuous ceremonies for their own pleasure and that of their
> gods – and now in addition for the delight of tourists.
>
> (1993: 75–76)

In the late colonial period educated Balinese also began to contemplate what constituted 'Balineseness' and to come to terms with and understand the changes affecting Balinese culture. Schools and religious foundations for the study of Balinese culture were established and periodicals were founded to serve as a forum for debates and discussions about the nature of Balinese religion and society. Interestingly these were written not in the Balinese language, but in Malay, which was subsequently to form the basis of the Indonesian national language (1997: 187). At this time there emerged the notion of a Balinese people, a distinct ethnic group, defined in terms of religion and custom; these two key elements of definition were also expressed separately by the Balinese in the Malay language as *agama* and *adat* respectively. What had been previously an island of considerable cultural variation, with a considerably modified Hinduism, highly localized religions based on ancestral deities, which were closely integrated with customary practices and social relations, became an island-wide identity focused on Hinduism as a world religion (as against Islam and Christianity), and comprising separately defined spheres of belief and action expressed particularly in vibrant artistic traditions (ibid.: 187–192). Yet, above all, the Balinese, particularly their political elite, embraced the popular construction of themselves and used it for their own purposes; they accepted that their culture was a precious asset which needed to be cherished and nourished.

Balinese identity was further transformed following Indonesian independence. The founders of the Indonesian state constructed a national ideology and identity based on the 'high civilizations' of the region, particularly that of the Javanese (the immigrant Chinese and less advanced ethnic minorities were excluded). The national motto of 'unity in diversity' was based on the notion of an overarching primordial Indonesian cultural pattern, and the national identity of Indonesia was importantly based on these common customs, as well as a shared language (*bahasa Indonesia*), a shared history and a shared territory. Assumed shared concepts of the social community, intra-community dependence, mutual obligations and reciprocity, decision-making by collective discussion and consensus, and the importance of the collectivity over and above the individual were emphasized (Hitchcock and King, 1997: 8–9). To forge and consolidate an enhanced sense of consciousness of belonging to an Indonesian 'ethnic group', the political elite also formulated a 'state philosophy' of Pancasila which stressed the birth of the Indonesian nation in the revolutionary struggle for independence from the Dutch and which interestingly drew inspiration from European political philosophies. It became the sacred cornerstone of Indonesian national unity, and linked to the Javanese sacred number five, it comprised five principles (belief in one God, democracy and sovereignty of the people, nationalism and national consciousness, social justice, and humanitarianism and equality among mankind) (Holtzappel, 1997). Thus, Indonesian ethnicity was primarily a post-war political construction melding together various elements of an imagined tradition and principles derived from European political philosophies.

With regard to the definition of ethnicity in terms of religion (an increasingly important dimension in Balinese identity), the Indonesian secular state, in its national principle of 'Belief in one God', acknowledged and constitutionally protected and supported only 'genuine' religions. Initially Balinese religion was not so classified and had only the official status of a 'tribal' religion because it was considered to be based on custom (*adat*). After much lobbying by the Balinese and a further formalization and codification of a Bali-wide Hindu religion, it was given presidential support as a true religion in 1958. At that time it was referred to as 'Hindu Balinese Religion', but when official recognition was finally given in 1965 it was designated as *agama Hindu* (Hindu religion) (Picard, 1997: 194–195). This resulted in the further separation of Balinese religion from custom, and the increasing importance of Hinduism in defining the Balinese, though Picard remarks that this official religion 'bears little resemblance to everyday religious practice in houseyard and village temples' (ibid.: 195).

In addition to these changes in Balinese ethnic identity and culture from the 1920s the most significant recent changes have been in the context of the increase of package and back-packer tourism to Bali since the 1970s. Its origin was in the opening up of Indonesia to foreign investment and the push for economic growth under President Suharto's New Order after the end of Sukarno's presidency in 1965. The *Master Plan for the Development of Tourism in Bali* was published in six volumes in 1971 as part of the Indonesian government's objective to formulate a national tourism policy and secure an increasing share of the rapidly expanding international tourist market (Picard, 1996: 45ff.). Tourism was also part of the New Order's political agenda to promote national integration and unity and, after the political and economic chaos of Sukarno's last years, to re-establish Indonesia's position and raise its image on the world stage in order to attract foreign investment (Adams, 1997: 156ff.). Bali was to be the 'showcase' and the promotion of cultural tourism there was to 'serve as a model for future development of tourism in the archipelago' (Picard, 1993: 79). In fact the expansion of tourism did not really get under way until the late 1980s when the Indonesian government relaxed its protective national airline policy and opened Bali's airport in Den Pasar to foreign airlines, supported in the 1990s by government promotional and advertising campaigns, specifically targeted to attracting wealthy tourists to luxury international standard hotels in beach resorts (ibid.: 81).

Whilst the Indonesian government focused on the development of tourism in Bali as a national project, Balinese politicians, senior administrators and intellectuals became increasingly concerned about the marginalization of the Balinese people in these plans and the potentially undesirable consequences of mass tourism (Picard, 1996: 127, 182ff.). Their priority was to secure economic benefits for the Balinese and to spread these as widely as possible throughout the island, and, though not explicitly expressed, to promote the identity and status of the Balinese within the Indonesian nation–state. In addition, they argued that Balinese culture, essential to the tourism enterprise, should be protected and sustained. However, the concerns of the Balinese about the deleterious effects of international tourism and consequently the need to protect Balinese culture diminished during the 1980s. What began to be proclaimed by both foreign and Balinese observers, and McKean was an avid supporter of this position, was a tourism-generated cultural renaissance (cf. Picard, 1993: 88–89).

Yet Picard draws our attention to the way in which the conception of Balinese culture has changed during the Suharto years, a process which had been begun by the Dutch in the 1920s. The definition of culture in terms of basic values governing social, economic and political relations and moral behaviour has progressively shifted to a focus on tourism-focused 'artistic expressions' and 'cultural arts' (dance, music, costume, handicrafts, architecture) under the pressure of the official view promoted by the Indonesian Ministry of Education and Culture (1993: 90; 1996: 167–171, 198–199). Vickers too argues that public discussions of Balinese culture are not about culture as 'meaningful behaviour' but instead about 'the more narrow idea of formal religious and artistic activity' (1989: 195). The culture of the Balinese as an ethnic group has also been assimilated to the notion of a 'regional culture' or one which is not attached to a particular ethnic identity but to a province or an administrative unit. Balinese regional culture based on cultural display is then joined with others of a similarly officially sanctioned 'aesthetic' status to form an Indonesian national culture. Thus, Balinese culture is being sifted and arranged into those elements appropriate for the national culture which are then supported and financed by government (Picard, 1996: 171–179). Picard argues that it is this 'Indonesianized', 'folklorized' and 'provincialized' Balinese culture, assimilated by the Balinese themselves and presented as genuinely Balinese, which is experiencing a renaissance (1997: 203). Nevertheless, the 'frames of reference deliberately provided by the state as safe outlets for the expression of ethnicity in Indonesia' are subject to negotiation and debate, and though the Balinese are the weaker contestants in their relations with the state, they have rejected certain elements of 'Indonesianization', changed others and used some to their own advantage in expressing Balinese identity (ibid.: 202–206).

McKean's conclusion, and one originally embraced by the Balinese intelligentsia, that the Balinese have been able to sustain their traditional culture by distancing entertainments for tourists from genuine rituals for themselves and their gods, is difficult to accept when Balinese culture has been so thoroughly 'touristified' during the past eighty years or so. What is more, even before the influence of tourism became pronounced it was difficult to separate out the ritual and theatrical aspects of Balinese dance. In an analysis of dance Picard demonstrates that there are indeed certain performances such as the Legong Dance and the Ramayana Ballet which are 'modern creations', designed specifically for non-Balinese audiences, but these have then been re-incorporated into the regular Balinese repertoire. There are also various other performances staged for tourists, elements of which are used in Balinese exorcism and ritual, and still others derived from Balinese religious performances which have been adopted as tourist attractions (1996: 134–163). One dance, the *panyembrana*, started its life in a ritual context, became an entertainment and returned to ritual use (Picard, 1990: 62). Picard demonstrates very clearly that the development of cultural tourism in Bali encouraged a Balinese awareness of the value and importance of their own culture, and its role in defining Balinese ethnic identity, but that that culture is rather different from what it was in the early part of the twentieth century because 'tourist performances are now acknowledged as Balinese traditions' (ibid.: 73). In addition, 'for the Balinese, commerce and art, entertainment and ritual, are not clearly distinct categories – and ... the content of a cultural performance overflows from one category to another' (1996: 198).

In order to demonstrate that it is not only in the context of tourism development that the interaction between local communities and representatives of the state, colonial and postcolonial, shape and transform ethnic identities and cultures, let us now turn to Joel Kahn's examination of the constitution of Minangkabau identity (1993, 1995). Kahn himself says:

> While the intense touristic encounter between Bali and the West in the 1920s and 1930s makes the processes involved in the creation of the modern discourse about Balinese culture unique, it is interesting to note that very similar processes were at work at much the same time elsewhere in the Netherlands Indies, in places where tourism was of negligible significance.
>
> (1997: 110)

In other words, the creation of identities was part of the general encounter between Western colonial powers and those 'others' who were administered by them.

The creation of Minangkabau identity

As we saw in Chapter 5, Kahn undertook field research in West Sumatra in the early 1970s and later on among Minangkabau migrants in Negeri Sembilan. Subsequently he wished to understand how the situation he observed in the 1970s had come to be, and therefore he analysed a substantial historical literature on the Minangkabau from the perspective of globalism and cultural theory, noting that they had been increasingly incorporated into a wider economic system during the European mercantile period, and then become subject to processes of 'modernization' during the Dutch colonial period proper, particularly since the late nineteenth century. He attempted to understand why some observers were anticipating the demise of Minangkabau culture, and hence their traditional identity, in the face of global forces of change, while others saw the Minangkabau as remaining 'stubbornly premodern', 'self-contained' and 'other' (1993: vii, 21). How could this contradiction between modern images of the Minangkabau as individualistic, competitive, commercialized and rationalist, and traditional images focused on matrilineal kin groups, 'village republics', rice cultivation, handicraft production and forest gathering be explained (ibid.: 3–4)?

Kahn's main conclusion, echoing as we have already seen the findings of anthropologists like Picard for the Balinese and Pemberton for the Javanese, is that the origins of Minangkabau tradition are to be found in the Dutch colonial period not in a distant pre-colonial past. He also indicates that his task of historical analysis was made much more difficult because of the change in

227

thinking in anthropological circles, and the criticism of previously accepted premises, concepts and methods, especially the doubts cast in postmodern social science on an outsider's ability to analyse, explain and represent another culture. Even the presumption that anthropologists should seek to speak on behalf of others was questioned as 'ethnocentric' and 'Orientalist'. In this spirit Kahn argues that his account of Minangkabau culture is itself a 'created image', but one that needs to be evaluated in its social and historical contexts (ibid.: ix).

Kahn draws attention to the fact that the Minangkabau cannot be demarcated objectively and unambiguously as a discrete, unchanging, homogeneous unit (ibid.: 16–19). More generally, 'it has never been possible to treat Indonesian "societies" as "tribal isolates"', not least because of 'the centuries of contact with the West' (ibid.: 22). For him the images which have been used to represent the Minangkabau have been generated by particular social and historical processes. The major ones were generated by changing Dutch colonial ideologies, policies and practices from the late nineteenth century onwards with regard to land and village administration (ibid.: 32); the colonial bureaucracy increased in size, power, influence and range of functions, villages had to establish councils as administrative contact points and fund them from local levies, supra-village organization was undermined, and native rights over permanently cultivated land were 'protected' while 'waste ground' could be alienated on long lease, in mining concessions, and as forest reserves (ibid.: 187ff.). These processes, according to Kahn, in both West Sumatra and Negeri Sembilan, have comprised both what he calls 'modernization' (social differentiation and class formation, commoditization of production and social relations) and 'traditionalization' or 'peasantization' (formation of non-class relations, communalization) but within an overall 'modern' context (ibid.: 62–67). The deployment of non-capitalist, non-commoditized ('peasantist') strategies is merely one set of responses to technological innovation and the commercialization of agriculture, and households adopted various combinations of response depending on their circumstances.

From the late nineteenth century onwards Dutch writers constructed a highly selective 'stock of images' of a 'traditional' Minangkabau peasantry. An influential observer was the Dutch sociologist Bertram Schrieke (1955, I: 13), who represented the nineteenth-century Minangkabau as operating a small-scale, household-based, closed economy, largely self-sufficient and oriented to subsistence and not profit, personalized, dependent on rice agriculture on family-owned fields, with some barter, and governed overall by customary law. This system had then been increasingly undermined by commercialization, including the introduction of money taxation from the turn of the twentieth century onwards. Schrieke was of the view that the Minangkabau were on the path to modernization. Broadly, Dutch views were informed by evolutionist assumptions, but there was a variety of positions taken, some in favour of the capitalist transition for Indonesians, others opposed to it. Some argued for the desirability of liberal colonial policies of free trade, wage labour and freedom for capital to enable Indonesian societies to progress towards modernity; others – the 'ethical' movement – maintained that either the colonized peoples were unable to achieve modernity at a pace sufficient to justify liberal policies or Indonesian communities were 'developing according to their own logics, their own cultural dynamics' and they questioned the Western-led route to modernity (Kahn, 1993: 78). It was mainly the critics of liberalism who contributed to the construction of a uniquely Indonesian society and culture and this cultural uniqueness was also espoused by educated Indonesians, including Minangkabau intellectuals and political activists, who began to write about their own premodern, pre-colonial traditions from the 1920s (Kahn, 1995: 66–69, 94–98).

Yet, as Kahn demonstrates, the Minangkabau during the nineteenth century were involved in various ways and to varying degrees with commodity production and markets and there was considerable variation between communities as well as changes in the same communities through time (1993: 173ff.). Therefore, the discrete, traditionally defined Minangkabau cultural unit described by Dutch officials and academics and Minangkabau junior officials, merchants and intellectuals alike was primarily a twentieth-century creation (ibid.: 186). What is more, it was constructed in the context of the actions of a colonial bureaucratic state which was extending its power and range to local communities but without transforming the Dutch East Indies into a thoroughly capitalist economy. The importance of the bureaucratic state and individuals' and groups' relationships to it in determining life-chances, wealth and power has continued in the post-independence period. Kahn argues overall that the debates between those functionaries of the state who advocated the extension of liberal policies of development and the sweeping away of the relics of tradition and those who opposed it and constructed 'other cultures' was also a debate about 'what would constitute the most effective modes of domination' (ibid.: 278). Those who criticized Eurocentric and ethnocentric programmes for the modernization of traditional communities and attached importance to the uniqueness of Indonesia's communities and to a self-sustaining peasantry tended to see government as being more effective if defined ethnic groups maintaining certain traditional lifeways were the main elements in governance and administration.

Conclusion

What we have done in this chapter, specifically through a variety of case studies, is to demonstrate that ethnicity and identity are best understood as part of social and historical processes, and as being created and transformed as a result of interactions and encounters. Most notably for the minority populations in South-East Asia their identities have been formed in their interaction with powerful state systems: the civilizations of the lowlands, European colonial regimes and most recently the postcolonial independent governments of the region. Pluralism was also very much a product of the bringing together of different groups by colonial powers in the interest of trade and profit. Like the concept of culture we have focused on the dynamic aspects of identity and its variable, flexible and negotiated character. In the recent literature on ethnicity there is a very noticeable emphasis on what has been called a postmodern or postcolonial perspective, concerned with the analysis of 'discourses and practices' on such matters as tradition, culture, identity and authenticity and how certain discourses achieve a position of authority in relation to structures of power and hierarchy.

7

ECOLOGY AND ENVIRONMENTAL CHANGE

The study of the diverse environments of South-East Asia has been especially important in anthropology. Early post-war studies paid particular attention to the ways in which communities perceive, classify, use and adapt to their environment and the 'rationality' of resource use. However, during the past three decades there has been a noticeable shift in emphasis to the examination of human-induced changes in the context of the intensive exploitation of the natural resources of the region and the rapid transformation of natural landscapes for commercial agriculture, infrastructural development, tourism and industrialization (King, 1998, 1999: 123–129). There has also been an increasing sensitivity to historical analysis and to the processes and consequences of incorporation of local communities into wider economic and political systems (Bates and Lees, 1996: 1–3). As we saw in Chapters 5 and 6, anthropologists have had increasingly to address processes of change generated by global cultural, economic and political forces, and this is especially so in environmental research, and in relation to such fragile ecosystems as tropical forests, coral reefs and beaches, and coastal mangroves.

In this chapter we shall be concerned principally with rural habitats and ecosystems and how human communities change themselves in order to change the ways in which they use the natural environment; urban ways of life will be considered in Chapter 9. Anthropologists have undertaken major studies of a range of ecosystems in South-East Asia and we shall examine the main characteristics of these with an eye to the kinds of changes which have affected them. These include hunting-gathering (Hoffman, 1986; Rousseau, 1990; Endicott, 1984); horticulture (Ellen, 1978, 1979b; Morris, 1953; Fox, 1977, 1979); shifting cultivation of rice (Brosius, 1990; Condominas, 1977; Conklin, 1957; Dove, 1985; Frake, 1955; Freeman, 1955a, 1955b; Leach, [1954] 1970; Padoch, 1982); irrigated rice agriculture (Bray, 1986; Geertz, 1963a; Hanks, 1972; Scott, 1985); and artisanal fishing (Fraser, 1960, 1966; Nimmo, 1972; Sather, 1997).

Introduction

A very important concept in anthropological analyses of the environment is that of 'ecology' or 'human ecology' (Frake, 1962; Ellen, 1978: 1–3; 1979a, 1982). In detailed local studies the emphasis has been on the ways in which cultural values, world-views and perspectives, and technology shape and have shaped human adaptation to the environment and the exploitation of natural resources. In securing and sustaining their livelihoods, human communities use and manipulate the natural world. Very importantly, and in contrast to other species, humans occupy and exploit a wide range of habitats, primarily because of their ability to develop and use technology in novel and varied ways. Therefore, using technology they 'transform a vast variety of materials – including some rather unlikely ones – into sources of usable energy' and 'they tend to strongly affect the life chances and reproductive rates of the other populations' in a given habitat (Bates and Lees, 1996: 4).

As Ellen noted some time ago, there is a lack of consensus in anthropology about what constitutes an ecological approach (1979a: 1), but there is agreement that the study of human ecology focuses on the dynamic interrelationships or interdependencies between the natural environment, resource use and production, cultural perceptions and values and socio-economic organization. It is concerned with 'systems', and it was Clifford Geertz's study of processes of ecological change in Indonesia which was primarily responsible for bringing the concept of ecology to prominence among students of South-East Asian societies and cultures, although Hanks's eminently readable account of the ecology of rice agriculture also made an undoubted contribution (1972). Both Geertz and Hanks, in their concern to understand the precise relationships between rural production, social organization, culture and environment have provided a rather different historical perspective on change and transformation than that of the economic historian or the political economist.

Geertz in particular argues strongly for the advantages of an ecological approach in that the researcher can 'achieve a more exact specification of the relations between selected human activities, biological transactions, and physical processes by including them within a single analytical system, an *ecosystem*' (1963a: 3). This perspective overcomes the problem occasioned by treating culture and environment as two separate and independent domains which relate to one another as wholes by identifying the key social, cultural and environmental interdependencies – 'a patterned interchange of energy' – within a system (ibid.: 3; Bates and Lees, 1996: 3–4). In this concept of ecosystem the division between humankind and nature is seen as an artificial and arbitrary analytical device. Geertz says, for example, 'A Javanese peasant's [rice] terrace ... is both a product of an extended historical process of cultural development and perhaps the most immediately significant constituent of his "natural" environment' (1963a: 9). Ellen also in recognizing the complexity of human ecosystems emphasizes that the elements which comprise them are linked processually in two interrelated ways, first in terms of 'flows of matter and energy' and, second, in terms of 'flows of information' (1978: 1). He elaborates on this by defining an ecosystem as 'a relatively stable set of organic relationships in which energy, material and information are in continuous circulation, and in which all processes are seen in terms of their system-wide repercussions' (1982: 74).

In his own analysis and broad comparison of the ecosystems of irrigated rice cultivation in Java and swidden agriculture in Indonesia's outer islands, Geertz identifies those socio-economic and cultural elements which are intimately and crucially interrelated with environmental ones. He further argues that a focus on environmental and cultural interrelationships or transactions helps avoid the extremes of environmental determinism (or 'environmentalism'), on the one hand, and cultural determinism on the other. In other words, he sees the environment as providing certain constraints, opportunities and raw materials for human action under certain conditions and mediated by social and cultural systems which in turn furnish a range of resources for using the environment. The stress is on system, connection, links, interaction, reciprocal and mutual causality, process and change. But neither environmental nor cultural variables are straightforwardly determinant, and they interact in complex ways so that, for example, what appear to be 'natural' phenomena or 'cultural' artefacts are the very result of human–environmental interaction (and see Ellen, 1979a: 2–9; 1982: 1–20, 73–78). The significance of Geertz's study is that it also combined ecological and historical analysis in order to demonstrate how external influences which were generated in the course of the establishment and extension of a Dutch colonial politico-administrative and economic system had led to changes in local agricultural practices and resource use (and see Ellen, 1979b and Fox, 1979).

Another dimension of the anthropological study of human–environment relations is what Brosius *et al.* refer to as 'ethnoecology' (1986), and Ellen 'ethnobiology' (1993: 1). This field of study, though part of the broader interest in the interrelationships within an ecosystem, focuses specifically on the ways in which indigenous communities 'organize and classify their knowledge of the environment and environmental processes' (Brosius *et al.*, 1986: 187–188). It has a distinguished pedigree in research on South-East Asia and was used effectively in work on shifting agriculture in the Philippines by Harold Conklin on the Hanunóo of south-eastern Mindoro (1954, 1957) and Charles Frake on the Sindangan Subanun of Zamboanga del Norte, western Mindanao (1955), and more recently Roy Ellen on the ecology of the Nuaulu of Seram, central Moluccas (1978, 1993; and see Gianno, 1990). Conklin, for example, examines the native categorization of food and swidden land usage, climate, soils, terrain, vegetation and plants (1957: 29–138) and argues that agriculture must be understood in its cultural context and as a way of life; and Ellen presents, among other things, a detailed analysis of Nuaulu classification of vegetational types, soils, plants, cultivated land, land-forms and animals (1978, 1993). For example, in his study of Nuaulu zoological knowledge, he shows how animal categories were not only 'ordered' but also 'manipulated', and discovers that knowledge about animals was unevenly distributed within the population and was 'situationally adapted' (1993: 2–3). Crucially Ellen interprets classifications of the natural world as 'dynamic devices of practical importance to their users' (ibid.: 3), and argues that an understanding of folk classifications of the environment is essential for the analysis of ecological relationships (1978: 190–193; 1982: 204–235).

The cultural extent, complexity and core relevance of ethnoecological knowledge are also indicated in Paul Michael Taylor's intensive study of Tobelo folk biology (1980, 1990). Taylor discovered – and was able to take advantage of it in his fieldwork (total of thirty-seven months) – that 'ethnobiological classification is an important and integral part of Tobelo culture' (1990: 10). 'The Tobelo seemed to enjoy being studied' and spontaneously organized their dozens of field research assistantships, created by Taylor for collecting and preserving thousands of biotic specimens, to nominate positions such as 'Head of Birds', 'Head of Genealogy Transcription', 'Head of Sea Life', and so on (ibid.: 10). The result of this harnessed enthusiasm was, according to Taylor, 'probably the most comprehensive such study [folk biological knowledge in its ecological context] ever undertaken by a single individual'. And 'to document the conclusions presented here, the author assembled the world's largest collections of Halmahera's flora and fauna, and distributed them to specialists at many institutions . . . an international effort on the part of hundreds of specialists' (ibid.: 1).

Environmental history

More recently anthropologists interested in environmental issues have emphasized the importance of understanding longer term environmental change. As Bates and Lees say, 'Human ecologists are increasingly interested in documenting change and its sources, both in environmental events . . . and in the historical processes of population growth, technological development, economic expansion, and political change' (1996: 11). Of course, the opportunity to accomplish this in South-East Asia is dependent to a large extent on the quality and range of the published and archival materials. Nevertheless, for certain parts of the region the data are considerable, though uneven in detail and scope, and have enabled the reconstruction of environmental transformations going back to the early seventeenth century. Knapen, for example, in his environmental or 'green' history of Southeast Borneo, is able to examine changes as far back as 1600, though for the early period the data are much less detailed, continuous and reliable, requiring some speculation and 'guesstimates'. It is also worth noting that Knapen prefers not to use the term 'ecological history' in his study. He points out that, in its original meaning, 'ecology' refers to 'the scientific study of the relations between organisms and their biological environments' (2001: 3). He argues that it has been employed confusingly in studies which do not have much to do with ecology in this strict scientific definition of the term, and he is of the view that its use is best reserved for investigations by biologists, other than where the data permit the examination of 'human beings as an integral part of an ecosystem' (ibid.: 4). Knapen points out that in historical studies information is often patchy; very often there is little material on the beliefs, attitudes and values which influence the human use of the environment, and therefore it is difficult to adopt a truly ecological perspective. Nevertheless, it has to be emphasized that the concept of 'ecology' does enjoy relatively wide currency in anthropological studies of the environment and environmental change, including earlier studies of Indonesia (see, for example, Ellen, 1978; Geertz, 1963a and Fox, 1977), and with due acknowledgement to the reservations expressed by Knapen, we propose to continue to use it here.

Knapen (2001) makes several other points worth noting. First, he demonstrates that the popular notion that significant impacts on the environment really only commenced with the integration of South-East Asia into a global system during late colonialism is misleading and that important changes were already occurring at least from the seventeenth century. He says that even 'an isolated and out-of-the-way area [such] as Southeast Borneo has long been influenced by outside forces' (ibid.: 5–6). Second, the idea that tropical rainforest ecosystems in Borneo are relatively uniform also needs considerable qualification in that vegetation cover, habitats, fauna, rainfall, soils and terrain are diverse and variable (ibid.: 30–59). Third, and following on from the last point, 'the potential for human exploitation varies greatly from place to place, and some zones clearly have more to offer to mankind than others'; in addition, 'some environments are more resilient than others after transformation or degradation, either by human action or natural phenomena' (ibid.: 59). Finally, there is also the influence of 'uncertainties', 'disasters' and 'natural calamities' (such as storms and whirlwinds, drought, pestilence, earthquakes, volcanic ashfalls, natural fire, floods and epidemics), as well as human-induced crises (like wars and raiding, forest fires, over-exploitation of resources, and the collapse of markets for commercial crops) and those resulting from a combination of natural and human factors which can cause sudden and rapid changes to the environment and human activities (ibid.: 41–46, 367–388).

The dramatic and unexpected events are not so easily contained within the framework of ecosystem analysis, and indeed might occasion the breakdown of a system which is broadly in balance or equilibrium. Nevertheless, the human response to 'uncertainties' is addressed in ecological studies as 'risk-coping' behaviour and strategies, and the adaptation to 'the vagaries of the environment, economy or political systems' (ibid.: 386). Knapen suggests that generally human actors will take steps 'to contain the risk in order to minimize the occurrence and the severity of the impact' (ibid.: 369). One means of accomplishing this is to exploit a range of different environments and resources to spread risks; and, as Knapen says, in south-east Borneo 'people not only exploited the existing natural diversity, but expanded this diversity as well' by creating new environments and adopting new crops and products from outside (ibid.: 387). The important issues of environmental diversity, mixed cropping patterns and the building of contingencies into agricultural systems appear commonly in anthropological studies of resource use and it is given particular prominence in the work of Michael Dove to which we now turn.

Dove and ecological analysis

One of the most detailed studies of South-East Asian agriculture using an ecological perspective is undoubtedly Dove's analysis of swidden agriculture among the Kantu' of West Kalimantan (1985, 1993a, 1993b). Dove's work is really the culmination of a number of excellent studies of shifting cultivation undertaken in South-East Asia among upland minorities, and we shall refer to some of these later. Yet even at the time of his own research in the 1970s, Dove pointed out that the study of non-Western agricultural systems was 'a relatively new field' (1985: 1).

Dove analyses Kantu' swidden agriculture as a functioning ecological system and he examines in detail the relationships between culture and environment. His working hypothesis is that 'most behaviour is likely to contribute to the success of the swiddens', especially because this system of agriculture 'seemed ill able to tolerate nonfunctional or dysfunctional behaviour' (ibid.: 5). Nevertheless, the Kantu' had to overcome two major problems; first, environmental diversity in terms of drainage (dryland versus swampland), elevation, soil, vegetation cover and fauna, and the great uncertainty in relation to changes and variations in heat, winds, rainfall and river levels, and, second, the time constraints of intensifying labour in shifting agriculture, particularly as the demands on labour are concentrated at specific times of the year in such operations as planting, weeding and harvesting. Dove focuses on understanding the reasons for the various practices involved in cultivation and for their form and content, and in doing this he concludes that shifting agriculture is adaptive, sophisticated and rational. Furthermore, he presents a defence of it against the technocratic and administrative perspectives of government planners and officials who have usually argued that it is a primitive and wasteful form of cultivation and the expression of a traditional, subsistence-oriented and communal way of life (1983). On the contrary, Dove shows how the Kantu' act to minimize risk and maximize both the opportunities presented by environmental diversity and interdependence between households through the exchange of labour and goods (1985: 377–384). He also examines the ways in which the Kantu' have modified their farming system in response to changing environmental and other factors.

Dove attempts to understand the purposeful nature of shifting agriculture from the perspective of the Kantu' themselves and from his own external analytical perspective using the framework of cultural ecology and viewing the system as an interrelated whole. An important finding is that the Kantu' culti-vate two or more separate swidden fields each year which serves as a means of minimizing risk, exploiting different microenvironments and using labour resources more productively. This extensive system of cultivation in contrast to irrigated rice agriculture tends to achieve higher returns to labour, although yields per unit of land are lower so that 'the typical Indonesian swidden may well yield more kilograms of rice per workday than the typical Indonesian wet rice field' (ibid.: 383). Dove therefore advises that development practitioners should proceed cautiously in attempting to change, 'modernize' or, more dra-matically, eliminate shifting cultivation, and that the accumulated wisdom, skills and expertise of swidden farmers should be both 'appreciated and utilized' (ibid.: 384). The higher levels of return to labour may also help explain why a swidden farmer may resist government attempts to intensify agriculture and introduce irrigated rice cultivation, though from research undertaken in Palawan in the Philippines it would appear that in the short term the switch from a declining, relatively undiversified short fallow system to small-scale irri-gation agriculture increases labour efficiency, and crop reliability and diversity (Conelly, 1996: 306–309).

Revisions of the ecological paradigm

Although the shifting cultivation system of the Kantu' appears to be 'func-tional', Dove does tend to over-emphasize the functionality and stability of resource use, and the boundedness of a particular ecosystem. After all, adapta-tion and interaction with the environment are often processes of compromise and they might not lead to results which are all necessarily useful, purposeful or advantageous. Nor are communities contained in a closed and defined ecosys-tem; they trade and exchange goods, invade others' territories and engage in relations of domination and subordination. Ellen says, for example, in his study of the ecology of the Nuaulu of central Seram, that this has to be understood partly in relation to 'the exploitative processes and land use pattern of their neighbours' (1978: 19; and 1982: 185–186); and 'societies are rarely closed reproductive units' (1979a: 9). Furthermore, in understanding processes of 'adaptation' to an environment one has to acknowledge that, though for a social unit as a whole certain practices might be 'adaptive', they may also place some groups and individuals which comprise the unit at a disadvantage, or over time 'functioning' relationships may become 'maladaptive' (Ellen, 1979a: 10–14). Given these difficulties, some anthropologists have abandoned the notion of 'adaptation' altogether, or if they use it they recognize that 'adapta-tion is a temporary condition' (ibid.: 12) and that '[c]ultural adaptations are seldom the best of all possible solutions and never entirely rational' (1982: 251).

In some cases, resource use, mediated by culture, has resulted in the under-mining of environmental sustainability. Brosius, for example, in his study of the Ayta of the Zambales region of Luzon concludes that their swidden system, which has been highly productive, has also 'resulted in considerable deforestation', although this has also been occasioned by the extreme seasonality of rainfall and the rugged, steeply sloping terrain (1990: 153–155). Frake's study too of the Subanun demonstrates that on steep slopes, the practice of clearing large adjoining swiddens which are not surrounded sufficiently by forest, though effective against pest and animal depredations, may well encourage the growth of grasslands (1955: 93–95). The situation in Zamboanga has been exacerbated by the in-migration of lowlanders and increased population pressure (ibid.: 96). Geddes's study of the Miao or Hmong opium poppy cultivators of the northern uplands of Thailand counters exaggerated claims that their agricultural methods have resulted in widespread destruction of timber resources and soil erosion (1976). Nevertheless, poppy cultivation on steep slopes has led to 'adverse effects' in some areas which require ameliorative action, and it can only be sustained in the long term if the Hmong have access to new land or if population pressure is reduced by other means (ibid.: 5, 263). Geddes suggests that it is difficult to see what alternative cash crops, which can produce good yields and a viable economic return, are available to those in the remotest communities.

Padoch also, in her study of Iban agriculture in long settled areas of hinterland Sarawak, suggests that rather than a condition of balance and equilibrium, ecosystems have probably been more generally characterized by 'constant change and disequilibrium' (1982: 2). What has tended to happen, according to Padoch, is that the anthropological defence of shifting cultivation as a nondestructive and adaptive land use system, for example in the work of Geertz, has been translated into notions of equilibrium and changelessness. For Padoch, change, whether gradual or rapid, is the major characteristic of shifting agriculture and it is therefore important to examine how people have responded dynamically and flexibly to changing environmental and other conditions, especially to changes in the availability of resources (ibid.: 3–9).

What is more, adaptation to a particular set of environmental circumstances involves not only relationships to a physical environment but also to other neighbouring human groups. We have already referred to Ellen's study of the interrelations between the Nuaulu and their neighbours (1978); his work on sago and spices in the Moluccas is similarly concerned with the ways in which localized production units are linked increasingly into wider networks of exchange (Ellen, 1979b). Sather also demonstrates, in his study of the maritime-oriented Bajau Laut, that their specialized sea-nomad adaptation to specific habitats – either coral reefs or coastal mangroves – should be understood in relation 'not only to a group's interaction with its natural environment, but also of equal importance, to its interrelationships with other communities within an encompassing socio-economic and political order' (1997: 329). In other words, sea nomad groups do not live in a closed ecosystem and rather than exploit a generalized marine environment, historically they sought certain resources in demand in the sea-based trading states of which they had become a specialized constituent part.

Dove's ecological approach therefore helps us to understand the rationale of local level behaviour and practices in an integrated, relatively stable shifting agricultural system, but it becomes more problematical in situations of rapid change such as deforestation, large-scale physical migrations, marked social, cultural and environmental variation, and fluid relations between groups. A widespread practice in South-East Asia where there are pressures on land is secondary or supplementary shifting cultivation where land-hungry lowland farmers move into foothills and uplands and slash and burn land for planting as a step towards the introduction of more permanent forms of agriculture. In addressing transformations of this sort across large unbounded regions containing culturally and socio-economically different yet interrelated communities, Vayda has formulated the concept of 'progressive contextualization' in ecological analysis, specifically in his research on people–forest interactions in East Kalimantan (1981, 1983). In this approach Vayda argues that researchers should not only select specific human–environment interrelationships for scrutiny but also adopt research approaches and methods that are much more open-ended, flexible and dynamic. Instead of operating with the assumption of a bounded ecosystem or 'human use system' which is purposive, functioning and self-regulating, one starts by examining 'specific activities . . . performed by specific people in specific places at specific times' (1983: 266). One then widens the investigation socially, spatially and temporally to examine these activities as part of unbounded networks of dynamic, flexible, changing interactions.

This approach accords with the increasing emphasis in ecological studies on variations and changes in knowledge about the environment, variations in resource use within local and regional settings, and the importance of individual experience, experimentation and decision-making, and actor-driven outcomes (Ellen, 1978: 2, 22; 1979a: 9–10; and see 1982: 177–203). Vayda accepts that ultimately limits have to be set to the investigation. However, this is done in terms of the practical and common-sense requirements of the research, the time and resources available and 'the thoroughness or detail that the investigators [feel] to be useful or necessary for explaining the occurrence of certain activities to themselves' (1983: 272). Vayda led the multidisciplinary UNESCO Man and Biosphere (MAB) Program in East Kalimantan from the late 1970s. Its context was the rapid increase in mechanized log production and the damaging effects on the environment despite the official policy of selective logging. Vayda's team undertook region-wide research and used both quantitative and qualitative methods.

Three major locations were chosen to examine different uses of the environment:

1   a remote interior region of the Apo Kayan where the indigenous Kenyah population continued to practise a stable shifting cultivation system; farmers were mainly cultivating secondary forest areas which had first been cleared towards the end of the last century. It was discovered that a

carefully balanced cropping and forest fallow cycle had enabled agricultural practices to be sustained without reversion to grasslands or serious environmental degradation (Vayda, 1979: 26). It was concluded that contrary to government assumptions these swidden farmers were not 'uniformly ... nomadic destroyers of the forest' (1983: 277).

2   a resettlement area for Kenyah communities from the interior which was accessible to commercial loggers. Contrary to government expectations, these settlers had adopted a more extensive system of shifting agriculture which was causing damage to the environment. They had access to technology in the form of chainsaws, rice hullers and outboard motors; it enabled the Kenyah to gain access to more primary forest and clear it more rapidly. They were therefore farming larger areas and, in the short term, securing higher crop yields and having sufficient surplus labour resources to divert these to other income-generating activities (Colfer, 1983a, 1983b). They sold surplus rice, cut timber for sale and collected minor forest products such as rattan for the market. Other forms of land use in this area were expanding with the influx of commercial loggers and transmigrants.

3   a region in close proximity to the coastal conurbation of Samarinda and accessible by road. Here unlicensed loggers as well as commercial farmers were felling trees and clearing land in already logged areas, especially near the roads (Vayda, 1981: 10–11). Forest clearance for farming was undertaken mainly by Bugis migrants who were cultivating cash crops such as pepper. Vayda indicated that these activities were 'part of a well-organized long-term colonization process with the potential for moving Bugis to almost all accessible areas of East Kalimantan where pepper can be profitably grown' (1983: 274). What is more, this forest conversion was not undertaken by poor, landless shifting cultivators, but rather by 'better off, enterprising rural and urban residents interested more in making profits from land speculation and from cutting and selling timber than in farming' (ibid.: 274).

Overall, Vayda's research team demonstrated that shifting cultivation is a very variable and flexible system of agriculture and that no single government response in the interests of rural and agricultural development could embrace all these variations. In some cases, a long-term forest-fallow rotation can be operated; in other cases, where populations have been resettled or encouraged to move to other locations, and where there is pressure on land and access to modern technology, shifting agriculture can cause damage to the environment. In yet other cases, migrant farmers are using shifting agriculture as a stage in the conversion of forests to permanent cultivation.

A multidisciplinary region-wide research programme in the Bintulu area of Sarawak, Malaysian Borneo in the early 1990s revealed very similar processes at work (King, 1996b). A team of researchers examined the environmental and other effects of a range of processes including plantation development, the expansion of small-scale commercial agriculture, forest clearance and logging, urbanization and industrialization in coastal areas, the development of infra-structure such as roads, and population growth particularly from in-migration to take advantage of expanding employment opportunities in towns, logging camps, plantations and land schemes. Increasingly, shifting cultivation was being abandoned and replaced by permanent agriculture, including the growing of crops for sale. Former swidden farmers were also involved in the freelance cutting of remaining timber for sale to local agents, dealers and shopkeepers, and in wage work both in the countryside and increasingly in the towns. Stable and integrated systems of shifting cultivation had all but disappeared in this region and there were clear signs of environmental deterioration.

The Bintulu area has also long been an important source of forest products for sale, and Iban migrants who began to move into the region from the turn of the twentieth century were involved in the collection of such items as rattan, resins and ironwood. The forest also served as a source of food, medicines and materials for the manufacture of tools, domestic equipment and household fur-niture. Recent commercial logging has led to a depletion of forest resources while the expansion of the market economy and the increased demand for such items as rattan have resulted in the intensification of exploitation (King, 1999: 152). Some products were no longer used because they had been replaced by modern materials, but an interesting development was that some households had begun selectively to cultivate plants, which had formerly been gathered wild, on nearby fallow land or in home gardens, so that a reliable source of food, medicines and raw materials was at hand. Various plant fibres and rattan used for mat- and basket-making, as well as bamboo and wild ferns, were now avail-able from plants which were tended.

It is important to keep these changes in mind as we consider a range of studies of different kinds of ecosystems in South-East Asia undertaken by anthropologists. General trends have been the increasing integration of local level economic activities into the market-place, sedentarization of previously mobile hunter–gatherers, fishing communities and swidden agriculturalists, mechanization of various fishing and agricultural operations, and, in some cases, the abandoning of rural subsistence operations altogether in favour of wage work and urban-based employment. In this connection it is also useful to refer back to Chapter 5 for details of some of the organizational changes affecting small-scale agricultural and fishing communities. An overall corresponding trend has been the increased exploitation of the environment seen most directly in the rapid depletion of the South-East Asian rainforests, the decrease in wild animal populations and fish stocks, and the scarcity of various raw materials which forest dwellers used for construction and domestic products. In some cases there has been some replacement of non-domesticated resources with their deliberate cultivation and domestication.

We shall highlight the main characteristics of these rural ecosystems, but we should also note that, though we consider them separately, they were often interrelated in practice. In some cases the same community undertook a combination of activities such as hunting–gathering and horticulture, or rice agriculture and artisanal fishing, or communities moved from one ecosystem to another through time so that hunter–gatherers might settle down and adopt horticulture and then rice agriculture, or horticulturalists might move to hunting–gathering or to the shifting cultivation of hill rice, or, as Hanks demonstrates in Bang Chan, lowland shifting cultivators took up broadcasting of rice and then its transplantation in irrigated paddies (1972, and see below). An excellent ecological study of a mixed economy is that of Ellen of the Nuaulu of central Seram (1978). The Nuaulu hunt wild animals (pig, cuscus, deer, cassowary) and gather vegetables, fruits, other foods and non-edible products (especially construction materials) from the forest, they fish, sometimes plant sago palms as well as cut wild sago, clear swiddens and cultivate garden crops such as manioc, taro, sweet potatoes, sugar-cane, bananas and plantains, and grow cloves and coconut palms (for copra) for the market.

We shall first consider hunting–gathering and then move on to various forms of agriculture, and finally fishing economies. Our summaries of different ecosystems are pitched at a deliberately simple level and our categories of activity are broad-brush, though we recognize fully Ellen's advice that 'describing and analysing different patterns of human subsistence is a complex matter' (1982: 123), and, as Hanks says, 'technological evolution may well proceed in different directions and at different rates than social evolution' (1972: 2). For an introduction to this complexity we refer to Ellen's examination of three broad kinds of ecosystem based on the degree of human manipulation of the environment: 'pristine ecosystems' (food collection, hunting and fishing), 'partially altered ecosystems' (some fixed field horticulture and swiddening and elementary husbandry), and 'artificial ecosystems' (including irrigated rice cultivation) (1982: 124–176). Hanks's study of different modes of rice production in Bang Chan and the social and economic changes which accompanied 'a succession of agricultural techniques' is also invaluable (1972: 2), as is Dentan's study of the mixed shifting agricultural and hunting–gathering economy of the Semai of Peninsular Malaysia (1968).

Varieties of ecosystems

Hunting–gathering

Forest-based activities dependent on hunting, gathering and fishing were much more widespread in the region, even some thirty years ago, than they are today. As rainforests have been cleared and governments desire to resettle and modernize forest nomads, this form of ecological adjustment to the environment has been placed under severe pressure. Many nomads have, in contact with neighbouring farmers, settled down and adopted horticulture or rice agriculture, or have been resettled in government land schemes. Sometimes, chiefs and headmen in settled villages have also encouraged nomads to relocate near to them in order to control more easily sources of forest products or gain ready access to their labour resources and jungle expertise. In former times nomads met most of their everyday needs from the forest.

We should also note that, prior to the domestication of rice and its cultivation and in areas where species of wild rice flourished, seeds were gathered by relatively mobile populations (Hanks, 1972: 25–28). However, once agriculture or horticulture was introduced, a vital characteristic of those who remained as hunter–gatherers was that they have never been isolated populations, but have always lived in contact with agriculturalists with whom they have traded and are culturally related (Eder, 1996; King, 1993: 167). With regard to Borneo nomads, usually designated generally as 'Punan', Rousseau says that they 'form a distinct socio-economic sector, but they are not a separate society' (1990: 216). Through time there were also 'shifts from agriculture to hunting–gathering and vice-versa' (ibid.: 219).

Borneo nomads traditionally occupied primary forest and formed settlements in caves, shelters, lean-tos and raised farm-houses, near sources of drinking water. There were also variations in the degree of permanence of camps and settlements. Generally, population densities were very low and nomads were organized in bands varying in size from 30 to 40 people up to 150 or 200. These roamed separately over recognized territories, though they did not move at random but in a cyclical fashion around a base-camp. From time to time nomads also migrated long distances to new territories (ibid.: 220–223).

Nomadic economy in Borneo was based on the felling of the inland sago palm (*Eugeissona utilis*) and extracting flour from the edible pith which is eaten with sago and other palm shoots; it is calculated that a band of 25 people needed 20 palms per week for a normal diet (ibid.: 223), and that, given that a palm stand usually comprises 50 to 100 trees, of which about half are mature, bands would have to move to a new stand every week or two weeks (Sellato, 1989: 461–462). Other food comprised forest vegetables such as yams and mushrooms, ferns, honey, vegetable tallow, wild fruits like durian, mangosteen and rambutan, and animal protein from wild boar, deer, macaques, civets, squirrels, reptiles, jungle fowl and birds, as well as from fish, molluscs and crustaceans. Hunting of ground animals was undertaken by men using spears and dogs, or traps, while tree-dwelling creatures and birds were killed with poisoned darts from the blowpipe. Women usually gathered forest products near the camp.

As we have said, although traditionally nomads were to a large extent self-sufficient, they usually had long-standing trade relations with agriculturalists. They traded both goods for local consumption and jungle produce which was sought after in international markets. The nomads themselves acquired such trade items as rice, cloth, iron, copper wire, salt, tobacco, beads, necklaces and bracelets, metal earrings, tattooing needles, ceramic jars and brass gongs (Rousseau, 1990: 234; Eder, 1996: 88; Endicott, 1984: 29–52). In return the hunter–gatherers supplied rattan, resins, wild rubber, medicinal plants, hornbill casques and feathers, birds' nests, honey, bezoar stones, gold, antler horns, clouded leopard skins and rhinoceros horns, many of them for a wider Asian market. Indeed, Hoffman argued that the explanation for nomadic life in Borneo lay in the specialization in the commercial collecting and hunting of forest products (1986). He went further by proposing that nomadic society arose specifically to service the Chinese market with luxury tropical goods, and to do so hunter–gatherers entered into relations with agriculturalists who served as intermediaries. For Hoffman trade was essential to the nomadic way of life. However, this rather one-sided view has been criticized by both Rousseau (1990: 237–239) and Sellato (1989: 153ff.), who contend that, though nomads trade, some do so more than others and they 'do not depend on agriculturalists for anything of importance'. It was often difficult for downstream intermediaries to persuade the nomads to collect produce because they were often too preoccupied with meeting their own subsistence needs (Rousseau, 1990: 237–238). Be that as it may, for many nomad groups trading relations with settled farmers did take on an increasingly important role through time, and during the colonial period these relations became closer as forest nomads were brought under the umbrella of colonial administration (and see Dunn, 1975, for information on forest product trade in Peninsular Malaysia).

Several recent studies have documented the process of sedentarization. Eder, for example, in his work on the Batak, a foraging community of central Palawan in the Philippines, finds that they

> no longer earn their subsistence exclusively by hunting and gathering. Rather, trade, shifting cultivation, and wage labor have come to be important sources of cash and subsistence, reflecting growing articulation with lowland Philippine economy and society over the past one hundred years.
>
> (1996: 86)

Nevertheless, hunting–gathering still comprised a significant part of Batak economic activity in the 1980s, undertaken on a seasonal basis as other activities, particularly rice agriculture, permitted (ibid.: 91–94). For some part of the year the Batak resided in forest camps, though their main residence was close to their rice-fields; the camps were also smaller in size and much more temporary than in the hunting–gathering past and the range of fauna and flora utilized much reduced (ibid.: 92–96). In this transitional phase from hunting–gathering to settled agriculture in which the Batak spread their energies over several activities, Eder argues that their part-time foraging 'is not as remunerative or successful as it once was' (ibid.: 101).

It should also be noted that communities that practise shifting agriculture or horticulture in rainforest environments also derive significant amounts of food and other products by hunting and gathering in the surrounding forests. Indeed,

Ellen's study of the Nuaulu, who practise both swidden agriculture and horticulture, reveals that they obtain a considerable proportion of their food needs from non-domesticated sources, especially flour from wild sago (of the species *Metroxylon*) and wild animal protein (1978: 61–80).

What of the overall relationship between hunting–gathering and the environment? Rousseau suggests that generally the traditional hunting–gathering way of life did not damage the rainforest if only because population numbers and densities were relatively modest and the demands on the forest correspondingly slight. Nevertheless, he suggests that with regard to trade items, particularly in recent years, there has been over-exploitation of certain animals, birds and forest products (1990: 234). What is more, nomadic society itself has been the object of exploitation by agriculturalists through the medium of trade and labour. Yet hunting–gathering does occupy a special niche in tropical ecosystems, and the gathering of palm products is especially closely related to the development of horticulture to which we now turn.

Horticulture and palm harvesting

In some cases hunter–gatherers have settled down and taken up the cultivation of sago, manioc, cassava, sugar-cane, sugar palms and bananas. It is likely that in rainforest areas horticulture, based on the deliberate planting and tending of sago palms, was an early form of agriculture. It is a small step from the gathering of sago in the wild to cultivating it, and some rice agriculturalists also grow sago or have only recently abandoned it in favour of rice. In effect, there is a rather fuzzy line between the gathering of wild sago and its deliberate cultivation, and Ellen suggests that its availability in the wild may have limited horticultural development because there 'is little incentive to alter a landscape at some effort and adopt new and untried techniques when a living can be had by simply extracting resources from an unmodified environment' (1979b: 50). In his study of the Nuaulu of Seram, Ellen presents a detailed description and analysis of the combination of a hunting–gathering economy and a horticultural system in which root tubers are cultivated by shifting agricultural methods (1978). For the Nuaulu sago gathering provides the most important source of staple food while gardens are planted with such tubers as taro, manioc and yams. Usually gardens are farmed for a year and then left fallow, though crops such as manioc and fruits such as banana and papaya continue to be taken from the same plot in the second and third years (ibid.: 164–165). In some cases garden land is turned over for the long-term cultivation of sago palms and cash crops such as cloves and coconuts, which Ellen terms 'silviculture', and which results in land being taken out of the swidden–fallow cycle altogether and, in effect, used for permanent cultivation of tree or palm crops (ibid.: 173–178).

Some populations such as the coastal Melanau of Sarawak are well known as sago producers, and Borneo has extensive tracts of lowland swamps which are ideal for sago cultivation (of the species *Metroxylon sagu*). Ellen also indicates that lowland sago is vitally important in the Moluccas (mainly on the islands of Seram, Halmahera, Buru, Aru and Bacan), and has been the primary source of carbohydrate since at least the fifteenth century (ibid.: 48–49). The palm frequently reaches a height of over 12 metres; it throws up stems in succession from rhizomes, and it is easily propagated by planting suckers. Sago can also be grown from seed. It is a remarkably productive palm, has 'year-round availability' (ibid.: 50), and has usually been planted on land where lowland swamp forest has been cleared and burned. This activity has also frequently been combined with some swamp and wet rice agriculture if there are suitable areas where water can be controlled. Often ancillary activities are swamp forest collection and inshore fishing, and the cultivation of fruits, vegetables and rubber. Vegetables can be intercropped with sago, and the palm also provides a source of liquor, firewood, medicines and raw material for utensils and other items (ibid.: 50). Usually among the Melanau there was a gender division of labour with men clearing, cutting and rasping the palms to obtain the sago pith, and women cleaning, processing and drying the flour, and making it into biscuits and other foodstuffs (Morris, 1953).

This cottage industry in Sarawak also used to provide flour for export, but rasping and processing subsequently became mechanized, factory-based and controlled by Chinese companies (Morris, 1974). It resulted in increasing unemployment in some of the sago districts and native sago producers became wage labourers for others, and tied into credit–debt relations with Chinese dealers. In the Moluccas, Ellen also draws attention to the importance of sago flour and biscuits in exchange networks, and from the fifteenth century its close relationships to clove production in that the areas which concentrated on spices for export needed to import sago to meet their basic food needs (1979b: 53ff.). Importantly both Morris's and Ellen's studies of sago cultivation demonstrate the ways in which its production is integrated into wider networks of exchange and how the relations of humans to their environment, as well as the social and cultural organizations necessary to exploit the environment, change through time.

A rather different ecosystem based on the harvesting rather than the cultivation of the sugar palm of the species *lontar* (*Borassus* sp.) has been described in great detail by James Fox for the eastern Indonesian islands of Roti, Savu and Ndao in the Lesser Sundas (1977, 1979). In Roti there is also a supplementary palm, the *gewang*, which grows extensively. Importantly, Fox presents a modification of Geertz's grand division between the intensive wet rice ecosystem of inner Indonesia, particularly Java, and the shifting cultivation ecosystem of the outer islands, though Geertz also allows for composites of the two and the adaptation of either to the market economy. Fox draws attention to 'the intensive utilization of certain productive species of palm' as another distinctive ecosystem (1977: 17), and the contrast in the Lesser Sundas between an 'efficient, flexible and adaptive' mixed economy based on the sugar palm, and an 'ineffective, deleterious, and increasingly nonadaptive' swidden system (ibid.: 51; and

Ellen, 1979b: 43). He also notes the important role that other kinds of palm play in other South-East Asian economies including another variety of the sugar palm (*Arenga pinnata*), the nipah (*Raphia vinfera*), coconut (*Cocos nucifera*) and areca (*Areca catechu*) (Fox, 1977: 200–201), and the fact that the *Borassus* is also found in parts of mainland South-East Asia, as well as in east Java, Madura and southern Sulawesi (ibid.: 204).

Fox characterizes sugar harvesting as a 'peculiar mode of food production' and points out that people 'drink more meals than they eat' (ibid.: 3). The palm produces a sweet juice which can be drunk immediately if desired, or it can be boiled down for syrup, treacle or brown sugar; fermented beer can also be produced. Fox contrasts this economy with the swidden system of the neighbouring islands of Timor and Sumba. He also pays particular attention to the effects of about 400 years of European presence (Portuguese and Dutch) in the area and fuses ecological, economic and historical perspectives in his analysis (ibid.: 4; 1979: 21–23).

The swidden system in the Lesser Sundas is constrained by the generally long dry season, low and irregular rainfall, and impermeable, erosion-prone soils, and Fox demonstrates that in the 1960s the palm economy was advancing at the expense of shifting cultivation (ibid.: 10) in that it was 'better adapted to present ecological conditions' and had 'the capacity to support far higher population densities' than Timor and Sumba (ibid.: 9). This contrast was complicated by the introduction of cattle some years before in Timor and Sumba (in addition to horses) primarily for export, and 'indiscriminate grazing' which had led to increased vegetational deterioration and erosion (ibid.: 19). The environmental conditions in Roti, Savu and Ndao are if anything more severe, but there the palm economies support a higher population density (ibid.: 23). Fox says, 'The lontar is among the most efficient of the world's sugar-producing plants' (ibid.: 25), and a palm can produce juice twice daily for three to five months in its fruiting season. It also provides material for thatching, fencing, rope, clothing, containers, and other products and timber. It permits palm-tappers to develop a mixed economy which variously comprises inshore fishing, wet and dry rice agriculture, seaweed gathering, gardening, pig-, goat- and sheep-rearing and honey-gathering. Burned *lontar* leaves and animal manures are used in gardens as fertilizer, and pigs especially can be fed on palm products.

Interestingly, the success of the palm economy as against swiddening is also explicable in terms of the natural succession of vegetation after farming because overworked swidden fields are colonized not only by grasses but also by the *lontar* and *gewang* palms. What is more, Rotinese and Savunese palm-tappers also migrated to the larger islands of Sumba and Timor and took their preferred mode of production with them. Fox's study provides an excellent illustration of the ways in which different ecosystems are in dynamic relationships and that one form of production, in certain circumstances, can be superseded by another.

Shifting agriculture

Shifting or swidden cultivation as an agricultural system suited to tropical forest environments has been studied in detail by numerous anthropologists both in insular and mainland South-East Asia, principally because it is a widespread form of land use among minority upland and interior populations. A recent major area of contention in environmental studies has been the role of shifting agriculture in transforming tropical forests as against commercial logging, and the prospects for the sustainable use of resources. Invariably anthropologists have argued that shifting cultivation has been used as a scapegoat of governments, in some cases seriously misunderstood by government officials in others deliberately used to deflect attention from other much more damaging forms of land use such as logging and intensive cash-cropping. Indeed, it is a complex, varied, dynamic and sophisticated agricultural system, and, in favourable environmental and demographic circumstances, a sustainable form of cultivation in the long term.

Edmund Leach's study of the Kachin of Highland Burma in the late 1930s paid some attention to their ecology as a limiting but not a determinant factor of their social and political order. He argued that in general 'hill peoples can only be expected to yield a surplus under exceptional conditions of low population density and specially favourable terrain' ([1954] 1970: 21). He pointed to various agricultural adaptations such as terracing where physical and climatic conditions were unfavourable. Among the Kachin, Leach distinguished three kinds of upland agriculture which he calls monsoon *taungya* (the Burmese term for hill field), grassland *taungya*, and irrigated hill terraces. In the first type, which accords broadly with integrated tropical shifting cultivation systems, the vegetation was cleared, left to desiccate during the dry season and then burned. The burned debris provided an ash fertilizer of phosphates and potassium. The ground was dibbled or drilled among the ashes and sown with a variety of crops, principally hill rice, with maize, millet and buckwheat, and in this region the opium poppy as a cash crop. Usually after one year's cultivation, the area was abandoned and allowed to lie fallow and recover. Gradually secondary forest established itself. After a suitable period of time, which in the Kachin Hills is said to be 12 to 15 years, it was farmed again. Leach says that if this cycle was followed 'then there is no deforestation and negligible soil loss' (ibid.: 24).

This is an extensive agricultural system because at any one time there are substantial tracts of fallow land in various stages of regrowth; in other words it is the fields rather than the crops which are rotated. Leach notes that Kachin villages were usually small in size, scattered and close to their fields (and see Frake for the Subanun, 1955: 14). Shifting cultivation therefore might be put under pressure with population growth and intensification. A shortening of the fallow period, especially on hill slopes prone to erosion, might not permit the land to recover sufficiently and the vegetation to provide adequate cover to prevent soil leaching and to yield sufficient amounts of ash fertilizer when burned. In some parts of the Kachin Hills there were local concentrations of population usually as a result of warfare and the need for security and defence, or of 'external administrative interference' (Leach, [1954] 1970: 25). In some of these areas the fallow period in shifting agriculture had usually been shortened and the land cultivated for more than one year at a time. Leach points out that these practices 'do definitely lead in the long run to erosion and declining fertility' (ibid.: 25). Hanks too quotes examples of a reduction of the fallow period to three to ten years among such highland peoples of northern Thailand as the Hmong (Meo), where 'weeds and bamboo' rather than timber were being cleared and burned yielding only 'one thin crop' (1972: 31).

In the grassland *taungya* regions of Burma described by Leach, the climate is different with lower rainfall and temperatures so that rather than monsoon forests there are stands of pine, scrub and grasslands. This environment made for difficulties in ensuring sufficient rain and heat for hill rice. Beans were a favoured crop on cleared grasslands, followed by various other crops such as maize, buckwheat, millet, wheat and barley, planted in rotation on the same piece of land. The fields were then left to revert to grasslands. The poorer prospects for food crops also resulted in the cultivation of cash crops such as tea and the opium poppy.

In some areas irrigated rice terraces had also been constructed, 'when local population densities are great enough to create a serious shortage of land' and where communities were relatively fixed, often for military and political reasons to control trade routes ([1954] 1970: 27–28). Nevertheless, these terraces required considerable effort and energy to construct and maintain, and wherever possible the Kachin preferred to practise shifting cultivation.

Leach in turn has commented on another study of shifting cultivation, which, in his capacity as adviser to the Colonial Social Science Research Council and the Government of Sarawak, he was instrumental in supporting (1955: iii–v). Derek Freeman's examination of Iban agriculture in the Baleh region of interior Sarawak in the late 1940s and early 1950s is probably one of the most detailed and widely quoted studies of the shifting cultivation of hill rice in South-East Asia. It has generated considerable debate about the sustainability of this system in pioneer conditions when the same plot of land is farmed for two or more years in succession. Leach offers a word of warning in relation to the study because in the Baleh primary forest was still 'plentiful' and this, he suggests, echoing Freeman's conclusions, helps explain the Ibans' 'prodigal' use of resources (ibid.: iv).

Freeman estimated that farming in pioneer areas was probably typical of about 50 to 60 per cent of the Iban population of Sarawak at that time. He provides an historical context for his study, noting that the basin of the Rejang river in Sarawak, which included the Baleh, was a sparsely populated region mainly comprising primary forest (*kampong*) when the Iban began to colonize it from the beginning of the nineteenth century (1955b: 11ff.). Freeman says of the Baleh at that time that 'it was covered with the virgin forest so dear to the Iban cultivator's heart' (ibid.: 17), and that the Iban had an 'insatiable appetite for fresh areas of virgin forest' (ibid.: 19; and see Ellen on the Nuaulu, 1978: 83–85). Given this ample supply of primary forest Iban practice was 'to exploit the stored-up fertility of virgin land by extracting from it two or three successive crops, and then to move on to fresh fields' (Freeman, 1955b: 26).

Let us now summarize Freeman's findings. He reveals that in these pioneer areas it was usual for each separate Iban family (*bilek*) to open a farm (*umai*) of between four or five acres and to cultivate part of it for two years in succession. In favourable weather conditions virgin areas would yield harvests of 'exceptional abundance' and provide a surplus (ibid.: 111–115). The first clearing of land also established individual rights of ownership over it. In addition, the rainforest furnished raw materials for making mats and baskets, for thatching, for roof-shingles, lighting and bark-linings. After a period of cultivation the family abandoned the site and moved on to open new land in the general vicinity of the longhouse, returning to the same site to re-open it once 'the secondary jungle (*damun*) there was deemed to have grown to a sufficient size' (ibid.: 22). The fallow period was variable and Freeman suggests that in the Baleh it ranged from anywhere between 11 to 30 years (ibid.: 120). Thus, any one family came to own parcels of land scattered throughout the longhouse territory. For example, in 1949 one family in Rumah Nyala, a longhouse community of the Sut river, a tributary of the Baleh, had rights over approximately 150 acres of secondary jungle in some twenty-four different lots dispersed in an area of four to five square miles (ibid.: 22). Nevertheless, if a family moved out of the district to a new area its rights in secondary forest lapsed and could then be taken up by any members of their kindred who remained behind.

In an extensive system of agriculture it was also necessary to construct subsidiary longhouses (*dampa*) near to the farms once it became difficult to reach lands which were distant from the main house. These smaller field-houses usually comprised between two to ten families who were farming in the same vicinity. Nevertheless, each *bilek*-family was an independent unit of ownership, production and consumption, and it cultivated its own fields, though at certain stages of the agricultural cycle it would form along with other families small cooperative work groups on the basis of a system of strictly reciprocal labour exchange.

Another important feature of the traditional cultivation of hill rice (*padi*), which the Iban shared with other tribal peoples of South-East Asia, was that it was also a religious undertaking, and the various stages and practices of agriculture were closely interwoven with ritual and ceremony 'based on an elaborate fertility cult' (ibid.: 28; and see Conklin, 1957: 4 and Frake, 1955: 82). The Iban believed that their rice possessed a soul and was watched over by rice spirits, and each family had strains of sacred rice (*padi pun*) said to be of supernatural origin, which were planted in the central part of the farm and formed the locus of various rites which were performed to secure a plentiful harvest.

The Iban treated their rice with great respect and were constantly vigilant in ensuring that, in both word and deed, they did not annoy or anger the rice spirits.

At this juncture it is worth referring to a debate on the close interrelationships between the ritual and practical aspects of rice cultivation which centred on the use by South-East Asian shifting agriculturalists (and lowland rice farmers) of the finger- or hand-knife (Iban *ketap*) for harvesting. Freeman argued that Iban rates of reaping could have been increased if sickles had been employed but 'such a method is ruled out because of the reverential attitude which the Iban adopt towards their *padi*' (1970: 208). In other words, a more vigorous mode of harvesting might scare away the rice spirits. On the other hand, there are those who have stressed the technological advantages of the hand-knife under certain economic and environmental conditions and with the use of certain strains of rice (Alexander and Alexander, 1982; Miles, 1979). However, for the Philippines, Res notes that replacement of traditional rice strains with higher-yielding, short-statured varieties has favoured the efficiency of the sickle as against the hand-knife (1980).

The stages of shifting cultivation comprised clearing the undergrowth, felling the large trees, firing the farm, reburning the remaining debris if the burn is incomplete, dibbling and sowing, weeding, guarding the farms against pests and animals, harvesting, carrying in the rice in baskets, threshing, winnowing, storing, selecting suitable seed for the following year's sowing, and periodic pounding of rice when needed for eating. There was a relatively well-defined gender division of labour with men primarily responsible for slashing and felling the forest, dibbling, and carrying in the rice, and the women for sowing, weeding, reaping, selecting seed, and processing and storing the rice, though in certain of the operations like harvesting and weeding, this was not a hard-and-fast division (Freeman, 1955b: 77–80). Freeman indicates that a family might possess up to 15 different varieties of rice, so that the farm was arranged 'in a predetermined order' to facilitate harvesting and to ensure that there was no interruption in the path of the reapers so that the souls of the rice could follow and did not get lost (ibid.: 51–52). The Iban planted glutinous rice (*padi pulut*) first, then quick-ripening rice (*padi muda*), followed by different varieties of ordinary maturing rice (*padi taun*), and finally the sacred rice. The Iban also cultivated a range of catch-crops which were interspersed with the rice on the farm; some were sown in the same dibbled holes as the rice; these secondary crops included mustard, cucumber, pumpkin, gourd, cassava, maize, chilli and pineapples. Padoch in her study of the Engkari Iban found over twenty different cultigens in a field (1982: 66) and Frake in his work on the Subanun between twenty to forty (1955: 64). Traditionally, Iban agriculture did not use draught animals or ploughs; instead the dibble stick was used; clearing the forest and undergrowth was accomplished with axe, adze and fire; ash was used as a fertilizer with no artificial application; and reaping was with a small hand-knife and not a scythe.

Freeman demonstrates that the shifting cultivation of hill rice at that time was 'a highly uncertain undertaking', given the uncertainties of rainfall and temperature and the incidence of attacks by insects and animals, though he points out that in Iban eyes these hazards were 'very largely the result of magical and supernatural forces' (1955b: 97). Variations in yields between families and between different fields were also substantial (ibid.: 98). However, the introduction of rubber cultivation provided an important subsidiary source of income and served 'as a valuable safeguard against rice shortages' (ibid.: 107).

In his evaluation of Iban land use practices, Freeman is critical of the cultivation of virgin territory for two years in succession; it is, he says, 'an entirely pernicious practice' (ibid.: 118), though he recognizes that this was in the context of an ample supply of primary forest, and the perception that it was 'an expendable resource' (ibid.: 117). It was also a rational use of the land in terms of the available labour supply, because the continuous clearing of virgin forest was very demanding of labour, and successive farming enhanced the chances of securing a good burn, because cleared secondary vegetation required a much shorter drying-out period prior to firing. Virgin land farmed for a second year also produced good yields and was not subject to much weed growth (ibid.: 117). If this system was not followed, then virgin land was 'almost always cultivated again after a fallow period of one to three years' (ibid.: 119). Sometimes the two methods were combined, resulting in land being cultivated three times in the space of five to seven years (ibid.: 119–120).

Overall Freeman concludes that if cleared virgin forest, following one year's cultivation, was left to regenerate without further immediate clearing then 'vigorous and healthy' secondary forest containing 'very few noxious weeds' quickly re-established itself (ibid.: 126), and soil erosion was 'very slight indeed' (ibid.: 127). Ideally he proposes that this land should then be left for a further twelve to fifteen years and then farmed again for one year. If this cycle is maintained and land cultivated for only one year in each instance then 'the land may be utilized virtually indefinitely without serious degradation' (ibid.: 130). However, in his view the practice of farming virgin forested areas for two or more rarely three years in succession resulted in a much more inferior kind of secondary vegetation as did the cultivation of young secondary growth, and, in Freeman's view, these methods of farming did inflict 'serious and permanent injury' on the land and should be judged 'wasteful and dangerous' (ibid.: 128, 131). He judged that the consequences of successive cultivation of established secondary jungle was even more serious and repeated burning and cultivation of secondary vegetation, either that which was derived from the farming of virgin land or secondary regrowth land, within a period of 5 or 6 years following cultivation progressively reduced the cover vegetation to low-grade scrub, ferns and grasses. In order to maintain a 12- to 15-year cycle, Freeman calculated that shifting cultivation could support between thirty-four to forty-six persons per square mile (ibid.: 134). Conklin indicated a 12-year cycle among the Hanunóo in the early 1950s and argued that this appears to have been a relatively stable practice over a 75- to 100-year period (1957: 154).

Nevertheless, other observers have suggested that Freeman's analysis of shifting agriculture tended to take a too pessimistic view of the prospects for sustainability, and that he had been too influenced by the opinions of a few very influential colonial officers in Sarawak. Cramb, for example, suggests that the negative evaluation of shifting cultivation was only firmly established during the inter-war years, at a time when permanent, settled cultivation, plantation agriculture and commercial logging had increasingly won official favour. These latter were seen as more efficient and importantly more administratively controllable forms of land use (1989: 31ff.). Cramb argues that these views reflected, and continue to reflect, the 'cultural biases of the ruling elite', and more recently 'it serves the interests of the ... government's political-economic programme' (ibid.: 43).

Contrary to government views, in areas of Borneo where shifting cultivation has been practised by the Iban for three to four hundred years, the land had not been exhausted. Instead where there have been pressures on resources the Iban have adopted alternative methods of cultivation (Padoch, 1982: 10–11), and Cramb argues that Freeman's conclusions about environmental degeneration following successive cultivation were 'entirely speculative' (1989: 34). Cramb also maintains that a fallow period of 7 to 10 years following a period of cultivation is sufficient to enable forest and topsoil regeneration (ibid.: 35). What is more, if savannah grasslands are not regularly burned over, then these too will eventually succeed back to forest. In his own research in Sarawak, Cramb discovered that there was no noticeable soil erosion and increased flooding in areas of prolonged shifting cultivation, nor did the Iban exhibit a general proclivity to clear virgin forest. Secondary forest was more usually preferred, and soil loss and runoff from secondary forested areas were less than under primary forest because of the density of the undergrowth.

Cramb's and his colleagues' investigations of shifting cultivation in Sarawak in the 1970s and the 1980s also indicated that one of the significant responses to population pressure in long-settled regions where Iban had been farming for several centuries was to reduce the annual swidden area farmed and to switch to cash crops such as rubber and pepper, secure more income from wage work, and, where suitable lower lying lands were available, to move into swamp rice cultivation (ibid.: 40). Padoch too in her detailed study of the Engkari Iban in the early 1970s argues that 'land use among all [Iban] groups is not predicated on constant migration' (1982: 10), and her work demonstrates similarities with Conklin's findings among the Hanunóo who also did not undertake pioneer agriculture but instead preferred to clear secondary forest in long-settled areas (1957: 4). Padoch shows that in an area which had been long settled and where there was little primary forest remaining, Iban had adjusted their methods of agriculture and related institutions. These included changes in cropping–fallow regimes, a greater intensification of land use, borrowing land or taking over forfeited land from families who had left the area, wage labour in urban areas, plantations and timber camps, market-trading and population control. She concludes that the Iban in her research communities were not 'destructive cultivators forced constantly to migrate' (1982: 15).

With regard to the cropping–fallow cycle after one season fields were usually left for at least four years, and the median period was seven to eight years (ibid.: 54–55), though as Padoch notes, it was not so much the number of years that was important but the composition and size of vegetation, and this varied on a piece of land depending on soils, steepness of slope, drainage and so on. She did not detect any significant environmental deterioration and soil erosion. She also studied Iban in a pioneering area, the Ensebang, and found that the practices identified in the Baleh by Freeman were not universal and that the Ensebang Iban 'appear to be largely innocent of the worst prodigalities that Freeman found among Baleh groups' (ibid.: 59).

However, as we have seen in Vayda's and other studies of shifting cultivation it is a system of agriculture which is particularly sensitive to external pressures, and although it is still widely practised in South-East Asia, it has been much more susceptible than wet rice agriculture to change and replacement. In many regions it has given way to plantation agriculture and other forms of settled cultivation, and it has been difficult to sustain in regions subject to large-scale commercial logging. It has also declined because of the movement of villagers, especially young people, into urban-based wage work and the lack of interest in forest-based farming as a viable mode of livelihood.

Irrigated rice agriculture

Geertz's account of the ecology of the Javanese rice terrace is perhaps the most succinct and illuminating description of its essential character as a 'functioning productive system' in the literature on South-East Asian wet rice agriculture. A rice terrace is, he says, 'an artificial, maximally specialized, continuous-cultivation, open-field structure' (1963a: 28). He contrasts this with a swidden field which succeeds by imitating the forest and providing a generalized, diverse, temporary, closed-cover structure. In irrigated rice cultivation it is the supply and control of water (its level and timing) which play a crucial role, protecting the soil, bringing nutrients onto the fields, encouraging the activity of nitrogen-fixing organisms and the decomposition of organic material, and the aeration of the soil (ibid.: 28–36). Maintaining a uniform level of water on the field by levelling the land, constructing embankments or bunds and terraces, and regulating the water by a system of irrigation and drainage channels are therefore essential. So, it is not so much the soil that yields crops, though soil fertility and its structure do play a part, but the water which rests and moves across it. This removes the absolute need for artificial fertilizers, though in modern forms of farming they are used as are animal manures, and land can be worked much more intensively without undue risk of critical deterioration.

It should also be noted that a mode of agriculture which was practised relatively extensively prior to and in conjunction with the development of irrigated cultivation and where there were extensive, flat river levees or shorelands, was 'broadcasting', which was not so demanding of labour. In this system, following ploughing and before the arrival of the rains, seeds are scattered and then covered with a light dust on open undyked fields on a mudflat or dried swampland (Hanks, 1972: 33–36). Broadcasting therefore depends on natural flooding and does not require an investment of labour in water control, though its success or failure is subject to the vagaries of river-flooding – its timing, extent and duration.

An important characteristic of irrigated agriculture on the other hand is that the regulation of water demands a substantial resource of labour, in constructing and maintaining waterworks as well as in preparing fields for cultivation. In addition, water control systems and their maintenance require cooperation between farmers as do the demands on labour at peak times of the year such as at harvesting. In response to the need for increased production wet rice farmers in South-East Asia have also tended to prefer to cultivate existing fields more intensively rather than invest a large amount of additional labour in constructing new fields and increasing the irrigated area. The process of extension of irrigation works has been a relatively slow process until the recent introduction of large-scale government-sponsored irrigation projects such as Muda and Kemubu in Peninsular Malaysia.

In contrast to shifting agriculture which enjoys only a rather precarious relationship with soil, terrain and vegetation, and broadcasting which enjoys only a precarious relationship with flood-water, irrigated agriculture, provided the water sources are controllable and carry suitably fertile nutrients, can 'respond to a rising population through intensification' and through working the fields more carefully and finely (improving water control and drainage, seed selection, growth and transplantation, planting patterns, weeding, ploughing and soil preparation, manuring, and protection against pests) (Geertz, 1963a: 32–35). A key process in wet rice cultivation which assists in raising production is transplantation rather than broadcasting. Rice seedlings start their growth and are nurtured in nursery plots; when they are sufficiently established and healthy they are then moved as individual shoots to open fields (Hanks, 1972: 36ff.). Quick-ripening rice varieties with a two- to three-month growing period can be double- and sometimes even triple-cropped on the same field, and single-cropping of rice also benefits if the land is used in the dry season for other crops such as soybeans or groundnuts. As in swidden agriculture wet rice farmers spread their risks by growing several different varieties of rice on their fields, particularly those with different ripening periods. They also undertake other economic activities, both farm and non-farm, though during the colonial period farmers in the rice bowl areas of mainland South-East Asia, particularly in the Irrawaddy Delta in Burma and in central Thailand, were placed in dangerous situations of dependence producing rice for the world market and reducing their other sources of subsistence and income (Bray, 1986: 128–131). More recently farmers in large irrigation projects in such places as Malaysia have also been pushed increasingly into rice monoculture.

What is clear is that irrigation is closely related to labour-intensive methods of cultivation and 'the intensification of rice-farming both permits and requires demographic increase' (ibid.: xv, 16). Geertz demonstrates that the contrasting ecosystems of shifting cultivation and irrigated agriculture and their differing potentials provide the main reasons for uneven population distribution in Indonesia (1963a: 37). Wet rice agriculture is capable of responding to population increase while swidden systems have either gradually been replaced by plantation and other forms of permanent agriculture or have led to environmental deterioration and been gradually abandoned. In his study of the lowland rice-growing settlement of Bang Chan, Hanks traces the step-by-step development of agriculture by means of improvement and expansion, and the successful response of small-holding rice-farmers in increasing their production. The population of Bang Chan, and indeed those in similar village communities in central Thailand, effected a positive evolutionary change in their agriculture, producing more by improved techniques and releasing surpluses into the national and international market. However, this is not the only direction of change in wet rice systems.

We have already seen in Chapter 3 the consequences of European intervention in the Indonesian islands and the involutionary rather than evolutionary processes which were set in train in the wet rice areas of Java which soaked up increased populations and led to progressive division of the land into smaller and smaller farms. Bray argues that the development of rice agriculture in Asia has generally taken a rather different direction from the development of Western cereal-based agriculture, in that in Asia rather than improving the productivity of labour by replacing labour with machines and realizing economies of scale, the productivity of land has been increased by increasing the application of labour to it (1986: 27). Broadly speaking, in the West labour is the scarce resource while in Asia it is land. She further suggests that Asian rice economies operate 'skill-oriented' technologies and depend much more on 'the development and intensive use of human skills', and Western agriculture tends to depend much more on 'mechanical' technologies using equipment and machinery (ibid.: 114–115). What is more, in many cases in Asia, terrain and soil, patterns of landholding, population density, lack of capital and size of farms have also made it difficult to introduce large-scale mechanization.

Yet in spite of the suitability of wet rice cultivation for small-scale farming and investment in labour, technological innovations have been introduced recently, especially in the context of the 'Green Revolution'. It is worth dwelling briefly on some of the changes which have been introduced to demonstrate the application of new and improved technologies to irrigated agriculture and the dramatic increase in rice yields. James Scott, in his detailed study of a Malay village in the Muda Irrigation Project in northern Kedah and southern

Perlis undertaken in 1978–1980, indicates that double-cropping with the use of new fast-growing, high-yielding seed strains and fertilizers was introduced from the late 1960s and combine-harvesting in 1976 (1985: xvii; and see Chapter 5). Tractors for land preparation and large-scale improvements in irrigation systems had been introduced prior to 1970 (ibid.: 74–75). The government also provided credit facilities and 'new milling and marketing channels' (ibid.: 64). The major government concern was to ensure that the rising demand for the basic foodstuff of rice was met increasingly from domestic rather than external sources. Furthermore, the Malay-based governing political party, UMNO, needed to direct resources to the countryside to retain the support of the Malay rural constituency, many of whom were rice farmers, and to address issues of poverty and deprivation there. Therefore, government policy towards rice agriculture has been based on 'increasing the productivity and incomes of rice growers' specifically in large irrigation projects (ibid.: 55). Scott's main focus was on the conflict and the 'ideological struggle' between the rich and the poor in Malay rural society but he also reveals much about the technological changes in rice agriculture and their effects. It demonstrates the close interrelationship between human innovation and the social and cultural dimensions of land use.

The Muda Irrigation Project organized by the Federal government began in 1966 and was fully operational by 1973, enabling the large-scale double-cropping of rice. However, Scott also shows that technological changes displaced labour. As Geertz's study demonstrates, the cultivation of wet rice is capable of absorbing a large amount of labour, particularly in such processes as land preparation, transplanting, harvesting and threshing. But, with the use of tractors for ploughing the land and combine-harvesters for reaping and threshing, a large part of the labour needs was removed. Scott finds that the 'Green Revolution' in Kedah, though almost tripling rice production in the space of some fifteen years, doubling average farm incomes and improving the general security, health and standard of living of most farmers – small and large, owner and tenant – had also resulted in increasing social and economic inequalities, increases in land prices which put land purchase outside the reach of only but the wealthy, growth in the percentage of small owner-operated farms producing 'a bare subsistence income' (ibid.: 71), a worsening income distribution, a decrease in tenancy and a growth of large capitalist farms. 'Double-cropping, higher yields, and mechanization have made it increasingly profitable and feasible for landlords to resume cultivation' and to displace tenants (ibid.: 71). Prior to the 'Green Revolution' the large farmers needed tenants to help work their land and labourers to assist in field preparation, transplanting, harvesting and threshing. Machines increasingly made these services and support dispensable and those who already had land and capital before the introduction of technological innovations could realize the benefits of these more readily. What is also interesting, and it is a trend which we have drawn attention to in some detail in Chapter 5, is that technological transformations do not necessarily lead in the overall direction of increasing class polarization and capitalist farming, but instead it may also result in the process of peasantization and the growth and/or consolidation of small owner-operators (Bray, 1986: xv). Scott observes in the Muda scheme that the result of the reorganization of village life in response to new technologies was 'a numerous, marginal, poverty-sharing class of small farmers at the bottom of the heap, a robust class of capitalist farmers at the top, and a still-significant middle peasantry in between', the major change being the fairly rapid 'liquidation' of the pure tenant class (1985: 71).

Fishing and strand-collecting

We have already seen in Chapter 5 in the examination of the work of Raymond Firth and his colleagues on small-scale peasant economies how artisanal fishing communities organize their production and marketing and the changes in the fishing industry resulting from the introduction of technology and the improvements in communications to markets. Artisanal fishing is on the decline, and there have been several anthropological studies of both the 'traditional' organization of fishing as well as its recent transformations. Generally, fishing communities readily enter into exchange relationships because the specialized production of fish requires them to secure supplies of other foodstuffs such as rice from land-based communities. Nevertheless, in some isolated cases fishing can remain 'largely unmediated by money', without middlemen and with the continued use of traditional equipment, as Barnes demonstrates in his study of the sea-hunting economy of Lamalera, a settlement on the eastern Indonesian island of Lembata (1996: 2). The Lamalerans hunt for whales, manta rays, porpoises, as well as fishing and gathering for turtles, oysters, sea urchins and edible seaweed. However, it should be noted that this is a quite unique way of life which Barnes sees as now under threat from processes of modernization, particularly from the outmigration of young people for wage work and education (ibid.: 344–345).

One of the best-known studies, aside from that of the Firths, of a fishing economy is Thomas Fraser's work on the Malay village of Rusembilan in the Pattani province of southern Thailand undertaken in the 1950s and the early part of the 1960s (1960, 1966). Fraser argues that ecological factors predispose or limit change but that changes 'are actually brought about in response to disequilibriums in the social or cultural organizations of the community' (1960: 234). From the subsistence cultivation of rice the village of Rusembilan had moved to offshore commercial fishing (ibid.: 234). What is more, on his first visit to the community Fraser noted that the villagers were considering the purchase of motorboats for catching small mackerel (*kembong*), and that subsequently motorboats were bought (ibid.: 45–49). The village was also close to the commercial and administrative centre of Pattani town, and this too was generating changes in Rusembilan with the increasing integration into a market economy (ibid.: 4, 77ff.). Importantly nearly every family in the community worked in rice cultivation so that fishing was only a part, though the most significant part of the local economy (ibid.: 32). Coconut- and rubber-growing were also gaining ground (ibid.: 57), and increasingly rice was being bought in the market because of salinization of some of the local ricefields and population growth (1966: 14). The main mackerel season was from April to September or October. Fishing was undertaken mainly at night and for three months during the monsoon season it stopped, and therefore time was available for the pursuit of other activities, particularly rice agriculture during the rainy season. After the monsoon period from late December or January until March large prawns (*udang uko*) were caught (1960: 35). Other fish were caught, often inshore, as and when they became available, but the main preoccupation was mackerel fishing.

Fishermen were organized into boat groups for mackerel and prawn fishing and the most important role in each group was taken by the steersman, who was usually but not invariably the owner of the large boats (*kolek*) suitable for deep-sea fishing (ibid.: 39). Some boats were owned by cooperatives. The use of motorboats to tow the groups of *kolek* to the fishing grounds began to make daytime fishing feasible and desirable and held out the promise of increasing catches; it also required cooperation between boats in net groups (ibid.: 40–41). Fraser discovered that increasingly the use of motorboats was setting up strains between crew-members because previously they had been used to fishing relatively independently (1966: 91–92). Subsequently individual *kolek* began to fit outboard motors and to fish independently, and innovations in net manufacture with the introduction of lighter nylon nets in place of heavier cotton nets also reinforced this independence (ibid.: 93). In any case, the village-based fishing industry seemed to be on the decline in the early 1960s suffering from changes in the shoal movements of fish and competition and over-fishing from the heavily capitalized large boats and refrigeration facilities of Chinese-Thai operations (ibid.: 94). The main responses of the Rusembilan fishermen were to turn to smaller-scale inshore fishing, employment on plantations, and wage work in towns (ibid.: 95–96).

Dramatic changes have also affected other fishing communities elsewhere in South-East Asia. Important studies have been undertaken on the 'sea nomads' or 'sea gypsies', boat-dwelling communities of the region, especially the Bajau Laut (Sather, 1997; Nimmo, 1972). The Bajau Laut are part of a much larger, fragmented and widely dispersed ethnolinguistic group, the Sama-Bajau, which is found in coastal and maritime zones in eastern Indonesia, the Moluccas, Sulawesi, eastern and north-eastern Borneo and the southern Philippines. The major changes affecting these populations comprised the process of sedentarization which was increasingly evident from the 1950s and the 1960s. Sather, who studied the Bajau Laut of Semporna of coastal south-eastern Sabah in the mid-1960s and subsequently in 1974 and 1979, found that previously independent boat-families who had lived on boats as fishermen and foragers in coastal forests, coral reefs and offshore islands had begun to settle on land in villages of pile-house dwellings, though at that time they still dispersed to their boats and spent extended periods at sea in 'ephemeral, variously organized fishing fleets' (1997: v). These either fished alone or joined groups of two to six families or larger drift-net assemblages drawn from several villages. They had therefore 'abandoned boat nomadism for a sedentary way of life' (ibid.: 1). Nimmo's study of the Bajau of southern Sulu discovered similar processes of sedentarization through the influence of proximity to markets, incorporation into administrative structures, and economic differentiation into other activities (1972: 1, 50–51).

Up to the 1970s there was only a small minority of Bajau who continued a nomadic existence moving from anchorage to anchorage to take on food, fresh water, firewood, and to dry nets; the trend increasingly was to settle down. However, some communities had for a long time practised mixed farming of wet rice, fruit and vegetables as well as cattle-rearing on land. Historically the Bajau were suppliers of maritime trade items to several Muslim states including Sulu (ibid.: 14). The most important products comprised sea cucumber (*tripang*), dried fish, turtle eggs, mother-of-pearl, tortoiseshell, shark fin and decorative shell. They traded in onshore markets in return for rice, cassava and other staples, as well as manufactured goods such as netting twine, fish hooks, sailcloth, lamps and ropes (ibid.: 79).

In a society and economy based on movement the primary unit of production was the conjugal family boat crew (*dabalutu*) of husband, wife and children, who owned their own boat. These came together in the process of sedentarization to form shore-based settlements (*lahat*), which were relatively fluid social groupings, and to form multi-family households (*luma'*) and household clusters. This in turn led to increasing economic and social differentiation and a move away from fishing for many households into farming and wage work in towns and plantations. Mechanization of the fishing industry and the manufacture of ice also resulted in the breakdown in the boat-family structure and the change to all-male crews on larger boats and groupings of boats directed to securing larger catches (ibid.: 80). With modernization there was also a greater need for cash and an increase in wage work. Overall, fishing has become a market-based activity, with the intervention of Chinese dealers in the market; some Bajau too have become fish-buyers and retailers (ibid.: 81).

As Sather demonstrates, this kind of ecological arrangement does not easily lead to the establishment of permanent social groups; membership was constantly changing, and social networks at sea were very fluid. There was considerable choice in the formation and activation of social ties, though movements of social groupings were determined by fishing cycles and the availability of other marine products. Furthermore, Sather says, 'Interpersonal relations among the Bajau Laut are shaped not only by their dependence on the sea, but also by the relationships they maintain with surrounding shore- and land-based peoples' (1997: 320). Nimmo also refers to a symbiotic relationship between boat people and land-dwellers in that they enter into exchanges of fish and marine products for rice, vegetables and fruit (1972: 13). Bajau Laut adaptation to specialized marine ecosystems was in part a response to their integration into wider commercial and exchange networks focused on Muslim Malay sultanates (Sather, 1997: 328–329).

Conclusion

We have tried to show how an ecological perspective has assisted anthropologists in exploring the complex and intimate interrelationships between human communities and their environments. Importantly a focus on ecosystems has emphasized how the interaction with and use of environmental resources are mediated through culture, how environments are classified and ordered in cultural terms, and the ways in which communities organize themselves to exploit particular ecological niches. Nevertheless, ecosystems are never in practice bounded units, and communities engage with each other, often in relationships of exchange, which in turn shape the use of the environment. As we have seen, the incorporation of communities into wider economic and political systems have had dramatic consequences for human–environment relations so much so that human ecologists have increasingly turned to examining the environmental processes which have been occasioned by population growth, technological innovation, the expansion of markets and political change (Bates and Lees, 1996: 11). In South-East Asia the environmental and economic consequences of, for example, the 'industrialization' of fishing, the destruction of the rainforests by commercial loggers, the development of beach resorts, golf courses and high-rise hotel complexes and the expansion of mechanized agriculture have been profound (see King, 1999, for some of the developmental dimensions of these changes).

8

GENDER AND THE SEXES

In this chapter we examine gender as a cultural construct and the importance of distinguishing biological (or natural) and cultural factors in defining and talking about the differences between men and women. In other words, cultures assign attributes – ways of dressing, behaving, working – to the cultural 'categories' male and female, and these cultural elaborations, symbols and values can vary considerably between different societies. Importantly, what it means to be a 'man' or a 'woman' and what 'manhood' and womanhood' might constitute are expressed in varied ways and they are not universal, homogeneous categories of identity. In addition, often the attributes of 'maleness', on the one hand, and 'femaleness', on the other, may not coincide exactly to form discrete and exclusive categories, rather they may overlap and constitute differences of degree. They may also not prescribe what men and women actually do and how they behave; they are subject to change through time and they interrelate with other modes of categorization such as class, age, family status and so on, so that the identity 'man' or 'woman' will also differ in a given culture depending on whether the individual is young or old, single or married, a cognatic relative or an affine, high or low class, a manual worker or a professional. We also explore in this chapter the issue of the relative gender equality, symmetry or complementarity which researchers have claimed for South-East Asia and the problems of defining female status in particular. Cases are selected from Burma–Thailand, Malaysia–Indonesia, the Philippines and Vietnam to examine both the socio-economic and psychocultural dimensions of gender and some of the consequences for gender relations of economic globalization and the increasing involvement of women in factory employment.

Introduction

In her overview of research on gender issues in South-East Asia, Rosemary Firth has stated that the detailed study of the role and position of women in society and the consequences for them of socio-cultural change and development have really only emerged during the 1980s (1995). Firth's own study of housekeeping among Malay fishing communities conducted in 1939–1940, with a revisit in 1963, 'was probably one of the first published studies of women in Southeast Asia' (1995: 3), although in the 1960s and 1970s the study of family life in the region primarily by women anthropologists has also increased our understanding of gender relations in domestic contexts (e.g. Hildred Geertz on Java [1961a]; Mi Mi Khaing on Burma [1962], Potter on Northern Thailand [1977]). One of the first studies of small-scale marketing in which women were heavily involved was that by Alice Dewey in Java (1962). More recently interest in the study of gender relations has increased rapidly with some major contributions to the literature (Atkinson and Errington, 1990; van Esterik, 1996; Laderman, 1983; Ong, 1987; Ong and Peletz, 1995; Rudie, 1994; Rutten, 1993; Stoler, 1989, 1991; Wazir Jahan Karim, 1992, 1995; Wolf, 1992), though the major focus has been women's status and roles and concepts and symbolism of 'femininity'; very little attention has been devoted to concepts of 'masculinity' (though for early examples see Siegel on Acheh [1969] and Renato Rosaldo [1980] and Michelle Rosaldo [1982] on Ilongot, Luzon).

An issue which has particularly exercised anthropologists interested in South-East Asian societies is the status of women in relation to men. In early sociological texts preoccupied with discerning common or distinctive features of South-East Asia, it was frequently claimed that women generally enjoyed a higher status there than their counterparts in the nearby countries of India and China (Burling, 1965: 2, 25, 47, 99–100, 114). This feature of gender relations was in turn related to such things as the widespread occurrence of bilateral kinship (Errington, 1990: 3–4), and the involvement of women in economic activities as traders and managers of domestic finances (ibid.: 4).

The problem with arguing in these general terms is to decide what female status is, since anthropologists and other social scientists often differ in their definition of it, concentrating usually on only one sphere such as economic organization, jural rights, behaviour, religious worth and spiritual potency, or on authority and power (Williams, 1990: 9ff.; van Esterik, 1996: 9). Furthermore, it is difficult to define status in absolute terms, especially in examining relations between men and women, since individuals and groups might occupy positions of high status and exercise power and influence in different areas of social and cultural life, and the categories 'man' and 'woman' are not unitary and homogeneous (Errington, 1990: 9–10).

In these circumstances anthropologists have tended to phrase their discussions in terms of the 'complementarity' or 'symmetry' of men's and women's responsibilities, rights and duties, and the 'lack of exaggerated opposition of male and female ideologies' (van Esterik, 1996: 9; Errington, 1990: 1). Margaret Mead has even remarked on the physical similarity of men and women in Bali (1962: 135). What is more, Wazir Jahan Karim argues that women in South-East Asia usually work through 'informal' structures and in a 'culture of informality' in which it is problematical to distinguish the domestic domain, in which women are more generally located, from the public world. This does not mean that South-East Asian women are conniving, calculating and manipulative using the public sphere through their sexuality to secure prestige and power. Rather they are merely conforming to proper and approved modes of behaviour (1995: 17ff.). Wazir Jahan Karim concludes that 'western themes of feminism cannot envisage a situation where male and female relations are managed in a way as flexible and fluid as they are in Southeast Asia' (ibid.: 26). In addition, Ong and Peletz, in a more recent postmodernist and postcolonialist mode, reinforce this view when they say 'gender is a fluid, contingent process characterized by contestation, ambivalence, and change' (1995: 1). Gender comprises 'contradictory ideologies constantly undergoing change' (ibid.: 4).

Bearing these complexities in mind appearances can be very misleading. Gloria Poedjosoedarmo (1983) lists five 'impressions' of modern Javanese life, including men's statements on the alleged inferiority of Javanese women and women's special responsibility for the hard chores of cleaning and washing at home, but she says that these male postures or attitudes do not convey an accurate picture of what happens in practice. In average Javanese villages, men may dominate political life but women control economic life:

> In village society, economics is almost exclusively the domain of women. Though men are in charge of agricultural production, it is the women generally who handle marketing. In addition to marketing their own produce, at all levels of society women are involved in buying and selling for profit ... Traditionally, though men dominated political life, it was the women who held a monopoly on the economy and this is still true at least on the village level.
>
> (ibid.: 7, 8)

As we have just seen, it is usual among observers to generalize about the similarity of the two genders in society but then to qualify the statement by pointing out that politics, especially at the higher levels, is emphatically male-dominated (i.e. the districts, towns and capitals are controlled by men in their roles as officials and rulers). Ingrid Rudie who has studied Kelantanese Malay society for over two decades concludes:

> As far as my Malay material is concerned, I think it is possible to argue that a fair balance between male and female in the restricted public field of the local community is counteracted on higher levels of sociopolitical and cultural integration, and this trend is growing.
>
> (1994: 83)

Or Michael Peletz who worked with the distinctive Negri Sembilan Malays whose traditional social organization is underpinned by matrilineal lineages says: these Malays live

> in a social and cultural environment that places relatively little emphasis on gender or gender difference(s) ... in most contexts of

society and culture there is relatively little concern with gender or gender difference(s); and that compared to many (perhaps most) other societies studied by anthropologists, gender does not constitute an important marker of social activities, spatial domains, or cultural knowledge.

(1996: 232f.)

But he adds: 'at the same time, there are various contexts in which villagers assert that males and females differ in certain fundamental respects and are of dissimilar status', for example, women are spiritually 'weaker' but, by contrast, more sexually demanding (ibid.: 233–234).

Such generalizations, including the usual qualification that gender 'equality' was never and will never be total and all-embracing, are widely found in the anthropology of South-East Asia and, as remarked by Peletz in the passage just quoted, South-East Asia is quite possibly the only region of the world as we know it which features such androgynous or at least sex-similar systems (cf. Winzeler, 1996: 167–168, who says 'it would appear difficult to find another comparable region of the world' where sex symmetry is as marked as it is in South-East Asia). Several South-East Asian societies are explicitly argued to be sex equal: Rungus Dusun (Appell, 1991); Central Thai (Hanks and Hanks, 1963); Bontoc (Bacdayan, 1977); Peninsular Malay (Wazir Jahan Karim, 1992) (cf. Brown, 1976). South-East Asia's distinctiveness on this point increases the challenge to Western and anthropological understandings of how this could be so. To be reminded that men still monopolize public office does not diminish the point, since in every human group the males also lead in other 'pathological' behaviours – war and homicide, head-taking, drug-use, tree-climbing and the manufacture of musical instruments. Yet equally, with parallel worthiness, women monopolize child-bearing. And, as has been observed in Malay society, married couples welcome children both female and male; in practice there is no discrimination. Indeed, Carol Laderman, who did fieldwork in Terengganu in 1975–1977 observes that 'Girls and boys are valued equally. No matter how many children a couple may have [and five or six is usual], if they are all of the same sex the family is considered incomplete, and a child of the unrepresented sex may be adopted' (1996: 66). As Ernestine Friedl has indicated (1978) the mystery is not how it is that males are superior, it is why women and men believe that they are.

In one of the most rigorous attempts to define female status cross-culturally, Whyte (1978) was forced to admit, in the course of his lengthy study of fifty-two indicators in a sample of ninety-three pre-industrial societies, that 'female status' requires better definition, but we do not yet know how to achieve this.

Already we can see that if we wish to make cross-cultural generalizations about the status of women relative to men, we will have to be *much more specific than some previous scholars* in stating precisely what aspects of the relative status of women we are talking about. Political leadership is highly skewed in favor of males, shamanism less so; polyandry does seem almost as rare as previous work has indicated, beliefs in stronger male sex drive do not seem to be as common as some have supposed.

(ibid.: 94; emphasis added)

He warns that in his study 'no coherent unitary scale could be constructed [for women's status]' (ibid.: 98). Any person who has fallen in and out of love can probably testify to the inherent unpredictability in the ways society manages the claims and behaviours of the sexes, indeed some lovers can even question how many 'sexes' there are (a relevant question for some parts of South-East Asia as we shall see).

Finally, and before turning to case studies, we should note that, despite the emphasis which has been given to the important position of women in both the domestic and public sectors, there are studies which point to the increasing exploitation, marginalization and oppression of women as a consequence of capitalist development and state formation, their lack of access to certain modern productive resources, their anonymity (at least until recently) in development planning and project implementation, and their displacement in agriculture as a result of the introduction of mechanization (Bell, 1991; Eviota, 1992; Heyzer, 1986; Scott, 1985). Van Esterik also lists several problems which women face in a rapidly changing South-East Asia: the need for legal protection for women in family law, for more fairly rewarded income-generating opportunities, for innovations to ease domestic burdens, and for more participation in development planning (1996: 11–12). However, the positive view of such developments points to the increasing availability of off-farm work for women, along with greater female mobility, education levels and autonomy (Wolf, 1992).

Gender relations through case studies

Despite the increasing range of perspectives on gender relations in South-East Asia and the debates about gender equality and inequality, accounts from anthropologists about gender systems reach us generally in two broadly distinct, though occasionally overlapping forms. One is socio-economic, and depicts gender as tending to an equivalence of the sexes, using evidence of the division of labour, property holding and control of life chances (for example, initiating divorce, or uxorilocal residence). The other focuses on gender concepts in a psychocultural perspective, highlighting sexual attributes expressed through folk biology and in social-symbolic constructions of gender. Thus, the first type of account tackles the question at the level of social and economic discrimination and divisions, the second purports to reveal self-esteem and personal symbols. Anthropologists should of course argue across the full range of data. Apart from a picture that may lack proper context or be incomplete in other ways, the *parti pris* elevates the parochial and so makes comparison difficult.

Any review of gender in South-East Asia is also limited by the perennial question of typicality. Illustrations are bound to be selective and arbitrary. There is as yet no modern ethnographic atlas or survey of this important region of the world as there is for its languages or at least aspects of its languages (see the survey on words for 'rice' in Revel, 1988; compare the distributional study by Driver and Massey, 1957, on North America). Ideally the hologeistic method of controlled ethnographic sampling could be applied to the South-East Asian region to establish the outlines of gender and the sexes. Unfortunately little if any such work is available (see Winzeler, 1996; the quasi-encyclopaedic survey of human families by Stevan Harrell, 1997, excludes island South-East Asia entirely) and it is necessary for the time being to rely on limited and chance comparisons (see, for example, Brown, 1976; Spiro, 1975; Helliwell, 1993; cf. Sanday, 1981) which may or may not prove to be sound. But they are all we have, and we shall draw on those studies that seem to us to have typicality and to offer valid comparisons.

Burma–Thailand

One of the most empirically intensive, analytically elaborate, and scholastically sustained bodies of work carried out single-handedly on gender in South-East Asia is the series of studies by Melford Spiro, whose work has already been referred to (see Chapter 3). It is possible that his results come as close as any thus far to an effective programme for the study of gender and thus a suitable starting-point for our review. The Burmese provide an example of a major indigenous South-East Asian society with a strongly developed pattern of sexual equality but one which also has generated gender-specific responses which serve to distance the genders from one another. The following outline paraphrases a section from Spiro's account (1997: 11–12).

In Burma, until recently anyway, women participate at all levels of the society. They control the domestic or household economy, they are prominent in retail trades as village hawkers and as proprietors of the stalls and shops in the larger markets, and figure noticeably in larger business enterprises. They are also well represented in the professions (such as medicine and college teaching, though not engineering). In the village economy, women perform many of the same tasks of agricultural production as men and receive an equal wage even while it is admitted by both sexes that women's output is usually less than men's.

Legally, Burmese women have the same rights as men. In Burma today – as in all other South-East Asian countries – women have the right to vote and sometimes occupy high political office. Local headships can in theory go to women where a suitable male candidate (usually the son of the headman) is not available. The family estate is divided equally between sons and daughters, women own property in their own name, and after marriage husband and wife own all property jointly. Girls are just as qualified as boys to decide when and whom to marry, the girl's family oversees the daughter's (first) marriage, the bride not the groom receives a marriage payment, and men and women have the same rights in initiating divorce. None of the typical East Asian, Southern Asian or South-West Asian traits of women's subjugation were found – veil, purdah, child betrothal, foot binding, female infanticide, widow immolation, the prohibition of widow remarriage – and polygyny, though not prohibited, was uncommon below the highest court circles.

In social life there are numerous signs of sexual symmetry. Many early European observers were struck by the freedom of women in Burma and Thailand to move, apparently securely, in public and to associate informally with men. Women were not prevented from speaking in public, from occupying a place of honour alongside their husbands, and in general going wherever he went in normal peacetime. The everyday picture is much the same today; it has been reinforced to some degree by modern education and the mass media.

So runs Melford Spiro's concise sketch of the Burmese gender system (cf. Mi Mi Khaing, 1963). An identical picture – if anything more concise – of the everyday life of men and women in the neighbouring Theravada Buddhist country of Thailand emerges also from writing by the anthropologist Herbert Phillips on Thai villagers of Central Thailand. He speaks of the sociological simplicity of the village of Bang Chan, describing with that phrase the villagers individualism and non-conformism at the personal level, the freedom to affiliate (the kinds of activity that gave rise to Embree's phrase 'loose structure' (1950): see Chapter 3) and how this simplicity and sexual egalitarianism is reinforced or 'supported' by the small or 'slight' differentiation that villagers make between the adult roles of the two sexes. Echoing what we have remarked above on the distinctiveness of South-East Asian gender systems, Phillips states:

> In contrast to all other known cultures, in Thailand both men and women may serve as midwives and do plowing. They both own and operate farms, inherit property equally, share equally in the property brought to a marriage and divide it equally in cases of divorce. It is not uncommon to find men tending babies while women are off on a business deal; nor is it unusual, as indicated earlier, to see women paddling right along with men as crew members in a boat race.
>
> (Phillips, 1965: 82 n.23; emphasis added)

In the face of so much affirmation it is still worth a reminder that symmetry and equality, though highly distinctive of so many of the South-East Asian gender systems, does not mean lawlessness, promiscuity, unfettered freedom in relations between the sexes. Women and men still face each other with expectations and stereotypes – they recognize a respectful distance between them – spiritual, ethical, emotional, occupational. Spiro has done as much as any anthropologist to analyse this dimension of the mutual gaze in gender concepts and attitudes. He argues that in religion and the domestic group – two pillars of village life – the Burmese have accepted an overlay of formal male superiority. In Spiro's discussion this overlay comprises two cultural systems which are in opposition to, if not in contradiction with, the socio-economic system of gender already outlined above. This cultural system not only projects males and females as different and distant from each other, it also endows the sexes with substantially – one might say dramatically – distinct interpsychic attributes. The ideology of masculinity makes men superior, the ideology of femininity makes women dangerous. In Burma as in Thailand women will sit in the western inferior side of the house at a formal, ritual gathering. Burmese women regularly (though Spiro says periodically) pay homage to their husbands by kneeling before them and touching forehead to the ground in the obeisance known in Burma as *shikkhou* (1997: 15). (See below for a ritual reversal of this action observed in modern Chiangmai, Thailand.) Buddhism allows men an overall spiritual monopoly through the institutions of monkhood; in contrast, opportunities for nuns in Buddhism are negligible since none of the spiritual benefits can be earned in this way. Women gain merit in Buddhism instead by 'giving' sons to the monastery and by donating food to monks for their daily meals.

An insightful summary of the complex gender situation in Thailand has been provided by Khin Thitsa, herself Burmese by birth; it is just as apt for the Burmese:

> Thai women had a strong position despite, not thanks to, Buddhism. Buddhist philosophy importantly denigrates the *de facto* position of women, propagating an image of her as inferior and dangerous, which has been instrumental in denying her legitimate power in the form of bureaucratic or official position, while allowing her unrestricted access to the realms of labour and the economy.
>
> (1983: 9–10; original emphasis)

Over and above their treatment as inferiors at the formal ritual occasions in the household and religious life, Burmese women are seen by men as 'dangerous' as the above quote reminds us. In other words, they are not simply passive partners, they are active threats. Spiro was able to make some field study of Burmese male sexuality and determined two extreme though unconscious sources of male fear and insecurity – of genital contact (fear of the vagina) and of too close a dependency on his wife. The Burmese male's sexual identity is the product of 'anomalous' (1997: 178) gender experience, of the impossibility of correlating his 'distance' from female alter (opposite). Burmese men (and possibly women too) have fashioned – unconsciously – a set of frankly superstitious beliefs in male superiority and female assertiveness as a psychological defence, integral to their everyday psychic success.

Whether or not this internal and highly graphic conflict in Burmese male gender perceptions is only to be found in Burmese society, or follows the same pattern in other parts of South-East Asia, where more muted expressions of the same incompatible male and female 'natures' occur, as Spiro duly notes, for example, in the Malay phrases *hawa nafsu* and *akal,* or female 'passion' and male 'reason', and in the spatial orientations left and right, higher and lower, etc., is hard to know at the present time. We will discuss it further below. The symbolic beliefs in gender asymmetry are cross-cultural (i.e. worldwide), but in gender systems in other parts of the world there is greater convergence or agreement between males' intimate learning on the one hand, and formal role models on the other. By contrast, in South-East Asia, with its distinct sociolegal and economic gender equivalence, there is a divergence, and the bridge to equanimity and happiness is, at least in Burmese society, on Spiro's hypothesis, too shaky by far. If Spiro's analysis were to hold more widely for South-East Asia, how would the discrepancy, as observed for Burmese, between the informal and the everyday (where sisters, daughters, wives and mothers hold sway as at least the equals of men), and the formal and sacred – where men are elevated – be contained, bridged, resolved?

We do not know much about Burma now. In Thailand, with population growth and increased economic hardship in the countryside, people have begun to move to towns and to the modern capital Bangkok. The problem is for unskilled villagers to get a foothold in these new environments. Many eke out a living as petty traders or hawkers, others find work in factories. They do not necessarily sever their ties with their home villages. Khin Thitsa, in her study just quoted, gives an insightful analysis of the ways northern Thai women have recently exploited traditional gender assignments in the male-dominated town of Chiangmai by redefining them in terms of economic opportunities. Women have occupied positions on the margins and in the interstices of the Buddhist traditions in the ancient Thai town of Chiangmai as it undergoes a recrudescence of its traditional place in the modern nation. Specifically they have variously become nuns (*mai chii*), mediums (*maa khii*), and prostitutes (*ying borikan* or 'entertainment women').

The nuns enter monasteries specifically to improve their lives; many are young unmarried women from the poor countryside around Chiangmai who give up home, marriage prospects and sexual activity, and in doing so approximate the life of holiness and abstinence of the male monks. The spirit-mediums in Chiangmai, of which there were an estimated 1,000 by 1981–1982 (Thitsa, 1983: 30–31) and growing, were over 80 per cent female, often from impoverished backgrounds and with a history of illness or marital failures. The stronghold of spirit mediums in the rural areas used to be the domestic matrilineal cults where the medium was possessed by female ancestors, but these are declining and the urban mediums are possessed mostly by individual male spirits. All classes of person consult the mediums, including prostitutes and masseuses, and monks (ibid.: 2). The mediums cater to a sector of people's lives – illness, infertility, misfortunes and bad luck – where Buddhism plays no role. In Burma too the spirit mediums (*nat kadaw* 'shaman' in Spiro's wording) can be either male or female 'but virtually all are female' (Spiro, 1997: 14).

Prostitution, though illegal in Thailand, flourishes. This sex industry in Thailand is not solely the product of demand from foreign visitors; Thai men were and are still the major customers. As Thitsa says, buying the services of women makes Thai men 'feel like Kings of Siam' (1983: 36). 'Chiangmai, with a population [1981–1982] of 150,000, has at least 70 brothels, seven massage parlours (two with over 80 women) and six nightclubs with [escort women] to say nothing of . . . restaurants, bars and beauty parlours' where women are available (ibid.: 33–34). And although a despised and dangerous occupation, prostitution in Thailand has yielded benefits for many of its women who do manage to turn it to their advantage in supporting themselves and often their poor rural relatives (ibid.: 40–41).

The interest of this case study on the changing strategies of women's lives in northern Thailand is not only about the division of labour in modern Thailand, where men and women succeed both through traditional rural skills and through education, and through the refashioning of orthodox beliefs and practices; it also informs us, in the latter instance, of the susceptibility of Thai sex roles to elaboration through symbolic antithesis. The monk (nun) and the prostitute (male client) represent two powers: respectively, spirituality through abstention, and domination through its opposite, profligacy. In between is the spirit medium:

> Usually possessed by the male spirits of warriors, princes and even kings, the *maa khii* is a [ritually defined] transvestite. Pure, undeniably Buddhist and feminine when free from possession, she is transformed into a belligerent, sexually aggressive and whisky-drinking social 'male' when possessed.
>
> (ibid.: 43)

In other words, when ritually 'entered' by male spirits she is a woman, yet when uttering her spirit messages, she becomes simultaneously a man who 'commands monk and general alike, who attends the rites of mediums for advice and consultations. The only time in Thai society when a monk may be observed kneeling before a woman is during such spirit medium sessions' (ibid.: 43). Sexual reversal, which may be subliminal, and sexual masquerade are characteristic in shamanism. For example, in central Sulawesi: 'Among the Bare'e Toradja the role of shaman was open only to women or to men who posed as women' (Downs, 1956: 47). 'Thus [Thitsa says] marginal roles emerge which offer women new opportunities to manipulate the images which have [traditionally] defined them [as subordinates and inferiors]' (1983: 44). In comparative view, Thai and Burmese women's social disabilities are relatively few but they can be increased by the stress of poverty and life crisis. In Chiangmai several roles enable them to stem the encroachment of a male-centred ideology which is itself unstable and inconsistent.

Malaysia–Indonesia

Even in South-East Asian societies where Islam is the dominant 'great tradition' the indigenous gender systems have until recently, as they have in Burma and Thailand, counteracted or diluted some if not many of the formal male-weighted prescriptions of ritual and the law. But there is a major difference between Islam and Buddhism (which as far as we know has never been discussed comparatively for South-East Asia) but which must affect the psychocultural aspects of gender in South-East Asia. Recall that a major profession of the faith in Buddhism lies in one of its particular ascetic practices, sexual abstention. In other words, celibacy – both temporary and permanent – is crucial to the true path of enlightenment and rebirth, the highest ideals of Buddhism attainable by all ordinary believers, even if, in the case of women Buddhists, at one remove. It is entirely the opposite in Islam. Islam nowhere accords merit or blessing to sexual abstention once a person reaches marriageable age. Only at certain points in the daily and annual ritual cycle are male and female Muslims bound to observe rules of ritual purity which may include sexual abstention. In fact Islam is neutral regarding sexual activity in the scale of the life cycle. No stage of a Muslim's life after puberty (the point when Islam allows marriage) should be celibate. If a Muslim marries late it is regarded as lost time in religious terms, not time well spent. As stated, to our knowledge this topic has not yet been investigated in the South-East Asian context but it seems plausible to suppose that sexual frustration of some kind, which Spiro, and others, single out as a hidden and troublesome component of gender in the Theravada Buddhist cultures, plays a far smaller role in the traditional Islamic cultures of South-East Asia.

As Rudie and Peletz, among others, have remarked, the gender balance in Malay societies shifts as its field moves from the informal to the formal, and from the mundane to the sacred, as hierarchies form and the economic sphere grows. Islamic law purports to govern the whole of social life and beliefs: its followers are usually known as 'believers' to carry the idea of total dedication. Islam originated in an Arabic-speaking society and incorporates that society's patrilineal descent bias, and so in appearance Islam favours males and gives no leeway for change in female status. The laws and rituals of Islam give the man most of the initiative in divorce, greater inheritance shares than the woman, a right, under certain conditions, to take more than one wife, greater freedom of travel, spiritual predominance in ritual and prayers, and so on. Gender inequality in Islamic law is a matter of degree. Muslims are quick to remind anybody who thinks the legal bias works 'against' females that the prophet Muhammad reformed the social practices of his time in Arabia and in propagating Islam immeasurably improved women's status.

In much the same way as in the Buddhist communities, and despite Islam's claim to be more precise and more 'just' in its governance of people's lives than the other great religions, the tenets of Islam in Malay and Javanese societies and in other South-East Asian Muslim societies are often taken up more or less selectively and in piecemeal fashion. For instance, the laws of marriage, divorce and inheritance are meticulously spelled out in Islam (as they are not in Buddhism) but until the last 30 years in Malaysia, Singapore, Brunei and Indonesia, the administration of Islamic law lagged far behind the state's secular administration and Muslims largely saw the strict letter of Islamic law as a last resort, only called into play when traditional and informal measures failed.

In the past 30 to 40 years the laws of Muslim divorce have been 'tightened' in the four countries mentioned (see Jones, 1994). While this strengthening of the role of Islam encourages more formal exercise of rights by both sexes and has very visible results in worship practices, it is still not the pervasive (or invasive) force its theological advocates claim for it. Since Islamic law allows women to hold and bequeath property it is not in strong contradiction with the bilateral inheritance pattern of most of the traditional South-East Asian societies, including the Muslim Malays and Javanese. One group of Malay speakers, the Minangkabau people, located in western Sumatra around modern-day Padang, and in the Malaysian state of Negri Sembilan, in the western Malay Peninsula, had, and have today, a system of matrilineal descent-groups. This inheritance system by definition confers property (clan land) exclusively through females and cannot be reconciled with Islamic law. The Minangkabau 'solution' has been to apply the Islamic ritual regulations and much of the rest of Islamic law as required for most of its affairs but to ignore inheritance as applied to customary law (adat) and estates. In this, both branches of the Minangkabau group were supported over the years, first by their colonial and later their national regimes.

As we suggested earlier, it is unsatisfactory at least in anthropological terms to reduce gender relations to the sexual division of labour or gender-specific property devolution. While in no way superficial or negligible (as would for instance be an exclusive focus on the gendered varieties of hairstyles, body adornment and dress), these two aspects of rights and power in community subsistence take us only so far. They seem to lead to a picture of the gender pattern in a region of the world exhibiting sex roles that are to some degree androgynous ('androgynous' – having the characteristics of both sexes, divided equally; see Zolla, 1981) or, at the very least, diffuse; as anthropologists have suggested, this picture is unlike any other region in the ethnographic record, regions where sex roles are usually sharply defined and distinguished and even more usually unequal.

Far more than ethnic identities, and more than kinship and friendship affiliations, gender relations depend on learned emotional routines – respect, love, avoidance and abstention, dependency, antagonism. This could be because gender ties are, if not uniquely then less susceptible of adoption (change of identity or affiliation) than the other ascriptive forms and are capable of more intimacy. And the muteness of sexual expressions in South-East Asian cultures

273

has often been noted (e.g. Errington, 1990: 2–5) and may even be responsible for the failure of anthropologists to pay sufficient attention to the various forms of sexual intimacy – etiquette, exchange, commensality, friendship, sex life – as specifically gendered forms. Studies of Malay communities in northern Peninsular Malaysia by Carsten, Wazir Jahan Karim and Rudie fortunately go some way to make up for this less-studied arena, as do the few studies of children and socialization. They go some way to bridging the disparate interests of scholars of the South-East Asian peasant 'moral economy' (shared poverty, notions of debt and obligation) and specialists in symbolic, psychological and structuralist anthropology.

The major populations of South-East Asia, and many of the so-called 'hill' or 'forest' people too, have long been familiar with markets and thus lived in a partly or wholly monetized economy. And yet, as one of us learned in his own fieldwork with Pahang Malays and reported by others, the men hold ambivalent feelings about money, and more specifically the handling of and identification with cash (see, for example, Brenner [1998: 134–170], writing on Surakarta/ Solo in Java). (The situation is not unlike the Freudian-tinged epithet 'filthy lucre' familiar to the European–American upper-middle classes of old – essential to demonstrate one's social repute but fatal to one's self-respect and public face to discuss it openly.) To earn, save and invest money from village pursuits – essentially self-employment in the domestic mode of production, the family farm – is respectable, but to hire oneself to an employer – to 'earn wages' (*makan gaji* in Malay) no matter how honest and necessary it may be, is a kind of failure in life, and risks cutting oneself off from village roots and an honourable reception. A salaried, pensionable post in government service is exempt, however, since it was a sign of achievement, bringing security both desirable and esteemed. Manual labourers, factory workers and taxi drivers, however, are likely to be thought of as failed farmers. (Not that farming, especially nowadays, is a desired even if esteemed occupation.) Traditionally women in the household context were also exempt since men delegated the holding and much of the budgeting of cash income to their wives, but more recently in Free Trade Zone industries young female wage-earners also come under this ambivalent gaze, as we shall see below.

Janet Carsten (1989) has developed an ingenious (or 'idiosyncratic' as one reviewer said, Cedercreutz, 1998: 480) argument showing how the mediation of women makes cash acceptable, in a sense the wife launders men's money by 'cooking' it, thus making men's gained income from fishing, conducted far away from the house and village and in a competitive, divisive atmosphere, into a spendable, handleable resource which helps and solidifies the household and farm village, rather than corrupting them. The key symbolic medium for effecting this transformation in the community's subsistence is the staple food, rice, which is insulated from the market: rice is produced solely for domestic consumption and provides no cash income (see also Carsten, 1997: 135, and Chapter 5 *passim*). While this is equally true of the Pahang Malay village with

which Wilder is familiar, it is not the case in other Malay villages, where rice
and other food crops may provide some cash income.

Cash from the sale of fish is put in charge of the woman of the house, it is
deliberately not divided up – shares are 'explicitly left uncalculated' (Carsten,
1989: 131) – in the female effort of 'socializing' it; some is put into the *kut* or
females' credit ring which provides useful capital to its members in turns; husbands who want some of the money they have earned for spending money must
ask their wives for it (Carsten, 1997: 154–155). On Pulau Langkawi labour is
strongly divided: housekeeping and rice-growing for the benefit of the household are aligned against the male fishing crew which is seasonal, avoids kin
involvement and is non-commensal: 'Fishermen, it seems, are neither of one
house [kin circle] nor even of one boat' (Carsten, 1989: 127). In other words, in
symbolic terms, rice feeds the house members and in doing so produces likeness
and a unity among them, but the fish catch that men bring back is an irregular
product of unlike persons, strangers. The agent in this process of commodity
transformation is the manager-wife not at the formal head but at the *de facto*
centre of the typical village dwelling house. Insofar as the domestic unit is the
most functional in the everyday economic pursuit it is the wife and mother who
leads it in actual practice.

What does this analysis tell us about female and male in Malay social life? It
suggests a life where women and men spend much time apart but are not separated, that is, they are united in spirit. The economy on Langkawi Island is
market-orientated, regional and well monetized, as befits a peasant economy,
but it remains small in scale because it is devoted to satisfying subsistence needs
in the village and in part because Langkawi is distant and isolated from the
mainland. (This account does not take into account the recent development of
the island as a tourist resort.) Would the same complementarity between the
sexes hold in a community more tied into its region and state? Rudie's research
on Malays in Kelantan may be cited here.

Rudie has tracked changes in the rural economy in Kelantan from 1965 to
1980: she states:

> Readers who are familiar with Malay ethnography know that it is a
> well documented feature that women administer the family's money
> and, by extension, are entitled to men's earnings. This was . . . part of
> normal expectations in Kelantan in 1965, and again in the 1980s.

except that in the more recent period the village and its households are more
and more part of the larger economy and at the expense of women's earning
power (Rudie, 1994: 113). While this new division of labour does not
totally change the picture, the earning community is gradually becoming less
uniform and predictable in terms of its financial decisions. 'This seemingly dis-
passionate acceptance by women of [husband's control over money] . . . is not
a sign of women's subjugation, but rather something quite different: a certain

separateness in marriage, coupled with equality in the project of running a household' (ibid.: 113). Rudie calls this 'separate-but-equal and cooperative' ethos duocentric (ibid.: 108–109).

Where they lose control over money

> the women have [in such cases] lost control over the total process of acquiring commodities and transforming them into gifts ... Instead of being responsible for the whole chain of production as well as the preparation of food, more and more women are now responsible only for preparing it.
>
> (ibid.: 114)

And too, 'Small plots of [village] land are distributed approximately evenly among men and women. When this land was used for market gardening, it activated women's productive capacity ... The women–food–resource link was complete' (ibid.: 114–115), but this land is now being used less for kitchen produce and more as building land, with a growing tendency for married sons of the house, rather than daughters, to build on it. And yet Rudie argues that the 'duocentric' form of the Malay household continues, while in some cases women's financial autonomy has diminished, their expectation of separateness and cooperation from their husbands – both of which are compatible with equality – may be unabated (ibid.: 116– 117).

We have looked at gender roles and more specifically women's roles in some of the major ethnic populations – Burmese, Thai, Malay, Javanese and Minangkabau. There is much in the ethnographic data which shows that women acting in their roles as wives, mothers and married daughters in these major populations handle the cash brought in by men, women and even children to the domestic kitty or 'circle'. Women in these roles are mainly responsible for 'liquidity' in household units, and, in Malay and Javanese societies, women may also support the rotating credit rings (*arisan* or *kut)* to increase their local financial power. In a southern Luzon fishing village, a comparable – though evidently gender-blind – savings scheme, known as *turnohan* (lit. 'taking turns') involves twenty or more persons or families and makes large cash sums available to its members (Illo, 1995: 213). Beyond the household, women may and often do engage in petty trade, shopkeeping and even own, if they do not actually run, businesses. They might, for instance, own craft shops, or a fleet of taxis on lease to male drivers. Female control of houses, land, shop and business enterprises, commercial licences and contracts is comparatively strongly aided in most parts of South-East Asia by the indigenous systems of property devolution – bilateral descent and the customary marriage and divorce arrangements giving women substantial rights of inheritance and control over wealth. The involvement of females and their households in craft production in the Philippines casts additional light both on gender concepts and on the economic system which activates them.

The Philippines

Lynne Milgram (1999) worked among the Ifugao, in the northern Philippine province of Luzon in 1995, on the management of income in eighteen artisan households, a study inspired in part by Rosanne Rutten's report on female hat and mat weavers in a lowland area of the Philippines (1993). The Ifugao artisans specialize in the weaving of cotton table runners for the local tourist market. They are mainly women. Women and men also work as woodcarvers and basket makers. Some seventeen Ifugao villages in the municipality of Banaue have developed significant craft production. While the major subsistence pursuit in this mountainous area is wet-rice cultivation on thousands of terraces built into the steep mountainsides, with secondary reliance on sweet potato (camote), Milgram reports that '[a]n average of 55 percent [sic] of each village's approximately 250 households have at least one member involved in craft production or trade (e.g. basketmaking, weaving, woodcarving)' (1999: 223). At the same time, cash income is required for households to support activities such as education, small craft enterprises, consumer wants and loan repayments. Milgram's study of the sexes in the tasks of household survival in these relatively remote and impoverished villages emphasizes the flexibility of their domestic economy and the active response of women and men in seizing productive work. It confirms both that women are free and able to work in a variety of ways, and that they contribute significantly and equally to household income.

Within the domestic group, the woman, as wife and mother, sees herself as the 'treasurer of the house' (ibid.: 226). This is a familiar South-East Asian theme. In this Ifugao community:

> Women control and allocate household cash, have a major say in decisions on work and expenditures, and assume an equally active part in productive work ... Married women collect most or all of the earnings of their husbands and children. The family's pooled income is collectively used first to meet daily subsistence needs and, if possible, to accumulate some reserves against setbacks.
>
> (ibid.: 226)

There is, also, a 'pooling' of duties between husband and wife and with older children of the house. Work within the household is 'highly interchangeable' (ibid.: 228); Milgram speaks of the 'fluid interchangeability of tasks' in response to chances of securing income. Craftwork is not the only cash-generating activity: wage labour, laundry service and petty trade in garden produce also produce income, and every adult calculates which activities he or she must and can afford to engage in. While craftwork yields an income, it only does so in the tourist season (December, March, April). At other times of the year, agriculture or other work must be sought. Yet between 10 and 50 per cent of household income can derive from one member's craftwork and such work is especially important in land-poor households which cannot rely on a harvest to reduce their outgoings. 'Income from handicrafts enables household members to purchase their daily necessities and in no way should be thought of as providing "pin" money for women' (ibid.: 145).

A prominent feature of the Ifugao domestic economy, though not as visible as the craft products and field harvests, is people's regular use of borrowed cash. The network of credit is not exceptional, since Milgram writes that the Ifugao have a 'respect for moneylending' (ibid.: 243). It is a chance for women especially to demonstrate their financial skills. Milgram once observed a quantity of harvested rice in an informant's house which did not come from her own fields but which, so the informant explained, consisted of part of the repayment, in kind, of a 20,000 peso loan made the previous year to relatives in the lowlands (ibid.: 243). (In lowland Bicol, Fenella Cannell was surprised to find the house of one of her non-farmer informants 'filled with sacks of unmilled rice'; these were revealed to be a loan repayment and not her own harvest [1999: 103].) The household had also made cash loans to neighbours and was receiving repayment plus 10 per cent interest. As Milgram reports, 'Each of the artisans in the survey continuously borrowed small amounts of cash without interest from their personal connections' and the use of these kinship-inspired social relations in access to money supports household enterprise, including the commoditization of crafts (1999: 254). The willingness in this community to enter into and to discharge debts reliably is shown to be a strong force for stability and for economic survival.

In lowland Filipino culture the notion of the obligation to repay is known as *utang* which we will discover again in Chapter 9. It can be argued that *utang* as understood in the Philippines is a strongly feminized notion (and see the discussion of *utang* in Cannell [1999: 102–104] where it is observed that strict debt accounting is infused with and constrained by the idea of debt as 'remembrance' and 'respect', *utang na loob*).

Gender relations in the Philippines have been extensively documented, and not only by anthropologists. In accordance with what we said in the discussions of gender in the Buddhist and Muslim societies of South-East Asia, the overwhelmingly Christian, and within that the largely Roman Catholic, component in Philippine culture deserves mention as do the cultural, social and academic alliances with America (see Chapter 3). What we have given here is only a sketch but is we hope close, as far as it goes, to most of the anthropological descriptions. It has been noted that the Philippines is a highly urbanized culture, probably a result of long commercialized plantation development, the 'comprador' export economy, and a comparatively robust infrastructure for South-East Asia. The Philippine gender theme reappears in Chapter 9 where the rural–urban continuum will be discussed and illustrated.

Vietnam

Vietnam's historical experience helps explain its distinctive, and divergent, social characteristics in comparison with the other parts of the region. Vietnam has existed in proximity to China for centuries and its direct exposure to Chinese influences is evident in religion and society. Confucianism, Taoism and Chinese Buddhism have blended with Vietnamese folk beliefs, and in the precolonial era Chinese men (or more precisely 'peasant-class males') periodically migrated from southern provinces of China, and married local women in Vietnam (O'Harrow, 1995: 168–169). In a similar way to other indigenous South-East Asian local societies, the Vietnamese domestic group is strongly dependent on female management and is expected to be so. The official, polite characterization of wife is that of 'interior helper' (*noi tro*) (ibid.: 172), but vulgar concepts such as 'general'-ship (*noi tuong*) and the dominion of a 'Lioness' in domestic groups come into play also.

Female domination, even where it exists only in aspiration and ideal, is obtrusive enough in O'Harrow's eyes to indicate a 'dysfunction' in Vietnamese gender systems (ibid.: 168). O'Harrow's approach draws on the psychocultural interpretation of gender relations mentioned at the beginning of the present chapter. Vietnamese peasant life is seen to be subject to shame – as opposed to guilt – sanctions (ibid.: 173). More than in the other large South-East Asian lowland or 'valley' peoples, in which ambilocal or matrilocal postmarital residence prevails, Vietnamese postmarital residence is strongly patrilocal (in common with southern Chinese traditional culture, see Wolf, 1972) and the introduction of the new bride to her husband's parents' house leads to a power struggle as the husband's mother attempts to control the new bride and the new bride attempts to maintain her autonomy.

Institutionalized though not necessarily inevitable domestic conflict, where it occurs, is a manifestation, in miniature, an outgrowth, of a long-standing 'peculiarly Vietnamese social dichotomy, in which the two layers of social ethic co-existed: the sinicised ethic [among the men] and the Southeast Asian female ethic [among the women]' (ibid.: 169). Another aspect of this dichotomy is that the 'massive hypocrisy' (ibid.: 168) which occludes and ostracizes the unmarried young female within the extended Vietnamese domestic group emphasizes the wider division (and divisiveness, leading to 'dysfunction') in Vietnamese culture between the Confucian male-dominated public sphere and the female-dominated domestic sphere (ibid.: 162–163). During the Vietnamese wars (roughly 1946–1976) the practical role of females in Vietnamese economic life became essential, but, in the years of Vietnamese independence following, the patriarchal ethic has measurably re-asserted itself (Albee, 1995), partly as a consequence of the decollectivization of agriculture since 1981 (Tran, 1999: 112–114).

'Factory girls'

Globalization of the economy in South-East Asia has come to mean for many of its people assembly plants (generally called factories) making components whether in the form of garments, electronic parts, or smaller consumer durables and consumables. The mostly light industries require a numerous semi-skilled local workforce, rather than robots or fully-automated production lines. They have developed rapidly since the early 1970s in West Malaysia, Java, Thailand, the Philippines and Singapore and more recently in Vietnam and even Cambodia. They are an economic response to price competition in the developed, consumerist world which finds a supply of cheap labour in these countries of South-East Asia (Brunei, Laos, East Malaysia and Burma do not yet come into the industrialization picture). The traditional demand for extraction of raw materials and for agricultural exports is thus beginning to be eclipsed though it continues to contribute to national incomes for the time being. Another response is seen in the growth of regional and overseas labour migration from South-East Asia, in which women are as, or more, prominent than men.

In one respect, the rural-based workforce – Malay, Javanese, Thai and Filipino – is already attuned to the new environment of mass production technology through its experience with the rudiments of money and markets, institutions long familiar to both males and females in the villages of South-East Asia. This knowledge does not mean, however, that the pathways to manufacturing plants and overseas employment are smooth ones. The very speed of the transition from field to factory makes for dislocation and uncertainty at the grassroots. There have been a number of anthropological studies of the ways in which predominantly rural communities have responded to new forms of work, and the incomes new work generates, or in Diane Wolf's epiphany, responses to the incursions of 'early industrial capitalist proletarianization on a rural area' (1992: 251). The inscription of factory industry on a rural landscape can be surprisingly literal:

> in this site [in Central Java], ten large-scale 'modern' factories, driven by Western machinery and technology and organized to run at a rapid, efficient pace, squat in the middle of the agricultural land of two [Javanese] villages that still have neither running water nor electricity and where most technology is driven by human labor or animal power. Some of these factories nest in rice fields, disrupting neat rows of rice shoots with metal fences and guards.
>
> (Wolf, 1992: 109)

Two of the most thorough, and best-known, analyses of the 'feminized' workforce are by Aihwa Ong (1987) and Diane Wolf (1992) and, since they reach broadly similar conclusions on the place of young women workers in the 1980s, during the early stages of South-East Asia's entry into the globalized manufacturing economy, we will look mainly at Ong's. From one point of view the rapid expansion, in Malaysia, Thailand and other countries, of industrial wage labour and of higher education has culturally enfranchised the young (defined for our purposes as persons roughly 18–30 years of age). This youth cohort enlarges an already existing plantation and urban workforce or proletariat and an educational elite, bequeathed to society by the colonial era, but in Ong's thesis the new entrants occupy a special role in Malaysia's rise to economic prosperity. They, and more particularly the unmarried female factory workers in Malaysia's Free Trade Zones, officially represent, as first-generation wage-earners, hope for the future but popularly they are also seen as a disruption to the national culture. Why, Ong asks, 'should sexuality become a key image/construct in Malay transition to industrial capitalism?' (1987: 4).

The popular and tabloid image of young female wage-earners as sexually aware (although in conservative Malaysia there is little study of their sexual activity) is a sensationalized exposure of the repressed gender theme of the passionate female, as noted earlier in this chapter. Thus, 'A heightened sexuality attributed to Malay female workers by the Malaysian public can be considered the contradictory cultural constructions of a society intensely ambivalent about the social consequences of industrial development' (ibid.: 4). In its approach to the hypothesis, Ong's *Spirits of Resistance and Capitalist Discipline* treats two crucial aspects of female industrial work: the 'capitalist discipline' of the workplace and its impact on Malaysian employees, and the florid public images, perceived at a distance by others, of an unrestrained new sexual and social class. Yet to begin to understand the genesis of these outpourings, we have only to consider the magnitude of the changes occurring in the short space of a few years in the semi-rural Malay settlements on the west coast of Peninsular Malaysia. First-time employment of village girls at low 'female' wages in foreign-owned and usually foreign (Japanese)-managed shopfloors requires, simultaneously, the move (usually only a few miles geographically – see the vignettes of factories in rural Java quoted above) from village house to global factory (ibid.: xiv), peasant to proletarian, village time to clock time (ibid.: 10), subsistence to cash, equal to unequal, alter-identity (within *adat* or world of custom) to self-identity (the world of wages), and sexual security (village) to sexual danger (mass society).

There is some dispute as to the saliency, and very meaning, of reported outbursts of spirit-possession or spirit-attack and of 'haunted' factory buildings among female factory workers (Ong, 1987: 204–213; Wolf, 1992: 201) in the early years. Since 'spirit attacks' naturally cause disruption of the factory work, it is tempting to interpret them as veiled acts of resistance, of the kind James Scott has analysed (Scott, 1985). They may be found to be genuine, though transitory, signs of the traumatic entry of Malays and Javanese into the globalized workplace. It seems that Thai and Filipino workers are not susceptible in these ways, perhaps because their protests are more active and direct than is customary in Malaysia, Singapore and Java (see Margold, 1999: 9). In her intensive examination of the villages which supply cheap labour to the Malaysian Free Trade Zone factories, Ong brings out the fact that rural villages have undergone a steady depletion of their landholdings throughout the twentieth century. Land and cash crops used to be the village assets, but increasingly human labour and skills, backed by greater mobility and education, took their place. By the time of Ong's fieldwork in 1979, only 15 per cent of village households depended wholly on farming (Ong, 1987: 83) and she saw that 'more families come to depend on [cash] incomes derived not from joint production effort on the land but from the wage employment of individual members' (ibid.: 107): Not only income but family relations are affected. 'In effect the employment status of working daughters [has] repercussions: [it] has loosened many [daughters] from father-brother control, connecting them instead to male power institutionalized in bureaucratic systems external to the *keluarga* [family household]' (ibid.: 108).

Direct or indirect protests against rural impoverishment might be expected. Not one but two forms of stress, first, on the factory floor owned and managed by Japanese or other foreigners, and, second, the relentless loss of traditional agricultural land to wealthy Malay outsiders, are consequences of 'capitalist discipline'. Malay parents in the village and their daughters who have gone to work outside it are subject to the insecurity and disruptive forces produced by these two forces. With the loss of family order and the village comes the threat to *adat* or Malay custom which stems from the increasing sense, for village daughters, of their own 'personal aspirations and acquired interests' (ibid.: 116), a psychocultural development we will see more of in Chapter 9 in James Siegel's interpretation of change in urban Solo (Surakarta). The effect is not selective. According to Ong:

> Young women's perceptions of self, and of men, are increasingly refracted through the prism of the cash register. Daughters from well-to-do families are clear-eyed about emotions and personal interests when marriage has become the key to *their* social mobility. Daughters of poor families also evince self-reflection in their handling of relationships with parents, lovers, and husbands.
>
> (ibid.: 135; emphasis Ong's)

As hinted above, the changes in female self-image and behaviour elucidated by Aihwa Ong, and in a similar way by Diane Wolf, for Malaysia and Java respectively, are replicated in some ways all over industrializing South-East Asia in the sense that factory work constitutes an extension of an otherwise largely traditional life cycle. Factory work offers several years of immersion in the commodified world of money and world labour markets but conventional marriage, though more delayed than in the past, remains a key aspiration for females and males alike. While agricultural functions of village land contract and 'As rural society became firmly woven into the circuit of capital production, more *kampung kebun* [tree plantations] were reduced to housing lots for a migratory labour force fanning across the country and overseas' (ibid.: 218) 'This decentering of rural Malay society was manifested in the marked emphasis on individual interests and the acquisition of symbolic capital by the young in matrimonial negotiations. Marriage strategies became increasingly conditioned by the wage earning capacity of a potential spouse, acquired tastes, and an expanded marriage circle. For what was negotiated were not merely relations among villagers but social relationships in a wider field which could facilitate upward mobility' (ibid.: 219). The case of Thai factory workers cited in Chapter 9 also illustrates this framework of youth aspirations.

The persisting role of 'tradition', for instance in marriage and householding, has been suggested. While many features of male and female roles have clearly shifted in the context of migration, urbanization, commodification and so on, it seems that we can still discern a baseline gender system. This can be summed up in the 'cognation argument' as presented by Wazir Jahan Karim.

A broad view of gender: the cognation argument

The most sustained and wide-ranging analysis in support of claims for the prevalence of sexual equality in a South-East Asian group is Wazir Jahan Karim's (1992) on the Malays of West Malaysia. She argues that Malay *adat*, or custom, way of life, underlying beliefs, is so organized as to equalize the gender balance in Malay society. Western anthropological research on women relies heavily on well-worn dichotomies – nature and culture, domestic and political, private and public, masculine and feminine (ibid.: 218–219) – which are descriptive of Western and some other gender systems but only subvert the analysis of hitherto unknown or unimagined gender systems such as those found in South-East Asia. She says:

> A basic area of investigation is the way in which constructions of Western knowledge have been superimposed on indigenous non-Western knowledge systems rendering reinterpretation of relationships of gender and sex. These reinterpretations, surfacing in formal education, media, legislation and political processes may be demonstrated through articulations of opposition between the two systems or alternatively, continuity and accommodation.
>
> (ibid.: 4)

Western dichotomies are not analytically or comparatively sound and only serve to prejudge the gender issue and leave it undiscovered by confining it in the limited universe of rigid dichotomies (see also Wazir Jahan Karim, 1994).

Adat is a Malay concept of civilization, a force for conservation and continuity. As Wazir Jahan Karim states, summarizing her discussion of Malay women in West Malaysia through history and in contemporary life:

the dominant view upheld in this study is that throughout history, Malay culture, in *adat*, has ensured women a position equal to men and that *adat* constructions of gender regularly attempt to redefine and reaffirm women's social contributions in the long term (to trends of development in the political process, and in major contributions to social and political history). . . . Malay *adat* as an 'equalizer' actively attempts to formulate women's position vis-à-vis men in non-hierarchical ways despite Islamization and other allied processes (capitalism, industrialization and modern bureaucracy) which become subject to male interpretations which are usually made to favour men rather than women.

(1992: 129, 281)

While Malay society has in common with other large-scale social systems differentiation and ranking by age and by class – and even here to a limited degree only – it conspicuously lacks or underemphasizes another of the usual modes of hierarchy, that of gender (Errington, 1990: 2–5) and that special, almost exceptional feature, is the issue Wazir Jahan Karim vigorously unravels. Even Islam in its recent revivalist form has largely failed to unseat the conserving effect of Malay *adat* with respect to women's role. It remains to be seen how far the other world-revolutionizing forces, those of capitalism, 'Western' (as opposed to 'Asian') values, and urban living (see Chapter 9), will be resisted by *adat*. (So far, in her view, the signs are good, she is optimistic.)

Until recently, in those – still many – Malay villages where income and livelihood derived from agriculture whether in subsistence or cash crops, it was common for land to be *worked* by both women and men, and for land to be *owned* by women to the tune of 40 per cent or more (Wazir Jahan Karim, 1992: 124 referring to Province Wellesley-Kedah, 1983) and there was still a tendency to allocate land equally between sons and daughters, a procedure consciously attributed to *adat* and not Islam. Wilder's own fieldwork in Pahang 1964–1976 bears this point out (Wilder, 1997; cf. Stivens *et al.*, 1994). Malay kinship and marriage is strongly reflective of the descent rule anthropologists call 'bilateral' or 'cognatic' which means that neither parent receives the greater preference in aligning relatives (cf. Wilder, 1991, on diverse and co-existing forms of descent Malays recognize: cognatic, patrilineal, matrilineal). Conversely, as mentioned above, children of both sexes are equally desired and a birth-group of one sex only is regarded as incomplete.

And, at other levels of action, Wazir Jahan Karim generalizes that women and men are equally allocated by age and seniority, matrimony except for the sometimes distorting (but rare) effect of polygyny, socio-economic ranking, which is sex-neutral, personal attributes – the expression of character, initiative, and charisma and morality – *maruah* and *nama* together (1992: 6–7) a need for 'reputation, commanding respect'. Malay *adat* and its essential component of bilaterality (which is the structural feature of kinship systems all over lowland South-East Asia) become for Wazir Jahan Karim a vehicle for a set of Malay

values – balance, flexibility, interchangeability and fluidity extending to relationships of any kind.

> I see bilaterality as a wider abstraction of kinship and gender and a
> popular Southeast Asia[n] mode of conceptualizing relationships of any
> kind. Whether the context of reference is gender, class, religion or the
> state, the creation or the need to create flexible boundaries of action
> and interaction seems to be valued.
>
> (ibid.: 9)

Bilaterality, she says, is

> a convenient abstraction to denote rules of 'balancing' or harmonizing
> intersexual ties and relationships [and] . . . a rule of social relations in
> society, obscuring clear distinctions of rank and class amongst unequals
> . . . male–female, patron–client, elite–peasant, elders–youth. Malay
> *adat* minimizes power differences wherever they are found.
>
> (ibid.: 11)

Thus, in history 'Malay kingships were formed through patriliny but ordered
through bilaterality' (ibid.: 50), reciprocity and bilaterality went together and
cooperation and domestication threaded through Malay history rather than
deliberate oppression and extermination (ibid.: 52, cf. 72 'Malay families freely
left villages [to escape oppression]'). Bilaterality was and is 'a mediatory mode of
thought and action' (ibid.: 113). Indeed, weak kingship seems to have been the
usual state of Malay kingdoms (Gullick, 1958); Joseph Conrad's novels *Outcast
of the Islands* and others illustrate the scene of Malay parlousness in this respect
as well as any). In South-East Asia power can be theatrical, not material, a topic
not touched on by Wazir Jahan Karim [but see 1992: 80 'sense of powerlessness
of Malay rulers' and ibid.: 83], but discussed by other scholars such as Clifford
Geertz and Stanley Tambiah (see Chapter 3).

As observed already in Spiro's work on Burmese sexual relations viewed from
a psychocultural angle, Malay sexuality is gendered but is also strongly
complementary. Peletz (1996) and Wazir Jahan Karim (1992: 143–146) are
among the few writers to tackle the subject for Malays. Wazir Jahan Karim
remarks on the mutuality of needs and concerns of Malay married couples
where, as we have seen already, 'The maintenance of equal roles and duties in a
Malay marriage reflects the principle of bilaterality – mutual responsibility and
rights between men and women on the domestic and community level' (ibid.:
146). Partners view each other as 'sparring partners' engaged sexually in a tussle
or confrontation (*lawan*) (ibid.: 144): 'A woman who participates actively in
lovemaking is said to be a good "sparring partner" (*melawan*)' (ibid.: 144) and a
man if unable to meet the sexual demands of his wife may be the butt of jibes –
one who *tenggelam* or *mati lemas* 'sinks' or 'drowns' when he performs poorly

(ibid.: 143). From gossip and anecdote overheard in Pahang we can confirm this picture of women and men as equal and complementary sexual partners. Sexual fitness is not only highly valued but often is public knowledge (see also Peletz, 1996).

Thus, looking across the spectrum of social relations in modern Malaysia, a spectrum including urban and industrial settings, Wazir Jahan Karim contends that there is a persistence of a marked Malay egalitarianism, and – what is more distinctive than that – a sexual symmetry.

> Viewed comparatively, systems of separation of role, rights and status according to gender are not significantly evident among the Malays, save what has developed in urban industrial employment or recent Islamic movements (either Western or Arabic norms have been applied in ordering roles and positions respectively).
>
> (1992: 226)

Gender as a heterogeneous category

Wazir Jahan Karim has enlarged the field of debate further since her 1992 book, but has still largely confined her discussions to feminism as applied to South-East Asia and this limited scope has two disadvantages: it introduces an arguably 'Western' viewpoint in the notion of 'feminism' (cf. her own criticism above on Western-inspired dichotomies), and it sticks with the socio-economic viewpoint which, as suggested at the beginning of this chapter, is only half the story. There is great confusion, both in the West and in the East as a result of Western influences, over what we can call gendered demeanour, that is, the boundaries of the set of characters which shall be normative for the sexes, in gendered roles, just what characters should be included and what excluded. Fortunately an abundance of anthropological work is available in the literature on this question of gendered demeanour and in particular on the gender-expression of mixed sexes (see Morris, 1994). Not just division of labour, or house-ownership and landholding, can be complementary elements, symmetrical or even substitutable – which is the South-East Asian violation of Western and most other world gender concepts as discussed above, but we must also consider blurred genders, transitional genders, what the West in its blinkered way tries to reduce to 'bisexuality' or merely to perversions. Much has been written on the West's historical preoccupation with fixed sexuality, for which a much-quoted case is the medical diagnosis and 'correction' (or normalization) of the hermaphroditic state (see Garfinkel, 1967). And much is known of the domination by Darwinian and medical ideologies of the West's sexual knowledge and awareness.

In this connection Morris's examination of mixed sexes requires a little more attention. She notes how she and other visitors and fieldworkers in Thailand were 'astounded by the plasticity and heterogeneity of Thai gender and sexual identity' (1994: 18), and she speaks of 'ambiguous gender'. (To which we could add the blended, fluid characteristics of Thai gender roles, seen in the cross-dresser, the androgyne, the hermaphrodite.) The historic Thai gender system, she argues, is carried in the Tai-Buddhist text *Pathamamulamuli* (ibid.: 20, 41). It reports a triadic gender logic, a 'sexual trinity' (ibid.: 20). While the three sexes – male, female and neuter – are not explicitly detailed sexually, they are given sex-linked characteristics in terms of Buddhist 'suffering'. Males suffer unfulfilled sexual longing, females the pain of childbearing, and the neuter or hermaphrodite the troubles of a 'too sensitive heart' (ibid.: 21). For Morris, the three gender types are indigenous Tai (embracing the Tai-speaking peoples of Laos, Thailand, south-western China and parts of Vietnam and Burma) and are of equal standing. Locally, today, Thai boys seen as 'effeminate', even when very young, are natural candidates for the role of *kathoey* (which includes trans-vestite, transsexual, hermaphrodite). On the positive side, *kathoey* are, in modern Thailand, admired for their excellent imitations of femaleness. Nega-tively, they are beginning to be cast as homosexuals.

Morris argues that a modernized binary gender system (which recognizes male, female, male-to-female [a form of the *kathoey*] and female-to-male [les-bians] and which sees them in 'contradiction') has been imposed on top of, or parallel with the historical 'three-sex system'. In place of the triadic ideology, a male-weighted, male-biased gender construct has emerged in which males are seen as elastic and mutable, whereas females are immutable, inviolable, irre-versible and unified (ibid.: 26). Morris suggests that the *kathoey* role has a new form, not neuter as before, but segmented, and signifying a new social–sexual strategy by which *kathoey* males seek access to the 'female domain' (ibid.: 26) rather than subverting the binary gender logic.

Secondary sex characteristics now, in modern times, in the visual and state-dominated age, define genders. Sex is now bounded into 'correct' and 'incor-rect', or 'deviant' behaviours. The rise of modern medicine, and modern anatomical knowledge under the aegis of the state which legitimizes it, has imposed a strictly binary set of secondary characteristics, and with it a binary set of 'desires' (ibid.: 27–28). But surprisingly, Thai society still retains a third sex, the *kathoey*, though in a modified conception; they are 'now as likely to be "passing" for gay men as for women, and they frequently move back and forth between ... these systems' (ibid.: 28). *Kathoey* is being redefined as 'an extremely effeminate form of gay identity' (ibid.), now having the sense of a confused, subordinate form of sexual expression, no longer equal. The more the public state defines attitudes and behaviour, the more anxiety-ridden and unequal non-binary types become.

As in Malaysia (see Wilder, 1998), we could argue, in modern Thailand, there is a growing revulsion against and alienation from the body, a fear and anxiety resulting from the medicalization of society, the reduction of desires to the monosexual reproductive act (i.e. legal marriage with reproduction as the only 'normal' possibility). People's bodies are more and more controlled by capitalism and the state in the form of, among other institutions, medical knowledge and practices (ibid.: 34–35). Thais feel they must accept medicine's definition of 'health' as 'normal' and its narrowed and simplified concepts of gender so removed from the village-centred universe of intimacy and the whole person. People are not whole any more and to retain some of their personal wholeness they have to accept a bureaucratically defined sexual monoculture (binarism), under 'sumptuary laws' of the state which 'crystallize' 'ideally dualist visions of male and female appearance' (ibid.: 33), and discrepant gender concepts, which cannot be abolished, are pushed aside. One suspects Thailand, Indonesia and the Philippines are able to retain some gender tolerance – to avoid the 'panoptic gaze of Western modernity' (ibid.: 36) – because of the incomplete achievement of their states, whereas Malaysia and Singapore, much more advanced in statehood, have made binarism more nearly absolute. Johnson's study of transsexualism and gays among the Sama-Tausug of the southern Philippines explores many of these issues of the definition and crossing and transcending of gender boundaries (1997; and Jackson, 1999).

Given these detailed explorations of gender relations and the symbolization of gender in South-East Asia, we can more fully appreciate that, at least in many traditional societies in the region, gender is far more subject to passage and transformation, partly through the simple and honest biological recognition that the sexual drives wax and wane through the course of the human life cycle. What is more, anthropological studies are exceedingly well placed to elucidate the change of gendered demeanour and characteristics through the life cycle of even the most strictly defined males and females.

9

URBAN WAYS OF LIFE

In this chapter we consider anthropological studies which have concentrated on the ways in which urban-dwellers adapt to life in rapidly changing, densely settled, cosmopolitan, open communities. We do not provide a comprehensive review of South-East Asian urban anthropology but instead focus on case studies of domestic life in different urban settings in Dagupan City in the Philippines, Singapore, Surakarta in Central Java and Bangkok in Thailand, specifically the importance of the dimensions of gender and age in understanding responses to the expansion of the market economy, factory work and national projects for development. We also briefly consider the importance of Clifford Geertz's distinction between the bazaar (informal) and firm (formal) sector in urban social organization. Studies of urban areas by anthropologists, sociologists and psychologists find that social life is predictably impersonal rather than personal, but that urban life is not in general depersonalized. In the new urban communities of South-East Asia, where urban ways are still being formed, the Western individualistic rootlessness and lack of a sense of order (a state of anomie) is not a feature. While it is almost self-evident that commoditization, through the general and global use of cash prevails in almost all areas of high urban life, field studies tend to confirm that people can adapt to and incorporate a cash nexus in their relationships within modified forms of cultural traditions.

Informal and formal sectors

Probably one of the most important and influential early contributions to urban anthropology in South-East Asia was Clifford Geertz's *Peddlers and Princes* (1963b) in which he compares experiences in two small towns in Java (Modjukuto) and Bali (Tabanan), and the related volume *The Social History of an Indonesian Town* (1965) where he considers the changing interrelationships between ethnicity and other principles of social organization in Modjokuto (and see Chapter 3). In *Peddlers and Princes* Geertz presents a modified version of Boeke's concept of 'dual economy' (see Chapter 2) in order to explore, among other things, the characteristics and dynamics of small-scale urban economic activity, and to identify potential growth points or elements of economic dynamism in Indonesian society which will assist in the modernization process. Geertz divided the urban structure into a 'bazaar' and a 'firm'-type economy and then examined the relationships between them and the ways in which 'modern' entrepreneurs might emerge from small-scale business. A central problem was how petty traders might increase the volume of their operations and their level of profits, and transform the organization of their businesses.

Given that the communities which Geertz studied were relatively small urban centres, he and his collaborators were able to employ established anthropological methods of data collection, particularly participant observation, and to concentrate on the face-to-face relationships and the operation of social networks in changing urban situations. In exploring the nature of the bazaar (*pasar*) economy, Geertz identifies a key feature of the activities of petty traders and that is the need to spread risks across numerous transactions, given that the level of capitalization and profits are low. The sector also has the capacity to absorb a large amount of labour. These commodity traders 'relate to one another mainly by means of an incredible volume of ad hoc acts of exchange' (1963b: 29). The turnover of goods is high and exchanges are of small volume. Trading networks are also ramifying, complex, personal and social as well as economic in content. Alice Dewey, in her work on peasant marketing in Java, also reveals that economic exchanges are located in a social and cultural matrix (1962) (and see Chapter 5). The firm economy, on the other hand, is large-scale, comprising mainly impersonal, specialized contractual and commercial relationships. Its economic advantage lies in its ability to reinvest profits in the expansion and, in some cases, diversification of the business operations.

Although the terminology has tended to change and anthropologists and others increasingly talk about the 'informal' and the 'formal' sectors of the urban economy and society, Geertz's characterization of small-scale and large-scale organizations and activities has proved remarkably enduring and of continued analytical value. However, interests have tended to shift towards exploring the linkages between the two sectors and the ways in which the informal sector rather than disappearing in the face of modernization is increasingly integrated into, though at the same time marginalized by the formal sector. In other words, petty trading and production become dependent on the market and large-scale activities and there is a constant interchange of goods, services and labour between small family-based enterprises, self-employed workers and artisans, and casual workers and the larger scale capitalist producers and suppliers. In these analyses the focus has turned towards understanding the dynamic processes of formalization and informalization (van Dijk, 1986), as well as the ways in which the informal sector and its expression in urban squatter settlements, slums and shanty towns develop and sustain viable organizational forms. The social and cultural organization of poor, low-class urban residential areas has been explored, especially in the Philippines (see the work of Jocano [1975] and Laquian [1969] on the slums of Manila and Feldman on the squatters of Davao City [1973]) and in Indonesia (see Jellinek on urban *kampung*-dwellers in Jakarta [1991]). A general conclusion is that social life in these communities is organized, dynamic, variegated and meaningful.

Another dimension of the anthropological analysis of urban social life has been the focus on ethnicity and the ways in which ethnic identity manifests itself in urban communities. Geertz examines the principle of ethnic difference in his *The Social History of an Indonesian Town* and the change from a colonial town organized principally along ethnic lines to a post-war one which is based on 'strategic groups' and 'second-order groups' of a religio-political kind (1965). We have already discussed the importance of ethnicity in Chapter 6, but in an urban context we should mention E.M. Bruner's pioneering work on multi-ethnic social systems in Indonesian urban areas and the conditions under which identities are lost, changed, negotiated or maintained (1961, 1973). A key variable is whether a given urban centre is dominated by a majority population from one ethnic group or comprises several ethnic communities with no one group serving as a cultural referent for the others. Clammer too addresses in considerable detail the importance of ethnicity in Singapore (1985b). He argues that rather than it being a product of majority–minority relations in which the minority uses ethnicity to assert or protect itself against the majority, ethnic identity has been chosen by the ethnic majority – the Chinese – as the main means of national social classification (ibid.: 107–108). We shall see in a moment the ways in which ethnicity influences urban life.

Case studies and urban fieldwork

In our case studies below it is clear that urban-dwellers, using the various social and cultural resources at their disposal, can energetically and imaginatively adapt to the operation of a market economy. This accommodation between cash and custom may emerge especially in those situations where there is a strong ethnic awareness, as in the cases of the Lowland Filipinos, Singapore Malays and Solo Javanese to be discussed. Where ethnicity, and social life itself, are undermined by grinding poverty, the effect can be a kind of social starvation and exclusion, where affluence, government policies and local planning initiatives combine to reduce the urban potential for some people. Thus Malay hawkers in urban Singapore may not be as successful as their Chinese counterparts but they are still able to survive (Li, 1989: 159), in Jakarta, Manila and Bangkok, on the other hand, uncompromising new regulations enacted in the name of beautification and sanitation (related to what is known in planners' jargon as 'slum clearance') may drive small street traders off the streets entirely and condemn them to even more limited means of livelihood (see, for example, Jellinek, 1991; Askew, 1996).

Anthropologists are, understandably, less at home in cities than in rural and small-scale habitats. People in cities often are not born in, nor expect to die in, the city where they live. Their abode is speculative. Cities do not observe seasonality in the more rigorous way villages do, as does life on the land, and so the rhythm of social life reduces to daily rounds. And, as mentioned, a greater impersonality and anonymity in the city contribute to the closed-off, speculative, more insecure and unpredictable style of life to which city residents have to adjust. A consequence of the city's greater mass, shortened chronicity, and reduced sociality is that the anthropologist cannot use the textbook anthropologist's direct, all-embracing, long-term data-gathering techniques which are so fruitful in the countryside. In modern Singapore, men and often women do not work in or near their homes, their income is monetary, may fluctuate by the day or hour, and can be concealed, and experience such as that in formal education is impersonal and remote. As Clammer says, in his research in the city-state, '[t]he classical methods of fieldwork still continue to be applicable, but they clearly have limitations' (1985b: 4). Much of the actual experience of social life in cities remains hidden from the anthropologist's immediate gaze, which in a village could not only be *talked* about with the villagers but directly *observed* as well. It is the task of the urban anthropologists or social researchers, to devise, through the compromise forced on them by urban ways, something approximating the directly observed, insider's picture.

Tania Li's experience in her fieldwork with families in high-rise Singapore in 1983–1984 is indicative. She says, 'Singapore is an urban society where about 80 per cent of the population live behind the closed doors of high-rise flats. Street-corner or casual observation is therefore not a very productive source of data, particularly on household questions' (1989: vii). To get around this narrowed accessibility of social and personal data in modern Singapore, Li chose to engage in a form of interview technique, or survey sample, to ensure that the homogeneity, and any variations that existed would be reflected in the interview data. Instead, she organized a sample of seventy households located in three districts of the city, and from this cross-section collected

> basic data on personal history, subgroup origins, household compositions, education, occupation, income, monthly budget, association memberships, and neighbourhood ties. These data were usually obtained from the woman of the house during the day when the husband was absent, as part of a strategy to ensure that women's, as well as men's, perspectives would be obtained.
>
> (ibid.: vii)

She then focused on a smaller number of households to obtain substantial life histories and other narratives, and to accompany people in their social activities as a guest or family friend, and in these ways to produce a picture of everyday and family life in urban Malay households.

In her study of social networks in Dagupan City in the Philippines, Lillian Trager (1988) combined observation of and interviews with Filipino city

dwellers both in the city and in the rural settlements where many of them origi-
nate. Through personal contact, she eventually chose seven migrants or migrant
couples and compiled extended case studies of their 'dispersed households', the
family-kin networks to which they belonged and which they supported from
their urban base. Further field research tactics in urban fieldwork have been
worked out as well, as we will see below. In effect they are researchers' attempts
to elucidate the positive, adaptive role of face-to-face behaviours and domestic
units in the 'anthropologically unfriendly' environment of the metropolis. We
will look at the anthropological results of these compromise studies in the
diverse cityscapes of Dagupan City, Singapore, Surakarta and, briefly, Bangkok.

Dispersed family networks in the Philippines

The conceptual problem broached in Lillian Trager's analysis of the position of
Filipino migrants in Dagupan City is the linkage of the broad 'structural'
context particularly the socio-economic context of the city and its region and
the heterogeneous initiatives of many local Filipinos who use the city as a base
for their resource-enhancing activities (survival, employment, education, class
mobility). It is not simply a report on the micro-economics of economic
advancement, as the phrase 'resources' might suggest, but is about the modern
form of the (mainly rural) domestic unit for many Filipino families whose lives
are spent in, and depend on, urban pursuits. Urban dwelling is 'therefore considered not solely with respect to a particular individual' who adopts a strategy
and migrates to the city 'but also in terms of the social context from which he
or she comes *and to which he still belongs*' (Trager, 1988: 3; our emphasis). Trager
seeks a middle position which 'would link the examination of structural forces
with that of individual behavior' (ibid.: 8) by examining the emergence in this
sector of Filipino society of 'dispersed family networks [that] function to some
degree as households' (ibid.: 79). The monetary and other rewards the city
offers its successful members do not dissolve but rather sustain family and
kinship ties and reciprocal obligations within personal networks (ibid.: 3). How
does this come about?

Dagupan City in Central Luzon about 150 kilometres north of Manila has a
population of 100,000 and is 'the only fully urban center' in the province of
Pangasinan (pop. 1,520,000). Dagupan City is a commercial and administrative
centre, with major educational and health services as well ('many migrants first
come to the city as students', ibid.: 27), but has little industry, a factor which
probably keeps the city's population fairly constant (as the city's in- and out-
migration are in balance). The commercial centre of Dagupan is dominated by
Chinese-owned businesses, but elsewhere the businesses are Filipino-owned
(ibid.: 29). Economically the region of Pangasinan relies heavily on agriculture,
mainly rice production, and, as in so much of the Philippines, this means widespread poverty and the need to migrate or emigrate, not only to Dagupan,
within the province itself, but to Manila and overseas. The province as a whole

shows a net out-migration (ibid.: 64). Migration to Dagupan itself may be facilitated by the fact that migrants are not discriminated against, since both Dagupan natives and migrants are found in approximately equal numbers in all the city's occupations (ibid.: 33). If migrants do not live with relatives in the city, they may stay in boarding-houses.

Trager acknowledges the emphasis in Filipino society, which holds for the Philippines at large, on nuclear family households, i.e. parents and their unmarried children. This unit not only embodies strong loyalties but may, if with less regularity, develop external ties. Filipino kinship includes not just 'nuclear' or primary ties but develops 'multiple equivalent bonds between adults and children' through various wider relationships (ibid.: 77, citing E. Yu and W.T. Liu, 1980). These bonds are made up of alliances and attachments beyond the immediate family, through kinship ties maintained by the older generations in fosterage and in the fictive kinship called *compadrazgo* or *compadrinazgo* (godparenthood and ritual coparenthood). Filipinos see in these family-kinship ties a series of debts, obligations and reciprocities. 'Both within the nuclear family and in other kin and fictive kin relationships, relationships of mutual obligation and reciprocity develop and are maintained' (ibid.: 77). The notion of debt, *utang na loob*, has been translated as 'debt of prime obligation' and is not confined in Filipino society only to kinship, but for most Filipinos whose personal, intimate circle of relationships is defined by mutual dependence and obligation it is a central concern. Unstinting help and support of all kinds are ideally expected in that circle. This lifelong expectation, of generosity and its return (*utang na loob*), is most strongly expressed in Filipino parent–child ties. (The notion of a 'debt of gratitude', in Negros dialect *utang nga buot*, applies in the employer–employee relationship in the sugar plantation studied by Rosanne Rutten (1982: 37).) Not to be able to reciprocate brings shame (*huya*) – the employee feels ashamed (*nahuya*).

Geographical distance does not alter the internalized sense of obligation to parents and other kin. The migrant's job may have been found through the kin network. One of Trager's subjects found her first two jobs in Dagupan this way. She comes from a municipality next to Dagupan where her family farms rice but cannot make ends meet. She and her brother, two of eight children in the household, work and live in Dagupan, not just to support themselves but to help finance the family household. At age 22 when interviewed, she was unmarried. Her first job came through working with her cousin in the central market area ('Dagupan Supermarket') and living with her and her husband. Her second job was in a hardware store owned by her mother's godmother (*ninang*, sponsor at her mother's wedding, 1988: 155) and she lived above the store with the owners. For her third job which she held at time of interview she had replied to a notice in a window of a large shop, passed the exam as required by the firm, and was hired. She visits her family home at weekends, even at Christmas time when she works seven days a week. In Dagupan she visits not just her brother but her mother's brothers and sisters who live in the city (ibid.: 89–91).

The dispersed kin network described here is simplified; it understates the volume of ties and the many ways they can be activated, created and optimized, as Trager's personal histories show. Another of her histories relates the growth of a cloth-selling business run by a migrant couple who married and set up home in Dagupan in 1960. Three years after their marriage they moved into their present house which belonged to a *comadre* (co-sponsor) of the wife and eventually bought the house. Regular suppliers or customers (*suki*) (ibid.: 136, 141, 202 – *suki* means both) may become ritual kin (*comadre, compadre*) (ibid.: 142). *Compadrazgo* ties are brought into being by sponsorship, the choice of a person (and *ipso facto* a couple) as ritual sponsor at birth, confirmation and marriage, choices which may assume the quality of alliances, that is, to fuse business and social ties. Whether constituted by ties of descent, marriage, adoptive, fictive or ritual kinship, the social networks serve as what we might call 'instructions' for advice, favours, gifts of goods and services, and visits, but are especially adapted for remittances, that is, urban incomes for the support of rural households.

Monetary remittances in the Dagupan region area are variously described as supplementary, as periodic assistance, or as indispensable in shoring up domestic incomes in the impoverished rural sector. The specific organization of these remittances is the dispersed family networks. These networks are not formally established as corporate units, with a thoroughgoing scale of obligations and with exclusive rights to income. Something of that (i.e. pre-emption on joint income) would occur in marriage and the early stages of child-rearing and it is surely no accident that the remittance networks are biased in favour of unmarried sons and daughters (a new generation-specific role which will be noted below). Lillian Trager's survey included 176 migrants, 50 per cent of whom sent money to family members elsewhere. Only seven migrants did not visit or send remittances to relatives elsewhere (ibid.: 79, 200). She therefore estimates that 'Overall, the majority of migrants do retain strong ties with family elsewhere and a large proportion fulfil reciprocal obligations through monetary gifts' (ibid.: 79).

Furthermore, remittances tend to be greater and more regular from unmarried daughters. This is an aspect of women's role in Filipino society (and in South-East Asia generally as we saw in Chapter 8). In the Philippines, women are not discouraged from receiving education and so are highly educated, and are not discouraged from seeking work of many kinds and so their participation in paid work is high although the level of women's wages is often lower than men's (ibid.: 80–81). Women are traditionally seen as good budgeters, better than men. Both by default and by preference, women, including young unmarried women (or 'daughters'), play a major role in migration to and as earners in cities and, because they are thought of (and perhaps are) better planners and providers than men, are more reliable as remitters in the dispersed family unit (ibid.: 82–83, 190–192).

The outwardly rural or suburban (or residential) appearance of Dagupan City is similar to that of other South-East Asian cities (that is, until the 1980s when large-scale 'renewal' of the more major city-centres began to take off in the wake of the region's prosperity). Beneath this geo-aspect, however, is the family-based intermingling and interconnection of urban and rural lives and their economic support systems. As Trager remarks:

> It is easy to give undue emphasis to a contrast between the 'urban' members of the family and the 'rural' members. In fact, the women considered here do not make this kind of strong distinction between themselves and others in the family.
>
> (ibid.: 127)

While poverty, as a form of economic 'crisis', undeniably plays a part in the flow of cash from city to country, anthropologists are concerned to discover the social principles or 'instructions' that underlie and give form to the dispersal of these city incomes in a variety of circumstances. How does an increased role and flow of cash, which in the Philippine data used here stems from the city system, change people's roles and life cycles?

One of Trager's findings, which seems to be repeated in other studies, is that while age at marriage is rising (predictable with rising education levels and prosperity), marriage is still seen by many young women and men as the next step after work. For women migrant-workers in cities, and in many new factory industries, newfound wages are seen as a prelude to (more or less traditional) marriage. One of Lillian Trager's subjects saw her time in Dagupan 'as a sojourn, an interlude before marriage and settling in the barrio like her parents' (ibid.: 127). She saw her new wages as wealth to be shared, in accordance with Filipino family values. We next explore a comparable situation in urban Singapore but one in which the repayment from child to parent is more explicitly cast in the idiom of the gift.

Domestic life in Singapore

In the late 1960s, the Singapore government embarked on an urban development programme which aimed, among other things, to re-house its citizens in modern flats and to ensure that all its citizens would be provided with education, amenities and facilities leading to employment. The housing programme explicitly supported marriage and family and discouraged single-person households. The full-employment objective meant that the majority of adults earned a wage or salary and could expect to control that income for themselves. Tania Li's study, carried out in the early 1980s, focused not on the Chinese majority but rather on Singapore's second-largest ethnic group, the Malays who comprise 14.6 per cent of the population, to discover recent changes in their family units and how far these changes fitted the social transformation of the wider – and unavoidably Chinese-dominated – society.

In examining as it does the role of cultural ideas, specifically Malay ideas, in the formation of Singapore urban households, Li's anthropological study falls somewhere between sociology and political economy. She examines Malay conceptions of cash-flow in families against the background of muscular state intervention, amounting to large-scale social reform, and she examines in particular the reception of money income in Singapore domestic life. She shows how some of this income functions as 'gift-giving' and how that conception conforms to the 'real exigencies' of the economy, which for most Malays are mainly those of the lower-income wage-worker (1989: 4). She says, 'Features of the economy, such as the availability of work for individuals of different age and sex, and rates of pay, form the practical conditions of daily life, and yet they do not have a mechanistic or determining effect upon social life because they are perceived, interpreted, and acted upon in the light of cultural knowledge' (ibid.: xv).

The analytic distinction between household form and composition, on the one hand, and the organization, through cultural knowledge, of relationships within the family, on the other hand, proves essential. Specifically, Li found Malay household form and composition in modern Singapore to be similar to their rural counterparts in Malaysia and Java, but that Malay 'practice', in domestic families in Singapore, has been radically transformed by the Singapore Malays' entry into the fully-monetized and meritocratic national economy. Malay cultural ideas have formulated new priorities in response to major changes in social patterns. Chief among the socio-economic changes for Singapore Malays are the increased frequency of the following:

1   waged daughters, in 1980 comprising some 67.8 per cent of the female population in the 15–24 age bracket [NB *boys* were employed at a lower rate because Malays were excluded from national service, ibid.: 109];
2   'own' as opposed to adopted children in families [and reduction in divorces];
3   better-educated offspring with the attendant costs of education;
4   older first-marrieds, specifically for females, and, Li claims, the virtual extinction of 'arranged' marriages;
5   the concept of 'own time' figured in terms of own wages;
6   the overt (as opposed to hidden) 'calculation' (*berkira*) of material and sentimental resources offered by family ties;
7   the 'upward flow' (child to parent) of support within families.

These are the bare bones of changes produced by the marked and rapid socio-economic development which has touched every family in Singapore, Malay, Chinese and others, since 1965. As a general trend, Li observed in 1983–1984 a 'remarkable similarity' in the household composition patterns of Singapore Chinese and Malays. Like Malay households, Singapore Chinese households are predominantly elementary in form (ibid.: 150). The dramatic reduction in divorce among Malays since 1960 (Djamour, 1966) has given them family stability closer to that of Chinese among whom the divorce rate was always low.

The economic development of Singapore makes employment and enterprise available to all and especially to the unmarried daughters of a household (Li, 1989: 105, *passim*).

The convergence of form in Malay and Chinese households is not complete, however. 'Like Malays, Chinese have come to rely on their daughters both before marriage and also in old age, yet Chinese still place much greater conceptual significance on the role of sons' (ibid.: 156–157). Chinese households continue to reflect the patrilineal bias of traditional mainland China, with its tendency to patrilocality and a preference for sons, whereas Malay households preserve a bilateral emphasis, and husband and wife, sons and daughters receive a more or less equal share of affection and rights to property (and this despite Islamic law which strictly applied would favour males). They do so even against the policies of the Singapore state which makes minimal concession to customary laws. But Li argues that any seeming convergence in Malay and Chinese domestic groups is misleading, in the sense that it distracts our attention from the much more significant inner workings of the respective units. In themselves the 'pre-given' notions and ideals, whether of descent, or of gender, do not necessarily predispose households one way or another. However, by focusing on the different 'cultural logics' associated with Malay and Chinese, Li shows how these logics both create and constrain practice in families and ultimately reveal significant differences.

The two cultural logics are summed up by Li as 'gift' (Malay) and 'debt' (Chinese) and played out between parents and children. In modern Singapore these notions are embodied in the new phenomenon of parents' call on the younger generation's earnings, acquired independently of parents and yet codified in such a way as to preserve a balance between parents and children. 'The Chinese stress a clear-cut obligation of children towards parents, which is engendered by a debt, while the Malays view the relationship in terms of more diffuse obligations engendered by gifts. In both Malay and Chinese households, notions of kinship derived from the deeper cultural heritage, have been reassessed and applied in new ways to the practical circumstances of Singapore life' (ibid.: 156). Li does not say notions of debt are absent from the Malay set of ideas about the obligations of young jobholders living at home, nor that any discretionary attitude in young Chinese working women is entirely lacking, but that the construction of the offspring's economic position at home leads to a definite contrast in the economic performances in the two cases. One implication of the gift concept among Malays is that households do not manifest joint economy, instead the domestic economy reflects Malay individualism, in which money transfers and fund accumulation are voluntary, discretionary, conditional. Singapore Malay daughters contribute about one-third of their income to their mother (ibid.: 50). Chinese families, on the other hand, show a degree of corporate organization in which unmarried sons and daughters are expected to contribute a half or more of their wages to the parental household fund. Another correlate of the two sets of cultural ideas is that Chinese daughters begin paid work outside the home earlier and continue longer in that work.

Malay daughters tend to find less secure work (e.g. in factories) and marry earlier.

The two economic patterns contain key elements for modern Singapore society. Chinese concepts of filial piety and family name reinforce the parental expectation of return of the 'debt' as against Malay concepts of 'care and concern' (*kasihan*) which reinforce personal funds and small if any expectation of return in later life. But Li perceptively remarks on a tendency to convergence of the two patterns in the new urban conditions, for Malays to accept an obligation to care for aged parents (a Chinese trait), a practice largely absent in rural Malay villages, and for Chinese parents to lack the authority to enforce obligations to repay 'debt' (in the absence of landed wealth in their new urban setting) and to rely more, as do Malays, on diffuse emotional ties to their children to persuade them to contribute a share of their earnings to household finances (ibid.: 156).

The Malays in Singapore, according to Li's findings, have adapted their domestic life to these changes in a distinctive way according to what she calls their 'culture of individualism', and in contrast to Chinese response with their culture of 'familism' (see Wilder, 1982b). Despite similar forces of policy and change – since the changes, shown above, apply broadly to both Malays and Chinese, and have led (although by different paths) to a 'nuclearization' of family in both Malay and Chinese societies in Singapore – their ethnically distinct traditions, such as a traditionally older age at marriage for Chinese females than for Malays and a Chinese facility for handling of money (Freedman, 1959), have led to stubbornly contrasting outcomes in modern urban family fortunes. In some ways it looks as though Chinese have a cultural head-start for (and pre-adaptation to) commodified, monetized social relations and this predisposing trait still keeps the ethnic communities unequal today, despite major government development policies to even them up.

In Li's Singapore study we see how the steady infiltration of monetization into social relations with all its tendencies to homogenization of relationships, through the globalizing forces of modern technology, planning and education, wages and employment, and market systems, has been localized through a 'creative' reorganization of local culture to accommodate the generations of people living together in households. In Li's words:

'Although the structural economic conditions of the urban wage economy in Singapore which prompt these changes in the Malay and Singapore [sc. Chinese] households are common to both groups, there remain very significant differences in the way they organize and perceive their household relationships. These differences between Malay and Chinese households are related to the distinct cultural heritage of the two groups, which has been revised and restructured, but not eradicated or changed in any uniform, predetermined way by the economic conditions prevailing in Singapore.

(1989: 157)

Urban life in Surakarta, Central Java

Cities are not all made up of 'imports', they are 'new' but the people are not and cities do not impose a message on all of 'their' inhabitants. Cities are scenes of struggle between, on the one hand, the local urban order, changed though it is in so many ways from the life of the countryside, and on the other hand the demands of nationalism and global hegemony which offer people – through possessions, language, bureaucracies, mobility – a new, and alternative, sense of power. James Siegel's experiential account of language and meaning in Surakarta (1986) shows that society and culture in Surakarta in 1980–1981 when Siegel made his observations was beginning to see the local transformation of well-known institutions such as Javanese theatre and music but also the innovation of (no less local) life styles such as youth culture. Like Li in elucidating the Malay variant of social life in urban Singapore, through what we can, accurately, call the Malays' own chrematistical ideas ('on the acquisition of wealth'), Siegel argues for the 'Javaneseness' of Surakarta (or Solo as it is also called), with its population of a half a million, through their own ideas of hierarchy. Unlike Li, however, he does attempt something like an all-embracing, participant-observation approach. While living in Kemlayan, a small district of Solo, a *kelurahan* or 'headman's settlement', he learned Javanese and acted as far as possible as any ordinary resident of the city would, sleeping in a Javanese house, eating with a Javanese family, talking with and visiting a wide variety of people and places.

Solo in the New Order unavoidably owes much to the Geertzes' and their collaborators' studies of Javanese in east Java over twenty years earlier. (Also to his Cornell colleague Ben Anderson's thorough knowledge of Java [see, for example, 1990], and to the deconstructionist Jacques Derrida.) The monograph studies on the one hand those aspects of Javanese culture and society which are to some extent common to both town and country (language use and etiquette, domestic values in dwelling-houses and in the neighbourhood, schools and literacy, folk arts in stories, dance, music, magic and belief, and death and funeral customs), but on the other hand it goes further, to treat forms and arenas of behaviour more specifically urban, including streets and traffic (Chapter 5), crime (Chapter 3), an anti-Chinese riot (Chapter 9), mass media such as magazines, cinema, television (Chapter 7), and the manifestations of money in consumption, gambling and enterprise.

Siegel's study is unusual in the breadth of its ethnographic aspirations and in its attempt to adapt conventional single-handed ethnographic techniques to a group of people numbering hundreds of thousands and in that, like Michelle Rosaldo's well-known study of Ilongot headhunters (1980), it relies very much on language use and language texts to 'explain' actions (in contra-distinction to the more standard ethnographic categories and their chapter headings, economy, kinship, marriage, religion, life cycle, change and so on). To make his field observations manageable over such a wide empirical catchment area,

Siegel views the Javanese of Solo through their language or more precisely lan-guages. The Javanese spoken language in particular is not used only to convey information but it is also a social medium. Javanese in its spoken form has speech-levels, one called *Ngoko*, spoken to inferiors, and one called *Kromo*, addressed to superiors. All Javanese learn *Ngoko* or 'Low Javanese' as children but it is the mark of the 'civilized, poised, refined (*alus*)' person to have learned *Kromo* or 'High Javanese' as well, because *Kromo* allows people to show respect, to prove deference and manners all of which is best done in the presence of superiors to whom, strictly speaking, *Kromo* must be addressed. The kinds of Javanese spoken – Low, Medium, High – in an encounter between Javanese speakers indicate distance and difference of rank between the speakers. The subordinate person speaks a formal, highly respectful dialect *Kromo* and in doing so shows the ability to defer and to do it in a 'refined' way (*alus*). Speaking Javanese is an elaborate routine of politeness in which, like actors on the stage or job applicants, one's demeanour feels under severe scrutiny. 'Nervousness about language is also nervousness about behavior' (1986: 16). Command of vocabulary, gentle tone of voice, careful phrasing and much more combine, if successful, to produce correct, courtly manners (ibid.: 16–17).

But *Kromo* is an acquired speech, a 'second language', and as Siegel stresses over and over again its reciprocal form of address, which labels the first (*Kromo*) speaker as inferior, is *Ngoko* or 'Low Javanese', is in effect a suppressed language since, in the social asymmetry, the first speaker may not use *Ngoko* his 'born' language (ibid.: 17). Instead he speaks to his superior using *Kromo*, an 'imitation' of a language (ibid.: 17) (as more recently and in a somewhat similar way the national language Indonesian is) and yet, as Siegel observes, High Javanese is (or was) highly prized, a prestigious social skill, showing the ability to be *alus*: on most occasions, 'people seem to delight in speaking High Javanese. Partly they delight in the ability to show that they are in control of that language, that they can, in fact, manage the highest forms of deference' (ibid.: 26).

Having fixed the urban milieu in the different languages spoken, and those not spoken, in Surakarta, Siegel is able to follow a network of meanings as understood in Javanese and in Indonesian by the Solonese. The far-reaching implications of this social asymmetry in the pair *Kromo* and *Ngoko*, and the decline of traditional forms of respect in modern Javanese cities, has a back-ground in the Javanese ideas of cosmos (the definitive explanation is in Ander-son, 1990). Siegel outlines this idiom as it operates in Surakarta as follows:

> To speak very well is to imagine an entire hierarchy, a state with a king and nobles. The fantasy of the state and the conception of reserve in language are linked. To speak properly is to hold something back; to pay respect is to be reserved; respect is the basis of hierarchy; hierarchy is imaged in the notion of the state.
>
> (1986: 230)

Surakarta is a composite city. It is a former royal capital and descendants of royalty still live there. It is also a municipality and a part of the Indonesian republic. The languages spoken in the city reflect this political duality, the 'indigenous' language is Javanese and Indonesian the imposed national language. Siegel's broadly sociolinguistic approach shows how each operates in relation to the other through the choices and strategies of its speakers. The linguistic picture of Surakarta is further complicated by the fact that Javanese itself is a divided language (as explained just now), as well as by the presence of non-Indonesian languages, chiefly English and Chinese, both of them international languages. The central point of reference for Javanese city life is the Javanese language itself. The over-riding claim of Siegel's analysis is that the Javanese spoken language creates a hierarchical social universe and that the crisis of spoken Javanese in the city is the demands made on it by Indonesian, its main language rival, and by money and mass media which operate in their most concentrated form in cities.

In the closed (and socially and ethnically mixed) residential neighbourhoods hidden behind the main shop-lined thoroughfares, a quasi-domestic intimacy prevails. The areas are generally bounded by the main roads but are seen as safe and tranquil places, chiefly due it seems to the neighbourhood watch groups of young men (*ronda*) who patrol against thieves. In daily life the residents use informal, intimate speech *Ngoko* reciprocally, in other words, in this concealed inward-looking place the hierarchy exists (ibid.: 126) but is suspended in an atmosphere of 'shared security' (ibid.: 51). (That is how we read, and give here in much simplified form, Siegel's account.) Surakarta as a city consists of many other kinds of social spaces and media (busy roads, crowds, the market and shops, the schools, fan magazines for teenagers, the local theatre troupes). In the classroom, for example, the pupils speak *Ngoko* (reciprocally) among themselves but Indonesian to their teacher both because that is the ordained medium of instruction and because by doing so they accord traditional respect to the teacher. Here the 'new' language Indonesian functions roughly as the 'old' language *Kromo* or spoken High Javanese in satisfying the needs still felt for observing the familiar ideas of hierarchy.

The city is not unified or homogeneous under a single stratification system. We believe the word stratification does not even appear in the book, nor does the term plural society, which must be a measure of the way James Siegel has tried to see Solo as much through Javanese eyes as possible (see his frequent remarks on methodology). Siegel's study is not simply a linguistic map of Solo in 1980–1981. Instead it attempts to show that Javanese society in Solo, in the first decade of the national government of Suharto or the 'New Order' (the whole period of roughly the thirty years to 1998 when he was forced to step down), filtered the changing elements of city life through its well-tried hierarchical notions. How, for example, city street traffic observes 'hierarchical assumptions' while largely ignoring public rights of way (ibid.: 237), how the apprehension of a thief and the prevention of prostitution in the neighbourhood are carried out in the idiom of hierarchy (ibid.: 41–50), how reproductions of popular art by Indonesian (Javanese?) contemporaries portray in Solonese homes a hierarchical exterior landscape (ibid.: 131–134), how even money, whether as prices or as wages is, though not successfully, 'domesticated' to fit the Solonese desire for hierarchy rather than profit through 'becoming a token of deference [and] a form of gift or sacrifice' (ibid.: 184), and through being concealed and therefore neutralized by women (ibid.: 187–202).

The indigenous notion of hierarchy, or, to put it more simply, traditional social power, underlies a very great deal of the city life of Surakarta which in appearance and atmosphere is a rapidly-developing urban centre. It is the 'suppressed' layer of the Surakartans' way of life that Siegel has unravelled through their language behaviour. Two groups in the city had, however, departed enough by 1980–1981 from the hierarchical notion to seem to undermine it; these are the Javanese youth (remaja) and a comedy theatre (Sri Mulat, a traditional troupe re-formed in 1966 just as Suharto was assuming power). The comedy theatre, by definition, used Javanese language to expose its formal rigidities and by exposing them releasing the Javanese audience from the tensions of its formality. Its most popular character is a 'Mrs Draculla' [sic], a creature from some distant place outside Java. This comic and frightening character represents 'spontaneity' (spontan) and the 'odd' and unexpected (anéh), signs of a form of power wholly outside traditional ideas of hierarchy and potentially disruptive to it (ibid.: 98). It seems to be a premonition of violence, and of the kind of startle reaction that is recognized to produce in some cases the dissociative state known (in Malay) as latah, with echolalia, echopraxis and forms of disapproved speech and behaviour (ibid.: 109). It represents disorder at large but has no point of origin and no sense of deliberateness.

The city's youth are perhaps the most sensitive of all its people to new and distant influences, as would be expected. They are directly exposed in school to the orthodox ideas of the 'new', but they also read locally-produced 'fashion' magazines aimed at teenagers. Siegel notes the significance of remaja, an invented word rather than other Indonesian words, pemuda 'youth', pelajar 'student', bujang 'bachelor', a word that acknowledges a category beyond the reach of hierarchy with its 'old' terminology. Through teen fashions in music, clothes, readers' letter columns and stories of performers, an incipient consumer culture and an alien sense of 'taste' and moneyed selfhood develops in the young Javanese readers of these media. Whereas the traditional Solo-made batik cloth has a hidden layer, and the buyer/wearer can deny the wearer's 'coarseness' (kasar) through merging with the invisible 'spirit' somewhere in the batik medium and design, the archetypical teen T-shirt proclaims difference openly and 'loudly'. With batik one 'holds back', with teen gear one announces a public, sometimes worldwide, preference and this is in contradiction to the stable order of Javanese hierarchy. Siegel notes that the conflict is reiterated in the music.

The nature of the conflict [between local revived popular music and new 'national' pop music] is clear: popular music, like public education, sets up a system in which knowledge and forms of expression are nationalized. In doing so, there is an implicit claim that the 'new' takes shape in the interaction of talent [*bakat* or *bakat alam*], foreign influences, and chance. This contrasts with Javanese notions, which imply that everything that does not belong within the social hierarchy stems from the realm of the spirits. We have seen that Sri Mulat features 'Mrs Draculla from Abroad' and thereby pulls the foreign into the *anéh* [unnatural, unusual]. The continued strength of popular forms that are not part of the circuit of fans and celebrities seems to deny the claims of 'talent'.

(ibid.: 218)

While Siegel was living in Solo an anti-Chinese riot lasting several days served as one of those fortunate diagnostic incidents for the anthropologist in showing the fracturing of the tense negotiations of youth, the new values of money and consumption, and ethnicity. For young people (*remaja*) in 1980s Surakarta, 'newness comes accidentally and takes the form of commodities. The contemporaneity of commodities confirms what students learn in school: that their education guarantees them a special access to the future, that they are the figures in whom the future will be embodied. When, however, through the working out of the events of the [street] accident [touching off public disturbances in November 1980], commodities became identified with Chinese, the identification of *remaja* and commodities, already established, had to be disavowed. This is why rioting on a city-wide scale [in the commercial districts and involving only young Javanese males] began with the gathering of *remaja* at Chinese shops and why their first action was against the glass, behind which sat commodities' (ibid.: 249).

Several days of turmoil provided an opportunity. The social distinction of Javanese and Chinese had to be re-asserted, the exclusion of Chinese from Javanese hierarchy, but since this distinction and exclusion is well rehearsed already, in the daily life of the city and even in mixed residential neighbourhoods, the rebellion, the incensed reaction, of youth was to re-assert their own Javaneseness which they themselves threatened with their own growing consumerism (their music, clothes, stories of 'success', self-consciousness).

The richness of Siegel's account of tradition and change, the incursions of the new and the renewal of the old in a Javanese city can only be hinted at. It owes much to a formidable American interest in Java since the Second World War (see Chapter 3) but at the same time it deploys a formidable knowledge of Indonesian languages and techniques of cultural interpretation. One of the groups most strenuously undergoing change we have noticed in Dagupan City, Singapore and Surakarta is youth. This is not too surprising since adolescence is inherently and universally a time of accelerated, concentrated, and possibly stormy personal development but as though like attracts like youth also attracts the new forces of development, since, on the Javanese evidence anyway, they are the people nearest to the future. We have seen that young unmarried females in the Philippines and Singapore households and young popular music fans in Surakarta, even though they remain integrated with their conventional domestic surroundings and thus bound to 'traditional' ways of life, demonstrate the strongest, or at least most visible, departure from traditional norms of their culture. We will look further at this new social category next and ask about the impact of its emergence.

Bangkok factory workers: new lives in the old

A further example of an urban-generated 'youth culture' is that of Thai factory workers in Bangkok. We can learn anthropologically from a large-scale survey, conducted on workers' attitudes to health risks and sexual relationships in 1993–1994, by Nicholas Ford and Sirinan Kittisuksathit (1995). They and their co-workers attempted to situate their survey, of social characteristics and sexual attitudes of 2,033 young factory workers, in the Thai cultural context. While their study proceeds on a different path from that of the cultural semantics of gift and hierarchy reviewed earlier, it reveals the similar growth of a newly independent (or semi-independent) urban economic group, that of unmarried wage-earners. It indicates that these young Thai people, less than a generation removed from tradition and so, perhaps not unexpectedly, in search of a life-style, can subvert (or at least convert) modernity to meet their own ends. How far their lives do change in this way and how far tradition moderates biography we will remark on after briefly reviewing Ford's and Kittisuksathit's data.

Bangkok has many factories turning out cheap electrical goods, plastic ware and clothing. The factories employ women and men in large numbers at the factory benches and in the warehouses. The survey sampled unmarried workers aged 15–24 years – 1,469 female and 564 male – employed in 103 factories located in Bangkok and five neighbouring districts. The majority of the sampled workers (85 per cent) were migrants who had left their home areas (most but not all rural) in search of work. Over half were educated to some stage of secondary school standard. Both the women and the men were paid at broadly the same level but the men were slightly more likely to reach the higher income levels. Most (both females and males) lived apart from their parents or relatives, either in factory dormitories or with friends outside the factory and very few (5 per cent) lived alone or with their boy or girl friend.

In these circumstances of increased independence and freedom for both sexes through paid work in the city, it would be expected that friendship and love between the sexes would appear to the participants in a new light. Thai females and males aged 15–24 years were becoming both occupationally mobile and emotionally independent, through living away from their parents. But at the same time they were re-inventing their traditional social ideas, with emphasis on good marital prospects and conjugal stability on the part of the young women, although with a 'traditional' Thai male freedom to engage in extramarital sex with prostitutes, a view upheld it seems by both females and males. A point we must not forget: in all these countries marriage is still seen as the usual destination for females and males, consequently we should understand that young workers have added a pre-marital phase, not replaced it. (Of course the axiomatic status of marriage may well be the next thing to disappear, but family welfare policies in South-East Asia as well as traditional culture are against this, and we have seen that, in the Philippine case, how even distant migration to urban centres affirms rather than erodes family ties.) The ongoing changes do not mean that all of a sudden young people are in control of events but as wage-earners or as consumers they are able to adapt to them and control them within limits. The continued role of marriage as a general social ideal is one constraint on their new freedoms, as well as the limited time span of factory employment for the majority of workers.

In brief, the findings indicate a culture of expectations in which young urban Thais have considerable freedom to form sexual relationships of their own choosing. There is a gradual movement to the formation of boy–girl friendships, the relationships indicate a fairly high level of emotional commitment with an underlying expectation of marriage, and, while in the Thai case there is still an acceptance of the notion of women as subordinate, there is also evidence of a questioning of this position of lesser power. Ford and Kittisuksathit observe that the last point is perhaps suggestive of a shift taking place in perceived gender roles. As noted above, the attachment of the young people's age grade to a new pattern of work and social life could, but probably does not, signal a rupture with tradition. Rather it looks as though a particular group of Thai youth has added a 'window' of about ten years (assuming ten years to be the likely average time in factory work) to a traditional life cycle. Factory work does not offer utopia but seems to afford to both sexes a significant degree of affluence at a crucial stage in the life cycle.

Conclusion

The scenes treated anthropologically by Lillian Trager in Central Luzon, Tania Li in Singapore, James Siegel in Surakarta, and Nicholas Ford and Sirinan Kitti-suksathit in Bangkok are just four historical instants in a world of rapidly developing cities and may well be unrepeatable experiences for people in their footsteps (though predictions would be unwise). We have seen in those two cases how a biographical moment, that of the age-grade (as anthropologists call it) which is defined by later adolescence and early maturity, assumes a new and more prominent place, both 'in' society and in 'breaking out' of it. Females and males living at this stage of life in the city are the first to undergo, in numbers and as a generation, the generation-specific accession of a cash income (unmarried daughters in Dagupan and Singapore), and a novel subculture (teenage fashion consumers in Solo). We have seen how the idioms of gift and hierarchy are moving their centres in response particularly to the transforming effects of cash or 'money-wealth'.

These studies demonstrate some of the themes urban anthropologists have taken up: the flow of cash, and commodification in general, and how persons in cities adapt in local terms to it; the questions of gender and of generation. Cities can of course be viewed as a total market-place in which legal tender is its lifeblood. We have extracted one set of social institutions, those of domestic life, as a measure of the form and function of social relations in different urban settings in contact with the monetary necessities bound up with the urban milieu. Cities present such a variety of social forms and rapidity of change we have not attempted to review them in their entirety. In cities we find wealth and poverty, crowds and solitary persons, bureaucratic control and informal control, sexual diversity and occupational specializations, and so on. By focusing on domestic life and intimate relations in the midst of many other possible urban performances and qualities, we may possibly see how humans adapt in the longer term.

10

CONCLUSION

This final chapter considers whether the anthropological study of South-East Asia has been characterized by a dominant tradition of work or a distinctive paradigm or whether there has been theoretical diversity in approaches and interests. Our overall view is that, given the institutional importance of certain American research institutions like the South-East Asia Program at Cornell University and the collection of studies by the Geertzes, certain strands of American anthropology have played an influential role in the development of the anthropology of the region, but they are not the only important traditions, and they have tended to differ considerably from the perspectives and concerns of various schools of European anthropology. We also provide some indication of the likely future development of work in the anthropology of South-East Asia.

Introduction

The anthropological study of South-East Asia has produced a notable literature, which has contributed both to our understanding of societies, cultures and socio-cultural transformations in the region and to the development of anthropology as a discipline. Indeed, there are outstanding studies which have marked crucial turning points in anthropological thinking and have excited the interest of scholars who have worked in other parts of the world. Among them (and in no particular order of precedence) are the work of Edmund Leach on the Kachin and Sarawak peoples; Stanley Tambiah on Thai Buddhism and the spirit cults; Melford Spiro on Burmese religion, kinship and personhood; Rodney Needham and several of his colleagues and students (particularly Andrew Beatty, Robert Barnes, Clark Cunningham, Kirk Endicott and James Fox), along with P.E. de Josselin de Jong on symbolic classification and social forms in the Malay–Indonesian archipelago; Raymond Firth and his colleagues and students on Malay peasant society and economy; Derek Freeman on Iban agriculture and cognatic social organization; Maurice Freedman and G. William Skinner on Chinese social organization and history; Clifford Geertz on Javanese and south Balinese culture, society, economy and history and his theoretical contribution to the study of culture; Fredrik Barth on the society and culture of northern Bali; Koentjaraningrat's contribution to Indonesian ethnography; Lauriston Sharp and Lucien Hanks on Central Thai society, economy and history; Charles Frake and Harold Conklin on upland Philippine social organization, agriculture and classification; Roy Ellen and Andrew Vayda on Indonesian ecologies; Jonathan Friedman and his interpretation of tribal social forms in mainland South-East Asia from a Marxist perspective; Aihwa Ong and Wazir Jahan Karim in the field of gender studies; Judith Nagata on Malaysian pluralism; John Pemberton on the construction of Javanese culture; and Joel Kahn on Minangkabau and Malay society, culture and history and his recent contribution to postmodernist studies of culture. There is also the anthropologically influenced work of such political scientists as James Scott on peasant 'moral economy' and Benedict Anderson on Javanese culture and 'imagined communities'. Finally, we should not forget the significant contributions to the earlier development of anthropology and ethnology, based on South-East Asian ethnography, of Alfred C. Haddon, Robert von Heine-Geldern, R.F. Barton, H. Otley Beyer, Robert Hertz, Margaret Mead and Gregory Bateson, Ruth Benedict, J.P.B. de Josselin de Jong and W.H. Rassers, Claude Lévi-Strauss, A.R. Radcliffe-Brown, Georges Condominas, and rather more loosely J.S. Furnivall and J.H. Boeke. It is worth noting that many of the prominent anthropologists of the post-war period who have established their reputations significantly on the basis of analyses of South-East Asian societies and cultures have also worked in other parts of the world and have seen themselves in the main not as South-East Asianists or anthropologists of South-East Asia, but as making a theoretical and ethnographic contribution to the general discipline of anthropology.

A dominant paradigm?

We saw in Chapter 1 that there are difficulties in defining South-East Asia as a cultural area, given its extraordinary cultural diversity, geo-political fragmentation, and openness to external influences and the cultural transformations and differentiation which have occurred during the past two millennia, although some anthropologists including Robbins Burling (1965) and most recently John Bowen (1995, 2000) have argued that there are common cultural 'threads' or themes which are found widely in the region. In addition to identifying a cluster of substantive social and cultural elements, institutions and principles (bilateral kinship, relative gender equality, flexible and charismatic leadership, exemplary centres), there is another way in which regional studies take shape, and this happens to be the main focus of Bowen's two recent papers. Regional definition can also be sought in common or shared theoretical questions, perspectives, approaches and methodologies, or, in Bowen's terms, 'styles' of analysis. He argues that there is such a dominant 'style' of anthropological analysis in the region which comprises 'interpretive approaches to culture' (1995: 1047), and most recently he elaborates on this argument and refers to a cross-disciplinary 'style' closely connected to 'cultural interpretation' and characterized as a 'historical anthropology of politics' and 'comparative studies of culture in context' (2000: 11–13). He qualifies his position by advising that he is not considering all South-East Asian anthropology – 'in any case an impossible task', he adds; his focus in both papers is principally on the work of American scholars, especially cultural anthropologists and most recently also political scientists and historians, who have worked in Indonesia, and he acknowledges that he has little to say about other traditions of analysis which examine, for example, social structure or ecology and which are much more characteristic of anthropology outside the United States (1995: 1047; 2000: 11–13).

Bowen then identifies this 'dominant style' in the search for symbolic systems imbued with 'meaning', an approach which draws largely on Franz Boas and Max Weber (and one might add Friedrich Nietzsche), filtered through the work of Talcott Parsons and Clifford Geertz. He, of course, emphasizes that earlier concepts of culture which concentrate on basic and unchanging cultural features and on cultural coherence have been subsequently modified to take account of the ways in which cultures are created, negotiated and transformed in the context of particular social and historical processes. In his own detailed historical study of the Gayo of northern Sumatra he examines changes in their poetic practices (ritual speaking, sung poetry and historical narratives) and politics from 1900 to 1989 and the ways in which Gayo verbal expression shapes and is shaped by political–cultural change (1991). In particular, he reveals the ways in which Gayo actors 'respond to change and conflict by representing and embodying alternative ideas and attitudes in speech, writing, and other forms of expression' (ibid.: 270). Nevertheless, overall he is convinced that the dominance of 'interpretive anthropology' and the concern with 'comparative cultural history' lends coherence to South-East Asian Studies in general and, in an appropriate response to the perceived socio-cultural particularities, commonalities or continuities of the region, has given a certain unity to the anthropological endeavour there. It should be noted that Bowen also recognizes that different research traditions have resulted in the construction of different kinds of South-East Asia (he refers to three such models: the Hindu-Buddhist or 'Indianized' kingdoms model; South-East Asia as the Austronesian or 'Malayo-Polynesian ethnological space'; and the region 'as part of the Muslim world'). However, he suggests that 'in all of these distinct traditions, certain regional continuities appear that constitute a shared point of departure for these several traditions' (2000: 4), and these shared regional features 'shape the disciplines that study them' (ibid.: 6).

We have already seen in Chapter 6 that from an anthropologically informed political science stance Benedict Anderson, in his seminal concept of 'imagined communities', has also contributed to this 'interpretive', historical and comparative perspective on culture. According to Bowen the 'interpretive style' comprises the analysis of 'culture into publicly accessible forms and the interpretations different actors give those forms' (1995: 1047). There is no doubt that both Anderson's and more particularly Clifford Geertz's work (see Chapter 3) in this genre has had an important influence on subsequent studies in South-East Asian anthropology, though largely in relation to Indonesia. But it would seem that at times Bowen's view of Geertzian 'interpretation' is so wide that it serves as an umbrella for what might be seen as significantly different kinds of anthropological analysis, especially some of those developed by European anthropologists, which have been critical of Geertz's analysis of cultural forms. Bowen's broad view of 'cultural interpretation' is not altogether surprising given that 'despite his Nietzschean (and Weberian) borrowings, Geertz can sound conventionally Durkheimian (and structuralist)' (Rapport and Overing, 2000: 210). Yet if one widens the conception of 'interpretive anthropology' too widely, as Bowen seems to do, to include elements of Lévi-Straussian structuralism, and its British and Dutch variants, and various studies of gender, ethnicity, patron–clientship and agrarian change which are much more social structural (and in some cases political-economic and ecological) than cultural in orientation, then the notion of a defined and identifiable style becomes almost meaningless (King, 2001b). Interestingly, in his recent article, Bowen is rather more modest in his aims and concentrates very specifically on a cross-disciplinary approach which brings together the study of culture, politics and history in South-East Asian Studies and is associated mainly with 'a Cornell perspective' (2000: 12). Although he adds by way of qualification that the Cornell studies have 'not gone without strong criticism . . . [which] is generally rooted in analytic traditions that have historically been stronger outside the United States, and, in particular conflict-oriented approaches, whether inspired by Marx or Weber' (ibid.: 13).

The differentiation of 'styles': colonial and postcolonial?

Colonial anthropology

In our examination of colonial anthropology in Chapter 2 we noted the preoccupation of Western observers with the peripheries or frontier areas of expanding colonial empires and the insecure and undemarcated buffer zones between competing imperial interests. In the political and economic context of Western expansion overseas it is hardly surprising that colonial ethnologists concentrated on sub-regions and culture areas within expanding colonial dependencies, and in postcolonial discourse 'created' pagan races or non-Christian 'tribes' in specific colonial territories (Central Borneo, Highland Sumatra, Central Sulawesi, Upper Burma and the Shan States, Interior Malaya, Mountain Province in Luzon, the Central and Southern Philippines, and the Central and Northern Highlands of Vietnam). Anthropologically oriented colonial observers tended to pay less attention to the lowland populations, a focus which was to change in post-war American cultural anthropology as we shall see.

During the colonial period one might be tempted to suggest that there were certain distinctive paradigms in South-East Asian ethnology or anthropology, developed in response to specific socio-cultural commonalities, which might have been employed to define South-East Asia as a region. The one that immediately comes to mind was that provided by the so-called 'Leiden school' or 'Dutch school of structuralism' as it was developed by F.D.E. van Ossenbruggen, J.P.B. de Josselin de Jong, F.A.E. van Wouden and W.H. Rassers. This seems to us to be an excellent example of the very close association between a set of ideas and principles about social and cultural organization and a specific set of colonial interests, relations and activities tied very closely to the training in East Indies studies or Indology of colonial officers. But, and this is the important point, it was specific to the Dutch East Indies, expressed in the Dutch language, and was not adopted elsewhere in the region prior to the Second World War. Indeed, if anything, it served to reinforce the divide between the island and mainland worlds, and in its post-war form it continued to focus primarily on Indonesia.

There are two other pre-war concepts which deserve our attention, and which might indicate the possibility of a more general sociological or anthropological orientation to South-East Asia: J.H. Boeke's dual economy thesis (as applied to the Dutch East Indies) (1953) and J.S. Furnivall's plural society (as applied to Burma and the East Indies) (1939, 1956), both of which saw colonial or tropical society as deeply divided. Yet these ideas were generated mainly in debates within economics and political economy and not anthropology. Furthermore, they did not seem to capture the imagination of scholars who concentrated on other parts of colonial South-East Asia. What they did do, however, was to help create, along with Dutch reconstructions of ancient Indonesian social structures, a unique 'otherness' different from that proposed by those Western writers (mainly British and French) of the 'modernist' (techno-rationalist, instrumentalist, utilitarian, evolutionist) tradition who argued for both the inferiority and backwardness of the colonialized populations and also the need to protect, civilize and develop them. Indeed, Indonesian societies in particular were seen in Dutch ethnology as having their own inner logic and dynamics, their own non-Western rationale and integrity, and the capacity to domesticate outside influences. These portraits of otherness establish interesting connections with certain post-war representations of South-East Asia's cultural diversity, especially in the emphasis on the receptiveness and adaptability of local communities to external cultural ideas and practices, which in turn and paradoxically are claimed to produce a kind of cultural unity.

Aside from the partial and heavily qualified exception of Dutch structuralism, there seems to have been no other dominant pre-war paradigms or methods – colonialist, modernist or those anticipating the postcolonial critique – to mark South-East Asia off as a region in its own right. All the anthropological frameworks deployed were not specific to the region, and most of them responded to South-East Asia's diversity rather than any assumed unity. As we have seen in Chapter 2 these include evolutionism; racial or ethnic categorization and ethnographic encyclopaedism; functionalism or structural-functionalism, and variants of them, particularly that stemming from Durkheim's concept of social structure; diffusionism; culture and personality studies; and studies of acculturation, socio-economic change and conflict. In any case, research tended to be divided between and oriented to the circumstances of particular colonial dependencies, using the appropriate metropolitan language (English, French or Dutch).

Post-war anthropology

After the Second World War the prospects for defining South-East Asia as a region in ethnographic or cultural terms and on the basis of a dominant anthropological style of analysis (in tune with assumed region-wide characteristics) began to look more unrealizable in spite of the fact that this was precisely the time that the concept of the region had decisively entered academic discourse. American and European anthropologists tended to go their separate ways, despite the efforts of trans-Atlantic arbiters like F.K. Lehman and James Peacock, and we witnessed the development of at least two strongly competing paradigms, neither of them clearly dominant, which were largely focused on different kinds of South-East Asian society. This had already been prefigured in the colonial period: Koentjaraningrat noted many years ago that the pre-war work of various American anthropologists including Margaret Mead (with Gregory Bateson), Jane Belo and Cora du Bois 'did not receive much attention from Dutch Indologists' (1967: 15), nor, we assume, were these American cultural anthropologists enamoured of Indology, given the subsequent criticisms of Dutch studies of Indonesia by Hildred Geertz (1961b, 1965) and Clifford Geertz (1961) and the sharp Dutch response (de Josselin de Jong, 1965).

Despite Clifford Geertz's Durkheimian tendencies, there was a developing division between post-war American, largely Boas- and Weber-inspired cultural anthropology and European, largely Durkheim- and Lévi-Strauss-inspired structuralism, both of which had their roots in colonial anthropology. However, these were tendencies and there were also considerable variations and differences within both American and European anthropology and several cross-cutting ties, expressed not least in the work of Americans trained in Europe. We should note that the studies of native South-East Asian anthropologists tended to embrace the models of their university mentors in the United States or Europe or in local institutions (which in the 1950s and 1960s were still staffed by senior expatriates). American anthropologists, unlike most of their European counterparts, primarily directed themselves to the study and representation of South-East Asia from the perspective of its 'peasant' heartlands. In this connection Ruth McVey suggests, in her general evaluation of American scholarly endeavour in South-East Asia, that following the liberation of the region from both Japanese and colonial domination, the USA saw South-East Asian peoples as beginning a journey on the road to 'national self-realization' and 'progress to modernity' (1995: 2). The twin concepts of nation-building and modernization were to form the core of so-called modernization theory, the post-war, social science paradigm dominant in American scholarship on developing regions of the world including South-East Asia.

As we saw in Chapter 3, several influential American anthropologists of the time translated this focus into an examination of small-scale, agrarian societies, mainly so-called lowland 'peasant', cognatically organized communities, in the context of modernizing nation–states; they also focused on syncretic religions as a product of interactions between great and little traditions, as well as child-rearing practices, socialization and personality formation (the obvious high profile research comprised the Cornell programme in Thailand, and in Indonesia, mainly under the direction of Lauriston Sharp and Lucien Hanks [the tradition on which Bowen concentrates]; the MIT team's research in Java, dominated by the Geertzes with support from Robert Jay, Alice Dewey and others; Yale's work, inspired by Raymond Kennedy and Karl Pelzer, primarily in Indonesia; and Chicago [and Illinois] researchers, particularly Melford Spiro and Manning Nash, who worked mainly in the Mandalay region of Burma). We should note that 'schools' of study or common analytical perspectives owe much to institutional factors, funding policies, graduate training and so on, and this was certainly the case in the United States (as it was to a lesser extent in Europe).

Interestingly the Philippines was something of an exception to this focus on peasant societies in that the pre-war American colonial interest in upland pagan minorities or non-Christian tribes (which replicated the interests of other colonial powers in their minorities), continued (mainly through Fred Eggan, a Radcliffe-Brownian, at Chicago) with an important focus on traditional legal institutions and practices, as well as on cognatic kinship and folk religions. Nevertheless, even in America's former colony there was a noticeable shift to lowland Filipino peasant communities, especially in Luzon and the central Philippines in the work of Chicago-, Yale- and Cornell-trained anthropologists.

Some of the major research questions which American anthropologists who were interested in processes of modernization addressed were: How will local communities develop in the context of modernization? What directions will they take? What are the prospects for a democratic transition? What facilitates and hinders modernization? What roles do values play in modernization and how are people socialized into these values? How have modern values been diffused to traditional societies and what forms has acculturation taken? There was also emphasis in some studies on the practical value of anthropological research in the context of nation-building and development. Out of this research on peasant societies came notions of 'loose structure', 'involution' and 'multiple societies', and the concepts of dualism and pluralism were further evaluated. The paradigms of modernization, evolution and acculturation were also transferred to local graduates who pursued their further studies in the USA or in Manila (among them Moises Bello, F. Landa Jocano, Mary Hollnsteiner, Koentjaraningrat and Selosoemardjan).

Generally, American anthropological studies worked within or in response to certain assumptions about change and progress, and these perspectives of course were not specific to South-East Asia. The main assumption to be tested was that small-scale communities – mainly the peasant 'others' and also in some cases 'tribal' minorities – would be increasingly incorporated into the world system via the newly independent nation–state and would follow the path of Western modernity, individualism, rationalism and liberal democracy. Nevertheless, given the sensitivities of anthropologists to cultural difference, they did not perceive the road to modernity to be entirely straightforward and unidirectional (see Nash, 1965). Clifford Geertz, for example, was by no means a mainstream modernization theorist, though he framed certain of his analyses within traditional–modern parameters. Very familiar with the main ideas of pre-war Dutch scholars on the uniqueness of Indonesian culture and its adaptive capacities, Geertz's conclusion on his field-site of Modjokuto (Pare) in the 1950s was that it was 'a curious mixture of borrowed fragments of modernity and exhausted relics of tradition' in which 'the future seemed about as remote as the past' (1983: 60). The transition to a modern society had commenced but 'whether – or perhaps better, when – it will be completed is far from certain' (1963b: 4). A key Geertzian concept for exploring this in-betweenness and rendering it comprehensible was, as we have seen in Chapter 3, 'involution'.

There were important exceptions to studies within this dominant American modernization/nation–state paradigm, among them F.K. Lehman, James Peacock, and Oxford-trained American structuralists (Clark Cunningham, R.H. Barnes, Kirk Endicott among others). In addition in the Philippines, where American colonial anthropology continued to exercise some influence, Harold Conklin and Charles Frake, for example, studied marginal hinterland shifting cultivators using ecological perspectives (see Chapter 7) and, through detailed analyses of language in the emerging field of cognitive anthropology, examined native classifications and taxonomies (see especially Frake, 1980). But overall the study of peasant communities was pursued single-mindedly, and when field-sites became over-subscribed or inaccessible in the long-established heartlands, then several American anthropologists shifted their attention to the Malay peasant lowlands and coasts of Malaysia and Brunei (see, for example, Brown, 1970, 1976, 1998; Nash, 1974; Provencher, 1971).

In Europe, on the other hand, structuralism took the lead, and the immersion in symbolic classification directed British, Dutch and French anthropologists principally to 'tribes' and away from the heartlands, particularly to societies which were organized not on a cognatic basis but on principles of unilineal descent (see Chapter 4). Here we have a quite radical representation of cultural 'otherness'; the communities studied were not generally 'peasants becoming modern'. Structural anthropology was in many respects a continuation of the colonial tradition of focusing primarily on 'exotic' minorities in the marginal uplands, hinterlands and outer islands. The inspiration came from the Durkheimian sociological tradition, filtered primarily through Claude

Lévi-Strauss and translated for an English-speaking audience by Rodney Needham and Edmund Leach and for both English- and Dutch-speaking students by the de Josselin de Jongs. However, Lévi-Straussian structuralism was not an all-consuming passion and variants of functionalism and structural-functionalism, which concentrated mainly on social and economic organization, continued to flourish under Raymond Firth's tutelage at the London School of Economics; a considerable body of work was undertaken by London-based anthropologists on majority lowland populations like the Malays (see Chapter 5), and on the Singapore Chinese by Maurice Freedman and his students in particular. Occasionally structuralists also strayed into the lowlands; but even here European-based scholars did not usually move into the territories which had already been claimed by American researchers. The Cambridge- and Leach-trained Stanley Tambiah, for example, went nowhere near the Central Thai Plain and ended up in the distant Lao-speaking borderlands of North-East Thailand.

Looking back on this structuralist literature, some of it meticulous and thought-provoking, there is something of a timelessness and quaintness about it, rather remote from the realities of political and economic development and change generated in the heartlands and addressed by American anthropologists in the main. Yet concerns with grammars of culture, right and left hands, 'bad death', male and female gifts, mother's brothers' daughters, and 'circulating women' were not something which exercised most American anthropologists; structural analyses of these cultures, especially the total structural analyses of Rodney Needham and several of his Oxford colleagues, which provided a powerful and influential paradigm in European anthropology, served to mark out the distinctive characteristics of particular categories of society and culture in South-East Asia. These studies also gave further expression to cultural diversity and otherness and to the broad distinction between the majority lowland populations of the region and the minorities of the uplands, hinterlands and outer islands (see, for example, Needham, 1962).

From the 1970s onwards there is evidence of some continuity in American cultural anthropology and European structural anthropology in South-East Asia, but the past 30 years have witnessed an increasing diversification of approaches and paradigms. Some European-based anthropologists continued with a broadly structuralist view of the world, though others converted to various strands of Marxism, including structural Marxism and political economy, again under the influence of the French (see Chapter 5). In Britain it was London-based anthropologists, particularly at the LSE and University College London, who embraced Marxist variants of anthropology, including Maurice Bloch (1975). As we have seen, Joel Kahn, a London-trained American, was one of the foremost and eloquent exponents of neo-Marxist analyses of South-East Asia (1975, 1980, 1982) as was Andrew Turton in a Marxist-influenced political economy perspective (1989a, 1989b; Taylor and Turton, 1988). It should be noted that this radical literature, though critical of various studies which employed concepts and perspectives from American cultural anthropology as well as from British functionalism and structural-functionalism, made very little impression on these approaches and these latter continued to be employed, albeit often in modified form.

Much of the neo-Marxist effort was spent re-evaluating earlier work, subjecting the anthropologies of the colonial period to critical scrutiny, and castigating post-war American social science, including anthropology, for its close association with the perceived international hegemonic position and role of the United States. Geertz's work on Java and Bali came in for special attention as did American 'conservative' sociology and anthropology in Thailand and the Philippines (see King, 1996c). From Talal Asad's neo-Marxist critique of the colonial roots of anthropology expressed most fervently in his *Anthropology and the Colonial Encounter* (1973), and Kahn's gradual movement away from 'modes of production' and 'social formations' to the construction of culture and the constitution of identity (1993, 1995) we have edged recently into postmodernism and postcolonialism, illustrated most clearly in Tsing's subtle appreciation of the culture of the Meratus Dayaks of Kalimantan (1993), Pemberton's brilliant study of Java (1994), and most recently Spyer's complex analysis of the Aruese of Eastern Indonesia (2000), and Cannell's intriguing excursion into the cultural idioms of the Bicolanos of South-Eastern Luzon (1999). Yet these are not the only approaches to be adopted in the anthropology of South-East Asia as we shall see.

During the past two to three decades there seems to have been no dominant schools, centres, programmes or paradigms which might provide the study of South-East Asia with a distinctive profile in anthropology or indeed in South-East Asian Studies. In current scholarly work there is, happily, a healthy mix of the old and the new. Some anthropologists continue to fill in ethnographic gaps with structural-functionalist treatments of communities; others have gone to the archives or to collect oral traditions to reconstruct ethnic histories and identities. There is still a considerable attention to symbolisms, often using culturally focal elements – rice-meals, houses, cloth, marriages, funerals – to build up more general cultural images of 'community'. There are also those who, using variants of structuralism, continue to explore classification systems, alliances and ritual processes.

What is also apparent is the increasing anthropological attention to development and change in the region, neglected by Bowen, though this does not provide any coherent paradigm or focus in South-East Asian anthropology. Many anthropologists have become involved in the field of development, either taking advantage of it or denouncing the increasingly close relationships between social science knowledge and practice and the national development plans of the various governments in the region (King, 1999). Policy-relevant and applied research has also been an especially important area of activity for local anthropologists. However, aside from those who have deconstructed development and those who conceptualize it as discourse and as a symbolic

317

system, much of the work has been quite practical and down-to-earth. Allied to these concerns, and given the crucial significance of natural resource exploitation and technological development in South-East Asia, there has also been growing interest among anthropologists in the study of ecology and environment, often with attention to indigenous knowledge of the natural environment (Dove, 1985; King, 1998). Local level studies of agrarian differentiation in the context of technological change and commercialization, and of local power structures and their relationships with wider political and economic processes, have also fed into debates about development (Hart, Turton and White, 1989).

Finally, and aside from these concerns with development and change, more and more studies are being undertaken by anthropologists on gender relations, ethnic identities, tourism, leisure and consumption, material culture, and the media and performance; these subjects are bound to continue to command our attention. However, they are being increasingly examined from the perspectives of postmodernism and postcolonialism, and significantly from within multi-disciplinary (cultural, media, communication, film, tourism, ethnic, gender, museum) 'studies' rather than from within the discipline of anthropology. In other words, debates which were conducted much more decisively within anthropology up to about the 1980s have now moved into a much more multi- and interdisciplinary arena, and even beyond the confines of multidisciplinary area studies programmes. Within anthropology Joel Kahn's recent contribution has been significant in his attention to the processes by which cultural otherness and identities are constructed, specifically with regard to the Minangkabau (1993), and the relationships between culture, politics, the state and identity in the region (1998; Kahn and Loh, 1992). Yet even he remarks that in addressing these issues he has had to move beyond anthropology and area studies into 'the relatively new fields of cultural studies, globalisation theory and especially, postcolonial theory' (1995: xi). A recent volume edited by Yao Souchou on 'the relationship between discursive practices, modernity, and state power in Southeast Asia' in the context of multidisciplinary 'cultural studies' captures these current concerns beautifully (2000: 3–4).

If anything, the recent mood of self-reflection and self-criticism in anthropology has added to the perception of South-East Asia's cultural diversity. Anthropologists have become increasingly preoccupied with the exploration and implications of the concept of 'alterity' or 'otherness' in relation to specific identities and in response to postmodernist and postcolonialist critiques. One of the consequences of this self-analysis has been a profound ambivalence about the primary object of anthropological study which, in postcolonial discourse, is the 'Western imperialized other', the 'exploited', and the 'inferiorized' and serious concerns have been expressed about the issue of 'representation' and who speaks for or about local people and with what authority (Rapport and Overing, 2000: 9). There appears then to have been a recent shift in emphasis towards the contextualized, knowable local community or ethnic group and the ways in which it has been 'constituted' or 'constructed' in the context of colonialism, postcolonial state power and globalization (for example, Kipp, 1993; Spyer, 2000; Steedly, 1993; Tsing, 1993), and away from rather earlier more generalized categories of the 'other' such as Robbins Burling's 'peasant cultivator' or 'hill farmer'.

This 'crisis of representation' has led to what Raul Pertierra, in his examination of Philippine studies, has called the 'new ethnography' in which anthropologists address the personal dimension of their involvement in other people's lives while they are engaged in studying, recording and writing about those lives (1994). He says that

> [the] representation of the Other is becoming increasingly problematic in a world characterized by a global order where the local no longer possesses the autonomy of isolation [in that isolation] allowed a discipline such as anthropology to speak about its subjects without their express authorization.
>
> (ibid.: 121)

An example of this 'new ethnography' is Jean-Paul Dumont's account of a Visayan peasant fishing community (1992), described by Pertierra as 'deliberately self-conscious', a 'nuanced exploration of local life', a 'sensitive account' providing 'vignettes' or character portraits of local informants in the context of a fieldwork situation in which 'the ethnographer is justly overwhelmed with guilt over the generosity of the natives' (Pertierra, 1994: 125–128). Another is Renato Rosaldo's exploration of why Ilongot men traditionally hunted heads (see Chapter 8) and his search for explanations for head-taking in the emotional realms of grief and rage, emotions which Rosaldo himself experienced with the accidental death of his wife, Michelle, during fieldwork in the Philippines (1980, 1989).

Postscript

In our attempt in this text to provide an introduction to the anthropology of South-East Asia we have perforce had to range over a considerable amount of material. We recognize that there have been certain especially important themes, trends, issues and perspectives which have informed the understanding of the societies and cultures of the region and that South-East Asia merits attention in its own right. However, we should not then assume that the region can be defined straightforwardly in cultural terms and its boundaries easily identified nor that there has been a dominant 'style' of analysis which marks off South-East Asian anthropology decisively from studies of other parts of the world.

What is striking is the diversity of approaches and perspectives which the study of South-East Asia has occasioned. In addition, during the last decade there has also been an important focus not so much on the 'heartlands' and political centres of the region but rather on the 'margins' or 'peripheries' of the politically defined South-East Asia; this enterprise has involved examining cultures, social interactions, movements and networks across political boundaries. The work of James Fox and his colleagues on Austronesian-speaking populations in South-East Asia and the Pacific (Bellwood *et al.*, 1995; Fox and Sather, 1996; Fox, 1997) and studies of the minorities of northern mainland South-East Asia and southern China (Evans, Hutton and Kuah, 2000; Michaud, 2000b; Wijeyewardene, 1990) immediately come to mind. Early examples of the fruitfulness of this concern are Edmund Leach's now classic examination of the 'frontiers of Burma' (1960) and Peter Kunstadter's two-volume text on South-East Asian 'tribes, minorities and nations' (1967), which also looked beyond the region. We find the recent interest in re-exploring borderlands and 'margins' and examining ethnolinguistic groupings beyond borders to be of considerable importance for the study of South-East Asia.

Finally, Joel Kahn draws attention to, what for us seem to be our main and formidable tasks for the future when he asks how anthropologists can best represent the divergent cultures of South-East Asia, and how we should appropriately respond to divergent accounts of the same culture (1993: 5). If nothing else, his question serves to remind us that South-East Asia as commonly constituted and delineated is not what it seems, and that, despite our consideration of the anthropology of the region in this text we should acknowledge that most anthropologists, far from searching for regional unities or commonalities, have positively rejoiced in cultural diversity. We hope that we have conveyed some of the cultural richness and variety of South-East Asia and the range of perspectives and approaches which have been used to understand it, and, if we have achieved that objective, that readers will be persuaded to go on to find out more about this fascinating region of the world.

APPENDIX
List of ethnic groups

Peninsular Malaysia

Batek, Chewong, Jakun, Malay, Semai, Semang, Senoi.

Borneo States (Sarawak, Sabah, Brunei, Kalimantan)

Bajau Laut, Banjarese, Belait, Bisaya (Dusun), Dayak (general term for non-Muslim natives), Dusun (Kadazan), Iban, Kadayan, Kantu', Kayan, Kenyah, Land Dayak (Bidayuh), Ma'anyan, Malay (coastal, Brunei), 'Maloh', (Embaloh, Taman, Kalis), Melanau, Meratus Dayak, Murut (in interior Sabah), Murut (Lun Bawang, Lun Dayeh, in western Sabah, Brunei, Sarawak), Ngaju, Punan, Tutong.

Indonesia

Sumatra

Achehnese, Alas, Batak (Toba), Gayo, Kubu, Malay, Minangkabau, Mentaweians, Niasans, Rejang.

Java, Bali, Madura, Lombok, Sumbawa

Balinese, Bimanese, Javanese, Madurese, Sasak, Sumbawans, Sundanese, Tenggerese.

Eastern Indonesia, Lesser Sundas, Sulawesi, Moluccas (Maluku), Irian Jaya (West Papua)

Alorese, Ambonese, Atoni, Bemunese (Aruese), Bugis (Buginese), Kakean, Kapauku, Kédangese, Lamalerans, Makassarese, Ndaonese, Nuaulu, Rotinese, Savunese, Sumbanese, Toraja.

Philippines

Ayta, Bajau, Batak, Bontoc-Igorot, Filipino, Gaddang, Hanunóo, Ifugao, Ilocano, Jama Mapun, Kalinga, Kankanay, Malitbog, Panayan, Subanun, Sulod, Tausug, Tiruray.

Myanmar (Burma), Assam

Aimol, Arakanese, Burmese (Burman), Chawte, Chin, Garo, Kachin, Karen, Khasi, Lakher, Mikir, Mon, Naga, Purum, Shan.

Thailand (Siam)

Hmong (Meo, Miao), Lue, Malay, Thai, Yao.

Vietnam, Laos, Cambodia

Cham, Hmong, Khmer (Cambodians), Lao, Mnong Gar, Rhade, Sré, Vietnamese.

Other Asians

Arabs, Chinese (Baba/Peranakan/Straits, Cantonese, Foochow, Hainanese, Hakka, Hokkien, Teochiu), Indian (Bengali, Chettiar, Chitty, Chulia, Gujerati, Jain, Jawi Peranakan, Malayali, Parsee, Sikh, Tamil).

GLOSSARY

abangan	animistic subvariant of religion (Javanese)
adat	customary law, custom (Indonesian/Malay)
akal	reason (Malay)
aliran	politico-cultural groupings or streams (Indonesian)
alus	refined, civilized, poised (Indonesian)
anéh	odd, unexpected (Indonesian)
apa basi	metalsmith's workshop (Minangkabau)
arisan	rotating credit ring (Malay)
bahasa	language (Indonesian/Malay)
bajang	birth demon, vampire (Malay)
bakat (alam)	talent (Indonesian)
banjar	hamlet (Balinese)
banuaka	our people ('Maloh')
batik	tie-dyed textile (Indonesian/Malay)
berkira	calculation (Malay)
bhuvana agung	cosmos (Balinese)
bhuvana alit	human world (Balinese)
bilek	room, household, domestic family in longhouse (Iban)
bodong	peace pact (Kalinga)
bomoh	folk-doctor (Malay)
bujang	bachelor (Indonesian)
bumiputera	'sons of the soil' (Malay)
camote	sweet potato (Philippines)
comadre/compadre	co-sponsor (Philippines)
compadrazgo/compadrinazgo	godparenthood, ritual coparenthood (Philippines)
dabalutu	boat crew (Bajau Laut)
dampa	farmhouse (Iban)
damun	secondary forest (Iban)
daulat	attribute of kingship (Malay)
desa	village (Bali, Java)

dukun	magical practitioner (Javanese)
fedew	state of mind, rational feelings (Tiruray)
fiyo	'the way things should be' (Tiruray)
gumchying gumsa	gumsa paramount chief (Kachin)
gumlao	egalitarian organization (Kachin)
gumsa	ranked organization (Kachin)
haj	pilgrimage to Mecca (Malay/Arabic)
hantu	wandering, free spirit (Malay)
hawa nafsu	passion (Malay)
huya	shame (Philippines)
ilmu	esoteric knowledge (Malay)
imam	prayer leader (Malay)
jin	free spirit (Malay)
juruselam	fishing expert (Malay)
kadangyan	aristocratic families (Kalinga)
kamma/karma	the law of moral retribution (Pali; Burmese kan)
kampong	swidden field (Iban)
kampong/kampung	village (Malay)
kampung kebun	tree plantation (Malay)
kasar	coarse (Indonesian/Malay)
kasihan	care and concern (Malay)
kathoey	transvestite, transsexual, hermaphrodite (Thai)
kefeduwan	legal authority or specialist in customary law (Tiruray)
keluarga	family (Indonesian/Malay)
kelurahan	headman's settlement (Javanese)
kembong	small mackerel (Malay)
ketap	hand-knife (Iban)
ketua kampung	village headman (Malay)
khenduri	ritual feast (Malay)
kolek	kind of fishing boat (Malay)
konsi/kongsi	Chinese association (Chinese/Malay)
kromo	high speech (Javanese)
kuna	conservative (Indonesian/Javanese)
kut	women's rotating credit ring (Javanese)
lahat	settlement (Bajau Laut)
langsuir	birth demon, vampire (Malay)
latah	dissociative state (Malay)
lawan	confrontation (Malay)
lebai	person knowledgeable in Islam (Malay)
lontar	sugar palm species (Indonesian)
ludruk	proletarian drama (Javanese)
luma'	multi-family household (Bajau Laut)
maa chii	nun (Thai)

maa khii	medium (Thai)
maju	progressive (Indonesian)
makan gaji	earn wages (lit. 'eat money', Malay)
monca-pat	village pattern of central settlement and four settlements at cardinal points (Javanese)
mandala	circle of kings (Javanese/Sanskrit)
mangol	title of rank or status, brave warrior (Kalinga)
maruah	character, initiative, charisma (Malay)
mati lemas	drown (Malay)
melawan	sparring partner (Malay)
mong	state (Shan)
mukim	administrative unit (Malay)
nagari	township (Minangkabau)
nahuya	ashamed (Philippines)
nama	name, reputation, morality (Malay)
nangkodoh	head smith (Minangkabau)
nat	spirit (Burmese)
nat kadaw	shaman, spirit-medium (Burmese)
negara	state (Bali)
nibbana/nirvana	the state which transcends sentient existence, nothingness (Pali; Burmese neikban)
ninang	mother's godmother (Philippines)
ningan	inferior section or part (Purum)
ngoko	low speech (Javanese)
noi tro	'interior helper' (Vietnamese)
noi tuong	'generalship' (Vietnamese)
nyawa	breath of life (Malay)
orang kaya	'big man', rich man (Malay)
orang tua kampung	village elder (Malay)
padi	rice (dry rice, Iban)
padi muda	quick-ripening rice (Iban)
padi pulut	glutinous rice (Iban)
padi pun	sacred rice (Iban)
padi taun	ordinary rice (Iban)
pagta	peace pact provisions (Kalinga)
panyembrana	type of dance (Balinese)
pasar	bazaar, market (Indonesian/Malay)
pawang	magician (Malay)
pelajar	student (Indonesian)
pelesit	ghost, familiar spirit (Malay)
pemimpin/pimpin	leader, to lead (Malay)
pemuda	youth (Indonesian)
penanggalan	birth demon, vampire (Malay)
penggawa	government official (Malay)

penghulu	sub-district head (Malay)
petani	farmer (Malay)
phumlil	superior section or part (Purum)
polong	ghost, familiar spirit (Malay)
pontianak	birth demon, vampire (Malay)
priyayi	Hindu-Buddhist subvariant of religion (Javanese)
rajah	ruler (Malay)
ratus	one hundred (Indonesian/Malay)
remaja	youth (Javanese)
roh	aspect of human soul which leaves the body during sleep (Malay)
ronda	neighbourhood watch groups (of young men, Javanese)
santri	Islamic subvariant of religion (Javanese)
saohpa	prince (Shan)
sawah	irrigated wet rice field (Indonesia)
semangat	soul, vital principle (Malay)
shikkhou	obeisance (Burmese)
slametan	ritual or communal feast (Javanese)
spontan	spontaneity (Javanese)
subak	irrigation society (Balinese)
suki	regular suppliers or customers (Philippines)
taungya	swidden field (Burmese)
tenggelam	sink (Malay)
tiyawan	formal encounter between two or more kindreds (Tiruray)
tripang	sea cucumber (Malay)
tuan tanah	landlord (Malay)
turnohan	'taking turns' (saving scheme, southern Luzon)
umai	swidden farm (Iban)
umbun	swidden unit (Meratus Dayak)
ume	house (Atoni)
ustaz	religious teacher (Malay)
utang	debt, obligation to pay (Philippines)
utang na loob	debt of prime obligation (Philippines)
utang nga buot	debt of gratitude (Negros)
wayang kulit	shadow play (Javanese)
ying borikan	entertainment women/prostitutes (Thai)

BIBLIOGRAPHY

Adams, Kathleen M. (1997) 'Touting touristic "primadonas": tourism, ethnicity, and national integration in Sulawesi, Indonesia', in Michel Picard and Robert E. Wood (eds), *Tourism, Ethnicity, and the State in Asian and Pacific Societies*, Honolulu, University of Hawai'i Press, pp. 155–180.

Adas, Michael (1974) *The Burma Delta: Economic Development and Social Change on an Asian Rice Frontier, 1852–1941*, Madison, WI, University of Wisconsin Press.

Adriani, N. and Kruyt, A.C. (1912–1914) *De Bare'e-sprekende Toradja's van Midden-Celebes*, Batavia, Landsdrukkerij, 3 vols.

Albee, Alana (1995) 'Living in Transition: Women in Rural Vietnam', Unpublished paper, ASEASUK conference, University of Durham, March.

Alexander, J. and Alexander, P. (1978) 'Sugar, rice and irrigation in colonial Java', *Ethnohistory*, 25: 207–223.

Alexander, J. and Alexander, P. (1979) 'Labour demands and the "involution" of Javanese agriculture', *Social Analysis*, 3: 22–44.

Alexander J. and Alexander, P. (1982) 'Shared poverty as ideology: agrarian relationships in colonial Java', *Man*, 17: 597–619.

Andaya, Barbara Watson (1997) 'The unity of Southeast Asia: historical approaches and questions', *Journal of Southeast Asian Studies*, 28: 161–171.

Anderson, Benedict (1990) 'The idea of power in Javanese culture', in Benedict Anderson, *Language and Power: Exploring Political Cultures in Indonesia*, Ithaca, NY, Cornell University Press, pp. 17–77 (Chapter 1); first published in Claire Holt (ed.), *Culture and Politics in Indonesia*, Ithaca, NY, Cornell University Press, 1972, pp. 1–69.

Anderson, Benedict (1991) *Imagined Communities: Reflections on the Origin and Spread of Nationalism*, London, New York: Verso, revised and extended edition, originally published in 1983.

Appell, Laura W.R. (1991) 'Sex role symmetry among the Rungus of Sabah', in Vinson H. Sutlive (ed.), *Female and Male in Borneo: Contributions and Challenges to Gender Studies*, Phillips, Maine: Borneo Research Council, Monographs No. 1, pp. 1–20.

Arts, Henry (1991) 'Langko Soo. Het Langhuis bij de Taman-Daya: Continuïteit en Verandering', Nijmegen University, doctoraal thesis.

Asad, Talal (1972) 'Market model, class structure and consent', *Man*, 7: 74–94.

Asad, Talal (ed.) (1973) 'Introduction', in Talal Asad (ed.), *Anthropology and the Colonial Encounter*, New York, Humanities Press, pp. 9–19.

Askew, Marc (1996) 'The rise of Moradok and the decline of the Yarn: heritage and cultural construction in urban Thailand', *Sojourn: Southeast Asian Journal of Social Issues*, 11: 183–210.

Atkinson, Jane Monnig and Errington, Shelly (eds.) (1990) *Power and Difference: Gender in Island Southeast Asia*, Stanford, CA, Stanford University Press.

Baal, J. van (1971) *Symbols for Communication: An Introduction to the Anthropological Study of Religion*, Assen, van Gorcum.

Bacdayan, Albert S. (1967) 'The peace pact system of the Kalingas in the modern world', unpublished PhD thesis, Cornell University.

Bacdayan, Albert S. (1977) 'Mechanistic cooperation and sexual equality among the Western Bontoc', in Alice Schlegel (ed.), *Sexual Stratification: A Cross-cultural View*, New York, Columbia University Press.

Bachtiar, Harsja W. (1967) '"Negeri" Taram: a Minangkabau village community', in Koentjaraningrat (ed.), *Villages in Indonesia*, Ithaca, NY, Cornell University Press, pp. 348–385.

Bachtiar, Harsja W. (1968) 'Indonesia', in D.K. Emmerson (ed.), *Students and Politics in Developing Nations*, New York, Praeger, pp. 180–214.

Bachtiar, Harsja W. (1972) 'Bureaucracy and nation formation in Indonesia', *Bijdragen tot de Taal-, Land- en Volkenkunde*, 128: 430–446.

Barnes, R.H. (1976) *Kédang: A Study of the Collective Thought of an Eastern Indonesian People*, Oxford, Clarendon Press.

Barnes, R.H. (1996) *Sea Hunters of Indonesia: Fishers and Weavers of Lamalera*, Oxford, Clarendon Press.

Barth, Fredrik (1959) *Political Leadership among Swat Pathans*, London, The Athlone Press.

Barth, Fredrik (1969) 'Introduction', in Fredrik Barth (ed.), *Ethnic Groups and Boundaries: The Social Organization of Culture Difference*, Bergen and Oslo, Universitets Forlaget and London, George Allen and Unwin, pp. 9–38.

Barth, Fredrik (1993) *Balinese Worlds*, Chicago and London, University of Chicago Press.

Barton, Roy Franklin (1919) *Ifugao Law*, Berkeley and Los Angeles, CA, University of California Press, reprint 1969.

Barton, Roy Franklin (1949) *The Kalingas: Their Institutions and Custom Law*, Chicago, University of Chicago Press.

Bates, Daniel G. and Lees, Susan H. (1996) 'Introduction', in Daniel G. Bates and Susan H. Lees (eds), *Case Studies in Human Ecology*, New York and London, Plenum Press, pp. 1–12.

Bateson, Gregory and Mead, Margaret (1942) *Balinese Character. A Photographic Analysis*, New York, New York Academy of Sciences, Special Publication, II.

Bayly, Susan (2000) 'French anthropology and the Durkheimians in colonial Indochina', *Modern Asian Studies*, 34: 581–622.

Beattie, J.H. (1968) 'Aspects of Nyoro symbolism', *Africa*, 38: 413–442.

Beattie, J.H. (1976) 'Right, left and the Banyoro', *Africa*, 46: 217–235.

Beattie, J.H. (1978) 'Nyoro symbolism and Nyoro ethnography: a rejoinder', *Africa*, 48: 278–295.

Beatty, Andrew (1992) *Society and Exchange in Nias*, Oxford, Clarendon Press.

Beatty, Andrew (1999) *Varieties of Javanese Religion: An Anthropological Account*, Cambridge, Cambridge University Press.

Bell, Peter F. (1982) 'Western conceptions of Thai society: the politics of American scholarship', *Journal of Contemporary Asia*, 12: 61–74.

Bell, Peter F. (1991) 'Gender and economic development in Thailand', in Penny and John van Esterik (eds), *Gender and Development in Southeast Asia*, York University, Canadian Council for Southeast Asian Studies, 20, vol. II, pp. 61–82.

Bello, Moises C. (1967) 'Some observations on beliefs and rituals of the Bakun-Kankanay', in Mario D. Zamora (ed.), *Studies in Philippine Anthropology (in Honor of H. Otley Beyer)*, Quezon City, Alemar-Phoenix, pp. 324–342.

Bello, Moises C. (1972) *Kankanay Social Organization and Cultural Change*, Diliman, Community Development Research Council, University of the Philippines.

Bellwood, Peter (1985) *Prehistory of the Indo-Malaysian Archipelago*, Sydney, Orlando, London, Academic Press.

Bellwood, Peter (1995) 'Austronesian prehistory in Southeast Asia: homeland, expansion and transformation', in Peter Bellwood, James J. Fox and Darrell Tryon (eds), *The Austronesians: Historical and Comparative Perspectives*, Canberra, Australian National University, pp. 96–111.

Bellwood, Peter, Fox, James J. and Tryon, Darrell (eds) (1995) *The Austronesians: Historical and Comparative Perspectives*, Canberra, Australian National University, Department of Anthropology, Research School of Pacific and Asian Studies.

Belo, Jane (ed.) (1970) *Traditional Balinese Culture*, New York, Columbia University Press.

Ben-Ari, Eyal (1999) 'Colonialism, anthropology and the politics of professionalisation', in Jan van Bremen and Akitoshi Shimizu (eds), *Anthropology and Colonialism in Asia and Oceania*, Richmond, Curzon Press, pp. 382–409.

Benedict, Ruth (1952) *Thai Culture and Behavior: An Unpublished War Time Study dated September, 1943*, Ithaca, NY, Cornell University Southeast Asia Program, Data Paper No. 4.

Bernstein, Jay H. (1997) *Spirits Captured in Stone: Shamanism and Traditional Medicine among the Taman of Borneo*, Boulder, CO, Lynne Rienner.

Bloch, Maurice (1975) 'Introduction', in Maurice Bloch (ed.), *Marxist Analyses and Social Anthropology*, London, Malaby Press, pp. xi–xiv.

Blok, Anton and Boissevain, Jeremy (1984) 'Anthropology in the Netherlands: puzzles and paradoxes', *Annual Review of Anthropology*, 13, Palo Alto, CA, Annual Reviews Inc., pp. 333–344.

Boeke, J.H. (1910) *Tropisch-Koloniale Staathuishoudkunde: Het Probleem*, PhD dissertation, Leiden University.

Boeke, J.H. (1953) *Economics and Economic Policy of Dual Societies as Exemplified by Indonesia*, New York, Institute of Pacific Relations.

Boon, James A. (1977) *The Anthropological Romance of Bali 1597–1972: Dynamic Perspectives in Marriage and Caste, Politics and Religion*, Cambridge, Cambridge University Press.

Bowen, John R. (1991) *Sumatran Politics and Poetics: Gayo History, 1900–1989*, New Haven and London, Yale University Press.

Bowen, John R. (1995), 'The forms culture takes: a state-of-the-field essay on the anthropology of Southeast Asia', *The Journal of Asian Studies*, 54: 1047–1078.

Bowen, John R. (2000) 'The inseparability of area and discipline in Southeast Asian Studies: a view from the United States', *Moussons. Recherche en sciences humaines sur l'Asie de Sud-Est*, 1: 3–19.

Bray, Francesca (1986) *The Rice Economies: Technology and Development in Asian Societies*, Oxford, Basil Blackwell.

Breman, Jan (1982) 'The village on Java and the early colonial state', *Journal of Peasant Studies*, 9: 189–240.

Bremen, Jan van (1999) 'The Japanese and Dutch anthropology of insular South-East Asia in the colonial period 1879–1949', in Jan van Bremen and Akitoshi Shimizu (eds), *Anthropology and Colonialism in Asia and Oceania*, Richmond, Curzon Press, pp. 362–381.

Bremen, Jan van and Shimizu, Akitoshi (eds) (1999) *Anthropology and Colonialism in Asia and Oceania*, Richmond, Curzon Press.

Brenner, Suzanne April (1998) *The Domestication of Desire: Women, Wealth, and Modernity in Java*, Princeton, NJ, Princeton University Press.

Brosius, J. Peter (1990) *After Duwagan: Deforestation, Succession, and Adaptation in Upland Luzon, Philippines*, University of Michigan, Center for South and Southeast Asian Studies, Michigan Studies of South and Southeast Asia No. 2.

Brosius, J. Peter, Lovelace, George W. and Marten, Gerald G. (1986) 'Ethnoecology: an approach to understanding traditional agricultural knowledge', in Gerald G. Marten (ed.), *Traditional Agriculture in Southeast Asia: A Human Ecology Perspective*, Boulder, CO, Westview Press, pp. 187–198.

Brown, D.E. (1970) *The Structure and History of a Bornean Malay Sultanate*, Brunei Museum, Brunei Museum Journal, Monograph No. 2.

Brown, D.E. (1976) *Principles of Social Structure: Southeast Asia*, London, Duckworth.

Brown, D.E. (1998) 'Issues in the nature of Brunei society and polity', *Janang. Warta Akademi Pengajian Brunei, Universiti Brunei Darussalam*, 7: 85–90.

Bruner, E.M. (1959) *Kinship Organization of the Urban Batak of Sumatra*, New York, Transactions of the New York Academy of Sciences, 22, Series II.

Bruner, E.M. (1961) 'Urbanization and ethnic identity in North Sumatra', *American Anthropologist*, 63: 508–521.

Bruner, E.M. (1973) 'The expression of ethnicity in Indonesia', in A. Cohen (ed.), *Urban Ethnicity*, London, Tavistock, pp. 251–280.

Burling, Robbins (1965) *Hill Farms and Padi Fields: Life in Mainland Southeast Asia*, Englewood Cliffs, NJ, Prentice-Hall, reprint with new preface, 1992, Arizona State University, Program for Southeast Asian Studies.

Cannell, Fenella (1999) *Power and Intimacy in the Christian Philippines*, Cambridge, Cambridge University Press.

Carroll, John J. (1968) *Changing Patterns of Social Structure in the Philippines 1896–1963*, Quezon City, Ateneo de Manila University Press.

Carsten, Janet F. (1989) 'Cooking money: gender and the symbolic transformation of means of exchange in a Malay fishing community', in J. Parry and M. Bloch (eds), *Money and the Morality of Exchange*, Cambridge, Cambridge University Press, pp. 117–141.

Carsten, Janet F. (1997) *The Heat of the Hearth: The Process of Kinship in a Malay Fishing Community*, Oxford, Clarendon Press.

Casiño, Eric (1976) *The Jama Mapun: A Changing Samal Society in the Southern Philippines*, Quezon City, Ateneo de Manila University Press.

Catley, Bob (1976) 'The development of underdevelopment in South-East Asia', *Journal of Contemporary Asia*, 6: 54–74.

Cedercreutz, Sini (1998) 'Review of Janet Carsten, *The Heat of the Hearth: the Process of Kinship in a Malay Fishing Community*', *Bijdragen tot de Taal-, Land- en Volkenkunde*, 154: 479–485.

Chapman, Graham P. and Baker, Kathleen M. (1992) *The Changing Geography of Asia*, London and New York, Routledge.

Chayan Vaddhanaphuti (1993) 'Traditions of village study in Thailand', in Philip Hirsch (ed.), *The Village in Perspective: Community and Locality in Rural Thailand*, Chiang Mai University, Social Research Institute, pp. 9–38.

Christie, Jan Wisseman (1985) *Theatre States and Oriental Despotisms: Early Southeast Asia in the Eyes of the West*, University of Hull, Centre for South-East Asian Studies, Occasional Paper No. 10.

Chua Beng Huat (1998) 'Racial-Singaporeans: absence after the hyphen', in Joel S. Kahn (ed.), *Southeast Asian Identities: Culture and the Politics of Representation in Indonesia, Malaysia, Singapore, and Thailand*, Singapore and London, Institute of Southeast Asian Studies, pp. 28–50.

Clammer, John R. (1980) *Straits Chinese Society*, Singapore, Singapore University Press.

Clammer, John R. (1985a) *Anthropology and Political Economy: Theoretical and Asian Perspectives*, Basingstoke and London, Macmillan.

Clammer, John R. (1985b) *Singapore: Ideology, Society, Culture*, Singapore, Chopmen Publishers.

Clammer, John R. (1986) 'Ethnic processes in urban Melaka', in Raymond L.M. Lee (ed.), *Ethnicity and Ethnic Relations in Malaysia*, Northern Illinois University, Center for Southeast Asian Studies, Monograph Series, Occasional Paper No. 12, pp. 47–72.

Cohen, Erik (1988) 'Authenticity and commoditization in tourism', *Annals of Tourism Research*, 15: 371–386.

Cole, Fay-Cooper (1945) *The Peoples of Malaysia*, New York, D. van Nostrand.

Colfer, C.J.P. (1983a, 1983b) 'Change and indigenous agroforestry in East Kalimantan' (Parts I and II), *Borneo Research Bulletin*, 15: 3–21, 70–87.

Condominas, Georges (1977) *We Have Eaten the Forest*, New York, Farrar, Strauss and Giroux (translation of publication, *Nous Avons Mangé la Forêt de la Pierre-Génie Gôo: Chronique de Sar Luk, Village Mnong Gar*. Paris, Mercure de France, 1957).

Conelly, W. Thomas (1996) 'Agricultural intensification in a Philippine frontier community: impact on labor efficiency and farm diversity', in Daniel G. Bates and Susan H. Lees (eds), *Case Studies in Human Ecology*, New York and London, Plenum Press, pp. 289–310.

Conklin, Harold C. (1954) 'An ethnoecological approach to shifting agriculture', *New York Academy of Sciences, Transactions*, 17: 133–142.

Conklin, Harold C. (1957) *Hanunoo Agriculture: A Report on an Integral System of Shifting Cultivation in the Philippines*, Rome, Food and Agriculture Organization of the United Nations, FAO Forestry Development Paper No. 12.

Conklin, Harold C. (1967) 'Ifugao ethnobotany 1905–1965: the 1911 Beyer-Merrill Report in perspective', in Mario D. Zamora (ed.), *Studies in Philippine Anthropology (in Honor of H. Otley Beyer)*, Quezon City, Alemar-Phoenix, pp. 204–262.

Cooley, F.L. (1962) *Ambonese Adat: A General Description*, New Haven, CT, Yale University Southeast Asia Studies.

Cooper, Robert G. (1978) 'Poly-ethnic systems analysis; the relevance of Leach's *Political Systems* to the ethnography of Northern Thailand and Laos', *Journal of Sociology and Psychology*, 1: 56–64.

Cramb, R.A. (1989) 'Shifting cultivation and resource degradation in Sarawak: perceptions and policies', *Borneo Research Bulletin*, 21: 22–49.

Crystal, Eric (1989) 'Tourism in Toraja (Sulawesi, Indonesia)', in Valene L. Smith (ed.),

331

Hosts and Guests: The Anthropology of Tourism, Philadelphia, PA, University of Pennsylvania Press, pp. 139–168.

Cunningham, Clark E. (1958) *The Postwar Migration of the Toba-Bataks to East Sumatra*, New Haven, CT, Yale University Press, Southeast Asia Series, Cultural Report Series No. 5.

Cunningham, Clark E. (1973) 'Order in the Atoni house', in Rodney Needham (ed.), *Right and Left: Essays in Dual Symbolic Classification*, Chicago and London, The University of Chicago Press, pp. 204–238 (originally published in 1964)

Dalby, Andrew (1995) 'J.G. Scott (1851–1935): explorer of Burma's eastern borders', in Victor T. King (ed.), *Explorers of South-East Asia: Six Lives*, Kuala Lumpur, Oxford University Press, pp. 108–157.

Davis, William G. and Hollnsteiner, Mary R. (1969) 'Some recent trends in Philippine social anthropology', *Anthropologica*, ns 11: 59–84.

De Koninck, Rodolphe (1994) *L'Asie du Sud-Est*, Paris, Masson.

Dentan, Robert Knox (1968) *The Semai: A Nonviolent People of Malaya*, New York, Holt, Rinehart and Winston.

Dentan, Robert Knox (1975) 'If there were no Malays who would the Semai be?', in Judith A. Nagata (ed.), *Pluralism in Malaysia: Myth and Reality*, Leiden, E.J. Brill, pp. 50–64.

Dentan, Robert Knox (1976) 'Ethnics and ethics in Southeast Asia', in David J. Banks (ed.), *Changing Identities in Modern Southeast Asia*, The Hague, Paris, Mouton Publishers, pp. 71–81.

Dentan, Robert Knox (1997) 'The persistence of received truth: how the Malaysian ruling class constructs the Orang Asli', in Robert L. Winzeler (ed.), *Indigenous Peoples and the State: Politics, Land, and Ethnicity in the Malaysian Peninsula and Borneo*, New Haven, CT, Yale University Press, pp. 98–134.

Dewey, Alice G. (1962) *Peasant Marketing in Java*, New York, The Free Press of Glencoe.

DeYoung, John E. (1955) *Village Life in Modern Thailand*, Berkeley, CA, University of California Press.

Diamond, Stanley (1980) 'Introduction: Anthropological traditions: the participants observed', in Stanley Diamond (ed.), *Anthropology: Ancestors and Heirs*, The Hague, Mouton, pp. 1–16.

Dijk, Miene Pieter van (1986) 'Formalization and informalization processes in a small town in Central Java', in Peter J.M. Nas (ed.), *The Indonesian City: Studies in Urban Development and Planning*, Dordrecht and Cinnaminson, Foris Publications, Verhandelingen van het Koninklijk Instituut voor Taal-, Land- en Volkenkunde, pp. 237–249.

Diposiswoyo, Mudiyono (1985) 'Tradition et changement social: étude ethnographique des Taman de Kalimantan Ouest', unpublished PhD dissertation, Paris, Ecole des Hautes Etudes en Sciences Sociales.

Djamour, Judith (1959) *Malay Kinship and Marriage in Singapore*, London, The Athlone Press.

Djamour, Judith (1966) *The Muslim Matrimonial Court in Singapore*, London, The Athlone Press.

Dournes, Jacques (1972) *Coordonnées: structures Jörai familiales et sociales*, Paris, Institut d'Ethnologie.

Dournes, Jacques (1977) *Pötao: une théorie de pouvoir chez les Indochinois Jörai*, Paris, Flammarion.

Dournes, Jacques (1980) *Minorities of Central Vietnam: Autochthonous Indochinese Peoples* (translation by Mark Goetzke, Stephen Headley and Stephen Varro), London, Minority Rights Group Report No. 18.

Dove, Michael R. (1983) 'Theories of swidden agriculture and the political economy of ignorance', *Agroforestry Systems*, 1: 85–99.

Dove, Michael R. (1985) *Swidden Agriculture in Indonesia: The Subsistence Strategies of the Kalimantan Kantu'*, Berlin, Mouton Publishers.

Dove, Michael R. (1993a) 'Smallholder rubber and swidden agriculture in Borneo: a sustainable adaptation to the ecology and economy of the tropical rainforest', *Economic Botany*, 47: 36–47.

Dove, Michael R. (1993b) 'Uncertainty, humility, and adaptation in the tropical rainforest: the agricultural augury of the Kantu', *Ethnology*, 32: 145–167.

Downs, R.E. ([1955] 1977) 'Head-hunting in Indonesia', in P.E. de Josselin de Jong (ed.), *Structural Anthropology in the Netherlands: A Reader*, The Hague, Martinus Nijhoff, Koninklijk Instituut voor Taal-, Land- en Volkenkunde, translation series 17, pp. 116–149.

Downs, R.E. (1956) *The Religion of the Bare'e-speaking Toradja of Central Celebes*, 's-Gravenhage: Uitgeverij Excelsior, PhD thesis, University of Leiden.

Dozier, Edward P. (1966) *Mountain Arbiters: The Changing Life of a Philippine Hill People*, Tucson, AZ, University of Arizona Press.

Dozier, Edward P. (1967) *The Kalinga of Northern Luzon, Philippines*, New York, Holt, Rinehart and Winston.

Driver, Harold Edson and Massey, William C. (1957) *Comparative Studies of North American Indians*. Philadelphia, American Philosophical Society, Transactions, n.s. vol. 47, pt. 2.

Du Bois, Cora (1944) *The People of Alor: A Social-Psychological Study of an East Indian Island* (with analyses by A. Kardiner and E. Oberholzer), Minneapolis, University of Minnesota Press, reprint New York, Harper Torchbooks, 1961, 2 vols.

Du Bois, Cora (1964) *Social Forces in Southeast Asia*, Cambridge, MA, Harvard University Press, second printing, first published 1949, University of Minnesota.

Dumont, Jean-Paul (1992) *Visayan Vignettes: Ethnographic Traces of a Philippine Island*, Chicago and London, University of Chicago Press, London, Cohen and West.

Dunn, Frederick L. (1975) *Rain-forest Collectors and Traders: A Study of Resource Utilization in Modern and Ancient Malaya*, Kuala Lumpur, Monographs of the Malaysian Branch of the Royal Asiatic Society, No. 5.

Durkheim, Emile ([1912] 1995) *The Elementary Forms of the Religious Life*, (transl. Karen E. Fields), New York, The Free Press.

Durkheim, Emile and Mauss, Marcel ([1903] 1963) *Primitive Classification* (ed. and transl. Rodney Needham), Chicago, The University of Chicago Press, London, Cohen and West.

Durrans, Brian (1988) 'Introduction', in Charles Hose, *Natural Man: A Record from Borneo* [1926], Singapore, Oxford University Press, reprint, pp. vii–xvi.

Duyvendak, J.P. (1935) *Inleiding tot de Ethnologie de Indische Archipel*, Groningen, Batavia, J.B. Wolters.

Eder, James F. (1996) 'Batak foraging camps today: a window to the history of a hunting–gathering economy', in Daniel G. Bates and Susan H. Lees (eds), *Case Studies in Human Ecology*, New York and London, Plenum Press, pp. 85–102.

Eggan, Fred (1941) 'Some aspects of culture change in the northern Philippines', *American Anthropologist*, 43: 11–18.

Eggan, Fred (1954) 'Social anthropology and the method of controlled comparison', *American Anthropologist*, 56: 743–763.

Eggan, Fred (1960) 'The Sagada Igorots of Northern Luzon', in George Peter Murdock (ed.), *Social Structure in Southeast Asia*, Chicago, Quadrangle Books, pp. 24–50.

Eggan, Fred (1967) 'Some aspects of bilateral social systems in the northern Philippines', in Mario D. Zamora (ed.), *Studies in Philippine Anthropology: In Honor of H. Otley Beyer*, Quezon City, Alemar-Phoenix, pp. 186–203.

Eggan, Fred (1974) 'Applied anthropology in the Mountain Province, Philippines', in Robert J. Smith (ed.), *Social Organization and the Applications of Anthropology*, Ithaca, NY, Cornell University Press, pp. 196–209.

Ellen, Roy F. (1976) 'The development of anthropology and colonial policy in the Netherlands: 1800–1960', *Journal of the History of the Behavioral Sciences*, 12: 303–324.

Ellen, Roy F. (1978) *Nuaulu Settlement and Ecology: An Approach to the Environmental Relations of an Eastern Indonesian Community*, The Hague, Martinus Nijhoff, Verhandelingen van het Koninklijk Instituut voor Taal-, Land- en Volkenkunde, 83.

Ellen Roy F. (1979a) 'Introduction: anthropology, the environment and ecological systems', in P.C. Burnham and R.F. Ellen (eds), *Social and Ecological Systems*, London, Academic Press, pp. 1–17.

Ellen Roy F. (1979b) 'Sago subsistence and the trade in spices: a provisional model of ecological succession and imbalance in Moluccan history', in P.C. Burnham and R.F. Ellen (eds), *Social and Ecological Systems*, London, Academic Press, pp. 43–74.

Ellen Roy F. (1982) *Environment, Subsistence and System: The Ecology of Small-scale Social Formations*, Cambridge, Cambridge University Press.

Ellen Roy F. (1993) *The Cultural Relations of Classification: An Analysis of Nuaulu Animal Categories from Central Seram*, Cambridge, Cambridge University Press.

Elliott, Alan J.A. (1955) *Chinese Spirit-Medium Cults in Singapore*, London, Athlone Press.

Elson, R. (1978) *The Cultivation System and 'Agricultural Involution'*, Melbourne, Monash University, Centre for Southeast Asian Studies, Working Paper 14.

Elson, R. (1984) *Javanese Peasants and the Colonial Sugar Industry: Impact and Change in an East Java Residency, 1830–1940*, Singapore, Oxford University Press.

Embree, John F. (1950) 'Thailand, a loosely structured social system', *American Anthropologist*, 52: 181–193.

Emmerson, Donald K. (1984) '"Southeast Asia": what's in a name?', *Journal of Southeast Asian Studies*, 25: 1–21.

Endicott, Kirk Michael (1970) *An Analysis of Malay Magic*, Oxford, Clarendon Press.

Endicott, Kirk Michael (1979) *Batek Negrito Religion: The World-view and Rituals of a Hunting and Gathering People of Peninsular Malaysia*, Oxford, Clarendon Press.

Endicott, Kirk Michael (1984) 'The economy of the Batek of Malaysia: annual and historical perspectives', in Barry L. Isaac (ed.), *Research in Economic Anthropology*, Vol. 6, Greenwich, CT, JAI Press Inc., pp. 29–52.

Errington, Shelly (1990) 'Recasting sex, gender and power: a theoretical and regional overview', in Jane Monnig Atkinson and Shelly Errington (eds), *Power and Difference: Gender in Island Southeast Asia*, Stanford, CA, Stanford University Press, pp. 1–58.

Esterik, Penny van (1996) 'Introduction', in Penny van Esterik (ed.), *Women of Southeast Asia*, DeKalb, Northern Illinois University, Center for Southeast Asian Studies, Occasional Paper No. 17, pp. 1–12, first published 1982.

Evans, Grant (1993a) 'Introduction: Asia and the anthropological imagination', in Grant Evans (ed.), *Asia's Cultural Mosaic: An Anthropological Introduction*, New York, Prentice-Hall, pp. 1–29.

Evans, Grant (ed.) (1993b) *Asia's Cultural Mosaic: An Anthropological Introduction*, New York, Prentice-Hall

Evans, Grant (1999) 'What is Lao culture and society?', in Grant Evans (ed.), *Laos: Culture and Society*, Chiang Mai, Silkworm Books, pp. 1–34.

Evans, Grant, Hutton, Christopher and Eng, Kuah Khun (eds) (2000) *Where China Meets Southeast Asia: Social and Cultural Change in the Border Regions*, Singapore, Institute of Southeast Asian Studies.

Evans, I.H.N. (1922) *Among Primitive Peoples in Borneo*, London, Seeley Service, reprint 1990, Singapore, Oxford University Press.

Evans, I.H.N. (1937) *The Negritos of Malaya*, Cambridge, Cambridge University Press, reprint, 1968, London, Frank Cass.

Evans, I.H.N. (1953) *The Religion of the Tempasuk Dusuns of North Borneo*, Cambridge, Cambridge University Press.

Evans-Pritchard, E.E. (1960) 'Introduction', in Robert Hertz, *Death and the Right Hand* (transl. Rodney and Claudia Needham), London, Cohen and West, pp. 9–24.

Evans-Pritchard, E.E. (1962) *Social Anthropology and Other Essays*, New York, The Free Press, London, Faber and Faber.

Evers, Hans-Dieter (ed.) (1969) *Loosely Structured Social Systems: Thailand in Comparative Perspective*, New Haven, CT, Yale University Press.

Evers, Hans-Dieter (ed.) (1980a) *Sociology of South-East Asia: Readings on Social Change and Development*, Kuala Lumpur, Oxford University Press.

Evers, Hans-Dieter (1980b) 'The challenge of diversity: basic concepts and theories in the study of South-East Asian societies', in Hans-Dieter Evers (ed.), *Sociology of South-East Asia: Readings on Social Change and Development*, Kuala Lumpur, Oxford University Press, pp. 2–7.

Eviota, Elizabeth Uy (1992) *The Political Economy of Gender: Women and the Sexual Division of Labour in the Philippines*, London, Zed Books.

Fegan, Brian (1989) 'Accumulation on the basis of an unprofitable crop', in Gillian Hart, Andrew Turton and Benjamin White (eds), *Agrarian Transformations: Local Processes and the State in Southeast Asia*, Berkeley and Los Angeles, CA, University of California Press, pp. 159–178.

Feldman, K.D. (1973) 'Squatters and squatting in Davao City, the Philippines: the dynamics of an adaptive institution in the urbanization process of a developing country', unpublished PhD thesis, University of Colorado.

Firth, Raymond (1948) *Report on Social Science Research in Malaya*, Singapore, Government Printing Office.

Firth, Raymond (1966) *Malay Fishermen: Their Peasant Economy*, London, Routledge and Kegan Paul, second edition, first published 1946.

Firth, Raymond (1967) 'Themes in economic anthropology: a general comment', in Raymond Firth (ed.), *Themes in Economic Anthropology*, London, Tavistock Publications, pp. 1–28.

Firth, Raymond (1970) 'Foreword', in E.R. Leach, *Political Systems of Highland Burma: A Study of Kachin Social Structure*, London, The Athlone Press, LSE Monographs on Social Anthropology, No. 44 (reprint, originally published 1954 by G. Bell and Son), pp. v–viii.

Firth, Raymond (1975) 'The sceptical anthropologist? Social anthropology and Marxist views on society', in Maurice Bloch (ed.), *Marxist Analyses and Social Anthropology*, London, Malaby Press, pp. 29–60.

Firth, Rosemary (1966) *Housekeeping among Malay Peasants*, second edition, London, The Athlone Press, first published 1943.

Firth, Rosemary (1995) 'Prologue: a woman looks back on the anthropology of women and feminist anthropology', in Wazir Jahan Karim (ed.), *'Male' and 'Female' in Developing Southeast Asia*, Oxford, Berg, pp. 3–10.

Fisher, Charles (1962) 'South East Asia: the Balkans of the Orient?', *Geography*, 47: 347–367.

Fisher, Charles (1964) *South-East Asia: A Social, Economic and Political Geography*, London, Methuen.

Ford, Nicholas J. and Kittisuksathit, Sirinan (1995) 'Sexuality and gender of Thai youth', unpublished paper, ASEASUK conference, University of Durham, March.

Fox, James J. (1971a) 'Semantic parallelism in Rotinese ritual language', *Bijdragen tot de Taal-, Land- en Volkenkunde*, 127: 215–255.

Fox, James, J. (1971b) 'Sister's child as plant: metaphors in an idiom of consanguinity', in Rodney Needham (ed.), *Rethinking Kinship and Marriage*, London, Tavistock Publications, pp. 219–252.

Fox, James J. (1973) 'On bad death and the left hand: a study of Rotinese symbolic inversions', in Rodney Needham (ed.), *Right and Left: Essays in Dual Symbolic Classification*, Chicago and London, The University of Chicago Press, pp. 342–368.

Fox, James J. (1977) *Harvest of the Palm: Ecological Change in Eastern Indonesia*, Cambridge, MA and London, Harvard University Press.

Fox, James J. (1979) 'A tale of two states: ecology and the political economy of inequality on the island of Roti', in P.C. Burnham and R.F. Ellen (eds), *Social and Ecological Systems*, London, Academic Press, pp. 19–42.

Fox, James J. (ed.) (1980) *The Flow of Life: Essays on Eastern Indonesia*, Cambridge, MA and London, Harvard University Press.

Fox, James J. (ed.) (1997) *The Poetic Power of Place: Perspectives on Austronesian Ideas of Locality*, Canberra, Australian National University, Department of Anthropology, Research School of Pacific and Asian Studies.

Fox, James J. and Sather, Clifford (eds) (1996) *Origins, Ancestry and Alliance: Explorations in Austronesian Ethnography*, Canberra, Australian National University, Department of Anthropology, Research School of Pacific and Asian Studies.

Frake, Charles O. (1955) 'Social organization and shifting cultivation among the Sindangan Subanun', unpublished PhD dissertation, Yale University.

Frake, Charles O. (1962) 'Cultural ecology and ethnography', *American Anthropologist*, 64: 53–59.

Frake, Charles O. (1980) *Language and Cultural Description: Essays by Charles O. Frake*, selected and introduced by Anwar S. Dil, Stanford, CA, Stanford University Press.

Frank, André Gunder (1967) *Capitalism and Underdevelopment in Latin America*, New York, The Monthly Review.

Fraser, Thomas M. (1960) *Rusembilan: A Malay Fishing Village in Southern Thailand*, Ithaca, NY, Cornell University Press.

Fraser, Thomas M. (1966) *Fishermen of South Thailand: The Malay Villagers*, New York, Holt, Rinehart and Winston.

Freedman, Maurice (1957) *Chinese Family and Marriage in Singapore*, London, HMSO.

Freedman, Maurice (1959) 'The handling of money: a note on the background to the economic sophistication of Overseas Chinese', *Man*, 59: 64–65.

Freedman, Maurice (1960) 'The growth of a plural society in Malaya', *Pacific Affairs*, 33: 158–168.

Freedman, Maurice (1961) 'Immigrants and associations: the Chinese in 19th century Singapore', *Comparative Studies in Society and History*, 3: 25–48.

Freedman, Maurice (1962) 'Chinese kinship and marriage in early Singapore', *Journal of Southeast Asian History*, 3: 65–73.

Freeman, J.D. (Derek) ([1955a] 1970) *Report on the Iban of Sarawak*, Kuching, Government Printing Office, reprinted as *Report on the Iban*, London, Athlone Press.

Freeman, J.D. (Derek) (1955b) *Iban Agriculture: A Report on the Shifting Cultivation of Hill Rice by the Iban of Sarawak*, London, HMSO.

Freeman, J.D. (Derek) (1960) 'The Iban of Western Borneo', in George Peter Murdock (ed.), *Social Structure in Southeast Asia*, Chicago, Quadrangle Books, pp. 65–87.

Fried, Morton H. (1968) 'On the concepts of "tribe" and "tribal society"', in June Helm (ed.), *Essays on the Problem of Tribe*, Seattle, University of Washington Press, The American Ethnological Society, pp. 3–20.

Friedl, Ernestine (1978) *Women and Men: An Anthropological View*, New York, Holt, Rinehart and Winston.

Friedman, Jonathan ([1979] 1998) *System, Structure, and Contradiction: The Evolution of "Asiatic" Social Formations*, Copenhagen, Nationalmuset; second edition, Walnut Creek, CA, AltaMira Press.

Friedman, Jonathan (1987) 'Generalized change, theocracy, and the opium trade', *Critique of Anthropology*, 7: 15–31.

Furnivall, J.S. (1939) *Netherlands India: A Study of Plural Economy*, Cambridge, Cambridge University Press.

Furnivall, J.S. (1956) *Colonial Policy and Practice: A Comparative Study of Burma and Netherlands India*, New York, New York University Press, first published 1948, Cambridge University Press.

Furnivall, J.S. (1980) 'Plural societies', in Hans-Dieter Evers (ed.), *Sociology of South-East Asia: Readings on Social Change and Development*, Kuala Lumpur, Oxford University Press, pp. 86–96.

Garfinkel, Harold (1967) 'Passing and the managed achievement of sex status in an "intersexed" person, Part 1' (in collaboration with Robert J. Stoller), in H. Garfinkel, *Studies in Ethnomethodology*, Englewood Cliffs, NJ, Prentice-Hall, pp. 116–185 (and Appendix, pp. 285–288)

Geddes, W.R. (1954) *The Land Dayaks of Sarawak: a Report on the Social-Economic Survey of the Land Dayaks of Sarawak presented to the Colonial Social Science Research Council*, London, HMSO.

Geddes, W.R. (1976) *Migrants of the Mountains: The Cultural Ecology of the Blue Miao (Hmong Njua) of Thailand*, Oxford, Clarendon Press.

Geertz, Clifford (1956) *The Development of the Javanese Economy: A Socio-cultural Approach*, Cambridge, MA, MIT Center for International Studies.

Geertz, Clifford (1959) 'Form and variation in Balinese village structure', *American Anthropologist*, 61: 991–1012.

Geertz, Clifford (1960) *The Religion of Java*, New York, The Free Press of Glencoe.

Geertz, Clifford (1961) 'Review of *Bali, Studies in Life, Thought and Ritual*', *Bijdragen tot de Taal-, Land- en Volkenkunde*, 117: 498–502.

Geertz, Clifford (1963a) *Agricultural Involution: The Processes of Ecological Change in Indonesia*, Berkeley and Los Angeles, CA, University of California Press.

Geertz, Clifford (1963b) *Peddlers and Princes: Social Development and Economic Change in Two Indonesian Towns*, Chicago and London, University of Chicago Press.

Geertz, Clifford (ed.) (1963c) *Old Societies and New States*, New York, Free Press.

Geertz, Clifford (1965) *The Social History of an Indonesian Town*, Cambridge, MA, MIT Press.

Geertz, Clifford (1967a) 'Tihingan: a Balinese village', in Koentjaraningrat (ed.), *Villages in Indonesia*, Ithaca, NY, Cornell University Press, pp. 210–243.

Geertz, Clifford (1967b) 'The cerebral savage: the structural anthropology of Claude Lévi-Strauss', *Encounter*, April: 25–32.

Geertz, Clifford (1968) *Islam Observed: Religious Development in Morocco and Indonesia*, Chicago and London, University of Chicago Press.

Geertz, Clifford (1973) *The Interpretation of Cultures: Selected Essays*, New York, Basic Books.

Geertz, Clifford (1980) *Negara: The Theatre State in Nineteenth-century Bali*, Princeton, NJ, Princeton University Press.

Geertz, Clifford (1983) *Local Knowledge: Further Essays in Interpretive Anthropology*, New York, Basic Books.

Geertz, Clifford (1984) 'Culture and social change: the Indonesian case', *Man*, 19: 511–532.

Geertz, Clifford and Geertz, Hildred (1975) *Kinship in Bali*, Chicago, Chicago University Press.

Geertz, Hildred (1961a) *The Javanese Family: A Study of Kinship and Socialization*, New York, The Free Press of Glencoe.

Geertz, Hildred (1961b) 'Review of *Bali, Studies in Life, Thought and Ritual*', *Journal of Asian Studies*, 20: 391–392.

Geertz, Hildred (1965) 'Comment', *Journal of Asian Studies*, 24: 294–297.

Gennep, Arnold van (1960) *The Rites of Passage*, transl. M.B. Vizedom and G.L. Caffee, London, Routledge and Kegan Paul, first published 1908.

Gianno, Rosemary (1990) *Semelai Culture and Resin Technology*, New Haven, CT, Connecticut Academy of Arts and Sciences.

Goethals, P.R. (1961) *Aspects of Local Government in a Sumbawan Village (Eastern Indonesia)*, Ithaca, NY, Cornell University, Modern Indonesia Project, Monograph Series.

Gombrich, Richard (1972) 'Review of *Burmese Supernaturalism* and *Buddhism and Society*', *Modern Asian Studies*, 6: 483–494.

Goody, Jack (1977) *The Domestication of the Savage Mind*, Cambridge, Cambridge University Press.

Gough, Kathleen (1968) *Anthropology: Child of Imperialism*, London, SOAS, Third World Study Group, reprint from *Monthly Review*.

Guilleminet, Paul (1952) *Coutumier de la Tribu Bahnar, des Sedang et des Jarai de la Province de Kontum*, Hanoi, Ecole Française d'Extrême-Orient.

Gullick, John M. (1958) *Indigenous Political Systems of Western Malaya*, London, The Athlone Press, second edition, 1988.

Guthrie, George M. (1961) *The Filipino Child and Philippine Society*, Manila, Philippine Normal College Press.

Guthrie, George M. and Jacobs, P.J. (1966) *Child Rearing and Personality Development in the Philippines*, Pennsylvania, Pennsylvania State University Press.

Haddon, Alfred C. (1932) *Headhunters: Black, White and Brown*, London, Watts, abridged edition.

Haddon, Alfred C. and Start, Laura E. (1936) *Iban or Sea Dayak Fabrics and their Patterns*, Cambridge, Cambridge University Press.

Halim Hj. Salleh (1981) *Bureaucrats, Petty Bourgeois and Townsmen: An Observation on Status Identification in Kota Bharu*, Monash University, Centre of Southeast Asian Studies.

Halpern, Joel (1964) *Economy and Society of Laos: A Brief Survey*, New Haven, CT, Yale University Press.

Hanks, Lucien M. (1962) 'Merit and power in the Thai social order', *American Anthropologist*, 64: 1247–1261.

Hanks, Lucien M. (1972) *Rice and Man: Agricultural Ecology in Southeast Asia*, Chicago, Aldine-Atherton.

Hanks, Lucien M. (1975) 'The Thai social order as entourage and circle', in G. William Skinner and A. Thomas Kirsch (eds), *Change and Persistence in Thai Society: Essays in Honour of Lauriston Sharp*, Ithaca, NY, and London, Cornell University Press, pp. 197–218.

Hanks, Lucien M. and Hanks, Jane Richardson (1963) 'Thailand: equality between the sexes', in Barbara E. Ward (ed.), *Women in the New Asia: The Changing Roles of Men and Women in South and South-East Asia*, Paris, UNESCO, pp. 424–451.

Harmand, J. (1882) 'Les races Indochinoises', *Mémoires de la Société d'Anthropologie de Paris*, 2 (second series): 314–368.

Harrell, Stevan (1997) *Human Families*, Boulder, CO, Westview Press.

Hart, Donn V. (1954) 'Barrio Caticugan: a Visayan Filipino community', unpublished PhD dissertation, Syracuse University.

Hart, Donn V. (1977) *Compadrinazgo: Ritual Kinship in the Philippines*, DeKalb, Northern Illinois University Press.

Hart, Gillian (1986) *Power, Labor and Livelihood: Processes of Change in Rural Java*, Berkeley, Los Angeles, CA, University of California Press.

Hart, Gillian (1989) 'Agrarian change in the context of state patronage', in Gillian Hart, Andrew Turton and Benjamin White (eds), *Agrarian Transformations: Local Processes and the State in Southeast Asia*, Berkeley and Los Angeles, CA, University of California Press, pp. 31–49.

Hart, Gillian, Turton, Andrew and White, Benjamin (eds), with Brian Fegan and Lim Teck Ghee (1989) *Agrarian Transformations: Local Processes and the State in Southeast Asia*, Berkeley and Los Angeles, CA, University of California Press.

Hefner, Robert W. (1985) *Hindu Javanese: Tengger Tradition and Islam*, Princeton, NJ, Princeton University Press.

Hefner, Robert W. (1990) *The Political Economy of Mountain Java: An Interpretive History*, Berkeley and Los Angeles, CA, University of California Press.

Heine-Geldern, Robert von (1923) 'Südostasien', in Georg Buschan (ed.), *Australien und Ozeanien Asien, Illustrierte Völkerkunde*, vol. II, Stuttgart, Strecker and Schroder, pp. 689–968.

Heine-Geldern, Robert von (1928) 'Die Megalithen Südostasiens und ihre Bedeutung für die Klärung der Megalithenfrage in Europa und Polynesien', *Anthropos*, 23: 276–315.

Heine-Geldern, Robert von (1932) 'Urheimat und früheste Wanderungen der Austronesier', *Anthropos*, 27: 543–619.

Heine-Geldern, Robert von (1935) 'The archaeology and art of Sumatra', in Edwin M. Loeb, *Sumatra: Its History and People*, Vienna, Institut für Völkerkunde, pp. 305–331.

Heine-Geldern, Robert von (1963) *Conceptions of State and Kingship in Southeast Asia*, Ithaca, NY, Department of Asian Studies, Cornell University, Southeast Asia Program, Data Paper No. 18, originally published in *The Far Eastern Quarterly*, 1942, 2: 15–30.

Heine-Geldern, Robert von (1965) 'Some tribal art styles of Southeast Asia: an experiment in art history', in Douglas Fraser (ed.), *The Many Faces of Primitive Art*, Englewood Cliffs, NJ, Prentice-Hall, pp. 165–221.

Held, G.J. (1935) *The Mahabharata: An Ethnological Study*, London, Kegan Paul, Trench, Trubner.

Helliwell, Christine (1993) 'Women in Asia: anthropology and the study of women', in Grant Evans (ed.), *Asia's Cultural Mosaic: An Anthropological Introduction*, New York, Prentice-Hall, pp. 260–286.

Hertz, Robert (1960) *Death and the Right Hand* (transl. Rodney and Claudia Needham), London, Cohen and West, essays first published 1907–1909.

Heyzer, Noeleen (1986) *Working Women in Southeast Asia: Development, Subordination and Emancipation*, Stratford, Open University Press.

Hickey, Gerald Cannon (1964) *Village in Vietnam*, New Haven, CT, and London: Yale University Press.

Hickey, Gerald Cannon (1982a) *Sons of the Mountains: Ethnohistory of the Vietnamese Central Highlands to 1954*, New Haven, CT, and London, Yale University Press.

Hickey, Gerald Cannon (1982b) *Free in the Forest: Ethnohistory of the Vietnamese Central Highlands 1954–1976*, New Haven, CT, and London, Yale University Press.

Hickey, Gerald Cannon (1993) *Shattered World: Adaptation and Survival among Vietnam's Highland Peoples during the Vietnam War*, Philadelphia, University of Pennsylvania Press.

Higgins, Benjamin (1963) 'Foreword', in Clifford Geertz, *Agricultural Involution: The Processes of Ecological Change in Indonesia*, Berkeley and Los Angeles, CA, University of California Press, pp. vii–xv.

Higgott, R. and R. Robison (eds) (1985) *Southeast Asia: Essays in the Political Economy of Structural Change*, London, Routledge and Kegan Paul.

Hirschman, Charles (1992) 'The state of Southeast Asian Studies in American universities', in Charles Hirschman, Charles F. Keyes and Karl Hutterer (eds), *Southeast Asian Studies in the Balance: Reflections from America*, Ann Arbor, MI, The Association for Asian Studies, pp. 41–58.

Hitchcock, Michael and King, Victor T. (1997) 'Introduction: Malay–Indonesian identities', in Michael Hitchcock and Victor T. King (eds), *Images of Malay–Indonesian Identity*, Kuala Lumpur, Oxford University Press, pp. 1–17.

Hobsbawm, E. (1983) 'Introduction: inventing traditions', in E. Hobsbawm and T.O. Ranger (eds), *The Invention of Tradition*, Cambridge, Cambridge University Press, pp. 1–14.

Hocart, Arthur Maurice (1970) *Kings and Councillors: An Essay in the Comparative Anatomy of Human Society*, Chicago, Chicago University Press, Classics in Anthropology (originally published Cairo: Barbey, 1936)

Hoffman, C.L. (1986) *The Punan: Hunters and Gatherers of Borneo*. Ann Arbor, MI, UMI Research Press.

Hollnsteiner, Mary (1963) *The Dynamics of Power in a Philippine Municipality*, Quezon City, Community Development Research Council.

Holtzappel, Coen (1997) ' Nationalism and cultural identity', in Michael Hitchcock and

Victor T. King, *Images of Malay–Indonesian Identity*, Kuala Lumpur, Oxford University Press, pp. 63–107.

Homans, George Caspar and Schneider, David Murray (1955) *Marriage, Authority, and Final Causes: A Study of Unilateral Cross-Cousin Marriage*, Glencoe, ILL, Free Press; republished in G.C. Homans, *Sentiments and Activities: Essays in Social Science*, London: Routledge, 1962, Chapter 14 (pp. 202–256, notes on pp. 311–315)

Hooykaas, Christiaan (1974) *Cosmogony and Creation in Balinese Tradition*, The Hague: Martinus Nijhoff, Koninklijk Instituut voor Taal-, Land- en Volkenkunde, Bibliotheca Indonesica 9.

Hose, Charles (1926) *Natural Man: A Record from Borneo*, London, Macmillan.

Hose, Charles (1927) *Fifty Years of Romance and Research or a Jungle-Wallah at Large*, London, Hutchinson.

Hose, Charles and McDougall, William (1912) *The Pagan Tribes of Borneo*, London, Macmillan, 2 vols, reprint, London, Frank Cass, 1966.

Howell, Signe (1989) *Society and Cosmos: Chewong of Peninsular Malaysia*, Chicago and London, University of Chicago Press, first published 1984, Singapore, Oxford University Press.

Hudson, A.B. (1972) *Padju Epat: The Ma'anyan of Indonesian Borneo*, New York, Holt, Rinehart and Winston.

Hunt, Chester L. and Dizon, Dylan (1978) 'The development of Philippine sociology', in Donn V. Hart (ed.), *Philippine Studies: History, Sociology, Mass Media and Bibliography*, Northern Illinois University, Centre for Southeast Asian Studies, Occasional Paper 6, pp. 98–232.

Huntington, Richard and Metcalf, Peter (1979) *Celebrations of Death: The Anthropology of Mortuary Ritual*, Cambridge, Cambridge University Press, second edition, revised 1991.

Hurgronje, C. Snouck (1906) *The Achehnese*, transl. A.W.S. O'Sullivan, Leiden, E.J. Brill, 2 vols, first published as *De Atjèhers*, 1893–1894.

Husin Ali, S. (1964) *Social Stratification in Kampong Bagan: A Study of Class, Status, Conflict and Mobility in a Rural Malay Community*, Singapore, Malaysian Branch, Royal Asiatic Society.

Husin Ali, S. (1975) *Malay Peasant Society and Leadership*, Kuala Lumpur, Oxford University Press.

Hüsken, F. (1979) 'Landlords, sharecroppers and agricultural labourers: changing labour relations in rural Java', *Journal of Contemporary Asia*, 9: 140–151.

Hutton, J.H. (1921a) *The Angami Nagas*, London, Macmillan.

Hutton, J.H. (1921b) *The Sema Nagas*, London, Macmillan.

Huxley, Tim (1996) 'International relations', in Mohammed Halib and Tim Huxley (eds), *An Introduction to Southeast Asian Studies*, London, I.B. Tauris Publishers, pp. 224–246.

Illo, Jean Frances (1995) 'Redefining the *maybahay* or housewife: reflections on the nature of women's work in the Philippines', in Wazir Jahan Karim (ed.), *'Male' and 'Female' in Developing Southeast Asia*, Oxford, Berg, pp. 209–225.

Inglis, Fred (2000) *Clifford Geertz: Culture, Custom and Ethics*, Cambridge, Polity Press.

Iwabuchi, Akifumi (1994) *The People of the Alas Valley: A Study of an Ethnic Group of Northern Sumatra*, Oxford, Clarendon Press.

Jackson, Peter A. (1999) 'Review of Mark Johnson, *Beauty and Power*', *Journal of Asian Studies*, 58: 894–896.

Janlekha, Kamol Odd (1957) *A Study of the Economy of a Rice Growing Village in Central Thailand*, Bangkok, Division of Agricultural Economics, Ministry of Agriculture.

Jay, Robert R. (1969) *Javanese Villagers*, Cambridge, MA, The MIT Press.

Jellinek, Lea (1991) *The Wheel of Fortune: The History of a Poor Community in Jakarta*, Sydney, Allen and Unwin for Asian Studies Association of Australia.

Jenks, A.E. (1905) *The Bontoc Igorot*, Manila, Bureau of Printing.

Jensen, Erik (1974) *The Iban and their Religion*, Oxford, Clarendon Press.

Jocano F. Landa (1968) *Sulod Society: A Study in the Kinship System and Social Organization of a Mountain People of Central Panay*, Quezon City, University of the Philippines Press.

Jocano, F. Landa (1969a) *Growing Up in a Philippine Barrio*, New York, Holt, Rinehart and Winston.

Jocano, F. Landa (1969b) *The Traditional World of Malitbog*, Quezon City, Community Development Research Council.

Jocano, F. Landa (1973) *Folk Medicine in a Philippine Municipality: An Analysis of the System of Folk Healing in Bay, Laguna, and its Implications for the Introduction of Modern Medicine*, Manila, The National Museum.

Jocano, F. Landa (1975) *Slum as a Way of Life: A Study of Coping Behavior in an Urban Environment*, Quezon City, University of the Philippines Press.

Johnson, Mark (1997) *Beauty and Power: Transgendering and Cultural Transformation in the Southern Philippines*, Oxford, New York, Berg.

Jones, Gavin W. (1994) *Marriage and Divorce in Islamic South-East Asia*, Kuala Lumpur, Oxford University Press.

Josselin de Jong, J.P.B. de ([1935] 1977) *De Maleische Archipel als Ethnologisch Studieveld*, Leiden, J. Ginsberg, reprinted as 'The Malay Archipelago as a field of ethnological study', in P.E. de Josselin de Jong (ed.), *Structural Anthropology in the Netherlands: A Reader*, The Hague, Martinus Nijhoff, Koninklijk Instituut voor Taal-, Land- en Volkenkunde, pp. 166–182.

Josselin de Jong, J.P.B. de (1977) 'Lévi-Strauss' theory on kinship and marriage', in P.E. de Josselin de Jong (ed.), *Structural Anthropology in the Netherlands. A Reader*, The Hague, Martinus Nijhoff, Koninklijk Instituut voor Taal-, Land- en Volkenkunde, pp. 253–319; originally published in 1952.

Josselin de Jong, P.E. de (1951) *Minangkabau and Negri Sembilan: Socio-political Structure in Indonesia*, Leiden, Eduard Ydo.

Josselin de Jong, P.E. de (1965) 'An interpretation of agricultural rites in Southeast Asia, with a demonstration of use of data from both continental and insular areas' and 'Reply to Professor Geertz', *Journal of Asian Studies*, 24: 283–291, 297–298.

Josselin de Jong, P.E. de (1977) 'Introduction: structural anthropology in the Netherlands: creature of circumstance', in P.E. de Josselin de Jong (ed.), *Structural Anthropology in the Netherlands: A Reader*, The Hague, Martinus Nijhoff, Koninklijk Instituut voor Taal-, Land- en Volkenkunde, pp. 1–29.

Josselin de Jong, P.E. de (ed.) (1984) *Unity in Diversity: Indonesia as a Field of Anthropological Study*, Dordrecht-Cinnaminson, Foris Publications, Verhandelingen van het Koninklijk Instituut voor Taal-, Land- en Volkenkunde, 103.

Kahn, Joel S. (1974) 'Imperialism and the reproduction of capitalism: towards a definition of the Indonesian social formation', *Critique of Anthropology*, 2: 1–35.

Kahn, Joel S. (1975) 'Economic scale and the cycle of petty commodity production in West Sumatra', in Maurice Bloch (ed.), *Marxist Analyses and Social Anthropology*, London, Malaby Press, pp. 137–158.

Kahn, Joel S. (1978) 'Ideology and social structure in Indonesia', *Comparative Studies in Society and History*, 20: 103–122.

Kahn, Joel S. (1980) *Minangkabau Social Formations: Indonesian Peasants and the World-Economy*, Cambridge, Cambridge University Press.

Kahn, Joel S. (1981) 'Mercantilism and the emergence of servile labour in colonial Indonesia', in Joel S. Kahn and Josep R. Llobera (eds), *The Anthropology of Pre-Capitalist Societies*, London and Basingstoke, Macmillan, pp. 185–213.

Kahn, Joel S. (1982) 'From peasants to petty commodity producers in Southeast Asia', *Bulletin of Concerned Asian Scholars*, 14: 3–15.

Kahn, Joel S. (1985) 'Indonesia after the demise of involution: critique of a debate', *Critique of Anthropology*, 5: 69–96.

Kahn, Joel S. (1992) 'Class, ethnicity and diversity: some remarks on Malay culture in Malaysia', in Joel S. Kahn and Francis Loh Kok Wah (eds), *Fragmented Vision: Culture and Politics in Contemporary Malaysia*, Sydney: Allen and Unwin, pp. 158–178.

Kahn, Joel S. (1993) *Constituting the Minangkabau: Peasants, Culture, and Modernity in Colonial Indonesia*, Providence, RI, and Oxford, Berg Publishers.

Kahn, Joel S. (1995) *Culture, Multiculture, Postculture*, London, Sage Publications.

Kahn, Joel S. (1997) 'Culturalizing Malaysia: globalism, tourism, heritage, and the city in Georgetown', in Michel Picard and Robert E. Wood (eds), *Tourism, Ethnicity, and the State in Asian and Pacific Societies*, Honolulu, University of Hawai'i Press, pp. 99–127.

Kahn, Joel S. (1998) 'Southeast Asian identities: Introduction', in Joel S. Kahn (ed.), *Southeast Asian Identities: Culture and the Politics of Representation in Indonesia, Malaysia, Singapore, and Thailand*, Singapore and London, Institute of Southeast Asian Studies, pp. 1–27.

Kahn, Joel S. and Llobera, Josep R. (1981) 'Towards a new Marxism or a new anthropology?', in Joel S. Kahn and Josep R. Llobera (eds), *The Anthropology of Pre-Capitalist Societies*, London and Basingstoke, Macmillan, pp. 263–329.

Kahn, Joel S. and Wah, Francis Loh Kok (eds) (1992) 'Introduction: fragmented vision', in Joel S. Kahn and Francis Loh Kok Wah (eds), *Fragmented Vision: Culture and Politics in Contemporary Malaysia*, Sydney, Allen and Unwin, pp. 1–17.

Kaufman, Howard Keva (1960) *Bangkhuad: A Community Study in Thailand*, Locust Valley, New York, J.J. Augustin.

Keesing, Felix M. (1962) *The Ethnohistory of Northern Luzon*, Stanford, CA, Stanford University Press.

Kemp, Jeremy (1989) 'Peasants and cities: the cultural and social image of the Thai peasant village community', *Sojourn*, 4: 6–19.

Kemp, Jeremy (1993) 'On the interpretation of Thai villages', in Philip Hirsch (ed.), *The Village in Perspective: Community and Locality in Rural Thailand*, Chiang Mai University, Social Research Institute, pp. 81–96.

Kerkvliet, Benedict J. (1977) *The Huk Rebellion: A Study of Peasant Revolt in the Philippines*, Berkeley and Los Angeles, CA, University of California Press.

Kessler, Clive S. (1992) 'Archaism and modernity: contemporary Malay political culture', in Joel S. Kahn and Francis Loh Kok Wah (eds), *Fragmented Vision: Culture and Politics in Contemporary Malaysia*, Sydney, Allen and Unwin, pp. 133–157.

Keyes, Charles F. (1977) *The Golden Peninsula: Culture and Adaptation in Mainland Southeast Asia*, New York, Macmillan, revised edition, 1995, Honolulu, University of Hawaii Press.

Keyes, Charles F. (1992) 'A conference at Wingspread and rethinking Southeast Asian Studies', in Charles Hirschman, Charles F. Keyes and Karl Hutterer (eds), *Southeast*

Asian Studies in the Balance: Reflections from America, Ann Arbor, MI, The Association for Asian Studies, pp. 9–24.

Kiefer, Thomas M. (1972) *The Tausug: Violence and Law in a Philippine Moslem Society*, New York, Holt, Rinehart and Winston.

King, Victor T. (1978) 'Moral economy and peasant uprisings in South-East Asia', *Cultures et développement*, 10: 123–149.

King, Victor T. (1981) 'Marxist analysis and Highland Burma: a critical commentary', *Cultures et développement*, 13: 675–688.

King, Victor T. (1983) 'Imaginary Kachins', *Man*, 18: 405–406.

King, Victor T (1985) *The Maloh of West Kalimantan: An Ethnographic Study of Social Inequality and Social Change among an Indonesian Borneo People*, Dordrecht-Cinnaminson, Foris Publications, Verhandelingen van het Koninklijk Instituut voor Taal-, Land- en Volkenkunde, 108.

King, Victor T. (1993) *The Peoples of Borneo*, Oxford, Blackwell.

King, Victor T. (1994) 'What is Brunei society? Reflections on a conceptual and ethnographic issue', *South East Asia Research*, 2: 176–198.

King, Victor T. (1996a) 'Reflections on the nature of Brunei society', *Janang. Warta Akademi Pengajian Brunei, Universiti Brunei Darussalam*, 6: 145–161.

King, Victor T. (1996b) 'Environmental change in Malaysian Borneo: fire, drought and rain', in Michael J.G. Parnwell and Raymond L. Bryant (eds.), *Environmental Change in South-East Asia: People, Politics and Sustainable Development*, London, Routledge, pp. 165–189.

King, Victor T. (1996c) 'Sociology', in Mohammed Halib and Tim Huxley (eds), *An Introduction to Southeast Asian Studies*, London, Tauris Academic Studies, pp. 148–188.

King, Victor T. (ed.) (1998) *Environmental Challenges in South-East Asia*, Richmond, Curzon Press.

King, Victor T. (1999) *Anthropology and Development in South-East Asia: Theory and Practice*, Kuala Lumpur, Oxford University Press.

King, Victor T. (2001a) 'A question of identity: names, societies, and ethnic groups in interior Kalimantan and Brunei Darussalam', *Sojourn*, 16: 1–37.

King, Victor T. (2001b) 'South-East Asia: an anthropological field of study?', *Moussons: Recherche en sciences humaines sur l'Asie du Sud-Est*, 3: 3–31.

King, Victor T. and Wilder, W.D. (1982) 'Southeast Asia and the concept of ethnicity', in Victor T. King and W.D. Wilder (eds), Special focus volume on *Ethnicity in Southeast Asia* in *Southeast Asian Journal of Social Science*, 10: 1–6.

Kingshill, Konrad ([1960] 1965) *Ku Daeng, The Red Tomb: A Village Study in Northern Thailand*, Bangkok, Bangkok Christian College, 2nd edition, revised 1965.

Kipp, Rita Smith (1993) *Dissociated Identities: Ethnicity, Religion, and Class in an Indonesian Society*, Ann Arbor, MI, University of Michigan Press.

Kirsch, A. Thomas (1965) *Notes on Thai Religion*, Ithaca, NY, Cornell University, Southeast Asia Program.

Kirsch, A. Thomas (1973) *Feasting and Social Oscillation: A Working Paper on Religion and Society in Upland Southeast Asia*, Ithaca, NY, Cornell University, Southeast Asia Program, Data Paper No. 92.

Kloos, Peter (1975) 'Anthropology and non-Western sociology in the Netherlands', in Peter Kloos and Henri J.M. Claessen (eds), *Current Anthropology in the Netherlands*, Rotterdam, Anthropological Branch of the Netherlands Sociological and Anthropological Society, pp. 10–29.

Knapen, Han (2001) *Forests of Fortune? The Environmental History of Southeast Borneo, 1600–1880*, Leiden, KITLV Press, Verhandelingen van het Koninklijk Instituut voor Taal-, Land- en Volkenkunde, 189.

Koentjaraningrat (1961) *Some Social-Anthropological Observations on Gotong Rojong Practices in Two Villages of Central Java*, Ithaca, NY, Cornell University Press.

Koentjaraningrat (ed.) (1967) *Villages in Indonesia*, Ithaca, NY, Cornell University Press.

Koentjaraningrat (1968) 'Javanese data on the unresolved problems of the kindred', *Ethnology*, 7: 53–58.

Koentjaraningrat (1975) *Anthropology in Indonesia: A Bibliographical Review*, The Hague, Martinus Nijhoff, Koninklijk Instituut voor Taal-, Land- en Volkenkunde.

Korn, V. (1924) *Het Adatrecht van Bali*, Den Haag, Martinus Nijhoff.

Korn, V. (1932) *Het Adatrecht van Bali*, Den Haag, G. Naeff, second revised edition.

Kroeber, A.L. (1928) *Peoples of the Philippines*, New York, American Museum of Natural History, second revised edition.

Kruyt, A.C. (1906) *Het Animisme in den Indischen Archipel*, The Hague, Martinus Nijhoff.

Kruyt, A.C. (1938) *De West-Toradjas op Midden Celebes*, Amsterdam, Verhandelingen der Koninklijke Nederlandsche Akademie van Wetenschappen, Afd. Letterkunde, 40.

Kuchiba, Masuo, Tsubouchi, Yoshihiro and Maeda, Narifumi (eds) (1979) *Three Malay Villages: A Sociology of Paddy Growers in West Malaysia*, trans. Peter and Stephanie Hawkes, Honolulu, The University Press of Hawaii.

Kunstadter, Peter (ed.) (1967) *Southeast Asian Tribes, Minorities and Nations*, Princeton, NJ, Princeton University Press, 2 vols.

Kunstadter, Peter (1969) 'Hill and valley populations in Northwestern Thailand', in P. Hinton (ed.), *Tribesmen and Peasants in North Thailand*, Chiangmai, Tribal Research Centre, pp. 69–85.

Kuper, Adam (1983) *Anthropology and Anthropologists: The Modern British School*, London, Routledge and Kegan Paul, revised edition.

Laderman, Carol C. (1983) *Wives and Midwives: Childbirth and Nutrition in Rural Malaysia*, Berkeley and Los Angeles, CA, University of California Press.

Laderman, Carol C. (1996) 'Putting Malay women in their place', in Penny van Esterik (ed.), *Women of Southeast Asia*, DeKalb, Northern Illinois University, Center for Southeast Asian Studies, Occasional Paper No. 17, pp. 62–77, first published 1982.

Lafont, Pierre-Bernard (1963) *Toloi Djuat: coutumier de la tribu Jarai*, Paris, Publications de l'Ecole Française d'Extrême-Orient.

Laquian, Aprodicio A. (1969) *Slums are for People: The Barrio Magsaysay Pilot Project in Urban Community Development*, Manila, College of Public Administration, University of the Philippines.

Larkin, John A. (1971) 'The causes of an involuted society: a theoretical approach to rural Southeast Asia', *Journal of Asian Studies*, 30: 783–795.

Lasker, Bruno ([1944] 1945) *Peoples of Southeast Asia*, London, Victor Gollancz, and 1945, 2nd edn, New York, Alfred A. Knopf.

Leach, E.R. (1947) 'Cultural change with special reference to the hill tribes of Burma and Assam', unpublished PhD dissertation, University of London.

Leach, E.R. (1950) *Social Science Research in Sarawak*, London, HMSO.

Leach, E.R. (1952) 'The structural implications of matrilateral cross-cousin marriage', *Journal of the Royal Anthropological Institute*, 81: 23–55.

Leach, E.R. ([1954] 1970) *Political Systems of Highland Burma. A Study of Kachin Social Structure*, London, Athlone Press, LSE Monographs on Social Anthropology No. 44 (reprint of 1954, G. Bell and Son, reprint of 1964, Introduction by E.R. Leach).

Leach, E.R. (1955) 'Foreword', in J.D. Freeman, *Iban Agriculture: A Report on the Shifting Cultivation of Hill Rice by the Iban of Sarawak*, London, HMSO.

Leach, E.R. (1960) 'The frontiers of Burma', *Comparative Studies in Society and History*, 3: 49–68.

Leach, E.R. (1962) 'Pulleyar and the Lord Buddha: an aspect of religious syncretism in Ceylon', *Psychoanalysis and the Psychoanalytical Review*, 49: 81–102.

Leach, E.R. (ed.) (1968) *Dialectic in Practical Religion*, Cambridge, Cambridge University Press.

Leach, E.R. (1977) 'In formative travail with Leviathan', *Anthropological Forum* 4: 54–61, 190–197.

Leach, E.R. (1983) 'Imaginary Kachins', *Man*, 18: 191–199.

Lebar, F.M. (ed.) (1972, 1975) *Ethnic Groups of Insular Southeast Asia, Vols I and II*, New Haven, CT, Human Relations Area Files.

Lebar, F.M., Hickey, G.C. and Musgrave, J.K. (eds) (1964) *Ethnic Groups of Mainland Southeast Asia*, New Haven, CT, Human Relations Area Files Press.

Lee, Raymond L.M. (1986a) 'Introduction', in Raymond L.M. Lee (ed.), *Ethnicity and Ethnic Relations in Malaysia*, Northern Illinois University, Center for Southeast Asian Studies, Monograph Series, Occasional Paper No. 12, pp. iv–viii.

Lee, Raymond L.M. (1986b) 'Symbols of separatism: ethnicity and status politics in contemporary Malaysia', in Raymond L.M. Lee (ed.), *Ethnicity and Ethnic Relations in Malaysia*, Northern Illinois University, Center for Southeast Asian Studies, Monograph Series, Occasional Paper No. 12, pp. 28–46.

Lehman, F.K. (1963) *The Structure of Chin Society: A Tribal People of Burma adapted to a Non-Western Civilization*, Urbana, IL, The University of Illinois Press.

Lehman, F.K. (1967) 'Ethnic categories in Burma and the theory of social systems', in Peter Kunstadter (ed.), *Southeast Asian Tribes, Minorities and Nations*, vol. 1, Princeton, NJ, Princeton University Press, pp. 93–124.

Leong, Laurence Wai-Teng (1997) 'Commodifying ethnicity: state and ethnic tourism in Singapore', in Michel Picard and Robert E. Wood (eds), *Tourism, Ethnicity, and the State in Asian and Pacific Societies*, Honolulu, University of Hawai'i Press, pp. 71–98.

Leur, Jacob van (1955) *Indonesian Trade and Society: Essays in Asian Social and Economic History*, The Hague, W. van Hoeve.

Lévi-Strauss, Claude ([1956] 1963) 'Do dual organizations exist?' In C. Lévi-Strauss, *Structural Anthropology*, vol. 1, New York: Basic Books, Chapter VIII, pp. 132–163; first published in French in *Bijdragen tot de Taal-, Land- en Volkenkunde*, 1956, 112: 99–128, in an issue dedicated to J.P.B. de Josselin de Jong.

Lévi-Strauss, Claude (1966) *The Savage Mind*, London, Weidenfeld and Nicolson.

Lévi-Strauss, Claude (1967) *Les structures élémentaires de la parenté*, Paris, Mouton, Maison des Sciences de l'Homme. Collection de Rééditions II, second edition.

Lévi-Strauss, Claude ([1949] 1969a), *The Elementary Structures of Kinship*, London, Eyre and Spottiswoode (transl. of the second French edition 1967 by James Harle Bell, John Richard von Sturmer and Rodney Needham [ed.])

Lévi-Strauss, Claude (1969b) *Totemism*, Penguin, Harmondsworth (transl. Rodney Needham, with an Introduction by Roger C. Poole) (originally published in Paris, 1962, and in translation, London, Merlin Press, 1964).

Li, Tania Murray (1989) *Malays in Singapore: Culture, Economy and Ideology*, Singapore, Oxford University Press.

Lieberman, Victor (1995) 'An age of commerce in Southeast Asia? Problems of regional coherence – a review article', *Journal of Asian Studies*, 54: 796–807.

Locher, G.W. (1961) 'De antropoloog Lévi-Strauss en het probleem van de geschiedenis', *Forum der Letteren*, 2: 201–216.

Loeb, Edwin M. (1935) *Sumatra: Its History and People*, Vienna, Institut für Völkerkunde.

Lounsbury, Floyd (1962) 'Review of *Structure and Sentiment: A Test Case in Social Anthropology* by Rodney Needham', *American Anthropologist*, 64: 1302–1310.

Lynch, Frank (1959) *Social Class in a Bikol Town*, Chicago, University of Chicago Press.

Lynch, Frank and Hollnsteiner, Mary (1961) 'Sixty years of Philippine ethnology: a first glance at the years 1901–1961', *Science Review*, 2: 1–5.

Lyon, M.L. (1970) *Bases of Conflict in Rural Java*, Berkeley, Los Angeles, CA, Center for South and Southeast Asian Studies.

McKean, Philip Frick (1976) 'Tourism, culture change, and culture conservation in Bali', in David J. Banks (ed.), *Changing Identities in Modern Southeast Asia*, The Hague, Mouton Publishers, pp. 237–247.

McKean, Philip Frick (1989) 'Towards a theoretical analysis of tourism: economic dualism and cultural involution in Bali', in Valene L. Smith (ed.), *Hosts and Guests: The Anthropology of Tourism*, Philadelphia, PA, University of Pennsylvania Press, pp. 119–138.

McVey, Ruth (1995) 'Change and continuity in Southeast Asian Studies', *Journal of Southeast Asian Studies*, 226: 1–9.

Maitre, Henri (1909) *Les régions moï du Sud-Indochinois: le plateau du Darlac*, Paris.

Maitre, Henri (1912) *Les Jungles moï*, Paris, Larousse.

Malinowski, Bronislaw (1929) 'Practical anthropology', *Africa*, 2: 22–38.

Mandelbaum, D.G. (1966) 'Transcendental and pragmatic aspects of religion', *American Anthropologist*, 68: 1174–1193.

Mandelson, E.M. (1960) 'Religion and authority in modern Burma', *The World Today*, 6: 110–118.

Maran La Raw (1967) 'Toward a basis for understanding the minorities in Burma: the Kachin example', in P. Kunstadter (ed.), *Southeast Asian Tribes, Minorities and Nations*, vol. 1, Princeton, NJ, Princeton University Press, pp. 125–146.

Margold, Jane (1999) 'Reformulating the compliant image: Filipina activists in the global factory', *Urban Anthropology*, 28: 1–35.

Marx, Karl (1964) *Pre-Capitalist Economic Formations*, trans. and ed. Eric Hobsbawm, London, Lawrence and Wishart.

Mauss, Marcel ([1924] 1954) *The Gift: Forms and Functions of Exchange in Archaic Societies*, transl. Ian Cunnison, London, Cohen and West.

Mead, Margaret (1928) *Coming of Age in Samoa*, Magnolia, MA, Peter Smith.

Mead, Margaret (1962) *Male and Female: A Study of the Sexes in a Changing World*, Harmondsworth, Penguin Books, first published by Morrow and Co., 1949.

Metcalf, Peter (1982) *A Borneo Journey into Death: Berawan Eschatology from its Rituals*, Philadelphia, PA, University of Pennsylvania Press.

Michaud, Jean (2000a) 'A historical panorama of the Montagnards in northern Vietnam under French rule', in Jean Michaud (ed.), *Turbulent Times and Enduring Peoples: Mountain Minorities in the South-East Asian Massif*, Richmond, Curzon Press, pp. 50–76.

Michaud, Jean (ed.) (2000b) *Turbulent Times and Enduring Peoples: Mountain Minorities in the South-East Asian Massif*, Richmond, Curzon Press.

Miksic, John N. (1995) 'Evolving archaeological perspectives on Southeast Asia, 1970–95', *Journal of Southeast Asian Studies*, 26: 46–62.

Miles, Douglas (1979) 'The finger knife and Ockham's Razor', *American Ethnologist*, 6: 223–243.

Milgram, B. Lynne (1999) 'Crafts, cultivation and household economies: women's work and positions in Ifugao, Northern Philippines', in Barry L. Isaac (ed.), *Research in Economic Anthropology*, vol. 20, Stamford, CT, JAI Press Inc., pp. 221–261.

Mi Mi Khaing, Daw (1962) *Burmese Family*, Bloomington, IN, Indiana University Press.

Mi Mi Khaing, Daw (1963) 'Burma: balance and harmony', in Barbara E. Ward (ed.), *Women in the New Asia: The Changing Roles of Men and Women in South and South-East Asia*, Paris, UNESCO, pp. 104–137.

Moerman, Michael (1965) 'Ethnic identification in a complex society: who are the Lue?', *American Anthropologist*, 67: 1215–1230.

Moerman, Michael (1968a) *Agricultural Change and Peasant Choice in a Thai Village*, Berkeley and Los Angeles, CA, University of California Press.

Moerman, Michael (1968b) 'Being Lue: uses and abuses of ethnic identification', in June Helm (ed.), *Essays on the Problem of Tribe*, Washington, DC, Washington University Press, pp. 153–169.

Moerman, Michael (1975) 'Chiangkham's trade in the "old days"', in G. William Skinner and A. Thomas Kirsch (eds), *Change and Persistence in Thai Society: Essays in Honor of Lauriston Sharp*, Ithaca, NY, and London, Cornell University Press, pp. 151–171.

Mohammed Halib and Huxley, Tim (eds) (1996) *An Introduction to Southeast Asian Studies*, London, I.B. Tauris Publishers.

Moore, Barrington (1966) *Social Origins of Dictatorship and Democracy*, Boston, Beacon Press.

Morris, H.S. (1953) *Report on a Melanau Sago Producing Community in Sarawak*, London, HMSO.

Morris, H.S. (1974) 'In the wake of mechanization: sago and society in Sarawak', in Robert J. Smith (ed.), *Social Organization and the Applications of Anthropology*, Ithaca, NY, and London, Cornell University Press, pp. 273–301.

Morris, Rosalind C. (1994) 'Three sexes and four sexualities: redressing the discourses on gender and sexuality in contemporary Thailand', *positions* 2: 15–43.

Moubray, G.A. de C. de (1931) *Matriarchy in the Malay Peninsula and Neighbouring Countries*, London, Routledge.

Muijzenberg, Otto van den (1975) 'Involution or evolution in Central Luzon?', in Peter Kloos and Henri J.M. Claessen (eds), *Current Anthropology in the Netherlands*, Rotterdam, Netherlands Sociological and Anthropological Society, pp. 141–155.

Mulder, Niels (1989) *Individual and Society in Java: A Cultural Analysis*, Yogyakarta, Gadjah Mada University Press.

Murdock, George Peter (ed.) (1960a) *Social Structure in Southeast Asia*, Chicago, Quadrangle Books.

Murdock, George Peter (1960b) 'Cognatic forms of social organization', in George Peter Murdock (ed.), *Social Structure in Southeast Asia*, Chicago, Quadrangle Books, pp. 1–14.

Nagata, Judith A. (1974) 'What is a Malay? Situational selection of ethnic identity in a plural society', *American Ethnologist*, 1: 331–350.

Nagata, Judith A. (1975a) 'Introduction', in Judith A. Nagata (ed.), *Pluralism in Malaysia: Myth and Reality*, Leiden, E.J. Brill, pp. 1–16.

Nagata, Judith A. (1975b) 'Perceptions of social inequality in Malaysia', in Judith A. Nagata (ed.), *Pluralism in Malaysia: Myth and Reality*, Leiden, E.J. Brill, pp. 113–136.

Nagata, Judith A. (1979) *Malaysian Mosaic: Perspectives from a Poly-Ethnic Society*, Vancouver, University of British Columbia Press.

Naroll, Raoul (1964) 'On ethnic unit classification', *Current Anthropology*, 5: 283–291, 306–312.

Naroll, Raoul (1968) 'Who the Lue are', in June Helm (ed.), *Essays on the Problem of Tribe*, Washington, DC, Washington University Press, pp. 72–79.

Nas, Peter J.M. (ed.) (1998) 'Globalization, localization and Indonesia', special issue of *Bijdragen tot de Taal-, Land- en Volkenkunde*, 154: 181–364.

Nash, Manning (1963) 'Burmese Buddhism in everyday life', *American Anthropologist*, 65: 285–295.

Nash, Manning (1964) 'Southeast Asian society: dual or multiple', *Journal of Asian Studies*, 23: 417–423.

Nash, Manning (1965) *The Golden Road to Modernity: Village Life in Contemporary Burma*, New York, John Wiley.

Nash, Manning (ed.) (1966) *Anthropological Studies in Theravada Buddhism*, New Haven, CT, Yale University Press.

Nash, Manning (1974) *Peasant Citizens: Politics, Religion, and Modernization in Kelantan, Malaysia*, Ohio University, Center for International Studies.

Needham, Rodney (1957) 'Circulating connubium in Eastern Sumba: a literary analysis', *Bijdragen tot de Taal-, Land- en Volkenkunde*, 113: 168–178.

Needham, Rodney (1958) 'A structural analysis of Purum society', *American Anthropologist*, 60: 75–101.

Needham, Rodney (1959a) 'An analytical note on the Kom of Manipur', *Ethnos*, 24: 121–135.

Needham, Rodney (1959b) 'Vaiphei social structure', *Southwestern Journal of Anthropology*, 15: 396–406.

Needham, Rodney (1960a) 'Alliance and classification among the Lamet', *Sociologus*, 10: 97–118.

Needham, Rodney (1960b) 'A structural analysis of Aimol society', *Bijdragen tot de Taal-, Land- en Volkenkunde*, 116: 81–108.

Needham, Rodney (1960c) 'Chawte social structure', *American Anthropologist*, 62: 236–253.

Needham, Rodney (1962) *Structure and Sentiment: A Test Case in Social Anthropology*, Chicago and London, University of Chicago Press.

Needham, Rodney (1963) 'Some disputed points in the study of prescriptive alliance', *Southwestern Journal of Anthropology*, 19: 186–207.

Needham, Rodney (1969) 'Editor's note', in Claude Lévi-Strauss, *The Elementary Structures of Kinship*, London, Eyre and Spottiswoode (transl. James Harle Bell, Richard von Sturmer and Rodney Needham [ed.]).

Needham, Rodney (1973a) 'Prescription', *Oceania*, 43: 166–181.

Needham, Rodney (ed.) (1973b) *Right and Left: Essays on Dual Symbolic Classsification*, Chicago and London, University of Chicago Press.

Needham, Rodney (1976) 'Nyoro symbolism: the ethnographic record', *Africa*, 46: 236–246.

Needham, Rodney (1977) *Essential Perplexities*, Oxford, Clarendon Press.

Needham, Rodney (1979) *Symbolic Classification*, Santa Monica, CA, Goodyear.

Niel, Robert van (1992) *Java under the Cultivation System: Collected Writings*, Leiden, KITLV Press, Verhandelingen van het Koninklijk Instituut voor Taal-, Land- en Volkenkunde, 150.

Nieuwenhuis, A.W. (1900) *In Centraal Borneo: Reis van Pontianak naar Samarinda*, Leiden, E.J. Brill, 2 vols.

Nieuwenhuis, A.W. (1904–7) *Quer durch Borneo. Ergebnisse seiner Reisen in den Jahren 1894, 1896–97 und 1898–1900*, Leiden, E.J. Brill, 2 vols.

Nimmo, H. Arlo (1972) *The Sea People of Sulu: A Study of Social Change in the Philippines*, London, Intertext Books.

Nugent, David (1982) 'Closed systems and contradiction: the Kachin in and out of history', *Man*, 17: 508–527.

Nugent, David (1983) 'Imaginary Kachins', *Man*, 18: 199–206.

Nurge, Ethel (1965) *Life in a Leyte Village*, Seattle, University of Washington Press.

Nydegger, William F. and Nydegger, Corrine (1966) *Tarong: Ilocos Barrio in the Philippines*, New York, John Wiley and Sons.

Ogden, Charles Kay (1932) *Opposition: A Linguistic and Psychological Analysis*, Bloomington, ILL: Indiana University Press, reprint, 1967.

O'Harrow, Stephen (1995) 'Vietnamese women and Confucianism: creating spaces from patriarchy', in Wazir Jahan Karim (ed.), *'Male' and 'Female' in Developing Southeast Asia*, Oxford, Berg, pp. 161–180.

Okuno, Katsumi (1997) 'Wazawai no setsumei to wazamai eno taisho: Boruneo-tou Kalis ni okeru seirei, dokuyaku, jajutsu', [Explanation of and treatment for misfortune: spirits, poisoning, and sorcery among the Kalis of Borneo], unpublished PhD thesis, Hitosubashi University.

Ong, Aihwa (1987) *Spirits of Resistance and Capitalist Discipline: Factory Women in Malaysia*, New York, State University of New York Press.

Ong, Aihwa and Peletz, Michael G. (1995) 'Introduction', in Aihwa Ong and Michael G. Peletz (eds), *Bewitching Women, Pious Men: Gender and Body Politics in Southeast Asia*, Berkeley and Los Angeles, CA, University of California Press, pp. 1–18.

Osborne, Milton, 1985, *Southeast Asia: An Illustrated Introductory History*, Sydney, George Allen and Unwin, first edition 1979, second edition, 1983.

Ossenbruggen, F.D.E. van (1918) 'De oorsprong van het Javaansche begrip montja-pat, in verbond met primitieve classificaties', *Verslagen en Mededeelingen der Koninklijke Nederlandsche Akademie van Wetenschappen*, 5: 6–44; translated as 'Java's monca-pat: origins of a primitive classification system', in P.E. de Josselin de Jong (ed.) (1977) *Structural Anthropology in the Netherlands: A Reader*, The Hague, Martinus Nijhoff, Koninklijk Instituut voor Taal-, Land- en Volkenkunde, pp. 32–60.

Padoch, Christine (1982) *Migration and its Alternatives among the Iban of Sarawak*, The Hague, Martinus Nijhoff, Verhandelingen van het Koninklijk Instituut voor Taal-, Land- en Volkenkunde, 98.

Parkin, Robert (1996) *The Dark Side of Humanity: The Work of Robert Hertz and its Legacy*, Amsterdam, Harwood Academic.

Peacock, James L. (1968) *Rites of Modernization: Symbolic and Social Aspects of Indonesian Proletarian Drama*, Chicago and London, The University of Chicago Press.

Peacock, James L. (1973) *Indonesia: An Anthropological Perspective*, Pacific Palisades, CA, Goodyear Publishing Company.

Peacock, James L. (1975) *Consciousness and Change: Symbolic Anthropology in Evolution-ary Perspectives*, Oxford, Blackwell.

Peletz, Michael G. (1996) *Reason and Passion: Representations of Gender in a Malay Society*, Berkeley and Los Angeles, CA, University of California Press.

Pels, Peter and Salemink, Oscar (1999) 'Introduction: locating the colonial subjects of anthropology', in Peter Pels and Oscar Salemink (eds), *Colonial Subjects: Essays on the Practical History of Anthropology*, Ann Arbor, MI, The University of Michigan Press, pp. 1–52.

Pemberton, John (1994) *On the Subject of 'Java'*, Ithaca, NY, and London, Cornell University Press.

Perry, W.J. (1918) *The Megalithic Culture of Indonesia*, Manchester, Manchester University Press.

Pertierra, Raul (1994) 'Philippine studies and the new ethnography', in Raul Pertierra and Eduardo F. Ugarte (eds), *Cultures and Texts: Representations of Philippine Society*, Diliman, Quezon City, University of the Philippines Press, pp. 120–137.

Phillips, Herbert P. (1965) *Thai Peasant Personality: The Patterning of Interpersonal Behavior in the Village of Bang Chan*, Berkeley and Los Angeles, CA, University of California Press.

Picard, Michel (1990) '"Cultural tourism" in Bali: cultural performances as tourist attraction', *Indonesia*, 49: 37–74.

Picard, Michel (1993) 'Cultural tourism in Bali: national integration and regional differentiation', in Michael Hitchcock, Victor T. King and Michael J.G. Parnwell (eds), *Tourism in South-East Asia*, London, Routledge, pp. 71–98.

Picard, Michel (1996) *Bali: Cultural Tourism and Touristic Culture*, Singapore, Archipelago Press.

Picard, Michel (1997) 'Cultural tourism, nation-building, and regional culture: the making of a Balinese identity', in Michel Picard and Robert E. Wood (eds), *Tourism, Ethnicity, and the State in Asian and Pacific Societies*, Honolulu, University of Hawai'i Press, pp. 181–214.

Picard, Michel and Wood, Robert E. (eds) (1997) *Tourism, Ethnicity, and the State in Asian and Pacific Societies*, Honolulu, University of Hawai'i Press.

Piker, Steven (1968) 'Sources of stability and instability in rural Thai society', *Journal of Asian Studies*, 27: 777–790.

Poedjosoedarmo, Gloria (1983) 'The position of women in Java', *Indonesia Circle*, 32 (November): 3–9.

Popkin, Samuel L. (1979) *The Rational Peasant: The Political Economy of Rural Society in Vietnam*, Berkeley and Los Angeles, CA, University of California Press.

Pospisil, L. (1958) *Kapauku Papuans and their Law*, New Haven, CT, Yale University Publications in Anthropology.

Potter, Jack M. (1976) *Thai Peasant Social Structure*, Chicago and London, University of Chicago Press.

Potter, Sulamith (1977) *Family Life in a Northern Thai Village: A Study in the Structural Significance of Women*, Berkeley and Los Angeles, CA, University of California Press.

Pouwer, J (1966) 'The structural and functional approach in cultural anthropology: theoretical reflections with reference to research in western New Guinea', *Bijdragen tot de Taal-, Land- en Volkenkunde*, 122: 129–144.

Prager, Michael (1999) 'Crossing borders, healing wounds: Leiden anthropology and the colonial encounter (1917–1949)', in Jan van Bremen and Akitoshi Shimizu (eds),

Anthropology and Colonialism in Asia and Oceania, Richmond, Curzon Press, pp. 326–361.

Prasithrathsint, Amara (1993) 'The linguistic mosaic', in Grant Evans (ed.), *Asia's Cultural Mosaic: An Anthropological Introduction*, New York, Prentice-Hall, pp. 63–88.

Provencher, Ronald (1971) *Two Malay Worlds: Interaction in Urban and Rural Settings*, Berkeley, CA, University of California, Center for South and Southeast Asia Studies.

Provencher, Ronald (1975) *Mainland Southeast Asia: An Anthropological Perspective*, Pacific Palisades, CA, Goodyear Publishing Company.

Radcliffe-Brown, A.R. (1922) *The Andaman Islanders*, Cambridge, Cambridge University Press.

Radcliffe-Brown, A.R. (1931) 'Applied anthropology', *Proceedings of the Australian and New Zealand Association for the Advancement of Science*, Brisbane, 20th Meeting, pp. 267–280.

Rajah, Ananda (1999) 'Southeast Asia: comparatist errors and the construction of a region', in Amitav Acharya and Ananda Rajah (eds), 'Special focus: reconceptualizing Southeast Asia', special issue of *Southeast Asian Journal of Social Science*, 27: 41–53.

Rapport, Nigel and Overing, Joanna (2000) *Social and Cultural Anthropology: The Key Concepts*, London and New York, Routledge.

Rassers, W.H. (1959) *Panji, the Culture Hero: A Structural Study of Religion in Java*, The Hague, Martinus Nijhoff.

Rawson, Philip S. (1967) *The Art of Southeast Asia: Cambodia, Vietnam, Thailand, Laos, Burma, Java, Bali*, London, Thames and Hudson.

Reid, Anthony (1988–1993) *Southeast Asia in the Age of Commerce: 1400–1680*, vol. 1, *The Land below the Winds* (1988); vol. 2, *Expansion and Crisis* (1993), New Haven, CT, Yale University Press.

Reid, Anthony (1999) 'A saucer model of Southeast Asian identity', in Amitav Acharya and Ananda Rajah (eds), 'Special focus: reconceptualizing Southeast Asia', special issue of *Southeast Asian Journal of Social Science*, 27: 7–23.

Res, Lyda (1985) 'Changing labor patterns of women in rice farm households: a rainfed rice village', Iloilo Province, Philippines', in IRRI, *Women in Rice Farming*, Aldershot, Gower Publishing Co., pp. 91–117.

Revel, Nicole (ed.) (1988) *Le riz en Asie du sud-est: atlas du vocabulaire de la plante*, Paris, Editions de l'Ecole des Hautes Etudes en Sciences Sociales.

Rigg, J. (2001) *More than the Soil: Rural Change in Southeast Asia*, Harlow, Prentice-Hall.

Rivers, W.H.R. (1914) *The History of Melanesian Society*, Cambridge, Cambridge University Press.

Robinson, Kathryn May (1986) *Stepchildren of Progress: The Political Economy of Development in an Indonesian Mining Town*, Albany, NY, State University of New York Press.

Rosaldo, Michelle Zimbalist (1980) *Knowledge and Passion: Ilongot Notions of Self and Social Life*, Cambridge, Cambridge University Press.

Rosaldo, Renato (1980) *Ilongot Headhunting, 1883–1974: A Study in Society and History*, Stanford, CA, Stanford University Press.

Rosaldo, Renato (1989) *Culture and Truth*, Boston, Beacon Press.

Roth, Henry Ling (1896) *The Natives of Sarawak and British North Borneo*, London, Truslove and Hanson, 2 vols, reprint, Kuala Lumpur, University of Malaya Press, 1968.

Rousseau, Jérôme (1975) 'Ethnic identity and social relations in Central Borneo', in Judith A. Nagata (ed.), *Pluralism in Malaysia: Myth and Reality*, Leiden, E.J. Brill, pp. 32–49.

Rousseau, Jérôme (1990) *Central Borneo: Ethnic Identity and Social Life in a Stratified Society*, Oxford, Clarendon Press.

Rudie, Ingrid (1994) *Visible Women in East Coast Malay Society: On the Reproduction of Gender in Ceremonial, School and Market*, Oslo, Scandinavian University Press.

Rutten, Rosanne (1982) *Women Workers of Hacienda Milagros: Wage Labor and Household Subsistence on a Philippine Sugarcane Plantation*, Amsterdam, University of Amsterdam, Anthropology-Sociology Centre, South and Southeast Asia.

Rutten, Rosanne (1993) *Artisans and Entrepreneurs in the Rural Philippines: Making a Living and Gaining Wealth in Two Commercialised Crafts*, Quezon City, New Day Publishers, first published Amsterdam, VU University Press, 1990.

Salemink, Oscar (1991) 'Mois and Maquis: The invention and appropriation of Vietnam's Montagnards from Sabatier to the CIA', in George W. Stocking (ed.), *Colonial Situations: Essays on the Contextualization of Ethnographic Knowledge*, Madison, WI, University of Wisconsin Press, pp. 243–284.

Salemink, Oscar (1999) 'Ethnography as martial art: ethnicizing Vietnam's Montagnards, 1930–1954', in Peter Pels and Oscar Salemink (eds), *Colonial Subjects: Essays on the Practical History of Anthropology*, Ann Arbor, MI, The University of Michigan Press, pp. 282–325.

Sanday, Peggy Reeves (1981) *Female Power and Male Dominance: On the Origins of Sexual Inequality*, Cambridge, Cambridge University Press.

Sartono, Kartodirdjo (1973) *Protest Movements in Rural Java*, Singapore, Oxford University Press.

Sather, Clifford (1971) 'Kinship and domestic relations among the Bajau Laut of Northern Borneo', unpublished PhD dissertation, Harvard University.

Sather, Clifford (1997) *The Bajau Laut: Adaptation, History, and Fate in a Maritime Fishing Society of South-Eastern Sabah*, Kuala Lumpur, Oxford University Press.

Schaik, Arthur van (1986) *Colonial Control and Peasant Resources in Java: Agricultural Involution Reconsidered*, Amsterdam, University of Amsterdam, Institute for Social Geography.

Schärer, Hans (1963) *Ngaju Religion: The Conception of God among a South Borneo People*, transl. Rodney Needham, The Hague, Martinus Nijhoff, Koninklijk Instituut voor Taal-, Land- en Volkenkunde.

Schiller, Anne (1997) *Small Sacrifices: Religious Change and Cultural Identity among the Ngaju of Indonesia*, New York and Oxford, Oxford University Press.

Schlegel, Stuart A. (1970) *Tiruray Justice: Traditional Tiruray Law and Morality*, Berkeley, Los Angeles, CA, University of California Press.

Schmidt, Johannes Dragsbaek, Hersh, Jacques and Fold, Niels (eds) (1997) *Social Change in Southeast Asia*, Harlow, Longman.

Schmidt, P.W. (1910) *Grundlinien einer Vergleichung der Religionen und Mythologien der Austronesischen Völker*, Denkschriften der Kaiserlichen Akademie der Wissenschaften in Wien, 53, Vienna, Alfred Hölden.

Schrieke, Bertram J.O. (ed.) (1929) *The Effect of Western Influence on Native Civilizations in the Malay Archipelago*, Batavia, G. Kolff, Koninklijk Bataviaasch Genootschap van Kunsten en Wetenschappen.

Schrieke, Bertram J.O. (1955–1957) *Indonesian Sociological Studies: Selected Writings of B. Schrieke; vol. 2, Ruler and Realm in Early Java*, The Hague, W. van Hoeve.

Schulte Nordholt, Henk (1999) 'The making of traditional Bali: colonial ethnography and bureaucratic reproduction', in Peter Pels and Oscar Salemink (eds), *Colonial*

Subjects: Essays on the Practical History of Anthropology, Ann Arbor, MI, The University of Michigan Press, pp. 241–281.

Schulte Nordholt, H.G. (1971) *The Political System of the Atoni of Timor*, The Hague, Martinus Nijhoff, Verhandelingen van het Koninklijk Instituut voor Taal-, Land- en Volkenkunde, vol. 60.

Schulte Nordholt, H.G. (1980) 'The symbolic classification of the Atoni of Timor', in James J. Fox (ed.), *The Flow of Life: Essays on Eastern Indonesia*, Cambridge, MA, and London, Harvard University Press, pp. 231–247.

Scott, James C. (1976) *The Moral Economy of the Peasant: Rebellion and Subsistence in Southeast Asia*, New Haven, CT, and London, Yale University Press.

Scott, James C. (1985) *Weapons of the Weak: Everyday Forms of Peasant Resistance*, New Haven, CT, and London, Yale University Press.

Scott, James C. (1992) 'Foreword', in Charles Hirschman, Charles F. Keyes and Karl Hutterer (eds), *Southeast Asian Studies in the Balance: Reflections from America*, Ann Arbor, MI, The Association for Asian Studies, pp. 1–7.

Scott, James George and Hardiman, J.P. (1900) *Gazetteer of Upper Burma and the Shan States*, Rangoon, Superintendent of Government Printing and Stationery.

Sellato, Bernard (1989) *Nomades et Sédentarisation à Borneo. Histoire Economique et Sociale*, Paris, Ecole des Hautes Etudes en Sciences Sociales.

Selosoemardjan (1962) *Social Changes in Jogjakarta*, Ithaca, NY, Cornell University Press.

Sharp, Lauriston and Hanks, Lucien M. (1978) *Bang Chan: Social History of a Rural Community in Thailand*, Ithaca, NY, and London, Cornell University Press.

Sharp, Lauriston, Hauck, Hazel M., Janlekha, Kamol Odd and Textor, Robert B. (1953) *Siamese Rice Village: A Preliminary Study of Bang Chan, 1948–1949*, Bangkok, Cornell Research Center.

Shway Yoe (J.G. Scott) (1882) *The Burman: His Life and Notions*, New York, Norton.

Siegel, James T. (1969) *The Rope of God*, Berkeley and Los Angeles, CA, University of California Press; second and extended edition, 2000, Ann Arbor, MI, The University of Michigan Press.

Siegel, James T. (1986) *Solo in the New Order: Language and Hierarchy in an Indonesian City*, Princeton, NJ, Princeton University Press.

Skeat, Walter William (1900) *Malay Magic: An Introduction to the Folklore and Popular Religion of the Malay Peninsula*, London, Macmillan.

Skeat, Walter William and Blagden, Charles Otto (1906) *Pagan Races of the Malay Peninsula*, London, Macmillan, 2 vols, reprint, London, Frank Cass, 1966.

Skinner, G. William (1957) *Chinese Society in Thailand: An Analytical History*, Ithaca, New York, Cornell University Press.

Skinner, G. William (1958) *Leadership and Power in the Chinese Community of Thailand*, Ithaca, NY, Cornell University Press.

Skinner, G. William (ed.) (1959) *Local, Ethnic and National Loyalties in Village Indonesia: A Symposium*, New Haven, CT, Yale University Press.

Skinner, G. William (1963) 'The Chinese minority', in R. McVey (ed.), *Indonesia*, New Haven, CT, HRAF Press, pp. 97–117, 491–498.

Skinner G. William and Kirsch, A. Thomas (1975) 'Introduction', in G. William Skinner and Kirsch, A. Thomas (eds), *Change and Persistence in Thai Society, Essays in Honor of Lauriston Sharp*, Ithaca, NY, and London, Cornell University Press, pp. 9–24.

Smith, A. (1981) *The Ethnic Revival*, New York, Cambridge University Press.

Smith, Ralph (1986) 'The evolution of British scholarship on South-East Asia

1820–1970: Is there a "British tradition" in South-East Asian Studies?', in D.K. Bassett and V.T. King (eds), *Britain and South-East Asia*, University of Hull, Centre for South-East Asian Studies, special issue, Occasional Paper No. 13, pp. 1–28.

Smith, Robert J. (1974) 'Introduction', in Robert J. Smith (ed.), *Social Organization and the Applications of Anthropology: Essays in Honor of Lauriston Sharp*, Ithaca, NY, and London, Cornell University Press, pp. 7–19.

Smith, Valene L. (ed.) (1989) *Hosts and Guests: The Anthropology of Tourism*, Philadelphia, PA, University of Pennsylvania Press, revised edition, first published 1977.

Spiro, Melford E. (1967) *Burmese Supernaturalism: A Study in the Explanation and Reduction of Suffering*, Englewood Cliffs, NJ, Prentice-Hall.

Spiro, Melford E. (1970) *Buddhism and Society: A Great Tradition and its Burmese Vicissitudes*, Berkeley, CA, University of California Press, second expanded edition, 1982.

Spiro, Melford E. (1975) 'Marriage payments: a paradigm from the Burmese perspective', *Journal of Anthropological Research*, 31: 89–115, reprinted in Melford E. Spiro, *Anthropological Other or Burmese Brother? Studies in Cultural Analysis*, New Brunswick and London, Transaction Publishers, 1992, pp. 113–143.

Spiro, Melford E. (1977) *Kinship and Marriage in Burma: A Cultural and Psychodynamic Analysis*, Berkeley, CA, University of California Press.

Spiro, Melford E. (1992) *Anthropological Other or Burmese Brother? Studies in Cultural Analysis*, New Brunswick and London, Transaction Publishers.

Spiro, Melford E. (1997) *Gender Identity and Psychological Reality: An Essay on Cultural Reproduction*, New Haven, CT, and London, Yale University Press.

Spyer, Patricia (2000) *The Memory of Trade: Modernity's Entanglements on an Eastern Indonesian Island*, Durham, NC, and London, Duke University Press.

Steedly, Mary (1993) *Hanging without a Rope: Narrative Experience in Colonial and Postcolonial Karoland*, Princeton, NJ, Princeton University Press.

Stevenson, H.N.C. (1943) *The Economics of the Central Chin Tribes*, Bombay, The Times of India Press.

Stivens, Maila, Ng, Cecilea and Jomo, K.S. (eds) (1994) *Malay Peasant Women and the Land*, London, Zed Books, The International Labour Office within the framework of the World Employment Programme.

Stoler, Ann L. (1977) 'Rice harvesting in Kali Loro: a study of class and labor in rural Java', *American Ethnologist*, 4: 678–698.

Stoler, Ann L. (1989) 'Rethinking colonial categories: European communities and the boundaries of rule', *Comparative Studies in Society and History*, 13: 134–161.

Stoler, Ann L. (1991) 'Carnal knowledge and imperial power: gender, race, and morality in colonial Asia', in Micaela di Leonardo (ed.), *Gender at the Crossroads of Knowledge: Feminist Anthropology in the Postmodern Era*, Berkeley and Los Angeles, CA, University of California Press, pp. 51–101.

Sturtevant, David R. (1976) *Popular Uprisings in the Philippines 1840–1940*, Ithaca, NY, and London, Cornell University Press.

Swift, M.G. (1965) *Malay Peasant Society in Jelebu*, London, The Athlone Press.

Swift, M.G. (1971) 'Minangkabau and modernization', in H.R. Hiatt and C. Jayawardena (eds), *Anthropology in Oceania: Essays Presented to Ian Hogbin*, Sydney, Angus and Robertson, pp. 255–267.

Takahashi, Akira (1969) *Land and Peasants in Central Luzon*, Honolulu, East–West Center Press.

355

Tambiah, S.J. (1970) *Buddhism and the Spirit Cults in North-East Thailand*, Cambridge, Cambridge University Press.

Taylor, John G. and Turton, Andrew (eds) (1988) *Southeast Asia*, Basingstoke and London, Macmillan.

Taylor, Paul Michael (1980) 'Tobelorese ethnobiology: the folk classification of "Biotic Forms"', unpublished PhD dissertation, Yale University.

Taylor, Paul Michael (1990) *The Folk Biology of the Tobelo People: A Study in Folk Classification*, Washington, DC, Smithsonian Institution Press.

Taylor, Robert H. (1987) *The State in Burma*, London, C. Hurst and Co.

Textor, Robert B. (1954) *Notes on Indonesian Villagers' Participation in Programs to Modernize Rural Life*, Ithaca, NY, Cornell Modern Indonesia Project.

Textor, Robert B. (1973) *An Ethnography of the Supernatural in a Thai Village*, New Haven, CT, Human Relations Area Files, 6 vols.

Thambun Anyang, Y.C. (1996) *Daya Taman Kalimantan: Suatu Studi Etnografis Organisasi Sosial dan Kekerabatan dengan Pendekatan Antropologi Hukum*, Nijmegen, Nijmegen University Press.

Thitsa, Khin (1983) 'Nuns, mediums and prostitutes in Chiengmai: a study of some marginal categories of women', in *Women and Development in South-East Asia*, Canterbury, University of Kent, Centre of South East Asian Studies Occasional Paper No. 1, pp. 4–45.

Thompson, E.P. (1966) *The Making of the English Working Class*, New York, Vintage Books.

T'ien Ju-K'ang (1953) *The Chinese of Sarawak: A Study of Social Structure*, London, The Athlone Press.

Trager, Lillian (1988) *The City Connection: Migration and Family Interdependence in the Philippines*, Ann Arbor, MI, University of Michigan Press.

Tran Thi Van Anh (1999) 'Women and rural land in Vietnam', in Irene Tinker and Gale Summerfield (eds), *Women's Rights to House and Land: China, Laos, Vietnam*, Boulder, CO, Lynne Rienner Publishers Inc., pp. 95–114.

Tsing, Anna Lowenhaupt (1993) *In the Realm of the Diamond Queen: Marginality in an Out-of-the-Way Place*, Princeton, NJ, Princeton University Press.

Turton, Andrew (1989a) 'Thailand: agrarian bases of state power', in Gillian Hart, Andrew Turton and Benjamin White (eds), *Agrarian Transformations: Local Processes and the State in Southeast Asia*, Berkeley and Los Angeles, CA, University of California Press, pp. 53–69.

Turton, Andrew (1989b) 'Local powers and rural differentiation', in Gillian Hart, Andrew Turton and Benjamin White (eds), *Agrarian Transformations: Local Processes and the State in Southeast Asia*, Berkeley and Los Angeles, CA, University of California Press, pp. 70–97.

Vayda, Andrew P. (1979) 'Human ecology and economic development in Kalimantan and Sumatra', *Borneo Research Bulletin*, 11: 23–32.

Vayda, Andrew P. (1981) 'Research in East Kalimantan on interactions between people and forests: a preliminary report', *Borneo Research Bulletin*, 13: 3–15.

Vayda, Andrew P. (1983) 'Progressive contextualization: methods for research in human ecology', *Human Ecology*, 11: 265–281.

Veth, P.J. (1854–1856) *Borneo's Wester-Afdeeling: Geographisch, Statistisch, Historisch, voorafgegaan door eine Algemeene Schets des Ganschen Eilands*, Zaltbommel, Noman, 2 vols.

Veth, P.J. (1875–1884) *Java, Geographisch, Ethnologisch, Historisch*, Haarlem, F. Bohn, 3 vols.

Veth, P.J. (1881–1897) *Midden Sumatra: Reizen en Onderzoekingen der Sumatra Expeditie*, Leiden, Brill, 9 vols.

Vickers, Adrian (1989) *Bali: A Paradise Created*, Berkeley and Singapore, Periplus Editions.

Visser, Rob and van der Wiel, Arie (1981) 'Anthropology and development cooperation', in Peter Kloos and Henri J.M. Claessen (eds), *Current Issues in Anthropology: The Netherlands*, Rotterdam, Anthropological Branch of the Netherlands Sociological and Anthropological Society, pp. 228–243.

Volkman, Toby Alice (1984) 'Great performances: Torajan cultural identity in the 1970s', *American Ethnologist*, 11: 152–169.

Volkman, Toby Alice (1985) *Feasts of Honor: Ritual and Change in the Toraja Highlands*, Urbana and Chicago, ILL, University of Illinois Press.

Volkman, Toby Alice (1990) 'Visions and revisions: Toraja culture and the tourist gaze', *American Ethnologist*, 17: 91–110.

Wadley, Reed L. (2000) 'Reconsidering an ethnic label in Borneo: The "Maloh" of West Kalimantan, Indonesia', *Bijdragen tot de Taal-, Land- en Volkenkunde*, 156: 83–101.

Wallace, Ben J. (1971) *Village Life in Insular Southeast Asia*, Boston, Little, Brown and Company.

Waterson, Roxana (1990) *The Living House: An Anthropology of Architecture in South-East Asia*, Singapore, Oxford University Press.

Wazir Jahan Karim (1992) *Women and Culture: Between Malay Adat and Islam*, Boulder, CO, Westview Press.

Wazir Jahan Karim (1994) 'A theory of a distinction of words roughly answering to sex', in Maznah Mohamad and Wong Soak Koon (eds), 'Feminism: Malaysia critique and experience', *Kajian Malaysia* (Journal of Malaysian Studies), special issue, 12: 160–184.

Wazir Jahan Karim (1995) 'Introduction: gendering anthropology in Southeast Asia', in Wazir Jahan Karim (ed.), *'Male' and 'Female' in Developing Southeast Asia*, Oxford, Berg, pp. 11–34.

Wertheim, W.F. (1974) *Evolution and Revolution: The Rising Waves of Emancipation*, Harmondsworth, Penguin Books.

Wertheim, W.F. (1980) 'Changing South-East Asian societies: an overview', in Hans-Dieter Evers (ed.), *Sociology of South-East Asia: Readings on Social Change and Development*, Kuala Lumpur, Oxford University Press, pp. 8–23.

White, Benjamin (1983a) *'Agricultural Involution' and its Critics: Twenty Years after Clifford Geertz*, The Hague, Institute of Social Studies.

White, Benjamin (1983b) '"Agricultural Involution" and its critics: twenty years after', *Bulletin of Concerned Asian Scholars*, 15: 18–31.

White, Benjamin (1989) 'Problems in the empirical analysis of agrarian differentiation', in Gillian Hart, Andrew Turton and Benjamin White (eds), *Agrarian Transformations: Local Processes and the State in Southeast Asia*, Berkeley and Los Angeles, CA, University of California Press, pp. 15–30.

Whyte, Martin K. (1978) *The Status of Women in Preindustrial Societies*, Princeton, NJ, Princeton University Press.

Wijeyewardene, Gehan (ed.) (1990) *Ethnic Groups across National Boundaries in Mainland Southeast Asia*, Singapore, Institute of Southeast Asian Studies.

Wilder, William D. (1982a) *Communication, Social Structure and Development in Rural Malaysia: A Study of Kampung Kuala Bera*, London, The Athlone Press.

Wilder, William D. (1982b) 'Psychosocial dimensions of ethnicity', *Southeast Asian Journal of Social Science*, 10: 103–115.

Wilder, William D. (1991) 'Kinship, community, and the structure of Pahang Malay kindreds', in Frans Hüsken and Jeremy Kemp (eds), *Cognation and Social Organization in Southeast Asia*, Leiden, KITLV Press, Verhandelingen van het Koninklijk Instituut voor Taal-, Land- en Volkenkunde, 145, pp. 125–136.

Wilder, William D. (1997) 'On the gender of land: rural Malays in the 20th century', in T.C. Chang, Shirlena Huang, Jessie P.H. Poon and Brenda S.A. Yeoh (eds), *Proceedings of the International Conference on Women in the Asia-Pacific: Persons, Powers and Politics*, University of Singapore, Department of Geography, South-East Asian Studies Programme and Centre for Advanced Studies, pp. 714–726.

Wilder, William D. (1998) 'Bodies in the East: cosmic images in Malay tradition', *Ecumene: A Journal of Environment, Culture, Meaning*, 5: 167–185.

Wilken, G.A. (1912) *Verspreide Geschriften*, edited by F.D.E. van Ossenbruggen, Semarang, G.C.T. van Dorp, 4 vols.

Williams, Linda B. (1990) *Development, Demography, and Family Decision-making: The Status of Women in Rural Java*, Boulder, CO, Westview Press.

Willmott, W.E. (1970) *The Political Structure of the Chinese Community in Cambodia*, London, The Athlone Press.

Wilson, Peter J. (1967) *A Malay Village and Malaysia: Social Values and Rural Development*, New Haven, CT, HRAF Press.

Winstedt, R.O. (1925) *Shaman, Saiva and Sufi: A Study of the Evolution of Malay Magic*, London, Constable and Co.

Winstedt, R.O. (1947) *The Malays: A Cultural History*, London, Lowe and Brydone, sixth edition, 1961.

Winzeler, Robert L. (1976) 'Ecology, social organization, and state formation in Southeast Asia' (with discussion and response), *Current Anthropology*, 17: 623–640.

Winzeler, Robert L. (1996) 'Sexual status in Southeast Asia: comparative perspectives on women, agriculture and political organization', in Penny van Esterik (ed.), *Women of Southeast Asia*, DeKalb, Northern Illinois University, Center for Southeast Asian Studies, pp. 139–169, first published 1982.

Winzeler, Robert L. (1997) 'Introduction', in Robert L. Winzeler (ed.), *Indigenous Peoples and the State: Politics, Land, and Ethnicity in the Malayan Peninsula and Borneo*, New Haven, CT, Yale University Press, pp. 1–29.

Wolf, Diane Lauren (1992) *Factory Daughters: Gender, Household Dynamics, and Rural Industrialization in Java*, Berkeley and Los Angeles, CA, University of California Press.

Wolf, Eric (1966) *Peasants*, Englewood Cliffs, NJ, Prentice-Hall.

Wolf, Eric R. (1969) *Peasant Wars of the Twentieth Century*, New York, Harper and Row, London, Faber and Faber..

Wolf, Jan de (1999) 'Colonial ideologies and ethnological discourse: a comparison of the United Faculties at Leiden and Utrecht', in Jan van Bremen and Akitoshi Shimizu (eds), *Anthropology and Colonialism in Asia and Oceania*, Richmond, Curzon Press, pp. 307–325.

Wolf, Margery (1972) *Women and the Family in Rural Taiwan*, Stanford, CA, Stanford University Press.

Wolters, O.W. (1999) *History, Culture and Region in Southeast Asian Perspectives*, Ithaca,

NY, Cornell University, Southeast Asia Program Publications, Studies on Southeast Asia 26, revised edition in cooperation with the Institute of Southeast Asian Studies, Singapore, originally published by I.S.E.A.S., Singapore, 1982.

Wood, Robert E. (1984) 'Ethnic tourism, the state and cultural change in Southeast Asia', *Annals of Tourism Research*, 11: 353–374.

Wood, Robert E. (1993) 'Tourism, culture and the sociology of development', in Michael Hitchcock, Victor T. King and Michael J. G. Parnwell (eds), *Tourism in South-East Asia*, London, Routledge, pp. 48–70.

Wood, Robert E. (1997) 'Tourism and the state: ethnic options and constructions of otherness', in Michel Picard and Robert E. Wood (eds), *Tourism, Ethnicity, and the State in Asian and Pacific Societies*, Honolulu, University of Hawai'i Press, pp. 1–34.

Woodward, Mark R. (1989) *Islam in Java: Normative Piety and Mysticism in the Sultanate of Yogyakarta*, Tucson, AZ, University of Arizona Press.

Wouden, F.A.E. van (1968) *Types of Social Structure in Eastern Indonesia*, The Hague, Martinus Nijhoff.

Wouden, F.A.E. van (1977) 'Local groups and double descent in Kodi, West Sumba', in P.E. de Josselin de Jong (ed.), *Structural Anthropology in the Netherlands: A Reader*, The Hague, Martinus Nijhoff, Koninklijk Instituut voor Taal-, Land- en Volkenkunde, pp. 184–222.

Yao Souchou (ed.) (2000) *House of Glass: Culture, Modernity, and the State in Southeast Asia*, Singapore, Institute of Southeast Asian Studies.

Yengoyan, Aram A. (1984) 'Values and institutions in the Philippines: The social anthropology of Frank Lynch', in Aram A. Yengoyan and Perla Q. Makil (eds), *Philippine Society and the Individual: Selected Essays of Frank Lynch, 1949–1976*, University of Michigan, Center for South and Southeast Asian Studies, pp. 11–19.

Yengoyan, Aram A. and Makil, Perla Q. (eds) (1984) *Philippine Society and the Individual: Selected Essays of Frank Lynch, 1949–1976*, University of Michigan, Center for South and Southeast Asian Studies.

Yu, Elena S.H. and Liu, William Thomas (1980) *Fertility and Kinship in the Philippines*, Notre Dame, University of Notre Dame Press.

Zamora, Mario D. (ed.) (1967) *Studies in Philippine Anthropology (in Honor of H. Otley Beyer)*, Quezon City, Nemar-Phoenix.

Zamora, Mario D. (1976) 'Cultural anthropology in the Philippines – 1900–1983: perspectives, problems and prospects', in David J. Banks (ed.), *Changing Identities in Modern Southeast Asia*, The Hague, Mouton Publishers, pp. 311–339.

Zolla, Elémire (1981) *The Androgyne: Fusion of the Sexes*, London, Thames and Hudson.

AUTHOR/NAME INDEX

Page numbers in **bold** signify an extended discussion

SUBJECT INDEX

Page numbers in **bold** signify an extended discussion